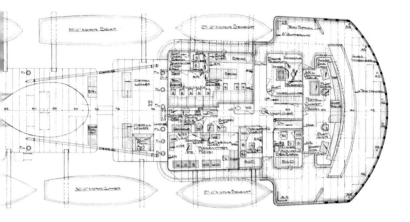

COMPASS PLATFORM

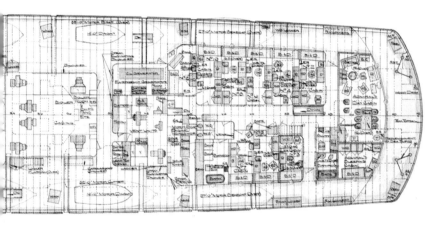

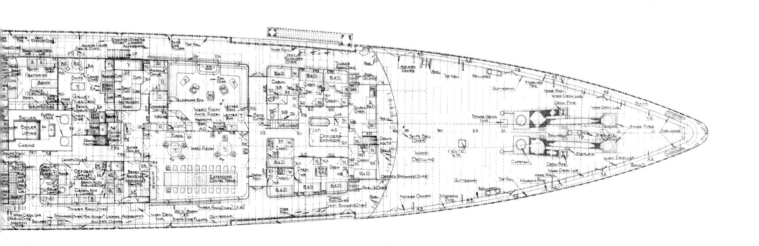

THE ROYAL YACHT
BRITANNIA
THE OFFICIAL HISTORY

THE ROYAL YACHT
BRITANNIA
THE OFFICIAL HISTORY

Richard Johnstone-Bryden

Foreword by HRH The Duke of Edinburgh

CONWAY

ABOVE: *HMY Britannia entering Dartmouth, 1992.*

(© British Crown Copyright / MOD)

TITLE PAGE: *The Queen and Prince Philip step ashore from Britannia to be greeted by President Mandela, thus beginning the Yacht's 85th and final State Visit.*

(© British Crown Copyright / MOD)

© Richard Johnstone-Bryden 2003

This edition first published in Great Britain by Conway Maritime Press,
a division of Chrysalis Books plc
64 Brewery Road
London N7 9NT

Distributed in North America by Casemate, 2114 Darby Road, Haverton, PA 19083

A member of Chrysalis Books plc

www.conwaymaritime.com

ISBN 0 85177 937 9

British Library Cataloguing in Publications Data
A CIP catalogue record for this book is available from the British Library.

Richard Johnstone-Bryden has asserted his moral right under the Copyright Design and Patents
Act 1988, to be identified as the Author of this work.

Editor: Alison Moss
Design and typesetting: Champion Design

Printed and bound in Spain

CONTENTS

ACKNOWLEDGEMENTS

I have been extremely fortunate to enjoy an unprecedented level of assistance in writing this book. I would like to thank first and foremost Her Majesty The Queen and HRH The Duke of Edinburgh KG KT for allowing me to write the Official History of HM Yacht *Britannia*. Their support for this project has enabled me to gain access to a wide range of official documents relating to all aspects of *Britannia*'s story. They have also allowed me to interview a representative cross section of those involved in *Britannia*'s story including members of the Royal Household as well as those who served in the Yacht. Without this level of backing these people would not have granted me an interview for this book or contributed in any way to my research. I would also like to thank HRH The Duke of Edinburgh for writing the Foreword as well as contributing directly to this book and personally checking each chapter. Her Majesty Queen Elizabeth The Queen Mother kindly read through Chapter One for which I am particularly grateful especially as she was the last person alive who was involved in many of the events the chapter covered. I would like to thank HRH The Prince of Wales KG KT, HRH The Duke of York CVO and HRH The Princess Royal KG KT who each granted me an audience and contributed directly to the book with their memories of this great ship.

I would like to thank President Ford and Mrs Reagan for sharing their memories with me of their visits to *Britannia*. Their contributions were important because they provided an impression of how *Britannia* was seen by foreign Heads of State when she was used in support of The Queen's State Visits.

HRH The Duke of Edinburgh's family have also provided me with valuable assistance. I interviewed The Countess Mountbatten of Burma CBE CD JP DL, The Lord Brabourne CBE, and Lady Pamela Hicks who each told me about their memories of *Britannia*.

I would like to make a special mention of Sir Brian McGrath GCVO, Rear Admiral Sir Paul Greening GCVO, Rear Admiral Sir John Garnier KCVO CBE, Rear Admiral Sir Robert Woodard KCVO DL, Commodore A J C Morrow CVO RN, and Mrs David Griffiths CVO who, in addition to describing their experiences of the Yacht, have provided me with a constant source of advice, assistance and encouragement throughout the three years it has taken me to produce this book for which I am especially thankful.

I would like to thank everyone who gave up their time to talk to me about their memories of this great ship and check through the drafts of their quotes to ensure the highest levels of accuracy. In addition to each contributor checking their quotes each of the surviving FORYs and CORY have checked through the chapter that covers their time in command of the Yacht. For those chapters where the Admiral is no longer alive I asked the Commander in his time to check through the text to provide an additional check on the overall accuracy of the material. Although it is not possible to include the stories of everyone who was involved in *Britannia*'s long and varied career I hope the following account provides an insight into life on board HM Yacht *Britannia*.

In particular I would like to thank Rear Admiral Sir Richard Trowbridge KCVO as well as the following former members of the Yacht's company: Admiral Sir Jock Slater GCB LVO DL, Admiral Sir Brian Brown KCB CBE, Vice Admiral Sir Cameron Rusby KCB LVO, Vice Admiral Sir Michael Moore KBE LVO, Vice Admiral Sir Peter Berger KCB LVO DSC, Vice Admiral Sir Philip Watson KBE LVO, Vice Admiral Sir James Weatherall KCVO KBE, Rear Admiral J Adams CB LVO, Rear Admiral J P Edwards CB LVO, Rear Admiral Sir Patrick Rowe KCVO CBE, Rear Admiral C H Layman CB DSO LVO, Rear Admiral D Lammiman CB LVO QHS, Captain N Dalrymple-Hamilton CVO MBE DSC DL RN, Captain I R Bowden LVO RN, Captain L A Bird LVO RN, Captain R A Worlidge LVO RN, Captain C Page RN, Captain D Hart Dyke CBE LVO RN, Captain R A Cosby LVO RN, Captain W R Canning DSO RN, Captain N Blair CVO RN, Captain C H H Owen RN, Captain R T Love RN, Captain D T Smith OBE RN, Captain G J M Andrewes LVO RN, Captain M E Barrow CVO DSO RN, Captain P I F Beeson LVO RN, Captain H B Daglish LVO RN, Captain C F B Hamilton RN, Captain N P Wright LVO RN, Captain D G Roome LVO RN, Captain P B Archer RN, Captain G M A James RN, Captain M A Jones MVO RN, Captain F P Brooke-Popham OBE RN, Surgeon Captain D G Dalgliesh LVO OBE RN, Surgeon Captain T R Douglas-Riley RN, Commander J M Child LVO RN, Commander J L Lees LVO RN, Commander H L Foxworthy OBE RN, Commander

G J T Creedy LVO RN, Commander I Fergie-Woods MVO RN, Commander R K Easson RN, Commander J L L Prichard RN, Commander C Howeson RN, Lieutenant Colonel P J Neville OBE MVO FRAM RM, Lieutenant Colonel J R Mason OBE MVO LRAM ARCM LGSM RM, Lieutenant Colonel G A C Hoskins OBE MVO ARAM RM, Lieutenant Commander C H Knollys DSC RN, Lieutenant Commander V J W Crompton MVO RN, Lieutenant Commander G Ford RN, Lieutenant Commander T Brydon MBE RN, Lieutenant Commander T Young RN, Major J Perkins Mmus ARAM ARCM LGSM RM, Lieutenant A Baker MVO RN, Lieutenant A W Eve RN, Captain E P Whealing MVO BA ARAM ARCM LTCL MIMgt RM, Captain D C Cole MVO Mmus ARAM RM, Mr E V Norrell MVO RVM, Mr A Deane MBE RVM, Mr H M Cain RVM, Mr L L Fuller MVO RVM, Mr G R King RVM, Mr D Morris BEM, Mr W Bennett, Mr R A Field RVM, Mr J A S Field, Mr J Masters, Mr T Gregory RVM, Mr I Denny RVM, and Mr L Marsh MVO RVM.

Inevitably with the passage of time some of the people I would have liked to interview for this book are no longer alive so I am especially grateful to the families of those who were part of Britannia's story for granting me access to relevant papers and photographs within their possession. In particular, I would like to thank Lady Janion, Lady Morgan, Lady Lewin, The Hon. T Lewin, Mrs R Wolrige-Gordon, Mrs E Dalglish, Mrs A Mott, Mrs Madden, Mrs E Hewitt, Mr P Gilbride, Mr D McVicar, and Mrs C Zogolovitch.

As part of Britannia's story it was important to cover the background to the Government decisions that directly effected the Yacht. It was also important to cover the perspective of former Foreign Secretaries and Foreign Office Ministers as well as those Ministers directly involved in the drive to attract inward invest to the UK through the various Sea Days held in Britannia. I would therefore like to thank the following former Ministers who helped me:

The Rt Hon. the Viscount Younger of Leckie KT KCVO TD DL, The Rt Hon. the Lord Carrington KG GCMG CH MC, The Rt Hon. the Lord Callaghan of Cardiff KG, The Rt Hon. the Lord Owen CH, The Rt Hon. the Lord Howe of Aberavon CH QC, The Rt Hon. the Lord Hurd of Westwell CH CBE, The Rt Hon. the Lord Waldegrave of North Hill, The Rt Hon. the Lord Forsyth, The Rt Hon. Sir Malcolm Rifkind KCMG QC, and The Rt Hon. W Hague MP.

In addition to the material from former Government Ministers about Britannia's effectiveness in promoting British industry I found the memories of Ms G Murdoch MBE who organised Sea Days in Britannia for British Invisibles and The Hon. P Benson who was the Chairman, International Privatisation Group, Coopers & Lybrand very helpful. Captain D Peters MN's memories of the Sea Day in China were also useful. As part of my research into the various proposed schemes for

Britannia's replacement in the 1990s I found the assistance given by Mr M Drummond OBE JP DL Hon. DSc of help.

Another important aspect of Britannia's story was how the use of Britannia supported the work of the various Royal Households during Royal Tours. I am therefore grateful for the help I have received from The Rt Hon. the Lord Moore of Wolvercote GCB GCVO CMG QSO, The Rt Hon. the Lord Fellowes GCB GCVO QSO, The Rt Hon. Sir William Heseltine GCB GCVO AC QSO, The Rt Hon. Sir Robin Janvrin KCVO CB, Lieutenant Colonel Sir Edward Ford GCVO KCB ERD DL, Sir Kenneth Scott KCVO CMG, Captain Sir Alastair Aird GCVO, Major General Sir Simon Cooper GCVO, Professor Sir Norman Blacklock KCVO OBE FRCS, Vice Admiral Sir David Loram KCB CVO, The Hon. Mary Morrison DCVO, The Lady Susan Hussey DCVO, Mr M C W M Jephson LVO, Mr L T Mann MVO RVM, and Mr F A Holland RVM.

I am grateful to the following members of the Royal Household who have helped me with various aspects of my book, Mrs P Gee, Miss P Russell-Smith LVO, Commander W N Entwisle MVO RN, Captain A R M Spry.

As part of my research into the building and preservation of Britannia I would like to thank Mr J Brown, Mr S Irvine, Mr J Carney, Mr T Biggins, Sir Robert Smith CBE, Mr R S McNeill CBE, Rear Admiral N Rankin CB CBE, Mr T Smith, Mr R Downie, Mr I Jones, Mr D Campbell.

Acknowledgement is also due to the following Government Departments and archives, Mr D A Belson, Crown Copyright Administrator, Commodore H Edleston RN, DCC(N), Lady de Bellaigue LVO, Miss P Clark MVO, Mrs J Kelsey MVO, Miss F Diamond MVO and Miss H Grey, The Royal Archives, Miss J Wraight, The Admiralty Library, Ms M McQuaide, Ministry of Defence, Mr D A Daellenbach and Mr W H McNitt, Gerald R Ford Library, Mrs L Wenden, Fleet Photographic Unit, Mr W Hunt, CS Photos, Mr R Sheild and Mr J Constantine, DML, Mr G Shore and Mrs J Keohane, The Fleet Air Arm Museum, Mr G Gardner, University of Glasgow. I would especially like to thank the Controller of Her Britannic Majesty's Stationery Office for granting me permission to use the official British Crown Copyright and Ministry of Defence photographs and drawings reproduced throughout this book.

Sadly, with the passage of time some of those who have helped me with this project are no longer with us. I would like to make a special mention of the help that the following gave me: Sir John Brown, Commander R L Hewitt LVO RN, Commander J M A Parker CVO RN, Lieutenant Commander C L Cheffings BEM RN.

Last and by no means least I would like to thank my father for patiently reading through the various drafts of the book. I would also like to thank John Lee of Conway Maritime Press for his help, guidance and patience through this, my second major book.

BUCKINGHAM PALACE.

When Her Majesty's Yacht 'Britannia' was finally paid off in Portsmouth on 11 December 1997, it signalled the end of an unbroken succession of Royal Yachts dating back to the reign of King Charles II. Commissioned in 1954, 'Britannia' was the first of that long line to be thoroughly ocean-going and that capacity was fully exploited during her 44 years in service. It made it possible for members of the Royal Family to visit Commonwealth and foreign states from the Antarctic to Russia, from Africa to the Caribbean and both North and South America. In home waters, she took part in major State and Naval occasions and visited all the major, and several of the minor, seaports around the British Isles.

'Britannia' was lovingly maintained by a company of dedicated officers and ratings of the Royal Yacht Service, ably backed up by a multitude of craftsmen in the Naval Dockyards. Her graceful lines and immaculate appearance never failed to generate interest and admiration wherever she visited and the 'Yachties' always did their very best to maintain the highest standards of seamanship in all circumstances.

The combination of her ocean-going capacity and efficient management reflected our long maritime traditions and made an invaluable contribution to the prestige of this country. She managed to project the very best British characteristics to people all over the world, which also produced significant tangible and intangible contributions to the British economy. Now that she has completed such valuable services to Britain, it is only right that the story of this very special ship should become the subject of an official history. It is also well timed, as it has enabled the author to interview many of the people who have first-hand experience of the different aspects of her story to supplement the numerous official and private documents. He has produced a full and fascinating account of the career of this remarkable ship.

HMY Britannia.

(© British Crown Copyright / MOD)

Chapter One

THE KING'S YACHT

The Royal Yacht Replacement Programme 1936–1952

For over four decades the Royal Yacht *Britannia* played an important role in the reign of Queen Elizabeth II. Despite this close visible and personal link to both The Queen and Prince Philip the project that resulted in *Britannia's* construction was conceived during the short and troubled reign of King Edward VIII in 1936.[1] However, his abdication, coupled with the deteriorating international situation leading to the Second World War, followed by hard economic times, resulted in considerable delays in building a replacement for the antiquated Royal Yacht *Victoria & Albert*.

The keel of Queen Victoria's final Royal Yacht, known affectionately as *V&A*, was laid on 15 December 1897 in Pembroke Dockyard. She was launched on 9 May 1899 by The Duchess of York (later Queen Mary), and became the third Royal Yacht to carry the name *Victoria & Albert*. The fitting out work progressed swiftly with the installation of her engines and the stepping of her three masts before she was moved into dry dock to free up Pembroke's only fitting out berth for the completion of HMS *Spartiate*. When the final fitting out work was finished, preparations were made to ease *V&A* out of dry dock when disaster struck on 3 January 1900 while the dry dock was being filled with water. As the water level rose *V&A* started to float and took on a progressive list to starboard which increased to 20 degrees until further movement was arrested by the docking wires. When two of these wires were slightly slackened her list increased by a further 5 degrees until they once more stopped her movement. The dockyard workers managed to hold *V&A* in position overnight until she could be righted on the following morning's tide. To do

this they had to flood her double bottom with 200 tons of water and place 105 tons of pig iron near the keel. This temporary solution succeeded in correcting the list to 10 degrees and she was moved out of dock and secured to a mooring buoy until a permanent solution was devised. Although quick thinking by the dockyard workers managed to save *V&A*, the damage had been done to her reputation as questions were asked about her future and whether the safety of the Royal Family should be risked on board her. Queen Victoria quickly made up her own mind after she heard about the incident and apparently vowed never to step on board the new Royal Yacht.

Despite public concern about safety, she was taken in hand for further work to eliminate the stability problems. This included the removal of 260 tons through the lightening of items such as the masts and the funnels. In addition, 250 tons of iron ballast was placed in the double bottoms. During subsequent trials *V&A* proved to be a seaworthy vessel, and she was finally commissioned at Portsmouth on 23 July 1901. By that time, Queen Victoria had died and was succeeded on the throne by King Edward VII. Compared to the busy annual programme later undertaken by *Britannia*, *V&A* enjoyed a relatively sedate existence. During the reign of Edward VII, which saw her busiest years of service, she was used for cruises to Europe and the Mediterranean as well as voyages in home waters, including The King's annual visit to Cowes Week. Essentially, these duties were of limited duration and for the more ambitious tours either a warship was converted, or a liner was chartered to fulfil the role of Royal Yacht.

Victoria & Albert (III) was the last Royal Yacht to be built for Queen Victoria. Although The Queen never stepped on board, V&A went on to serve four Monarchs.

(© FAA Museum)

During King George V's reign (1910–36) V&A's programme became progressively confined to UK waters, although Queen Alexandra continued to make use of her for European and Mediterranean cruises before the outbreak of War in 1914. During the First World War V&A was laid up, together with the other Royal Yachts, in Portsmouth under the care of the Keeper & Steward of the Royal Apartments and a small team of shipkeepers. The bulk of the Royal Yacht Service, from which the Royal Yachts were manned, was drafted to form part of the ship's company of the battleship HMS *Agincourt*. At the beginning of the War she was under construction for the Turkish Navy as the *Sultan Osman I*. When Turkey entered the War on the side of Germany in November 1914 she was seized by the Admiralty and completed for the Royal Navy. The Royal Yachtsmen remained on board *Agincourt* for the duration of the War returning to Portsmouth in 1919 to recommission V&A under the command of Rear Admiral the Hon. Sir Hubert Brand. In the years that followed the Armistice V&A's programme

increasingly featured commitments centred round two of King George V's personal passions – sailing and the Royal Navy. Like his father before him, King George V regularly attended Cowes Week where he raced his father's legendary yacht *Britannia*. He also used V&A for reviews of the Fleet and observing naval manoeuvres first hand.

The question of replacing V&A was first raised during the brief reign of King Edward VIII. From the outset it was considered essential that a new Royal Yacht should have a secondary wartime role. When the initial discussions began in May 1936 about the type of vessel to replace V&A it was suggested that the new ship could be built as a hybrid cruiser. The idea was that in time of war the ship would be converted into an operational cruiser. This scheme was quickly dismissed by the Admiral Commanding HM Yachts, Rear Admiral Dudley North CB CSI ADC, who instead suggested that the new ship's secondary role should be to act as a hospital ship. This combination would enable the new ship to have more comfortable accommodation for the Royal Family and yet help to fill an urgent Royal Navy requirement for additional hospital ships.[2]

In July 1936 King Edward VIII instructed Admiral North to begin discussions with the Admiralty about the building of a new Royal Yacht. The King felt that the new ship should be of approximately 4000 tons and have a speed of between 25 and 30 knots.[3] By the end of the month the First Lord of the Admiralty, Sir Samuel Hoare had discussed the matter with the Chancellor of the Exchequer. The Chancellor felt that a good case could be made for the new Royal Yacht in Parliament providing that The King gave a firm undertaking to make use of the ship when she was completed.[4] This point was further underlined by Sir Samuel when he saw The King after the summer recess of Parliament in October 1936.[5] This concern was hardly surprising, because V&A had only undertaken a limited programme in home waters since the end of the First World War, the only major exception being King George V's recuperation cruise around the Mediterranean in 1925. King Edward VIII's first visit to V&A was on 30 June 1936 when he embarked for just half an hour to inspect the Yacht's company.[6] The following day he embarked for lunch and left in the afternoon to return to London by car.[7] When The King visited France on 26 July 1936 he sailed in the Admiralty Yacht HMS *Enchantress* instead of V&A. In fact King Edward only used V&A for one period of Royal duty during his reign. This was when she sailed to Portland to be used as a floating base for his two-day visit to the Home Fleet on 12 and 13 November 1936.[8] In contrast he spent between the 10 August and 6 September on board the steam yacht *Nahlin*. King Edward charted *Nahlin* from Lady Yule for a private holiday cruising around the Mediterranean. Interestingly, *Nahlin* was one of the last great steam yachts to be completed. She was designed by G L Watson who had designed King Edward VII's racing yacht *Britannia* and she was built by John Brown & Co., who later built HMY *Britannia*. *Nahlin* subsequently became the Royal Yacht of King Carol II when she was purchased by the Romanian Government for £120,000 in 1937 and renamed *Luceafural*.

Despite the promising start to the procurement process of a new Royal Yacht the abdication crisis soon engulfed the programme. King Edward VIII abdicated on 11 December 1936 and was succeeded on the Throne by his brother The Duke of York as King George VI. Six days later the new King met with Sir Samuel Hoare and they decided to suspend the immediate activity to replace V&A and to reconsider the issue in a further six months.[9] Although this decision by the new King was politically prudent, the issue could not be ignored for long. V&A was by this time clearly showing her years and had become a relic from another age. Her hull and machinery were rapidly deteriorating while the accommodation for her crew was cramped and old fashioned by the Royal Navy's standards of the day.[10] To keep her in commission she needed an expensive major refit, which may have extended her service by only a few more years.

Although the Coronation of the new King in May 1937 brought much needed stability to the British Monarchy in the wake of the turmoil created by the abdication of King Edward VIII, international events looked as though they would overshadow the attempts to resurrect the project to build a new Royal Yacht. When the issue of replacing V&A was raised again in 1938 King George VI wanted to ensure that the decision would gain public support. He recognised that an announcement to build a new vessel to be used exclusively as a Royal Yacht at that time could create unnecessary difficulties for the monarchy. Therefore, The King told the Admiralty that he wanted the design of a future Royal Yacht to incorporate the capability for rapid conversion into a hospital ship in the event of war.[11]

To help prepare the way for a new Royal Yacht the First Lord of the Admiralty, Duff Cooper, circulated a memorandum to his Cabinet colleagues on 30 June 1938 to set out the situation and the options.[12] Its contents were then fully discussed by the Cabinet who gave their unanimous backing to the replacement of V&A on 6 July.[13] Their decision enabled the Admiralty to set the design process in motion. Two days later King George VI met the Controller of the Navy, Vice Admiral Sir Reginald Henderson KCB to discuss the design of the new Yacht.[14]

During the summer months the process moved forward smoothly until the autumn when the deteriorating international situation, in particular, the aftermath of the Munich Crisis of September 1938, once again called the timing of this programme into question. The Government had already significantly increased the naval budget as part of the re-armament programme and The King felt that spending £800,000–£900,000 on a new Royal Yacht would be politically unwise at that time. In November The King's Private Secretary, Sir Alex Hardinge, wrote to the newly appointed First Lord of the Admiralty, Earl Stanhope, to make him aware of these views.[15] In his response Earl Stanhope stated that from a practical point of view the building of a new Royal Yacht would not affect the re-armament programme in any way because there was no need for the Royal Yacht to be built in a shipyard engaged in building warships. On the other hand he agreed that politically such an announcement could be unhelpful. However, he felt that by waiting until the naval budgets began to drop again he could introduce the building of a new Royal Yacht as a positive measure especially if it was billed as part of the Government's policy of maintaining employment in the shipbuilding industry despite a decline in the number of orders for new warships.[16]

Without a firm commissioning date for a successor in sight the veteran V&A continued to soldier on in service and began what turned out to be her last 'season' in service in 1939. The fragile state of her machinery was once more highlighted during her annual steam trials held at the beginning of June. Due to the continual overheating of the port crosshead bearing it was decided to reduce her top speed from 15 knots to 13 knots.[17] This was not the first time that it had been necessary to reduce the maximum speed of V&A as a result of concerns over the safety of her machinery. In 1930 it was decided that in view of the boilers' age the maximum pressure of their safety valves should be reduced, thus resulting in a drop of just over 3 knots from a top speed of 20.6 knots to 17.5 knots.

V&A's only Royal cruise that year was a four-day voyage to the west country beginning on 20 July when she left Portsmouth.[18] She anchored overnight in Weymouth Bay[19] where The King and Queen, accompanied by the two Princesses and Lord Mountbatten, embarked in the Yacht the following afternoon. V&A weighed anchor at 1730 and sailed for Torbay to spend the night[20] prior to The King's visit to the Royal Naval College (RNC) at Dartmouth on 22 July. Having visited the RNC in the afternoon the Royal Family hosted a dinner party on board V&A to which Prince Philip, who was a naval cadet at the RNC, was invited.[21] The following morning while The King and Queen attended morning chapel at the RNC Prince Philip was sent to the Captain's House to

The Admiralty prepared this design in 1939 as a suitable replacement for V&A. However, the outbreak of the Second World War led to the suspension of the Royal Yacht replacement programme. When the programme was resumed after the War this was used as the starting point for a design which eventually culminated in the construction of Britannia.

(The Royal Collection © HM Queen Elizabeth II)

look after the two young Princesses who enjoyed his company. This was not the first time that Prince Philip had met Princess Elizabeth as they had both been present at Princess Marina's wedding in 1934 and Prince Philip had attended a number of family gatherings since then. When V&A left Dartmouth on the evening of 23 July she was escorted by a flotilla of 250 boats, including Prince Philip alone in a small rowing boat.[22] Having anchored in Start Bay for the Royal party to enjoy dinner V&A weighed anchor and made her way overnight to Cowes arriving there at 1000. The Royal party disembarked for a couple of hours to pay a short visit to the Isle of Wight before the Yacht resumed her voyage back to Portsmouth where she arrived that afternoon.[23]

V&A began her final spell of Royal duty on 8 August 1939 when she sailed from Portsmouth bound for Portland and The King's review of the Reserve Fleet under the command of Vice Admiral Sir Max Horton.[24] The King embarked in the Yacht the following morning, and little did anyone know that when he disembarked at 1730[25] it marked the end of V&A's service as a Royal Yacht. When she returned to Portsmouth for the last time on 10 August[26] V&A was expected to see further service as a Royal Yacht so she did not fly the traditional paying off pennant. However, international events were to dictate otherwise with Great Britain declaring war on Germany on 3 September 1939.

The outbreak of war immediately arrested the procurement process for the new Royal Yacht despite its planned secondary wartime role as a hospital ship. By the time that the new Royal Yacht programme was suspended, the Admiralty had produced, in close collaboration with The King and Queen, a basic design for the new vessel together with a set of requirements. These formed the basis for the 'invitation to tender' documents which were issued by the Admiralty on 10 August 1939 to 11 prominent ship-

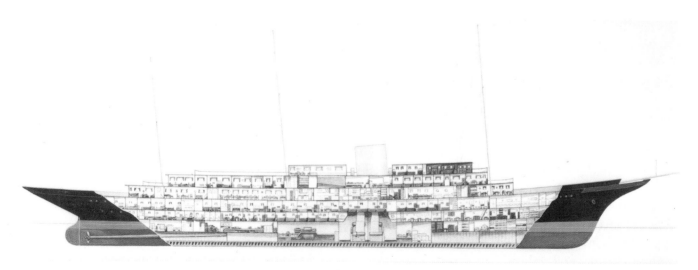

yards. The list of shipyards approached included well-known firms such as John Brown & Co. Ltd of Clydeside and Cammell Laird of Birkenhead. The responses to the eight-page document were to be delivered no later than 12 September 1939. Outlining the Admiralty's specification for rig and appearance the document said: 'it is emphasised that a well-balanced, graceful and dignified appearance, suitable for the ship's service, is essential.' It also stated that a single funnel and three masts were core requirements. Other requirements were that the fully loaded displacement should not exceed 5000 tons and that the waterline length should be 406 feet. The draft was not to exceed 16 feet while the Yacht was to be capable of 22 knots yet have a range of 3750 miles at 12 knots.[27] Although a Royal Yacht was never built to these plans they provided a valuable point of reference for the resurrection of the project after the War.

For V&A the outbreak heralded a rapid change in status. Within four days she had been moved out of the dockyard at Portsmouth and placed on G moorings in Fareham Creek. Many of the Yachtsmen were discharged from the Royal Yacht Service to take up appointments in the Fleet while the Royal Marine detachment was discharged to Eastney.[28] The return to the mainstream service for many of the Yachtsmen did not work out well because they initially resumed their naval careers with the rank they had held before they were accepted into the Royal Yacht Service. However, this was later sorted out so it only proved to be a short-term problem.[29] With the effective disbandment of the Royal Yacht Service the Vice Admiral Commanding HM Yachts, Vice Admiral Sir Dudley North visited the Commander-in-Chief Portsmouth on 16 September 1939 to discuss his own future.[30] They concluded that the time had come for his flag to be struck. Thus at sunset on 18 September 1939 the flag of Vice Admiral Commanding HM Yachts was hauled down and the post fell dormant.[31] The following day the Yacht's complement was reduced to a care and maintenance party. The motor boats and the stores were returned to the dockyard for storage while the Wardroom silver was packed into boxes to be held in the store rooms of the Royal Apartments. As part of her change in status V&A was now classed as a tender to HMS Victory and cared for by a complement of three officers and 49 ratings.[32] For nearly three years the old yacht sat at her moorings until April 1942 when the Admiralty asked for The King's permission to use V&A as an accommodation vessel for WRNS serving in the Gunnery School on Whale Island HMS Excellent.[33] The King willingly gave his approval to both this request and the subsequent one to accommodate male officers and ratings when it was found impractical to accommodate WRNS on board[34].

The issue of a replacement Royal Yacht remained dormant until the closing months of the Second World War. The former Vice Admiral Commanding HM Yachts, by then Admiral Sir Dudley North KCVO CB CSI CMG, wrote to The King's Private Secretary, Sir Alan Lascelles on 30 April 1945 about the reformation of the Royal Yacht Service. Describing the state of the V&A during a recent visit Admiral North wrote: 'Although now probably unfit for long sea trips (she was getting a bit bed ridden before the war) she is I think perfectly capable of providing comfortable accommodation for Their Majesties in harbour and also has extremely suitable and stately rooms for entertaining.' To ensure that there would be a cadre of experienced Yachtsmen to commission a new Royal Yacht, Admiral North felt that it was important for the RN to allow the former Yachtsmen to return to V&A at the end of their wartime commitments. As he was approaching the end of his time as the Flag Officer Great Yarmouth he suggested that he could resume his former duties as the Admiral Commanding HM Yachts until a permanent successor could be appointed.[35] Both The King and the First Sea Lord agreed to this suggestion[36] and Admiral North was officially appointed to HMS President for special duty to reconstitute the Royal Yacht Service on 2 August 1945.

Unofficially, Admiral North began to take up his new duties during July attending meetings on the reformation of the Royal Yacht Service and establishing a base for himself on board V&A. The Royal Yacht Service was formally reconstituted in September 1945 so that the most valuable Yachtsmen could be guaranteed employment until the age of 50. On their return to V&A, the Yachtsmen once more donned their old uniforms and started work to tidy up the elderly Yacht.[37] All appeared to be going smoothly until October when the navy condemned V&A as being no longer seaworthy. Judging by her deteriorating condition before the War this should not have been a major surprise but it did bring V&A's future into question. Admiral North maintained that V&A still had an important role to play by housing the Royal Yacht stores, HM's furniture and to act as the base for the Ship's company of a new Royal Yacht until its completion.[38] The King endorsed this view informing the Master of the Household that his personal stores were to remain on board.[39] For the time being, this view prevailed as work continued to spruce up V&A. By November the media were beginning to take an interest in the activity on board V&A. The most visible sign of this work was the repainting, which was triggered by the Commander-in-Chief Portsmouth, Admiral Leighton, who felt that the old Yacht should be smartened up. Seeing this work a reporter from the *Evening Standard* contacted Admiral North to find out if it was an outward sign of *V&A* being brought forward for further service. He of course explained to the reporter that it wasn't and nothing should be read into the current surge of activity[40]. As normality began to return to the rejuvenated *V&A* Admiral North hoped that she would be released from her accommodation duties before the end of 1945. Such orders were not forthcoming and *V&A* continued to be classed as a tender to HMS *Excellent*. When those duties finished on 1 May 1946 *V&A* was transferred to the RN Barracks at Portsmouth HMS *Victory* to perform the same role.[41]

Having survived condemnation by the navy in October 1945 *V&A*'s future was once more called into doubt the following May when, in response to enquires from the Admiralty, The King informed them that he did not

During the first half of the twentieth century the Admiralty either chartered a liner or converted a major warship to support long overseas Royal tours. The battlecruiser HMS Renown was used to support a number of tours by the Prince of Wales (later King Edward VIII and The Duke of Windsor), and is seen here steaming through the Panama Canal with His Royal Highness embarked.   (CPL)

intend to use *V&A* again.[42] The navy therefore approached The King to seek approval for her to be scrapped because they no longer had a requirement for her either.[43] Initially The King agreed to the request providing that Admiral North and the Master of the Household were given enough time to select which items should be removed.[44] On hearing this news Admiral North became very concerned. Although he recognised the difficulties of justifying the continued retention of *V&A*, as a hulk he felt her demise would threaten the immediate future of the Yachtsmen who had returned to the Royal Yacht Service. He was also worried that the scrapping of *V&A* without a successor would dramatically reduce the chances of a new Royal Yacht being built in future. He therefore advised The King to authorise the scrapping of *V&A* only if he was given a definite documentary promise to build a new Royal Yacht.[45] In light of this wise advice The King asked the Admiralty to delay making a decision about *V&A*'s fate.[46]

While the future of the new Royal Yacht programme seemed to be as uncertain as ever there were developments towards the provision of a suitable vessel for the Tour of South Africa which was due to begin in February 1947. This was an important commitment for The King who was going to be accompanied by The Queen and the two Princesses, because it was his first visit to a

Commonwealth country since the War and the first tour of South Africa by a reigning British Monarch. The RN's most powerful battleship, HMS *Vanguard* was chosen in 1946 to fulfil this important role. Interestingly, the Royal Family already had close links with the battleship because Princess Elizabeth had launched *Vanguard* in 1944 and attended the Commissioning ceremony of the ship on 12 May 1946. After only a few months in commission *Vanguard* entered dockyard hands in Portsmouth to begin the work to adapt her for her new role in August 1946. This was not the first time that a major RN warship had been used for a tour. The Prince of Wales had used the battlecruisers HMS *Renown* and HMS *Repulse* separately for major tours in the 1920s while The Duke of Connaught sailed to India in the battleship HMS *Malaya* in 1920–21 to open the Indian Provincial Council. As Duke of York, The King, together with The Queen, had sailed in the battlecruiser HMS *Renown* to open the Australian Parliament and visit New Zealand.

The quarters for the Admiral and his staff on the shelter deck were chosen as the location for the Royal Apartments. Queen Elizabeth was closely involved in the appearance of these quarters, choosing the colour scheme and appointing Miss Margot Brigden to supervise the interior decorating. The Apartments were fitted out with new items of furniture which had been specially commissioned for the Tour as well as many items of furniture and stores from V&A. Men from V&A were to be involved, both in the preparations on board *Vanguard* and for the Tour itself, including the provision of the Royal Barge with its crew and the embarkation of the Keeper & Steward of the Royal Apartments, Mr Pardy.

The 45,000-ton battleship HMS Vanguard *shortly after she left Portsmouth in December 1946 to begin sea trials following her conversion for King George VI's Tour of South Africa.*

(CPL)

Although the use of *Vanguard* between February and May 1947 provided some positive future employment for members of the Royal Yacht Service there was still little immediate prospect of a new Royal Yacht being ordered. At the end of November 1946 the Admiralty wrote to The King's Private Secretary, Sir Alan Lascelles to advise him that they would be informing Admiral North to suspend his work for the time being.[47] Whilst Admiral North's work was far from finished he had, in just over a year, secured the services of 36 pre-war Yachtsmen and developed a scheme for the entry, training and enrolment of future Yachtsmen.[48] Admiral North's work ultimately made a significant contribution towards the successful commissioning of *Britannia*. His work provided the framework for the future expansion of the Royal Yacht Service to commission a new Royal Yacht. Without this work many of the lessons gained through generations of Yachtsmen manning previous Royal Yachts, including almost four decades of service by *V&A*, would have been lost. His quick thinking at the end of the War in rounding up former Yachtsmen before they were demobilised ensured that there was an experienced cadre of men to train the next generation of Yachtsmen.

Following Admiral North's departure, responsibility for the Royal Yacht Service passed to the Commodore RN Barracks Portsmouth.[49] *V&A* continued to be used as an accommodation ship, although the Royal Apartments were maintained so that they could be used by either members of the Royal Family or the Household. While it seemed very unlikely that she would ever be used by the Royal Family again she did perform a vital role as a store ship for items that might be required by Their Majesties when they embarked in other ships. The Admiral's quarters were also maintained on board *V&A* as it was anticipated that the post of Admiral Commanding HM Yachts was only temporarily in abeyance.[50]

While *V&A* awaited her fate in Portsmouth moves continued behind the scenes to re-ignite the Royal Yacht replacement programme, but it was not until 1949 that any significant progress was made. In June 1949 the Admiralty were tentatively considering two options. First, to build a new Royal Yacht to the 1939 design or to design a new smaller Royal Yacht of 3500 tons. Given the requirement to accommodate a Royal party of 40 the Admiralty doubted if a vessel of less that 3500 tons would be large enough to meet the requirements of a Royal Yacht. As ever the cost was still the major issue. The original estimate for the 1939 design stood at £825,000[51] but this had increased to between £1,250,000 and £1,500,000. Even the smaller Royal Yacht design was estimated as costing between £850,000 and £900,000.[52] As with the pre-war programme it was felt that the new vessel should be designed to undertake an operational role during wartime. The 1939 design had been drafted to include the capability for rapid conversion into a hospital ship. While this remained the principle option for either design, consideration was given to the adoption of an alternative secondary role including employment as a HQ ship for combined operations, or as a small submarine depot ship, or as a mobile base HQ ship.[53]

Although the primary focus of this programme was to build a new vessel, the conversion of an existing vessel into a Royal Yacht was evaluated as an economic and expedient solution. In March 1946 The King firmly rejected the Admiralty's offer to convert the *Dido* class cruiser HMS *Scylla* into a hybrid Royal Radar Yacht. Commenting about this suggestion, Admiral North wrote on 19 March 1946: 'I have heard since that that class of ship roll like hell. But perhaps the re-construction would reduce that.'[54] In 1949 the Admiralty reviewed a number of private yachts in UK waters. Of these the most suitable was Sir Bernard and Lady Docker's yacht *Shemara*, which could only accommodate a Royal party of 10 or 12. Due to this very limited capacity an approach was never made to the Dockers.[55]

However, the Turkish Government's desire to sell the elegant *Savarona*, which had been purchased for the late President Mustafa Kemal Ataturk, presented a realistic option for conversion. She was designed by Walter F Gibbs of Gibbs & Cox for the American heiress Mrs Emily Roebling Cadwalader and built by the Hamburg shipyard Blohm & Voss in 1931. With a displacement of 5710 tons and a length of 408 feet *Savarona* was the largest private yacht in the world before she was sold for $1,200,000 to the Turkish Government in 1938. By 1950 they were keen to part with her for both political and economic reasons, although it looked as though the asking price would be in the region of $3,000,000. However,

undercover research by officials from the British Embassy in Istanbul revealed that she could possibly be purchased for about $1,000,000. Despite being nearly 30 years old *Savarona* had undertaken very little cruising and was in remarkably good condition.

With investigations underway into the possibility of buying *Savarona* another suitable candidate emerged when the German yacht *Grille* was purchased by a US ship-breaker for £35,000. With a displacement of 4100 tons and a length of 377 feet she was not much smaller than either V&A or the 1939 design.[56] Politically, the decision to convert *Grille* into the next Royal Yacht would have caused enormous controversy. She was described as Hitler's 'Royal Yacht', although no evidence existed at the time to prove that Hitler had actually ever used her in such a capacity. She was laid down in March 1934 at Blohm & Voss as an Admiralty Yacht and commissioned on 19 May 1935. On the outbreak of War she was used as a minelayer before being decommissioned in July 1942. She spent the remainder of the War at Narvik as a staff ship for the Commander-in-Chief and Com Sub Arctic. Interestingly, she was transferred to Great Britain after the War prior to being passed on to the US in 1947. Soon after transfer the US Government sold *Grille* to private owners before she ended up in the American scrapyard.

The Ship's company of HMS Vanguard *man ship for King George VI's ceremonial arrival in Cape Town.* (CPL)

Despite the Admiralty's misgivings about public acceptance of *Grille* The King confirmed that he would accept a rebuilt *Grille* if there really was no other way of providing him with a seagoing yacht.[57] From the financial perspective *Grille* was an attractive option because it was anticipated that her refurbishment would cost between £400,000 and £500,000 which was half the cost of building a new 4000-ton yacht and only a third of a 5000-ton yacht.[58] As part of this refurbishment *Grille* would have been fitted with new engines, boilers and electrical arrangements. Prompted by the need to completely redecorate and update *Grille*'s accommodation, serious thought was given to making the best use of the available space. During discussions about the revised layout The King suggested that *Grille*'s speed could be reduced by 4 knots to 22 knots (the required speed of the 1939 design), which would eliminate the need for one of her boiler rooms. This space could then have been reclaimed for additional accommodation. He also felt that the number of cabins needed for civilian members of staff could be reduced by the increased use of RN stewards who would be accommodated in standard mess decks thus freeing up more space.[59] It was assumed that the revenue generated by the sale of *V&A* for scrap would balance the money needed to pay for the purchase of *Grille* from the American scrapyard.[60]

The deteriorating health of The King during 1951 led to fresh progress in the moves to build a new Royal Yacht as it was hoped that he would be able to take a convalescence cruise in the Yacht. This would not have been the first time that a Royal Yacht had been used for this purpose as both King Edward VII and King George V had used *V&A* for convalescence cruises. King George VI's failing health had already led to the cancellation of his Commonwealth Tour of 1951. Originally, he was due to have undertaken the Tour with Queen Elizabeth and Princess Margaret but arrangements were later made for the Tour to be undertaken by Princess Elizabeth and The Duke of Edinburgh. In the absence of a new Royal Yacht the cargo liner SS *Gothic* of the Shaw Saville Line was chartered by the Admiralty and converted by Cammell Laird at their Birkenhead shipyard in 1951. The Royal couple were due to join *Gothic* in Mombasa on 7 February 1952. *Gothic* was one of four IC class passenger/cargo liners and she was launched at the Tyneside yard of Swan Hunter on 12 December 1947. With a displacement of 15,902 tons and a speed of 17 knots she was used for passenger and cargo traffic between the UK, South Africa, Australia and New Zealand.

Towards the end of May 1951 The King, together with The Queen, discussed the issue with the Prime Minister, Clement Attlee, who was not unsympathetic towards his desire for a new Royal Yacht.[61] Following this meeting events moved quickly. It appears that the *Savarona* proposal had by then been dropped, presumably because the relatively high purchase price did not present a major saving over the building of a new vessel. This left a straightforward choice between a modernised *Grille* and the building of a new vessel. Before the middle of June the Prime Minister accepted the recommendation of The First Lord of the Admiralty, Lord Pakenham. He suggested that a 4000-ton hospital ship should be included within the re-armament programme. In peacetime this hospital ship would be used by The King as a Royal Yacht.[62] However, it was to be another four months before the Admiralty announced the decision to the press on the evening of Monday, 8 October 1951. In these intervening months the Prime Minister consulted the leaders of the other political parties who were enthusiastic about the proposal and thus the decision was taken with the concurrence of the Opposition. With a General Election on 25 October it was important to avoid the possibility of the Royal Yacht becoming a major election issue. With the defeat of Attlee's government this proved to have been a wise precaution as the incoming Prime Minister, Winston Churchill was equally committed to the swift completion of the new Yacht.

While the political process got underway to prepare the way for the announcement of the new Royal Yacht the Government was able to begin the process of implementing its decision. The first step was to secretly approach seven shipyards during August 1951 to see if they were interested in building the new vessel. At the same time the Admiralty began work on a sketch design using a scaled down version of the 1939 design as the basis. However, the Admiralty significantly reviewed the direction of this work as a result of the sketch design submitted in November 1951 by J Thornycroft & Co. Ltd. Their design, which was prepared as a private venture, had a displacement of 4500 tons. The building cost was estimated as £2,110,000 which included £331,000 for the decoration of the Royal Apartments, Retinue and Admiral's quarters. In response to this design the Admiralty scaled down their requirements to help keep the costs under control. Despite their intentions their room for manoeuvre was strictly limited by the requirement for the Yacht to perform the role of hospital ship as well as having the seaworthy capability to undertake long ocean voyages. In a paper delivered to the Institute of Naval Architects in London on 7 April 1954, the Director of Naval Construction, Sir Victor Shepheard KCB RCNC, explained the difficulties experienced in designing the new Royal Yacht to meet its two different roles.

'Designs had to be developed simultaneously for the Royal Yacht and hospital ship roles and the best arrangements worked out which would meet both requirements and at the same time ensure that the work and cost of conversion in wartime would be kept to a minimum. For example, certain features have been embodied in the design which add to the value of the ship as a Royal Yacht, but which are not altogether essential for that purpose. They would, however, be necessary if and when the ship is used as a hospital ship. Such features include ship's stabilisers, certain air-conditioning, large laundry facilities and comparatively high speed, none of which could be added on conversion as a hospital ship except at considerable additional expense and long delay in completion.'

The consultation with the shipyards brought to light an opportunity to bring the date of the keel laying forward from the end of 1952. The Clydebank shipyard John Brown & Co. Ltd revealed that they had the capacity to build the new ship immediately. Because a major part of the Admiralty's case for pushing the Royal Yacht through the Treasury at such short notice was built around the state of The King's health it seemed foolish not to take advantage of this opportunity. By the end of the year the Admiralty were engaged in detailed discussions with John Brown & Co. about the design of the new ship. Prior to these discussions the Admiralty still favoured the construction of a Royal Yacht that followed the outline of the 1939 design. While such a vessel would have looked very elegant, the long overhangs meant that the usable internal space of such a vessel was considerably less than a similar sized merchant ship. Therefore if this shape remained as a key requirement a much bigger hull would have to be built to successfully meet all of the operational requirements. This in turn directly affected the construction costs, which were finally estimated as being upwards of £3,000,000.

Clearly such a figure would have attracted an enormous amount of criticism and so an alternative approach needed to be found and quickly. The Assistant Director of Naval Construction, Mr A N Harrison felt that one of John Brown & Co.'s recent projects could provide an alternative approach as the John Brown & Co. Naval Architect, Dr John Brown (later Sir John Brown) explains.

'We had already built the two North Sea steamers *Amsterdam* and *Arnhem* for the Harwich to the Hook of Holland Service. They thought that those steamers would meet their requirements for size and thus Mr Harrison from the Admiralty and I worked hand in glove on the development of these steamers into what would become the Royal Yacht. The main hull itself required little change because we were essentially adapting what we already had in the form of the cross channel steamers apart from the development of a semi-bulbous bow. The bulbous bow effect was to give extra speed due to pressure effects around the hull. The Admiralty did not want to include a full bulbous bow within *Britannia*'s design so a modified version was adopted instead. The public rooms were altered to suit the Royal requirements which in turn meant that we had to redevelop the superstructure to accommodate those changes.'

Having seen Amsterdam *the Admiralty felt her design could form the basis of the design for the new Royal Yacht.*

(The University of Glasgow Archives)

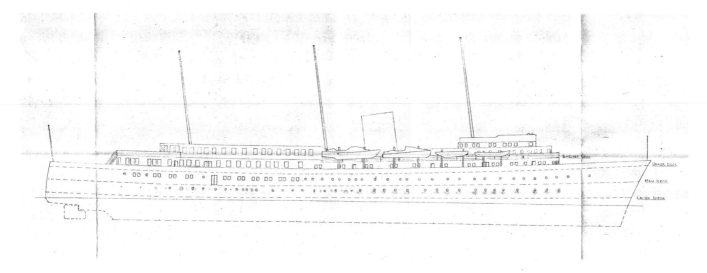

These plans, dated October 1951, clearly show the inspiration of both V&A and the North Sea Ferries Arnhem *and* Amsterdam *in the design of the new Royal Yacht.*

(© British Crown Copyright / MOD)

The new design also benefited internally from the steamers as Sir John Brown continues: 'The Admiralty wanted a steam turbine arrangement rather than anything experimental. These steamers had been fitted with this type of machinery, which proved acceptable.'

By the end of 1951 the Admiralty had prepared a new design together with a firm set of requirements which they presented to The King for his approval. These plans met his wishes for a Royal Yacht that was of a modern appearance but not unnecessarily futuristic. Having gained The King's approval the Admiralty were in a position to agree a timetable with John Brown & Co. for the construction of the new Royal Yacht. The Admiralty formally triggered the implementation of this programme with the telegram they sent to the Clydeside shipyard on

4 February 1952 informing them 'To proceed forthwith with detailed design and construction on fair and reasonable price basis of hull machinery of vessel referred to in your letter McN/MK dated 24th November.' These instructions were followed up in writing the next day. Interestingly, the desire to secure the vacant space within John Brown's meant that a final price had yet to be agreed. Sadly, this major milestone towards the commissioning of a new Royal Yacht was quickly overshadowed by the untimely death of the project's principal supporter, King George VI, only one day after his new ship had been formally ordered.

These plans, dated March 1952, show that by the time the order for Britannia *had been placed with John Brown & Co. her design had taken on a more recognisable profile, although there were still many changes to be made, such as the moving of the position of the mizzen mast.*

(© British Crown Copyright / MOD)

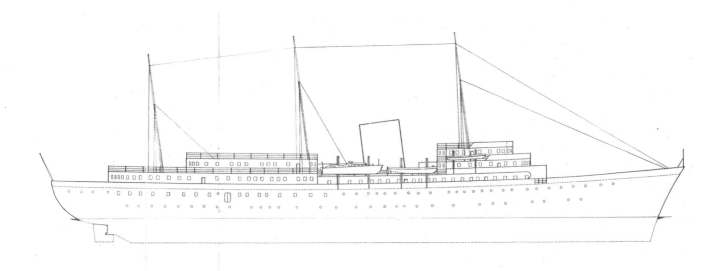

Chapter Two

THE YACHT WITH NO NAME

Building the Royal Yacht 1952–1954

On hearing of her father's death Princess Elizabeth – now Queen Elizabeth II – flew back to the UK. The Commonwealth Tour that she had just begun with Prince Philip was immediately suspended for the foreseeable future, thus leading to the recall of *Gothic* from Mombasa where she had been waiting to receive the Royal couple. As *Gothic* made her way to the UK, discussions were already underway about when the Tour should resume. Initially, it looked as though the Tour could be reorganised to begin early in 1953 thus requiring the services of *Gothic* again.[1] In the meantime *Gothic* underwent further work at Cammell Laird which was restricted to the minimum amount necessary for her to resume her normal commercial duties.

Among the early issues to be reviewed by the young Queen when she returned to London was the construction of the new Yacht. The Director of Naval Construction, Sir Victor Shepherd KCB RCNC, was given the honour of being granted an early audience with the new Queen. When she received him on 29 February 1952 they discussed the design of the Yacht. This marked the beginning of the close involvement of the Royal couple in the building of what was to become one of their homes for the next 44 years. The construction of the Yacht presented them with a unique opportunity to influence the design of a Royal palace because their other residences had all been built and fitted out by their predecessors. As a recently serving Naval Officer, Prince Philip

was able to inject new ideas into the project, drawing on his own practical experience. As he explains, some of these suggestions led to major revisions:

'Fortunately, the design had not been set in concrete so when the late King died I was able to get hold of the plans. I then looked at them to see if it was practical to accommodate the party that we were going to have in *Gothic* and thus big changes were made to the layout. There were also various practical details in need of change such as the lack of a pantry near the main saloon. They didn't have a main capstan aft which seemed to me to be essential. The two aft ladders were essentially the same as those carried by battleships. They each had to be dismantled by hand and hoisted onto the Verandah Deck. So I managed to persuade the Admiralty to redesign them so that power could be supplied to hoist them to deck level and then folded into the ship's side.

'The davits were to be manually operated as they were in *V&A* which meant that the lower deck had to be cleared to man the davits. So I told them that I thought it was a little out of date. So they said, "Well what do you suggest?" I told them that every merchant ship has got mechanical davits so put them in. "They will look terrible," came the reply.

"They may do but it will make life much easier."

Then I was asked what should they do with the fid-

dler. "What fiddler?" I inquired. They told me that in
V&A there was a fiddler who played while they hoisted the boats. So I told them the best thing they could
do was give him a pension as I didn't think he would be
needed anymore.'

By the time *Gothic* arrived in Liverpool docks on 19 May
1952[2] to be partially reconverted, her involvement in the
postponed Tour had yet to be confirmed. Ideally, the
revised Tour would be planned to include the use of the
new Yacht but the Prime Ministers of Australia and New
Zealand wanted The Queen to complete her Tour by
April 1954 so that they could hold elections. Whilst theoretically the new Yacht could be in Australia by the first
week of March 1954 it didn't leave any room for manoeuvre to allow for the inevitable minor delays that usually
result during the construction and work up of a new ship.
This left three other options. First, to use *Gothic* and
release her for commercial work in the meantime.
Secondly, to use a cruiser of the Australian or New
Zealand Navies. Thirdly, to charter a liner nearer the time
without converting it. If this third option had been pursued it would not have been the first time that an unconverted liner had been used to undertake the role of Royal
Yacht. In 1939 King George VI had planned to use the
battlecruiser HMS *Repulse* for his Tour of Canada and the
USA. However, as the departure date drew closer The

King grew more concerned about the withdrawal of a
powerful warship from the Fleet with the looming threat
of war. The Admiralty agreed with these concerns and
chartered the Canadian Pacific liner *Empress of Australia*
at short notice for The King's voyage across the Atlantic.
This time the use of an unconverted liner seemed financially and practically to be the most attractive option
because the use of *Gothic* would involve a holding fee of
£125,000 while a cruiser would offer a much lower standard of accommodation.[3] In the end, having discussed the
matter with the Cabinet, Winston Churchill favoured the
continued retention of an option on *Gothic* and releasing
her in the meantime for trade purposes.[4]

In Clydebank the building of the new Yacht, known
simply as ship No. 691, began with the laying of the keel
on 11 June 1952. As John Carney, who worked at John
Brown's as a shipwright, recalled, 'I set up the keel blocks
and the keel plates. On the day of the keel laying we simply lifted a keel plate and then laid it in place.' The conditions on board the embryonic hull form were quite difficult as Joe Brown, who worked as a ship's plumber at
John Brown's, explains:

'We put in a lot of the service pipes from when the keel
was laid and we would work within the claustrophobic
confines of the double bottom which only had about 3
feet of space. To ensure that the weight figures were

*The laying of the keel on 16
June 1952 for ship No. 691
– the future Royal Yacht*
Britannia.

(Courtesy of Forth Ports Plc)

accurate every pipe was weighed and numbered. If we trimmed a pipe to length the excess was taken to the weighbridge so that the weight of the off cut was taken off the Yacht's figures.'

Going on to describe more about those early days, Joe Brown continues:

'Nobody had a choice about working on the Yacht they were drafted on to her by the yard foreman. Although it was a Royal Yacht she was just another ship to us. If you looked at the keel and the double bottoms as they initially were she didn't look much. Therefore, when we went to work on her at that level it was no different from working on any other ship, starting work at seven thirty on a cold November's morning. However, one of the major differences between working on the Yacht, and some of the larger ships built in the yard, was that on board a larger ship there were longer periods working in an enclosed area in a degree of relative comfort. Whereas on ships like the Royal Yacht we were very exposed as she took shape. This was not helped by where they built the Yacht which was a semi-covered building berth. In the winter it became like a wind tunnel because the wind would come up the river and go through this place and I remember it being a pretty cold place in which to work.'

While the hull of the new Yacht was beginning to grow the Vice Controller (Air), Rear Admiral E M C Abel Smith CB CVO (later Vice Admiral Sir Conolly Abel Smith GCVO CB) was chosen as the first Flag Officer Royal Yachts (FORY) in July 1952. Admiral Abel Smith had entered the Royal Navy in 1912 and served during the First World War on board the battlecruiser HMS *Princess Royal* as a Midshipman. He became one of the first Fleet Air Arm pilots when he gained his wings in 1924 and spent most of his subsequent naval career in aircraft carriers, including HMS *Courageous* as the Commander (Air), and HMS *Triumph* as the Captain. He was not unknown to the Royal Family before his appointment as FORY because he had been appointed as King George VI's Equerry in 1939 and become a Naval ADC to The King in 1949, in which year he was also promoted to Rear Admiral before taking up his appointment as Vice Controller (Air) in 1950. In September 1952 his promotion to Vice Admiral became effective just as he was beginning to take up the reigns of the Royal Yacht Service. Describing what Admiral Abel Smith was like as FORY Captain Michael Barrow CVO DSO RN, who served in the Yacht between 1954 and 1956 as a Lieutenant recalled:

'Admiral Abel Smith was a real courtier and an extremely good Naval Officer in every sense of the word. Although he was a Vice Admiral and a Knight of the Realm he was very much one of us but we looked up to him enormously. He joined in absolutely everything and he was frequently in the Wardroom. He dressed, behaved and spoke like a courtier but one never thought that he had any airs or graces but he was just perfect for the job of FORY. As a ship's Captain he was everything one could wish for; he made himself scarce while we were in Portsmouth but he was never inaccessible and always available at the end of the phone. He would come back from his estate in Scotland about a week before starting a period of Royal duty. He had that very special quality of being fun in every sense of the word. He could be serious when he needed to be but usually there was a good twinkle in his eye whatever we were doing and one knew instinctively if things weren't going quite right because that twinkle wasn't there and he would momentarily look concerned. This didn't happen very often because he was very well served and he took the rough with the smooth.'

Although Admiral Abel Smith began to take up his duties as FORY towards the end of 1952 the post of Flag Officer Royal Yachts was not formally established until 2 February 1953 when the flag of Vice Admiral C Abel Smith CB CVO was hoisted in *V&A*.[5] Just as Admiral North had foreseen in 1946, *V&A* was to prove very useful over the coming year as the focal point for the rebirth of the Royal Yacht Service. One of the early priorities was to get the recruitment process underway as quickly as possible. An Admiralty Fleet Order was issued on 20 March 1953 appealing for volunteers to man the new Yacht and set out the conditions of service. One of those early recruits was Leading Seaman Tom Brydon (later Lieutenant Commander Tom Brydon MBE RN). Describing the state of *V&A* at that time he recalled:

'*V&A* was no longer being used as an accommodation ship but it wasn't quite the Royal Yacht either. The pre-war yachties who had returned to the *V&A* after the War were old by naval standards especially when you think that sailors retired when they were 45 years old. They were by this time in their upper fifties and early sixties because as a yachtie they could remain in the Royal Yacht Service until the age of 65. When I went on board for my interview I was one of three Leading Seaman who were interviewed for the job of Admiral's Coxswain. We sat in an anteroom and did not speak to each other. The anteroom itself was palatial compared to the Naval Barracks and I thought it was extremely ostentatious but in retrospect it was tastefully furnished.'

The interview went well for Leading Seaman Brydon as he was selected to become the Admiral's Coxswain and was sent to join the other Yachtsmen on board *V&A*. Looking back at those transitional days on *V&A* he said:

'When I joined *V&A* the complement consisted of the CO Lieutenant Commander R Woodford, the Engineer Officer Lieutenant Commander E J Sawdy, the Supply Officer Commander H L Cryer, Mr Pardy the Keeper & Steward, eight Chief Petty Officers, four sailors, and two Royal Marines. Because there were so few men on board, the four members of the Royal Barge's crew had their own cabin which previously had been a double cabin for two Petty Officers and was very comfortable. We used to play uckers (ludo) in one of the large passageways. In the Royal Apartments there was a carpet with a centre made up of black and white squares. We had two dice made out of leather which were filled with cotton waste. A cane waste paper basket was used to shake up the dice. The sailors, Chief Petty Officers and the two Royal Marines would play uckers about once a week usually on a Friday afternoon when there were no Barge duties. Although *V&A*'s 18 boilers were no longer operational, the walk along the centre walkway of the boiler room was like something out of science fiction. By then, we had diesel electric generators which provided the power not least to keep the bilge pumps working as by then she leaked like a sieve. When she had been used as an accommodation ship during the War a large number of empty tins had been dumped over the side. I soon discovered during one of my early dives under *V&A* that the sea bed was quite deep in these cans consisting mostly at sea bed level of Hits [herrings in tomato sauce], Pusser's Beans, Babies' Heads [steak and kidney puddings] all topped off with tons and tons of empty beer cans. At every low water she sat on the tins and the hull had made her own grave in the mud. If she settled on one of these tins on an old inlet it caused a leak, so rounds had to be done once an hour every night and I was on duty every fourth night.'

Although the new Yacht's hull had been taking shape over the winter months of 1952, the final design of the Royal Apartments had yet to be agreed. Prince Philip wanted the experience gained from both *V&A* and the preparation of *Gothic* for the forthcoming Commonwealth Tour to be incorporated into the layout of the new yacht, as he explains:

'Having been on board *V&A* and then looking at the layout sketches for the new Royal Yacht of where the cabins were and how they were arranged and who was accommodated where and how many there were provided an interesting comparison with what we were about to have on board *Gothic*. We came to the conclusion that what was needed was accommodation that would accommodate the party that we would have in *Gothic* as a broad concept of the numbers that would be required in the Yacht for that sort of occasion. Equally, there was not much in the way of office accommodation in *V&A* and there wasn't much provision made for women.'

To turn these objectives into reality the Admiralty supported John Brown's recommendation to appoint Patrick McBride, of the Glasgow based firm McInnes Gardner & Partners, to design the Royal Apartments. Patrick McBride seemed an obvious candidate for the job because he had been closely involved in the design work for the Royal Apartments in *Gothic*.[6] The Queen agreed to his

The embryonic hull form of the future Royal Yacht, 12 September 1952.   (John Brown & Co.)

appointment in a letter from her Private Secretary, Sir Alan Lascelles, to the Admiralty on 24 June 1952. However, before McBride could start work in earnest The Queen wanted to see him so that she could discuss her requirements for the Royal Apartments personally.[7] Describing McBride, and how he worked, the designer Sir Hugh Casson later recalled:

'He was a very splendid man and always wore a bowler hat, like all ship people. He didn't do many drawings, he used to say, "Dining room, French seventeenth century, 30 brocaded chairs, two pianos", and he'd specify things and then the contractors would produce ideas for him, people like Heals and the big furnishers, Waring and Gillows. Then he would make alterations, and then they'd do it. His fee per ship was £1000. I remember, he told me.'

However, when The Queen and Prince Philip received McBride at Buckingham Palace on 4 March 1953 to discuss his drawings and ideas the Royal couple weren't entirely happy. They decided that the best way forward would be to invite another designer to inject some fresh ideas, as Prince Philip explains:

'McBride had been the interior designer for the *Queens* [the liners *Queen Mary* and *Queen Elizabeth*] and what he came up with was another *Queen*. Neither of us thought it was appropriate because it was so elaborate. I had been involved with the Design Council so I approached the Director of the Council, Gordon Russell, and asked him to find someone suitable to which he asked what about Hugh Casson? I had met Hugh Casson because he was the co-ordinating architect for the Festival of Britain. He turned out to be a man of exquisite tact and somehow managed to charm McBride into doing a complete re-design and making him feel he had done it himself. The result was a very simple interior which owed most of its detail to Hugh Casson.'

The Queen formally approved Sir Hugh Casson's appointment in a letter from Sir Alan Lascelles to the Admiralty on 17 March 1953.[8] One of Sir Hugh's early priorities was to discuss his plans with the Admiralty as he later recalled:

'I told them that Prince Philip wasn't too happy about the interior to which they replied, "well, it's too bad, because the whole thing's pretty well finished. You can choose the lampshades if you like." So then I went up to Glasgow at the beginning of April and saw Patrick McBride who couldn't have been nicer and so to speak, understanding and professional. I said I was going to do a new set of drawings, which was really running a lawn mower over the Louis XVII adornments. I was going to concentrate on one-colour carpet throughout, which was sort of lilac/grey, and all the walls would be white. The only enrichments would be a bit of gilding on, in grand places, and the doors would be polished mahogany. I then did 4-foot by 2-foot watercolour perspectives of all the main rooms – the sitting room, the drawing room, state dining room, Prince Philip's study, The Queen's study/office, their bedrooms, the Royal guest rooms, the passages and the landings.'

While Sir Hugh Casson concentrated on preparing his drawings for the revised Royal Apartments John Brown's were making good progress with the building of the new Yacht itself. By March 1953 the hull was ready for the painters to transform her from an ordinary looking ship into a yacht fit for a Queen. When the Royal couple discussed the colour scheme for the Yacht at the beginning of 1953 they decided not to follow the example of *V&A*, which had a black hull, white topsides and buff funnels. They also decided against the colour scheme used for *Gothic*, which consisted of white for the hull and topsides with a buff band 1-foot wide at sheer strake level. The funnel was buff and black to reflect the colours of the Shaw Saville Line while the boot topping at the waterline was green. Instead they decided to use the paint scheme applied to their Dragon class yacht *Bluebottle* which had been given to them in 1948 as a wedding present, as Prince Philip explains:

'She was painted dark blue with a red boot topping which I thought looked rather smart so I suggested that *Britannia* should be painted in the same colour scheme. It caused more trouble than I expected because they couldn't find a paint that had a fast die. It did all sorts of strange things, such as turning the paint purple and it took a few years before a paint which retained its colour could be found.'

To complement the dark blue, a thin gold leaf band was applied around the top of the hull. This attracted considerable criticism over the years because of its higher cost as opposed to a painted line. However, when Admiral Abel Smith first proposed the incorporation of the gold leaf band in place of the red painted band he said that it would last much longer than conventional paint. Therefore, although the application of gold leaf would involve a much higher initial outlay it wouldn't prove to

The Queen and Prince Philip arrive at John Brown & Co.'s Clydebank shipyard to perform the launching ceremony for the new Royal Yacht.

(Courtesy of Forth Ports Plc)

be significantly more expensive over the long term. *V&A* was originally given an elaborate brass rope around the top of the hull. However, it was removed as part of the work to reduce her topweight, following her heeling incident in January 1900, and replaced with a gold line.

The task of producing a smart hull finish was hampered by the fact that *Britannia* was one of the last fully riveted ships to be built. This problem was solved on *V&A* by cladding the hull with teak planks to create a smooth finish. To disguise the rivets of *Britannia*'s hull it was decided to countersink the rivets into the shell plates and then chamfer off the heads. When this had been done the painters applied a composition with knives, which was skimmed across the length of the hull to provide a sound foundation for the six coats of paint. Although the result was impressive, its production had not been entirely straight forward, as Sir John Brown recalled:

'The Admiralty were very keen on getting a polished surface effect. We had to buff down the surface until we had a basis for the paint and then there was a lot of trial and error with the paint. The Admiralty sent up a specimen of the finish they wanted on a wooden panel but it wasn't going to work on a ship. However, in the end after a great deal of experimentation the workers achieved a wonderful finish.'

Surprisingly, when the painters had finished their work the feelings of the men who had built the Yacht began to change, as Joe Brown explains: 'up until then the Yacht had seemed just like any other ship but as the final touches were made to the hull coating prior to launch we all began to realise what we had been involved in. It might sound a bit blasé but that was the way we felt.' Pat Gilbride, who worked at John Brown's as a shipwright, continues, 'two weeks before the launch when she was ready to go I looked down the berth where she was built and I thought I was looking at a washing board. On the day of the launch she was immaculate. The reason for that was the painters.'

On 8 April 1953 the future Commander of the Yacht, Commander J S 'fish' Dalglish (later Captain J S Dalglish CVO CBE RN) was appointed to stand by her at John Brown's. Although the future Commander (E), Commander J Mott, had been standing by the Yacht since 1 December 1952, when he became the first officer to be appointed to her, it was unusual for a senior seaman officer to be appointed to stand by a ship so early in her life. This move was a reflection of the enormous level of work that still had to be completed to establish how the Yacht would be run once she was commissioned. Although the recruiting process for the new Yacht's company was well underway, this operation needed to be completed and a comprehensive training programme needed to be worked out and implemented. Describing his first days at the yard Captain Dalglish later wrote:

'Plain clothes were worn by us in the yard. We spent a lot of time in the drawing office where all the plans were kept. This first period was spent mainly learning the layout of the ship but soon we became involved in details such as the ship's ladders and methods of handling them, the motor boats, the awnings, the bridge, etc.'

Eight days later it was finally time for the Yacht to be launched on 16 April 1953. As she sat on the slipway awaiting The Queen and Prince Philip she looked immaculate. The men of John Brown's had worked hard but there were still a few anxious moments, as Sir John Brown recalls: 'the launch calculations were my responsibility ensuring that the Yacht would act properly. Thus any launch is a nervous time for the Naval Architect. Things can happen: the ship can get stuck half way down or it might not start at all and the rams have to be operated.'

A Royal launch is always a special occasion but this particular event was also historic because it was the first time that a reigning Monarch had launched a Royal Yacht. Interestingly, the first launching ceremony for a Royal Yacht was held for *Victoria & Albert* (III) in 1899. Previously, Royal Yachts were launched and then blessed at a later date. The last such ceremony to be performed by the reigning King or Queen was held on 14 April 1670 when King Charles II's wife Queen Catherine named the Portsmouth-built *Saudadoes*.

One of those in the vast crowd at John Brown's was a 15-year-old Jock Slater (later Admiral Sir Jock Slater GCB LVO DL) who subsequently served in the Yacht as a Season Officer and as Equerry to The Queen and eventually became First Sea Lord. Describing the Royal couple's arrival at the shipyard he said, 'people like me had hardly ever seen The Queen and Prince Philip before. They walked down the side of the Yacht before the launch and I remember the Clydeside workers shouting, "come on Lizzie give us a smile."' The Queen and The Duke of Edinburgh then made their way to the specially erected dais by the bows of the Yacht. Although the launch day was a cause for celebration The Queen was dressed in black thus observing the formal period of court mourning for her grandmother, the late Queen Mary, who had died on the evening of 24 March.

After a short service which was conducted by the Rev. John Mackay The Queen answered the question on everyone's lips at 1430 when she uttered the words, 'I name this ship *Britannia*, I wish success to her and to all who sail in her.'

'In the crowd we heard the words, "I name this ship", but the cheer was so great that we didn't actually hear the name and it took some time for the word to get round that she was called *Britannia*,' Admiral Slater remarked. Amid those great cheers The Queen released a bottle of Empire wine, which smashed across *Britannia*'s bows, and simultaneously pressed the launching key.[9] The Yacht began to move slowly, picking up momentum as she slid gracefully down the slipway and into the cold waters of the River Clyde to the accompaniment of sirens which were sounded by ships in the river. Until that moment *Britannia* had been known at John Brown & Co. as ship No. 691. Despite the veil of secrecy surrounding the new name it appeared a few weeks before as though others may know more than they should as Captain Dalglish explains: 'John Mott was suspicious the secret had leaked because of a ship's bell he had seen in John Brown's boardroom where the last four letters were visible "...ANIA"; this we found on closer inspection had belonged to *Aquitania*!' The Queen's declaration ended months of speculation as Sir John Brown recalls: 'there was tremendous interest in what the name might be. Most people seemed to be backing Victoria as the possible name. I certainly thought that the name would end with the letters IA but I had no real idea of what it would be.'

When the issue of the Yacht's name was discussed by the Admiralty's Ships' Names Committee on 17 March 1952 a short list of five names was considered consisting of Britannia, Commonwealth, Prince Royal, Royal Charles, and Princess Anne. The Admiralty advised against the use of Britannia because they felt that it wouldn't be wise to link the Yacht quite so closely with the UK alone when a name with wider associations could be used. Instead the Admiralty favoured the name Prince Royal which had been used by three previous warships in the Royal Navy. All three had enjoyed distinguished careers, the first serving as Sir George Ayscue's flagship in

the Four Days Battle in 1666. The second was the flagship of The Duke of York at the Battle of Solebay in 1672, while the third wore the flag of Vice Admiral Broderick at Lagos in 1759.[10] Despite this advice from the Admiralty the Royal couple chose the name Britannia and this was passed on to the Admiralty in a letter from Sir Alan Lascelles dated 5 November 1952.[11] This decision resulted in the renaming of the Royal Naval College (RNC) at Dartmouth. Since 1922 the RNC had reverted to its original name of HMS *Britannia* following the loss of *The King Edward VII* class battleship in the First World War. Therefore, to avoid any potential confusion between HMY *Britannia* and HMS *Britannia* the RNC became known by its present title of Britannia Royal Naval College (BRNC).

Having come to a halt in the waters of the Clyde, *Britannia* lay motionless until the yard's tug had moved into position to tow the Yacht round to her fitting out berth. For the launch itself *Britannia* flew the Union Flag, the Admiralty Flag and the White Ensign. However, The Queen had instructed that the Royal Standard would not be flown in the Yacht thus following the established practice since 1907 for the launching of HM warships. After watching *Britannia*'s movement to the fitting out berth The Queen and Prince Philip attended a brief presentation when Lord Aberconway, the Chairman of John Brown & Co. Ltd, presented The Queen with a set of six glasses and an antique goblet as a souvenir of the occasion.[12] The Queen then made a brief speech in which she paid tribute to the part her father had played in the building of the Yacht by saying:

'I am sure that all of you who are present here realise how much the building of this ship meant to the late King, my father. For he felt most strongly, as I do, that a yacht was a necessity and not a luxury for the Head of our great British Commonwealth, between whose countries the sea is no barrier but the natural and indestructible highway. With the wise advice of the Admiralty and of your firm, he laid the plans of a vessel, which should wear the Royal Standard in days of peace and which, in the event of war, should serve the cause of humanity as a hospital ship. Had he been in Clydebank today he would have been as delighted as I am to see what a fine ship our yacht promises to be.'

As *Britannia* continued to take shape on the River Clyde the eyes of the British public turned towards the Solent for The Queen's Coronation Fleet Review on 15 June 1953. In the absence of *Britannia* a substitute ship was clearly needed so the despatch vessel HMS *Surprise* was chosen towards the end of 1952. *Surprise* was originally

Britannia *takes to the water for the first time as she waits in the River Clyde for the tugs to move her to her fitting out berth.*

(John Brown & Co.)

laid down as part of the *Loch* class of anti-submarine frigates on 21 April 1944. However, shortly before her completion in September 1946, it was decided to reduce her armament and provide extra accommodation so that she could be used as the despatch vessel/yacht for the Commander-in-Chief Mediterranean Fleet. Despite the high profile nature of *Surprise*'s role in the Mediterranean it was still felt necessary to bring her back to Portsmouth for a short refit to bring her up to the standard of a Royal Yacht. With this new status in mind the Admiralty felt that *Surprise* should receive a new colour scheme. When they asked The Queen about this she opted for *Surprise*'s normal colour of light grey rather than the overall white scheme and buff funnel proposed by the Admiralty.[13] As part of the refit *Surprise* was completely repainted and the brasswork polished, while many of the other fittings were either chromed or cleaned up.

While the issue of *Surprise*'s colour scheme was quickly resolved, the question of a suitable review platform on board *Surprise* took more time to settle. Both The Queen and Prince Philip felt strongly that they should use a position aft.[14] The Admiralty were concerned that a platform on the top of the deckhouse aft of the funnel would be exposed to smuts and fumes from the low funnel while very few people would be able to see the Royal couple.[15] They subsequently agreed to the Admiralty's suggestion of building a temporary low bridge in place of the twin 4-inch gun turret in B position.[16]

By 8 June 1953 *Surprise* was ready to begin her new temporary role, so Admiral Abel Smith transferred his flag from *V&A*.[17] Over the coming days the Ship's company of *Surprise* were joined by members of the Royal Yacht Service including Keeper & Steward Mr Pardy and the Barge's crew. Court flags were broken out on the evening of 14 June when The Queen and Prince Philip joined *Surprise* alongside in Portsmouth prior to the Fleet Review the following day.[18] Because *Surprise* only had two masts, the three court flags normally used for the Sovereign were dispersed as follows; flag of the Lord High Admiral was worn at the fore, the Royal Standard was worn at the main, and the Union Flag was worn at the peak on a specially lengthened gaff. Before *Surprise* sailed from Portsmouth at 1500 further members of the Royal Family embarked including Queen Elizabeth The Queen Mother, Princess Margaret, The Duke and Duchess of Gloucester, The Princess Royal, The Duchess of Kent, Princess Alexandra and Prince Michael of Kent. By 1530 *Surprise* entered the review lines to sail past 14 miles of ships.[19] The battleship had been the dominate warship at the 1937 Coronation Fleet Review held for King George VI with 10 British battleships and 2 battlecruisers present.

During the 16 years since that review the battleship had virtually disappeared from the strength of the RN with only HMS *Vanguard* left in commission, which was present as the flagship of Admiral Sir George Creasey. By 1953 the place of the battleship at the head of the RN had been taken by the aircraft carrier. This was reflected

HMS Surprise *with The Queen and Prince Philip embarked passes the cruiser USS* Baltimore *during The Queen's Coronation Fleet Review off Spithead on 15 June 1953.*

(© British Crown Copyright / MOD)

Britannia *alongside her fitting out berth. The superstructure housing the Admiral's quarters and the cabins for the senior officers is now in place.*

(John Brown & Co.)

at the Fleet Review by the presence of seven RN carriers including the wartime HMS *Illustrious* and the RN's latest carrier HMS *Eagle*, which had been launched by The Queen on 19 March 1946. Another major change since 1937 was the development of the Commonwealth navies which were acquiring major warships, such as the Royal Australian Navy represented by their aircraft carrier HMAS *Sydney*, and the Indian Navy by their cruiser INS *Delhi*. Foreign navies were also represented through ships such as the USS *Baltimore*, the Soviet *Sverdlov*, and the Swedish *Gota Lejon*. Having reviewed the assembled ships, *Surprise* dropped anchor at the head of the Fleet in preparation for the flypast of the FAA before an evening of functions for the Royal party, culminating in a major fireworks display and the illumination of the ships. The Queen and Prince Philip were the only members of the Royal Family to stay on board overnight.[20] The next morning *Surprise* returned to Portsmouth for The Queen

and Prince Philip to disembark at 0920 thus concluding her short spell of Royal duty.[21]

With the successful completion of the Fleet Review FORY was able to turn his thoughts towards the arrangements for the forthcoming Commonwealth Tour which was going to involve the use of both *Gothic* and *Britannia*. Since the middle of 1952 *Gothic* had resumed her normal commercial work, which continued until August 1953 when she returned to the Mersey for Cammell Laird to re-convert her for Royal duty. The use of both ships during the course of the Tour led to the need to carefully pool resources. For example, in 1951 it had been planned to embark the Barge in *Gothic* for the original Tour. However, by the end of 1953 John Brown's wanted the Barge in Clydebank to check that it was fully compatible with *Britannia*'s davits. Therefore, it wouldn't be available, so arrangements were made by the Admiralty to provide an interim Royal Barge. It was decided to use a standard Flag Officer's pinnace, which had previously been used by the Commander-in-Chief Portsmouth. Before the interim Royal Barge was delivered by road to Liverpool it was refurbished and painted in 'Britannia blue' and given highly varnished cabin sides.

During August 1953 Sir Hugh Casson submitted his ideas to revise the Royal Apartments in *Britannia* to The Queen and Prince Philip. While he was waiting to receive their reaction to his perspectives Sir Hugh went to Portsmouth to visit *V&A* as he explains:

'I had a wonderful time going through all the furniture, the pictures, the china and the light fittings deciding what to recommend for re-use. We kept virtually all the pictures, which were a very good collection comprising both oil paintings and water colours. We decided to use all the dining room chairs, which were in very good trim and we designed a new dining room table.'

Sir Hugh was not the only visitor to *V&A* to select items for inclusion within *Britannia*, as Prince Philip continues:

'The decision had been taken to scrap *V&A* so I travelled to Portsmouth to salvage various items including the two binnacles which had originally been fitted in *Royal George*. We decided to fit one of the binnacles on the Verandah Deck and the compass card was wired to a gyro compass repeater. All the silver, linen and glass was also transferred to *Britannia*. While many items were saved from *V&A* not all of them were transferred to *Britannia*. For example, *V&A* had four big silver lanterns decorated with rope work and anchors. We took one to *Britannia* to hang in the lobby outside our sleeping cabins. I gave the other three to the three naval depots namely Portsmouth, Devonport and Chatham. The silver four-poster bed was sent to the Captain's house of RNAS Lossiemouth.'

At the beginning of September 1953 The Queen and Prince Philip invited Sir Hugh Casson to Balmoral to discuss his drawings. The Royal couple were happy with his work and didn't want to make any changes although he wasn't able to get his way entirely, as he recalled:

'I had long arguments with the Admiralty about whether there should be a fireplace or not. Because under Naval Regulations, if you have a fire on a ship, in a fireplace, you have to have a sailor stationed beside it with a bucket, in case it gets out of hand, so they didn't want a sailor standing in the Drawing Room all day. So we decided on an electric fire inside a simple marble frame.'

Later in the month the three masts were stepped in *Britannia* which triggered a small ceremony, as Captain Dalglish explains:

'It is a custom when masts are shipped in a vessel to place a coin beneath each, and in wooden ships these coins would get squashed flat by the weight of the mast.

In *Britannia* we had hollow masts, at the base of each of which the firm welded small containers for the coins. On behalf of all officers then standing by the vessel I placed under the main mast a Coronation Crown, together with a Coronation Shilling from myself, and my fellow Commanders did the same for the fore mast and mizzen when they were shipped.'

By the beginning of October 1953 *Britannia*'s maiden voyage was within sight when steam was raised for the first time. This was soon followed by a basin trial on 15 October when the main engines were run while the ship remained securely alongside. Senior Commissioned Engineer Vic Crompton (later Lieutenant Commander Vic Crompton MVO RN) joined *Britannia* shortly afterwards.

'I was told by the yard that I was not to wear a cap because I would be mistaken for a workman. All the gaffers wore bowler hats and the officers were expected to do the same. We weren't allowed to actually do anything because *Britannia* was being built under Lloyds' supervision. Thus we were only appointed to the Yacht as she neared completion so that we could get to know her systems.'

Fellow Warrant Engineer C L Cheffings (later Lieutenant Commander C L Cheffings BEM RN) continues, 'although we spent most of the time poring over plans if we had any comments that we felt were vital we told the Admiralty overseer and let him sort it out with the shipyard.'

In this view Britannia *is beginning to take on a recognizable profile. Her three masts have been stepped while the funnel has been craned on board and the superstructure is now in place.*

(John Brown & Co.)

By mid October *Gothic*'s re-conversion was finished and she sailed from the Mersey on 13 October 1953 to undertake a week of trials off Greenock. The machine for ironing stiff collars and dress shirts presented about the only problem during these trials when it developed an appetite for unsuspecting items of clothing, but this was soon fixed. On completion of the trials *Gothic* returned to Liverpool for a few days to load cargo before sailing to London on 26 October wearing FORY's flag which had been shifted from V&A that day.[22] FORY had joined the night before and his flag was to remain in *Gothic* until he joined *Britannia* the following year. In the intervening months FORY accompanied The Queen for the duration of her Commonwealth Tour in *Gothic*. For this Tour, *Gothic* was manned by a combined Ship's company consisting of Shaw Saville Line officers and ratings supplemented by the RM Band and a small naval party led by FORY. While this combination could have resulted in major problems due to the very different methods used by the RN and Merchant Navy the mixture worked very well, as Captain North Dalrymple-Hamilton CVO MBE DSC DL RN who served in *Gothic* as the Royal Cypher Officer recalls:

'Initially, the Shaw Saville Line officers found it strange to have Admiral Abel Smith and Commander

Still wearing the Red Ensign, Britannia *is put through her paces during her sea trials in November 1953.*

(© British Crown Copyright / MOD)

Madden (his Staff Officer) coming up on to the bridge from the passenger accommodation and telling them what to do; furthermore they had never had the experience of the importance of the precise timing, position, course and speed of a ship with The Queen embarked particularly when ships were joining the escort, firing salutes, etc. However, the Master, Captain David Aitchison, and his officers adapted very well to the "strange" ways of the RN, although the same could not always be said vice-versa. In the RN, when the ship was in sight of land or entering harbour her position was fixed constantly by taking bearings on points of land or prominent objects on shore, but this was not necessarily the practice in the Merchant Navy. I remember in particular our arrival at the Cocos Islands in the Indian Ocean where the approach to the anchorage is surrounded by coral reefs. Commander Madden was walking round the bridge taking bearings and plotting them on the chart and saying to Captain Aitchison, "do you realise that a reef is just off there?" However, Captain Aitchison, having looked at the chart and with his many years of experience knew exactly what he was doing and judged his approach perfectly by eye.'

The absence of FORY meant that the day-to-day responsibility for the final stages of *Britannia*'s fitting out and work up had to be delegated to another officer. The Admiralty was initially planning to appoint a Captain but Admiral Abel Smith was opposed to this, as Captain Dalglish explains:

As Britannia *was not due to be completed in time for the main part of The Queen's 1953/1954 Commonwealth Tour, the Shaw Saville cargo liner SS Gothic was chartered by MOD to be used for the Tour.*

(© British Crown Copyright / MOD)

'He did not want any stranger coming into an organisation which he had so carefully indoctrinated with Royal Yacht ideas and customs and anyway, he argued, it was the custom of the service that the second in command takes over if the Captain is not there. So the unbelievable happened and I received a new appointment: "…to serve in the acting rank of Captain while holding the appointment of *Victory* additional for HMY *Britannia* in continuation…to take effect from 10.11.53. You are also appointed HMY *Britannia* in temporary command on commissioning 7.1.54." What an astonishing stroke of fortune this was.'

However, before FORY finally left the UK in *Gothic*, *Britannia* began her Contractor's Sea Trials on 3 November 1953, thus making her first voyage under her own power. Explaining the objective of these trials Sir John Brown said: 'the trials were essentially machinery trials as the ship was complete by then. Any comments which the Admiralty had to make by then were merely relating to fine detail.'

On 9 November Prince Philip, accompanied by FORY and his Private Secretary Lieutenant Commander M Parker, joined *Britannia* off Fairlie, Ayrshire to witness the trials,[23] as Sir John Brown continues:

'Prince Philip was very definite in his opinions. A minor incident illustrates this. We were on trials bound for the Clyde. We had to pick him up early so one of the barges was sent to collect him. He came on board via an accommodation ladder. The barge was then lifted on board. The winch which was supposed to lift the barge stuck. Prince Philip who had been watching this said, "that's out anyway."'

The accommodation ladder arrangements also came under close scrutiny from Prince Philip as the temporary Navigating Officer for this period, Lieutenant Commander Hugh Knollys DSC RN, recalls: 'Prince Philip asked, "what is the delay in leaving?"

We told him, "We are hoisting the gangway Sir." The gangway was in fact being hoisted by about 25 Yachtsmen.

"Have you no electric winch?"

"No Sir, we have indented for one but we weren't allowed one."

"Oh rubbish, I'll see to that."'

Talking about the reason for his visit, Prince Philip said:

'I wanted to go to sea in her and see what she felt like. As we were in the Clyde there was no seaway to test the stabilisers so someone suggested that we could make the Yacht roll by switching on the stabilisers. This was not my first experience of using stabilisers because the frigate HMS *Magpie*, which I had commanded in the Mediterranean, had been fitted with them. It was also interesting to see how she reacted at speed, although she suffered from severe vibration between 12 and 18 knots all through her time in service. As a result we would cruise at 18 knots during the day at which speed she rumbled and 10 knots at night.'

In addition to the vibration the sea trials also revealed further noise which could be eliminated as Tommy Biggins, who was an engineer at John Brown's, recalls: 'while doing the speed trials on the measured mile off Arran we discovered the propellers were "singing". So we took her back to the Clyde and into dry dock. The propellers were removed and sent back to the machine shop.'

Following his brief visit to *Britannia* to observe the sea trials FORY returned to London to rejoin *Gothic* ready for her departure from London the next day. In the Admiral's absence the selection of future Yachtsmen continued apace. As before the interviews were held on board *V&A* with Acting Captain Dalglish presiding in place of the Admiral. As can be expected the interview process was a daunting prospect for many of the sailors. Surprisingly, it also presented the interview board with a few problems, as Captain Dalglish recalls:

'Our crew were all volunteers recruited by Admiralty Fleet Orders, and we had to interview them all and pick those who were to become Yachtsmen with us. The five Commanders formed the interview board and we had sessions at the three home ports after we had examined all the service certificates and weeded out those we did not think we wanted. We were able to be choosy, avoiding for example those who were not VG Superior [VG means Very Good Character, and Superior means Superior Professional Efficiency. Each was the highest assessment possible on a man's service record.] The interview process was intriguing and, with the senior ratings in particular, we had plenty of choice and found ourselves looking for people with unusual interests such as football referees, concert party experts, those who liked sailing or who played a lot of games or who had distinguished themselves in some way.'

One of those called forward for an interview at this time was Able Seaman Ellis Norrell (later Mr E Norrell MVO RVM), who later became the Coxswain and, after 34 years of continuous service, achieved the distinction of being the longest serving Yachtsman in *Britannia*.

'My father told me to put in for it but I didn't think I would stand a chance. I wasn't an outstanding Able Seaman just a solid steady plodder. My father who had served in *V&A* as a Boy Seaman told me it would be a quiet number – something which couldn't have been further from the truth! I was drafted to Singapore and I thought that I had missed my chance. However, after a month I got a signal calling me for interview back in the UK on board *V&A*. I nervously walked along the precarious pontoon to *V&A*. I didn't see anyone else there for interview and I was met by a kindly Chief Petty Officer and taken below decks to wait outside a door. I was then taken into what had been a stateroom with a large red carpet. At the end of the room was a long polished table behind which sat four Commanders. A single chair was placed several feet from the table and I was invited to sit down. Without thinking I brought the chair closer to the table. I wasn't asked about my seamanship, instead the questions were mainly about what my hobbies and sports were.

After the interview I did remember to replace the chair and returned to the Naval Barracks at HMS *Victory* to hear whether I had been selected. It was a very anxious period because each day certain people were being selected for the Yacht. For example, the laundry crew were selected early so that they could attend courses.'

Unlike the early Yachtsmen who were chosen, these later men were not accommodated on board *V&A*, instead they remained in the Naval Barracks at HMS *Victory*.

As the commissioning date drew ever closer the preparations for Royal duty continued apace. One of the aspects of *Britannia*'s routine, which would become a hallmark, was the execution of orders without verbal commands. As Captain Dalglish explains it required some imagination to achieve an effective system:

'Everything on deck had to be done in silence which demanded a lot of initiative. I introduced various gimmicks for signalling orders including hand-held wooden pads coloured red one side (for stop) and green the other (hoist or lower or go). I made all Seaman Officers become proficient in the quick semaphore used by signalmen for the passing of instructions. The Yacht would usually be required to dress ship as well as lowering boats and getting out booms on entering harbour. Instead of the customary G on a bugle, we had a G flag raised for standby and dipped for action. Perhaps my craftiest idea was the red hot notice board on which stop press notices could be displayed, e.g. "Muster for anchoring at 1200 instead of 1230". To draw attention to this, coloured discs were located at important points such as near the heads, dining room, messes, rec space, etc. One coloured disc could be replaced by a different one if circumstances changed again. The disc meant "Go at once to the red hot notice board". Chaps had to be on the ball. We did of course use telephones below decks as well. One forgets how much noise goes on in a ship until one has to stop it! All these plans were entirely worthwhile as we found out when entering Malta and going up the Thames where verbal orders would never have been heard above the sirens and cheering and fireworks and all that which greeted Her Majesty.'

As Peter Cain RVM, who joined the Yacht at this time as a Petty Officer, explains the Yachtsmen were able to see how impressive this silent talent was very early on.

'During the work up we were involved in a towing exercise with HMS *Termagent*. We had laid out all the wires and as *Termagent* approached from astern we could hear their Tannoy system chirping away because we were working so quietly. It was from that moment that we realised how impressive that was.'

Another procedure to require a little thought was the method of actually dressing and undressing ship as Lieutenant Commander Knollys explains: 'we all agreed that undress ship was very messy with flags lying about everywhere waiting to be cleared away. Someone had the ingenious idea of all the amidships flags appearing from and then subsequently being recovered back into the funnel. We tried it and it worked very well.'

Having made his final inspection of *Britannia*, Vice Admiral Sir Ralph Edwards KCB, Third Sea Lord and Controller, signed the form D.448 on 7 January 1954. With his signature on the paper the advance party could embark in *Britannia* and formally commission her.

'On assuming command I requested FORY by signal to convey to Her Majesty the following message:

"On behalf of the Officers and Yachtsmen who have commissioned Your Majesty's Yacht *Britannia* may I with humble duty assure Your Majesty of the pride with which we assume our duties and of our determination to make the ship happy and worthy of her task. James Dalglish, Captain."

'To which The Queen replied:

"I am very pleased to hear *Britannia* is now in commission and I look forward to joining her in Tobruk for, I hope, the first of many voyages in her. Elizabeth R.'" Captain Dalglish recalled.

That evening the rest of the Yacht's company travelled up from Portsmouth to Glasgow by train to join *Britannia* the following morning after breakfast.[24] As Peter Cain explains, the new Yachtsmen were in for a few surprises when they went down to their messes for the first time.

'In the Petty Officers' mess there were triple bunks and tables just like we had left in the RN. The bulkheads were typically RN bare with no form of decoration. The sailors being sailors went into the dockyard later on and fiddles were worked to obtain things to improve the standards of the messes. In our mess we wrote to the Mayors of major cities to ask for plaques which progressively filled in the deckhead. We then later built a bar so gradually over a number of years the messes became very comfortable.'

Captain Dalglish continues:

'We left Clydebank on 11 January, being seen off by vast crowds of shipyard workers and their families. They did so in complete silence, which is a custom dating back to when the departure of a ship from the yard inevitably meant men being laid off to unemployment. We did the requisite two hours steaming and I myself then signed the form accepting the Yacht from the builders on behalf of the Admiralty.'

Britannia at anchor in Scottish waters shortly after commissioning.

(© British Crown Copyright / MOD)

As part of Britannia's *work up she was taken in tow by the* T *class frigate HMS* Termagant *for an exercise.*

(© British Crown Copyright / MOD)

Thus the Officers and Yachtsmen were fallen in on the Verandah Deck and at 1530 the White Ensign was hoisted in place of the Red Ensign as the Yacht formally became HM Yacht *Britannia*.

Four days later *Britannia* hit the headlines when she was caught in a full gale. She had been anchored in the Clyde and the anchors began to drag. Captain Dalglish decided the best course of action was to ride out the gale at sea and thus spent the night cruising off Arran.

The period following her commissioning was very busy as Ellis Norrell recalled:

'It was very hard work when the Yacht came out, there was a lot of cleaning to be done – the brass had to be polished, the decks scrubbed. All of the various drills, such as man overboard, boat drills, and fire drills, had to be practised. We worked solid from morning to night with very little relaxation.'

Describing a few of the many tasks to be completed during this intensive period Captain Dalglish said:

'Our early trials were to do with our radio – especially the world-wide radio telephone capability. Other trials allowed the designers to check on conditions which had been calculated from wind tunnel and other trials on models, and trials of the Yacht's handling qualities, such as turning circle trials, and speed trials over a measured mile to find what engine revolutions gave what speeds. We lost no opportunity of manoeuvring at sea. I found a small, white, mooring buoy in Kilchattan Bay which would give me a ship-handling opportunity. The first time we approached it I was going too fast, being used to the astern power of a *Battle* class destroyer, we smacked it on the starboard bow and it scraped the full length of the Yacht. There were anxious moments waiting for it to come to the surface astern of us but it did "watch" all right. I at once turned and made another approach, going astern much sooner, and this time somewhat naturally we stopped a bit short.'

For the first three weeks of her time in commission, the Yacht worked up in her native waters of the Firth of Clyde, before heading north to round the top of Scotland for further trials and exercises at Invergordon and later Rosyth. During her final day in Rosyth a trial was carried out – the embarkation of the Rolls Royce. The garage for the Rolls Royce was located on the Boat Deck inboard of the Barge and had to be stowed on a tailor-made transporter some 20 feet long and weighing 2½ tons,[25] which ran on a trackway sunk into the teak deck. To embark or disembark the Rolls Royce, the Barge had to be lowered on the davits so that the transporter could be craned on board or ashore.

On the afternoon of 15 February Britannia slipped her moorings in Rosyth to head south for the next stage of her work up at Portland. Interestingly, it was noted in the Admiral's Diary that, as she passed under the Forth Bridge, a penny landed on the Flag Deck from the train crossing the bridge.[26] Discussing Britannia's work up at Portland Captain Dalglish said:

'One of the objectives of our working up plan was to make sure that we practised every possible routine or manoeuvre we expected to have to do in the months ahead. We had, for instance, to rehearse the arrival in Grand Harbour, Malta, where one turns between two buoys and ends up secured to both, also the straight securing to two buoys in a tideway as when we reached the Pool of London. We would often need to refuel from a tanker at sea. Jackstay transfers of mail, or stores, or personnel, at sea would be required. Some of this we had practised in the north, especially during a day we had with a destroyer in company, but our eight days at Portland were earmarked to complete it all. We were lucky to have wonderful co-operation there from Captain Frank Hopkins in HMS Tyrian, and we worked with other ships, and a tanker, and a lot was achieved. We came in for a lot of press attention from boats and helicopters but it was good to get used to being in the public eye because people were critical of how we looked and what we did. Michael Dunlop achieved a nice bit of one-upmanship the first time we went to a buoy in Portland when many in other ships after we arrived asked how we had painted the bridles when they had not seen us do it. Ships normally put a chap over the side and do this after securing, but Michael had had the bridles ready painted before we entered harbour. Simple when one thinks of it.'

At the end of an eventful cruise from the Clyde and work up off Portland, Britannia entered her home port of Portsmouth for the first time on 26 February 1954.[27]

Although Britannia was essentially complete, the Royal Apartments still required a lot of finishing work to make them habitable for the Royal party when they joined in Tobruk. The principle problem was that some of the furniture and fittings identified by Sir Hugh Casson for the final layout were actually in use on board Gothic, so additional items of furniture had to be found for the voyage to Tobruk and back. While the dockyard men finished off Britannia, Captain Dalglish gave two weeks leave to both watches. By the end of March Britannia was finally ready and it was time for the various officials from both the RN and Buckingham Palace to carry out their own inspections to ensure that she was ready for her first Royal assignment.

Britannia's first Commanding Officer, Acting Captain Dalglish, who oversaw the final stages of Britannia's fitting out, followed by her work up and the voyage to Malta, where he was relieved by Vice Admiral Conolly Abel Smith and reverted to his former role as The Commander.

(©British Crown Copyright / MOD)

Prince Charles and Princess Anne wave to The Queen Mother and Princess Margaret as the Yacht leaves her moorings in Portsmouth. Their Governess, Miss Peebles, and The Queen's Naval Equerry, Lt Cdr D Loram RN, can be seen in attendance on the Royal children.

(© British Crown Copyright / MOD)

During the voyage out to Malta Prince Charles was invited to take the helm of Britannia *using the wheel which came from King Edward VII's racing yacht of the same name. From left to right: A/PO Dobson, CPO Breach and Prince Charles.*

(© British Crown Copyright / MOD)

While The Queen and Prince Philip were away in *Gothic* they had left the young Prince Charles and Princess Anne in the UK with Queen Elizabeth The Queen Mother and Princess Margaret. It was decided that the Royal children would join *Britannia* when she sailed from Portsmouth so that they could be reunited with their parents in Tobruk and accompany them home. The voyage from Tobruk was to include the final stages of The Queen's extensive Commonwealth Tour, with visits to Malta and Gibraltar, before returning to the Thames to disembark the Royal Family in the Pool of London.

At last the moment the Yachtsmen had been waiting for arrived on 14 April 1954 when *Britannia* began her first spell of Royal duty. Captain Dalglish took the opportunity to have a final few words with the Yachtsmen before the arrival of the Royal party as he recalled:

'On the great day of commencing Royal duty I said a few final words to the Yachtsmen about how I wanted them to conduct themselves when The Queen was with us. I explained the formal kind of Royal bow, with just the head alone, and how one should proffer an elbow with one's hand on one's hip if Her Majesty needed it, e.g. getting out of a boat (and not grab her by the hand!); and particularly I wanted them not to be shy when meeting her, as they inevitably would round the Yacht, but greet her with a bow and always with a smile. They should not speak until she spoke to them and one always had to say ma'am.'

The first members of the Household arrived at 1130, including the Master of the Household, Major Mark Milbank, and Prince Philip's Treasurer, Lieutenant General Sir Frederick Browning. The Royal children travelled to Portsmouth with their Grandmother and Aunt, arriving at Pitchhouse Jetty at 1535, where they were met by Commander-in-Chief Portsmouth before embarking in *Britannia* shortly afterwards. Once on board, The Queen Mother and Princess Margaret were taken for a tour of the Yacht. For The Queen Mother it must have been a bittersweet moment because, as Queen she had been closely involved in the development of the project that resulted in the Yacht's construction. After their tour The Queen Mother and Princess Margaret took tea with the Royal children before disembarking at 1650 and leaving them in the capable hands of the Yacht's company.[28]

Watched by The Queen Mother and Princess Margaret from the quayside, *Britannia* let go her moorings at 1700, making her way past the battleship HMS *Vanguard* which had been used for the 1947 South African Tour. Crowds gathered along the sea front at Portsmouth to get a glimpse of the new Yacht and cheered as she sailed past them. To underline the enormous scrutiny that *Britannia* was exposed to, Captain Dalglish recounts the signal he was sent by the Commander-in-Chief Portsmouth about her departure. 'The signal read: "Your getaway was first class but completely spoiled, to a seaman's eye, by three members of the Household staff loafing about without even a cap on! It is as well to look to this on future occasions. Bon voyage."'

Although Captain Dalglish had the unenviable responsibility for the safety of the Royal children until the embarkation of FORY, he was physically unable to discharge this duty as well as commanding the Yacht. Therefore, he had to delegate this responsibility during the voyage to Malta as he explains:

'I chose two seamen and two stokers formally by name as lifeguards, one seaman and one stoker for Prince Charles and ditto for Princess Anne, one of them to be in close attendance whenever his child was outside the Royal Apartments. Mr Pardy was to have one of the Royal Stewards doing the same in the Royal Apartments but he could be withdrawn by arrangement with either Miss Peebles (Governess) or Mrs Lightbody (Nurse) or Miss Mabel Anderson (Asst Nurse) or the children's detective.'

Describing some of the activities that were organised for the Royal children, Ellis Norrell remembered: 'the children were made very welcome and they were all over the Yacht. Treasure hunts were organised and they washed the paintwork. The nannies kept an eye on it all not least to ensure they didn't hear the wrong words!' Talking about

To keep the Royal children fully occupied during the eight-day voyage to Malta, they were given various tasks such as cleaning one of the Yacht's life rafts.

(© British Crown Copyright / MOD)

Escorted by landing craft, Britannia *enters her first port outside UK waters as she arrives in Grand Harbour, Malta.*

(© British Crown Copyright / MOD)

her own memories of this trip Princess Anne recalled: 'they had an amazing model of the Yacht that I peddled around the deck which was an astonishing piece of kit, and a rubber swimming pool. I don't ever remember having a shortage of things to do.' As he explains, this trip gave The Prince of Wales an insight into some of the RN's customs: 'I went down to watch the rum being rationed. I always remember being hugely taken by the smell of rum and I have always had a thing about rum ever since because it smelt so delicious. It was so much a part of the old navy.'

During the passage to Malta, The Queen's new Naval Equerry, Lieutenant Commander D Loram RN (later Vice Admiral Sir David Loram KCB CVO), took the opportunity to carry out some last minute checks, as he recalls:

'We were very conscious of the fact that *Britannia* was going to be a hospital ship in times of tension. However, until she was completed the plans for her conversion were based entirely upon the drawings. So we were asked to evaluate the number of beds to be accommodated, etc., and come up with preliminary plans that could be made to work having seen the ship for real. Therefore, Lieutenant General Sir Frederick "Boy" Browning, Major Mark Milbank and I carried

The Queen and Prince Philip embark in the Yacht for the first time on 1 May 1954 for the final stages of their extensive Commonwealth Tour.

out a recce of every Royal and Household cabin and space to produce plans for further consideration. We also checked the cabins for creaks and groans, etc.'

On 22 April at 0900 *Britannia* sailed into her first overseas port as she entered Grand Harbour, Malta at the start of a six-day visit. Describing the entrance Captain Dalglish said: 'we were preceded by the QHM in his barge and escorted by 10 landing craft and witnessed by vast crowds everywhere. I made a sternboard up Dockyard Creek to secure between two buoys there. Halfway up harbour I received a signal from Mountbatten that he intended to come on board immediately.' As the Commander-in-Chief of the Mediterranean Fleet, Admiral Earl Mountbatten of Burma's HQ was in Malta. During *Britannia*'s visit to the island both the Earl and Countess Mountbatten spent time with the Royal children. Despite their young age they had an active programme which included visits to the aircraft carrier HMS *Eagle* and the cruiser HMS *Gambia*. Talking about his own memories of this visit The Prince of Wales recalled:

'We went on board *Eagle* and the Ship's company arranged the most marvellous diversions such as fishing out of port holes. I remember that there was a tug on the line and I wound it in and there was a present on the end of the line. I also remember looking out of the porthole at one stage and seeing a sailor's arm coming out of a porthole on a lower deck tying something on to the line, which was quite funny. They had also made large models of a destroyer or cruiser which my sister and I could sit in and pedal around the flight deck of *Eagle*.'

The Royal children also had a tour round the harbour in one of the landing craft which was being used to guard the Yacht. There were engagements ashore as well, including tea with the Governor of Malta, Sir Gerald Creasy, and a picnic with the Mountbattens at St Peter's Pool.[29]

On 27 April *Gothic* anchored off Aden at 0700 and FORY, together with Commander Madden and Commander Mackinzie, left to fly to Malta to join *Britannia*. Thus at 0750 the next morning Admiral Abel Smith embarked to relieve Captain Dalglish as the Commanding Officer of *Britannia*. FORY's flag was hoisted for the first time in *Britannia* at 0800 and Captain Dalglish removed his fourth stripe to revert to his former role as the Commander of the Yacht. That afternoon *Britannia* headed south for Tobruk.[30] Two days later *Britannia* arrived in Tobruk Harbour on 30 April and anchored to await the embarkation of The Queen and Prince Philip.[31] While he waited to be reunited with his parents, Prince Charles took a keen interest in the unfamiliar landscape as he recalls: 'I can just remember the desert scene with all the detritus of war which was still there in great rusting heaps. Through my binoculars I could see a camel train in the distance.' The following morning The Queen and Prince Philip inspected war graves and had coffee with King Idris of Libya in his Palace before travelling in the Barge to embark in *Britannia* for the first time. Thus at 1146 court flags were broken for The Queen as she stepped on board and, within half an hour, *Britannia* had weighed anchor and was heading north for Malta.[32] For the majority of the Yachtsmen on board *Britannia* this was their first taste of Royal duty with The Queen, as Peter Cain recalls: 'it really hit us because none of us had been prepared for the retinue and the staff and the high powered people that accompanied The Queen and Prince Philip. Because we were naval personnel we weren't used to having civilians on board, not least the ladies.'

The next morning on 2 May Admiral Abel Smith took the church service in the Royal Dining Room as there was no embarked Chaplain as part of the Yacht's company. The issue of a Chaplain had been discussed in 1953 but the matter was quietly dropped at the express wish of The Queen. She felt that the appointment of a Chaplain was not a good idea on several grounds. Instead she said that if she required the services of a Chaplain one could be embarked from the escorting warship.[33] During the course of the service Admiral Abel Smith said a prayer for the Royal Family which didn't mention everyone by name, as Lady Pamela Mountbatten (later Lady Pamela Hicks), who was The Queen's Lady-in-Waiting recalls:

'When the Admiral read the prayer he said, "…we humbly beseech thee to bless our gracious Queen, Queen Elizabeth The Queen Mother, Philip Duke of Edinburgh, Charles Duke of Cornwall and all the Royal Family…" When he came to the end he paused and a furious small voice from Princess Anne was heard to say, "he hasn't prayed for me, Mummy." Everyone had such giggles the service nearly came to an end.'

Shortly after the morning church service, the sight of the Mediterranean Fleet, thundering over the horizon at 25 knots led by the Commander-in-Chief Lord Mountbatten, came into view. The handling of the Mediterranean Fleet at such speed as it greeted the Yacht was a truly impressive sight. Describing the background to this Fleet manoeuvre and its subsequent execution, the Navigator of HMS *Chaplet* of the 1st Destroyer Squadron, Lieutenant David Smith RN (later Captain D T Smith OBE RN) recalled:

'Lord Louis assembled the Commanding Officers and the Navigators of the ships taking part in the steam past in the Manoel Island Theatre for a briefing where he told us exactly how he intended to manoeuvre the Fleet. The Fleet would be arranged in two columns with the cruisers in the van and the destroyers and fast

Britannia, as seen from one of the warships as they execute their steam past. The Queen and Prince Philip are standing next to the box on top of the Compass Platform. This box was only erected for this occasion and the passage up the Thames.

frigates astern. The columns were to be only two to three cables apart as they steamed towards the Yacht at 25 knots. Lord Louis said that the frigates and destroyers were to be stationed one and a half cables apart and he had no objection to Commanding Officers being within this distance but God forbid anyone being outside as this would make each line that much longer and more difficult to manoeuvre. When I originally read these orders I was horrified, but when Lord Louis stood up and told us what he wanted us to do it was quite clear that was how we were to behave. Therefore, any sense of fear disappeared because we knew that we would be doing what we had been told to do.

'So on the day we had ships very close together at high speed converging on the Yacht with one column going down each side. My own ship was half way down one column and I recall how the washes of the ships and the wash of the Yacht were interacting and bouncing off *Britannia*. The Yacht was rolling quite heavily. During the approach we had two occasions when we had to order stop engines and order a momentary astern movement which caused the necessary propeller drag to slow the ship down before steaming forward again. Obviously, this had a knock on effect down the line but we all survived and nobody disgraced themselves. We then reversed direction and came back with Lord Louis deploying one column on each side of the Yacht for the ceremonial approach to Malta. It was a very interesting Fleet manoeuvre that worked very well on the day and was high speed manoeuvring in the traditional sense.'

Describing the scene from on board the Yacht Captain Dalrymple-Hamilton recalled: 'we were steaming at 15 knots and while the cruisers were passing very close up our starboard side we had to keep 20 degrees of port helm on to counter the suction effect and to keep the Yacht on course. It was a most dramatic manoeuvre.' Talking about his own impressions of the steam past The Prince of Wales remarked:

'One of my most vivid recollections of this trip was the steam past of the Mediterranean Fleet. It was incredible standing on the Verandah Deck. Lord Mountbatten was determined to do the steam past faster and closer than anyone else. Even as a small person I found it unbelievably stirring with every Ship's company cheering as they steamed past. Even thinking of it now moves me greatly.'

In Philip Ziegler's biography *Mountbatten* he quotes Admiral Abel Smith as having remarked: 'at no time during this World Tour either before or afterwards, had quite the same thing been seen. The dash, timing and setting were things quite different and superior to other occasions. Her Majesty and The Duke of Edinburgh went out of their way to remark on the magnificent exhibition.' After the steam past the Commander-in-Chief transferred from his flagship HMS *Glasgow* to *Britannia* by jackstay to report the Mediterranean Fleet to The Queen. Once on board the Yacht The Queen gave Lord Mountbatten permission to exercise tactical command of the Fleet and in the afternoon the Royal party were treated to a series of

Britannia passes the aircraft carrier HMS Eagle *while the port column of the Mediterranean Fleet can be clearly seen in the background.*

(© British Crown Copyright / MOD)

diving manoeuvres by submarines close to *Britannia*. These were followed by flying displays by aircraft from *Eagle* and a flypast of RAF Shackletons based at RAF Luqa. The next morning the Mediterranean Fleet, which had been escorting the Yacht overnight, reduced its speed for *Britannia* to pass between the two lines of warships to enter Grand Harbour. As *Britannia* passed the St Elmo breakwater at 0900 on 3 May vast crowds were waiting on every available vantage point to watch her arrival, which was most impressive, as Admiral Sir David Loram recalled: 'Admiral Abel Smith went straight to the two mooring buoys and moored the Yacht without any problems. It was all the more impressive when you consider that he had had virtually no experience of handling *Britannia* beforehand.'

A day later *Gothic* entered Grand Harbour with the RM Band playing on her deck for the last time. She secured to a buoy close to *Britannia* so that the Yachtsmen could transfer the furniture from *Gothic's* Royal Apartments and the last of the Royal baggage to *Britannia*. At the same time Prince Charles and Princess Anne were taken for a look round *Gothic* while their parents were doing official engagements ashore. After a few hours of hard work the Yachtsmen had reduced her Royal Apartments to an empty shell enabling *Gothic* to get underway again at 1530.[34] Although most of her cargo was bound for Liverpool, *Gothic* was heading for London first to land The Queen's presents and the two Barges which had been embarked for the Tour. For those who transferred from *Gothic* to *Britannia* there was a significant change in pace, as Lieutenant Commander Brydon who had served as part of the Barge's crew in *Gothic* remarked:

'In the seven months we had been in *Gothic* there had been very little naval routine as the ship had been run by her normal Merchant Navy sailors. In all we only had 15 trips in the Barge so the pace of life on board wasn't exactly hectic for the Barge's crew but this changed when I joined *Britannia* in Malta. I arrived on board *Britannia* with a kit bag over my shoulder, a hammock under my arm and a suitcase in my hand. At 1100 I was shown to my mess deck and by 1400 I was sitting in a bosun's chair clearing a halyard that had fouled the sheave in the truck at the top of the main mast.

'Perhaps one of the biggest adjustments for me between the two ships was the absence of verbal instructions – a fact which hit me while I was suspended about 122 feet above the water clearing the main halyard. Suddenly we were confronted with a system of no verbal orders and a minimum of noise. Instead we had to rely on the Yacht's daily routine with the published Daily Orders amended as necessary by red hot notices pinned to squares of red baize on the main notice boards.'

As can be imagined the requirement to complete one's work without verbal instructions required the use of other methods to convey what was required of the Yachtsmen, as Lieutenant Commander Brydon continues:

'If the Yachtsmen were fallen in on either the forecastle or the quarterdeck while entering or leaving harbour they normally stood at ease. However, if we passed another ship and they piped the side or dipped their Ensign the Yachtsmen were brought to attention by a series of hand claps. One clap to draw their attention, two claps to come to attention, three claps to stand at ease. On occasion, throwing a heaving line from ship to shore could present problems. Later as the Forecastle Petty Officer one particularly difficult manoeuvre springs to mind. This was going alongside at Halifax, Nova Scotia when the ship stopped in the water with the bows too far away from the jetty. With the strong tidal stream pushing the bow of the Yacht farther away from the jetty Able Seaman Dennis Ivory and I resorted to our party trick of jointly throwing an extra long heaving line to the shore party of Canadian dockers. This evolution consisted of me with a large coil of line with the monkey's fist attached in my left hand, and Dennis with his coil in his right hand. With a good synchronised throw, the line almost at full extent landed on the jetty with a thud, but the weight of the line was gradually pulling the rope back off the dockside. The dockers were too interested looking at the occupants of the Royal Deck to notice the heaving line and in sheer frustration I shouted "Oi!" Immediately, I could feel every pair of eyes on me and I was afraid to look up at the Bridge not least because the Royals were invariably up on the Royal Bridge going in and out of harbour – the matter was never raised.'

After five full days of engagements around Malta for The Queen and Prince Philip, *Britannia* sailed on 7 May[35] for Gibraltar and a two-day stopover before returning to England and the tremendous welcome that awaited her. As *Britannia* sailed up the Channel on 14 May the Home Fleet replaced her previous four-ship escort for the voyage round to the Thames. This encounter was carefully recorded, as Captain Dalrymple-Hamilton explains:

'Lady Pamela Mountbatten was one of The Queen's Ladies-in-waiting. I found her taking notes on the upper deck so I asked her what she was doing. She replied, "Oh Daddy has told me that I have got to let him have a full report on what the Home Fleet did when they met the Yacht."'

As part of her report Lady Pamela wrote:

'We were joined by 18 ships of the Home Fleet. *Vanguard* had managed to limp along and looked very lovely but they were all far too far away to be able to see them properly without peering through binoculars. There was not the faintest glimmer of excitement or dash about their arrival. In fact they remained so far away that although they were our escort a busy little coastal tanker was able to puff its way down between us and them.'

Among the many craft that had turned out to greet the new Yacht were two rather special sailing craft as Lieutenant Commander R L Hewitt (later Commander R L Hewitt LVO RN), who was to subsequently serve in *Britannia* as the Commander (E), recalls:

'*Bluebottle* sailed in company with Uffa Fox in *Coweslip* to meet *Britannia*. We arrived at Yarmouth in time for an excellent lunch at the George Hotel and left again at 1445, slipping out through the Needles Channel with the last of the ebb. *Coweslip* lowered her sails and was taken in tow, while her crew came aboard *Bluebottle* for tea. By 1700 both yachts were in station on *Britannia*'s anticipated track. Owing to poor visibility we kept closer to the Bridge Buoy than was originally intended and consequently failed to make our rendezvous with Prince Philip's aircraft – as we had previously planned with Peter Horsley. Soon *Britannia* loomed through the mist, looking quite magnificent. Some yachtsmen have criticised the lines of the Yacht, but as she steamed towards us with deceptive speed she appeared an elegant, yet purposeful ship. There was barely time to complete the formalities of our greeting before she had swept past, only a few feet away, with The Queen and Prince Philip waving from the deck above us. We heard Prince Philip shout, "Don't get your feet wet!" They had been warned of our presence by Mike Parker, who had spotted two likely blips on the radar screen – right in *Britannia*'s path. In fact we had quite a job to avoid the close escort of Fast Patrol Boats, who had not been told of our intentions!'

In the waters of the Solent off Yarmouth, Isle of Wight, *Britannia* slowed down at 1815[36] to embark a small party, including the Prime Minister, Sir Winston Churchill and the designer of the Royal Apartments, Sir Hugh Casson, for the remainder of the voyage to London.

'I had received a telegram from Tobruk saying, "We love the ship. Please join us on the trip home, from the Isle of Wight." At 1755 *Britannia* came into view looking impossibly tall and heraldic with escort. In five minutes she was on top of us. At 1910 Southsea Castle fired a Royal Salute as *Britannia* approached more vessels. We passed down a double line of yachts, motor boats, crowded paddle steamers and finally warships, to the sound of gun salutes and cheers,' Sir Hugh Casson recalled.

Although the Royal couple were happy with Sir Hugh Casson's work, his presence on board for the final stages of the voyage home provided a good opportunity for them to discuss some of the finer details of his work which needed to be reviewed, as he explains:

'By 2300 the film was over when we repaired to the anteroom for drinks. Prince Philip then took me off to his Sitting Room for half an hour's discussing of points to alter or reconsider. The Queen joined us after 10 minutes, explaining that Winston was the centre of attraction (curious how even in the presence of Royalty he dominated the scene) and she could safely leave him. We all three sat on the main stairs and discussed various suggestions for improvements, then had a quick go round some of the main rooms before finishing in the Sun Lounge, which apparently was a room they used a great deal and which they wanted to be given a more domestic character. By then it was midnight and The Queen said she was going to bed as we passed her door. Prince Philip and I continued in Household cabins two decks down for half an hour more before he disappeared.'

In the early hours of the morning of 15 May *Britannia* anchored in Margate Roads for a few hours before weighing anchor to begin the final leg of her passage into London.[37] Describing the atmosphere on board the Yacht as the Royal party neared the end of a long, exhausting, yet successful Commonwealth Tour, Sir Hugh Casson wrote in his diary:

'Everyone obviously very happy to be nearly home. HM and HRH occasionally disappear to wave or salute on top platform, but usually return as the wind outside is very cold. Children absorbed for nearly one hour in telephoning to each other on the ship's telephone, with occasional forays outside. Through HM's binoculars I can see Norman Wilkinson sketching our progress up river on bridge of escorting FPB. Parker and I agree to send him an encouraging signal, which is gracefully acknowledged. Traffic by now much thicker, noise of cheering and hooting almost continuous.'

As the Yacht passed RNC Greenwich the officers and staff lined the College terrace and gave three cheers. This was just typical of the enthusiastic welcome experienced that day, as Captain Dalglish recalls: 'every bit of land we passed was crowded with people and we must have seen millions that day; hundreds of boats crammed to the gunwales; everyone cheering and waving; sirens hooting and general noise (which made us thankful once more that we could do our stuff in silence).' Sir Hugh Casson continues:

'By Greenwich the entourage kept more in the background to avoid confusing the crowds. The Queen and Prince Philip disappeared for good to the top platform. The noise was by then deafening – almost impossible to speak on the upper deck. Two men in trilby hats boil-

ing shrimps in a small boat took a few moments to give us a wave. I continually crossed from port to starboard in fear of missing something. The Swedish liner *Orcades*, crammed to the davits, Finnish timber boats, gas colliers, the occasional change of note in cheering indicated convoys of flag-waving children. The whole experience was at once deeply moving and yet I felt completely detached and dreamlike.

'I then retired inside the Royal Bridge for the final dramatic moments of passing through Tower Bridge, which spelled out the words "Welcome Home". The Lord Mayor was visible in an open boat, with upturned oars and fur hat upraised in greeting. The Queen Mother and Princess Margaret were just visible on the landing stage.'

Captain Dalglish continues: 'I particularly remember Vivian Dunn, Principal Director of Music of the Royal Marines conducting the Royal Yacht Band, played "Rule Britannia" as we passed under Tower Bridge as he had promised me he would do.' It was at that moment that the cranes lowered their jibs in salute to the new Yacht. 'It really was a wonderful homecoming. We got secured fore and aft, dressed overall, and two ladders down precisely eight minutes after passing Tower Bridge. We had never done it so fast before and that set the seal on everything we had been training for,' Captain Dalglish concluded.

Reflecting upon the impression made by the new Yacht The Queen's Assistant Private Secretary of the time, Lieutenant Colonel Edward Ford CB MVO (later Lieutenant Colonel Sir Edward Ford GCVO KCB ERD DL) said, 'the effect of *Britannia* was that she was a real prestige maker and that one felt that a country whose Head could travel in that way was really worth something.'

The arrival of *Britannia* in the Pool of London successfully concluded The Queen's first major overseas tour and made her the first reigning British Monarch to circumnavigate the world. Before disembarking, The Queen knighted Admiral Abel Smith with his own sword in the Royal Dining Room. He was invested as a Knight Commander of the Royal Victorian Order (KCVO). The following day the press were given their long awaited opportunity to look round *Britannia*. The press had not been allowed on board until The Queen had seen the completed Yacht for herself. A total of 200 reporters accepted the invitation to look around the Yacht and photograph anything they wanted except the private apartments on the Shelter Deck.[38] On 19 May *Britannia* sailed from the Thames and headed south, undertaking an overnight passage to Portsmouth,[39] arriving there the following morning to successfully complete her first spell of Royal duty.[40]

Chapter Three

THE MAIDEN CIRCUMNAVIGATION

Vice Admiral Sir Conolly Abel Smith
GCVO CB 1954–1958

Britannia's return to Portsmouth after the final stages of the Commonwealth Tour provided the first opportunity to complete the Royal Apartments. The Queen's Sitting Room was completed by the installation of the wheatsheaf pattern sconces and the elegant gilt mirror, which came from Gothic.

(©British Crown Copyright / MOD)

On *Britannia*'s return from the Pool of London on 20 May 1954, workers from Portsmouth Dockyard came back on board to implement the list of minor modifications required in light of the experience gained during her initial period of Royal duty. While this work was being undertaken, the task of preparing her predecessor for the final voyage to the scrapyard got underway in earnest. Since the beginning of *Britannia*'s construction V&A had been progressively stripped of items that could be incorporated into the new Yacht. However, the use of V&A as a focal point for the reformed Royal Yacht Service during 1953 meant that this process couldn't be completed until after the commissioning of *Britannia*. Not surprisingly, there were many organisations that wanted items from the former Royal Yacht, so Prince Philip travelled to Portsmouth on 29 May[1] to see for himself what was left on board and decide what should be salvaged.

A large collection of these artefacts were donated during 1953 and 1954 to the National Maritime Museum (NMM) including the large wheel and second binnacle which were first used in the *Royal George*. The initial items of this collection were featured within the NMM's Special Coronation Year Exhibition of Royal Yachts which was opened by Prince Philip on 8 May 1953. However, not all of these items remained with the NMM because, after the launch of *Britannia*, it was proposed, that in view of her name, the wheel from King George V's racing yacht should be used to steer the new Yacht. Prince Philip agreed to this suggestion and thus the wheel left Greenwich to be installed within *Britannia*. The NMM received further items in 1954, such as the Royal Arms and scrollwork from the stern as well as the mizzen mast. When *V&A*'s masts were removed on 2 September 1954 they revealed the coins that had been placed beneath them in 1899. These coins were donated by Queen Victoria, The Prince of Wales (later King Edward VII) and The Duke of York (later King George V). Reflecting their seniority Queen Victoria's sovereign, 5 shilling piece and 1 penny were placed under the main mast, and The Prince of Wales's sovereign, 5 shilling piece and 1 penny went under the fore mast, while The Duke of York's half sovereign, 5 shilling piece and 1 half crown had been placed underneath the mizzen mast. The coins were encased in wax so they were first cleaned and then mounted in a specially made tray that was subsequently placed within the mahogany bookcase (also from *V&A*) in *Britannia*'s anteroom. Among the other items transferred from *V&A* to *Britannia* were the spy cartoons of

Prince Louis of Batternberg and King George V. The silk White Ensign that was made by Captain Scott's wife to fly from his sledge which was hung in King George V's cabin on board *V&A* was also moved across to *Britannia*.

It wasn't just the grand fittings that were eagerly pursued. For example, the Electrical Engineering Manager at Portsmouth wanted to acquire for his department the ship's main switchboard (80-volt Clarke Chapman design) as an example of electrical equipment dating from 1900. Another such recipient was the Petty Officer's School at Corsham, HMS *Royal Arthur*, where Prince Philip had served as an instructor, which received the aft capstan, a pair of davits, mess tables and a quantity of chain. Once the main fixtures and fittings had been removed the final

The Royal Dining Room laid out for a dinner. Over the years the walls of the Royal Dining Room were decorated with souvenirs from Britannia's travels, including the broadsword presented to The Queen by the Swedish Navy in 1956 and a 7-foot rib bone of a whale found by Prince Philip on Deception Island in 1957.

(© British Crown Copyright / MOD)

round of work concentrated on the fabric of the ship itself with the main staircase and two doors from the Royal Apartments going to HMS *Excellent* and the figurehead being sent to the Commodore of the Naval Barracks Portsmouth. Although some of the wooden panelling was presented to HMS *Dolphin*, some of it was retained within the Yacht stores to be turned into souvenirs of *V&A*, such as cigarette boxes. As the process of carving up *V&A* continued in Portsmouth Dockyard, *Britannia* sailed on 9 July 1954 for Prince Philip's visit to Cowes and Dartmouth, returning to Portsmouth on 13 July.[2]

On 30 July 1954 *Britannia* left Portsmouth to begin the first voyage across the Atlantic Ocean by a British Royal Yacht.[3] While there was nothing remarkable about sailing across the Atlantic Ocean by 1954, the trip served to underline the significant step change between *Britannia* and her predecessors. The new Yacht was the first such ship to possess a true world-wide capability, thus eliminating the need to use either major warships or liners for long Royal voyages. The journey itself was uneventful apart from a request by the Canadian authorities on 5 August to search for a missing tug. The search proved fruitless, although the Canadian escort HMCS *Micmac* discovered a 7-foot dory which wasn't linked to the tug.[4] During his Canadian Tour Prince Philip attended the Commonwealth Games in Vancouver and visited a number of remote districts in the north, before joining *Britannia* in Goose Bay on 17 August.[5] The next morning the Yacht sailed for the UK to take Prince Philip to Aberdeen where *Britannia* arrived on 23 August.[6] Her entry into Aberdeen was watched by many people who had gathered along the headlands and the harbour. Once alighting, Prince Philip travelled to Balmoral to join the rest of the Royal Family for the summer break, while *Britannia* headed to Rosyth for a six-day visit before returning to Portsmouth on 31 August.[7] The rest of the year was taken up with a short refit followed by two sets of sea trials. When *Britannia* entered Portsmouth at the end of her second batch of sea trials on 16 December[8] she passed the empty hulk of *V&A* alongside South Railway Jetty. At the time, the United Towing Co.'s tugs *Englishman* and *Airman* were manoeuvring into position to take *V&A* in tow to Faslane to be broken up for scrap.

The year 1955 began with further sea trials and a work up during which Admiral Sir Dudley North joined *Britannia* in Portland for three days. Having played such a crucial role in her building it must have been very satisfying for the old Admiral to finally stand on the decks of *Britannia* and go to sea in her. Before long *Britannia* began her next major deployment, leaving Portsmouth on 18 January 1955[9] for Trinidad where Princess Margaret

would embark for her Tour of the Caribbean. By the time the Yacht reached Trinidad on 29 January[10] much of the blue paint around the waterline and the bows had been washed off. Fortunately, Princess Margaret wasn't due to embark until 5 February which gave the Yacht's company enough time to complete the repainting.

Within half an hour of Princess Margaret joining the Yacht off Tobago on 5 February, *Britannia* was underway for the overnight passage to Grenada, and this was typical of the pace of this Tour, which had been dismissed by some parts of the press as the 'Royal Calypso Cruise'. During the course of the next 21 days Princess Margaret visited the islands of Grenada, St Vincent, Barbados, Antigua, St Kitts, Jamaica and the Bahamas. The Tour was well received in the Caribbean. For example, when she arrived in Barbados on 9 February, a fleet of 50 fishing boats came out to greet the Princess and escort *Britannia* to its anchorage at Carlisle Bay off Bridgetown.[11] Equally, the presence of the Yacht during the Tour provided the Princess with some much needed relaxation between visits, as the Commander of *Britannia* at the time, later Rear Admiral J H Adams CB LVO explains:

'The whole trip, like other tours, was planned at break-neck speed and there was no doubt to us that it was essential to have spare time at sea for members of the Royal Family to relax between their arduous round of engagements. The Yacht was very good at allowing an extra hour or so when sailing from A to B so that we always had a couple of hours spare. Therefore, if we saw a little island we would be able stop have a picnic and then go on again. The visit to Conception Island during the voyage from Trinidad to the Bahamas was a perfect example of this and I remember as we approached the island the water shelved very rapidly from 800 fathoms to 8 fathoms in what seemed like a minute. The Admiral asked for an echo sounding and as the reading was being given he said, "I can see the rocks under the bow!"

'Of course the other benefit of allowing extra time for a passage was that it enabled us to keep the Yacht looking at her best for every arrival. One of the tricks of the Yacht would be to sail towards a rainstorm if we saw one and sit under it turning first one side and then the other to the rain. Thus the whole of the Yacht's side was given a quick rinse and the salt washed off before we entered harbour. This is how we got our reputation for our shining sides.'

Britannia's role in the Princess's tour came to an end on 26 February when she left the Yacht at Nassau. Two hours later the Yacht began her passage to Villefranche via Bermuda and Gibraltar.[12] A few days later as *Britannia* steamed across the Atlantic the Canopus aircraft taking Princess Margaret back to the UK passed overhead some miles to the north. Not wishing to let the event go unnoticed the Yacht sent the Princess a message together with a short rhyme. Before the Princess could reply to the Yacht's message, air traffic control told *Britannia* to stop making signals as it was interfering with operational safety waves. As a result, they did not receive their reply from Princess Margaret until *Britannia* reached Gibraltar on 7 March. Despite the time it took the reply to catch up with *Britannia* it did reveal the Princess's affection for the new Yacht.

'Here fly the bodies of us poor old five,
Praying we will all get home alive,
We wish we were floating in your old steam packet,
And we're all of us clutching our yellow lifejacket.
Safe journey and best wishes to you all.
Margaret'

Following her overnight visit to Gibraltar *Britannia* sailed for Villefranche on 8 March to participate in exercise Sealance with ships of the Home and Mediterranean Fleets.[13] Shortly after the Yacht anchored off Villefranche on 10 March the First Lord of the Admiralty, The Rt Hon. J P Thomas, The Fifth Sea Lord, Rear Admiral Bingley, and the Naval Secretary, Rear Admiral Luce, embarked followed half an hour later by Prince Philip.[14] The addition of the First Sea Lord, Admiral of the Fleet Sir Rhoderick McGrigor three days[15] later meant that dur-

ing the course of the exercise six Admirals lived on board *Britannia* causing one Yachtsmen to ask who the duty Lord was today! The exercise provided an opportunity to try out a new type of stretcher for transporting cot cases from ship to ship by jackstay or from ship to helicopter. Once *Britannia* had played the role of hospital ship during the replenishment of the Fleet underway facing the threat of an atomic attack she simulated a merchant ship for the rest of the exercises with FORY in effect becoming the Convoy Commodore. Prince Philip and the Admirals spent a lot of time in the Royal Charthouse, which had been converted into an operations room. Sealance was concluded with a simulated wartime entry into Malta on 15 March followed by the usual round of official callers. During the week in Malta Prince Philip visited a number of ships and various military units ashore as well as playing polo in the Keyes Cup.[16] On 22 March *Britannia* sailed to observe an anti-submarine exercise and manoeuvres with NATO aircraft carriers, before returning to Portsmouth via Gibraltar, where she arrived at South Railway Jetty on 1 April and Prince Philip disembarked.[17]

Britannia then entered dockyard hands for repainting. Since *Britannia* had commissioned the original blue paint supplied by British Paints Ltd had become a constant problem suffering from extensive peeling, in particular during the voyage to the West Indies earlier in the year. It was therefore felt, despite the expense of an additional docking period, that the only option left was to strip the hull back to bare metal and try some new paint supplied by

During Exercise Sealance the Royal Charthouse was converted into a temporary operations room.

(© British Crown Copyright / MOD)

Ripolin.[18] The work was completed by the end of May and on 18 June *Britannia* sailed for Rosyth to embark The Queen and Prince Philip for their State Visit to Norway.[19] As the Yacht sailed past the Norwegian islands and mainland off Arendal, she was brought close inshore for The Queen to see the bonfires that had been lit in accordance with Norwegian custom to mark midsummer's night.[20] Shortly after *Britannia* anchored off Oslo The Queen and Prince Philip landed amid the thunder of saluting canons and the cheers of the Oslo crowds to live ashore as guests of The King for the next couple of days. They returned to the Yacht at the end of their State Visit on 26 June to host the dinner for King Haakon, who was, incidentally, a Honorary Admiral in the RN. When The King embarked in *Britannia* from the Norwegian Royal Barge his Standard was broken at *Britannia*'s main mast alongside the Royal Standard. Although this was common practice for such occasions it was the first time it had happened in *Britannia*. Over the years this honour was to be extended to all of the heads of state who were received on board *Britannia*. After dinner The King and his family left *Britannia* in their Royal Barge and the Yacht sailed for Dundee,[21] as Admiral Adams commented: 'it was a lovely summer's evening with small craft racing here and there on Oslo Fjord. The Queen stayed up until midnight waving to boats and the people onshore. We floodlit The Queen at her own request so that people onshore could see her.'

As *Britannia* approached Dundee on the morning of 28 June two familiar sailing boats came out to greet the Yacht. *Bluebottle* and *Coweslip* had been taken north to compete in Tay Week where *Bluebottle* had won each of the three Dragon class races. Sadly, while they were trying to keep station under the lee of *Britannia*, *Coweslip* lost way and the heavier *Bluebottle* kept moving causing the two boats to collide. Although this caused some damage to *Coweslip*, she was quickly repaired by *Britannia*'s shipwrights after her arrival in a rather wet Dundee.[22] There The Queen's bodyguard in Scotland, The Royal Company of Archers, were lining the jetty for The Queen's visit. Despite the rain The Queen decided to carry out the dry weather routine to enable more people to see her. 'When The Queen had left I invited the rather bedraggled looking Archers to come on board for a well-deserved drink in the Wardroom,' Admiral Adams remarked. Two days later *Britannia* sailed for Granton to spend six days before returning to Portsmouth on 7 July 1955.[23]

On 29 July *Britannia* sailed from H Moorings to make her debut at the Cowes Week Regatta, securing to the Royal Yacht Buoy at 1748.[24] The sight of *Britannia* in Cowes Roads provided visible evidence of the strong links that have existed between the Royal Family and yachting at Cowes since the early nineteenth century. This long association began in 1817 when The Prince Regent (later King George IV) indicated that he wanted to join The Yacht Club, which subsequently became the Royal Yacht Squadron of today. Two years later he went to Cowes in August 1819 to watch the yacht racing from the Royal Yacht, which helped to generate interest in both the sport of yachting and Cowes itself. These links were strengthened in 1865 when The Prince of Wales (later King Edward VII) decided that he wanted to take a more active role in the Royal Yacht Squadron and compete in the racing. Over the years he owned eight racing yachts, beginning with the 36-ton *Dagma*, which was launched in 1866. She was followed by the *Princess* in 1869, the *Alexandra* in 1871, the *Zenobia* in 1872, the *Hildegarde* in 1876, the *Formosa* in 1880, the *Aline* in 1882 and finally, the most famous of them all, *Britannia* in 1893.

Following the death of King Edward VII on 6 May 1910 the racing yacht *Britannia* passed to his son King George V, who was also a keen sailor, and he continued to race at Cowes until his death in 1936. None of King George V's sons wanted to take on *Britannia* so, in May 1936, it was announced that she would be stripped of all her equipment and scuttled. Thus shortly before midnight on 9 July 1936 the two destroyers HMS *Amazon* and HMS *Winchester* came out from Portsmouth to collect *Britannia* and take her out of the Solent for the last time. She was taken to the south of the Isle of Wight where charges were detonated in her bilges and she slowly slipped below the waters of the Channel. Although King George VI enjoyed sailing, he disliked the atmosphere of Cowes Week, so it wasn't until after the Second World War that Royal patronage of yachting was re-established by his son-in-law Prince Philip.

The revival of yachting after the Second World War took on a more modest form with the disappearance of the magnificent J class yachts of the pre-war years. In keeping with this new mood, Princess Elizabeth and Prince Philip began to make enquires about buying a second-hand Dragon class yacht as building licenses for new boats were still restricted. This interest was soon picked up by a member of the Cowes based Island Sailing Club (ISC) who approached the Commodore of the ISC with the proposal that the club could present a Dragon as a wedding present to the Royal couple. Agreeing to the suggestion the Commodore, J C W Damant, sent a letter to Clarence House on 2 April 1948 formally making the offer which was quickly accepted by the Royal couple. To ensure that all of the members who wanted to contribute could do so, the donations were limited to £5 per member resulting in the target being met within a week! In the meantime the club had arranged to buy a Dragon on order from Camper & Nicholson which had been commissioned to participate in the Olympic trials that summer. Not being able to use his new yacht, the owner readily agreed to sell the Dragon to the ISC and her keel was laid on 12 May 1948. It took the Royal couple some time to decide upon a name for the Royal Dragon. In the end Prince Philip came up with the name *Bluebottle* which attracted a certain amount of criticism along the lines that it was a flippant choice and an insult to the donors. In fact, the name was carefully arrived at through an association of Dragon – Dragonfly – Blue (her colour) – Blue Fly – Bluebottle. Because of the Royal couple's various commitments the Admiralty agreed to supply a Naval Officer to act as the sailing master. This enabled *Bluebottle* to be seen at as many regattas as possible and help to generate a wider interest in sailing. Thus the Royal Dragon made her racing debut on 10 July 1948 in the Solent at the hands of her sailing master, Lieutenant Commander Michael Crichton, who finished third out of 10 starters.

Prince Philip's busy programme meant that he didn't actually race her for the first time until 5 September 1948 when he participated in the Lee-on-Solent Regatta. The following year the Royal couple attended Cowes Week but the weather was so bad on the day of their arrival at Beaulieu that the racing at Cowes was cancelled. *Bluebottle* had been sailed across the Solent to meet them so the Royal couple opted to stay there for the rest of the day and sail *Bluebottle* on the Beaulieu River together. It was the only time that The Queen sailed in *Bluebottle*. In 1949 Prince Philip was posted to the Mediterranean, so it was not until 1951 that he was able to race again during Cowes Week, this time in his Flying Fifteen *Coweslip* in which he recorded his first Cowes Week victory.

After the accession of The Queen, Prince Philip became a regular competitor at Cowes Week, racing in both *Coweslip* and *Bluebottle* during the early years. The use of *Britannia* from 1955 onwards during Cowes Week not only enhanced the regatta itself but provided a secure base for Prince Philip and the other members of the Royal Family who wanted to participate. As can be imagined there was never a shortage of offers to take members of the Yacht's company racing. However, Cowes Week was always a busy time for those on board the Yacht not least due to the large amount of boat running.

And so back to 1955, having raced in *Coweslip* and *Bluebottle* in the regatta Prince Philip left *Britannia* during the afternoon of 4 August and she sailed the next day to conclude her first Cowes Week. *Britannia*'s next destination was Spithead where Prince Charles, Princess Anne and Prince Philip's mother, Princess Andrew of Greece,

embarked for the start of the first Western Isles Cruise.[25] The idea for the regular Western Isles Cruise was suggested by Prince Philip to provide enough time for the Household to move from Buckingham Palace to Balmoral so that they were in position by the time the Royal Family reached Scotland for the summer break. This, combined with the Royal Family's desire to see outlying parts of Scotland, formed the basis of the first Western Isles Cruise to which visits to Milford Haven and the Isle of Man were added. The Queen always looked forward to the Western Isles Cruise because it was the only opportunity that she had within the year to unwind away from the constant stream of public engagements and visitors. In spite of this, the ability of *Britannia* to take The Queen to visit remote parts of the UK meant that The Queen invariably included at least one public engagement within each Western Isles Cruise. Once the Royal children and their grandmother had joined *Britannia*, she weighed anchor and steamed overnight to Milford Haven securing to a buoy there the next morning.[26] The Queen and Prince Philip arrived in Milford Haven during the day and took the Royal children for a picnic, as Admiral Adams recalls:

'I had the privilege of going on their first picnic. We had Mr Gwyther from The Queen's Harbourmaster's boat crew who came with us to show us where the best sandy bay was. We grounded in 2 feet of water in Lindsway Bay and everyone jumped over the side and paddled ashore. Mr Gwyther picked up Prince Charles and carried him ashore. Someone turned to him and said, "do you realise that you are carrying the future Prince of Wales for his first time to Wales?" which brought tears to his eyes. Once ashore the children went for only their second swim in the sea – the first had been during their visit to Malta in the previous year which was something that really struck me. The Queen told me that every time the Royal Family tried to go on the beach a crowd would gather. So they didn't go on the beach for the sake of the children. However, The Queen realised that with the Yacht's boats she could go to any sheltered bay and hopefully nobody would be there. It was during these early picnics that we quickly learnt to make an elaborate check-off list before the Royal party went ashore. Otherwise we would find ourselves in the position of being ashore for a barbecue without any matches. Thus as soon as the bell was rung for us to arrange a picnic people started to dart off in every direction to get things organised. It was up to the Household Stewards to provide the food but somehow the heating of the food became the Yacht's responsibility!'

Once the barbecue was lit Prince Philip would personally cook the food himself. While the Royal children enjoyed further picnics ashore during the stay at Milford Haven, their parents undertook a programme of engagements on 7 August and then Aberystwyth on the 8th, returning on board that evening for the Yacht to set sail for the Isle of Man.[27]

During the voyage the Yacht's seamanship skills were given an impromptu exercise, as Admiral Adams explains:

'Prince Charles was playing with a football on the Verandah Deck when he kicked it over the side. The Yachtsman normally assigned to keep an eye on Prince Charles around the Yacht said, "Shall we go back for it?"

The Prince replied, "Yes please."

So I ran up to the bridge and asked the Admiral if we could turn round and launch the sea boat to get the ball, which we did. Prince Charles thought this was enormous fun so as we got underway again the Prince took the ball and kicked it over the side again. But I said, "Sorry, we're not going back a second time."'

When the Yacht dropped anchor in Douglas Bay on the morning of 9 August, the Isle of Man was shrouded in mist, in keeping with the local legend that a curse brings down the cloud every time the Sovereign visits the island. While The Queen and Prince Philip went ashore the children remained on board playing games and telephoning each other in the afternoon. After the conclusion of the reception that The Queen hosted for people from the Isle of Man, Britannia weighed anchor for Cairn Ryan[28] and the Scottish part of the cruise, which included a visit to upper Loch Torridon. It was while Britannia lay at anchor in Loch Torridon that The Queen went ashore for a walk by herself, as Admiral Adams explains:

'As I greeted Her Majesty at the gangway on her return, I asked whether she had had a good walk. She was obviously amused and replied that she had met two people who had not recognised her despite seeing the Yacht in the loch. She remarked that it was rather disconcerting – should she tell them or laugh it off? She walked on and later met a shepherd, who as he passed The Queen, lifted his hat and said, "A grand evening for a walk, your Majesty." Those were the only people she met on her walk and to this day I wonder if that couple ever realised who they met.'

On the last full day of the cruise the Yacht paid her first visit to Scrabster Roads so that the Royal Family could go ashore and spend the afternoon with The Queen Mother at the Castle of Mey. The castle was originally built by the 4th Earl of Caithness between 1566 and 1572. By the time The Queen Mother purchased the castle in 1952 it had fallen into disrepair and so during the early years of The Queen Mother's ownership the castle and its surrounding gardens were given an extensive restoration. All too soon it was time for the Royal Family to return to Britannia to resume their voyage to Aberdeen. The Queen invited the officers to join her on the Verandah Deck as Britannia passed the illuminated Castle of Mey at 2215.[29] To mark the occasion the Yacht fired a series of rockets to which the castle responded with a salvo of its own. As the Yacht slipped out of sight and into the darkness of the night signals were exchanged between Britannia and the castle as follows:

To: Castle of Mey
From: FORY
'The Castle of Mey,
Looks Terribly Gay,
We've all lost our hearts to it,
We're sad to depart from it,
To the end from the start of it,
We've had a most glorious day.'

To: FORY
From: Castle of Mey
'We've all been very glad to have you with us.
Please come back again soon.'

The next morning Britannia entered Aberdeen and the Royal Family left to go to Balmoral, as Princess Anne recalls: 'At the end of the trip I didn't want to get off. History has it that I had to be carried off kicking and screaming from the Yacht!' When Britannia sailed for Portsmouth on 15 August 3 officers and 20 airmen from The Queen's Flight had embarked to see what life was like on board, while a similar number of Yachtsmen were flown south in an aircraft of The Queen's Flight.[30] Over the years this became a regular arrangement, as did occasional visits by parties from the Yacht to the Royal Palaces and the Royal Train, and vice versa.

Three days before Britannia sailed from Portsmouth on 6 October to embark Prince Philip in Dundee, Bluebottle and five other Dragon class yachts were craned on board Britannia for the voyage across to Denmark.[31] The Dragons had been invited by the Danish Dragon Club to participate in a series of races organised to coincide with the British Trade Exhibition in Copenhagen. Prince Philip was already due to travel in Britannia to visit the exhibition so he offered to take the Dragons in the Yacht. Thus, carrying her unusual cargo, Britannia arrived in Copenhagen on 12 October watched by King Frederick. As soon as the first brow was secured The King stepped on board *Britannia* to personally welcome Prince Philip to Denmark before driving himself back to Fredensborg Castle. Having visited the exhibition in the afternoon Prince Philip had dinner with The King and Queen at the castle.[32] The next day The King and Queen visited *Britannia* to have lunch with Prince Philip. Afterwards they were taken for an extensive tour of *Britannia* including the mess decks.[33] The day of 14 October was taken up with further engagements before Prince Philip left to spend the weekend with The King and Queen prior to leaving for Germany on 17 October.[34] When the Yacht sailed for Portsmouth two days later The King and Queen, together with Princesses Benedikte and Anne Marie, turned out to watch *Britannia*'s departure.[35]

Britannia reached Portsmouth after lunch on 21 October and proceeded up the harbour to her moorings off Whale Island.[36] Unfortunately, the normally effective execution of instructions without verbal commands experienced a rare glitch, as Admiral Adams explains:

'Coming into Portsmouth we were going to send off our boats to the dockyard's boatyard. I arranged with the Admiral to slow down as we passed HMS *Dolphin* to drop off the four boats and then speed up again to Whale Island. At the last moment we decided it was too rough and that we would take the boats with us. I went to the back of the bridge and signalled with my hand, "cancel" which looks remarkably like "slip". I should explain that as few orders as possible were given

aloud in the Yacht, dependence being given to visual, silent ones. In this case it clearly didn't work for as I turned round to go to the front of the bridge again I heard three boats crash into the water! I should have run my finger horizontally across my throat – roll on the day of the walkie talkie!'

Britannia spent the rest of the year undergoing her annual refit in Portsmouth, which was followed by sea trials and a work up in January 1956.

On 1 March 1956 Prince Philip joined *Britannia* in Portsmouth shortly before she sailed to observe Home Fleet exercises off Gibraltar.[37] On conclusion of the exercises the Yacht parted from the Home Fleet and headed into the Mediterranean to embark The Queen and Princess Alexandra at Ajaccio Harbour for a private cruise on 10 March.[38] The eight-day cruise off Corsica followed a similar pattern to the Western Isles Cruise, with the Royal Family landing each day for picnics on remote beaches. At the end of the cruise the Royal Family left the Yacht at Ajaccio Harbour and *Britannia* headed off to Gibraltar to participate in further exercises, as Admiral Adams remarked: 'there was really foul weather during Exercise Dawn Breeze. We acted as a raider for three days and had fun in two "night actions" dodging aircraft and Force 11 squalls. In the exercises we jammed transmissions with musical recordings of "Britannia Rules The Waves!"' At the end of the exercise *Britannia* returned to Portsmouth on 26 March.[39]

During The Queen's State Visit to Sweden she was presented with some furniture by the Swedish Royal Family, which was later used in the Ante Room.

(©British Crown Copyright / MOD)

As part of the preparations for The Queen's visit to Sweden The Queen's Rolls Royce was embarked on 29 May.[40] Two days later the Yacht left Portsmouth to collect The Queen, Prince Philip and Lord Mountbatten from Middlesborough and take them across the North Sea to Sweden.[41] As the Yacht neared the end of her voyage to Stockholm on the morning of 8 June the fog became so thick that *Britannia* had to drop anchor for over an hour until the visibility improved enough to be able to resume the journey. The unforeseen delay meant that *Britannia* had to increase her speed in a bid to make up for lost time, as Admiral Adams explains:

'It was important not only from the obvious point of arriving in the centre of Stockholm on time but because the Swedish Air Force had planned a very impressive air display for our arrival. So we came in at full speed and the escorting *Daring* class destroyers increased their speed to 26 knots to catch up. Despite the Admiral's concern the pilot said that it would be all right to go in at full speed adding, "Swedish destroyers go as fast as they like here." But the result was that we caused £100,000 of damage to private boats all the way down into the harbour. The Ambassador went on local TV that night to apologise and explained the need to arrive on time. He also said that the British Government would repay anyone who claimed that their yacht had been damaged by our arrival. When we arrived the two buoys given to us were 700 feet apart as opposed to the 520 feet we had asked for. It took us two and a quarter hours to secure.'

While *Britannia* was still being secured The Queen and Prince Philip were taken ashore in the Swedish Royal Pulling Barge *Vasa Orden* and escorted ashore by The Duke of Halland who had joined *Britannia* during the final stages of her voyage into Stockholm.[42] The official part of the State Visit was concluded by the dinner held on board *Britannia* on 10 June.[43] The next day Princess Margaret and The Duke and Duchess of Gloucester arrived in Stockholm to join The Queen and Prince Philip. The second part of the visit, which lasted until 17 June, was essentially an informal event for the Royal Family to watch the Olympic Equestrian Games and to spend some time with the Swedish Royal Family.[44]

Having returned to Portsmouth on 20 June, *Britannia* sailed a week later for the Clyde and the centenary celebrations of the Royal Clyde Yacht Club.[45] Prince Philip participated in the regatta, by racing *Bluebottle* on 30 June, and finished fourth. The day after, he sailed the new *Fairey Fox*, and took part in a fleet cruise organised by the Royal Clyde Yacht Club. Describing the background to

Fairey Fox's design Prince Philip explained:

'I suggested to Uffa Fox [the Cowes-based yacht designer and boat builder who crewed for Prince Philip for various regattas, including Cowes Week] that it might be interesting to see whether a sailing craft could make use of "hydrofoil". He thought it might work and designed a 24-foot gunter-rigged dinghy and Fairey Marine designed and made the foils. Uffa had a go with the foils, but the experiment did not work and the foils were never used again.'

Prince Philip concluded his involvement by racing *Coweslip* on 2 July before leaving the next morning. Shortly afterwards the Yacht weighed anchor and made an overnight passage back to Portsmouth.[46] In view of the forthcoming major deployment to the southern hemisphere leave was given to the Yachtsmen during July. However, it wasn't a period of total relaxation because trials were conducted with a rubber raft to transport a Land Rover from *Britannia* to a beach where it could be driven ashore. Previously, during the first Western Isles Cruise the two jolly boats were secured together side by side and the Land Rover was placed on top of them which was a rather precarious arrangement. The trials were so successful that they created interest with the Chief of Amphibious warfare.

August began with the visit to Cowes Week between 3 and 9 August in which Prince Philip sailed *Fairey Fox*. During the recent State Visit to the UK of King Faisal of Iraq, Prince Philip had discovered that the young King was an enthusiastic sailor, so he invited The King to spend a couple of days on board *Britannia* during Cowes Week. At the end of the regatta *Britannia* sailed to Southampton to drop off Prince Philip and embark Prince Charles and Princess Anne, before heading north to Barrow-in-Furness where The Queen, Prince Philip and Princess Margaret would join for the Western Isles Cruise. By the time *Britannia* reached Barrow-in-Furness on 11 August the prevailing conditions presented FORY with a dilemma,[47] as Admiral Adams explains:

'The Admiral had the difficult decision as to whether he should pick up The Queen and her party or go to another port further along the coast like Liverpool. The combination of a narrow harbour, strong winds and poor tugs meant that when the Admiral asked for my views I recommended that we shouldn't go in as we "sailed" in the wind thanks to only 12,000 horsepower, a 16-foot draft and a very high freeboard for the wind to catch hold of. However, the Admiral said he wouldn't let The Queen down and fortunately did no more damage than bump a quarter on the jetty and put three dents in the ship – the tugs' fault not ours. The Yacht was often asked to go into difficult places to pick up Royalty and the Admiral took risks which I wouldn't have liked to take in a destroyer. But the Admiral's view was that the Sovereign's requirements were paramount. It is difficult to fault that.'

Having embarked the Royal party, *Britannia* sailed from Barrow-in-Furness and headed north for a cruise round the west coast of Scotland and the Western Isles, including the annual visit to Scrabster Bay on 18 August. Earlier in the day the Yacht had entered Stornoway for the Royal party to carry out a busy day of engagements including visits to the herring canning station, Lews Castle College and Triumphan lighthouse. By the time the Royal party returned and the Yacht left Stornoway she had to steam at 21 knots to reach Scrabster in time for The Queen Mother to come on board that evening,[48] as Anne Stevenson (later Mrs David Griffiths CVO) who was one of Prince Philip's Lady Clerks at the time recalls:

'The Barge was sent ashore to collect The Queen Mother who came on board for dinner. She arrived with the Vyners and left again about 2230 and the Yacht weighed anchor passing the Castle of Mey, which was floodlit. It was a lovely evening – very calm sea and nearly a full moon.'

As before there was an exchange of rockets between the castle and *Britannia*:

'Four salvos of rockets were fired. The last rocket was lying on deck; someone had taken its plug out and it was ignited by the flames of the previous one. It went off along the Flag Deck between our feet and then expired. Roars of laughter from the Royal Bridge where The Queen and the rest of the Royal Family heard us stamping on deck. Although treated as an amusing incident, it could have been more serious and was a sharp lesson to all of us,' Admiral Adams remarked.

From Scrabster, *Britannia* headed not for Aberdeen but for Leith because The Queen was due to attend the first two days of the Edinburgh Festival. Because of its close proximity to the Scottish capital of Edinburgh, Leith has been the arrival point of kings and queens in Scotland for centuries. Despite this proud tradition The Queen was in fact the first reigning British Monarch to arrive in Leith by sea since Queen Victoria in 1842. Interestingly, Queen Victoria's voyage to Leith brought the era of British Royal Yachts powered by sail to an end. For this journey Queen Victoria embarked in the 25-year-old *Royal George* which was overtaken during the passage north from Woolwich

by a number of steamships. The young Queen was so dismayed by this that the paddle steamer *Trident* was chartered for the return trip and the first *V&A* was subsequently commissioned as a replacement for the *Royal George*. Over a century later the welcome was just as enthusiastic for Queen Victoria's great great granddaughter. However, much to the disappointment of the crowds in Leith, Prince Charles, Princess Anne and Princess Andrew of Greece were taken out of sight of the cameras by the Barge from Leith to Rosyth from where they travelled to Balmoral. At the end of The Queen's visit to Leith on 21 August *Britannia* sailed across the Firth of Forth to Rosyth to disembark the Royal party before heading south back to Portsmouth, where she arrived on 22 August to take on stores and provisions ahead of her first major deployment.[49]

On 28 August 1956 *Britannia* left Portsmouth to begin her first world cruise. Over the next 110 days she would steam a total of 39,549 miles and visit many of the most remote communities in the southern hemisphere. Describing the background to the voyage Prince Philip said:

'It all started with the 1956 Olympic Games in Melbourne and the Commonwealth Trans Antarctic Expedition. I had already agreed to go to the Games when I heard about the plans for the Trans Antarctic Expedition from Sir Vivian Fuchs. He was to start from the Weddell Sea and Sir Edmund Hillary was to begin his trek from the Ross Sea. Sir Edmund was due to leave Christchurch in New Zealand in December, not long after the end of the Games. I had visions of visiting both ends of the expedition but they soon faded. However, in discussing these ideas and looking at charts and maps, it soon became obvious that there were a good many island communities and outposts in the Indian Ocean, the South Pacific, Antarctic and Atlantic which cannot be visited by air and which are too remote and too small to get into the more usual tours. Although it meant being away from home for three months, including Christmas and New Year, I decided to try to arrange the journey out to Australia and back by sea in the Yacht.'

Prince Philip's plans were later adjusted and he began the first part of his outward journey by air to Mombasa where he joined the Yacht, thus enabling *Britannia* to be used to support part of Princess Margaret's Tour of East Africa. This, together with the necessity to sail to Mombasa via the Cape of Good Hope, due to the deteriorating relations between the Egyptian and British Governments following the nationalisation of the Suez Canal by Egypt, and the incorporation of The Queen's State Visit to Portugal meant that the length of the Yacht's deployment was extended from four to six months.

However, before *Britannia* sailed from her Hampshire home port there were extensive preparations for the trip, including the installation of a suitable radio so that Prince Philip could make a Christmas Day broadcast, and a Bathythermograph to collect information for the Royal Oceanographic Society. As part of this information gathering process, a log was also kept throughout the deployment by the Officer of the Watch recording details of all whales and sea birds sighted by the Yacht as well as separate logs recording details of the weather and echo soundings. Describing some of the other preparations Admiral Adams said: 'we took a Land Rover, my scooter, photographic goods by the dozen, *Coweslip*, extra fridges, beer, wind scoops, extra cable and 101 other things. We also took a great deal of long life milk and stowed it everywhere. It was much appreciated in the months to come.' When she sailed, *Britannia* had her largest complement to date, with 22 officers and 268 Royal Yachtsmen, which included six Australian and New Zealand ratings, for the World Tour. The numbers had increased thanks to the embarkation of the RM Band, an extra RM detachment, an extra shipwright, Physical Training Instructor (PTI), the Australian and New Zealand contingent, extra cooks for Princess Margaret's Tour and a writer in the office. Among those who turned out to watch the Yacht's departure were two former Royal Yacht officers who witnessed the event from FORY's yacht *Mariota*. During his time as the Navigating Officer, Commander Robin Graham had planned most of the forthcoming voyage while Lieutenant Mike Barrow had only just left *Britannia* that day. Because of the changes in the programme *Britannia* could not afford to lose any time so, once she had slipped through the Solent, her speed was increased to 19 knots and it was important that she maintained an average speed of 18 knots for most of the voyage to Mombasa.

Apart from brief refuelling stops at Freetown, Luanda, and a slightly longer visit to Cape Town, the main highlight of *Britannia*'s outward bound voyage to Kenya came on 7 September when she crossed the equator for the first time. The ceremonies connected with Crossing-The-Line are in fact linked to earlier pagan rituals held when sailors entered unknown waters during the days of early maritime explorers. Even as late as 1675 Chaplain Teonge refers to the ducking from the yardarm of men entering the straits of Gibraltar for the first time. In more recent times the crossing of the equator in RN ships has become an excuse for a day of good-natured revelry to break the routine of a long passage. Before the Yacht left the UK the Crossing-The-Line certificates were produced by the drawing

office in HMS *Vernon* and incorporated crests and emblems associated with the Tours of Prince Philip and Princess Margaret. Apart from compiling the list of novices nothing else was done until the week before when a series of 'intercepted signals' were distributed around the Yacht to whip up enthusiasm on board, culminating in the visit of Dolphinius, Clerk of the court to His Oceanic Majesty King Neptune on the evening of 6 September to read the proclamation of King Neptune to the Yacht's company in which he said:

'We send greetings to you Admiral Sir Conolly Abel Smith, Knight Commander of the Victorian Order, Companion Of The Bath and to all Royal Yachtsmen of HM Yacht *Britannia* on this her first visit to our Equatorial Waters.

'In accordance with the custom you are instructed that our court will be convened on board at 0930 tomorrow 7 September 1956.

'You are strictly charged to offer at our court the courtesies by custom decreed and to assemble for our purposes those novices under your command who have not been initiated into our mysteries and also those who are charged with offences against our decrees and whose names are contained in the list I bear. We further charge you to observe and execute such directions as to the apprehension and indictment of malefactors as we shall require and to afford our police and bears such assistance as is necessary for the proper performance of their duties.

'Given under our hand and seal this doomsdate eve at our court on the Equator.

'Signed Neptunus Rex.'

Because the weather was rather cold and wet the Crossing-The-Line ceremony was postponed until after lunch when approximately 130 members of the Yacht's company who had never crossed the line were ducked as part of their initiation. In addition to the duckings a number of people were presented with awards including FORY, who was created Lord of the Telegraph and presented with an engine room telegraph, the Surgeon Commander who was awarded the Order of the Bilge Pump, and Leading Seaman Forge who was made a member of the boat busters order (Scottish Division). Describing his own encounter with the court of King Neptune Admiral Adams said:

'I was dragged up to the platform and heard all the dreadful things I had committed against King Neptune during the past few years – dodging a foreign commission, spying on the birds and fishes by instituting a log on the bridge for this cruise, of issuing too many orders about swimming baths, etc. Then I was given a ghastly pill and doughnut soaked in soap to eat, soaped, shaved, hair cut and well and truly tipped up and ducked. About 130 novices out of a Yacht's company of 268 plus 22 officers followed me. It was great fun, everyone behaved extremely well and everyone got ducked in the end regardless of who he was except FORY. It then started to heat up with hoses playing everywhere and the only way to stop the party one and a half hours after it began was to turn the ship back into wind and get on with the voyage to Luanda.'

As *Britannia* continued to steam towards Mombasa it looked increasing likely that there would be a military operation to recover the Suez Canal. In light of these circumstances FORY asked the Commander to draw up

Princess Margaret is seen talking to FORY, Vice Admiral Sir Conolly Abel Smith, prior to going ashore.

(© British Crown Copyright / MOD)

some proposals about how *Britannia* could be used in a future conflict. Although FORY felt it was unlikely that the Tour would be cancelled in the event of a Suez conflict he thought it would be prudent to be prepared for all eventualities. Some of the issues considered included the minimum number of men required to steam the Yacht back to the UK. What action would be required by the Yachtsmen if *Britannia* was to become a hospital ship or a troop ship or a headquarters ship?

Regardless of these preparations the deployment proceeded as planned with *Britannia* arriving in Mombasa on 21 September ahead of Princess Margaret's embarkation the following evening. After a full day of engagements ashore on 23 September Princess Margaret returned to *Britannia* and she sailed that night to a tremendous send off,[50] as Admiral Adams recalls: 'it was rather eerie sailing in the dark with ourselves floodlit and the shore near but in the dark. There was a lot of cheering from the crowds onshore and the Princess waved back from the floodlit Royal Bridge.' During the voyage to Mauritius it was decided to make a slight detour, as Admiral Adams continues:

'We decided to go to Aldabra Island to let Princess Margaret go ashore for a swim. When we got there the surf was coming in from the wrong direction and made boat work quite impossible. The other end of the island had a small settlement where copra was made and was thus unsuitable. There were quite a lot of natives waving from the beach who shared the island with giant tortoises which grow to 3 feet high and live well over 100 years. The island itself was 12 miles long in the shape of a horseshoe, the lagoon inside being the most wonderful light emerald green colour and mangrove trees growing out of the water. There were a few very small beaches on which we could see the tracks of the turtles where they had come in from the sea to lay their eggs.'

Without a suitable beach in sight the Yacht headed off towards Assumption Island in the hope of finding some privacy for the Princess, as Admiral Adams explains:

'Since these coral atolls come sheer out of the sea from 1000 fathoms, it was almost impossible to anchor without going aground. Thus the Admiral decided to remain underway and stay on board while I took charge of the bathing party. So on arrival Mr Croker (the detective) and myself carried out a reconnaissance in a jolly boat. Five natives came out in a boat from a small settlement and greeted us in good English. When we explained that we wanted privacy they were first class, showed us the best bathing position on the beach and said they would remain away.

'So back to the Yacht and away in the motor boat with the Royal party. We towed a dinghy as the water was very shallow – with coral – for the last 100 yards and we had to row in. The beach was about 2 miles long and lovely everywhere until one stood on coral. There were, however, sandy bits every so often under water and we all had a glorious swim of 30 minutes or so. We also landed 30 or so men along the beach as a scouting party but no natives ever turned up which demonstrated a rare understanding so lacking everywhere else we had been. The natives said that there were no sharks but I saw one big barracuda and kept to seaward of the Princess the whole time on the Admiral's special instructions so that I could get eaten first! After a swim we explored the rocks and I produced hermit crabs out of dry sand and dug deep for land crabs. These dug as quickly as I could but they were fascinating to catch and turned out to be quite big. They had huge eyes which popped up and down into a recess and looked like two little horns when they ran across the sand at very high speed.'

By 1700 all the boats had returned to the Yacht and *Britannia* resumed her passage stopping the next day at the Farquar Islands.

'These islands were another little speck in the ocean. We arrived at 1215 and I went ashore in the jolly boat to explore. It was a beautiful island about 200 yards long with lagoons and white sand all round. I radioed back to the Yacht that I thought it was OK and *Britannia* anchored by the remains of a wreck on the reef. The Admiral took the Royal party ashore after lunch and three boats went away to fish but we did better from the Yacht's side. Able Seaman Clench caught a beautiful red and blue spotted wrasse of about 10 pounds. Several huge Manta rays, about 12 feet across from wing to wing, circled us. The island was so different from the long coral sand of the previous day. While they were ashore the Royal party had some young fledglings brought to them by four natives while they were there. The natives hadn't a clue who anyone was although the word *Britannia* rang a bell somewhere!' Admiral Adams remarked.

After a further two days at sea, *Britannia* arrived off Mauritius, which is also known as the star and key of the Indian Ocean, as Admiral Adams recalls:

'The approach to Mauritius was simply lovely. The island was small only 36 by 28 miles wide and we could see nearly all of it from the sea. The centre has many jagged peaks, none going above 2700 feet high but seeming far more in perspective. Port Louis is the harbour at the foot of it all and although dirty and dishevelled by the standards of the rest of the island, attractive from seaward with waving palm trees, etc. White coral beaches with white surf thundering against the jade green reef.'

The yacht secured at 0800 in Port Louis with Princess Margaret disembarking at 1030 to live ashore in Government House for the duration of her visit. Once the Princess had left the Yachtsmen got on with their normal routine, as Admiral Adams explains:

'We spent the rest of the morning getting straight as we always did in a new harbour. Where does the sullage go? What liberty boats were required? Which parts of the town were the vice centres? What drink is bad? Entertainment programme? Uniform for libertymen? What are the police doing to help us? Ceremonial sentry for the jetty? Cars for the Admiral and the Wardroom – and so on.'

On 1 October Princess Margaret returned and half an hour later the Yacht sailed for Zanzibar being given another superb send off by the locals.

'The visit was a very great success and in particular all the French were widely excited about Princess Margaret and wanted to know everything. The French were also the most appreciative people that any of us had shown round the Yacht. We sailed at 1900 in the dark with the Yacht floodlit. The entrance was narrow with ships loading sugar either side of the channel. Then suddenly two enormous bonfires flared up very brightly and fireworks started everywhere. With the flares, lights of Port Louis and all the cascading stars and cheers from all the ships and masses of small boats it was the most impressive departure I had seen during my time in *Britannia*,' Admiral Adams remarked.

After a few days at sea, which included a ship's concert for Princess Margaret given by the Yachtsmen, *Britannia* arrived in Zanzibar on 5 October, which lived up to the expectations of those on board, as Admiral Adams recalled:

'Zanzibar was all that the romanticists would have it. The smell of cloves comes over the water before anchoring, the small sailing dhows with their triangular sails and the fast native catamarans called *ngawalas* all made a wonderful picture. There were coral sands and palm trees with a most attractive-looking city coming right down to the water's edge. All the Arab boats had their drummers going full blast and chanting so that everywhere there seemed to be the hot rhythm falling and rising. When the Princess went ashore she had the most wonderful welcome. She then spent the whole day ashore doing various functions.'

On 7 October the Yacht left Zanzibar for Dar-es-Salaam stopping en route at another small island for a picnic organised by the Wardroom for Princess Margaret. While the Royal party was ashore the Yachtsmen were engaged in a fishing competition on the forecastle and one Yachtsman managed to catch an octopus which glided along the deck with effortless grace. The next morning the Yacht secured in Dar-es-Salaam for Princess Margaret to disembark at 1020 to continue the rest of her East African Tour ashore. When the Yacht sailed at 1800 she was watched by Princess Margaret from Government House.[51] The following morning Britannia arrived at Mombasa to wait for Prince Philip to arrive a week later, thus providing an opportunity for the Yachtsmen to take some leave ahead of their next period of Royal duty.

Prince Philip joined the Yacht on 16 October having flown into Kenya. Although his arrival was kept low key, so that it didn't overshadow Princess Margaret's continuing Tour of the area, his journey to the Yacht was slightly unusual in that he was driven in a vintage Rolls Royce which had been borrowed from a former police superintendent. At 2200 Britannia slipped her moorings, bound for Mahe Island, capital of the Seychelles Islands.[52] Despite watching the Yacht's arrival from the Governor's summer residence, Sans Souci, the island's most famous resident at the time, Archbishop Makarios, did not meet Prince Philip during his short visit on 19 October. From there the Yacht sailed for Ceylon for a three-day visit. During this time reports were received that riots had broken in Singapore's Chinese schools, which lead to a rapid change in the Yacht's programme. Prince Philip had been due to pay a visit to Singapore next. However, the Foreign Office advised him that it would be unwise to proceed with the original plan. In a hasty revision planned over the radio telephone it was decided to go to Langkawi Island on 30 October, followed by Penang on 31 October, and then resume the original programme.

While Prince Philip spent the night of 31 October ashore in Kuala Lumpur the Yacht sailed round to Port Swettenham arriving there on 1 November.[53] That night Prince Philip hosted a dinner on board for the rulers of the Malay States, prior to Britannia's departure at 2300 to begin the 3000-mile voyage to Australia. When Britannia arrived nine days later at Port Moresby, Papua New Guinea, Prince Philip took the opportunity to keep up his ship-handling skills and berthed Britannia himself.[54] He

then went aft to receive the Australian Governor-General, Field Marshal Sir William Slim, who joined Britannia for the voyage across the Coral Sea to Brisbane. Prince Philip left the Yacht early on 11 November to complete his Tour of New Guinea visiting Lae and Rabaul, before flying to Australia where he would rejoin the Yacht in Melbourne at the end of the month. In the meantime Britannia sailed later that afternoon for Australia to visit Brisbane and Sydney before arriving in Melbourne on 29 November.

When Prince Philip embarked again the following day, Britannia was moored in the River Yarra, which runs through the centre of Melbourne. Between 1 and 8 December Prince Philip spent the days ashore undertaking engagements linked to the XVIth Olympic Games and often drove himself in his Lagonda. On board Britannia there was particular interest in the progress of Bluebottle, which had been chosen as the British Dragon for the Olympics. The races were held in Port Phillip Bay, which is a roughly circular shaped stretch of water, about 30 miles across and virtually tideless. In her final race of the Games with her sailing master, Lieutenant Commander G H Mann RN at the helm, the Royal Dragon seized the Bronze Medal from the grasp of the Argentinean Dragon Pampero. While a number of Yachtsmen were able to get tickets to watch the Games, those required for duty on board watched them on one of the six TV sets kindly lent to the Yacht during her visit.

After a day of relaxation Prince Philip went to the Royal Australian Air Force graduation parade at Point Cook on 10 December. While he was away, two of his guests joined Britannia as part of the Royal party for the long voyage ahead. Sir Raymond Priestley was a distinguished explorer and had gone to the Antarctic with both Shackleton and Scott.[55] He later held a number of prestigious appointments, including that of Vice Chancellor of the Universities of Melbourne and Birmingham and Chairman of the Royal Commission on the Civil Service between 1953 and 1955. He enjoyed his time in Britannia, as Admiral Adams recalls: 'he had a big sense of humour and he used to give us all nicknames based on birds.' Anne Griffiths continued: 'he entered into all aspects of life on board, lecturing the Yachtsmen on his previous Antarctic experiences and was usually seen wearing a bandanna handkerchief tied over the top of his head.'

The second guest was Edward Seago who had spent his early adult life travelling and painting with circuses. During the Second World War he became the personal war artist to General Alexander in the Italian campaign. After the War he became a visitor to Sandringham, and members of the Royal Family including The Queen

Mother and Princess Margaret visited his studio in Ludham, Norfolk. Discussing why he invited Edward Seago for the Antarctic Tour Prince Philip said:

'I had no idea what to expect, but I knew that no artist of any repute had done any work in the Antarctic since Wilson did his marvellous watercolours while he was with the Scott Expedition. I hoped that Ted would find something to challenge his remarkable talent for landscape painting. Neither of us was disappointed. We could hardly tear him away from his easel to come to meals. He was fascinated by the icebergs, the colour of the sea between the drifting pack ice and the background of glaciers and snow-covered hills. We were fascinated by his almost miraculous technique. He had a knack of capturing a scene with speed and dexterity that rivalled that of a conjurer.'

On the morning of the 11th Prince Philip was due to leave for New Zealand by air. However, his flight was delayed due to engine problems, and thus Britannia left Melbourne half an hour late. The Yacht was towed stern first down the River Yarra to the basin where she was turned with the assistance of a tug before she could head back to sea. The four-day voyage to Lyttelton provided a good chance for the two new guests to be given a thorough tour of Britannia by FORY. Ted Seago also began painting, including one picture of the islands of the Tasman Sea by memory. He subsequently had to alter it when Sir Raymond pointed out that he had omitted the main feature of the depicted scene, which was a square fortress like rock!

Britannia's arrival in Lyttelton on the morning of 15 December was marred by a minor berthing incident when the cross wind briefly strengthened at the wrong moment and pushed the Yacht's stern hard against the wharf. Despite a request from the Yacht to have adequate catamarans between the wharf and Britannia, the Harbour Authorities had only provided a pair of logs strapped together. They promptly capsized the moment Britannia touched them, providing no protection between the hull and the wooden piles of the jetty. Although a number of plates were buckled and the lower gangway doors were stove in, a water test, using high pressure hoses, proved that her seaworthiness for the voyage ahead had not been affected. However, the lower gangway doors would not be usable again until the frame could be straightened back in the UK. The following morning many of the Yachtsmen turned out to see the arrival of HMNZS Endeavour which was due to take the New Zealand element of the Trans Antarctic Expedition under Sir Edmund Hillary down to McMurdo Sound.

Having joined the Yacht the night before, Prince Philip spent 17 December undertaking a programme of engagements in Lyttelton and Christchurch. The day started well when he was presented with the Glass Reinforced Plastic (GRP) sailing dinghy, White Heron, by the New Zealand Manufacturers' Federation, which was subsequently craned on board Britannia for the voyage. Prince Philip then went on board Endeavour to be taken around the ship by Sir Edmund Hillary. The rest of the Royal party were entertained in the mess by the expedition team who were fascinated by Sir Raymond's tales of his own departure from Lyttelton on board Nimrod in 1907 as part of Shackleton's first expedition. Sir Raymond recalled that when they left in Nimrod they were given a tremendous send off by a crowd of 50,000 people. While Prince Philip then went off to complete the rest of his programme, the Yachtsmen were busily embarking the final stores for their Antarctic adventure, including fresh and frozen food, prior to their departure that night.

Two days later Britannia arrived at the Chatham Islands. Describing this short visit Prince Philip said:

'The Chatham Islands are not unlike the Shetlands – rolling, windswept, grassy hills, the only trees stunted and bent by the wind. We attended a race meeting there and an outdoor Maori cook up for the whole population. Huge pieces of beef and mutton, cabbages and potatoes were cooked in a large pit in the ground, covered with a sheet and the earth heaped over the top. A most effective way of cooking for a large number of people, and the results were certainly eatable, though I can't imagine the comments of a French chef.'

Britannia sailed from the Chatham Islands on 19 December to begin the Roaring Forties part of the voyage. In recognition of this Prince Philip agreed that beards could be grown on board and he joined in the spirit by growing one himself. About 150 of the Yachtsmen also started to grow beards as did Admiral Abel Smith and most of the officers. Later that day the Yacht crossed the International Date Line which enabled the Commander to enjoy his birthday twice over, so he generously threw two parties to celebrate. As the Yacht headed south the preparations for potential rough weather were made, as Admiral Adams explains:

'We put up all the storm shutters. Boats were tied down with extra lashings. Some of the furniture was lashed in place to stop it crashing about. Fortunately, there was to be no need for any of these precautions because the weather was very good. Sir Raymond Priestley went round the Yacht looking at our superstructure and kept saying, "We're going to turn turtle if it freezes up."'

The artist Ted Seago at work in the Antarctic.

(© British Crown Copyright / MOD)

So I said, "Sir, please can you stop putting the fear of death into the Yachtsmen.'"

During those long days at sea both Prince Philip and Ted Seago got on with their painting. Prince Philip spent the first two days painting Ted Seago, Sir Raymond Priestley and Mike Parker while Seago painted the Chatham Islands and, on 21 December, used the Replenishment At Sea (RAS) with *Wave Chief* as the subject for another painting. Surprisingly, the weather continued to be kind despite Sir Raymond Priestley's earlier gloomy predictions. About the only wintry weather recorded in the Tour Diary for this period was a snow storm during a game of deck hockey on 23 December. However, on Christmas Day itself this spell of good weather was broken as the sea became rough and the sunshine gave way to dull skies. Because of the time difference with the UK it was an early start for the Yachtsmen so that they could listen to the BBC's hour-long Christmas Day broadcast from around the world. The final instalment of this programme was Prince Philip's speech live from the temporary radio studio in The Queen's Sitting Room on board the Yacht at 0656 local time (1456 in the UK). There had been some concerns about whether the BBC in London would be able to receive the broadcast from the Yacht 9000 miles away. As a precaution Prince Philip had made a recording in Christchurch on 16 December which was flown back to the UK. Half an hour before he was due to speak it looked as though the recording might be need-

ed because the Yacht's radio was being jammed by another station but thankfully the Communications Department came up with a solution and Prince Philip was able to make his speech as planned. Appropriately enough Prince Philip's broadcast was immediately followed by The Queen's traditional Christmas broadcast to the nation in which she mentioned the Yacht's company and their families, which was greatly appreciated by those on board.

By the time most of the Yachtsmen sat down for their breakfast they had already opened the presents their families had given them four months ago. Lieutenant Commander Wall's present to the Communications Department was perhaps the most imaginative of all. Shortly before *Britannia*'s departure from Portsmouth he had arranged for a tape recording to be made for each man within the branch by their wife, girlfriend or mother, which he played to them on Christmas morning. The Wardroom also exchanged presents with the Household, as Admiral Adams recalls:

'The Wardroom as a whole gave mechanical toys to the Household with a wonderful walking and talking cat to Prince Philip. Mike Parker was given a similar thing like a monkey while Viscount Cilcennin was given a frog with a coronet on his head and its mouth wide open. Sir Raymond got a Penguin with flapping wings.'

Soon after breakfast it emerged that there was a new Vice Admiral on board together with his Commander and Secretary and that they were busy conducting thorough rounds of 'their' new command. In fact the new arrivals turned out to be a team from the Engineer's Department who were following naval traditions for Christmas Day by impersonating senior officers. After the well-attended church service in the Royal Dining Room Prince Philip, accompanied by the Household, officers, and the youngest Yachtsman, Steward Gibson, who was dressed up in one of the Admiral's uniforms, conducted rounds and visited every mess on board. Describing some of what they saw during their rounds Admiral Adams recalled:

'The Royal Steward's mess had a bar in place of the hammock netting, the Chief Petty Officers mess had a drop down cloth of the Yacht, icebergs, penguins and Merry Christmas spelt out in rope, the Petty Officers used plenty of streamers and sticky labels left over from the cocktail parties at Melbourne, the Royal Marines had made up a motif of koala bears on a tree while the Communications mess had one of Winston Churchill. The stokers had completely closed in their mess with bunting, made a fireplace out of hammock netting and put the side of a house the size of a window at one end of the mess. The seamen weren't very enterprising but

had a large meteorological balloon with "Happy Christmas Dukie" written on it. The Supply Department made a cottage out of hammock netting with Father Christmas dashing over it driven by two carved antelopes from Mombasa. So we went round with neat rum being forced on to us although we tried to share it out which wasn't always successful as Prince Philip, the Admiral and myself were obvious targets.'

The winner of the best-decorated mess was judged by Prince Philip to be the Communications mess for which they were summoned to the Wardroom to receive 10 cigars. Following a cold buffet lunch in the Wardroom, Prince Philip and Ted Seago began work on drawing and cutting out a wooden block for the 'Red Nose' certificates

It is a naval tradition that on Christmas Day the youngest sailor on board a ship becomes the 'Commanding Officer' for the day. On this occassion Steward Gibson was elevated to the rank of Vice Admiral and was lent one of Vice Admiral Sir Conolly Abel Smith's uniforms. He is seen here conducting rounds with Prince Philip.

(© British Crown Copyright / MOD)

Prince Philip inks up the wooden block for the 'Red Nose' certificates designed by His Royal Highness and Ted Seago.

(© British Crown Copyright / MOD)

which were later printed on old charts and issued to the Yacht's company on entering the Antarctic Circle. The festivities continued later in the day with a smoking concert after tea and the Wardroom being invited aft to join Prince Philip's Christmas night party. By the time the last of the celebrations died down after midnight everyone had had a very enjoyable day despite being thousands of miles from their loved ones.

On Boxing Day the Yachtsmen sighted their first tabular iceberg. It was about 3½ miles long and 150 feet high and was followed the next day by the sighting of a further two icebergs. However, on 28 December it was discovered that the fuel taken on from *Wave Chief* after Christmas had been contaminated by sea water and thus it all had to be returned to *Wave Chief* before a fresh load of fuel could be transferred. This operation lasted into the next day before *Wave Chief* was able to leave the Yacht in the afternoon and head north to the Falkland Islands. Her place as escort was taken by the Ice Patrol ship HMS *Protector*, which rendezvoused with the Yacht at 1830 wearing the flag of the Governor of the Falkland Islands, Mr O R Arthur CMG CVO. During the voyage towards the Antarctic Circle the Bathythermograph was dipped to measure the underwater sea temperatures. When the Yacht crossed the Antarctic convergence on 30 December the temperature dropped from 44°F to 37°F degrees within 12 hours.

The following day at 0630 *Britannia* became the first Royal Yacht to enter the Antarctic Circle[56] while Prince Philip's Lady Clerks, Anne Stevenson and Ione Eadie, became the first two British ladies ever to cross the

Antarctic Circle and received a signal from the Governor in HMS *Protector*. At 1030 the Yacht came across the whale factory ship *Southern Harvester*. In 1956 the UK was still a whaling nation and at that time the whale population was not under threat. Therefore it was only natural that Prince Philip should take an interest in *Southern Harvester's* activities. Describing the meeting with *Southern Harvester* Prince Philip said:

'The method of transfer was quite interesting. A whale catcher, towing a dead sperm whale alongside as a fender, came alongside the Yacht. On the catcher's deck was a large round wicker basket which was attached to a rope which went to the top of the catcher's mast and then down to its winch. There were also two steadying lines. The basket was hauled up and then across to the Yacht; each member of the party in turn climbed into the basket, was hauled up off the Yacht's deck and lowered on to the catcher.

'This sounds quite reasonable, but there was quite a swell running and the catcher's mast reached only a short way above the Yacht's deck. The result was that as the ships rolled apart the basket was snatched away from the Yacht, and then swung gaily about the catcher's mast. The return journey was done the same way and was even more perilous. Added to this, each time the ships rolled together the sperm whale fender was given a hefty squeeze and as it was not altogether freshly killed the waves of stench that arose at intervals cannot be described.'

Southern Harvester was the depot ship for about 15 whale

A whale catcher towing a dead sperm whale as a fender comes alongside Britannia *to embark Prince Philip for his visit to the whale factory ship* Southern Harvester.

(© British Crown Copyright / MOD)

catchers which closely resembled a typical East Coast fishing trawler. Once a whale had been caught and killed markers were attached and the whale catcher would leave the body drifting in the sea to go and catch the next whale. When the catcher had caught enough whales it would use the markers to locate the drifting whales and tow them back to the factory ship for processing. Describing what he saw on board *Southern Harvester* Prince Philip continued:

'There was an enormous square hole at the waterline in the stern and a ramp which led from the hole up to the flensing deck, covering about three quarters of the ship's space. The deck was divided into two parts. On the first part the flensers got to work with long curved knives on the ends of broom handles and cut the blubber off the flesh. It was cut into strips and the strips were torn off by a wire and a steam winch while the flenser neatly separated the blubber from the flesh as the strip peeled off. The long strips were then cut into roughly 1-foot squares and pushed into the tops of boil-

ing vats. These holes were level with the deck, so I had to look where I was going on the flensing deck as the blood and blubber made it as slippery as an ice rink.

'The remainder of the whale, that is the flesh and bones after the blubber had been stripped, was dragged by winches on to the second part of the deck, where it was, so to speak, butchered. The flesh was sliced off in huge hunks, cut up and pushed into one set of boiling vats, and the bones into another.

'All of the parts of the whale were perfectly recognisable, but their size comes as a bit of a shock. The vertebrae, for instance, were the size of side drums and were wrenched apart by steam winches. The ribs were up to 10 feet; as an ordinary butcher's saw wouldn't have got very far on those bones, they used a steam driven saw with a blade 8 feet long. The intestines looked very similar to a heap of inner tubes for tractors' tyres.

'Apart from accommodation, the rest of the ship was given over to the machinery for processing the whales to oil, and bone and blood meal and the necessary storage tanks and holds.'

Prince Philip and his party returned to the Yacht at 1700, including Mr Arthur who had joined the visit to *Southern Harvester* by helicopter from *Protector*. The Governor's New Year celebrations began on a high note because the BBC had just broadcast the New Year's Honours list, which included the news that he was to be made a Knight Commander of the Order of St Michael and St George, thus making him Sir Raynor Arthur KCMG CVO. Just before midnight the Royal party returned aft from the Wardroom to see the youngest officer on board, Lieutenant Malcolm Baird RAN, ring in the New Year 16 times on the ship's bell in broad daylight! The temperature was unbelievably mild allowing the officers and members of the Royal party to sing 'Auld Land Syne' on the Verandah Deck while still in their mess jackets without the need for greatcoats. At 0900 the Yacht rendezvoused with the RRS *John Biscoe* in thick fog in the Marthe Strait off the tip of Adelaide Island. Prince Philip transferred by jolly boat to the *John Biscoe* to make the voyage through pack ice to Base W, which was the most southerly of the bases that he was due to visit.

While Prince Philip was visiting the southerly Falkland Islands Dependency Survey (FIDS) Bases, the Yacht, together with *Protector*, steamed around the outside of the ice to rendezvous with *John Biscoe* at Port Lockroy the next day, where Prince Philip was due to visit the oldest of the FIDS Bases which also acted as the centre of their radio network. The voyage south towards Port Lockroy took *Britannia* and *Protector* through the Neumayer Channel which was only a mile wide at times. As she approached Wiencke Island the Yachtsmen were given their first sight of the Antarctic mountains and glaciers. *Britannia*'s arrival ahead of *John Biscoe* provided the Yachtsmen with the chance to go ashore and visit a penguin rookery inhabited by gentoo penguins. However, it was soon time to resume official duties as *John Biscoe* emerged from the Bismarck Strait. During the Prince's tour of the southernmost bases the American observer Mr Crawford insisted in playing a game of tennis with Sir Raymond Priestley to claim the honour of playing the first such game in the Antarctic Circle. From Port Lockroy the three ships headed north again through the Neumayer Channel to visit Base O located on the southern side of the island of Ronge. However, because of ice in the narrow channel leading to the recently established Base O, between the mainland and the island, the Yacht and *Protector* had to lay off the northern end of Ronge while *John Biscoe* took Prince Philip to the base. With his southernmost visits complete Prince Philip transferred back to the Yacht at 2300 enabling *John Biscoe* to set sail for the Falkland Islands while *Britannia* and *Protector* sailed through the Schollaert Channel towards Deception Island to visit Base B.

When they arrived off Neptune's Bellows, which was shrouded in fog on 3 January 1957, it was decided to abort the passage through the narrow channel that leads to the horseshoe-shaped harbour. The island was once an active volcano and the remains of the crater form a relatively sheltered harbour. While the Yacht remained at anchor off the harbour, the Royal party went ashore in a jolly boat that was conned through Neptune's Bellows by *Britannia*'s radar. When the fog cleared in the afternoon the Yacht was able to enter the harbour and drop anchor. In addition to the FIDS Base, Hunting Aerosurveys Ltd also had a base from which they operated a pair of Catalina flying boats to conduct aerial surveys in the region. As Admiral Adams recalled the local wildlife were very curious about their neighbours:

> 'There was a man working on one of the Catalinas with a spanner. When he put it down a penguin saw this lovely shiny thing and rushed up and took it off to his nest. The engineer got up and retrieved it; he then put it down again and back came the penguin.'

When the Royal party visited the FIDS Base they discovered that the inhabitants collected tails of the ties of visitors. Each member of the party had the tail of his tie cut

Prince Philip and Sir Raymond Priestly (right) look round the whale factory ship Southern Harvester.

(© British Crown Copyright / MOD)

off and nailed to the bar. As Prince Philip's Private Secretary, Lieutenant Commander Mike Parker didn't have a tie he lost the tail of his tartan shirt, while Anne Stevenson lost two handkerchiefs and a headscarf as did Ione Eadie. Prince Philip returned the hospitality of both bases and invited them on board the Yacht for a Wardroom supper and to watch the film *Seven Brides for Seven Brothers* in the Royal Dining Room.

Prince Philip had hoped to have seen Deception Island from *Protector*'s helicopter the following morning, but the weather prevented this, so *Britannia* set sail at 1100 for the four-hour passage to King George Island of the South Shetland Islands. On her way across to Base G the Yacht stopped off St Thomas's Point so that Prince Philip could visit a vast penguin rookery, populated by an estimated 250,000 birds including chinstraps, gentoos and adelies, as well as a colony of elephant and weddell seals. Prince Philip and Sir Raynor Arthur decided to have a closer

look at the birds and climbed up the steep hill. The Yacht then steamed across Admiralty Bay to anchor in the Martel Inlet for Prince Philip's visit to Base G. At 2230 *Britannia* weighed anchor bound for the Falkland Islands thus concluding Prince Philip's tour of the Grahamland Peninsula. During 5 and 6 January the Yacht crossed the Drake Passage below the notorious Cape Horn, once again experiencing remarkably calm weather which had been a pleasant feature of the entire Antarctic Tour, except for a couple of relatively rough days over Christmas.

Early on 7 January the Yacht paused to fit kelp strainers over the main condenser inlets before entering the outer harbour of Port Stanley and passing the tanker *Wave Chief*. As she approached the inner harbour the two FIDS ships, *John Biscoe* and *Shackleton*, which were moored alongside the abandoned sailing ships being used as store ships, oil hulks and jetties, came into view as they each fired a salute before *Britannia* anchored just 400 yards off the town of Port Stanley. One of the abandoned ships in the harbour was the hull of *Great Britain*, which was eventually brought back to this country and is now

Britannia lying off Deception Island.

(© British Crown Copyright / MOD)

Prince Philip used a horse to visit a remote beach on the Falkland Islands. Note the rather unusual sheepskin saddle.

(© British Crown Copyright / MOD)

preserved in Bristol. The Falklands Islands Company had been using her to store wool. At 0930 Prince Philip went ashore in full dress uniform for the formal welcoming ceremony before being driven to Government House in the Governor's London Taxi to change for the afternoon's horse racing. The annual Sailors Race had its most distinguished list of jockeys in its history, which included Prince Philip, Admiral Abel Smith, Lieutenant Commander Parker and Sir Raynor Arthur among the nine starters. Prince Philip was given a tremendous ovation by the islanders when he passed the post, a length in front of Lieutenant Commander Parker, who was in turn a length in front of the Admiral.

The following morning Prince Philip was taken for a flight in a Beaver float plane to see more of the island at the start of another busy day of engagements, which culminated in a reception on board the Yacht for the people of Port Stanley, before *Britannia* sailed for Fox Bay, West Falkland. After a morning ashore to see the meteorological station and local farming a lunchtime reception was held on board the Yacht before she headed towards South Georgia. Despite warnings of bad weather from the islanders the passage to South Georgia was calm and relatively uneventful. The Yacht arrived at first light on 12 January and anchored in Leith harbour at 0900.

Prince Philip transferred from *Britannia* to *Busemann* to be taken ashore for a tour of Salvesen's whaling factory before embarking in the whale catcher *Southern Jester* for the 20-mile voyage to Grytviken. *Southern Jester* was com-

manded by Nochart Neilson who, at the age of 63, was reputed to be the oldest and best gunner in South Georgia.[57] During the short voyage he demonstrated his marksmanship to Prince Philip by dropping a box over the side and shooting it to bits at a range of 70 yards. In honour of Prince Philip's visit five whale catchers were neatly moored up in Grytviken and dressed overall. As he arrived the whale catchers fired a 21-gun salute with their harpoon guns. After lunch the Royal party went to see the plain white cross which had been erected as a memorial to Sir Ernest Shackleton who died on the island in 1922. The Royal party then moved on to the Compania Argentina de Pesca's whale factory to watch it in action as it dealt with two fin whales and experienced the foul series of rich and nauseating stenches that are an unforgettable part of the process. Before Prince Philip returned to *Britannia* he went with Sir Raymond Priestly to visit the grave of Sir Ernest Shackleton which lies in the cemetery at Grytviken marked by a large granite block. After a brief visit to The King Penguin Rookery in the Bay of Isles *Britannia* got underway to Gough Island.

Early the next morning the Yacht discovered three whale catchers in the middle of hunting whales among 25 icebergs. Those on board *Britannia* witnessed their first kill, as Admiral Adams recalls: 'It was a horrible sight. I

From left to right: Prince Philip, Sir Raymond Priestly and Ted Seago visit the memorial to Sir Ernest Shackleton on South Georgia.

(© British Crown Copyright / MOD)

At Grytviken the Royal party witnessed the process of dealing with two fin whales and experienced the foul series of rich and nauseating stenches that were an unforgettable part of the process.

(© British Crown Copyright / MOD)

never realised that the whales made a noise and that there was so much blood. The sea was red with blood for about 100 yards around the whale.' After witnessing a second kill the Yacht resumed her course for Gough Island which, apart from the small South African weather station, is inhabited only by penguins, seabirds and mice. The island was first discovered by the Portuguese in the sixteenth century who named it Diego Alvarez. The island was given its present name in honour of Captain Gough who came across the island in 1731. Since then Gough has been visited by a variety of people including diamond miners, sealmen and whalemen. Many of these visitors have carved details of their landings on stone slabs.

The passage between South Georgia and Gough Island witnessed a major achievement in *Britannia*'s short history when she completed her first circumnavigation in longitude 17° 43' West at 1030 on 15 January. This feat had been completed in 135 days, during which time the Yacht had crossed the equator three times and steamed 31,430 miles. To mark the occasion the Yacht's siren sounded four long blasts. The following day the greenery of Gough Island began to emerge over the horizon after 1300 and its landscape made a dramatic change to the icebergs and landscape of the Antarctic.

Prince Philip and his party went ashore by dinghy to visit the weather station which was located in the hut built by the 1955–56 Gough Island Scientific Expedition. Prince Philip had been Patron of the expedition so he was keen to see the island, including the 2986-foot peak which was named Edinburgh Peak in his honour by the survey team. Unfortunately, the peak remained shrouded in cloud for the duration of the visit but the Royal party returned to the Yacht in time to see the two southern right whales which had been swimming around *Britannia* during the afternoon. By the time *Britannia* weighed anchor at 1800 she had acquired an additional passenger.

When the Yacht arrived the Surgeon Commander was asked to examine Lukas Henning of the weather station party who was experiencing abdominal pains. He quickly concluded that he would need an operation to remove his appendix, which was successfully conducted later that evening during the voyage to Tristan Da Cunha.

Tristan Da Cunha is the furthest island from another populated land in the world and was discovered in 1506 by the Portuguese Admiral who gave his name to the island group. The island was then left undisturbed until the Dutch explored it in 1643. The island was later used by pirates, sealers and whalers, and in 1810 Jonathan Lambert of Salem proclaimed himself King of the three islands which he renamed the Islands of Refreshment. By the time the British deployed a garrison from South Africa to the island in 1816, to prevent any attempts to rescue the exiled Napoleon on the nearby St Helena, Lambert and his shipmate Williams had disappeared leaving Thomas Currie as the last of the trio, who claimed he had lived alone for the last six years. Within a year Britain felt that the threat posed by Napoleon had eased so they recalled the garrison. However, Corporal William Glass asked for permission to remain behind and he founded the colony of Tristan Da Cunha together with his family and two other soldiers who left shortly afterwards. Subsequently, the population started to grow through the survivors of shipwrecks and sailors who deserted or asked to be dropped off. The main settlement was named Edinburgh in honour of Prince Alfred, Duke of Edinburgh, who visited the island in 1867.

Shortly after the Yacht dropped anchor on 17 January off Big Beach, Prince Philip was collected by the islanders using one of their canvas-hulled long boats. Dressed in the uniform of an Admiral of the Fleet Prince Philip took the helm of the long boat while the Chief of the Island, Willie Repetto, took on the role of pilot. 'Conolly Abel Smith brought his shooting stick with him and I only just stopped him in time from using it on the canvas hull!' Prince Philip remarked. Once ashore Prince Philip was greeted by many of the 250 islanders. As part of his programme ashore Prince Philip was shown around the canning factory, which had been built in 1949 to can crawfish, and a short tour of a few of the small thatched cottages inhabited by the islanders. While this was going on the Yachtsmen played football against the Island's XI

on a pitch that sloped down to the cliffs. Great care had to be taken to keep the ball on the island. The day ashore culminated in the RM Band providing the music for an island dance in the school hall before Prince Philip returned to the Yacht in a long boat to enable *Britannia* to weigh anchor bound for St Helena.

After two days at sea *Britannia* received a signal on 20 January from the Argentinean ship SS *Mabel Ryan* stating that the First Engineer, Carlos Heine, was in need of immediate medical attention. Interestingly, the *Mabel Ryan* was owned by Compania Argentina de Pesca, which also owned the whaling station that Prince Philip had visited at Grytviken on South Georgia.[58] On receiving the signal the Yacht's course was changed and the speed increased to 17 knots to rendezvous with the *Mabel Ryan* which was 250 miles away. The two ships met at 0100 the next morning and Carlos Heine was transferred to *Britannia* to have his appendix removed. Despite the detour *Britannia* still arrived off St Helena at 0930 as planned for Prince Philip to visit the former home of the exiled Emperor Napoleon. When King George VI and Queen Elizabeth, accompanied by the two Princesses, had

During the voyage from South Georgia to Gough Island Britannia *came across this whale catcher in the course of hunting a whale.* (© British Crown Copyright / MOD)

visited the island in 1947 on their way home from South Africa, Napoleon's house at Longwood was virtually a ruin due to the white ant which had eaten nearly all of the woodwork. Afterwards Queen Elizabeth discussed the state of Longwood with the French Ambassador in London. This led to the French Government's restoration of Longwood which was completed by the time of Prince Philip's visit. From Longwood Prince Philip went to see the site of Napoleon's original tomb which the former Emperor had chosen himself. At the time of his death in 1821 the British would only allow the words General Bonaparte to be inscribed on his tomb. In a final act of defiance the French decided to leave the flat white stone covering the grave completely blank. When Napoleon's body was later taken to France for internment at Les Invalides in 1840 the stone slab was left as a reminder of his initial resting place. Before *Britannia* set sail for Ascension Island at 2300 Prince Philip hosted a dinner party for some of the islanders on board the Yacht.

After an uneventful passage *Britannia* dropped anchor off Ascension Island at 1000 GMT on 25 January. However, a misunderstanding about which time zone was observed by the islanders meant that the Yacht was in fact one hour late! This didn't seem to spoil Prince Philip's brief visit to the island. As *Britannia* headed north towards Gambia she crossed the equator for the fourth time at 2100 on 26 January. Two days later *Britannia* was joined at midday by the *Egret* class frigate HMS *Pelican* as escort. The following day the Yacht entered the Gambia River in poor visibility. As the Yacht made her way up the river Prince Philip took

over the handling of the Yacht and brought her alongside in Bathurst for the start of a three-day visit to the Gambia. To mark the Yacht's arrival the Governor, Sir Percy Wyn-Harris let off a fireworks display, as Prince Philip recalls:

'The fireworks were fired from a pair of old guns outside Government House. The Governor developed a technique of lighting the fuse of a "thunderflash" and putting it down the barrel of the gun. He then lit another thunderflash and dropped that into the barrel. The first fired the second into the air, which then went off and scared all the kites in the fig trees. He described the effect as a "double drambuie".'

During his day ashore Prince Philip was given a display of native dancing which was followed in the evening by a torchlight parade through the main street. At the head of the parade there was a series of illuminated models depicting ships from many different eras. The following morning the Yacht sailed to begin the 75-mile journey up river towards Sankwia. Along the way the Yacht stopped to enable Prince Philip to go ashore at Salekeni for a crocodile shoot before resuming her voyage past the mangrove swamps. That evening the local chiefs were invited on board for a reception hosted by Prince Philip.

Prince Philip attended the 14th conference of Chiefs of the Gambia Protectorate on the morning of 31 January before having lunch on board the Governor's yacht *Mansa Kila Kuta*. In the afternoon *Britannia* began the voyage back down the Gambia River towards Bathurst stopping off at Tendaba Creek where Prince Philip went ashore to see some of the rice fields. Shortly after Prince Philip returned to the Yacht Admiral Abel Smith tried to turn *Britannia* but briefly ran aground on one of the projecting mud flats. The passage up and down the Gambia River was very challenging for both the Admiral and Commander (N) as there was only 3 or 4 feet beneath the keel at times. When the Yacht reached Bathurst she paused for the Governor to be disembarked before resuming her voyage out to the open sea.

The following morning the SS *Uganda* performed a close sail by with her decks crowded with passengers. Prince Philip watched her manoeuvres with interest from the Verandah Deck and waved to the passengers as she sailed by. Now that Prince Philip had effectively completed his World Tour it was decided to hold the final of the beard growing competition that evening. The competitors, who had had a month and a half to grow their beards since *Britannia* left the Chatham Islands on 19 December, gathered on the forecastle to be judged by Sir Raymond Priestley, Commander Adams, Lieutenant Commander Parker and Chief Writer Barrett. The judges decided to split the contest into five categories namely the bushiest, the handsomest, the most distinguished, the most colourful, and the one that didn't quite make it. The panel decided to award the prize for the most handsome beard to Petty Officer Mander and judged Musicians Casseldon and Fitzgerald to have the bushiest and most

distinguished beards respectively, while Leading Seaman Ward's beard was the most colourful. Abel Seaman Solbach secured the dubious honour of having the beard that didn't quite make it with a single hair about 18 inches long! He was awarded the prize of razor, razor blades and shaving soap. By the following morning most of the Yachtsmen had shaved off their beards just in time for the round of official group photographs to be taken. Prince Philip caused some amusement by shaving off his beard one day but keeping a moustache for a further 24 hours. The final three days at sea before *Britannia* reached Gibraltar provided a last chance to pursue the various deck games such as tug-of-war and squat football.

On 6 February Prince Philip brought the Yacht alongside in Gibraltar to conclude his World Tour which had seen the Yacht steam 39,000 miles since she left her Hampshire home in August 1956. However, there was no rest for the Yachtsmen because they had to prepare *Britannia* so that she was immaculate for The Queen's State Visit to Portugal. Shortly after *Britannia*'s arrival Prince Philip's party began to disperse, with Lieutenant

Prince Philip is met by the islanders of St Helena. Even in these remote island communities the full ceremonial formalities were observed. The Governor wears his uniform and Prince Philip is dressed in the uniform of an Admiral of the Fleet.

(© British Crown Copyright / MOD)

On the final visit of Prince Philip's extensive 1956–57 World Tour he visits a small community in Sankwia, Gambia.

(© British Crown Copyright / MOD)

Commander Parker flying home that day, followed by Sir Raymond Priestley and Edward Seago the next day, and Viscount Cilcennin on 14 February. Prince Philip remained on board ready to accompany The Queen in Portugal. In the intervening days Prince Philip took the opportunity to visit ships from the Home Fleet and enjoy some private sailing. When *Britannia* sailed from Gibraltar at 0800 on 15 February Prince Philip once more handled the Yacht and took her out of the harbour himself.

The following morning the Yacht anchored off Setubal to await the embarkation of The Queen that afternoon and subsequently sailed the short distance to Lisbon on 18 February to begin her formal State Visit which was well received by the Portuguese. The culmination of *Britannia*'s involvement in this short visit was to act as the venue for the dinner on the 20 February before setting sail at last for Portsmouth the next day where she arrived on 24 February to conclude *Britannia*'s first major global deployment.

On 11 April 1957 Captain John Adams was relieved as the Commander of the Yacht by Commander Terry Lewin DSC (later Admiral of the Fleet the Rt Hon. the Lord Lewin KG GCB LVO DSC). Because of the changes in the programme for the World Tour, Admiral Abel Smith was unable to interview Commander Lewin personally so he wrote to Commander Lewin on 23 August 1956 to ask for his reaction to the news that he was to become the next Commander of the Yacht. As the Commander later recalled the news was not entirely welcome:

'I didn't know much about the new Yacht and what life was like on board her. I'd spent about a fortnight accommodated in *V&A* during the War and my impression of the Yacht was it spent most of its time swinging around a buoy at Portsmouth Harbour and once a year went over to Cowes for Cowes Week. The idea of becoming a courtier and exchanging my fine, fighting destroyer HMS *Corunna* for this sedentary life did not appeal. I agonised for about 24 hours on what on earth I should say and I eventually wrote out a letter saying, Dear Admiral Abel Smith, I am indeed very honoured to be on the short list of three for the Yacht but I am in the middle of my first command of a destroyer, enjoying it immensely and I would really rather not be considered for the appointment.'

Despite this reluctance Commander Lewin was selected for the job and when he joined *Britannia* he was pleasantly surprised to find that his preconceptions about the Royal Yachtsmen were in fact wrong, as he explains:

'I expected that the Yacht's company would be mostly transferred from *V&A* and be elderly and set in their ways. However, I discovered that some 40 *V&A* Riggers had indeed commissioned *Britannia* but they found the pace of life far too hot and they had all gone. So instead of the elderly Yacht's company that I had expected I had a very young Yacht's company with people like the Chief Boatswain's Mate and the Coxswain of the Barge and the Coxswain of the ship acting Chief Petty Officers at the age of 29 or 30 and desperately keen to do anything.'

When Commander Lewin joined *Britannia* she was undergoing a short maintenance period which included docking for a repaint.

As the maintenance work continued more new officers were appointed to *Britannia*, including Commander P Watson (later Vice Admiral Sir Philip Watson KBE LVO), who joined *Britannia* as the new Commander (L). Describing the role of the Electrical Officer he said:

'I was in charge of all the electrical installations in the Yacht including all the communications equipment like the radio, etc. However, my principal role was to set up the communications links by voice which were necessary wherever the Yacht was. Today the process of long-range communications is easy with satellites that enable direct links to be made between any two points. But in those days we didn't have satellites so things were more difficult for instance when we were in the South China Sea with Prince Philip we had to establish communication by radio from the Yacht to Singapore. From there it was transmitted by land line across Asia and Europe back to London. These set ups had to be planned carefully before we went anywhere to make sure that on no occasion would we be out of touch with Whitehall. Therefore, everyday we were at sea we would establish this circuit in order to make sure it was there in case it was necessary to use it in an emergency. This process would lead to some amusing incidents.

'One day the engineers needed some spares so they spoke to the stores in Portsmouth using this link from a position about 200 miles off Hong Kong. They told the store keeper what they wanted and he asked where the items should be sent thinking that the Yacht would be on H Moorings or nearby. He was told to dispatch the parts by air to Hong Kong because *Britannia* was 200 miles away. Of course at this time that type of voice communication was virtually unheard of in the course of ordinary business in the RN. Interestingly, the position of Electrical Officer on board *Britannia* was filled by a Commander in the early years not because of the work load but because Admiral Abel Smith felt he needed five Commanders in order to help The Queen's programme of entertaining so he wanted one from each Branch.'

On 17 May *Britannia* left Portsmouth for Hull to embark The Queen and Prince Philip for their State Visit to Denmark.[59] The passage round to Hull was Leading Telegraphist A Deane's (later Mr A Deane MBE RVM) first voyage in the Yacht since he had joined as a temporary replacement for another Yachtsman. Describing his first impressions of *Britannia* he said:

'I had the preconceived idea that the Yacht would be full of boffins and goodie goodies. However, when I joined it was a complete eye-opener because these sailors played hard and they worked hard. There was no beer rationing as such whereas in the general service ships there was. Everything was done on trust and we were treated like grown-up people. And as a result the moral of the Yacht's company was incredible. When we set sail I found the Yacht had a peculiar motion that it took a while to get used to. It was different from a warship movement in a rough sea – it was like a corkscrew. We could immediately feel the difference when the stabilisers were housed for maintenance because she would cork screw all over the place.'

Once *Britannia* had arrived in Hull on 18 May she anchored in the River Humber to await the embarkation of The Queen. As Lord Lewin explained, the morning didn't get off to the best of starts:

'The officers of the local Royal Naval Volunteer Reserve (RNVR) division had invited themselves on board for a drink before lunch and they came out proudly in their former battleship launch. They didn't make a very good alongside the starboard forward ladder and smashed the right hand stringer, which is the side of the ladder that holds the steps in. Earlier on in

During the voyage from Gambia to Gibraltar at the end of His Royal Highness's World Tour the educational liner SS Uganda carried out a close sail by with her decks crowded with passengers. (© British Crown Copyright / MOD)

the morning we towed a barge inshore to pick up some of the Household staff and even our expert Barge's crew were finding it difficult to get alongside the starboard after ladder. They were hovering off the starboard after ladder, sweeping in against it and then away again. There was a mature lady waiting to step on to the ladder with what looked like a rather expensive jewel case. She came into a very favourable position but was dithering about getting out so I shouted out to her "jump". She came up the ladder and gave me a look, which went absolutely through me like a knife. I later discovered that this was the renowned Margaret Macdonald, The Queen's personal maid so I had started off by making an enemy of her. The Admiral returned ahead of The Queen after lunch in a very good mood and the first thing I had to say was that the starboard after ladder was smashed, and he said, "Don't worry about that Commander, the chippies will have that mended overnight", which it was. This was the sort of thing that made me realise that the Yacht was rather different to other ships.'

When The Queen and Prince Philip embarked at 1650[60] they were met at the top of the gangway by FORY and then the new Commander as Lord Lewin recalled:

The Admiral said, "Ma'am this is the new Commander." I of course had known her when she was Princess Elizabeth while Prince Philip was serving in HMS *Chequers* (the leader of the 1st Destroyer Flotilla) and I was the Flotilla Gunnery Officer. She looked me straight in the eye and said, "Oh yes Commander, you're the chap who didn't want to come to my Yacht", with a twinkle in her eye.'

Following a routine passage across the North Sea, *Britannia* arrived in Copenhagen Harbour escorted by a large number of small boats on the morning of 21 May. Just over half an hour later the Danish King and Queen embarked from their Royal Barge. Shortly afterwards the four of them went ashore in the Danish Royal Barge to begin The Queen's State Visit.[61] The Queen and Prince Philip lived ashore at the Amalienborg Palace in Copenhagen for the duration of the visit. Like the Portuguese State Visit earlier in the year, *Britannia*'s principle role was to act as the venue for the dinner to mark the conclusion of the visit on 23 May. At the end of the dinner The Queen and Prince Philip left the Yacht again to spend a couple of days privately with the Danish Royal Family rejoining *Britannia* at Helsingor on 25 May for the voyage back across the North Sea to spend three days with the Home Fleet.[62]

Britannia rendezvoused with the warships off the Cromarty Firth on the morning of 27 May in glorious weather. On completion of the steam past, the aircraft carriers *Ark Royal* and *Albion* broke off from the Home Fleet to launch their aircraft for a flypast in formation spelling out the letters ERII. Afterwards the Home Fleet anchored in Cromarty Firth for the dinner hosted on board HMS *Ocean* by the Commander-in-Chief Fleet, Admiral Sir John Eccles KCB KCVO CBE. The second day consisted principally of visits to the ships anchored in Cromarty Firth by The Queen and Prince Philip. Their time with the Home Fleet was rounded off on 29 May with a morning at sea in HMS *Ark Royal* to watch aircraft operations. This was the first such visit by The Queen since she became Sovereign. Having returned to *Britannia* for lunch The Queen and Prince Philip went ashore in the Barge to drive to Royal Naval Air Station (RNAS) Lossiemouth and depart by air leaving the Yacht to return to Portsmouth.[63]

As Admiral Abel Smith's time as FORY was approaching its conclusion, *Britannia* was used by The Queen and Prince Philip for a three-day visit to the Channel Islands in late July before attending Cowes Week at the beginning of August. *Britannia*'s arrival in Portsmouth on 10 August signalled the end of the Admiral's seagoing career.[64] For his remaining five months in command Admiral Abel Smith delegated much of his responsibilities to his senior officers, as Lord Lewin explains:

'He would come down from Scotland on the night sleeper on Tuesday having done his hunting on Tuesday, go to his club and arrive for dinner on the Wednesday, spend Wednesday night with us having dinner and spend Thursday with us and would leave on Thursday to catch the night train home so that he could get his hunting in on Friday. I was left as the Commander to run the Yacht and deal with the correspondence. The Navigating Officer, Commander Mitchell dealt with the planning for the next State Visit and we sent all our correspondence up with a flimsy copy to the Admiral already typed there and he always sent the flimsy back saying "signed and dispatched" and he never altered a single word.'

While the Yacht was in Portsmouth she underwent a short refit which included the stripping of the Royal Apartments. The objective was to try and cure the vibration problem. The areas affected included The Queen's bedroom when *Britannia* was cruising at 16 knots or more. As part of the remedial work stiffeners were added around the stairwell leading up to the Royal bedrooms.

Chapter Four
THE ST LAWRENCE SEAWAY

Vice Admiral Sir Peter Dawnay
KCVO CB DSC 1958–1962

At morning colours a sailor on board HMS *Vigo* announced a change in FORY when he hoisted the Flag of an Admiral who would never actually step on board his temporary flagship. A few hours later on 30 January 1958 Rear Admiral Peter Dawnay CB MVO DSC walked on board the Yacht to assume command of *Britannia* and relieve Vice Admiral Sir Conolly Abel Smith GCVO CB of his duties as FORY. After five very eventful years, during which he oversaw the rebirth of the Royal Yacht Service, it was time for Admiral Abel Smith to hand over the reins of the Royal Yacht Service, and retire to his estate in Scotland. At sunset his flag was finally struck in *Britannia* and replaced, the next morning at colours, by that of Admiral Dawnay to complete the hand over.[1]

Whereas his predecessor had been one of the FAA's first pilots Admiral Dawnay was a signals officer and had accompanied King George VI and Queen Elizabeth on their Tour to Canada in 1939. He was awarded the DSC for his part in the sinking of the German battlecruiser *Scharnhorst* in December 1943 while serving as the Fleet Wireless Officer in Admiral Sir Bruce Fraser's flagship HMS *Duke of York*. After the War he commanded the destroyer HMS *Saintes*, the signals school HMS *Mercury* near Petersfield and the cruiser HMS *Glasgow*, before being promoted to Rear Admiral and becoming the Deputy Controller of the Navy in 1956. Describing

Admiral Dawnay, his second Commander, later Captain N Dalrymple-Hamilton CVO MBE DSC DL RN, who had also served under Admiral Abel Smith in *Gothic* remarked:

> 'Admiral Abel Smith was much liked and respected by the whole Yacht's company and after nearly four highly successful years in command of *Britannia* it would not have been easy for his successor. Admiral Dawnay was a completely different character, highly strung, reserved in manner and not easy to get to know.'

Professor Sir Norman Blacklock KCVO OBE FRCS, who served on board as an additional doctor in 1959 and subsequently became The Queen's Medical Officer for visits abroad, continues: 'Admiral Dawnay was an old aristocrat in its best possible sense. He had very pronounced views on people some of which wouldn't pass muster these days but he was absolutely appropriate for the role of FORY. He had the greatest admiration and respect for Royalty.'

Admiral Dawnay had a reputation for very skilful ship handling, as his final Commander, later Captain D Roome LVO RN, explains:

> 'He had a fine reputation for ship handling which he continued to exhibit in *Britannia*. In particular, I remember when we entered Tunis Harbour with The Queen Mother embarked. There was a strong cross wind

across a very narrow channel of at least a mile through which he had to enter. Many a Captain of other ships would probably have decided not to risk it and tried on another day but Admiral Dawnay pressed on and managed to enter the harbour without incident.'

As Vice Admiral Sir David Loram explains, this ability was clearly evident in earlier appointments.

'I had seen him while I was serving in the 1st Flotilla in Malta during his time as Captain D of 3rd Flotilla while he commanded HMS *Saintes*. These large *Battle* class destroyers used to be steamed astern down Sliema Creek and he would perform this manoeuvre in HMS *Saintes* at quite a rate of knots. I had never seen anything like it before. We would actually come up on deck to watch such fine ship handling.'

When the Yacht was at sea Admiral Dawnay would relax by doing woodwork, as his Senior Engineer, later Captain P Archer RN, recalled: 'He was slow but his joints were

Vice Admiral Sir Peter Dawnay KCVO CB DSC, who served as Flag Officer Royal Yacht between 1958 and 1962.

(© British Crown Copyright / MOD)

perfect. When the weather was reasonable at sea he would have his workbench set up on the upper deck in the afternoon by the shipwright officer and there he would work.'

During Admiral Dawnay's first year as FORY *Britannia* undertook a limited programme in home and European waters. After the usual round of trials and work up, during February and early March 1958, *Britannia* was ready for her first spell of Royal duty under Admiral Dawnay. Thus on 21 March the Yacht sailed from Portsmouth to Harwich to embark The Queen and Prince Philip and take them across the North Sea to Amsterdam where they arrived on 25 March for the State Visit to Holland.[2] The conclusion of the two-day visit was marked by the dinner held on board the Yacht which involved some careful attention to detail, as Admiral Watson remembered:

'The Queen had decided to substitute the painting of *Britannia* in the Pool of London by Norman Wilcox, which was normally kept over the fireplace in the Royal Drawing Room, for a painting of King William III leaving Holland to take the British Throne. This was felt to be a more appropriate painting for the Dutch State Visit. On the day of the dinner for The Queen of Holland I returned on board *Britannia* to be told by the officer of the day that The Queen wanted to see me in the Royal Drawing Room. So I went down there to find her with two angle-poise lamps which she had obtained. One had come from her Sitting Room and the other from Prince Philip's Sitting Room. She had arranged these lamps to shine up to the painting. When she saw me she turned and said, "Oh, I'm pleased to see you because we have taken the trouble to bring this painting but it is so dark that I feel it needs some more light. I have been trying to light it with these lamps." I explained we had some proper fittings and asked if she would like me to install them, which I did. I thought it was interesting that even after a busy day ashore The Queen was still taking the time to make sure that everything was right for that evening's event.'

At the end of the dinner, Queen Beatrix and her family left *Britannia* and the Yacht sailed for Dover, where The Queen disembarked on 28 March, before the Yacht returned to Portsmouth the next day.[3]

On 5 May *Britannia* sailed for Liverpool to embark The Queen Mother, who was to use the Yacht for the first time in support of her work.[4] From Liverpool, *Britannia* sailed across the Irish Sea to provide a secure base for The Queen Mother's short visit to Northern Ireland between 8 and 10 May.[5] During the voyage back home the Yacht anchored off Lundy Island, to enable The Queen Mother to spend a few hours ashore, before resuming the passage back to Portsmouth where Her Majesty disembarked on 12 May.[6] At the end of June *Britannia* headed north again, this time for the River Humber to embark The Queen and Prince Philip on 27 June. During the course of the next five days *Britannia* supported The Queen and Prince Philip's Tour of the north east visiting Grimsby, Holy Island, the Farne Islands, Rosyth and finally Leith. Although it would have been possible to visit the mainland towns without the Yacht, it made the visits to Holy Island and the Farne Islands possible and enhanced the profile and sense of occasion for the visits to the mainland.

The end of July saw another voyage in home waters, this time to Cardiff for the 6th British Empire and Commonwealth Games. The Queen had been due to perform the Opening Ceremony but illness resulted in Prince Philip deputising for her. The Queen chose the Closing Ceremony on 26 July to announce in a pre-recorded message that she had created Prince Charles The Prince of Wales. The largely Welsh crowd greeted the announcement with enthusiasm and a large number of local people turned out for *Britannia*'s departure from Cardiff that evening to give Prince Philip a memorable send off.[7] After the cheers and Welsh songs of Cardiff, the next day off the Scilly Isles was a very different affair as *Britannia*'s arrival was greeted by strong winds and drizzle which led to the cancellation of Prince Philip's planned tour in the Barge. Despite this, Prince Philip still managed to complete most of his programme before the Yacht weighed anchor for Dartmouth.[8] Shortly after *Britannia* secured to two buoys in the River Dart on the morning of 28 July, Prince Philip was joined on board by the First Lord of the Admiralty, The Earl of Selkirk and the First Sea Lord, Admiral of the Fleet Earl Mountbatten of Burma. The two men accompanied Prince Philip ashore for his day-long visit to BRNC, which included the presentation of a Queen's Colour to the college.[9] From Dartmouth, *Britannia* returned to Portsmouth via Plymouth where Prince Philip spent the day ashore in Devonport Dockyard.

At the beginning of August The Prince of Wales accompanied his father on board *Britannia* to attend his first Cowes Week. As he explains, dinner at Uffa Fox's house in Cowes was an integral part of Cowes Week for the Royal Family:

'Uffa's dinners were legendary. He would cook an entire salmon in a copper fish kettle and also a baron of beef. We would wait hours while everything cooked and everyone would go into the kitchen and then roar with laughter at it saying it would never work. While it all cooked he would tell ruder and ruder stories and yet he was one of the very few people who had the ability to get away with incredibly rude stories in front of ladies but he was such a funny man that no one ever minded.'

At the end of Cowes Week, *Britannia* sailed to Southampton to embark The Queen and Princess Anne for the regular Western Isles Cruise. Large crowds lined the banks of Southampton Water to watch the Yacht's departure from Southampton accompanied by pleasure steamers and a large number of small boats.[10] Once clear of the Solent the Yacht headed north for The Queen's visit to Holyhead on 9 August.[11] As part of his preparations before sailing the deputy Supply Officer, later Captain C H H Owen RN, arranged for a bakery in Holyhead to provide the Yacht with fresh bread:

'In their letter of reply the bakery said, "it would be an honour to supply the Royal Yacht once again." As *Britannia* hadn't been to Holyhead before, I asked them what they meant and I discovered that they were in fact referring to an occasion in 1911 when *V&A* visited Holyhead for the investiture of The Prince of Wales (later King Edward VIII and then Duke of Windsor).'

From Holyhead the Yacht continued to head north for Scottish waters visiting Loch Ryan on 10 August.[12] Describing some of his own memories of these early Western Isles Cruises Prince Charles said:

'I remember visits to the NAAFI [Navy, Army and Air Force Institute] to buy things, visits to the Laundry which was always fascinating, not least because of the tremendous temperature down there and I always admired those characters who worked in such heat. There were always visits to the various messes with some jolly games. When I was even smaller I would go round the Yacht helping the Yachtsmen do various things such as cheesing down the ropes on the Verandah Deck, getting involved in the putting up of awnings and steering the Yacht from the wheelhouse. For me it always seemed to be another home, like Balmoral or Sandringham. We had always known the Yacht and the people on board made it so special. These people were always so loyal and had such high standards down to every last detail. They could turn their hand to almost anything and do it properly – it was incredible. I was lucky enough to be transported in this living, working, sailing demonstration of the best of Britain – at least that is what I think.'

As Princess Anne explains, the Yachtsmen were always coming up with new ways to keep the Royal children occupied:

'The Yachtsmen created a slide which was used until the end. It came down the steps beside the Verandah Deck and the fire hose was turned on at the top of the slide. Because the slide had a kink at the bottom we would come down much faster with the water on and hit this puddle and go straight on across the deck pretty well on towards the end. There was only just enough room collecting splinters along the way.'

However, while the Royal children enjoyed themselves exploring the Yacht a few of their questions required some quick thinking, as Captain Owen remarked:

'One morning I was getting the money out of my safe in order to put up pay for the Yachtsmen when Prince Charles walked past and examined in detail everything in the safe – he wanted to know whose money it all was, and I was just about to give the normal answer of "The Queen's" when I realised that might lead to endless difficulties! So I rather lamely said, "it belonged to the Admiralty," and quickly diverted his mind to the sheets of postage stamps, all with 240 postage stamps and each with his mother's picture on them.'

Following official visits to Rothesay and Campbeltown for The Queen and Prince Philip on 11 August the Yacht sailed to West Loch Tarbet and then Applecross Bay where she anchored for four days. During the passage to Applecross Bay on 13 August The Queen went for her first 'Walkabout' in the Yacht which was a very popular gesture among the Yachtsmen.[13] The Walkabout included visits to the mess decks and the galley, as Captain Owen recalls:

'The Chief Cook gave her a very detailed Cook's tour which amused her and thrilled him. The Chief Cook, who normally lived up to his surname of Merrie, told me afterwards: "Everything was going lovely, Sir. We'd gone right through the fridge and I was just describing the bacon slicer when THAT BOY let me down terribly – he lifted the lid of the gash bin. I wished the floor would open and swallow me up because you can't have The Queen seeing the gash. But all was all right in the end, and I could see The Queen was on my side because she turned to him and said, "Charles, don't touch things you shouldn't ought to," and I breathed again."'

During the course of their stay in Applecross Bay the Royal Family indulged in a little lobster fishing which produced a surprise for them, as Captain Owen recorded:

'About six of us from the Wardroom, with Lieutenant Commander Peter Campbell, The Queen's Equerry, went off fishing from a boat at about 0530, put a bottle

The Land Rover used by the Royal Family is brought ashore in Applecross Bay during the 1958 Western Isles Cruise on the specially constructed inflatable raft.

of brandy in one of the Royal lobster pots and then caught 12 mackerel which we had for breakfast. At breakfast, Peter Campbell told the Royal children, Prince Charles and Princess Anne, about the film shown the night before and how naughty the men had been who had smuggled by using lobster pots. Then after breakfast, Prince Philip, the children and Peter Campbell went off to see what they had caught, and the first thing they found was the bottle of brandy. The children were quite shocked and said, "Oh Papa, we must send for the police." However, all was explained and Prince Philip thought it a huge joke. By the time the children got back they were very proud of their "catch" (and there were no lobsters!).'

The Western Isles Cruise concluded with a visit to Fort William for The Queen and Prince Philip, from where they were driven to Gair Locky to join the Barge for a passage up the Caledonian Canal as far as Cullocky. There they disembarked to be driven on to Balmoral Castle for the summer break.[14] Once the Barge had returned to *Britannia* she weighed anchor for the voyage back to Portsmouth, arriving there on 20 August.[15]

The rest of the year was taken up with preparations for the very busy 1959 programme. On 8 October the Yacht entered dry dock for routine maintenance and some modifications required for the opening of the St Lawrence Seaway in June 1959.[16] Unlike the Panama Canal, ships entering the locks of the St Lawrence Seaway have to do so under their own power without the benefit of steadying wires. However, in a strong cross wind there would be the very real risk of the Yacht being blown into the rough concrete sides of the lock. While this risk might have been perfectly acceptable for the cargo ships that normally use the canals, it was not for the Yacht where a high standard of finish was required at all times. As such, it was decided to fit a 9-inch thick, 120-foot long elm rubbing strake to the hull each side at the waterline. This in conjunction with use of inflatable rubber fenders would keep the precious side of the Yacht away from the rough concrete sides of the dock walls and thus preserve the paint. Equally, it became apparent that *Britannia* would not be able to get under all of the bridges on the St Lawrence Seaway because the fore and main masts were too high. When *Britannia* was designed, the height of her masts were carefully worked out so that she would have the right proportions and thus the obvious solution of shortening the masts was rejected on the grounds that it would have given her a stumpy appearance. Installing telescopic top sections was also rejected because of the cost, which left the option of hinging the radio aerial on the fore mast and the top 20 feet of the main mast that was subsequently adopted. Having settled on the method of reducing the height of the masts there was still the issue of what the manoeuvre was going to be called, as Admiral Watson explains:

'The Admiral was giving a lot of consideration to what order could be adopted to initiate the lowing of the main top mast. I suggested that we should say scandalise the main top mast. I felt it would be the most appropriate term as it had previously been used to initiate the scandalising of the yards in sailing ships.'

Seven days into the New Year *Britannia* left Portsmouth to begin her second round-the-world voyage which was to last for the next four months and see the Yacht steam a total of 29,000 miles. As she made her way down Portsmouth Harbour she was flying a new flag at the fore mast to signal the promotion of FORY to the rank of Vice Admiral. As Captain Owen remembered, FORY received a number of congratulatory telegrams to mark the occasion: 'Admiral Dawnay had very nice telegrams from The Queen and Prince Philip – the latter's obviously written by himself as there was nobody else in the Palace who would have known the naval phrase he used: "Am looking forward to wetting the new stripe in Rangoon."' From Portsmouth the Yacht headed for Vizagapatam via Gibraltar, Malta and the Suez Canal. Because of the deteriorating relations between the Egyptian and British Governments in 1956, *Britannia* had been forced to sail around South Africa during her first world-wide deployment. Thus this was her first transit through the canal, which was watched with interest locally. When the Egyptian pilot embarked off Port Said on 21 January he told FORY that the Chairman of the new Canal Company was watching from his car ashore. As the Yacht made her way through the canal the Yachtsmen observed the work which was being undertaken both to widen and deepen the canal. Having cleared the canal at 0145 the following morning, the Yacht continued her journey to Vizagapatam for a nine-day self-maintenance period. Describing her arrival on 6 February Captain Owen said:

'On our way to the harbour entrance we passed through hundreds of small fishing boats which were mostly two carved logs tied together, some with tiny sails. The entrance to the harbour reminded me very much of Dartmouth – a high green hill on one side, and a sharp bend a short way up river. The entrance to the harbour was natural, though much dredged, but all the harbour proper was artificial and was fairly big containing several wharves, and India's only shipbuilding yard capable of building 10,000-ton ships.'

Once the Yacht had been refuelled she was moved alongside the Indian Navy's Boys Training Establishment INS *Circars* which was run along almost identical lines to the RN's own Boys Training Establishment HMS *Ganges* at Shotley, Suffolk. While the Yachtsmen enjoyed their first period of leave in Vizagapatam their families back in the UK were also being looked after. FORY's wife, Lady Angela Dawnay, organised a number of social events for the Yachtsmen's wives in the Home Club at Portsmouth. She wanted to ensure that the wives received the support they needed while *Britannia* was away. Over the years these links were built upon and in effect created a wider family of the Yacht, which still exists to this day.

In the Far East the first of Prince Philip's guests for the forthcoming tour arrived in Vizagapatam on 13 February. Admiral of the Fleet, The Lord Fraser of North Cape GCB KBE had enjoyed a distinguished naval career. During the Second World War he had held a succession of senior appointments including that of Commander-in-Chief Home Fleet, Commander-in-Chief Eastern Fleet and finally Commander-in-Chief British Pacific Fleet. Prince Philip himself had served under Lord Fraser in the Pacific as a junior Naval Officer while FORY had been his Fleet Wireless Officer in the *Duke of York* when the *Scharnhorst* was sunk. After the Second World War Lord Fraser served as First Sea Lord between 1948 and 1951. As Admiral Watson recalls, Lord Fraser quickly settled into life on board the Yacht:

'When he arrived on board a note was left as usual in his cabin to say that the Wardroom would be very pleased if he would consider himself an honorary member of the Wardroom. The Commander received a message from

Lord Fraser to say that he would come up to the Wardroom at 1800 and have a drink with us, which he did. When he arrived in the Wardroom for this drink he said, "I'm not going to announce my arrival every time I want to come to the Wardroom. You have asked me to be an honorary member so I will come and go as I like if you don't mind." Then he told us the other thing that had been exercising him was the fact that he was just a passenger in the Yacht with no official status at all. So he said, "What should I be called?" Then having thought about it he said, "I think the best thing would be to call me Uncle Bruce." So from that moment he was known on board simply as Uncle Bruce.'

The Rangoon market.   (HRH The Duke of Edinburgh)

As the Yacht arrived at Singapore she was given a traditional Malayan Escort.   (HRH The Duke of Edinburgh)

This might sound unusual for a man of his status to adopt such an informal title within the environment of the Yacht but Viscount Cilcennin had made a similar statement during the 1956 cruise when he was known on board simply as Uncle Jim.

After nine days alongside INS *Circars*, *Britannia* sailed for Rangoon on 14 February arriving there three days later to embark Prince Philip and the rest of his guests on 18 February. In addition to Lord Fraser, Prince Philip invited Sir Alexander Grantham and Dr Wolfgang Breitling to accompany him for the Pacific Tour. Sir Alexander Grantham had served in the Colonial Administrative Service, serving as Governor of Fiji and High Commissioner for the Western Pacific between 1945 and 1947, and finally as the Governor of Hong Kong between 1947 and 1957, where he was revered by the Chinese. Dr Breitling was an old school friend of Prince Philip and a talented photographer, artist and cook. He was already known on board the Yacht because he had accompanied Prince Philip on the 1956 Tour as far as Melbourne. That night *Britannia* sailed at 2330 for Singapore. Thankfully, there were none of the problems that had curtailed the 1956 programme and the Yacht was greeted by warships of the Far Eastern Fleet on 21 February, led by the cruiser HMS *Ceylon*, ready for the next day's entry into Singapore. The appearance of the dressing lines was done so quickly and smoothly when the Yacht dropped anchor that the local newspaper thought the procedure had been executed by an automatic device. Prince Philip lived ashore at Government House during his visit, which enabled the Yachtsmen to enjoy a run ashore before *Britannia* sailed from Singapore on the morning of 25 February. She was given a rousing send-off complete with a flypast of nine Canberra bombers and fireboats blowing coloured water from their hoses. The day after, *Britannia* arrived off the Kuching River, Sarawak, as Captain Owen recorded:

'We entered Kuching River which was lined by a very thick jungle leading to the water's edge on both sides, with occasional villages of a few houses on stilts. All these houses flew coloured flags and fired crackers as we passed. About an hour later we anchored off the small village of Tanjong Sadap where there was a great concourse of local boats full of people to welcome Prince Philip. When he landed he had to go about 4 miles up river in the Barge, but he first went very slowly through all these boats which of course was a most popular gesture. The few with engines followed him all the way up the river. It was all very colourful – but they had gone by the time it got dark.'

Britannia stayed at this anchorage overnight and sailed the next morning, leaving Prince Philip to carry out his programme in Sarawak and North Borneo while the Yacht made her way to Sandakan in North Borneo where she arrived on 1 March. Prince Philip arrived there the following day and embarked in the Governor's Barge to watch the local regatta, which was an impressive event. Captain Owen remarked, 'we had a grandstand view from the bridge. Eight-men paddling canoes were the best – just like a film of African warriors!' There were many colourfully decorated boats and various events, including tug of war between rowing boats, pillow fights on a greasy pole and races for speed boats and canoes. On 3 March the Yacht left for Hong Kong just as the sun was rising.

The journey into Hong Kong on 6 March was dogged by the threat of the fog closing in but all went to schedule and *Britannia* reached the mooring buoy as planned. Normally ships of the RN employ one of the side-parties to clean the ship's sides and take away their 'gash' food whenever they visit Hong Kong. Obviously, *Britannia* was a prestigious ship to clean and there was some fierce rivalry between Jenny's side-party and Susie's side-party to obtain the honour. Susie felt she had a good claim to the job because as a 9-year-old girl she had worked on the side of the W Class Destroyer HMS *Whelp* while Prince Philip was serving in her as First Lieutenant. However, Jenny had written to the Commander, later Captain Dalrymple-Hamilton CVO MBE DSC DL RN, shortly after the Yacht left the UK. Because he had known her from his time in the cruiser HMS *Birmingham* Captain Dalrymple-Hamilton was pleased to give her the job, as he explains:

'We had scarcely secured alongside at Hong Kong when Jenny came on board to get her orders and I saw Susie standing on the jetty looking as though she could cheerfully murder someone. There was of course tremendous "face", so important to the Chinese, in getting the Yacht job even if it was only for two days, and I felt sorry for Susie. I had scarcely packed Jenny off with the Petty Officer responsible for the appearance of the Yacht's side to draw paintbrushes, etc., when Prince Philip walked by. He asked me whom I had taken on for side-party and when I said, "Jenny, Sir," he said, "Why haven't you taken on Susie? She used to work for me."

There was not much answer to this except to tell him that Jenny was an old friend of mine. Clearly this didn't cut much ice, however nothing more was said. I decided that I had better do something about Susie if Jenny wasn't going to get a knife in her back, so I got her on board and managed to fix her up with a personal interview with His Royal Highness. I think that this went some way to restoring her wounded pride.'

Despite the best efforts of the Commander that wasn't quite the end of the rivalry, as Captain Owen wrote:

'Jenny's girls gave us a great farewell from their junk when we sailed on 8 March with plenty of especially loud crackers. Susie's side-party had even louder crackers from their junk, and also a large banner saying, "Bon voyage, Your Highness, from Susie side par" (there wasn't room for the "ty")!'

During the course of the visit many of those on board the Yacht had indulged in a little shopping including Prince Philip who purchased some wicker furniture for the Sun Lounge (although the plans showed the space as the Sun Lounge it was always known as the Verandah). By late afternoon the Yacht was on her own as she embarked upon the long passage across the vast expanse of the Pacific Ocean to the island of Gizo. During the first few days of the voyage the Yacht changed course a number of times to avoid the path of the tropical storm Sally which later passed 300 miles to the south west. By 16 March the

The small boat used by Jenny's side-party is dwarfed by the side of the Yacht as they begin their work to clean the Yacht's hull during her stay in Hong Kong. In the background the cruiser HMS Belfast *can be seen.*

(HRH The Duke of Edinburgh)

Even after nearly 14 years of peace Guadalcanal was still littered with the debris left by the fierce fighting between the Allies and the Japanese, such as this Japanese troop ship sunk close to the beach. (HRH The Duke of Edinburgh)

Yacht had reached the Bismarck Archipelago and Prince Philip asked the Admiral to anchor off one of the islands for a picnic resulting in the visit to the small Tench Island. Describing the remote island and its small community of people Captain Owen said:

'It was quite a circular island, barely a mile in diameter, and out of sight of any other land. Even in the distance, as we approached it, it was just like the desert island one sees in films – palm trees and a white beach, with breakers all round. It was a perfect day, flat calm, and on one side there was a gap in the reef so that boats could land on the beach. Quite a lot of the Yacht's company went ashore, ferrying in the dinghy when the motor boat could go no further. The Royal party took a large barbecue picnic with them. There were 53 inhabitants who live in a village where we landed. To our surprise, one or two spoke quite a bit of English, taught by missionaries. Their "houses" are beautifully made of matted leaves, on stilts. We visited the church, which also acts as the school and meeting house. We then went round the eight-bed hospital, which was also built like their houses. There was a well-stocked dispensary, or at any rate there were several bottles marked "the mixture" or "poison" and some bandages which badly needed to go to the

laundry! One of the men wore a skirt with a red cross on it – he was a trained nurse, and also the missionary-cum-parson – but he spoke very little English. They lived on fish, coconuts, eggs, nuts and other fruit. Ships call about every three months to collect the surplus copra from the coconuts and very occasionally a ship collects cowrie shells for sale in America. They have a few fine outrigger canoes which they use to go across the 20 odd miles to New Hanover. Prince Philip went round everywhere in the village and we gave them some of our matchboxes and postcards of the Yacht so that when the missionary next visited he could explain. We also gave them some fish hooks which were very popular.'

Shortly after the Yacht weighed anchor that evening to resume her voyage Dolphinius, the Clerk to King Neptune's Court arrived on board ahead of the next day's Crossing-The-Line ceremony which had been delayed by the visit to Tench Island. As usual the week before the ceremony had seen a flurry of 'intercepted signals' that were posted around the Yacht to whip up enthusiasm among the Yachtsmen. This included one that disagreed with the official reason for the delayed ceremony. Instead it stated that the delay was due to the Senior Engineer who had allowed two empty oil drums to be thrown over the side a couple of days before. These damaged a shadowing dolphin and the 'Dolphin Dockyard' had come out on 24-hour strike in sympathy, refusing to man King Neptune's Barge! Among those to receive summons for the next day's festivities were Prince Philip, Lord Fraser and FORY as well as 75 novices. The next morning the ceremony began on the forecastle, as Captain Owen noted:

'Prince Philip, the Household and the Admiral were on the dais to watch the beginnings and to receive their awards. The Wardroom formed the guard of honour for King Neptune, wearing rugger shirts and bathing trunks, and bowlers or cooks caps, with dolphins on them, carrying tridents and shields. We were inspected by the King (a CERA) and Queen Aphrodite (Superintendent Kelley) and they then went on the dais. After being introduced to the Royal party, we fired a *feu-de-joie* of Chinese crackers. We then joined the crowd, to watch the proceedings. All the Household received awards – Prince Philip was made a Grand Master of the Order of Penguins and received a garland of penguin chocolates round his neck and a tot. Lord Fraser received his award for, amongst other things, being the senior bachelor on the active list, and he brought the house down by promptly kissing The Queen [Aphrodite]. After the awards the "persons of august rank", as they were called, left the dais, and the normal soaping and ducking proceedings carried on for the rest of the morning, with individual warrants for about half the novices. Needless to say a lot of us "old hands" were also thrown in by the "police" for good measure!'

Early on the morning of 18 March the island of Gizo appeared over the horizon for the start of Prince Philip's tour of the British Solomon Islands Protectorate. The passage into Gizo Harbour looked a little daunting when the Yacht first approached the island because of the need to sail through the gap in the reefs that lay off the coast. To help the Yacht navigate safely through this potentially hazardous route the survey ship HMS *Cook* had laid some navigational buoys to mark the route during a recent visit to the island. Once through the reefs the Yacht was met by an escort of four war canoes each propelled by 24 oarsmen as *Britannia* anchored for Prince Philip's short visit to the island which included a display of native dancing on the village green. As a result of this visit the normal population on the island had swelled from less than 500 to nearly 6000 as people from the various outlying islands travelled up to 150 miles by canoe to welcome Prince Philip. From Gizo *Britannia* sailed that afternoon for the next day's visit to Honiara on Guadalcanal, the biggest of the Solomon Islands. During the Second World War Guadalcanal marked the southernmost part of the Japanese advance towards Australia and witnessed some of the fiercest fighting between the Allied and Japanese forces. Even after 14 years of peace there were still constant reminders of this recent history with wrecked ships, aircraft and vehicles littering various parts of the island. At one point 250,000 allied troops had been stationed on the island which at that time supported a population of a mere 3000 people. After a successful day ashore for Prince Philip the Yacht sailed at 2300 to the sound of a bamboo band and the cheers of the islanders as *Britannia* headed for Malaita Island.

As the Yacht approached Malaita's Bina Harbour on the morning of 20 March the sad sight of the High Commissioner's vessel *Coral Queen* aground on a reef loomed into view. Soon after the Yacht's arrival a team from *Britannia*, headed by the Navigating Officer, Commander Peter Berger, went over to the *Coral Queen* and helped her crew in their efforts to re-float her. During Commander Berger's absence a telegram was received on board the Yacht to inform him that he had become the father of a baby girl. Rather than wait for his return Commander N Dalrymple-Hamilton contacted him by radio to inform him of the news and that the champagne was being held on ice. There was soon cause for a double celebration as the *Coral Queen* was re-floated at high

water. Meanwhile, during Prince Philip's tour of the island he was shown the production of shell money, which was used on the island for the purchase of certain items including wives and pigs! In the afternoon Prince Philip was taken to see the buildings of the Malaitian Council which had been established to teach the natives how to govern themselves. While Prince Philip's tour continued throughout the day and into the evening some of the Yachtsmen managed to spend some time ashore and see the island for themselves, as Captain Owen wrote:

'It had rained during lunchtime, so the village was a bit of a swamp. There were a lot of people there, many having come from a village a day's march away to see Prince Philip that morning. The inhabitants of the village spoke a little English and they took us round it – we saw the church (South Sea Evangelical Mission), and watched them carving out their dug-out canoes. We also distributed sweets and cigarettes. We managed to get smiles out of even the fiercest looking warriors and they posed for photographs with great dignity. After an hour or so with them, we asked them if they would take us back to the Yacht in their large canoe. So in we got – there were 7 of us and 14 natives. We sat two abreast and paddled back. It seemed a long way and was hard work. Fortunately there weren't enough paddles to go round and so we had periodical breaks so that everyone had a chance to paddle! We came alongside the gangway much to the amusement of the Yacht's company,

This village on Malaita was typical of the small villages seen by Prince Philip during his tour of the Solomon Islands. Interestingly, the islanders still used dug-out canoes.

(HRH The Duke of Edinburgh)

and presented our "crew" with various presents – photographs of the Yacht, cigars, cigarettes and matches. Interestingly, their bailer was a Japanese helmet!'

After a quiet day at sea *Britannia* anchored in Graciosa Bay off Santa Cruz Island for the final day in the Solomon Islands. Despite the small island community's lack of money the islanders had gone to a great deal of trouble for Prince Philip's visit, as Captain Owen explains:

'Graciosa Bay is a long, narrow bay and we anchored at the far end – a most attractive anchorage with high mountains all round. Three of us landed ashore about half an hour after Prince Philip at a wonderful bamboo jetty with pontoon attached which had been built specially. All the way along Prince Philip's route was marked with a border decorated with bamboo leaves. There were villages every few hundred yards along the coast and Prince Philip had walked about a mile from where he landed through all the villages to the main one. By the time we reached these villages most of them were empty as all the people had gone to the main village to wait for the feast. Practically the only life we saw was a kingfisher. One village had an Anglican church, with altar, font and lectern, inlaid with mother-of-pearl Bible and prayer books in a native language. We got to the main village in time to see the beginning of the feast for about 600 people – it was on bamboo leaves on the ground, and the food was fat roast pig and yams – a great delicacy apparently. The Royal party had to join in and we soon went off for our own picnic. Whilst we

Prince Philip watches the grading of copra on Betio Wharf.

(HRH The Duke of Edinburgh)

were having it a man passed with bow and arrows, which he demonstrated for us – it was still the way they shoot their game. After lunch there was native dancing – quite attractive– some very fierce men from the outermost island of all called Tikopia, with hair like a lion's mane, did a wild dance with wooden spears.'

During his tour of the island Prince Philip was presented with feather money which, like the shell money found on Malaita Island, was still used for the purchase of wives and pigs. In the afternoon Prince Philip went for a sail in one of the island's ocean-going outrigger canoes, Describing the canoe and the experience of sailing it, Prince Philip said:

'It must have been about 30 feet long, but at no point was the beam greater than 18 inches. The outrigger was a solid spar not quite as long as the canoe, suspended about 15 feet from the side of the canoe by a number of struts and braces. It had one large lug sail and it was steered by a long oar. There was a crew of four or five and the thing went extremely fast, throwing up clouds of spray. The art consists of keeping the canoe upright and this is achieved by two or three members of the crew climbing out towards the outrigger as it is lifted out of the water in a puff, and then back towards the canoe as the outrigger drops back into the water again. This needs very careful timing; if they get too far out they are in danger of being swept into the sea; if they don't go far enough the canoe goes over. At times we must have been doing well over 15 knots.

'As the outrigger is on one side of the canoe it always has to be on the windward side, which means that it is impossible to go about in the ordinary way by bringing the wind on to the other bow. In this con-

Prince Philip's final day in the Solomon Islands began with a display of native dancing on Santa Cruz Island while the Yacht lay at anchor in Graciosa Bay.

(HRH The Duke of Edinburgh)

Having laid a wreath, Prince Philip salutes the simple yet dignified war memorial at Betio.

(HRH The Duke of Edinburgh)

traption you have to sail it in the opposite direction, which means shifting the sail and the steering oar from one end to the other; quite a lengthy process. I had a go at steering the canoe, but soon realised that the steering oar had very little effect and that the direction was controlled almost entirely by the trim of the sail.'

After his sail in the canoe Prince Philip returned to *Britannia* and took his yacht *Fairey Fox* for a sail. However, it was soon time to go and the Yacht weighed anchor to conclude the tour of the Solomon Islands and set sail for Tarawa. On the morning of 25 March *Britannia* was joined by the New Zealand Frigate HMNZS *Rotoiti* as escort for the islands of the Gilbert and Ellice Colony. Prince Philip had recently been appointed as an Admiral of the Fleet in the RNZN and thus when he transferred by jackstay to *Rotoiti* later in the morning he became the first such New Zealand Naval Officer to fly his flag in a ship of the RNZN. Prince Philip was transferred by jackstay and spent about one and a half hours on board the frigate before he was transferred back to the Yacht.

A couple of hours later the Royal Squadron arrived off Tarawa. Describing what he saw and how it compared to the Solomon Islands Captain Owen said:

'From the sea Tarawa looked like a long line of long, low islands, coconut trees on white sand – and this is really all it is, about 20 small islands forming a semi-circle round the lagoon, nowhere more than about 10 feet above sea level. There is a passage through the outer reef into the lagoon so that we could anchor in the semicircle, but we were still about 3 miles from the island on which the headquarters of the colony called

Bairiki were located. The island of Bairiki is tiny – only half a mile long and 150 yards wide, and at low tide it is joined by a causeway to the next islet and so on to all the string of islets round the lagoon which looks like open sea. We inspected some sailing outrigger canoes on the beach and then wandered about the village – of course everyone from Tarawa and many islands further away were there for our visit. Prince Philip's route was decorated with strings of cowrie shells. The houses (made of coconut leaves, and some with a form of brick) were very smart and laid out in rows with neat gardens round them, with banana bushes and an occasional flower – everything looked smart and prosperous compared with the Solomon Islands.'

Like Guadalcanal, Tarawa had witnessed fierce fighting between the Allied and Japanese forces during the Second World War. As part of his programme on 26 March Prince Philip visited Betio, the islet at the extreme western end of the east-west base of the Tarawa atoll. In October 1942 Betio was the scene of the Battle of Tarawa in which more than 1000 American and 4000 Japanese servicemen were killed in four days of fighting. The remains of Japanese concrete bunkers and rusting landing craft served as graphic reminders of the island's recent history. For the Keeper & Steward, Lieutenant Pardy, it was the first time he had been back to the island for 40 years. In 1919 he had been part of Admiral of the Fleet Earl Jellicoe's staff during his round-the-world cruise in the battlecruiser HMS *New Zealand*. He was heard to comment that little had changed since his last visit. The day's programme was concluded by

During his visit to Tarawa Prince Philip was invited for a sail in this ocean-going outrigger canoe and is seen at the helm.

(HRH The Duke of Edinburgh)

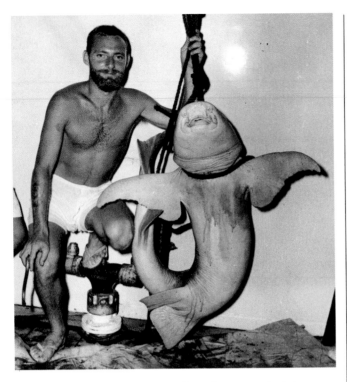

Electrician Hughes proudly displays the young shark he caught while fishing from the forecastle during the voyage from Ocean Island to Vaitupu. The shark weighed about 180 pounds.   (HRH The Duke of Edinburgh)

The moment Prince Philip's canoe touched the beach at Vaitupu the islanders walked into the surf and carried it ashore to the accompaniment of singing and the slapping of the canoe.   (HRH The Duke of Edinburgh)

a display of native dancing before the Royal party returned to the Yacht about midnight for the overnight voyage to Ocean Island.

The mooring buoy that *Britannia* secured to off Ocean Island was reputed to be the deepest laid buoy in the world at a depth of some 240 fathoms. Despite the depths of the surrounding waters there was no grounds for complacency as the clearly visible wreck of the large freighter SS *Kelvinbank*, firmly embedded in a reef, demonstrated. The island itself, which rises to 200 feet and is 2 miles square, is an extinct volcano. By 1959 Ocean Island had effectively become one large phosphate mine controlled by the British Phosphate Commission. The phosphate mined from the island, together with that found on Nauru and Christmas Island, was of the highest grade found in the world. At the time, Ocean Island was producing 300,000 tons a year, which was loaded direct on to ships moored off the island. The source of the phosphate was still a cause of much discussion with the two principle theories being that it was created by millions of bird droppings or that it was dead marine animals that had filled up an enclosed lagoon. The indigenous population of Banabans had left the island after the War and moved to the Fijian island of Rambi because much of their once fertile land had been turned into useless coral rock by the mining operations. Prince Philip hosted a lunch on board for some of the islanders and the RM Band played music in the background out of sight. Not realising that a real orchestra was playing outside one of the guests were heard to remark: 'they've got a good re-diffusion system on the Royal Yacht. It was so

good that it sounded just like a live orchestra!'

In the afternoon the Yacht left for Vaitupu, which was the only Ellice Island to be visited during this Tour. As the Yacht approached the island on 30 March (Easter Monday) she crossed the International Dateline, so it was decided to have a second Easter Monday. As Captain Owen explains, Vaitupu was a contrast to the rest of the Ellice Islands:

'It was much more typically Polynesian. There was no anchorage so we had to lie off, but some of us were able to get ashore in long boats, towed up to the reef, then paddled over until the boat went aground – there was then a hundred yard walk through shallow water until we reached the beach – so gym shoes and rolled up shorts was the rig for landing. The Polynesians were much more enthusiastic even than the Gilbertese, and their children gave us a great welcome as we waded ashore, mostly laughing! It was the usual attractive village, houses of coconut leaves all decorated'

Prince Philip's arrival ashore was rather more dignified and drier than that of the Yacht's officers. The moment his canoe touched the beach the men of the island walked into the surf to pick up the canoe with His Royal Highness still on board and carry it ashore to the accompaniment of singing and slapping of the canoe. Once ashore the Prince went to the *maneaba* (meeting place) for a feast preceded by the *alofa* (presentation of gifts) which truly lived up to its name with 107 mats, 100 baskets and 24 shirts being presented to Prince Philip. The rest of the Royal party, including some members of the Yacht's company, were also presented with gifts but they had to stand up and identify themselves to the assembled audience before they accepted them. Even those left on board the Yacht weren't forgotten, with the presentation of 2000 drinking coconuts. The various events were presided over by Vailele who was described in the Tour Diary as 'a natural humorist and orator and, despite his 70 odd years, still no mean dancer'. As the feast progressed music was provided alternatively by local guitarists accompanying their own singing and the RM Band. After lunch Prince Philip travelled in a lorry bedecked in flowers, which was the island's only motor vehicle, to visit the school before attending a *fatele* (local dancing and singing). Before Prince Philip left he was taken by the District Officer Penetala to catch flying fish in a canoe, as he recalls:

'The technique was for two or three outrigger canoes to drive a shoal of flying fish towards the reef and when the fish took off to get back to sea, the idea was to catch them in what were effectively salmon landing nets attached to long poles. As it all took place in an ocean swell close to the breakers on the reef, I never got anywhere near a fish.'

In a final gesture of goodwill the islanders tried to give Prince Philip the canoe, but he tactfully suggested that they should keep it and name it after him which was very popularly received. The islanders in the canoes that accompanied Prince Philip back to *Britannia* marked his return to the Yacht by leaping into the sea many times to bring a very happy day to a close.

During the second day at sea the Yacht approached Hull Island which is part of the Phoenix Island Group administered by the Gilbert and Ellice Islands Colony, as Admiral Watson recalled:

'Prince Philip was on the Bridge looking at the charts as Hull Island was just coming into view over the horizon so he turned to the Admiral and asked him if there was time to visit the small island as it wasn't on the programme but it was a British possession. The Admiral said we could and altered course accordingly.

Once ashore Prince Philip's programme began with a visit to the maneaba (meeting place) *for the* alofa (presentation of gifts), *which was presided over by the natural humorist and orator Vailele.*

(HRH The Duke of Edinburgh)

The chart had not been updated since Captain Cook first discovered and surveyed the island in the late eighteenth century and therefore the Admiral was naturally a bit nervous that the bottom could have changed dramatically. So we sent a motor boat ahead with a sailor and a lead line to take lead line soundings just as they would have done in Captain Cook's time to find if there was enough water for us. Just as we were doing this we noticed activity ashore. Because the population was so small the only official was the local Magistrate. An outrigger canoe was launched and in the stern was this important looking figure dressed in a white shirt, blue shorts and a black leather belt with a large buckle displaying the Royal Coat of Arms on it. The buckle turned out to be his badge of office and he seemed quite undisturbed by the circumstances in which he found himself. He was met at the bottom of the ladder and escorted up to meet Prince Philip. His Royal Highness told this man that he was quite surprised to see him because the visit wasn't planned.

'The man replied, "I knew the Royal Yacht would arrive here one day."

"But how did you know it was the Yacht?" Prince Philip inquired.

"Because we have a book with an illustration of the Royal Yacht inside so I compared what I saw with the photograph and knew it was the Royal Yacht."

'One of the things that struck me about visiting these small islands was that however small and insignificant an island might seem we always went through the full ceremonial process.'

After his discussions with the Magistrate it was decided that the Royal party would go ashore in the island's surf boat which was found to leak like a sieve and there was never less than 6 inches of water in the bottom during the short trip ashore. Despite this the Royal party arrived safe-

Part of the feast prepared by the islanders in honour of Prince Philip's visit to Vaitupu.

(HRH The Duke of Edinburgh)

Britannia *and HMNZS* Rotoiti *provide an impressive backdrop for Prince Philip's departure from Vaitupu.*

(HRH The Duke of Edinburgh)

ly. When he landed Prince Philip was given an enthusiastic and spontaneous welcome, with the villagers forming two lines to greet him. Following a brief walk around the island the Royal party enjoyed a barbecue before returning to the Yacht for the journey to Christmas Island where she arrived on 3 April.

Christmas Island was discovered on Christmas Day 1777 by Captain Cook, hence its name, and it is the largest atoll in the Pacific Ocean. Since 1954 it had been the British nuclear weapons test site. The island never had an indigenous population because of the erratic rainfall ranging from 5 to 100 inches a year. Before the nuclear test programme was launched a number of coconut plantations were cultivated. However, the infrastructure required to support the test programme meant that all of the work force brought in from the Gilbert Islands was required to support the military establishment. At the time of Prince Philip's visit, 2500 servicemen were stationed on the island, with the largest contingent being supplied by the RAF and the combined RN/RM contingent being the smallest. Despite the real danger of boredom the morale of those serving on the island seemed to be high. The arrangements for the visit from the firing of a Royal Salute to mark the Yacht's arrival and the formal dinner in the Officers' mess were a sharp contrast to the greeting ceremonies and island feasts encountered by the Yacht since leaving Hong Kong nearly a month before. In between these periods of 'normal' arrangements the Royal party was treated to one final *batere* when they visited the Gilbertese village of London on Christmas Island. Surprisingly, this turned out

to be the best *batere* of the Tour. As the islanders sang the song 'Tiparere' it sounded very familiar and turned out to be the classic First World War song 'Tipperary', sung in English although the singers didn't understand the words.

After lunch on the second day of the stopover at Christmas Island Prince Philip went to see the bird sanctuary, as he recalled:

'While I was stalking and snapping the local birds I noticed that the five Gilbertese boatmen who had brought us to the island were engaged in catching fish in a net. Judging by the shrieks and splashes, it sounded as if they were really enjoying themselves. As I was only wearing bathing trunks I went and joined them. We walked in line parallel to the shore, about waist deep until someone spotted a shoal of very pale silvery fish. The procedure was then to run out the net to seaward of the shoal and for those not actually holding the net to jump about and splash in an effort to keep the fish between the net and the shore. A great many got away despite our noisiest efforts, but by the time the net was hauled on to the beach we had usually captured between 10 and 20 very active, bright, shiny, white fish of about 1 pound each.'

After two days exploring Christmas Island *Britannia* let go from the mooring buoy and began the 15-day voyage across the eastern Pacific to Balboa and the Yacht's first transit of the Panama Canal. Five days into the voyage a bird, which seemed to be blind in one eye, landed on the

Prince Philip disembarks from the Royal Barge at Christmas Island.

(HRH The Duke of Edinburgh)

bridge. Over the course of the following days the progress of its recovery became a source of great interest among the Yachtsmen with updates given over the Sound Reproduction Equipment (SRE) and reports in the Yacht's own newspaper *Brag* (the paper's name was an abbreviation of Britannia's Rag). The bird was named Percy by the Yachtsmen and stayed for seven days until it had recovered enough to fly off again. The long period at sea provided an opportunity for those on board to pursue a number of deck sports, including deck quoits, deck tennis, deck hockey and uckers as well as another opportunity to practice the scandalising of the masts ahead of the St Lawrence Seaway deployment.

After two weeks at sea, the Yacht berthed in Balboa on 19 April. The timing of the visit coincided with a period of very high tension, with the threat of revolution looming over Panama. A past Ambassador to London, Roberto Arias and his wife, the former ballerina Dame Margot Fonteyn, were implicated in the suspected plot to overthrow the Government. Despite these fears nothing happened and warrants for the couple's arrest were issued after the Yacht's departure the following morning to begin the transit. Describing the journey through the canal Captain Owen said:

'The first 8 miles were rather dull (though higher banks than Suez). We then arrived at the first lock, which like all locks was a double lock (side by side) so that ships can go through in both directions at the same time. The "mule" system was extremely efficient. As our bows arrived at the lock entrance, we took in wires from the mules on the jetty (three on each side) –

there was a boat on each side waiting for us with the ends of the wires for us to pick up with heaving lines (or rather for the six Panamanian wire handlers, whom we had on board, to pick up). Our engines were then stopped and the Yacht was pulled into the lock by the mules. The pilot on board operated them by hand signals and the mules adjusted their wires on each side so that we were always in the centre of the lock. As soon as we were in the lock, the gate shut behind us without delay and immediately the lock started flooding up – and very quickly the water came in. As soon as it was full, the gate ahead opened and the mules pulled us into the next lock, waited for it to flood up and pulled us out into the canal again. It only took about 15 minutes for each lock. These two locks lifted us 55 feet altogether and we then crossed a small artificial lake, which was about a mile across, to the next lock, where the same process was repeated. This lifted us another 30 feet. From then on we were in level water until we went down three locks to the level of the Atlantic Ocean. The first part at the top level was about 8 miles of the Gaillard Cut, which was named after the American Colonel who died just before he completed the cut. The cut went straight through a small mountain and cost as much to excavate as the rest of the canal put together. It was narrow with high banks and still needs continual dredging to keep it from silting up, especially after the rains. This cut leads into the Gatun Lake which is a large artificial lake caused by damming the Chagres River and was needed to provide water to fill the locks. It is dotted with islands, which were once the tops of hills, and many tree

Britannia enters a lock in the Panama Canal. One of the lock's 'mules' can be seen on the right. As each ship enters a lock lines are passed to the mules, which move the ship through the lock. For Britannia *this was especially useful because the mules also kept the Yacht in the centre of the lock thus preserving the appearance of her hull.*

(© British Crown Copyright / MOD)

stumps still appeared above the waterline. The route of the canal followed the bed of the Chagres River. After 24 miles we reached the three locks which took us down to the Atlantic Ocean. The three locks were joined on to each other so one set of mules took us right through.'

Having cleared the locks the Yacht steamed another 6 miles to Limon Bay to drop anchor for Prince Philip's short visit to the town of Cristobal. That evening the Yacht weighed anchor for the Bahamas stopping at Conception Island on 23 April for a picnic before arriving the next day in Nassau where Prince Philip brought *Britannia* alongside in a strong wind. Later in the morning a familiar face returned to the Yacht when the Governor of the Bahamas, Sir Raynor Arthur, who had been the Governor of the Falkland Islands during the 1956 World Tour, came on board to call on Prince Philip. After lunch Prince Philip disembarked to carry out further engagements before flying on to Bermuda.[17]

Two days later the Yacht sailed to Bermuda to take on fuel for the Atlantic crossing back to Portsmouth. During the short stopover Prince Philip briefly re-embarked for a dinner party for the Governor prior to his flight home to the UK thus bringing his extensive Tour to a close.[18] Looking back on what was achieved by this Tour the final entry in the Tour Diary provides an interesting insight:

'To say that the tour has been enjoyable, especially in *Britannia*, would be a considerable understatement. But pleasure was not the object of the exercise. The object of the exercise was serious, to bring the Crown, in the person of Prince Philip, to the peoples of this diverse Commonwealth of ours. That the object has been achieved was made evident by the reactions of the people themselves, in India, in Pakistan, in Rangoon, in Singapore, in the Borneo territories, in Hong Kong, in the Solomons, in the Gilberts, in the Ellice Islands, in the Line Islands, in the Phoenix Islands, in the Bahamas and in Bermuda: places with vast populations and of importance in world affairs, places with minute populations and of no importance in world affairs. But one and all they are people and that the humblest of them was made to feel by the highest in the land that he was genuinely interested in them is perhaps the secret of the success of this tour: the human touch.'

On 29 April *Britannia* finally headed for home and reached Portsmouth on 7 May to conclude a deployment that had lasted for 120 days of which she had been underway for 107 days.

While the return to Portsmouth enabled many to take

leave, FORY and the Navigating Officer, Commander Berger flew to Canada to carry out a quick reconnaissance of the St Lawrence Seaway, where they met up with Commander C Rusby (later Vice Admiral Sir Cameron Rusby KCB LVO), the CO of the escort HMS *Ulster*. Because of the unusual design of the locks the three officers embarked in a lake steamer to see the arrangements for the handling of ships themselves and go through the fine detail for the forthcoming trip. As soon as he returned from Canada Commander Berger started making the detailed navigational plans for the visit, together with Lieutenant Commander D Smith (later Captain David Smith OBE RN) who had been temporarily seconded to the Yacht to assist with the navigation on this trip. They each had a set of charts for the voyage from Halifax to Port William in Ontario covering a distance of some 2800 miles. Commander Berger planned the voyage from Halifax to Port William while Lieutenant Commander Smith planned the return passage. Meanwhile, the Yacht was taken into dry dock and given a fresh coat of paint so that by the time she sailed for Canada on 6 June she looked immaculate.

When *Britannia* left Portsmouth the Yacht's company was swelled by a contingent from the Royal Canadian Navy, which had joined *Britannia* for the deployment, consisting of 2 Naval Officers and 15 Ratings. Once in Canada they would be joined by Petty Officer Auger of the WRCNS who would make history by becoming the first woman to wear the cap ribbon and flash of a Royal Yachtsman, when she embarked as the clerk to the acting Press Secretary. The Atlantic crossing was dogged by bad weather, beginning with high winds, rain and a heavy swell, followed by the unusual combination of fog and high winds off the Grand Banks. These factors had all conspired to slow down the Yacht so that, by the time she arrived in Prince Edward Island Naval Base on 14 June 1959, she was 24 hours late. President Eisenhower was due to embark in *Britannia* for the opening of the St Lawrence Seaway, so as soon as the Yacht was alongside, the Household Liaison Officer, Lieutenant H Foxworthy (later Commander H L Foxworthy OBE RN) had to liaise directly with the President's staff. Their discussions revealed the very different approach by the two nations towards protecting their Head of State, as Commander Foxworthy explains:

'When I spoke to the President's staff they told me that they would only be requiring accommodation for 54 people! Because of the limited amount of accommodation available I had to tell them that we were thinking of only two or three people. They said that this would

be totally inadequate to guard the President of the United States so I had to go back to the Yacht to discuss this with my superior officers. The discussions were re-established at a much higher level very quickly. It was pointed out to the President's security men that while President Eisenhower was on board his security would be a matter for the British Government and The Queen and that there would be no problems.'

Following the three-day visit to Prince Edward Naval Base, the Yacht sailed across to the northern side of the St Lawrence Estuary on 18 June to wait for The Queen and Prince Philip in Sept Iles. While the Yacht waited her side soon became covered in a film of brown iron ore dust from the nearby iron ore loading facitility, which the local fire chief kindly removed with the hoses of his fire engine. Almost immediately after The Queen's embarkation on 20 June *Britannia* sailed overnight for Gaspe Bay where the following morning she reviewed the Canadian Atlantic Fleet anchored there. The assembled warships, which included submarines and minesweepers, were headed by the recently commissioned frigate HMCS *Gatineau* wearing the flag of Rear Admiral H F Pullen Flag Officer Atlantic Coast. After engagements ashore in Gaspe for The Queen and Prince Philip the Fleet of 18 Royal Canadian Navy (RCN) warships accompanied the Yacht out of Gaspe Bay before reducing to an escort of nine ships for the next part of the tour.

On 22 June the Yacht left the St Lawrence Estuary to sail up the Saguenay River for the visit to Port Alfred. As Captain Owen remarked, the scenery along the Saguenay River had a familiar feel about it:

> 'The river was rather like going through the Kyle of Lochalsh, except that we went 50 miles up river before we berthed at Port Alfred in Ha Ha Bay. It was misty – just like Scotland and in fact often pouring hard. It was about the width of the Kyle, but very deep, and higher mountains on each side (1400 feet).'

Port Alfred itself was dominated by timber and the paper mill with a large number of floating logs appearing to fill Ha Ha Bay. However, timber wasn't the only local industry as The Queen and Prince Philip landed to visit the aluminium plant at Arvida. From Port Alfred the Royal Squadron sailed back to the St Lawrence Estuary for the visits to Quebec on 23 June, and Montreal where she arrived on 24 June accompanied by a tremendous local escort, as Captain Owen wrote:

> 'Our "close escort" of outboard motor boats really began – hundreds of them following us all the way, with RCMP [Royal Canadian Mounted Police] motor boats keeping them from getting too near the Yacht. Sometimes the RCMP were too conscientious and Prince Philip would beckon them to allow the boats to come closer.'

The Queen and Prince Philip spent 25 June ashore in Montreal carrying out engagements prior to the start of the main Seaway events the following day which were described in the Yacht's Daily Orders as Seaway Day One.

Because the St Lawrence Seaway is largely on the St Lawrence River, which is the border between Canada and the US, The Queen was joined on board the Yacht by the Prime Minister of Canada and Mrs Diefenbaker at 0855. Twenty minutes later The Queen and Prince Philip left for the Royal Canadian Air Force (RCAF) base at St Hubert to welcome President Eisenhower and his wife who would join the Royal party for the opening ceremonies. While The Queen was away the Yacht moved to the St Lambert Special Jetty, which had been built for the occasion, and passed under the Jacques Cartier bridge thus performing the scandalising manoeuvre in public for the first time. Describing the experience Captain Owen said:

'It was very frightening going under as there didn't look as though there would be anything like enough clearance – and there was only just enough. It was a very slick operation – strike the Standard on the main and Admiralty Flag at the fore, and at the same time break out the Standard on the fore, scandalise, go under the bridge, re-hoist mast, and then reverse procedure with flags. It all took less than four minutes for the whole operation. When the President was embarked, his Standard was flown alongside the Royal Standard, so they both had to come down on the main and be broken out on the fore at the same time – and it always looked most impressive. I always wondered whether the bridges were going to be high enough – power cables looked the worst.'

Having performed the shore-side ceremonies at the Seaway Ceremony Platform, The Queen and President Eisenhower embarked in the Yacht. At 1155 *Britannia* sailed to make her way between the two pontoons which marked the symbolic gateway to the St Lawrence Seaway. On the Royal Bridge The Queen, Prince Philip, President Eisenhower and Mrs Eisenhower, together with Mr Diefenbaker and his wife, watched as *Britannia* passed through the tape linking the two pontoons at noon, to open the St Lawrence Seaway. At this moment the crowds cheered while coloured balloons and fireworks were let off. With the spotlight of the media firmly focused on *Britannia* during the day's historic events it was essential that the Yacht was in the right place at the right time, which required good team work on board the Yacht, not least between the two Navigating Officers, as Captain Smith explains:

'There were times when both Commander Berger and myself were on the bridge at the same time, for example, during the ceremonial periods when Commander Berger would be conning the Yacht. I would then be checking the Yacht's position and altering the revolutions to make us go a little faster or slower. While it may sound simplistic it was very important because we had a radio at the back of the bridge tuned into the local radio network. We would hear the radio commentator saying that the Yacht had reached a certain position, which was crowded, and that we were 20 sec-

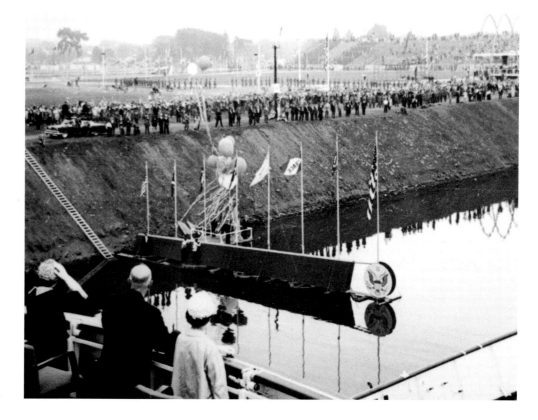

The Queen and President Eisenhower watch from the Royal Bridge as Britannia *passes through the symbolic gateway to open the St Lawrence Seaway.*

(© British Crown Copyright / MOD)

onds early would we be early at the next point? All the time I was adjusting the speed so that the public who had driven so many miles to see The Queen saw her exactly at the right time as we passed. Once we got out into the Lakes it was necessary, because of the different rules of the road on the Lakes, for the Officer of the Watch to have a back up with one of the two Navigators on the bridge or readily available in the charthouse to provide advice when needed. When fog closed in, as it did from time to time, Commander Berger remained closed up at the pelorus on the bridge whilst I provided blind pilotage advice from the charthouse. The sole radar set on board was crucial to safety under these conditions and thanks to the maintainers it never let us down.'

To reflect the international nature of the occasion the escort for this stage of the tour consisted of HMS *Ulster* from the RN, HMCS *Gatineau* from the RCN and USS *Forrest Sherman* from the USN. Shortly after the Yacht passed under Victoria Bridge at 1210 she entered the St Lambert Lock, as Lieutenant Commander T Brydon remembered.

'It was like driving into a tunnel 90 feet high. We got into the lock and the gate shut behind us. The Yacht came up at an alarming rate and the rubber fenders were getting squashed when suddenly there was a huge bang like a gunshot. I had never seen so many hands disappearing into jackets to grab revolvers, etc., as the security men reacted to what they thought was an assassination attempt on Eisenhower's life. In fact the culprit was not an assassin but one of the rubber fenders that had burst under the pressure and created a gunshot-like noise within this cavern. The security men quickly realised this and all was well.'

As the Yacht continued to make her way to Lake St Louis she passed a lake steamer which gave the Royal party a very enthusiastic welcome, as Captain Owen continues:

'We passed a Lake Liner called *North American* which had been chartered by the Chicago Chamber of Commerce for a St Lawrence Seaway Dedication cruise. As she approached we heard her loud speaker blare out, "passengers, guests and crew stand to attention and give three cheers for The Queen of Canada and the President of the United States." And there they all were, fallen in as for divisions almost! I never thought I'd see passengers in a liner so well disciplined!'

Having negotiated three more bridges *Britannia* entered Lake St Louis to be greeted by a line of 16 warships from the USN and RCN headed by the US guided missile cruiser USS *Macon*. There was also a salute by private yachtsmen with two lines of yachts all cheering and dipping their ensigns. From Lake St Louis the Yacht entered the Lower Beauharnois Lock where the President landed at 1710 to embark in one of the three helicopters waiting by the side of the lock and disappeared into a cloud of dust as they took off. After another lock and two bridges *Britannia* secured to a buoy in Couteau anchorage at 2025 for the night enabling The Queen and Prince Philip to go for a short cruise in the Barge in the Valley Field area.[19]

While the Royal couple were away Captain Dalrymple-Hamilton was asked to deal with a rather unusual problem, as he recalls:

'At 2140 I was in my cabin when I was rung up by Bobo Macdonald who announced, "there is a bat in The Queen's bedroom and Her Majesty does not like bats." I collected the First Lieutenant, Don Morison, and we rushed aft armed with tennis rackets. Bobo was there to meet us and let us into The Queen's bedroom. We downed the bat, much to Bobo's satisfaction and were just congratulating ourselves on a job well done when another bat was reported in the Royal Drawing Room. By then the Barge was in sight on its way back to the Yacht and we had about five minutes. The Royal Drawing Room, being a lot bigger than The Queen's cabin, this bat was much more elusive. However, we got it just as the Barge was approaching the ladder and, having thrown my tennis racket to Don who made a hasty retreat, I reached the top of the ladder just as the Barge came alongside. I discovered afterwards that there were bats everywhere, no doubt having been attracted by the Yacht's lights, and some of them were jammed in the ventilation trunking. I had to turn out the "duty part of the watch" and we had a job extracting them all, done in silence as The Queen had gone to bed.'

The Queen's programme for Seaway Day Two was severely disrupted by dense fog leading to some hasty changes to her programme as she left the Yacht at Snell Lock and rejoined that night at Iroquois Lock. On 28 June the voyage continued between Brockville and Kingston. Throughout the day the Yacht was surrounded once again by an armada of small boats, with many people taking advantage of the fact it was a Sunday and joining in the occasion, although it provided a headache for the RCMP and US Coastguard launches who were trying to keep them under control. At Kingston the Yacht anchored for The Queen to go ashore to watch a short display by the Fort Henry Guard at Old Fort Henry. In the evening

Britannia weighed anchor for Toronto where she arrived the next morning. After two days of engagements ashore The Queen and Prince Philip left to fly to Ottawa, leaving the Yacht to make her way through the eight locks and 30 miles of the Welland Canal on 1 July. Being Dominion Day it was a public holiday and about 500,000 Canadians decided to come out and watch *Britannia's* transit of the canal which was simply incredible, as Captain Owen remarked:

'They cheered, clapped and waved to us all the way through. Their enthusiasm, happiness and loyalty were tremendous. They all knew The Queen wasn't on board, but they wanted to see the Yacht come up into the Great Lakes. Nobody on board had seen anything like it, even when The Queen had been on board! The canal was very narrow most of the way so we were very close to the crowds who were on the edge of the canal, and some of us answered waves by waving back, particularly to the old and the children, and it gave them all a terrific thrill. There had been a lot of talk in the Canadian papers about Canadian indifference to the Tour but our passage through the Welland Canal completely squashed such comments. The Yacht in herself caused far more interest there than anywhere else I had been before. In the papers as many advertisements showed pictures of the Yacht as they did of The Queen.'

In addition to dismissing the Tour some of the newspapers made some extraordinary comments including the reporter who thought the Yacht had borrowed her Canadian flag from the Parliament Buildings, while another commentator claimed the Yacht carried a gardener to produce the flowers in the Dining Room and the Drawing Room! Both claims were of course quite wrong and in fact the Canadian Flags had been drawn specially for the tour from Portsmouth Stores as had the two Presidential Standards.

After an eventful day steaming through the Welland Canal the Yacht cleared the last of the locks and entered Lake Erie to continue with the passage to Windsor, where she arrived the next morning.[20] While *Britannia* had made her way to Windsor, The Queen and Prince Philip had visited Ottawa and arrived in Windsor by train to re-embark in the Yacht in the afternoon which promptly sailed for Sarnia. Once more the Yacht was followed by a large escort of private boats as she made her way along the Detroit River to Lake St Clair and up the Sarnia River. Describing the passage up the river Captain Owen said:

'It was very narrow, and twisty and wherever there was a house, the whole family and all their friends and relations were there. A lot of the American river bank is a great summer resort, and every house had its private motor launch, and everyone on the lawn waving flags and firing miniature cannons.'

Britannia reached Sarnia and berthed alongside for The Queen and Prince Philip's short visit before sailing again, as Captain Owen noted:

'It was too dark to see the crowds on each bank for this passage but we could certainly hear them. One party had

The passengers of the Lake Liner North American *were asked to stand to attention and given three cheers for The Queen of Canada and President Eisenhower. The Queen and Prince Philip watch the liner sail past* Britannia *from the Verandah Deck.*

(© British Crown Copyright / MOD)

a large bonfire, and the words "OUR QUEEN" spelt out in flames – it served as a very loyal welcome, and perhaps as a little dig at their friends across the water!'

The next day *Britannia* anchored off Penetanguishe in Georgian Bay and shortly afterwards The Queen and Prince Philip landed to catch the Royal Train to Parry Sound. There they rejoined the Yacht accompanied by the Prime Minister and Mrs Diefenbaker. Five minutes later the Yacht sailed for Chicago. By the time *Britannia* reached Lake Michigan on 5 July she was 2000 miles from the sea and 580 feet above sea level The outline of the American city of Chicago was first visible on board the Yacht an hour before she arrived on 6 July. Having secured to a buoy the Barge was lowered to take The Queen and Prince Philip ashore. As it made its way towards the city, the Barge was over flown by 70 bombers indicating that the Royal couple were in for a big welcome from the world's eighth biggest city. Their day ashore was rounded off by a banquet hosted by the Mayor of Chicago at the Hilton Hotel and a massive fireworks display along the waterfront. The Queen and Prince Philip returned to *Britannia* just before midnight and soon *Britannia* made her way into the night and the illuminated skyline of Chicago began to fade into the distance. On 8 July the Yacht arrived in Sault Ste Marie for the Royal party to pay a brief visit to the Canadian side before sailing for Port Arthur.

That evening The Queen invited the Captains of the three escorting warships to dine on board *Britannia* as she steamed across Lake Superior. As Admiral Rusby remarked:

'It was planned that we should transfer to *Britannia* by jackstay but, in order to simplify matters, the Captain of HMCS *Gatineau* and I went on board the third escort, HMCS *Kootenay*, beforehand so that all three of us could be transferred in one operation. Sadly, fog came down and our invitation was altered to coffee after dinner. Still the fog persisted and a message came across saying that Her Majesty would like to see us before she disembarked next morning. Realising that two of us were not in our own ships and only had mess dress available, FORY included the statement that "any rig will do". I spent the night in *Kootenay's* sickbay and, after anchoring on the morning of 9 July, we went on board *Britannia* to be presented to The Queen with two of us wearing stiff shirts and bow ties from the evening before. This prompted a signal from FORY which read, "I have always regarded a return to one's ship at 0930 in the morning in Mess Dress to be just a little decadent." To which we replied, "Concur. In order to avoid

any scandal we will return disguised as reporters."'

Britannia's arrival off Port Arthur required a degree of diplomacy because of the fierce rivalry that existed between Fort William and Port Arthur. To avoid favouring either town it was decided that *Britannia* would anchor off the breakwater. However, at the special request of the two Mayors, it was agreed that the Yacht would steam through both harbours before anchoring so that the local people could see the Yacht and her escorts, which called for some quick thinking from FORY, as Captain Smith recalled:

'As the Yacht closed the breakwater entrance so did the many small escorting power boats whilst others remained poised in the gap between the breakwaters. The latter were clearly showing no sense of urgency as the distance closed which caused close inspection through several pairs of binoculars by observers on the bridge and a realisation that these boats were stern towards and lying at anchor. I was reporting to Admiral Dawnay at this instant when he calmly ordered "full astern both engines", which brought the Yacht to a stop just in time – and with the after end of the Yacht gently pumping up and down due to the commotion in the water from the propellers it was not surprising to see the effect it had on the Verandah Deck! The Queen and Prince Philip suddenly appeared on deck. The small boats safely passed clear down the port and starboard sides and the Yacht resumed her dignified progress.'

The incident caught the eye of the local papers, as Captain Owen noted.

'The Admiral's feelings weren't improved when we got the local afternoon paper, which had three stories on the front page. One said we went aground and produced a photograph of us showing the bottom churned up by our screws as we extricated ourselves; one said we were too big to take the sharp corner after passing through the breakwater; and, fortunately, the third said we had to stop because a lot of local boats had anchored across our path! Suitable protests were made in the right quarters and all ended happily when the Admiral joked about it very well in a speech at a dinner given by both towns in the evening.'

Together with HMS *Ulster*, the Yacht was probably able to claim an altitude record within the RN of having reached a height of 600 feet above sea level during her visit to Port Arthur. Half an hour after anchoring The Queen and Prince Philip disembarked from the Yacht to begin their visit to Western Canada leaving *Britannia* to make a speedy passage back through the locks to Halifax. Like the first passage through the Welland Canal, large crowds gathered throughout this trip to see the Yacht even though The Queen was not on board. The main incident of the return voyage happened on 25 July after the visit to Montreal when the Yacht anchored in Murray Bay, as Captain Smith explains:

'Admiral Dawnay was temporarily confined to his bunk with flu and the Commander, Commander North Dalrymple-Hamilton took command. It was a dark wet night: the approach was across the stream, which was ebbing fast and the anchorage was to be found in deep water, close inshore. In the final stages of the approach, always slightly tense on such an occasion, the Navigator reported the distance to go and, at the appropriate moment he gave the order "go". On the forecastle the anchor was let go and the rattle of chain in the hawse pipe was clearly heard as the Yacht ran out her cable. Reports from the First Lieutenant indicated the amount of cable run out; the third joining shackle was reported as it disappeared through the hawse pipe, followed by the noise of more chain and then there was a deathly hush – no more noise from the forecastle. This was followed by a report that we had lost our port cable and the order "let go starboard anchor" was passed from the bridge and the Yacht was anchored safely. Once the Yacht was lying at anchor the investigation into what happened began, and the obvious starting point was to interview the officer who had witnessed the cable being secured to the cable clench in the bottom of the cable locker. Since it was nearing midnight the obvious place to look for the Lieutenant, who was off watch, was in his bunk! I gave Lieutenant Foxworthy a robust shake from his slumbers and sought an assurance that he had seen the cable properly secured. Relieved this was the case I told him to report to the Navigator on the Bridge.'

As Commander Foxworthy continues:

'I was summoned to see Commander Berger who told me that the cable had parted and then he asked me, "Did you check that the inboard end of the cable had been secured to the ship?" It was the responsibility of the Navigator to ensure that the inboard end of the cable was secured to the ship. Commander Berger hadn't been able to do it himself so he delegated the task to me. I was pleased to tell him that I had been down there myself with the dockyard worker when the cable was put back in the Yacht prior to our departure from Portsmouth. I knew for a fact that the inboard end was properly secured to the Yacht because I had hammered in the lead pellet to the shackle to clench it in the Yacht. When it broke no one knew what had happened and they thought that the whole cable had gone but a few minutes after I had spoken to Commander Berger it was found that the inboard end of the cable had been secured properly as only part of the cable had been lost.'

Before *Britannia* resumed her voyage to Halifax several attempts were made to recover the missing anchor. HMS *Ulster* sent a couple of divers down to locate it but the tidal conditions were such that they could only dive for a few minutes in every tide. In between dives Lieutenant Commander Smith spent much of the next day in a jolly boat with a grapnel trying to snag the cable. Unfortunately, it was a soft bottom and the anchor and nearly four shackles of cable had disappeared into the sludge. With half of a broken link to prove the cable had parted, subsequent analysis proved that the incident was caused by metal fatigue. This of course meant that the Yacht was now an anchor short, which was deeply embarrassing because there was an empty hawse pipe on the portside where the anchor should have been which couldn't be filled before the next period of Royal duty. The Queen and Prince Philip rejoined the Yacht in Shediac on 29 July for the voyage during the early hours of the next morning to Charlotte where they disembarked while *Britannia* sailed to Halifax arriving on 31 July. Once The Queen and Prince Philip had returned to the Yacht that evening and the press had dispersed, the Yacht quietly took on its new anchor.

'The First Lieutenant lowered some chain through the port hawse pipe which we hauled up to the corner of the jetty. At the corner was lying an Admiralty pattern anchor painted Royal Yacht blue and looking as though it was part of the scenery. We shackled the chain to the new anchor and quietly hauled it on board thus filling the hole! The media never noticed the absence of the port anchor, which would have provided them with an interesting snippet for them to enlarge upon. We got away with it and were rather pleased!' Captain Smith remarked.

After a busy programme ashore in Halifax, The Queen and Prince Philip left Halifax on the night of 1 August to fly back to the UK and *Britannia* sailed shortly afterwards, bound for the Shetland Islands and The Queen's visit. As *Britannia* made her way across the Atlantic a signal was received from Buckingham Palace at 1130 on 7 August to say that The Queen's Tour of the Shetland and Orkney

Islands was cancelled and that at 1230 a full announcement would be made on the BBC. At 1230 the news was announced that The Queen was expecting a baby in the New Year and that all her public engagements were being cancelled in the meantime. The news allowed *Britannia* to head straight for Portsmouth and the Yachtsmen received their leave a little earlier than planned. The arrival of *Britannia* at H Moorings on 10 August brought a very busy and eventful year to a successful conclusion, which had seen the Yacht steam a total of 40,232 miles visiting 21 countries and 56 ports. In the 243 days since her departure from Portsmouth in January she had been underway for 155 of them. The Queen's happy news meant that *Britannia* spent the rest of the year in Portsmouth, including a month in dry dock for repainting.

The New Year marked a return to Royal duty when Princess Mary, The Princess Royal, joined *Britannia* on 15 January 1960 for the voyage across the Atlantic Ocean and her Tour of the Caribbean.[21] Unfortunately, the Yacht encountered heavy weather during most of the passage giving the Princess quite a rough ride. However, the Yacht reached the British colony of British Guiana on 27 January for the start of the Tour which lasted for the next two months as *Britannia* crisscrossed the Caribbean visiting British Guiana in South America, Belize in Central America and 18 islands in the Caribbean before returning to Portsmouth via the Azores on 7 April. During this Tour FORY addressed the Yachtsmen on the forecastle on 19 February to inform them that The Queen had safely delivered a son (Prince Andrew) to which they responded by giving three cheers for The Queen and Prince Philip.[22]

On 3 May *Britannia* sailed from Portsmouth for the Pool of London for the wedding of Princess Margaret to Anthony Armstrong-Jones. After the wedding service the Yacht was to take them on their honeymoon but no one on board except FORY knew where the Yacht would be heading. This need for secrecy was essential if the Yacht was to achieve its aim of providing the Royal couple with a brief escape from the pressures of media interest and have some time to enjoy a true holiday. As the saying goes, time and tide wait for no one and this was especially true on the wedding day as the Royal couple were delayed in their journey to the Pool of London. Thus with the tide ebbing the Yacht slipped the mooring buoys as soon as the Royal couple were embarked and the Barge was hoisted as the Yacht got underway. By the time she reached the Blackwell Tunnel the clearance was marginally on the side of the Yacht and she was able to clear the Thames Estuary that evening and make her way into the English Channel. Now that there was no way of the news escaping, the Yachtsmen were informed that

Britannia was going to cross the Atlantic for a cruise in the Caribbean. The next day The Queen sent a message to the Yacht's company to congratulate them on the speed and efficiency with which the London departure had been performed.[23] Ten days later the Yacht had arrived off Tobago to land the Royal couple at an isolated cove for a picnic. Between 17 May and 8 June the Yacht anchored off different islands most days to enable the Royal couple to spend the day ashore enjoying picnics and a little exploring. At the end of the Caribbean cruise the Yacht weighed anchor on 8 June and sailed back across the Atlantic to Portsmouth, where she arrived on 18 June.

At the beginning of August *Britannia* sailed from Portsmouth to attend Cowes Week before heading north via Cardiff for the annual Western Isles Cruise. When she returned to Portsmouth she entered dockyard hands to begin the planning for a quadrennial refit which was started in November. Originally, the refit had been scheduled for the autumn of 1961 but, because of the need to reduce the vibration problems that were still being experienced in the Royal Apartments at certain speeds, the refit was brought forward by one year. Therefore, the Royal Apartments were completely stripped out again and further stiffening work was undertaken. During this time Commander Freeman became the last Commander (L) when he left the Yacht without relief on 2 December 1960. This move came as little surprise because, strictly speaking, the Yacht did not justify an Electrical Officer in the rank of Commander. The duties were subsequently undertaken by a Lieutenant serving under Commander (E).

During the course of the refit the Senior Engineer, later Captain Peter Archer RN, decided to make a minor unplanned addition to the Engine Room, as he explains:

'It is said that every great ship is given a golden rivet when it is being built which is driven into place amid great secrecy in the dead of night. Whenever we had visitors on board there always used to be sniggers about "oh one of the Engineer Officers will take you down to the Engine Room and show you the golden rivet". In the end I got fed up with this so during the refit I acquired some gold leaf and painted a rivet. Therefore, in future when people were told about the golden rivet I was able to take them down to the Engine Room and show them this gold rivet. However, when I went down to the Engine Room on the day of the decommissioning nearly four decades later to find the golden rivet I noticed that it had moved to the other side of the ship!'

Even without its golden rivet the Engine Room was very

different to any other ship's Engine Room, as Captain Archer continues:

'There was a mat outside the Engine Room and I remember remarking to my predecessor, "Oh I suppose that's there to wipe your feet when you leave the Engine Room."

"No," he replied, "we ask people to wipe their feet *before* going into the Engine Room because it is kept cleaner than any other part of the ship!"

There was something in that comment because it was absolutely immaculate. When one looked down into the bottom of the machinery spaces of a warship, only bilge water was usually visible. However, in the Yacht one looked down and saw white enamel – immaculate. I looked at this sight and remarked to my predecessor, "I suppose you have to keep it continually pumped out to keep it looking like that."

"No," he said, "we just wipe it out with a damp sponge once a week."

But of course no ship is like that and it was due to the hard work of the Engineers. The Engine Room lent itself to this. All the auxiliaries were electrically driven as opposed to a warship in which they were all steam driven and steam engines leak oil, muck, and water.'

As the refit approached its conclusion, the Yacht's company was brought back up to the full Ocean Complement which was completed by 6 March 1961.[24] When *Britannia* was originally commissioned it was decided to introduce a scheme whereby if the Yacht was going to be in Portsmouth for four months or more, the Yacht's company would be reduced by a third to the Harbour Complement. These proportions reflected the ratio of the Yacht's company made up by the Permanent Royal Yacht Service. The remaining third of the Yacht's company were drafted from the general service for a period of up to two years' service. Once a Yachtsman had been on board *Britannia* for six months he was able to volunteer to join the Permanent Royal Yacht Service. Provided there was a vacancy, and he was still recommended, he would be accepted into the Royal Yacht Service at the end of a further six months' service, at which point he would be on probation for a further 12 months. Once a Yachtsman was fully accepted he was able to serve out the rest of his naval service on board the Yacht. However, the one major drawback of a long period in the Royal Yacht Service was that promotion was strictly through 'dead man's shoes', and thus it wasn't unusual in later years to find a very capable Leading Seamen in the Yacht who would have easily reached the rank of Chief Petty Officer, or above, in the general service within the same period. This fact was beautifully underlined in 1983 when *Navy News* carried a photograph submitted by a warship proudly displaying its four 'three badge killicks' (Leading Seaman who had served at least 12 years) as a rare distinction. Seizing on this someone in the Yacht decided to make a list of its own 'three badge killicks' which came to a total of 22 such men. As *Britannia*'s programme became increasingly hectic over the years the reduction to a Harbour

Princess Margaret and Lord Snowdon on the Royal Bridge as the Yacht enters Portsmouth at the end of their honeymoon cruise.

(© British Crown Copyright / MOD)

Complement became a rare event seen principally during major refits.

One of those to be appointed to the Yacht as part of the Ocean Complement at this time was Lieutenant W R Canning (later Captain W R Canning DSO RN), who joined as the Commander's Assistant. Describing his feelings about the prospect of leaving the general service to serve in *Britannia* and his initial impressions of this new environment, he said:

'I had never entertained the thought of serving in *Britannia*. I wasn't wealthy, I didn't have a title, I was a young Lieutenant and I had a career focus of ultimately going to sea in command of a destroyer. Therefore, *Britannia* was in a sense outside this view. The novelty of associating with Royalty was a major challenge – I had never had that experience before. Perhaps one of the biggest challenges was the first occasion I dined aft in the Royal Apartments with members of the Royal Family. The three of us were given a briefing on how to behave, what to say and what not to do. It couldn't have been easier. All one's worries were baseless as the Royal Family were very good at putting us at ease. Another major adjustment was that when The Queen was embarked and I took the night watch I was conscious of the fact that my Monarch was sleeping aft. Whilst it didn't prey on my mind I devoted an extra special degree of attention to my duties. Looking back on my time in *Britannia* I wondered how I ever questioned the delights and privilege of serving in the Yacht. The beauty of serving in the Yacht was not just the privilege to serve closely the Royal Family but being in a ship with such superb people.'

Having completed her sea trials at the end of March *Britannia* was ready for her next period of Royal duty, which began on 17 April when The Queen Mother embarked in Portsmouth for her Tour of Tunisia. Shortly afterwards the Yacht set sail for Gibraltar, where she paid a three-day visit before heading south for Tunis. The Queen Mother's Equerry for this trip was Captain Alastair Aird (later Captain Sir Alastair Aird GCVO). Describing his role as Equerry and how the use of the Yacht for a Royal Tour enhanced the work of The Queen Mother's Household he said:

'As the Equerry I was the member of the Household who met the guests once they had arrived on board the Yacht and ensured that they had everything they wanted. I would be in attendance on The Queen Mother ashore during most of her engagements together with her Private Secretary and the Lady-in-Waiting. I also handled a limited amount of correspondence. The Yacht was always a wonderful base for office life. When we went on long overseas tours if the Yacht wasn't available we had to stay in Government House bringing the secretariat, luggage, and everything else. Therefore, every time we moved from state to state we had to take the whole Household with us and their luggage. There usually wasn't the level of office facilities in a Government House as there were in the Yacht. When on board the Yacht we could leave the secretaries typing away so that we simply had to sign letters when we came back at the end of the day's programme ashore. After dinner we were able to write the relevant thank-you letters which would be typed up the following day while we were ashore and this arrangement worked very well. In those early days there wasn't a great deal of work for members of The Queen Mother's Household while we were at sea so we would spend the day touring the Yacht and in the evening I would often play deck tennis with The Queen Mother's Private Secretary, Martin Gilliat and Admiral Dawnay together with one of the Yacht's officers. We would then have dinner parties in the Dining Room where officers would be invited to dine aft with The Queen Mother which ensured that we were always a party of 10 or 12. Once we got to Gibraltar and Tunis, correspondence was sent out to the Yacht and there was a backlog of work to catch up on. As the communications technology improved over the years everything seemed to arrive that much quicker and thus those first couple of days of tranquillity embarked in the Yacht seemed to disappear.'

During the Passage between Gibraltar and Tunis Lieutenant J Slater (later Admiral Sir Jock Slater GCB LVO DL) was invited to dine aft on the night of 23 April[25] which led to a surprise request by The Queen Mother, as he recalled:

'After dinner The Queen Mother asked me to sit with her on the sofa. She said, "I gather that you were in the National Youth Orchestra."

So I replied, "Yes Ma'am, but only for a short while."

"Oh, well we thought it would be nice if you entertained us this evening."

Shocked by the suggestion, I made some weak excuse that I really could not play without expert accompaniment and was immediately told, in Queen Elizabeth's inimitable way, that that was not a problem as the Lady-in-Waiting "played a little"; so I was dispatched to my cabin to get my flute. The Lady-in-

Waiting was in fact Lady Ruth Fermoy, a most accomplished pianist, and, thanks to her brilliant sight-reading, we successfully performed a Marcello Sonata.'

The Queen Mother enjoyed the event because the following year she asked Lieutenant Slater's successor Lieutenant Rowe (later Rear Admiral Sir Patrick Rowe KCVO CBE) about his musical skills, as he recalls: 'the Queen Mother asked me, "And what musical instrument do you play?" I had to confess that I didn't so she said, "Oh what a pity, we did so enjoy Jock and his flute."'

On 24 April the Yacht arrived off La Goulette with a Force 8 wind blowing down the narrow canal running from La Goulette to Tunis. Such conditions would have deterred many Captains from making the short passage but FORY decided to press on. Despite the wind veering to the Yacht's starboard side he managed to successfully negotiate the 150-foot-wide canal and enter Tunis for The Queen Mother to visit President M Habib Bourguiba.[26] The Queen Mother completed a further two days of engagements in the local area before leaving to visit the holy city of Karioran on the morning of 27 April. While The Queen Mother was away the Yacht sailed for Sousse having to steam at 21 knots to ensure she arrived in time for The Queen Mother's arrival by road there. When the Yacht arrived FORY saw a familiar ship in the harbour that turned out to be the destroyer HMS *Saintes* which he had once commanded. In his signal to *Saintes*, Admiral Dawnay said it gave him great pleasure as a former Captain to congratulate the Ship's company on her appearance. The next day President Bourguiba accompanied The Queen Mother for a drive through Sousse. Despite the President's fear of being assassinated The Queen Mother insisted in making the drive in an open top car. As The Queen Mother expected, the drive through the town went without a hitch and she returned safely to the Yacht, shortly before *Britannia* left for Cagliari where the Yacht arrived on 29 April.[27]

Unfortunately, when *Britannia* arrived in Cagliari she managed to wrap some 4-inch thick wire round the port propeller. The task of clearing the wire went on for most of the day with support from the Italian Naval Base at Cagliari and the Mediterranean Fleet, which diverted the tug *Mediator* to Cagliari from its passage to Spezia. Cutting equipment was flown to Cagliari from Malta. The Italian press picked up the incident and an amusing cartoon was published in the local paper the next day showing *Britannia* with a huge quantity of wire wrapped around its propeller with the heading 'Spaghetti'. Luckily, no damage was done to the propeller shaft so the Yacht was able to sail the next day as planned for the Lipari Islands.

By then The Queen Mother had flown back to London, while The Queen and Prince Philip had embarked for a couple of days cruising around the Lipari Islands prior to beginning their State Visit to Italy on 1 May when the Yacht berthed in Naples.[28] While The Queen and Prince Philip left for the duration of their State Visit, the Yacht sailed on the 3 May for Ancona on the Adriatic coast where she embarked The Duke and Duchess of Gloucester on 5 May. Interestingly, the Duchess was accompanied by her sister Lady Angela Dawnay as the Lady-in-Waiting, thus giving Lady Angela Dawnay the distinction of being the only FORY's wife to be embarked in the Yacht during a Royal tour in an official capacity. Having completed their State Visit, The Queen and Prince Philip also joined the Yacht that evening following their flight from Rome.[29]

Although the next day's visit to Venice was described as a private one for The Queen, it didn't seem to dampen the welcome that she received from the people of Venice who turned out in large numbers to greet her, including numerous gondolas manned by gondoliers in national and period costumes. After a day ashore the Royal Family went for an evening cruise in gondolas before returning on board to watch the 20-minute fireworks display, which included a float with fireworks spelling out 'Welcome To Venice'. The night was rounded off by an orchestra and choir in an illuminated gondola which came alongside the Yacht and serenaded The Queen.[30] On 7 May The Queen and Prince Philip left the Yacht to continue their private visit to Italy, and *Britannia* sailed in the morning for Athens to begin The Duke of Gloucester's Tour of Commonwealth War Graves.[31] As part of the Tour, on 17 May The Duke of Gloucester visited the site of the Gallipoli landings. The visit was unusual because the Dardenelles area was still highly restricted which meant that the former battlefields were virtually untouched since the Allied withdrawal in the First World War. From the Dardenelles the Yacht steamed across the Sea of Marmara to visit Istanbul, arriving there on 20 May, where The Duke and Duchess gave a dinner on board. As soon as the final guests left, the Yacht sailed for Rhodes, where *Britannia* met up with the Greek Royal Yacht *Polymestis*, which had served in the RN as the Algerine ocean minesweeper HMS *Gozo*, on 22 May.[32] The following morning the Commander of the Yacht, later Captain D Roome LVO RN, was woken up in the night by the sound of the anchor cable rattling, as he explains: 'I shot up to see what was going on and all looked fine. Normally, it would be the feeling one would get if the anchor was dragging. In fact we learnt the next morning that there had been a small earthquake!' For the next three days the Royal Yachts cruised in company together, with warships of the Greek Navy, including their flagship the cruiser *Elli*, visiting Heraklion and Suda Bay where The Duke and Duchess left the Yacht to fly home.[33] In the afternoon the Yacht began the voyage back to Portsmouth, via Malta and Gibraltar, arriving there on 5 June.[34]

In July 1961 the Yacht was used by The Queen to visit the RN's Boys Training Establishment HMS *Ganges* at Shotley, Suffolk, before being used for Cowes Week at the end of the month. From Cowes, *Britannia* sailed to Southampton to embark members of the Royal Family for the Western Isles Cruise, which included official visits by The Queen to Milford Haven and Belfast before the private part of the voyage could begin. By 1961 it had become traditional during the Western Isles Cruise for the Yachtsmen to put on a ship's concert for the Royal Family and this year was no exception. One of the acts was a most amusing impersonation of FORY to music by Sullivan and words adapted from Gilbert performed by his Flag Lieutenant Jock Slater. Admiral Slater recalls, 'as soon as the act was over, Admiral Dawnay secretly instructed his Steward to go to my cabin, pack up all my bags and put them by the boat – I got the message!'

On 18 September the Yacht entered dry dock in Portsmouth to have five-bladed propellers fitted in a further attempt to ease the vibration problems in the Royal Apartments.[35] This measure proved unsuccessful during the subsequent sea trials, when they were found to sing and cause more vibration at high speed, thus the Yacht was dry docked again to have the original four-bladed propellers refitted.[36]

Britannia began the final Royal tour under the command of Admiral Dawnay on 3 October when she left Portsmouth for The Queen's Tour of West Africa.[37] During the Tour The Queen and Prince Philip visited Ghana, Liberia, Sierra Leone, Gambia and Senegal. In Ghana The Queen and Prince Philip embarked in the Yacht at Takoradi for the last day of their visit on 20 November where she was used as the venue for the lunch attended by President Kwame Nkrumah. In the afternoon the formal farewell ceremonies on the jetty were watched by several tribal chiefs and their entourages, consisting of umbrella carriers, drummers, horn blowers and wives, who occupied the stands around the jetty. As the Yacht sailed she passed numerous Ghanaian schoolchildren waving flags at the entrance to the harbour while the Ghanaian Air Force flew over in salute.[38] Three days later the Yacht appeared off the Liberian coast, ready to enter Monrovia, when the President's Yacht approached from the starboard bow to fire a salute and then join the escort into the harbour where she berthed. The Queen's Press Secretary during this trip was William Heseltine, (later The Rt Hon. Sir William Heseltine GCB GCVO AC QSO). As he explains, when members of the Household accompanied The Queen ashore that day it was an uncomfortable experience:

'In Liberia it was a requirement imposed by the descendants of freed slaves that all civilians arriving for a formal State Visit should be clad in full morning coat and top hat. So in a temperature of 95°F and a humidity of 98 per cent those of us not in uniform had to disembark in black morning coats and black top hats and I have seldom been as hot in my life as on that occasion!'

The day's visit finished with a dinner on board the Yacht for President Tubman prior to *Britannia* sailing, just before midnight, for Sierra Leone.[39] When the Yacht approached Freetown on 25 November, a fleet of decorated native craft were waiting to greet The Queen and Prince Philip as *Britannia* made her way through the boats to berth.[40] Once in Freetown The Queen and Prince Philip left the Yacht, to undertake their Tour of Sierra Leone inland, returning to Freetown on 1 December ahead of the Yacht's departure, which was marked by the illumination of the shore by floodlights and a fanfare of bugles, as the Yacht headed into the night bound for Bathurst in Gambia.[41] During the following evening, as *Britannia* rounded the west coast of African, The Queen rewarded Admiral Dawnay for his services as FORY by investing him with a KCVO to mark his imminent retirement.[42] The next morning *Britannia* arrived in Bathurst for the four-day visit. When *Britannia* sailed on the night of 5 December Prince Philip remained behind to fly in the morning to Tanganyika and attend Tanzania's Independence Day celebrations. Meanwhile *Britannia* steamed overnight to Dakar, where The Queen landed to fly back to London while the Yacht sailed for Portsmouth via Gibraltar.[43]

When Vice Admiral Sir Peter Dawnay brought the Yacht alongside for the last time on 15 December[44] he continued to exhibit his flair for ship handling until the end, as Captain Archer observed:

'The Admiral was determined to bring the Yacht in faster than usual and perform a really flash motor boat type arrival alongside. Normally, with a ship like *Britannia* she would be brought in slowly with tugs standing by if necessary. Admiral Dawnay swung into H Moorings at Whale Island and gave us a full astern at the last minute followed by stop and we were alongside – it was a brilliant performance!'

Prince Philip's Sitting Room.

Prince Philip's Bedroom.

View of the Royal Drawing Room showing the fireplace.

A desk in the Royal Drawing Room.

The Queen's Sitting Room.

The Verandah.

Sir Hugh Casson produced this series of watercolours to provide The Queen and Prince Philip with a better impression of his ideas for the Royal Apartments in Britannia.   (© Sir Hugh Casson Ltd)

John Stobart's painting of
Britannia *during the open-*
ing of the St Lawrence
Seaway by The Queen and
President Eisenhower on 26
June 1959. The President's
Standard can be clearly
seen at the main mast
alongside The Queen's
Standard. Whenever The
Queen entertained a foreign
Head of State on board
Britannia *their Standard*
was broken alongside Her
Majesty's Standard.

(National Maritime Museum, Greenwich.
Reproduced courtesy of the artist.)

ABOVE: *The islanders of Santa Cruz Island prepare an ocean-going outrigger canoe to take Prince Philip sailing during his visit to Graciosa Bay on 22 March 1959.*

(© HRH The Duke of Edinburgh)

TOP LEFT: *Two of the four traditional war canoes that escorted* Britannia *to her anchorage off Gizo on 18 March 1959.*

(©HRH The Duke of Edinburgh)

ABOVE LEFT: *Edward Seago's painting of* Britannia *anchored in a bay off the Grahamland peninsula.*

(© HRH The Duke of Edinburgh)

LEFT: *Edward Seago's painting of the Verandah.*

(© HRH The Duke of Edinburgh)

*Britannia at speed wearing the Court Flags for
The Queen with the Lord High Admiral's Flag
at the fore mast, The Royal Standard at the
main mast, and the Union Flag at the mizzen
mast.*

*To keep Britannia looking at her best the hull is
repainted during a routine docking in Portsmouth
between April and June 1990.*

During his visit to Hong Kong in November 1989 The Prince of Wales painted this watercolour entitled 'View of Double Haven Bay, Hong Kong from After Deck of HMY Britannia'. (© A G Carrick Ltd)

Rear Admiral Greening escorts The Queen Mother ashore in the Venice water taxi which was used as a temporary Royal Barge during Her Majesty's visit to Venice in October 1984. (© British Crown Copyright / MOD)

*Princess Margaret followed by The Duke of York
embark in Britannia for the dinner to celebrate
The Queen Mother's 90th birthday held during the
Yacht's visit to the Pool of London in August
1990.*

*The Prince and Princess of Wales arrive on board
for the dinner to celebrate The Queen Mother's
90th birthday held during the Yacht's visit to the
Pool of London in August 1990.*

Britannia *lies at anchor as the Royal Barge heads inshore to embark The Queen during a Western Isles Cruise.*

C.
PORT SUEZ '86

After The Prince of Wales completed his visits to Oman and Saudi Arabia in November 1986 he remained on board the Yacht for the initial stages of her voyage back to the UK and disembarked when Britannia *reached Cyprus. While the Yacht was waiting to join the northbound convoy through the Suez Canal His Royal Highness painted this watercolour entitled 'Port Suez, Egypt'.*

Chapter Five

WESTABOUT

Rear Admiral Sir Joseph Henley
KCVO CB 1962–1965

Very nearly four years to the day since he became FORY, Vice Admiral Sir Peter Dawnay KCVO CB DSC was succeeded by Rear Admiral J C C Henley at noon on 25 January 1962. In recognition of his love of carpentry the Yachtsmen presented Admiral Dawnay with a wooden chest full of tools before he was rowed ashore in a gig by the Commanders. Once ashore the Chief Petty Officers towed his car to the gates of HMS *Excellent* in a manoeuvre more reminiscent of the Field Gun competition than the retirement of the Flag Officer Royal Yachts.[1] His successor was a gunnery officer who had served in the battleships *Ramillies* and *King George V*, as well as the battlecruisers *Hood* and *Tiger*. Admiral Henley commanded the *Daring* class destroyer HMS *Defender* between 1954 and 1955. The following year Henley was promoted to Commodore and appointed as the Naval Attaché in Washington. In 1958 he returned to the UK to become the Director of the Royal Naval Staff College at Greenwich. From there Henley went to the Mediterranean to become the Chief of Staff to the Commander-in-Chief Mediterranean Fleet in 1959. The following year he was promoted to Rear Admiral and remained there until his appointment as FORY.

A few days later the Yachtsmen turned out to say farewell to the longest serving officer in the Royal Yacht Service. By the time of his retirement on 1 February, the 69-year-old Keeper & Steward of the Royal Apartments (K&S), Lieutenant Fred Pardy MVO RN, was believed to be the last person afloat in the RN who had served in the Battle of Jutland.[2] His encyclopaedic knowledge of the Royal Yacht Service traditions had proved vital during the early years of *Britannia's* service as he had seen it all before and was thus able to advise the senior officers accordingly. During his four decades of service in the Royal Yacht Service he had personally served four British Monarchs and, in that time, had served in *V&A*, *Empress of Australia*, *Empress of Britain*, *Vanguard*, *Surprise* and *Britannia*. As a Chief Steward, Pardy had accompanied The Duke of Windsor when he sailed across the English Channel into exile on board HMS *Fury* in 1936. In June 1947 Pardy succeeded the 74-year-old Mr A Skipworth as K&S when Pardy was commissioned, placed on the Retired List and re-appointed as K&S in *V&A*. Lieutenant Pardy's attention to detail was legendary and he was described by *Britannia's* first Commander (E), later Captain John Mott LVO RN, as 'the height of perfection and discretion.' He wrote down all of the characteristics and foibles of the Royal and important guests so he would know for next time and would be able to anticipate their desire before they had even thought of it. For example, The Queen Mother could often be found in the Royal Drawing Room around noon telling some little story, when he would station himself immediately behind her. As she dropped her right hand to her side in some appropriate gesture in the story, she would clasp the glass of Champagne which Lieutenant Pardy had at the ready. His successor Lieutenant Albert Baker had a very hard act to follow but in Lieutenant Pardy he had found the perfect tutor.

When Princess Mary, The Princess Royal, embarked in the Yacht at Portsmouth on 12 February 1962, *Britannia's* planned departure had to be postponed because of gale force winds. Although the winds had moderated by the following morning the passage to Gibraltar was still dogged by rough weather.[3] After a week of engagements in Gibraltar, the Yacht sailed east into the Mediterranean for the Princess's visit to Cyprus, where she arrived on 1 March in Famagusta. The next day the Princess Royal hosted a lunch on board for the President, Archbishop Makarios, and the Vice President, Dr Kutchuk. In view of the sensitive political situation it was felt wise to fire an individual gun salute for both the President and Vice President when they arrived at the Yacht. Therefore, Admiral Henley had to seek special permission from the Admiralty to break the normal rules of protocol to enable the Royal Escort HMS *Scarborough* to fire the 19-gun salute as well. This permission was forthcoming and so, on the day of the lunch, the Chief Yeoman stood on the Bridge to look through his binoculars and watch for the official cars to arrive through the gates of the port, ensuring that the right salute was fired at the right time. As the Royal Cypher Officer at the time, later Commander I Fergie-Woods MVO RN, recalls:

'Things didn't quite go to plan. It had been arranged that the President would be the first of the two to arrive. At the expected time the Chief Yeoman spotted the presidential limousine arriving at the port gate and he ordered the 21-gun salute to be fired. This was well timed, for the salute ended as the car drew up at the gangway. But to the Chief Yeoman's utter dismay it was not Makarios who stepped out but Kutchuk. It seemed

that Kutchuk had intended to score a point over his President by deliberately arriving before him. Makarios's limousine was now approaching the port. The Chief Yeoman realised he could hardly order another 21 guns nor could Makarios be given only 19 guns. He got word to the Admiral who was awaiting the guests at the gangway and the Admiral with his customary charm greeted Makarios saying, "I am sure you will have heard your salute being fired, Sir, as you approached the port." I think presidential honour was satisfied.'

The Princess spent the rest of her Tour visiting Army Regiments stationed in Cyprus before going on to Libya where she visited the RAF base at El Adem. It so happened the garrison stationed in Tripoli was The Royal Scots of which Her Royal Highness was the Colonel-in-Chief. Before the Yacht berthed in Tripoli on 17 March a signal arrived in the Yacht arranging sporting events, as Captain Roome remembered: 'The Wardroom challenged the Army to polo. None of us had in fact played polo, and few had even watched it, so we were relieved not to have our bluff called when the challenge was declined!' At the end of the Princess's visit to Tripoli the Yacht returned to Portsmouth on 28 March where Her Royal Highness disembarked.[4]

At the end of April The Queen Mother joined the Yacht in Plymouth for a one-day visit to the Scilly Isles on 27 April, returning to Portsmouth the next day. *Britannia* then entered dockyard hands for a short refit until the end of June.[5] In late July The Queen and Prince Philip used the Yacht for a visit to the West Country, which included The Queen's first visit to BRNC in Dartmouth in a Royal Yacht since her 1939 visit in *V&A* with her parents.[6] On

5 August *Britannia* sailed from Portsmouth to attend Cowes Week which witnessed the public debut of a new Royal Yacht – *Bloodhound*.[7] At the end of the 1961 season Prince Philip had decided to stop racing *Bluebottle* and sent her to BRNC on long-term loan. *Bluebottle*'s Sailing Master, Lieutenant Commander M Jones (later Captain M Jones MVO RN), was summoned to Buckingham Palace in November 1961 to be instructed by Prince Philip's Treasurer, Rear Admiral Bonham Carter, to go and look for a good second-hand ocean-racing yacht for Prince Philip. Lieutenant Commander Jones came across the 63-foot Bermudan yawl *Bloodhound* lying at the back of the shed in Mashfords' yard in Plymouth. She had been built in 1936 by Camper & Nicholsons and enjoyed a successful racing career, including victory in the 1939 Fastnet Race. Lieutenant Commander Jones was subsequently given the go-ahead in February 1962 to go down to Plymouth, launch her and sail her back to Gosport, where she would be refitted by her original builders. The work was completed by June when she undertook sailing trials. Therefore, Cowes Week was one of the first regattas she attended since entering Royal ownership. One of those who joined the crew of *Bloodhound* during that Cowes Week was Commander Fergie-Woods, as he recalls:

'I enjoyed sharing the main sheet with Uffa Fox. He had a wealth of sailing experience, of course, plus a sense of humour and a little mischief. We were close on the wind when he said to Prince Philip, "You know, Sir, I find I can get closest to the wind if I lash my boom right down." Perhaps Prince Philip was only half lis-

tening, but Uffa found a line and tackle and he and I soon had the boom secured in no uncertain manner to a deck fitting. Uffa was pleased with the result but we were then upon the windward mark and Prince Philip was ordering "ready about". The main was in no way ready to go about and I well remember Prince Philip's immediate interest in what Uffa and I had been up to, to say the least.'

At the end of Cowes Week *Britannia* weighed anchor for Torbay on 10 August, arriving there in the afternoon for Prince Philip to start the Tall Ships Race the next day. High winds dominated the day, leading to the postponement of the race start until 1500, and delayed *Bloodhound*, which was making her way from Southampton to Torbay to embark Prince Philip on 12 August. From Torbay Prince Philip sailed in *Bloodhound* round to Campbeltown where he was joined by Prince Charles and Princess Anne for a family cruise in Scottish waters. Meanwhile, *Britannia* sailed back to Portsmouth on 13 August for the Yachtsmen to take leave and prepare the Yacht for her third global deployment at the end of the year.[8]

While the Yacht was in Portsmouth Commander Roome was relieved by Commander C Rusby (later Vice Admiral Sir Cameron Rusby KCB LVO) as the Commander of the Yacht on 8 October 1962.[9] As he explains, it took a little time to become accustomed to how everything was done on board the Yacht:

'Shortly after I arrived on board, FORY wanted to address the Yachtsmen. This was rather unusual but there was a major change in the programme, which he

Princess Mary,
The Princess Royal, is
taken ashore from
Britannia *in the Barge to*
begin her visit to Cyprus.

Rear Admiral Henley welcomes the Crown Prince of Libya on board the Yacht. For such formal occasions FORY wore a ceremonial day coat.

(© British Crown Copyright / MOD)

wanted to announce. There was no PA system on board so I couldn't pipe "clear lower deck". Instead this was usually pre-planned and published in the Daily Orders. I retired to my cabin and pondered how to achieve this as the Admiral wished to make the address ASAP. Almost immediately Leading Steward Bennet (later Councillor and Mayor of Kingsbridge) came into my cabin and said, "I believe Sir that it's clear lower deck."

"How did you know that?"

"It's all round the Yacht, Sir. If you look up on the forecastle I believe you will find the whole Yacht's company up there." I went up and had a look and sure enough they were all there. I was flabbergasted! I went back to the Admiral and told him that the Yacht's company were mustered on the forecastle. Nothing had been said and no written notices had been posted, it was quite remarkable, but as I later discovered, word got round the Yacht at incredible speed!'

Having embarked all of the necessary stores for the Tour ahead, including The Queen's Rolls Royce, the Yacht sailed from Portsmouth on 7 December.[10] In 1955 it was decided that whenever The Queen visited a Commonwealth country the host nation would provide a naval contingent of eight men to increase that country's sense of involvement in the tour. This deployment was no different and both the Australian and New Zealand navies sent personnel over to Portsmouth to sail out to the Pacific in *Britannia*, where further members of both navies would join the Yacht in Fiji. Unusually, the RM Band was joined for the outward voyage by the Director of Music, Captain Paul Neville (later Lt Col. P Neville OBE MVO FRAM RM). The RM Band for the Yacht was based in Eastney Barracks and formed part of the Portsmouth RM Band. The musicians joined the Yacht for each tour and spent the rest of the time working as part of the Portsmouth Band under the control of the Director of Music. Some people have likened the RM Band on board *Britannia* to the main armament of a RN warship, and certainly the RM Band was a fundamental part of the spectacle provided by the Yacht on ceremonial occasions. Typically, the Yacht's Band consisted of 24 musicians who were able to perform in a variety of environments, including ceremonial events such as Beating Retreat, informal events as a dance band and, most importantly, playing as an orchestra at formal meals and receptions.

The routine for playing at dinner was always the same. The Queen and her guests would walk into the Royal Dining Room and the doors would be closed. As soon as this happened the Band would be given the signal to come up from the deck below, take the piano out of the cupboard and set up their music stands, etc. Once they were ready to play the doors would be opened and the music would begin. The programme of music was always agreed personally by The Queen, or the member of the Royal Family undertaking the tour, before the Yacht left Portsmouth. As the meal came to an end the doors would be shut and the Band would disappear so that by the time The Queen emerged the area was clear.

In addition to playing music throughout these events it was the orchestra's role to play the National Anthems during State Visits. Sometimes the Band's rendition of a host country's National Anthem was recorded by local TV and radio stations and played instead of their own home-produced versions. The routine of the Yacht's Band differed from that of other RM Bands embarked in major RN warships because they would play irrespective of the hour for leaving or entering a port, whereas usually RM Bands only played between colours and sunset. To enhance the spectacle of a night-time departure by the Yacht, the Band would be illuminated on the upper deck so that they could be clearly seen.

The Band also played an important role in the life of the Yacht between periods of Royal duty. During long ocean passages the Band would often hold an impromptu concert for the Yachtsmen on the forecastle in good weather around lunchtime for half an hour. Whenever the Yacht met up with a Royal Fleet Auxillary (RFA) tanker for a Replenishment At Sea (RAS), the Bandmaster would position the Band in the waist so that the RFA tanker could be entertained as well. Shortly before a RAS the Yacht would send a signal to the RFA inviting requests for the Band and they would usually show their appreciation by sending a crate of beer across for the musicians. Equally, the Band played an essential part in the light-hearted events on board, such as Crossing-The-Line and the ship's concerts, where they provided all the music. The music for the Sunday morning church service held by FORY in the Royal Dining Room whenever the Yacht was at sea was also provided by the Band.

On long deployments the Director of Music normally remained behind in the UK and left the Band under the command of the Bandmaster, who would also be responsible for the Band during the return to the UK. While the Yacht travelled from Portsmouth the Bandmaster would rehearse the Band each morning in the Unwinding Room. (The Unwinding Room was also used by the junior Yachtsmen as their recreation space where they watched films and could have a drink off duty.) The Director of Music then flew out to join the Yacht shortly before the start of Royal duty. However, the Yacht's departure from Portsmouth in December 1962 coincided with a quiet period for the Portsmouth Band so Captain Neville decided to embark in the Yacht for the voyage out to the Pacific and work with the Band.

Having stopped for two days in Ponta Delgada the Yacht arrived in Kingston, Jamaica for Christmas. The weather had been kind to the Yacht so she was a day ahead of schedule by the time she arrived on 23 December. Christmas Day itself was marked by a service on the forecastle before the usual naval celebrations could begin, including rounds by the 17-year-old 'Rear Admiral' Urry, otherwise known as NAAFI Canteen Assistant J Urry, dressed in one of Admiral Henley's uniforms.[11] On 27 December the Wardroom hosted a reception for 150 guests on the Royal Deck, including several of the actors from the first James Bond film, *Dr No*, before setting sail the next day for the Panama Canal to spend New Year's Eve alongside the Rodman US Navy base at Balboa.

However, there wasn't too much time for New Year celebrations as *Britannia* set off for Tahiti at 1600 on New Year's Day.[12] The voyage across the Pacific was interrupted on the afternoon of 7 January 1963 when the SS *Glenmoor* transmitted a message asking for help in treating a member of her crew who had been badly burned by a flashback in the boiler room.[13] The Yacht responded to her distress signal and, once it had been established that she was the nearest ship with appropriate medical facilities, the Yacht's speed was increased to 18 knots while the *Glenmoor* turned back from her position 285 miles ahead of *Britannia* to rendezvous with her. This wasn't to be the Yacht's first meeting with the *Glenmoor*. During the Yacht's recent transit of the Panama Canal she had sailed past the *Glenmoor*, which hoisted signal flags to wish the Yacht *bon voyage*.

The 1962 Cowes Week regatta witnessed the debut of a new Royal Yacht. The 63-foot Bermudan yawl Bloodhound had been purchased by The Queen and Prince Philip at the beginning of 1962 and was subsequently refitted at the Gosport yard of Camper & Nicholson where she had been built in 1936.

At 0130 the next morning the Yacht caught up with *Glenmoor* and Surgeon Commander Haughton was sent across in the jolly boat to examine the injured man. Having assessed the condition of Joseph O'Connell, who came from South Shields, he was transferred to the Yacht and treated in the Sick Bay.[14] Although his condition was initially considered to be serious he demonstrated real resilience and continued to make a good recovery throughout the voyage to Tahiti. The fine weather throughout the long voyage across the Pacific provided the Yachtsmen with the perfect opportunity to pursue a range of deck sports. A new addition to the normal programme of activities was circuit training under the keen eye of Petty Officer Rogers from the RAN contingent.[15]

On 15 January 1963 *Britannia* reached Papeete on the South Pacific island of Tahiti and berthed stern to at Fare Ute Jetty. Once a brow had been put in place over the taffrail on the stern, the Yacht was boarded by Tahitian girls who gave the Yachtsmen a traditional greeting by placing garlands of flowers around the necks of FORY and the Yachtsmen. This was quickly followed by an impressive ceremony of welcome on the jetty consisting of Tahitian dancing and singing watched by the Yachtsmen from every available vantage point on the Yacht.[16] Over the next three days the Yachtsmen explored this Polynesian paradise and also discovered that the Yacht's diversion to assist the *Glenmoor* had made the headlines in the papers back home. A day after the Yacht's arrival FORY and the officers attended a reception and supper

party thrown by the Mayor and Madame Potoi. During the first of the Tahitian dances FORY was granted the Tahitian title of *Tehelariii*, which means crown of the Sovereign.[17] However, all good things must come to an end and shortly before the Yacht sailed on 18 January the Mayor and Madame Potoi came on board to give the Yachtsmen a traditional Tahitian farewell by presenting each of them with a garland of flowers and a string of shells. According to the local legend the garlands of flowers were to be thrown into the sea as the Yacht passed the reef outbound and if they were swept back to the shore it meant that the thrower would one day return to Tahiti.

From Tahiti the Yacht sailed for Lautoka in Fiji where The Queen and Prince Philip embarked for the start of their Tour. Two days into the voyage the Yacht closed in on Palmerston Island, which is part of the Cook Islands. The remote island was discovered by Captain Cook in 1774 and named after Lord Palmerston who was then serving as the First Lord of The Admiralty. The island's small community was founded nearly a century later by the former Gloucestershire ploughboy William Marsters who ran away to sea in 1858 shortly after his 21st birthday. However, William Marsters soon realised that life on board ship was even worse than the hardships of rural Gloucestershire he had left behind so he deserted his ship at Raratonga in the Cook Islands. There he met, fell in love with, and married one of the local girls, who he called Esther. Having heard about the uninhabited atoll of Palmerston Island William Marsters spent the rest of his money on a small sailing boat and set off from Raratonga with Esther and her 17-year-old sister Adelaine. By a stroke of remarkably good luck the intrepid three found the small island and established a home. Soon after their arrival Marsters married Adelaine as his number two wife and set off alone back to Raratonga to pick up supplies including chickens, tools, seeds and a Polynesian woman Naomi who subsequently became his third wife! Their community thrived with the birth of Marsters' first children and it was sustained by trading pearls and copra in return for supplies from the trading steamer that called every six months. In 1871 the Captain of HMS *Warspite* was amazed to find a community of 23 people of which 20 were children who all spoke English with a strong Gloucestershire accent and were all called Marsters. In 1899 William Marsters died and was succeeded as head of the island by his son William the Younger. By the time of *Britannia*'s arrival the island was ruled by William Marsters' grandson Ned who had become the 'Ruler' in 1946.

Soon after the Yacht appeared off Palmerston Island three boats were launched from the island to greet their visitors. FORY responded by launching the Gemini with the Principle Medical Officer (PMO) on board to see if any of the islanders required medical assistance ashore. Ned Marsters himself was taking a church service at the time of the Yacht's arrival so he was brought on board the Yacht when the Gemini returned an hour later. While Ned Marsters was being received by FORY the other

islanders were given refreshments by the Yachtsmen and taken to the NAAFI where they were given chocolate, toothpaste and other essentials of life. After four hours laying off this small island it was time to resume the passage to Lautoka. The visit was a major event for the islanders who had last seen a ship in September 1962 when a trading schooner called. The day was also to mark the beginning of a long running relationship between the islanders and the Yachtsmen.[18]

After these very enjoyable informal visits the Yacht finally arrived in Lautoka on 25 January to wait for The Queen and Prince Philip to arrive in Fiji for the start of their Tour. In the intervening days the Yachtsmen worked hard to touch up the paint where necessary and thoroughly clean the Yacht after her long voyage from Portsmouth. It was also at this time that the Yachtsmen finally said farewell to Joseph O'Connell who had made a good recovery from his burns and was walking again. The Queen and Prince Philip's flight from North America to Fiji experienced severe delays due to the weather. The first delay was caused by snow and poor visibility at Vancouver, which caused the flight to be diverted 400 miles to Edmonton. When the Boeing 707 resumed its flight it encountered near hurricane force winds and bad weather over the Pacific forcing the pilot to turn back and spend the night at Vancouver before making another attempt the next morning. By the time the aircraft finally landed at Nandi International Airport on 2 February the Royal couple were 24 hours late. As they were driven the 140 miles from the

Britannia is given a warm send off from Tahiti.

(© British Crown Copyright / MOD)

airport to the Yacht their arrival was greeted by the Fijians with silence which in Fiji denotes a high level of respect rather than a mark of protest. As soon as The Queen and Prince Philip had embarked in *Britannia* she made a flood-lit departure for Suva.

Whenever The Queen embarked in the Yacht she was always accompanied by members of her Household, including the chefs who manned the Royal Galley on board the Yacht. The menus for all the official entertainment were prepared and personally approved by The Queen before the Yacht sailed. Once her approval had been gained, the chefs would also work out how many other menus had to be produced for the Royal Family's private meals before they compiled their complete list of the produce required for the duration of the tour. Usually, all the frozen food was embarked in the Yacht before she left Portsmouth although, if they were able to purchase fresh produce of a high enough quality locally they would do so, and bring the frozen food back. Equally, one aspect which always had to be considered was how the use of embarked food in the Yacht might be affected by the regulations of a host nation while the Yacht was alongside. For example, the host nation might forbid the use of UK-produced lamb and require ships with stocks of UK lamb to keep the meat within a sealed fridge for the duration of their visit. Failure to observe the appropriate regulations could be the type of incident to cause embarrassment to the Royal Family and thus overshadow a State Visit. The Household's catering party would normally consist of a

Royal Chef supported by an assistant chef and a junior chef. There would also be a pastry chef, a staff chef and a kitchen porter. This team would be supplemented by the Yacht's Chief Cook who was responsible for the Admiral's catering so, when FORY dined aft with the Royal Household, the Chief Cook would work alongside the chefs from Buckingham Palace.

One of the chefs to join *Britannia* in Lautoka was Lionel Mann, later Mr L T Mann MVO RVM, who subsequently became the Royal Chef. Describing the catering facilities on board the Yacht and their typical routine he said:

'The conditions for preparing food were very cramped, very hot and in some of the places we visited it was very humid. On some trips the Royal Family would be presented with gifts such as a whole pig roasted in pine leaves. We didn't always know quite what to do with these gifts but if the host nation wanted to see their gift used as part of a State Banquet we sometimes changed the menus to include them. On an average day we would turn to at about 0630 and work through until 0900 generally preparing and serving breakfast as well as doing some other preparation work for later in the day. There would be one chef fully employed doing breakfast. The other chefs would be keeping an eye on the breakfast situation but mainly getting on with their preparation for lunch or dinner, or even the next day's meals. At 0900 we would knock off for our own breakfast for half an hour. Between 0930 and 1330 we would

The 'Ruler' of Palmerston Island, Ned Marsters, came on board the Yacht to personally welcome Rear Admiral Henley and the Yacht's company to his remote Pacific island. This visit marked the beginning of a warm relationship between the Yacht and the islanders.

(© British Crown Copyright / MOD)

be doing preparation and serving lunch for the Royal Family and their staff from 1200 onwards depending on the programme. There were sometimes days when there wouldn't be a lunch if they were all ashore. Sometimes we would leave one chef on duty during the afternoon depending on what had to be done. However, between 1345 and 1645 we were usually free and we would leave the tea things for the Footmen and Stewards to pick up. We would return about 1645 and prepare the evening meal. The staff would eat between 1830 and 1900. The senior officials ate at 2000 and the Royal Family would eat at any time from 2000 onwards. Usually we were finished by 2130 unless there was a reception and we would turn to and finish the reception. On those occasions we would have been preparing the canapés during the day and it would be somewhere between 2230 and 2330 before we finished.'

Fifteen minutes after the Yacht dropped anchor in Suva on 3 February, eight Fijian Chiefs came on board to perform the traditional Fijian ceremony of cavuikele (invitation to land) before The Queen on the Verandah Deck and present Her Majesty with the tasua (a sperm whale's tooth). The Royal couple then went ashore in the Barge and landed at the main wharf in full view of the British cruise liner Orsova.[19] The liner's decks were crowded with passengers who cheered as The Queen and Prince Philip landed. In a burst of enthusiasm one of the passengers yelled out, 'How about a wave for us Your Majesty?' The request was promptly granted by a wave in their direction before the Royal party went on to fulfil their engagements ashore. Meanwhile the Yacht was brought alongside the main wharf, and after lunch a lorry turned up beside the Yacht and out jumped 12 Fijian warriors. They then proceeded to carefully unload the whole roast pig and accompanying banquet that had been presented to The Queen and Prince Philip during the formal welcoming ceremony ashore in the morning, which was something of a surprise for the Royal Chef, Mr Aubrey! By mid afternoon the Royal couple had returned and the Yacht got underway for Waitangi.

When The Queen was embarked in the Yacht in home waters, she flew the Admiralty Flag at the fore mast (as Lord High Admiral), the Royal Standard at the main and the Union Flag at the mizzen. For visits to 'Realms' where The Queen is Head of State such as Canada, Australia and New Zealand the Yacht flew her appropriate Standard of the Realm being visited with the national flag at the mizzen. In countries which acknowledge The Queen as Head of the Commonwealth, the Yacht flew the Head of Commonwealth Flag at the main and the national flag at the mizzen. As such, when the Yacht entered New Zealand territorial waters on 5 February The Queen's Standard for New Zealand was broken at the main mast for the first time while the New Zealand National Flag was broken at the mizzen.

The Yacht arrived in the Bay of Islands on 6 February, which was a very significant anniversary in New Zealand history. On this day in 1840 Captain William Hobson RN signed, on behalf of Queen Victoria, a treaty with the Maori Chiefs in which they exchanged Sovereignty of New Zealand for the privileges of British citizenship. In the evening The Queen and Prince Philip attended the Waitangi Day celebrations which included a re-enactment of the original ceremony and a display of Maori dancing. Those left on board the Yacht listened intently to the radio commentary describing the celebrations. The day ended with the illumination of the Yacht and her RNZN escorts anchored in the bay. Following the dinner party on board, Britannia weighed anchor for Auckland, where The Queen was given a tremendous aquatic welcome by a large contingent of private boats that followed the Yacht into the harbour on 7 February. After a visit to Devonport in the morning the Royal couple spent the afternoon at the Tamaki Yacht Club where Prince Philip inspected 153 P class dinghies, all helmed by young people under the age 15. Once His Royal Highness had inspected the dinghies the youngsters launched their boats to bring the number of sailing boats racing in the bay to well over 700. Before the Yacht sailed the following night The Queen and Prince Philip spent the morning visiting factories in Auckland and the afternoon at the Horse of the Year Show. These first two visits set the pattern for the rest of the Tour of New Zealand with the Yacht making an overnight passage between locations and entering ports early in the morning to begin a packed one- or two-day programme of engagements ashore. By the time Britannia reached Port Chalmers on the final stage of the Yacht's involvement in the New Zealand Tour The Queen and Prince Philip had visited Tauranga, Napier, Wellington, Nelson, and Picton. At Port Chalmers The Queen and Prince Philip disembarked from the Yacht to continue their programme over land visiting Dunedin and Christchurch before flying to Canberra, Australia on 18 February.

Meanwhile, the Yacht sailed from Port Chalmers on 14 February for Adelaide, where the Royal couple would re-embark in Britannia on 19 February. For over a month the Royal couple made an extensive Tour of Australia. From the Yacht's perspective, the Tour was characterised by the people of each of the 12 places visited turning out in huge numbers, both on the water and ashore, to welcome The

The Queen Mother holds the Manx kitten Schickrys which was presented to her by the people of Castletown. Her Majesty subsequently presented the kitten to the Yacht and he was looked after by the family of Ian Denny, who served on board the Yacht as an Engineer.

(© British Crown Copyright / MOD)

Queen and Prince Philip. The interest taken by the Australian media in the Tour was immense, with live TV coverage of the Yacht's arrivals and departures. Like the 1959 opening of the St Lawrence Seaway, the Yacht became an attraction in her own right with people coming to see *Britannia* while the Royal couple were fulfilling engagements elsewhere.

The comprehensive Tour finished in Fremantle at the end of March. To mark the occasion The Queen made a farewell broadcast on 26 March to the people of Australia in which she spoke of the great pleasure it had given her to entertain so many Australians on board the Yacht. The following morning it was time for The Queen to say farewell to those who had supported her during those long weeks and pose for the customary end of tour group photographs on the Verandah Deck, as Commander Fergie-Woods recalled:

'Our escort, HMAS *Anzac*, who was berthed astern and up wind of us, had been raising steam and had not made an entirely clean job of it. Particles of soot landed embarrassingly on the Verandah Deck just as the Royal Household were assembling for their photograph. Word of this was not slow to get back to *Anzac*'s Captain, Commander Clarke: he was himself due shortly to be received by The Queen on the Verandah Deck! Commander Clarke got hold of his Chippie and he, in very quick time, made a neat little presentation box inside of which was placed a prize specimen of *Anzac* soot. Commander Clarke respectfully offered this to The Queen with his apologies.'

However, before Commander Clarke was presented to The Queen, she decided to invest Admiral Henley with the KCVO, to his enormous surprise and delight. After lunch The Queen and Prince Philip took off in a BOAC Boeing 707 bound for London.

On 30 March *Britannia* turned her nose for home, calling at Port Louis in Mauritius, Aden and Gibraltar, before arriving in Portsmouth on 6 May. However, there wasn't much time for relaxation as two days later The Queen Mother embarked for her visit to the Channel Islands. Her Tour included a visit to Guernsey to commemorate Liberation Day as well as calls on Jersey and Alderney before returning to Portsmouth on 13 May.

After just over a month in dry dock *Britannia*'s next period of Royal duty began on 4 July when The Queen Mother embarked in Holyhead for her visit to the Isle of Man, where *Britannia* arrived that afternoon. The Queen Mother's arrival was greeted by fine and calm weather.[20] Unfortunately, this wasn't to last because, while The Queen Mother was ashore during the third day of her visit, the fog rolled in over the sea, as Admiral Rusby explains:

'The Navigator conned the Barge back to *Britannia* by radio using radar. Because of the sea that was running I did not feel that it was safe for The Queen Mother to disembark from the Barge to the accommodation ladder in the usual manner. So I decided that we would hoist the Barge with The Queen Mother in it. The Barge was therefore hoisted to deck level where there was a convenient opening in the bulwark from which a small portable gangway was placed on to the Barge. The Queen Mother was thrilled because this was something that The Queen hadn't done!

'On another occasion when Her Majesty had returned on board during this visit she was holding a wicker basket which had a lid at both ends. When I greeted her The Queen Mother said, "I have brought you a present." I thought that perhaps it was some flowers she had been given but in fact she had a Manx kitten inside. No one had ever had animals on board so I wasn't quite sure how to deal with this unusual gift. I went to see her Private Secretary, Sir Martin Gilliat, and ask him for advice. With a broad grin he said, "You're jolly lucky it wasn't a race horse!"'

The kitten in question had been presented to Her Majesty by the town of Castletown. He was called Schickrys, which was the motto of Castletown and, translated roughly into English, means 'steadfast'.[21] After further deliberations about what to do with the Royal kitten it was decided that he should be looked after by the family of a permanent Yachtsman. Volunteers were called for and, in the end Ian Denny and his family became the custodians of Schickrys. Photographs were taken by the Yacht's photographer as Schickrys grew and were sent to The Queen Mother. His pedigree certificate was framed and displayed on board.

Shortly after The Queen Mother returned from her visit to Kirk Braddan on 7 July Britannia weighed anchor for Portsmouth via Falmouth Roads where The Queen Mother landed to have lunch with Mr Wilkins at St Mawes on 8 July.[22] Britannia's final spell of Royal duty for the year was at the beginning of August when she attended Cowes Week between 3 and 9 August.

On 31 December Britannia left Portsmouth for the start of another major deployment, this time to support The Queen Mother's Tour of Australia and New Zealand. As the Yacht steamed across the Atlantic, FORY held a very special party on 7 January 1964, marking the 10th Anniversary of the Yacht's commissioning, to which the 33 remaining members of the original Yacht's company were invited.[23] Over the next month the Yacht retraced much of her voyage from a year earlier by visiting Jamaica, passing through the Panama Canal, and proceeding to Tahiti and Lautoka. All was going to plan as Britannia sailed towards Lautoka until 3 February when a signal was received on board stating that The Queen Mother was suffering from appendicitis.[24] With only a week before the Tour was about to begin the short-term future looked very uncertain. However, until further plans could be confirmed Britannia continued to head towards Lautoka where she arrived on 8 February to await further orders.[25] By 12 February news had reached the Yacht that the Tour had in fact been cancelled rather than postponed so it was decided that Britannia would return to the UK via the Panama Canal.[26] Later that night she began her voyage back home across the Pacific, which included visits to Suva, Palmerston Island and Tahiti before heading back through the Panama Canal.

Two days after sailing from Tahiti lower deck was cleared so that FORY could inform the Yachtsmen that the Yacht's programme had been changed yet again. It had been decided that The Queen Mother would join the Yacht in Kingston on 12 March. From Jamaica the Yacht would take The Queen Mother on a 'convalescent cruise' for three weeks around the West Indies. As the Navigating Officer at the time, Commander J M Child LVO RN, explains, the Yacht was able to handle this kind of major change to the programme thanks to the routine precautions that were taken on board:

'We always carried an enormous number of charts for a world-wide deployment – far more than was normally carried in most HM ships. There were always a few extra charts just in case we deviated off somewhere. This paid off very well during The Queen Mother's convalescent cruise. Obviously, none of the programme had been planned in advance and this meant that the navigational planning was done virtually the night before, which isn't the easiest way to do such a trip.'

Equally, the normal perception of a convalescent cruise and The Queen Mother's interpretation of the term were

The Yacht's Communications Department, with Sam Fuller on the typewriter watched by 'Father' (RO) Buick who was the senior radio operator in the RN at the time.

Rear Admiral Sir Joseph Henley greets the Queen Mother as she steps on board in Barbados.

(© British Crown Copyright / MOD)

two very different things, as Admiral Rusby remarked:

'This cruise resulted in no less than 14 islands being visited in the space of three weeks! All visits were informal and picnics were arranged in most. As the Commander I felt it was necessary that the beaches where these picnics were to be held should be reconnoitred first. On one such occasion I embarked in the Barge myself. The idea was for the Barge to lie off the beach, while three of us would land using an inflatable dinghy, which it was towing. All went well until we pushed out from the beach to return to the Barge, and jumped into the dinghy. A wave caught us and the dinghy was upended, throwing us all into the water. The only solution was to drag it ashore, turn it over and try again. This time, despite a soaking-wet outboard motor, we were successful. I judged the beach unsuitable for that evening's picnic! However, I learnt later that The Queen Mother had been made aware of our capsizing, for she said with a twinkle in her eye, that she believed I had been having trouble. I had to admit to our ducking!'

At the end of her convalescent cruise The Queen Mother disembarked from the Yacht in Barbados on 1 April and *Britannia* sailed the next day for Portsmouth, returning home on 13 April.[27]

On 22 June the Yacht sailed for Thurso where the Queen and Prince Philip embarked for a short Scottish Tour including visits to Wick, Cromarty, Invergordon and Lossiemouth where The Queen disembarked before the Yacht sailed for Prince Philip's trip to Iceland. Prince Philip's visit was arranged to mark the restoration of peace after the Cod Wars between the UK and Iceland. During the passage through the Pentland Firth and out into the Atlantic *Britannia* encountered gale force winds and a heavy sea before the weather began to improve late on 28 June. The following morning *Britannia* sailed close to a group of trawlers fishing over the Kidney Bank off the east coast of Iceland. The rendezvous provided Prince Philip with an opportunity to watch trawlers at work. The interest in the trawlers' activities was rewarded with a gift for the Yachtsmen of fresh cod from the Grimsby-based trawler *Northern Reward* and a quantity of haddock from the trawler *Ross Kelly*. By 1330 it was time for the Yacht to increase speed again and resume the passage to Reykjavik. Early next day *Britannia* passed a new landmark as she closed to within a mile of the recently formed volcanic island of Surtsey, which had already reached a height of 400 feet above sea level. In a break with precedence the Icelandic Coastguard vessel *Odinn* joined the Yacht 3 miles off Gretta and led her into Reykjavik where she anchored at 1630. Previously, the only other vessel to have preceded *Britannia* was the Trinity House Vessel *Patricia*. On arrival Prince Philip landed to be met by President Asgeisson and subsequently attended a Presidential dinner at the Hotel Saga.[28]

During his second day in Iceland His Royal Highness toured the island, visiting Pingvellir, Uxatoryggir,

Nordura, Akureyri and Myvatn, where he spent the night. Before Prince Philip left Myvatn the next day he went bird watching prior to returning to Reykjavik in the afternoon and hosting a dinner on board the Yacht for the President. On 3 July Prince Philip left the Yacht in the Barge to visit the British Embassy before flying back to London. While this might appear to have been a perfectly routine event it in fact marked the end of the Barge's 26 years in service. To mark the occasion the Barge flew a paying off pennant as she returned to the Yacht. Once the Barge had been recovered, *Britannia* weighed anchor, returning to Portsmouth on 7 July.[29]

A week later the new 41-foot Barge was delivered by Camper & Nicholsons and embarked for davit trials before it was formally accepted by the RN.[30] When proposals to replace the original Barge were first discussed in 1961 both The Queen and Prince Philip made a number of suggestions which were subsequently incorporated into the design of the new Barge. The major change was the movement of the Coxswain from the bow to an elevated position amidships, from where he had good visibility of the whole Barge and he could easily communicate with the Royal party. Previously, the members of the Royal Family had to use a voice pipe, which meant the Coxswain had to bend down and couldn't see where he was going while he talked to the Royal party.

Two weeks later the Barge was used for her first period of Royal duty when Prince Philip and Princess Anne were embarked and taken from the Hamble to *Britannia*, which was secured to the Admiralty Buoy off Cowes for the start of Cowes Week.[31] At the end of Cowes Week *Britannia* returned to Portsmouth on 8 August to prepare for her autumn deployment to Canada.[32]

With about a week to go before the Yacht was next due to leave Portsmouth on Royal duty, the Commander (E),

Commander Hewitt, made an unwelcome discovery, as he later explained:

'I paused to admire the glistening hull of the new Barge when to my horror I looked at the starboard side and several long cracks were evident in the planking. It was later established that the moisture content in the timber was at fault, and much of the planking had to be reworked. But the immediate problem was that the old Barge was lying in the dockyard, stripped of all her ornamental fittings (which had been transferred to the new Barge), badly needing attention to her paintwork, and the engines needing some overhaul.'

Despite the limited amount of time available before the Yacht's departure the old Barge was given a reprieve as the Dockyard's Boathouse worked overtime to bring her back up to the required standard for Royal duty. Meanwhile, the new Barge was returned to Camper & Nicholsons for remedial work to be carried out.

On 11 September Princess Mary, The Princess Royal, embarked in *Britannia* at Portsmouth for the last time. She was due to visit the Royal Newfoundland Regiment in her role as Colonel-in-Chief for the Regiment's 50th Anniversary celebrations. Once again bad weather seemed to dog the Princess's passage in the Yacht across the Atlantic. Three days into the voyage the Yacht encountered the effects of an unusually widespread depression covering some 1200 miles of the north Atlantic. Although the new Navigating Officer, later Captain G Andrewes LVO RN, tried to avoid the worst of the weather, *Britannia*'s speed was still reduced to 7 knots because of the gale force winds and heavy seas. The metal storm doors were erected outside the Royal Apartments to protect the main doors to the lobby at the bottom of the staircase and the Yachtsmen were told that the upper decks were out of

Having taken Prince Philip ashore to fly back to the UK from Iceland the Barge hoisted a paying off pennant for the trip back to the Yacht to mark the end of her 26 years of Royal service.

The yacht encounters rough weather during her crossing of the Atlantic in September 1964.

The Princess Royal disembarks from the Yacht in St John's, Newfoundland wearing the uniform of an Honorary General in the British Army to carry out engagements to celebrate The Royal Newfoundland Regiment's 50th Anniversary.

bounds. Having survived the effects of Hurricane Ethel during 14 and 15 September *Britannia* had to sail through the remnants of Hurricane Dora on 16 September.[33] As Captain Andrewes explains, it was an interesting start to his appointment as the Navigating Officer:

'I had to see FORY and inform him that I thought we were going to be 24 hours late. This of course was something that shouldn't happen to the Yacht's programme. The arrival in St John's on 18 September was uneventful and thankfully on time which pleased me as my first landfall in the Yacht. One of the additional problems for the Navigating Officer of the Yacht was that unlike most HM ships the estimated time of arrival was actually the time alongside rather than the time passing the lighthouse or the breakwater.'

During her five-day visit to St John's, The Princess Royal attended regimental events for both serving and retired members of the Royal Newfoundland Regiment. She also hosted a dinner for the Prime Minister of Canada and visited Signal Hill where Signor Marconi received the first wireless signal from Europe in 1901. On 22 September *Britannia* left St John's for Cornerbrook where the Princess visited detachments of the Royal Newfoundland Regiment before flying back to the UK on 28 September.[34]

On 3 October *Britannia* sailed from Cornerbrook for Prince Edward Island where The Queen and Prince Philip embarked. The short passage was dogged by bad weather and, at 1745 the Yacht anchored in York Harbour to shelter from the high winds that were gusting to 60 miles per hour at times.[35] When Captain Cook had surveyed this part of the Newfoundland coast in 1763 he had named one of the local mountains Blowmedown Mountain. Two hundred and one years later it certainly lived up to its name, as the Senior Engineer at the time, later Captain G James RN, remarked.

'The second anchor had been let go to reduce the amount of yawing. During dinner that evening, one particularly heavy yaw ended with an almighty thump. The whole yacht vibrated to a major degree. When we came to weigh the starboard anchor later that evening we found that one of the flukes was missing!'

Once again the Yacht was in Canadian waters with only one usable anchor and, until a new one could be embarked, a wooden fluke was made by the shipwrights and added to ensure that nothing appeared to be out of place. *Britannia* arrived off Prince Edward Island on 5 October and at 1835 The Queen and Prince Philip embarked. The following morning *Britannia* weighed anchor to steam towards

Charlottetown arriving there at 1130.[36]

After a day and a half in Charlottetown the Royal couple were preparing to re-embark in the Yacht when the elements intervened, as Admiral Rusby recalled:

'It was planned that immediately after The Queen and Prince Philip had said farewell to local dignitaries on the jetty, the Yacht was to slip and sail away into the night. In order to expedite matters, I had told the First and Second Lieutenants to single up to just a head rope and stern rope. Unfortunately, we had recently been issued with nylon berthing ropes, in place of wires. The strong offshore wind that was blowing drove the Yacht away from the jetty and, frantically, I passed the word to both ends to heave in. All that happened was that the nylon ropes stretched further and further until the brow fell off the platform on which it was resting on the jetty. Fortunately, the Royal party was still saying good-bye, so the Boatswain and two of the side-party rushed down the brow and repositioned it on the platform, thus enabling The Queen and Prince Philip to get on board – no damage done. However, the press had seen it and the event became headline news in the following morning's papers. Later on in the Tour the local authorities hadn't provided a long enough red carpet to reach to the end of the Yacht's brow, so I sent some of the side-party out to pull the carpet back so that there wasn't a gap. This did not pass unnoticed by The Queen and she later said to me, "I see you're having trouble again Commander." I replied, "Yes Ma'am, I'm afraid I am. The red carpet wasn't long enough this time."'

From Charlottetown *Britannia* got underway for the journey to Quebec were she arrived on 10 October for the Royal couple's two-day visit. The berth at Wolfe's Cove, Quebec, was overlooked by the Heights of Abraham. There had been a lot of discussion beforehand about the suitability of this berth on account of the militant attitude of the Quebec separatists and the threat they posed to The Queen's safety. On the day, the Canadian Government took no chances and the Heights were closed to the public and heavily patrolled. When The Queen landed via a totally enclosed brow she was escorted on the inland side by nine RCMP Policemen who acted as a human shield. At the end of the second day in Quebec The Queen and Prince Philip flew from Quebec to visit Ottawa. Although Prince Philip would return in two days to begin his own separate visit it marked the end of The Queen's time on board as she would fly home to London direct from Ottawa.[37]

A day later the Yacht sailed for Isle aux Ruaux ahead of Prince Philip's arrival on 13 October. Following his day

During Britannia's *first visit to the Galapagos Islands Prince Philip was taken ashore to see some of the wildlife, such as this iguana.*   (© British Crown Copyright / MOD)

ashore shooting and fishing Prince Philip joined the Yacht that evening and *Britannia* set sail for Nassau arriving there on 20 October for Prince Philip's two-day visit. While the Yacht was alongside, *Britannia* was finally able to exchange her broken anchor for a new one which had been brought out from the UK by RFA *Wave Prince*.[38] His Royal Highness flew from Nassau to Mexico the next morning and half an hour later *Britannia* made a difficult departure, as Captain Andrewes recalled:

'When it came to leave there was a strong onshore wind blowing and there were no tugs only two powerful boats which pulled for several minutes taking us about 50 or 60 feet away from the jetty. I then turned to FORY and said, "I think we can go ahead as fast as possible." *Britannia* wasn't a very powerful ship but we cast off from these motor boats and shot ahead missing the ship on the berth ahead by about 10 yards which was close enough! It was interesting to say the least while we waited for the Yacht to gather speed and wondered how far the Yacht was going to be blown towards the shore.'

While Prince Philip began his Mexican Tour the Yacht sailed through the Panama Canal into the Pacific and headed for Acapulco where she anchored on 28 October. The next day Prince Philip returned to *Britannia* to host a dinner for the Mexican President to bring his Tour to a

In recognition of some comments made by Prince Philip about the Beatles the Yachtsmen present His Royal Highness with a suitable wig and guitar during the Crossing-The-Line ceremony on 5 November. In view of the date the ceremony also included an appearance by Guy Fawkes.

(© British Crown Copyright / MOD)

successful conclusion.[39] That night *Britannia* weighed anchor and steamed south towards the Galapagos Islands anchoring off Tower Island on 2 November. The Galapagos Islands presented the Navigating Officer with a few challenges, as Captain Andrewes remembered: 'these islands come straight up out of the sea and it is difficult to select an anchor berth that is shallow enough, but not too close to the shore. During the course of the next three days the Yacht anchored 10 times at different islands.' The Darwin Foundation's research ship *Beagle* was already lying at anchor in Darwin Bay when the Yacht arrived. His Royal Highness went across to the 50-foot brig to collect Captain Angemeyer, and Dr Perry, who was the director of the Charles Darwin Research Station on Santa Cruz Island. From *Beagle* the Royal party went ashore to spend the morning among the wildlife. Interestingly, they found that the animals were very approachable and in some cases they even came up to the visitors. When Prince Philip returned to the Yacht he was accompanied by the Captain and Dr Perry who became part of the Royal party for the rest of the visit. That afternoon *Britannia* dropped anchor off Isla San Salvador where the Royal party climbed a steep 300-foot hill before returning to the Yacht for the trip to Baltra Island. As *Britannia* approached the island the radar broke down prior to anchoring so the manoeuvre had to be done by stopwatch.

Having spent a few hours at anchor off Baltra Island *Britannia* made an overnight passage to Ferandina Island.[40] The following morning the Royal party went ashore to look round the island which consisted mainly of lava,

although there were some scrub and mangroves. During their time ashore the Royal party took the opportunity to photograph penguins, marine iguanas, land iguanas, sea lions and seals. Unfortunately, Prince Philip dropped his Hasselblad camera in the sea when he landed and it had started to buzz as the salt water got at the aluminium parts, as Captain Andrewes remembered:

'On returning to *Britannia* Prince Philip sought out Commander Hewitt to ask what should be done about his camera. Prince Philip was not a little astounded to have his camera immediately dropped in a basin of cold fresh water. The sequel to this tale is that when the camera was ultimately sent back to the makers, only two small springs needed replacement.'

In the Afternoon the Yacht moved across to Caleta Tagus where a few of the Yachtsmen had been enjoying some leave. At 1800 it was time for the Royal party and the Yachtsmen to return to *Britannia* ready for the overnight journey to Espanola Island. During his time on the island the next morning Prince Philip met a young couple, Mr and Mrs Nelson, who had been living on the island in a tent for four months bird watching. Prince Philip, who had previously met Mr Nelson, invited the couple to lunch on board the Yacht before *Britannia* sailed in the afternoon to Gardener Island for the final call of the visit. After a good afternoon ashore Captain Angemeyer and Dr Perry took their leave of Prince Philip to return to the *Beagle* as the Yacht prepared to get underway and sail back across the Pacific to Panama.[41] When *Britannia* reached the Panamanian coast she altered course towards the shore to enable the Royal party to watch birds migrating, as Captain Andrewes remembered:

'A blue-footed booby landed on the Flag Deck. It was obviously tired and reluctant to go on with its flight so the Yeoman of Signals introduced it to Prince Philip when he came up to the Bridge. Sensibly, in view of its serrated beak, Prince Philip declined to take it from the Yeoman.'

Britannia berthed in Balboa on 7 November for Prince Philip's two-day visit to Panama, which included an early morning expedition on 8 November to watch birds being caught and ringed. On 9 November Prince Philip left Panama to fly to the Windward Islands before rejoining *Britannia* in Barbados. In the meantime *Britannia* also left Balboa on 9 November to sail through the Panama Canal and on to Bridgetown, where Prince Philip embarked on 13 November.[42] Prince Philip's Caribbean Tour moved at a quick pace, as he visited an island a day, which required the Yacht to steam overnight so that she was able to appear over the horizon early the next morning to begin the day's programme of engagements ashore. This tightly packed programme looked as though it might be put in jeopardy when *Britannia* came to weigh anchor from Prince Rupert Bay, Portsmouth, Dominica, on 16 November, as Captain Andrewes explains:

'The anchor fouled a length of chain cable lying abandoned on the sea bed. This delayed the Yacht's departure by half an hour and so we had to steam at 19 knots all night to reach Anguilla by 1000 the following morning. In contrast to the storms in the early part of this Tour, it was a marvellous moonlit night and the dark shapes of the beautiful islands of Guadeloupe, Montserrat, Redonda, and Saba were clearly visible every 20 miles or so. The Yacht only stayed at anchor off Anguilla for three quarters of an hour so that Prince Philip could land. Then, after this short stay, she wound her way out through the shoals shown on the chart of 1870 and set sail for Montserrat where she came to anchor at dusk for Prince Philip to return on board after flying from Anguilla.'

That night the Yacht sailed overnight again to reach Antigua, the final call of Prince Philip's Tour. During the day Prince Philip was landed at St John's and driven to English Harbour to attend the annual Dockyard Day. The event was brought to a close by the Yacht's RM Band, which performed the sunset ceremony ashore while the Yacht lay at anchor in the background. That night Prince Philip flew back to the UK and *Britannia* returned to St

John's for a few days before setting sail for Portsmouth, where she arrived on 2 December[43]. When FORY ordered 'ring off main engines' it not only signalled the end of another successful major deployment but also his seagoing career as *Britannia* spent the last few months of his time as FORY in dry dock undergoing her quadrennial refit. As Admiral Rusby explains, the lead up to the refitting of *Britannia* was very different to that of a conventional RN warship:

'As the Captain of a normal warship I would be told that we were programmed to have a refit and the major items of work approved to be carried out. I didn't have much latitude or any idea of how much it all cost. But in *Britannia*'s case a sum was decreed. Each item was costed and we had to bargain with the dockyard to keep within the limit and so determine the scope of her refit at a pre-refit conference and we weren't to exceed it. I remember comparing the sum to the cost of refitting other ships and found that it equated to the amount spent on refitting a fleet tug!'

The Yacht was moved into No. 3 Basin to begin the preparations for the refit on 14 December. The following day the Labour MP, Emrys Hughes, who had been a frequent critic of *Britannia* since she was built, visited the Yacht together with the Minister of Defence (Royal Navy), Christopher Mayhew MP and the Naval Secretary, Rear Admiral O'Brien.[44] The purpose of the visit was to see the scope of the work to be done during the refit and look at the Royal Apartments. Despite saying to those on board that he was disappointed by the Royal Apartments he subsequently told the press that he had never seen such unparalleled luxury and that his visit confirmed his opinions that she should never have been built.

Despite the criticisms of Emrys Hughes the refit got underway in earnest in the New Year. When the Yachtsmen moved into RN Barracks ashore on 18 January 1965,[45] it was the first time they had been evicted from *Britannia* since she was commissioned. The move was necessary because the work of installing air conditioning meant that the Yacht was totally uninhabitable. As Admiral Rusby recalls:

'Having seen the state of their new accommodation the Yachtsmen decided to redecorate the whole place. By some miraculous means, and with the help of the Deputy Supply Officer and others the Yachtsmen acquired carpets and easy chairs for their quarters. The Commander of the Barracks was astonished at the transformation and voted their accommodation the best in the Barracks!'

Chapter Six

IN COOK'S WAKE

Rear Admiral Sir Patrick Morgan
KCVO CB DSC 1965–1970

With the Yacht hidden from view by scaffolding and her teak decks covered with plywood Rear Admiral Sir Joseph Henley KCVO CB walked ashore in plain clothes on 9 March 1965, shaking hands with each member of the Yacht's company. The Yachtsmen had turned out to say farewell to the third FORY, who had been succeeded at noon by Acting Rear Admiral P J Morgan DSC. Admiral Morgan was a navigating officer and had served in *V&A* as a Season Officer in 1938. During the Second World War he was awarded the DSC while serving in the cruiser HMS *Penelope* in the Mediterranean. In 1952 he became the Commanding Officer of the destroyer HMS *Constance* while she was still in Korean waters. From there he became the executive officer of the Navigation School HMS *Dryad*, before being promoted to Captain in 1956. He was subsequently appointed as the Naval Attaché in Ankara and Teheran before assuming command of the commando carrier HMS *Bulwark* in 1963. He was promoted to Rear Admiral on the day he formally became FORY. Describing Admiral Morgan his last Commander (E), later Rear Admiral Philip Edwards CB LVO, said:

'Admiral Morgan was a handsome, suave but very private Naval Officer, yet he was full of stature. He was a superb delegater and really trusted his Naval Officers and this feeling worked its way down the Yacht so that everyone trusted each other. He was a first-class ship handler and one of the first things he said to me on joining the Yacht was, "If I ever have to go full astern

I will invite you up for a glass of champagne." I only received the invitation once, when we were entering Gibraltar and needed full astern to take avoiding action; he kept his word.'

Admiral Sir Brian Brown KCB CBE, who served as his Deputy Supply Officer, added:

'He was in very many respects an archetypal old-fashioned Naval Officer. High standards, but quite a lot of fun about him – much more fun than you would first expect because the initial impressions were usually here is quite a daunting chap. He was often in the thick of all the fun with the Household, in particular The Queen Mother's Household, when they were embarked.'

Admiral Morgan's first concern on becoming FORY was that the Yacht's refit should be brought to a successful conclusion so that she was ready in time for The Queen's historic State Visit to West Germany at the end of May 1965. Because of the requirement for *Britannia*'s presence in West Germany it had been decided that the full upgrading of her communications equipment would be delayed until her next major refit.[1] However, a major component of the £325,000 refit[2] was the installation of air conditioning in the forward half of the Yacht for the benefit of the Yachtsmen. When *Britannia* was commissioned air conditioning was fitted aft in the Royal Apartments, not because of her Royal duties, but because of her secondary role as a hospital ship. By the mid 1960s it had become the Admiralty's policy to fit air conditioning where possible to existing ships that were likely to serve in the tropics. Despite the political sensitivities of any money being spent on *Britannia*, the Admiralty were keen to ensure that the standard of comfort for the Yachtsmen was not allowed to fall too far behind that of other HM ships. As the refit was coming to an end the Yachtsmen observed court mourning for Princess Mary, The Princess Royal, who died on 28 March. In recent years the Princess had been a familiar figure on board the Yacht during her long tours of the Caribbean, Mediterranean and Newfoundland.[3]

On 31 March the Yachtsmen moved back on board *Britannia* which had been moved out of dry dock the day before.[4] After conducting a series of post refit trials during the second half of April, *Britannia* set sail from Portsmouth for Royal duty on 12 May 1965. Her destination was Harwich to embark Princess Margaret and Lord Snowdon for their visit to Amsterdam in support of British Week – a trade promotional event.[5] Because *Britannia*'s design was influenced by the Harwich based North Sea ferries, *Amsterdam* and *Arnhem*, officials from Buckingham Palace were worried about unfavourable comparisons being made between them and the Yacht. Therefore, the Navigating Officer was involved in detailed discussions with the harbour authorities to keep *Britannia* away from the ferries during the course of the visit. This was just one of the more unusual problems to come the way of the Navigating Officer. It was also a curious situation, because if the officials from Buckingham Palace had taken a closer look at the ferries they would have realised that *Britannia* had a much better appearance both externally and internally!

Having embarked Princess Margaret and Lord Snowdon, *Britannia* arrived in Amsterdam on 14 May to find a strong RN contingent, headed by the cruiser HMS *Lion* wearing the flag of the Admiral Commanding Reserves. *Lion* and the 10 other ships formed the RN's contribution to British Week. Once the Yacht was secured to mooring buoys in Amsterdam Harbour, Princess Margaret and Lord Snowdon were taken ashore in the Barge for the Princess to perform the formal opening ceremony for British Week in Congress Hall which was attended by Queen Juliana of the Netherlands. After the ceremony the Royal couple spent the next three days attending events connected with the British Week. The embarkation of Queen Juliana for an informal dinner on 16 May caused an interesting re-arrangement of the Standards being flown on board. Being a Head of State The Queen's Standard took precedence and was thus broken at the main mast, displacing Princess Margaret's, which was broken at the fore mast, while FORY's flag was broken at the mizzen mast. During the final two days of

their visit the Royal couple visited Asscher's diamond factory and went for a short trip in a Westland Hovercraft before ending their visit with a ceremonial passage through the Amsterdam canals in the Barge on 18 May. At 1235 the Yacht sailed for Portsmouth, where she arrived the next day, and the Royal couple left.[6]

Five days after her return from Amsterdam *Britannia* sailed from Portsmouth on 24 May and once more headed east across the North Sea. This time her destination was Hamburg where she would embark The Queen and Prince Philip at the end of their historic State Visit. The trip was planned as a formal gesture of reconciliation between the two nations after the two World Wars. The last time a British Monarch had visited Germany was in May 1913, when King George V and Queen Mary went to Berlin for the wedding of Kaiser William II's only daughter Princess Luise of Prussia to Duke Ernst August of Brunswick-Luneburg. Before The Queen and Prince Philip joined *Britannia* they spent 11 days travelling some 1200 miles around West Germany and visiting 10 major

Flag Officer Royal Yachts between 1965 and 1970, Rear Admiral Sir Patrick Morgan KCVO CB DSC,

The Queen and Prince Philip walk past the German destroyers
Hamburg *and* Schleswig Holstein *on their way to embark in
the Yacht.*

(© British Crown Copyright / MOD)

cities. Meanwhile, *Britannia* berthed in Hamburg on 26
May to await the Royal couple. On the other side of the
jetty were moored the two German destroyers *Hamburg*
and *Schleswig Holstein* which were to form half of the
Royal Escort down the River Elbe alongside the RN
frigates *Lowestoft* and *Blackpool*.[7]

After the thorough inland part of their State Visit The
Queen and Prince Philip embarked in the Yacht in the
afternoon of 28 May prior to the State Banquet for the
President of the Federal German Republic that night.
One of those who accompanied The Queen as part of her
Household for this visit was her Press Secretary William
Heseltine (later The Rt Hon. Sir William Heseltine GCB
GCVO AC QSO). Describing the benefit of *Britannia's*
presence for such a high-profile State Visit for The Queen
he said:

'The Yacht brought a lot to any occasion because she
was a magnificent sight. She enabled The Queen to
entertain in her own surroundings in a magnificent
manner. *Britannia* also provided the opportunity for a
bit of military ceremony at the end of the evening
when the Royal Marines Beat Retreat on the jetty.
From the point of view of the Household *Britannia* also
provided office facilities and accommodation for all of
those who accompanied The Queen. Whilst this
aspect could be solved by other means on tours without
Britannia, the use of the Yacht was a very tidy solution
not least because we were all familiar with the available
resources. The Household was a very hierarchical
establishment when I first joined and the accommodation for them in the Yacht reflected this. The Queen
and Prince Philip lived in a degree of relative comfort
as did other members of the Royal Family and senior
members of the Household. Smaller cabins were allocated to those further down the ladder. For all of that it
was still a very happy existence for the Household and
I never detected any resentment among members of the
Household towards these arrangements.'

For The Queen's Lady-in-Waiting, Lady Susan Hussey (later Lady Susan Hussey DCVO), it was the first time she had been on board the Yacht. Describing her initial impressions of this new environment she said:

'I had no naval knowledge, I had never been in or near a warship before. When I joined *Britannia* I was expecting a cross between a channel ferry and a liner. Although I had already seen pictures of *Britannia* what first impressed me was the size of her, the extraordinary elegance of her, the extraordinary grace. I was still very young and I was somewhat overawed by it all. I was still learning how to do my job as a Lady-in-Waiting under the watchful eye of Lady Leicester. I wondered how I would ever find my way round the Yacht with all the different decks and the different parts where I should and shouldn't go. We were never allowed to go forward below decks from the Royal Apartments without an escort.'

After the State Banquet The Queen, Prince Philip and President Lubke watched the sunset ceremony performed on the quarterdeck of *Hamburg* as the ships were undressed. On completion of the ceremony the guests all landed from the Yacht and she slipped to begin her passage down the River Elbe, led by the German Pleasure Steamer *Wappen Von Hamburg* with the Senate of Hamburg embarked.[8] *Britannia*'s floodlit departure was the perfect way to end such a memorable occasion on a very high note, as Lady Susan Hussey explains:

'There were huge crowds on both banks of the River Elbe. Having only just hosted the farewell banquet The Queen was still dressed in full evening dress with tiara and jewels, and she came up on deck to wave to the crowds as we sailed by. Because of the size of these crowds The Queen was very worried about disappointing the crowds on one side of the Yacht or the other, so she was constantly crossing to and fro. The next day, as the Yacht arrived in the English Channel, there was this complete transformation from all the formality of The Queen's role as Head of State to a much more relaxed atmosphere. People wore slacks and played deck tennis. It was then that I saw the Yacht as being the place of recreation where the Queen and her party unwound, the place where she and the rest of us were restored after a very heavy, hard-working State Visit. The Queen was able to have a very necessary breathing space before returning to the UK and going straight into the next round of official engagements. This was always the value of the Yacht because The Queen was in her own home with people who guarded her privacy with their lives. Over the years no stories ever emerged from the Yacht about the Royal Family when they were on board as far as I can remember. Sadly the same can not be said about almost any other place in which they stay.'

After a day at sea *Britannia* returned to Portsmouth on 30 May where large crowds had gathered to watch The Queen's arrival.[9]

On 23 June the Yacht sailed for Cardiff for The Queen and Prince Philip to embark at the end of their visit to South Wales on 24 June, which included the Jubilee dinner for the Welsh Guards Old Comrades Association. From Cardiff the Yacht headed north for Kirkcudbright, and on 28 June *Britannia* visited the river of her birth by returning to Clydebank for the Royal couple's Dunbartonshire visit.[10] To mark *Britannia*'s return FORY was sent a telegram by the Deputy Chairman of John Brown's shipyard, Dr John Brown, who of course had originally designed the Yacht. In it he said, 'John Brown's salute an old friend. Delighted to see her looking so well. Best wishes from all at Clydebank.' The Yacht replied by saying, 'A great pleasure to visit our birth place again. We all wish you the best of luck in the future.' At the end of two full days of engagements the Royal couple left for Holyrood while *Britannia* sailed from the Clyde for Portsmouth, returning there on 1 July.[11] At the end of the month the Yacht sailed across the Solent on 25 July for The Queen and Prince Philip's visit to the Isle of Wight, which included the installation of Lord Mountbatten as the Governor of the Island on 26 July at Carrisbrooke Castle. The appointment allowed Lord Mountbatten to follow in the steps of both his uncle, Prince Henry of Battenberg, and his aunt, Princess Beatrice, who had both been Governors of the island.[12] As Captain Andrewes explains, the visit itself was perfectly straightforward until it came to the arrangements for The Queen's departure.

'Lord Mountbatten had the idea that The Queen would travel from Yarmouth in a SRN5 hovercraft of the Inter Service Trials Unit based at Lee-on-Solent to a suitable point where she could disembark on the Sussex coast and be driven to Goodwood. This involved me in a certain amount of planning and eventually I decided to place a boat every 10 miles from Yarmouth to the RAF Station at Thorney Island on the Sussex coast. If the hovercraft had broken down one of these craft would have taken The Queen off and still enabled her to arrive at Goodwood in time for lunch. The trip went well until the hovercraft's arrival at Thorney Island when it couldn't go up the ramp so The Queen was transferred to the boat lying off Thorney

Island and landed. Luckily, the press never got to know of this but it did demonstrate that it was worth having the safety boats deployed, otherwise she would have been late for her next engagement.'

Five days after The Queen's visit to the Isle of Wight the Yacht was once more secured to the Admiralty Buoy off Cowes for the annual Cowes Week Regatta on 31 July.[13] From Cowes the Yacht headed north again to embark the Royal Family for The Queen's visit to Kirkcudbright. This call was made at The Queen's own personal request because she had been unable to fulfil her engagements in Kirkcudbright when *Britannia* was there in June due to illness.[14] Having spent the day off Kirkcudbright *Britannia* sailed for the Clyde, where she rendezvoused with the Northern Lighthouse Board Tender *Pharos* on 10 August. Once the Commissioners of the Northern Lighthouse Board had paid their respects to The Queen, *Pharos* took up station ahead of *Britannia* to lead her to the anchorage off the Tail of the Bank. There, ships of the Home Fleet, headed by the cruiser HMS *Lion* wearing the flag of the Commander-in-Chief Home Fleet, Admiral Sir John Frewen KCB, had assembled for The Queen's first visit to the Home Fleet since she had become Lord High Admiral in 1964. The Office of Lord High Admiral was revived at the Restoration in 1660 when James, Duke of York was given the title. The duties of the Lord High Admiral were carried out by the Lords Commissioners For Executing The Office Of Lord High Admiral. These officials were more communally known as the Lords Commissioners of the Admiralty or the Board of Admiralty. When Lord

Mountbatten established the Ministry of Defence, the Board of Admiralty was abolished and replaced by a Navy Board. The title of Lord High Admiral therefore reverted to the Sovereign. During the morning the Royal party visited the *County* class destroyer HMS *Kent* and the *Leander* class frigate HMS *Dido*. The Ship's company of *Dido* had put together a display to illustrate the breadth of a modern frigate's activities, which included riot control, damage control and even pirates for a children's party. The Queen was so impressed by the display that in the afternoon arrangements were made for both The Prince of Wales and Princess Anne to visit *Dido* while their parents visited HMS *Dreadnought*, HMS *Maidstone* and the aircraft carrier HMS *Centaur*, where they were joined by the Prince and Princess. In the evening The Queen and Prince Philip joined the Commander-in-Chief Home Fleet for a formal dinner on board *Lion* to which all the Flag Officers and COs were invited. The Queen was preceded into dinner by the Master-At-Arms who carried the Verge of the Lord High Admiral. The Verge was made in 1660 for The Duke of York for use on state occasions and was normally carried on board *Britannia* except when it was used during Fleet Reviews and Lord High Admiral's Divisions at BRNC.[15] The following day the Royal party reviewed the eastern group of ships in the Barge, which consisted of smaller warships such as minesweepers and fast patrol boats. On completion, the Barge was hoisted and the Yacht weighed anchor to review the major warships as she made her way out of the Clyde to undertake the Western Isles Cruise before returning to Portsmouth on 18 August.[16]

The rest of the year was spent preparing for the New Year's major global deployment. As part of these preparations some serious thought had to be given about how the Yachtsmen were going to be entertained over the coming months especially during the long periods at sea between Royal duty. It was important that the entertainment programme ran smoothly because it was a key factor in maintaining a high morale. Responsibility for this work was always delegated to one of the Season Officers and thus in 1965 Sub Lieutenant Anthony Morrow (later Commodore A J C Morrow CVO RN) was invited to make the necessary arrangements for the forthcoming World Tour. Describing the role of the film officer he recalled:

'I had to plan for the entire period and then it was up to the Royal Naval Film Corporation as to whether we took the lot from Portsmouth or whether they re-supplied us during the deployment. Once we had these films on board it was up to us to share them around other ships we would meet. For example, in the Caribbean there was the West Indies Squadron so we could off-load some of the films we had watched and replace them with new ones. The films were shown in the Wardroom and the Yachtsmens' messes. The Royal Family also had their own cinema with two 35mm projectors mounted in the Royal Servery. It was one of those special occasions in *Britannia* when The Queen was embarked for any length of time that if the Royal party wanted to see a film after dinner the Royal Dining Room would be converted into a cinema. The officers and a restricted number of Yachtsmen would come in and watch the film with the Royal Family.'

On 19 January 1966 *Britannia* sailed from Portsmouth for The Queen and Prince Philip's Tour of the Caribbean. The Yacht's planned stop for fuel at Ponta Delgada had to be changed to Madeira because of continuing gales around the Azores which would have made it virtually impossible to berth. Due to the diversion and continuing gale force winds during the voyage across the Atlantic *Britannia* arrived 24 hours later than planned in Barbados on 30 January.[17] Two days later the Royal couple landed in Barbados in a VC10 from London and embarked in the Yacht for the overnight passage to Mustique, where they spent the next day ashore with Princess Margaret at her house, before resuming their journey to British Guiana for their two-day visit. From there the Yacht sailed for Trinidad to begin The Queen's Tour of the Caribbean Islands. Over the next month The Queen and Prince

The Yacht provided the only effective means for The Queen and Prince Philip to undertake a series of visits to island communities within a short period of time, such as their 1966 Tour of the Caribbean. Typically, the Yacht would sail between islands overnight.

(© British Crown Copyright / MOD)

Philip visited 14 islands. *Britannia* always came into her own during this type of tour because she enabled The Queen to visit a large number of small island communities in a relatively short period of time. Typically, The Queen would take one or two days to visit an island and then the Yacht would steam overnight to the next stop. The following morning The Queen would be able to step ashore at the next island and begin another full day of engagements. Not only did the use of *Britannia* in this way provide a practical way for The Queen to conduct a tour of island communities but it also provided a level of impact among maritime communities that would have been impossible without *Britannia*.

To record this Tour and all other aspects of life on board *Britannia* the Yacht's company included a Naval Photographer known as 'Snaps'. During the course of a tour the photographs taken by Snaps provided many of the Yachtsmen with their only glimpse of the main events of the tour. In 1966 the Yacht's Photographer was LA (Phot) Dave Morris (later Mr D Morris BEM). Describing the photographic facilities on board and his role Dave Morris said:

'The dark room was about 8 foot by 5 foot with a glazing machine and an enlarger in the corner plus two radio sets which got very hot. It was located above the throttles for the main engines while the Laundry Room was on the other side of the forward bulkhead. The temperature would routinely reach about 100° to 120° and thus I worked in there in just my underpants and flip-flops in the tropics. If I had a large number of enlargements to do I couldn't do them at sea because the enlarger was vibrated too much. Therefore, in port there was a great deal of work to be done. For example, when the principle guests came aboard for a State Banquet I would photograph them before they went in to eat. I would then process the film, produce the best print, which was signed by The Queen and framed, so that it was ready to be presented to the guests before they left the Yacht. However, I soon discovered that the Yachtsmen were very particular about how the Yacht looked in photographs as they were in real life. For example, I would take a cracking photograph of the Yacht only for the Yachtsmen to say that's not right one of the boats is missing or the ladders are down. Therefore, it was very rare to get a photograph of the Yacht where everything was really smart and the light was right.'

The Tour concluded in Jamaica on 6 March when The Queen and Prince Philip took off from Montego Bay airport to return to London. As the VC10 disappeared into the night *Britannia* weighed anchor to sail through the Panama Canal and into the Pacific. As the Yacht steamed across the Pacific the RM Band played a key part in keeping the Yachtsmen entertained. Lieutenant Colonel G Hoskins OBE MVO ARAM RM was serving on board as Bandmaster and subsequently returned in 1978 as the Director of Music. Describing a few of the ideas conjured up by the Band for the benefit of the Yachtsmen on long voyages he said:

'During the voyage we suddenly started putting up posters saying "The Flying Velluccis are coming". No

In addition to playing a key role in Britannia's *official duties the RM Band provided a major boost to the morale of the Yacht's company through their various concerts on the forecastle during long sea passages between periods of Royal duty. Here we see one of the Band's many impromptu acts, 'It's Trad, Dad! with The Utter Bilge Jazzmen'.*

When the Yacht anchored in Suva Harbour representative Fijian chiefs came on board to perform the ceremony of welcome in front of The Queen Mother on the Verandah Deck.

(© British Crown Copyright / MOD)

one knew what this meant and as successive posters appeared saying that The Flying Velluccis were definitely coming, interest among the Yachtsmen grew. One Saturday morning big red signs went up saying that the Velluccis would arrive on the forecastle at 1400. Off duty Yachtsmen gathered on the forecastle at the appointed time to see what it was all about when suddenly a group of about eight strangely dressed men clambered through the screen door. They appeared to be Italian strong men of the 1920s in black leotards and with long, black moustaches. They brought with them huge "weights" (actually made of black-painted cardboard and marked with size in kilos) which they proceeded to toss between themselves as part of a humorous tumbling routine. The Flying Velluccis proved to be members of the RM Band, who then went on to compete as the Band mess team in the sports afternoon that followed. It had been their plan to get everyone's full interest in this main event and it proved to be a great success.'

Despite their important role on board the Yacht the musicians didn't actually always have access to a mess deck until, in a refit, the on board RM Barracks was enlarged to accommodate their number. As Lieutenant Colonel Hoskins explains:

'Although we were always made most welcome on board the Yacht there was a shortage of accommoda-

Following The Queen Mother's visit to Fiji the Yacht's company put on a concert for Her Majesty entitled 'You Must Be Bluffing' as the Yacht steamed towards New Zealand. One of the acts featured the playing of this rather unusual instrument!

(© British Crown Copyright / MOD)

The Queen Mother clearly enjoyed this concert which was held on the forecastle.

(© British Crown Copyright / MOD)

tion when we were embarked. When the Yacht had been built no provision for a body of musicians had been made. The Director of Music, Bandmaster and Band Sergeants had accommodation within their respective messes but the ordinary musician was a bit of a cuckoo. Musicians had to bring folding camp beds with them when embarking, and every evening, having played for The Queen during dinner in the Royal Apartments, they had then to wait in a passageway right up in the fore part of the ship for the Unwinding Room to become available. Used nightly as a cinema and bar by off-duty Yachtsmen the musicians couldn't take their camp beds in and get their heads down until it had been vacated. By then it was a fairly foul-smelling and smoky place. To make matters worse, being so far for'ard in the forepeak, the rise and fall of the bows in even the mildest weather made for much discomfort.'

Once *Britannia* entered the Pacific she called at Tahiti, Bora Bora and Fiji where The Queen Mother embarked on 7 April.[18] On 9 April the Yacht anchored in Suva Harbour for representative Fijian Chiefs to perform the ceremony of welcome on the Verandah Deck in front of The Queen Mother. On completion of the ceremony The Queen Mother landed to begin two days of engagements ashore in Fiji before sailing for New Zealand the following night.[19] During the passage the Yachtsmen put on a ship's

concert for The Queen Mother entitled 'You Must Be Bluffing' on the forecastle. The voyage also provided The Queen Mother with the opportunity to walk around the Yacht and talk to many of the Yachtsmen. Such occasions always provided a great boost to the morale of those on board, especially the members of the Yacht's company who didn't come into direct contact with the Royal Family in the course of their work.[20]

On 16 April the Yacht arrived in Bluff, New Zealand for the start of The Queen Mother's Tour of New Zealand, which included visits to Dunedin, Timaru, Lyttleton, Wellington, Devonport and Auckland. On 3 May The Queen Mother hosted a dinner followed by a farewell reception on board the Yacht in Auckland. The end of the reception marked the closing stages of two long periods of Royal duty as Commodore Morrow recalled:

'The reception finished about 2100 and it had been a very successful formal occasion. Afterwards, we all felt very flat, here we were in all our mess kit and no one knew quite what to do as it was too late to go ashore. The Commander thought it would be a nice idea as The Queen Mother was still on board if we invited her down to the Wardroom. The Admiral was asked by the Commander to invite The Queen Mother and her Household to come to the Wardroom for an end of evening and end of tour drink. This invitation was conveyed and she graciously accepted. It was almost like an

end of term feeling for us because we had just completed two state visits and we now had a long passage back
home. The Queen Mother came to the Wardroom in
her long ballgown and tiara and we were all dressed in
our formal mess dress. As the evening drew on someone
said that they were rather hungry. The Queen Mother
picked up on this and said, "Oh yes, wouldn't it be nice
to have some bacon and eggs." Whereupon she led the
officers to the galley, put on an apron and proceeded to
assist us to cook bacon and eggs which we all then ate.'

The next morning The Queen Mother disembarked and
went straight to the roof of the Ocean Terminal to watch
the RM Band playing on the Royal Deck and wave
farewell to the Yachtsmen before finally being driven to
the airport to catch her flight home. On 5 May the Yacht
began the long voyage home stopping at Hobart and
Fremantle and then heading for Aden.

Prior to entering the Red Sea the Yacht was slightly
ahead of schedule so FORY decided to take advantage of
the good weather, as Captain James recalls:

'The Admiral said that we needed to mark time for a
bit so we lowered the two jolly boats. He organised a
seaman's team and an engine room's team to have a

race to the Yacht, which stopped 2 or 3 miles away.
After the race the Admiral organised a life raft drill by
ordering the life raft from number one station to be
thrown over the side. The Yachtsmen assigned to that
station were then invited to jump over the side, which
is a long way down from the forecastle! To set a good
example and to prove that we were all in it together
the Admiral told the Wardroom to go down to the
forecastle and then jump in to man the life raft after it
had been vacated by its crew. When we got back on
board he bought us all a drink.'

After a brief call at Aden the Yacht sailed through the
Suez Canal and anchored off Spithead on 15 June. By the
time *Britannia* dropped anchor she had steamed 32,230
miles and entered 56 different ports since she left
Portsmouth at the beginning of the year. Later in the
morning the families of the Yacht's company were
embarked for the short passage through the Solent and

*For many years the Yacht's home in Portsmouth was H
Moorings off Whale Island. In this 1966 view of H Moorings
the heavy cruiser HMS Belfast can be seen closest to the
Yacht.* (© British Crown Copyright / MOD)

into Portsmouth Dockyard. It was the first time that such an event, in effect a Families Day, had been held on board *Britannia* and it was greatly enjoyed both by the 400 guests and the Yachtsmen.[21]

After a few weeks in dockyard hands *Britannia* undertook a short period of trials at the beginning of August with a voyage to Falmouth where she anchored on 3 August. Sadly, the trip was overshadowed by the loss of the pleasure boat *Darwin*, which had been reported missing the previous day. During the morning of 4 August the search operation located a number of bodies and wreckage from the missing boat. *Britannia* had been dressed overall to mark The Queen Mother's birthday, but FORY gave the order to undress ship and when the Falmouth Lifeboat sailed past *Britannia* carrying some of the bodies the Yacht's colours were lowered to half mast as a mark of respect.[22] Five days later *Britannia* returned to Portsmouth for a period of leave and maintenance.

During The Queen Mother's visit to the West Country in May 1967 Her Majesty took the opportunity to walk round the Yacht and visited the NAAFI where she stopped to talk to the Canteen Manager, Mr Jackson, who had served in the Yacht since she was commissioned in 1954.

On 1 May 1967 The Queen Mother embarked in *Britannia* at Portsmouth for her Tour of the West Country and Northern France. As the Yacht made her way out of the Solent, she passed the Cunard Liner RMS *Queen Elizabeth* which Her Majesty had launched in 1938.[23] After the following day's visit to Penzance and St Michael's Mount the Yacht sailed past Portlevan so that The Queen Mother could see for herself the damage to Portlevan's beaches caused by the oil released from the tanker *Torrey Canyon* which went aground on the Seven Stones reef off Lands End on 18 March 1967. Although a major clean up operation was launched following the initial oil spillage, a number of beaches in Cornwall suffered a fresh round of pollution at the end of April.[24] On 3 May The Queen Mother visited Falmouth, and it had been planned to re-embark her in the Barge from Mevagissy but the gale force winds and heavy squalls led to a quick change in plans and the Yacht sailed on to Plymouth where Her Majesty re-joined the Yacht,[25] as the Deputy Supply Officer at the time, later Admiral Sir Brian Brown KCB CBE recalls:

'It was a wet and windy evening with a heavy swell and I can remember seeing the Barge emerge through the mist rolling heavily. As it did we could hear the faint sound of singing and then we realised it was The

Queen Mother leading her Household in a rousing chorus of the Eton boating song!'

The Yacht remained in Plymouth Sound secured to No. 1 Buoy while The Queen Mother undertook engagements in Plymouth, Tavistock and Stoke Climsland on 4 May. Having landed The Queen Mother the following morning, to continue her programme ashore, the Yacht weighed anchor for Brixham where Her Majesty re-embarked before heading across the English Channel to begin the French part of her Tour. As part of her programme The Queen Mother visited Ouistreham, Arromanches and the war cemetery at Bayeux on 6 May, and St Malo and Mont St Michael the following day, before *Britannia* weighed anchor that night for Portsmouth, arriving on 8 May where The Queen Mother disembarked.[26]

On 12 June 1967 *Britannia* left Portsmouth to cross the Atlantic for The Queen and Prince Philip's visit to Canada. After the Yacht passed the Irish coast she acquired four additional passengers in the form of four racing pigeons. One of the pigeons laid an egg under the Royal Bridge and it was taken down to the Engine Room where it was kept under simulated incubator conditions until it hatched. On 28 June *Britannia* arrived in Montreal and berthed alongside the site of the Universal and

Chief Yeoman Gerry King keeps an eye on the racing pigeons which decided to hitch a lift in the Yacht across the Atlantic for The Queen and Prince Philip's visit to Canada for Expo 67.

(© British Crown Copyright / MOD)

Britannia berthed alongside in the Bickerdyke Basin for the start of Expo 67. (© British Crown Copyright / MOD)

International Exhibition – Expo 67. The exhibition was staged on the islands of Ile Sainte Heline and Ile Notre Dame in the middle of the St Lawrence River opposite Montreal. The announcement of the exhibition in 1963 triggered a major construction programme, as only half of Ile Sainte Heline existed at that time and Ile Notre Dame had yet to be created. Work began in October 1963 and over the next 10 months 15 million tons of rock and earth was brought to the site. Expo 67 also led to an improvement in Montreal's transport infrastructure with the completion of the 15½ miles of subway lines that make up the Montreal Metro. *Britannia's* arrival in Bickerdyke Basin coincided with Expo 67's India Day. To mark the occasion the Yacht flew the Indian Ensign, which had been made on board, at the main mast.[27]

Despite carrying an average of 2000 flags on board the Yacht during a typical deployment, a certain amount of 'raw bunting' was always carried to cater for either a change of national flags, or major changes to the Yacht's programme, either of which could lead to the requirement for additional flags.

During the Yacht's two and a half days in Bickerdyke Basin many of the Yachtsmen took the opportunity to visit the exhibition, including the British pavilion which was dominated by a 200-foot tower set amid lagoons and moats in recognition of Britain's island heritage. The pavilion's theme was the Challenge of Change and it was divided into five sections namely, The Shaping Of Nations, Geniles Of Britain, Britain Today, Industrial Britain and Britain In The World. On 1 July *Britannia* sailed from Bickerdyke Basin, where she had become an attraction in her own right as thousands went past the Yacht on the Metro towards the pavilions. From Montreal the Yacht sailed through the St Lawrence Seaway to Cornwall, where The Queen and Prince Philip embarked for the passage back to Montreal to visit Expo 67 on 3 July. Like The Queen's previous visit to Canada in 1964 the authorities were very concerned about the safety of The Queen so, on the day of the Royal couple's visit, the area around the Yacht was put out of bounds to visitors. The Queen and Prince Philip returned to the Yacht in the late afternoon and *Britannia* headed back through the St Lawrence Seaway and embarked guests for the dinner at St Catherine's Lock. At the same time eight members of the press also came on board. It was a significant moment because it was the first time that members of the press had been embarked in *Britannia* to cover an official event. This move was part of a concerted campaign during the late 1960s by Buckingham Palace to reveal more about how the Monarchy worked, culminating in the successful film *Royal Family*. Despite this new mood of openness the press were restricted to taking pictures of the guests being presented to The Queen and Prince Philip and then entering the Royal Dining Room before the doors were firmly closed. After dinner both the guests and the press were landed prior to the Yacht entering the first Beauharnois Lock as she continued her passage to Kingston, Ontario.[28]

As *Britannia* entered US territorial waters on 4 July she was escorted by US Coastguard vessels. The fact that it was Independence Day didn't seem to dampen the enthusiastic welcome of the Americans, who turned out in large numbers to welcome The Queen and Prince Philip as the Yacht made her way through the Thousand Islands area of the St Lawrence Seaway. The Yacht reached Kingston at 1700 and dropped anchor. Shortly afterwards the press were once more embarked in the Yacht to cover Prince Philip presenting 50 young people with The Duke of Edinburgh Gold Award on the Verandah Deck[29]. The following morning The Queen and Prince Philip disem-

The Prime Minister, Harold Wilson, is greeted by The Queen's Private Secretary, Sir Martin Charteris. The Prime Minister had been invited on board for a cocktail party hosted by The Queen during her visit to the Scilly Isles.

barked by Barge to continue their Tour ashore before flying home. An hour later *Britannia* weighed anchor to sail back down the St Lawrence Seaway to St John, New Brunswick. The final stages of the passage into St John on 10 July were made very difficult by dense fog, which restricted visibility to just 40 yards and meant that the entry into St John had to be done by radar.[30] Four hours later The Queen Mother embarked to undertake her Tour of the Canadian Maritime Provinces. At the reception held on board on the evening of 11 July the spirit of openness with the press was once more in evidence as 10 members were invited on board to photograph guests being presented to The Queen Mother. Afterwards the members of the press also had the honour of being presented to The Queen Mother and, once they had left their cameras on the quarterdeck, they were allowed to join in with the reception.[31]

Two days later The Queen Mother visited Campobello Island to open the Campobello Island Recreation Centre. Having opened the centre The Queen Mother walked across the road to the Roosevelt International Park and the cottage once owned by the former US President, Franklin Roosevelt. There, members of the late President's family were waiting to greet Her Majesty.[32] After a visit to Halifax on 14 July the Yacht arrived at Canso Lock the next morning for The Queen Mother's programme of engagements ashore which included a visit to the Antigonish Highland Games. The origins of the Games dated back to 1863 and, like their Scottish counterparts, included Highland dancing, piping competitions as well as track and field events.[33] The Tour continued with visits to Prince Edward Island and Newfoundland where the Tour concluded on 22 July when The Queen Mother left *Britannia* in St John and flew back to London. An hour after Her Majesty's departure the Yacht slipped to begin her voyage back across the Atlantic.

Two days into the voyage *Britannia* picked up an emergency medical call from the bulk carrier SS *Container Forwarder*, which was 300 miles south east of the Yacht. It became clear that the ship wasn't receiving help from any other vessel so *Britannia* made contact with the bulk carrier and it was decided that she would turn round to enable the two ships to meet more quickly. When the two ships rendezvoused at 0245 on 25 July the PMO was sent over to the *Container Forwarder* to examine the Master, Captain Francis McCowie, who had collapsed the day before at 0730. The PMO decided to transfer Captain McCowie to the Yacht and the medical staff battled all day to save his life. Sadly, their efforts were in vain as he didn't regain conscious and died that night. When the Yacht reached Cornwall on 26 July she stopped off at Penzance to embark the coroner and two police officers. Half an hour later Captain McCowie's body was taken ashore in a motor cutter but the way in which its disembarkation should be handled provoked some serious thought. No one had ever died on board a Royal Yacht before and thus there wasn't a precedent to show how the landing of the body should be handled. In the end it was decided that Captain McCowie's coffin, draped in the American National Flag, would be accorded the rare honour of being piped over the side.[34] The following morning *Britannia* arrived in Portsmouth.

On 31 July *Britannia* headed across the Solent to secure to the Britannia Buoy in Cowes Roads for the Cowes Week Regatta. Prince Philip had travelled to Cowes ahead of the Yacht in the Barge to attend a meeting of the Royal Yacht Squadron in his capacity as the Commodore. During Cowes Week Prince Philip raced *Bloodhound* and was joined by Princess Anne. Discussing her memories of

Britannia leads a group of frigates and destroyers during Naval exercises off the west coast of Scotland at the beginning of April 1968.

sailing on board *Bloodhound* Princess Anne said, 'Bloodhound* was wonderful to sail on. I would see the other yachts thrashing about putting up their spinnakers and *Bloodhound* would be creaming along in a straight line. Although she wasn't competitive it was a good learning experience.' On 4 August the Royal Family left *Britannia* for the Hamble and the Yacht returned later in the day for Portsmouth, from where she sailed three days later to Southampton. At Southampton The Queen, Prince Philip, The Prince of Wales, Prince Andrew and Princess Anne embarked for the Western Isles Cruise. However, before the Yacht headed north she sailed for the Scilly Isles for the Royal Family to undertake official engagements ashore on the morning of 8 August. In the afternoon the Royal Family went for a cruise in the Barge around the Scilly Isles, before hosting a cocktail party on board in the evening, to which the Prime Minister, Harold Wilson, who had a holiday home in the Scillies, was invited. That night *Britannia* headed north for Campleton where Prince Philip, The Prince of Wales and Princess Anne left to enjoy a cruise in *Bloodhound* in Scottish waters. Following the usual visit to the Castle of Mey on 13 August The Queen and Prince Andrew left

the Yacht on 14 August in Aberdeen and the Yacht returned to Portsmouth on 16 August.[35]

By the beginning of 1968 the country was facing a difficult time economically and the Labour Government had embarked upon a tough round of public spending cuts. In a move designed to respond to these circumstances The Queen and Prince Philip made a secret offer to the Prime Minister to give up the Yacht as a clear example of the Royal Family's commitment to the nation's economy drive. Harold Wilson declined the Royal couple's offer which was kept confidential to avoid incurring public criticism of the Government at a time when they were driving through unpopular spending cuts. While *Britannia* was reprieved, her programme was carefully reviewed to see if there were ways of finding wider employment for her when she wasn't required for Royal duty. In the 1950s Prince Philip had managed to get her written into the spring manoeuvres of the combined Home and Mediterranean Fleets. Since then Prince Philip had tried without success to persuade the Navy to use *Britannia* for subsequent exercises. However, the need to find wider employment for the Yacht led to her renewed participation in exercises with the RN. The first of these exercises saw the Yacht being used as a submarine target ship off the West Coast of Scotland in April 1968. On 23 April *Britannia* left Portsmouth for a further round of naval exercises off the French coast before returning to Portsmouth on 3 May.

The guests who had embarked for the RN's Sea Days watch a bombing demonstration by 892 Squadron's Sea Vixens.

(© British Crown Copyright / MOD)

On 8 May *Britannia* resumed her Royal duties when The Queen Mother was embarked from the Barge at Spithead for her Tour of Scotland and the Western Isles. The Queen Mother's programme of engagements included a visit to the RN's submarine base at Faslane, which she formally opened, and the island of Iona. The Tour was concluded with a visit to Scrabster Bay so that Her Majesty could go ashore to spend a few hours at the Castle of Mey, before returning to the Yacht for the voyage to Aberdeen where The Queen Mother disembarked for Balmoral on 17 May. Two days later *Britannia* was back at H Moorings in Portsmouth.[36]

On 17 June Vice Admiral Sir Conolly Abel Smith joined *Britannia* shortly before she sailed to participate in a rehearsal for Sea Days. It was the first time the Admiral had spent a day at sea in the Yacht since his retirement as FORY in 1958. When *Britannia* anchored at Spithead that afternoon Admiral Abel Smith disembarked. For the final dress rehearsal, held the next day, The Queen granted permission for the families of the Yachtsmen to be embarked. The RN's Sea Days were a good opportunity for the RN to present its equipment and capabilities to a carefully selected audience of opinion formers including politicians, teachers, and students. Each day the 'Sea Day Forces' performed a series of exercises, including bombing runs by the FAA aircraft and anti submarine drills. The Yacht's participation in the series of Sea Days was useful politically not only because it clearly demonstrated the Yacht's wider employment beyond its Royal role but because it also enabled the decision makers of the present and the future to see the Yacht in action for themselves.[37]

On 2 August Britannia sailed for Cowes Week and had to anchor in Cowes Roads because the Admiralty Buoy, normally used by the Yacht, had been removed earlier in the year as part of a Government economy drive. As usual Cowes Week was followed by the annual Western Isles Cruise. However, in a break with tradition, The Queen and other members of the Royal Family joined the Yacht on 8 August while she was still at anchor in Cowes Roads. The Queen made the journey across the Solent in a British Rail Hovercraft and then undertook some public engagements in Cowes before embarking in *Britannia*. During the voyage round to Milford Haven the BBC film crew, who were making the TV Programme *Royal Family*, shot a number of sequences on board the Yacht. After a day of engagements ashore in Milford Haven Prince Philip took the opportunity to go and see the hulk of the former HMS *Warrior* which was commissioned in 1860 as the world's first iron, seagoing, armoured warship. Together with her sister-ship HMS *Black Prince* they were the most powerful warships in the world and in a single stroke rendered the world's wooden battlefleets obsolete. Since 1928 she had been used in Milford Haven as a floating pontoon to the oil depot. She was to remain there for another decade until she was released by the MOD and towed to Hartlepool where her restoration was masterminded by Sir John Smith. On completion of the work in 1987 *Warrior* was towed to Portsmouth where she was opened to the public.[38]

That evening *Britannia* sailed out of Milford Haven and headed north for the Western Isles Cruise. For the Royal children the Western Isles Cruise was always an adventure as they were allowed to explore the Yacht under the watchful eye of their 'Sea Daddy'. In 1968 Prince Andrew was 8 years old, and looking back on his early memories of *Britannia*, he said:

'I remember doing things like dropping the anchor which was one of the many activities laid on to keep the children occupied. We each had a "Sea Daddy" to ensure that we could go just about anywhere without

Prince Philip in Coweslip, *crewed by Uffa Fox, sails past* Britannia *during Cowes Week.*

Prince Andrew takes charge of the Yacht's would-be Cable Officers during the 1968 Western Isles Cruise. From left to right: Prince Andrew, Viscount Linley, Prince Edward and Lady Sarah Armstrong-Jones.

(© British Crown Copyright / MOD)

falling over the side. My "Sea Daddy" Michael used to live in the rope locker under the quarterdeck so I became quite nifty with monkey's fists and other things to do with ropes. We were accommodated on the main deck and I remember going down to the Sick Bay to collect the largest syringes we could find and having syringe fights up and down the passage which entailed lots and lots of water and people getting squirted followed by forever cleaning up afterwards.'

The Royal children were also allowed to try their hand at a little ceremonial work, as the Commander of the Yacht, later Captain Peter Beeson LVO RN, recalls:

'One afternoon Prince Andrew, Prince Edward, Viscount Linley and Lady Sarah Armstrong-Jones were asked if they wanted to try being cable officers. The four of them were on the forecastle and being the

senior one and the only one who had travelled in the Yacht before, Prince Andrew fell them in as I had told him to. I had explained that when the Yachtsmen come to attention so should they. They fell in and Prince Andrew took it upon himself and said, "salute". They all saluted with bare hands – in other words the army salute. I saw this from the Bridge so I sent for Prince Andrew and I asked him what he thought they were doing. "Oh," he said, "its not their fault. They have only seen the guards at Buckingham Palace!"'

While the Royal children explored the Yacht, The Queen would spend some time during the Western Isles Cruise compiling her private photograph albums, as Lady Susan Hussey observed:

'The Queen's day cabin would be strewn with photographs. It was a wonderful opportunity for her to get up to date with her photograph books without interruption. No one could get at her and she didn't have to keep stopping to see people. Sometimes she would consult one of us and ask if anyone could remember who this was? Or where was this? And when?'

The Western Isles Cruise also provided The Queen with

an excellent opportunity to find out what was going on in the RN, as Lady Susan Hussey continues:

'The Queen saw the Yacht as her strong personal link with the RN. The officers were there on average for about two years. During that time she would get to know most of them in their different fields and find out where they had come from, where they were going on to, and generally keep abreast of the naval gossip, which was always fun and sometimes a great help. Some of the senior Yachtsmen had been with the Yacht since she was commissioned and The Queen of course knew them well. Often she would be entertained in the Chief Petty Officer's messes during a cruise where people would talk freely to her of naval matters and of their lives and families. Therefore, over the years she built up a huge knowledge of what was going on in the RN. When she saw senior Naval Officers at Buckingham Palace or Ministry of Defence Officials, she had a lot of background information because of this personal link she had through the Yacht.'

At the end of another very enjoyable Western Isles Cruise the Royal Family disembarked at Aberdeen on 16 August to be driven to Balmoral. Three days later *Britannia* arrived back in Portsmouth for the Yachtsmen to take their annual summer leave.[39]

After another round of naval exercises in the North Sea and the Atlantic Ocean during the second half of September, *Britannia* left Portsmouth on 14 October for

The Queen and Prince Philip's State Visit to Brazil. Four days later the Yacht arrived alongside in Funchal, Madeira to take on fuel. Unfortunately, the contractor's hose burst spraying Furnace Fuel Oil (FFO) all over the Yacht's pristine port side, as Captain Beeson recalled:

'We were due to stop for only eight hours to refuel and the local hotel very kindly said that if we wanted to use the swimming pool please do so. I was coming back down the hill after my swim to return to the Yacht when I saw the most horrid sight – a fountain of thick black fuel oil. We watched in disbelief before running back to the Yacht. I was met on the way by the Chief Bosun's Mate who had come to meet me. He said you needn't worry we don't need to say a word and everyone was out there to clean the Yacht. The oil was 4 inches thick in places over the bright white paintwork and teak decks. We emptied the island of all detergents and despite the islanders kind offers of help we sorted the problem out ourselves. Every four hours for the next 10 days we worked hard to clean the Yacht. By the time The Queen and Prince Philip embarked there was only one spot left on the caulking in the deck to give the game away – no one else noticed.'[40]

On 29 October *Britannia* arrived in Recife to await the embarkation of The Queen and Prince Philip on 1 November. It was estimated that half a million people turned out to greet the Royal couple along their route to the Yacht. An hour later *Britannia* made a floodlit depar-

The Queen together with the Royal children watch the steam past of the Royal Escort HMS Eskimo during the Western Isles Cruise.

(© British Crown Copyright / MOD)

Princess Anne and Lord Mountbatten on the Verandah Deck during the NATO Fleet Review held off Spithead to celebrate the 20th Anniversary of the formation of NATO.

(© British Crown Copyright / MOD)

ture for Rio De Janeiro. Once at sea the Yacht was stopped for the arrival of King Neptune's Chief Herald, Davey Jones, to prepare the way for the next day's Crossing-The-Line ceremony which had been postponed so that the Royal party could enjoy the event as well.[41] The awards granted by King Neptune included the Order of the Noze to The Queen's Assistant Private Secretary, Sir Martin Charteris, in recognition of his love of snuff and the Order of the Tot.to four Yachtsmen to celebrate their birthdays. On the way to Rio the Yacht paused at Salvador for a few hours on 3 November for The Queen and Prince Philip to make a short visit before resuming the passage. Two days later Richard Cawston's BBC TV film crew embarked to film the Yacht's arrival in Rio De Janeiro that morning as the Royal couple formally began their State Visit.[42] At the end of the State Visit The Queen and Prince Philip left Brazil by air on 11 November for their State Visit to Chile. *Britannia* remained behind in Rio De Janeiro to carry out the first of two Sea Days held on the 12 and 13 November. These were the first such events to be held on board and were seen as another way of usefully extending *Britannia's* employment beyond her Royal role. Each day 80 guests were embarked and taken to sea for the day where they watched a number of displays by the escorting frigate HMS *Naiad*, including weapon firing and a flying display by her Wasp helicopter. Despite the success of these pioneering events it was to be another seven years before another trade day was held on board. At the end of the second trade day *Britannia* headed north along the Brazilian coast calling at Salvador on 16 November and

Recife on 18 November where The Queen and Prince Philip spent the night on board before flying back to the UK on 19 November.[43] From Recife *Britannia* sailed for home via Tangier and Gibraltar finally arriving in Portsmouth on 6 December.[44]

Royal duty began in 1969 with The Queen Mother's visit to the West Country and the Scilly Isles before the first of the year's two Fleet Reviews. To celebrate the 20th Anniversary of the formation of NATO it was decided to hold a Fleet Review of NATO's Naval Forces and The Queen was invited to review the warships off Spithead on 16 May. Thus ships of the RN were joined by warships from the USA, Canada, Holland, Norway, Turkey, West Germany, Greece, Denmark, Italy, Belgium and Portugal. At 1140 The Queen, accompanied by Prince Philip and Princess Anne, embarked and 15 minutes later *Britannia* sailed for Spithead, where she anchored at the head of the review lines at 1220. There followed a reception for the Flag Officers and Commanding Officers from the assembled Fleet prior to a lunch for the VIPs who joined in Portsmouth, including Lord Mountbatten, Defence Secretary Denis Healey and Supreme Allied Commander Europe, General Lyman L Lemnitzer. At 1500 *Britannia* weighed anchor for The Queen to review the Fleet from the Verandah Deck. Once the Yacht had steamed through the review lines she returned to Portsmouth where the Royal Family landed. That evening many of the NATO warships entered Portsmouth Dockyard and were opened to the public over the following couple of days.[45]

On 26 June *Britannia* left her Hampshire home port for Holyhead for the investiture of Prince Charles as the 21st

Prince of Wales at Caernarvon Castle on 1 July. After the ceremony itself, The Prince of Wales embarked together with Princess Anne in *Britannia* for a dinner party as the Yacht made her way to Llanduduo for the first day of the Royal progress through Wales on 2 July. Over the next four days the Yacht was used to support the Prince's Tour, culminating in the visit to Cardiff on 5 July which marked the end of a very successful investiture programme for the Prince.[46]

At the end of July the Yacht sailed to Torquay for the presentation by Her Majesty of The Queen's Colour to the Western Fleet in Torbay. The tradition of the Monarch presenting colours to the RN dated back to 1924 when King George V gave his approval for the RN to use The King's Colour. Colours were subsequently presented to the Portsmouth, Chatham and Devonport Commands and to each of the five major Sea Commands that existed at that time. King George VI presented the Home Fleet with its most recent King's Colour in 1937. With the abolition of all overseas stations, except the Far East Fleet, in 1967 the Home Fleet became the Western Fleet and thus it was felt appropriate that the new Fleet should be presented with a Queen's Colour. To mark the event 38 ships of the Western Fleet gathered in Torbay, headed by the aircraft carrier HMS *Eagle*, which The Queen had launched in 1946.[47]

After a brief stop at Swanage, where the First Sea Lord, Admiral Sir Michael Le Fanu and the Parliamentary Under Secretary of State for Defence (Navy), Dr David Owen embarked, *Britannia* anchored in Torbay on 28 July.

Later in the morning The Queen, accompanied by Prince Philip, The Prince of Wales, Princess Anne and Lord Mountbatten, embarked prior to the Yacht steaming through the review lines and anchoring at the head of the Fleet. The Royal party then dispersed with The Prince of Wales visiting RFA *Resource*, Princess Anne going to the frigate HMS *Eastbourne* and The Queen and Prince Philip inspecting the destroyer HMS *Hampshire*. After the lunch for the Flag Officers and Commanding Officers of the assembled ships, the Royal Family spent the rest of the afternoon visiting other warships. The day's events culminated in the dinner party given by the Commander-in-Chief Western Fleet, Admiral Sir John Bush on board HMS *Eagle* followed by a concert party. While the Royal party were in *Eagle* the wind increased in Torbay, as the Commander (E) at the time, later Rear Admiral Philip Edwards CB LVO, recalls:

'Thanks to the high winds the Barge had a very choppy trip back to *Britannia*. When everyone was safely on board and the doors to the Royal Apartments were closed, the tricky task of hoisting the Barge in a heavy sea started. The worst happened and before it could be hooked on, a block went right through the canopy making a jagged hole about 18 inches in diameter. Despite this the Barge was silently hoisted and secured on its davits immediately forward of The Queen's bedroom. Following a brief meeting in my cabin it was decided that the canopy would have to be repaired overnight, in situ. It was – despite almost continuous

The Prince of Wales and Princess Anne prepare to embark in Britannia *after the investiture of His Royal Highness as the 21st Prince of Wales on 1 July 1969.*

(© British Crown Copyright / MOD)

In a break with tradition the Royal Family did not use Britannia *for either Cowes Week or the Western Isles Cruise during 1969. Instead they decided to undertake a cruise around the Norwegian Fjords in* Britannia *and meet up with the Norwegian Royal Family in their Royal Yacht* Norge. *The two Royal Yachts are seen together during this cruise.*

(© British Crown Copyright / MOD)

wind and rain – and as far as I know no one was disturbed down aft and neither were they aware that there had been a problem because the Barge was in its usual pristine condition the next morning.'[48]

The second day of the Western Fleet gathering began with the presentation of the new Queen's Colour in *Eagle's* vast hanger, followed by the award of The Queen's Sword and telescopes to graduating Naval Officers from BRNC, Dartmouth. After the Royal Family had returned to the Yacht she weighed anchor and led the Fleet to sea for the warships to steam past *Britannia*. At the end of the steam past the recently converted helicopter cruiser HMS *Blake* closed in alongside the Yacht to embark Prince Philip, The Prince of Wales and Lord Mountbatten by jackstay so that they could be flown ashore by helicopter. *Britannia* then returned to Torbay where The Queen and Princess Anne landed. Having transferred the First Sea Lord to *Eagle* the Yacht headed back to Portsmouth where she arrived on 30 July.[49]

A day after the Yacht's return she sailed for Hull where the Royal Family embarked on 4 August before she went back down the River Humber preceded by the Trinity House Vessel *Patricia*. From Hull the Yacht sailed to the Shetland Isles for the Royal Family to undertake a day of public engagements on 6 August, culminating in a reception for 200 guests on the Verandah Deck. While the Royal Family entertained their guests 80 fishing boats steamed past the Yacht. In a break with tradition the Royal Family decided not to use *Britannia* for either Cowes Week or the Western Isles Cruise. Instead they

decided to go on a cruise of the Norwegian Fjords in company with the Norwegian Royal Family who were embarked in their Royal Yacht *Norge*. Thus *Britannia* crossed the North Sea that night and met up with *Norge* the following morning. Both Royal Yachts stopped for King Olav, Crown Prince Harald and Crown Princess Sonja to transfer to *Britannia* for the final stages of the passage into Bergen. After that night's official banquet at Hakoushallen hosted by the municipality of Bergen the next five days' programme resembled a typical Western Isles Cruise as both Royal Families went fishing and sightseeing. On the morning of 12 August Prince Philip, together with The Prince of Wales and Princess Anne, left *Britannia* to join *Bloodhound* for a final family cruise before she was sold by The Queen and Prince Philip. Meanwhile, *Britannia* headed west that afternoon and set sail for Aberdeen where The Queen, together with Prince Andrew and Prince Edward, would leave for Balmoral on 14 August

Having returned to Portsmouth on 18 August, *Britannia* was taken in hand by Portsmouth Dockyard a week later for a three-month refit, which included the upgrading of the Yacht's communications equipment. Despite the need to maintain an effective level of communications between the Monarch and her Government there had been very little improvement in the standard of *Britannia's* communications equipment over the years. The planned upgrading of the equipment in the 1965 refit had to be postponed because *Britannia* was required for The Queen's State Visit to West Germany that year. By 1969 *Britannia* wasn't able to maintain effective communication at all times and thus the new equipment was urgently required before the deployment to Australia the following spring. The refit was completed on time, which enabled the Yacht to undertake three days of trials before Christmas.

On 19 January 1970 the Yacht sailed from Portsmouth to begin another long deployment to the Southern Hemisphere. Among those on board the Yacht were Dr and Mrs Harris who sailed with the Yacht to the Galapagos Islands where Dr Harris was about to begin a two-year study into the preservation of bird life for the Charles Darwin Institute.[50] As part of the preparations for the long journey ahead, 35 tons of provisions were embarked, including 50,000 cans of beer, 400 gallons of rum, 2 tons of Royal baggage, and The Queen's Rolls Royce. The voyage coincided with the bicentenary of Captain Cook's first voyage of discovery in the Pacific and *Britannia*'s deployment was timed to culminate in a re-enactment in front of The Queen of Captain Cook's first landing in Botany Bay on 29 April. *Britannia*'s voyage to the Pacific was straightforward, with refuelling stops at Madeira, Barbados and Cristobel before sailing through the Panama Canal on 8 February.[51] Three days later the Yacht arrived off Tower Island which forms part of the Galapagos Islands. Dr Mike Harris was able to repay the hospitality of his hosts by showing members of the Yacht's company some of the island's wildlife before the Yacht moved on later in the morning to Santa Cruz Island. Shortly after the Yacht dropped anchor, the Director of the Charles Darwin Research Station on the island, Dr Roger Perry, came on board to welcome the Yacht to the Galapagos. Dr and Mrs Harris then left the Yacht after nearly a month on board. Many of the Yachtsmen took the opportunity to go ashore and see the research station. As part of their tour they were able to see the recently completed Tortoise House, which was built to incubate eggs and rear young tortoises.[52] After a fascinating day in the Galapagos Islands *Britannia* resumed her voyage across the Pacific Ocean stopping at Tahiti, Bora Bora and Palmerston Island, before arriving in Lautoka on 2 March.

As part of the preparations for the forthcoming period of Royal duty, The Queen's Rolls Royce was landed for the Coxswain to familiarise himself with the route he was to drive the Royal Family when he collected them from Nandi Airport and brought them to the Yacht. About an hour after The Queen, Prince Philip and Princess Anne embarked on 4 March the Yacht sailed for the overnight passage to Suva where The Queen received the traditional invitation to land from seven Fijian Chiefs who presented Her Majesty with a *tasua*. The Royal Family then undertook a busy programme of engagements, including witnessing Trooping the Colour by the 2nd Battalion Fiji Infantry Regiment, and the presentation of a charter to the University of the South Pacific. In the evening the Yacht sailed for Tonga as the Royal Family listened to the fading music of the band ashore accompanied by a large choir singing the Fijian song of farewell 'Isa Lei'.

After a day at sea the Yacht arrived off the Tonga Islands which were discovered in 1643 by Abel Tasman. When Captain Cook called at the Tonga Islands during his second and third major Pacific voyages he found the natives to be so friendly that he gave the islands their

Some of the Yachtsmen take the opportunity to go ashore in the Yacht's boats at Tower Island of the Galapagos Islands.

other name of 'The Friendly Islands'. Nearly two hundred years on and little seemed to have changed as both the Royal Family and the Yachtsmen were made to feel most welcome by the people of Tonga. The Royal Family were met by The King of Tonga, King Taufa 'ahau Tupou IV and Queen Mata 'aho and taken for a drive through the countryside including a visit to the site of Captain Cook's landing before being entertained to a Tongan feast. Members of the Household and the Yacht's company were invited to attend the feast of roast suckling pigs, chickens, lobsters, yams and a variety of local fruit. Those whose duties precluded them from attending weren't forgotten as The King sent a lorry load of food across to the Yacht for them to enjoy. The feast was followed with an entertaining display of Tongan dancing and singing before the Royal Family returned to the Yacht for that night's dinner and reception. At the end of a busy and enjoyable day in Tonga Britannia sailed watched by vast crowds in total silence. As in Fiji the silence was a mark of total respect by the local people and the 3000 children holding burning torches along the shore cast a flickering light to make an unforgettable farewell as the Yacht disappeared into the night.[53]

The much delayed Crossing-The-Line ceremony was finally held on 10 March as Britannia steamed towards New Zealand. Despite crossing the equator some 25 days earlier it was decided to postpone the event until after the Royal Family were embarked. For Princess Anne the time had finally come for her to appear before King Neptune and receive the ritual ducking that all novices receive when they cross the equator for the first time. However, before she was submerged by the bears, the Princess was presented with a sun hat which had been made by the sail maker.[54] Early the next morning land was sighted for the first time since Tonga as the Yacht approached the North Island of New Zealand. As Britannia made her way along the coast she steamed past Young Nick's Head which was named after the 12-year-old boy on board Captain Cook's Endeavour. The honour was part of Captain Cook's reward for the first man to sight land as they headed south across the Pacific Ocean in search of Alexander Dalrymple's great southern continent in 1769. In beautiful weather the Yacht entered the land-locked bay that forms the natural harbour of Wellington and berthed alongside the Overseas Passenger Terminal. The Yacht's early arrival meant that there was more time to land The Queen's Rolls Royce, which had to be steam cleaned underneath to comply with New Zealand's strict precautions against foot-and-mouth disease. The Royal Family landed for the formal welcome ceremony and lived ashore at Government House for the rest of their visit to Wellington. The Prince of Wales joined his parents at Government House that evening, having flown into Wellington from London.[55] The three-day visit to Wellington was significant because The Queen conducted the first of her informal 'Walkabouts' which became a popular part not only of the rest of this Tour but also of subsequent visits. Suddenly, a much greater number of ordinary people had the opportunity to meet The Queen and it helped to make the Monarchy seem less remote.

By the time The Queen and Prince Philip returned to the Yacht on 14 March The Prince of Wales and Princess Anne had left Wellington for a private weekend inland. Despite the strengthening winds the Yacht sailed as planned for Picton on 15 March. As the Yacht was passing through the heavy seas in the harbour entrance and the Barrett Reef the Yacht was hit by an exceptionally large wave which swamped the forecastle and trapped the First Lieutenant, Lieutenant Commander D J Bird in the eyes of the ship, as Admiral Edwards recalls:

'The anchor party had been caught unawares and although all the rest of the anchor party managed to escape, they were severely battered and bruised including one or two cracked ribs. The First Lieutenant desperately hung on to the Jack Staff and his life was certainly at risk, but no one seemed to panic. Prince Philip came up to the Royal Bridge where he was joined by FORY who explained the situation to him. I was called from the Engine Room and told about the problem, which was a build-up of water up to the height of the gunwales on the forecastle. The weight of the trapped water was making the Yacht unstable and it had to be dealt with quickly. I agreed to go down and have a look. When I got there I joined a Petty Officer

and two seamen trying to open the door to the forecastle from the starboard waist in order to release some of the water. Opening the door was extremely difficult as it opened on to the forecastle – against the weight of the water. Eventually we managed to get the door open and I was propelled some 30 yards towards the stern until I managed to grab a handrail. The rapid release of water did the trick and I returned to the Engine Room, drenched and bruised but otherwise unharmed and greatly relieved.'

The New Zealand escort HMNZS *Waikato* wasn't so lucky. As *Britannia* was being hit by the large wave three men were still working on *Waikato*'s forecastle and seconds later they were swept overboard when the same wave hit them. The weather conditions prevented either ship from turning so *Waikato* had to wait until she had passed through the narrows before her Wasp helicopter could be launched in very marginal operational conditions to recover the three men. The Wasp flown by Lieutenant Commander Burbury and supported by his crewman Sergeant Nicholson managed to safely recover Lieutenant Commander J Mair and Petty Officer Morley. Sadly, the third man Chief Shipwright Lindsay died before the Harbour Pilot Launch *Tiakina* could bring him back into Wellington.

Waikato turned back for Wellington while *Britannia* continued her voyage alone across the Cook Straits for Picton where the Royal couple watched an air display by

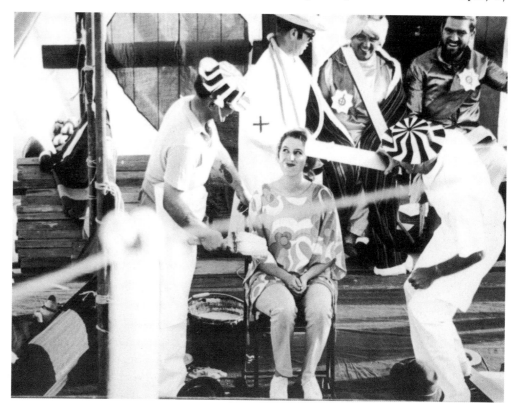

Even members of the Royal Family have to pay homage to King Neptune when they cross the Equator for the first time as Princess Anne is about to find out.

the RNZAF's aerobatics team the Red Chequers. At the end of the display the Royal Family returned to the Yacht and she moved round to Ship Cove where Captain Cook had refitted HMS *Endeavour* in January 1770. In view of the relative lack of shelter provided by Ship Cove The Queen and Prince Philip were embarked in the motor cutter at deck level and then lowered into the water for the trip ashore to watch the first of many re-enactments of landings by Captain Cook. Unfortunately, this first re-enactment was made very difficult by the gusty wind conditions. Once the Royal couple had returned, the Yacht weighed anchor and headed back through the Cook Straits for Lyttleton[56] where she arrived on 16 March. Among the guests invited to dinner was Captain Upham who was the only man alive to hold two Victoria Crosses. After the Yacht's visits to Lyttleton, Timaru and Dunedin, *Britannia* picked up the Cook trail again passing Cape Kidnappers, where the Maoris had attempted to abduct one of *Endeavour*'s Tahitian servant boys, before calling at Napier and Gisborne. The city of Gisborne stands on the

The Queen's Equerry, Lieutenant Commander Jock Slater, and The Prince of Wales perform an act in the ship's concert held on 28 March 1970.

(© British Crown Copyright / MOD)

site where Captain Cook first landed in New Zealand on 8 October 1769. Captain Cook was met with a hostile response from the Maoris and he soon returned to *Endeavour*, awarding the name Poverty Bay to the place because he hadn't managed to obtain anything he needed.[57] From Gisborne the Yacht sailed to Tauranga for a short visit on the morning of 23 March before weighing anchor for Mercury Bay at lunchtime. During the short passage the Yacht passed the rocky cluster that forms the Alderman Islands which had recently been presented to the Crown by Mrs Winiata. By late afternoon the Yacht had anchored in Mercury Bay where Captain Cook had set up a shore station to observe the transit of the planet Mercury on 9 November 1769. Not surprisingly, Captain Cook's landing there was re-enacted in front of the Royal Family before *Britannia* sailed that night for Auckland.

The next morning *Britannia* was given a tremendous welcome by an armada of small craft which needed 113 control boats just to manage them![58] The combination of the Yacht being escorted by lots of small boats and the dramatic setting of Auckland combined to turn the Royal Family's arrival into a major event which made a lasting impression on the local people. As Princess Anne explains, the use of *Britannia* for this type of tour made a very different impact on the people visited.

'Tours with *Britannia* were always much more personal because it was seen as Her Majesty's Yacht *Britannia*. Whether one thinks that Yacht is the wrong terminology doesn't matter. It's because Her Majesty lived there and used it herself that it had that special quality. As a result, there was a very special atmosphere on board which couldn't be described. A lot of people were surprised by the fact that she was nothing like as luxurious as the media made her out to be compared to some of the world's private super yachts. So much of the quality on board the Yacht was about the manpower and the way it was run. I have no doubt that because the Yachtsmen regarded it as a special privilege to serve on board that it ran in a way that nothing else does. From a personal point of view, if one is on a long trip being able to keep all one's kit in the same place and go back to a known bed fairly often is a huge advantage. To know that the quality of the entertainment and hospitality is guaranteed is again a huge advantage. There is nothing after that that would work as well. People felt that they were sharing someone's home rather than going to an official event and that was different too. It was possible to do all sorts of things on board and it would always be improved upon. In short it is difficult to evaluate and explain but it is impossible to replace.'

After three days in Auckland the Yacht sailed on the night of 26 March for the Bay of Islands so that the Royal Family could enjoy a couple of days of relaxation after their busy round of public engagements. At the end of the second day the Yachtsmen put on a ship's concert for the Royal Family on the forecastle which included two acts featuring The Prince of Wales, supported by The Queen's Equerry, Lieutenant Commander Jock Slater. Following the concert, *Britannia* weighed anchor for Waitangi, where she arrived the next morning. The Royal Family landed and attended a church service in the grounds of Waitangi Treaty House to celebrate Easter Sunday. After the service The Queen presented the people of New Zealand with the Portrait of Queen Victoria which had been brought from the UK in *Britannia*. While The Queen and Prince Philip embarked in *Britannia* for the short passage to Maturva Island, both The Prince of Wales and Princess Anne decided to join HMNZS *Waikato* and were seen standing on the wings of the frigate's bridge when she steamed past the Yacht just after midday. The Royal Squadron anchored off Maturva Island at lunchtime to enable the Royal Family to spend the afternoon ashore before heading off to Auckland from where they disembarked the next morning to fly to Australia. Within an hour of the Royal Family's departure, *Britannia* sailed from Auckland for Hobart, where she arrived on 3 April.[59]

Having embarked the Royal Family that afternoon the Yacht was given a tremendous aquatic send off by many yachtsmen as she headed north for the following day's visit to Inspection Head, Tasmania. When the Yacht arrived at Inspection Head there were so many people lining the wharf where she was due to berth that it was difficult to get a line ashore without injuring spectators. FORY subsequently discovered that it was the first time since the War that a ship of *Britannia*'s size had berthed there because the river wasn't considered capable of handling such ships! Despite this news the visit went without a hitch and the Yacht was able to sail that afternoon for Melbourne where she arrived on 5 April. During the second day of the stop at Melbourne the Royal Family went for a walk among the crowds outside the Melbourne Town Hall. This was the first time that this had been done in Australia and, like the similar events in New Zealand, it was very well received by the Australians. The Prince of Wales had to leave the Royal party on 8 April to fly back to the UK via Expo 70 in Japan to sit his university exams. That night the Yacht sailed back down the Yarra River to visit Port Kembla, Newcastle, Coff's Harbour and Brisbane where the Yacht enjoyed another spectacular entry on 12 April. An estimated 250,000 people lined the banks to greet The Queen while the Yacht was surrounded by countless small craft. The size of the welcome was helped by the fact it had been arranged for a Sunday so more sailors were able to join in. On the second day of the visit to Brisbane The Queen held an investiture for 50 people in the Royal Drawing Room. It was the first time that an investiture of this size had been held on board. Among those honoured was Warrant Officer K Payne who received the Victoria Cross for services in Vietnam, as The Queen's Equerry at the time, later Admiral Sir Jock Slater GCB LVO DL, recalls:

'Just before the investiture was due to begin, Warrant Officer Payne could not be found. I dashed around looking for him and eventually found him on the quarterdeck smoking a cigarette. I enquired if he was all right and he looked at me rather apprehensively and said, "Sir, I have never been so nervous in all my life."'

In another break with tradition the crowds were permitted on to the jetty alongside the Yacht to watch the arrival and departure of the Royal Family.[60]

From Brisbane the Yacht sailed to Scawfell Island where

Princess Anne, followed by The Prince of Wales, disembarks for an evening function in Melbourne.

(© British Crown Copyright / MOD)

the Royal Family rejoined *Britannia* having visited Mount Isa and Mackay. *Britannia* should have put into Mackay but the weather was too rough for her to enter the narrow harbour entrance, so the Australian Escort HMAS *Stuart* was instructed by FORY to embark the Royal Family at Mackay and bring them to Scawfell Island where they transferred back to the Yacht on 16 April.[61] The next three days were set aside for the Royal Family to enjoy a little relaxation before resuming their programme on 20 April with a day-long visit to Townsville, where the Australian Prime Minister and Mrs Gort joined to spend two days on board. The next day was a very special occasion because it was the first time that The Queen had spent her Birthday on board *Britannia*. To celebrate the event the Yachtsmen presented Her Majesty with a cool box, which would come in very handy for those barbecues that the Royal Family so enjoyed whenever they were in *Britannia*. In the morning the Yacht anchored off Green Island in the Barrier Reef. The Royal Family walked round the observatory which had been built at the end of the pier some 18 feet below the sea with windows looking out on to the Barrier Reef. At 1200 the Yacht weighed anchor for Snapper Island. In accordance with Royal Yacht tradition The Queen's health was drunk by the Wardroom on the day of her Birthday in champagne just after midday. As The Queen was embarked at this time the Royal Family joined the Wardroom for the occasion. After lunch *Britannia* arrived off Snapper Island and the Royal Family spent the afternoon ashore. In the evening the Royal Family attended a barbecue together with Mr and Mrs Gort which was cooked by members of the Wardroom. That night The Queen invested FORY with the KCVO, thus making him the first person to be knighted by The Queen on her Birthday.[62]

The following day The Queen's official duties resumed with the visit to Cookstown where the Prime Minister left the Royal party to return to Canberra. On 23 April the Yacht berthed in Cairns where the Royal Family disembarked to fly to Canberra. From Cairns the Yacht sailed the next day for Sydney where she arrived on 28 April and the Royal Family re-embarked ahead of the next day's major festivities. Finally, the focal point of the Tour had arrived with the bicentenary of Captain Cook's first landing in Botany Bay on 29 April. After engagements ashore in the morning the Yacht sailed for the passage to Botany Bay surrounded by a huge fleet of small boats to create the most striking images of the Tour. When the Yacht arrived in Botany Bay she had to ease her way through the waiting boats to her anchor berth. The Royal Family landed in the Barge to watch the re-enactment of Captain Cook's landing. While the crew of the 'official' Captain Cook were busily rowing him ashore from *Endeavour II*, a student dressed as Captain Cook arrived on the beach in a sports boat and then ran ashore to plant a Union Flag in the sand before he was arrested by the Police and taken away. At the end of the ceremony the Royal Family left Botany Bay by car to fulfil further engagements. Meanwhile, the Yacht sailed back to Sydney where the Royal Family re-embarked in the evening to watch the carnival of decorated boats, followed by a spectacular fireworks display.[63] After a further three days of engagements in the area it was time for the Royal Family to conclude their Tour and fly back to the UK on 3 May. Two days later *Britannia* began her own long voyage home via Pago Pago, Balboa, the Panama Canal and Bermuda, before finally reaching Portsmouth on 15 June 1970.

At the end of July *Britannia* sailed to Plymouth for Prince Philip to start the Tall Ships Race on 29 July. The Yacht returned to Portsmouth early on 30 July so that the Yachtsmen could mark the last day of the rum issue in true style on 31 July.[64] Over the years the daily issue of rum on board HM ships had evolved to the point where it had almost become a religious service. However, the continued daily issue of rum to sailors was seen as incompatible with the modern age where increasingly sophisticated equipment required clear headed sailors as operators. Despite the practical arguments in favour of the abolition of the Rum Tot it was still seen by many older sailors as just another sign of the 'old' Navy passing into the history books.

On 2 August Princess Anne joined the Yacht shortly before she sailed from Portsmouth for Cowes Week. In the absence of any other members of the Royal Family, Princess Anne's personal Standard was flown from the main mast for the first time. However, in the evening it was replaced by Prince Philip's Court Flags when he embarked. Following the sale of *Bloodhound* in 1969, Sir Owen Aisher kindly lent Prince Philip a succession of yachts to race in Class 1 at Cowes Week, beginning with *Yeoman XVI* in 1970. At the end of Cowes Week the Yacht returned to Portsmouth on 7 August following the Royal Family's departure earlier in the day. Three days later the Yacht sailed to Southampton to embark members of the Royal Family for the Western Isles Cruise. Having landed the Royal Family at Aberdeen at the end of the cruise, *Britannia* returned to Portsmouth for the last time under the command of Rear Admiral Sir Patrick Morgan on 20 August.[65]

Chapter Seven

THE LONGEST TOW

Rear Admiral Sir Richard Trowbridge
KCVO 1970–1975

As the fifth man to occupy the position of FORY, Rear Admiral Richard Trowbridge had enjoyed a remarkable naval career, which began in 1935 when he joined the RN as a Boy Seaman. Five years later he was commissioned as a Sub Lieutenant. During the later stages of the War he was appointed as the First Lieutenant of HMS *Wager* which was serving in the 27th Destroyer Flotilla alongside HMS *Whelp* in which Prince Philip was serving as First Lieutenant. By 1956 he had become the Commanding Officer of the destroyer HMS *Carysfort*. From there he went to the cruiser HMS *Bermuda* as the executive officer in 1958, followed two years later by the same position in the RN's Gunnery School at Whale Island, HMS *Excellent*. As a Captain, he commanded the Fishery Protection Squadron between 1962 and 1964, before subsequently becoming the Captain of the *County* class destroyer HMS *Hampshire* in 1967. In 1970 he was promoted to the rank of Rear Admiral, prior to taking up the appointment of FORY on 1 September 1970. When he became FORY Admiral Trowbridge was horrified to find that, with the exception of the NATO exercise Northern Wedding later in the month, there was nothing in *Britannia*'s forthcoming programme until the following July when she was due to attend Cowes Week. Admiral Trowbridge was very conscious that the sight of an inactive Royal Yacht lying in Portsmouth for months on end would provide *Britannia*'s critics with plenty of ammunition to call for her decommissioning. With the support of Prince Philip he started working on a proposal to deploy

the Yacht to the Pacific and Canada in the first half of 1971. The idea was for the Yacht to sail to Panama, where Prince Philip would embark, and take him across the Pacific to New Guinea, where he would leave the Yacht to fly home. The Yacht would then sail back across the Pacific to arrive in Vancouver in May for The Queen's visit to Canada, before returning to the UK via the Panama Canal.

Admiral Trowbridge's ideas came to fruition and on 15 January 1971 *Britannia* left Portsmouth at the start of a major six-month deployment, beginning with a passage across the Atlantic Ocean, stopping at Madeira and Barbados to take on fuel, before sailing through the Panama Canal and berthing in Balboa on 2 February. Over the next three days Prince Philip's party joined in three groups, with Princess Alexandra, Lord Mountbatten, together with Lord and Lady Brabourne (later Countess Mountbatten CBE CD JP DL), arriving on 3 February, Prince Philip and Sir Solly Zuckerman embarking on 4 February, and the Hon. Angus Ogilvy on 5 February shortly before the Yacht left Balboa to begin the passage to the Galapagos Islands.[1] To give the Royal party a foretaste of what they were to see on the islands, they sat down after dinner to watch the Galapagos films made for Anglia TV by Aubrey Buxton, who had accompanied Prince Philip to the Galapagos in 1964.

Two days later the Yacht entered Tower Island's Darwin Bay and, as the anchor was about to be dropped, a 12-foot-long shark swam slowly past the Yacht to provide everyone with their first glimpse of the local wildlife. Shortly afterwards the Director of the Darwin Institute, Dr Kramer, accompanied by Dr Mike Harris and Juan Black, came on board to greet His Royal Highness. Dr Harris knew the Yacht well, having taken passage in her the year before from the UK to begin his two-year study of the island's bird life. The Royal party spent most of the day ashore exploring the island and observing the fascinating variety of wildlife, which included frigate birds, red-footed boobies, masked boobies, land iguanas, marine iguanas and sea lions. Remarkably, the animals took very little notice of their visitors and only reluctantly moved out of their way when necessary.[2] After an interesting day ashore the Yacht weighed anchor for Albemarle Island, where she arrived on 8 February.

Once again the Royal party spent the day ashore, including a visit to Tortuga Bay in the afternoon where there was a beach of black lava. The bay's accumulation of driftwood proved very useful for that night's barbecue organised by the Royal party, to which the Wardroom were invited. Even in the moonlight there was much to see, with sea lions on the beach, and Galapagos penguins among the rocks.[3] The next morning the Yacht sailed across to Fernandina, during which time a large school of dolphins was seen, as were several sei whales. A large volcano still dominated Fernandina despite dropping 200 feet when it last erupted in 1968![4] After a further day of exploration the Royal party landed at Villamil on 10 February, while the Yacht went off to rendezvous with the tanker RFA *Blue Rover*. In addition to transferring fuel, *Blue Rover* sent across several bags of mail that had failed to reach Balboa in time for the Yacht's visit because of the postal workers strike in the UK. On completion of the RAS, *Britannia* returned to collect the Royal party and take them to Charles Island for the afternoon, before sailing to Indefatigable Island's Academy Bay where the Yacht spent the night at anchor.[5]

The visit to Academy Bay on 11 February began with the Royal party landing to visit the Charles Darwin Research Institute. The call coincided with a very special day for the Institute, which was celebrating the hatching of six tortoise eggs the day before in their recently completed Tortoise House. Each of the Galapagos Islands once had a subspecies of giant tortoise. The hood tortoise was on the verge of extinction with only two adults left, which were brought to the Institute in the hope that they would breed and provide the foundations for the survival of their species. The successful hatching of these eggs clearly demonstrated the importance of the Institute's work. At the subsequent lunch, held at the Galapagos Hotel, His Royal Highness presented the Institute with a number of gifts, including four sets of Comeal radio stations for communication between the islands. The day was rounded off by a dinner on board the Yacht for local and Ecuadorian people who were thrilled to be attending such an event in the Galapagos Islands.[6]

Having disembarked Sir Solly Zuckerman and the Hon. Angus Ogilvy at Isla Baltra to fly back to the UK, the Yacht sailed on to Hood Island for the last day of the Galapagos visit. As Lord Brabourne remarked, the sea lions were quite inquisitive:

'We were sitting on some rocks and this pool was full of sea lions which were very tame. I was sitting there filming Prince Philip with them and when I finished I put the cine camera down on the rock but kept hold of the strap. As I was picking up the other camera this large sea lion grabbed the strap of the cine camera and swam off with it. I managed to recover the camera but sadly both the camera and the film were a write off. When I returned to the UK I put in a claim to the insurance company for the lost camera and film. They came back to me and said, "we were most interested to hear about this sea lion taking your camera do you have any witnesses?" So I wrote back and explained that I had a number of very distinguished witnesses!'

Just before midnight the Yacht weighed anchor for the six-day cruise across the Pacific to Easter Island.[7]

After a day at sea Admiral Trowbridge decided it was time to break out the box of books he had been sent by the Admiralty Librarian as background information for the Royal party to prepare for their visit to Easter Island. Among the interesting, yet limited, collection of books there was a surprise, as Admiral Trowbridge recalls: 'the four copies of Robin Borwick's *People With Long Ears* was all about keeping donkeys rather than a history of the people of Easter Island as I had expected!' Later on, the Commander (E) was summoned to see Prince Philip, as Admiral Edwards explained:

'I found His Royal Highness sitting on a deck chair on the Royal Deck, facing aft. He beckoned me to sit in the chair alongside his. After some pleasantries he asked if I could see anything unusual about the wake. At first I could not see anything abnormal and said so. He asked me to look again and this time I commented that there was slightly more turbulence on the portside. He suggested that there might be something amiss with the stabilisers and of course he was right. I phoned the Engine Room and on being told that nothing untoward had been reported, I asked the Engineer Officer of the Watch to meet me in the stabiliser room where we

quickly noticed that the movements of the port stabiliser were somewhat exaggerated in comparison to
those of the starboard stabiliser. FORY agreed to stop
the Yacht whilst we sent down a diver to inspect the
two stabilisers. The diver found that the aileron on the
port stabiliser could be moved by hand and would obviously flap up and down uncontrollably in a seaway. A
bolt had dropped out of the operating link-arm joint.
Having diagnosed the problem we continued with our
voyage to Easter Island where the resourceful diver
effected an excellent temporary repair with the aid of
the Yacht's underwater welding equipment.'[8]

Back in the UK, 15 February saw the introduction of dec-
imal coinage and the disappearance of old pennies and
shillings. For the Yachtsmen Decimilisation Day had little
impact because the Yacht had moved on to the new system soon after she left the UK, so that the amount of old
coinage that had to be stored on board could be reduced.
Therefore, the main event of the day didn't occur until
the evening, when the RM Band finished their concert on
the forecastle. Shortly after the musicians stopped playing, the Yacht came to a halt and King Neptune's Herald
'mysteriously' appeared over the bows. He then read the
usual proclamation ahead of the following day's Crossing-
The-Line ceremony, which had been postponed by eight
days because of the visit to the Galapagos Islands.[9] Thus,
on 16 February the festivities got underway in earnest.
The first of the Royal party to be summoned by King
Neptune was Lord Mountbatten who listened to the
Herald read out,

'Some years ago our scouts would greet
Line upon line the Battle Fleet
That kept *Britannia's* homeland free:
The grey ships on the cold grey sea.
We do recall that in that time
A young Mountbatten crossed the line
And what is more we have heard tell,
Since then he has done rather well.
For many honours he has had
And just one more we would like to add
In honour of his deeds at sea
The "Old Sea Dog" or OSD'

Lord Mountbatten was then presented with a brightly
coloured toy dog on blue ribbon which failed to resemble
any known species. Princess Alexandra was the next to be
summoned and addressed by a Herald who said,

'Your Royal Highness, so they say
Was born upon a Christmas Day.
So we have set our chefs to make

A Birthday-Christmas-Pudding cake.'

However, just when the Princess thought she had escaped
a ducking the Herald continued,

'But wait! We have more things in store.
We hear you have crossed the line before,
Not openly across the Main
But out of reach by aeroplane.
You hope to pass us unawares
But now Ma'am you must meet the Bears.'

And so the Princess was lathered in the barber's chair
before being tipped into the tank and dunked by the
bears. The Brabournes experienced a similar fate after the
Herald told them,

'You are jointly charged with attempting to disturb
The balance of Nature,
Thereby invoking conservancy law Number 1
In that you did connive to feed dead fish,
Namely Herrings, in, out or somewhere,
To the seals of Hood Island
Thus threatening the well-being of King Neptune's
illustrious subjects.'

Prince Philip's Private Secretary, Lieutenant Commander
Willet was another victim who was dunked because 'he
did forsake his position as Sailing Master to take up the
despicable craft of quill driving without first appearing at
Neptune's Requestmen.' This highly memorable ceremony was concluded by the ducking of the novices among
the Yacht's company who had not crossed the line
before.[10]

With Easter Island less than a day's steaming away
Admiral Trowbridge decided to quiz the Royal party about
the last time the White Ensign had been seen in those
waters, as he recalled:

'Some days before I had sent a signal to the Admiralty
asking them the question. I got a signal back saying,
"No records of visits by HM ships in recent decades.
Records from 1919 to 1939 incomplete. Last visits that
can be traced were by Her Majesty's ships *Canbrian* and
Flora in 1906 and 1909." So I floated the question at
breakfast that led to a heated discussion which went on
for about an hour and a half with everybody giving eru-
dite reasons for why their guess might be right. I ended
up reading out my signal and I awarded a Mars bar to
the winner – sadly I can't remember who that was. I do
remember that the difference between Lord
Mountbatten's answer and Prince Philip's was about 35
years. Everyone present was astonished that an HM
ship had not been to Easter Island for over 60 years.'

Finally, after 1962 miles and six days steaming across the Pacific Ocean, the volcanic Easter Island was unveiled by the first rays of light on the morning of 18 February. As the Yacht approached, those looking through their binoculars spotted some of the 5000 feral horses and seven upright stone figures which had only been re-erected by archaeologists within the previous couple of years. On landing each member of the Royal party was presented with a garland made of string and shells before they were taken on a tour of the sights in four military trucks. As part of the tour the Royal party was given a lesson on the history of the island by the Chilean archaeologist Edmundo Edwards whose grandfather and great grandfather had been Ambassadors to London. Having seen the crater of Rano Raraku, which still contained about 100 unfinished stone figures, and the great ditch, as well as the burial platforms, the Royal party were entertained to a Polynesian style lunch at the Captain of the Port's house. The food was wrapped in banana leaves and placed in a hole in the ground on stones, which were heated by the fire below. The hole was then covered by earth and two hours later the food was dug up, by which time it was thoroughly cooked. Princess Alexandra accepted the invitation to join in with the dancing after lunch, although Prince Philip declined a similar invitation on the grounds he was suffering from archaeologists feet!

The tour concluded in the afternoon with a visit to the crater of Rano Kao which was the site of the religious rites of the island's last cult, the birdmen. As the rest of the Royal party re-embarked in the Yacht, Princess Alexandra remained on the island to catch a flight back to the UK so

that she would be present for the Rugby League Cup Final at Wembley.[11] From Easter Island, the Yacht headed west towards Pitcairn Island. The remote island was uninhabited until the eighteenth century when it became a safe haven for Fletcher Christian and his band of mutineers from HMS *Bounty*. They had seized the ship on 28 April 1789 while she was sailing near the island of Tofua of the Tonga group of islands. Having cast the Commanding Officer, William Bligh, and 18 other men adrift in one of the ship's boats the mutineers set sail for Tahiti where some of them decided to stay. The remaining mutineers were joined by several Tahitians for the voyage to Pitcairn Island. Soon after their arrival the mutineers ran *Bounty* aground and set fire to her to avoid being detected by any passing RN warships. Despite the odds Bligh and his men managed to make an epic voyage of 3600 miles in the open boat to reach the safety of Timor. When Bligh returned to Great Britain and informed the Admiralty of the mutiny they dispatched HMS *Pandora* to Tahiti to bring the mutineers back to stand trial. Of the 10 who were brought back 3 were hung for their part in the mutiny. As for those who chose the relative safety of Pitcairn Island they were faced with the daunting prospect of creating a sustainable community on an island just 2 miles long by 1 mile wide which rises to over 1000 feet. However, 182 years later the island was supporting a community of 92 people most of whom were direct descendants of the original mutineers.

The voyage to Pitcairn Island provided an excellent opportunity for the Yacht to perform some important survey work for the Hydrographic Office. By the early 1970s

Britannia had become a useful source of information for the Hydrographic Office because she was calling on so many remote places which other RN ships never had the chance to visit. In many cases the Yacht was able to supply information on areas which had last been surveyed by Captain Cook. Interestingly, when *Britannia*'s 'survey team' updated Cook's charts they found his work to be remarkably accurate. To enable *Britannia* to perform this role she was fitted with a deep water depth sounder and 1,000,000:1 plotting sheets. Describing some of the survey work completed by the Yacht during her voyage across the Pacific Ocean, Dick Field (later Mr R Field RVM), who was a Chief Electrical Artificer at the time said:

'Any time that we were outside the 100-fathom mark we plotted soundings every 15 minutes. During our voyage across the Pacific we ran with the shallow echo sounder on standby because in the Pacific there are a number of unexpected steep peaks that rise up because of the volcanic activity. On one occasion we charted a peak from a sea bed depth of 2000 fathoms to the summit at 600 fathoms. The deepest area I surveyed in *Britannia* was the Tonga trench. We were running along with an average depth of 2000 fathoms when suddenly I had a call, "Chief we've lost the echo!" I thought to myself, that's strange, so I started from scratch and then I found it was sounding a depth of 5800 fathoms which is deeper than the height of Mount Everest. I realised where we were and we kept going and an hour later the depth had dropped to just 43 fathoms as we came up the Tonga Plateau.'

Shortly after the Yacht anchored off Pitcairn Island on 21 February, two white motor launches, each flying a large Union Flag, set off from the small harbour in Bounty Bay carrying 50 islanders between them to take tea on board and listen to a concert by the RM Band.[12]

The following day Prince Philip, Lord Mountbatten and FORY went ashore dressed in White Naval Uniform for the formal welcome ceremony, but first they had to negotiate the tricky landing conditions, as the Commander of the Yacht, later Captain L A Bird LVO RN, explains:

'Getting ashore at Pitcairn is very difficult because of the long surf, but the locals are experts. We brought the Yacht's motor boats within about 200 yards offshore and transferred those going ashore to their long boats and they got us through the surf which we couldn't have done without them.'

Once ashore the Royal party were led to a pair of minimokes to take them 300 feet above the landing place to the village. Not surprisingly, Pitcairn's roads consisted of red, dusty, dirt tracks and in the open-topped cars the three Admirals' impeccable White Naval Uniforms soon showed the effects of the short journey. However, despite the initial progress they came to an abrupt halt when the wheels started to spin so everyone had to get out and push. Once the party reached the village they were met by 68 of the 83 islanders. After lunch the Royal party were taken for a tour of the island which included a visit to Thursday October Christian's house which is reputed to be the oldest house on the island and was once occupied by Fletcher Christian's son. Meanwhile, the RM Band, which was the first to perform on the island since 1937, gave a concert for the islanders, as the Director of Music, later Lieutenant Colonel J R Mason OBE MVO LRAM ARCM LGSM RM, recalled:

'I explained to the Island's Secretary, Ben Christian that I wanted to do a Beat Retreat but the only problem was that I needed a flat space to do it on. He told

When Fletcher Christian and his fellow mutineers from *HMS Bounty* came across Pitcairn Island the biggest attraction was the difficulty other boats would have in landing on the island. Two centuries later little had changed and the visitors to the island from the Yacht had to negotiate the tricky landing conditions before stepping ashore at the landing site.

Prince Philip, Lord Mountbatten, Lord and Lady Brabourne watch a Polynesian greeting ceremony in Raratonga.

(© British Crown Copyright / MOD)

me that I should use their village square. I asked him where it was and he told me that I was standing in it. It was exactly 7 yards by 3 yards which was tight for 26 of us marching up and down but we had to do it.'

Before leaving the island Prince Philip was presented with a wooden shark carved from mirowood. On accepting this gift he told them that the only thing the Pitcairn islanders had in common with sharks was their appetite, which they found amusing.

With the islanders farewell songs of 'Cling to the Bible My Boy' and 'The Sinking of the Vestris' still ringing in her passengers' ears, *Britannia* weighed anchor to begin the five-day voyage to the Cook Islands. During the long days steaming across the vast Pacific Ocean between visits the Royal party were able to unwind a little, as Countess Mountbatten explains: 'we did a lot of reading and there was a small collapsible swimming pool which as it got hotter it was nice to be able to sit in it.' The Yachtsmen also found various ways of keeping amused, such as the four-day knockout tug-of-war contest. Another popular activity was the crazy sports meeting held on 26 February.[13] The meeting included three relatively athletic three-minute events, which were performed in rotation by six-man teams from each mess. These 'sports' included darts, an obstacle course, and eating three buns washed down by a can of beer, which was completed in a record time of one minute thirty five seconds by one contestant! There was also the quick dressing competition in which each team had to find enough

clothes from the canvas bag to produce one commander, one marine, one stoker, one frogman, one fire fighter and one girl. Equally, the race to extract potatoes from the bottom of a water tank and then bouncing round a course on space hoppers provided the rest of the Yachtsmen with plenty of laughter. On a less physical note an inter-mess quiz was held every day in the early evening while at sea.

On the morning of 27 February the Yacht reached her next destination as she anchored off Raratonga for Prince Philip's one-day visit. Following the formal welcome, the Royal party went to the island's museum, which included a large cooking pot. Although the pot was in fact once used for boiling down whale blubber rather than cooking missionaries, Lord Mountbatten still couldn't resist the temptation of having his photograph taken in it! Chieftains came from across the Cook Islands to Raratonga to attend the various Polynesian greeting ceremonies held around the island throughout the day. The only exception was the islanders from Palmerston Island who sent a message of greeting and said their gift would be sent by post to London! However, as the Yacht was going to pass Palmerston Island on its way to Samoa it was decided to send a message to Ned Marsters to propose a visit. The suggestion was enthusiastically accepted so the following afternoon *Britannia* anchored off the Island for the Royal party to go ashore. Although the Yacht had visited the island a number of times, it was the first occasion that Ned Marsters had had the honour of receiving members of the Royal Family because the previous visits were made between periods of Royal duty. The Royal party were taken ashore in three boats provided by the islanders which were decorated with bright cushions and flowers. Following the brief formalities of welcome many of the islanders left to visit the Yacht, leaving their guests to explore the island, where they came across a surprise, as Countess Mountbatten explains:

'We were very taken aback because we were due to go ashore at 1500 so we thought that we would eat lunch on board and only be offered tea ashore. When we got ashore a table had been laid along the village street. This table was laden with food including their version of Cornish pasties. We had to do our best to eat this banquet on top of our lunch!'

The Cornish pasties were made to the same recipe that William Marsters had taught his wives when he first came to Palmerston Island based on his memories of the pasties cooked by his mother. Laden with gifts from the Yachtsmen, including sweets, tinned and fresh meat, the islanders returned ashore at the end of another brief yet enjoyable visit as the Yacht weighed anchor for Samoa.[14]

The following night the Royal party gathered on the forecastle for an entertaining ship's concert. One of the musical acts was an unusual performance of the 'Post Horn Gallop', as Prince Philip recalls:

'The Marine Bandsman appeared as a plumber with tools and a urinal in his bag. He took it out and fitted a piece of flexible hose to the outlet end and then put a bugle mouthpiece in the other end of the hose. No one was quite certain what he was doing at the time. He then proceeded to play the "Post Horn Gallop" on this curious instrument.'

On 2 March *Britannia* entered Apia escorted by the long *fautasi* boats powered by 50 Samoan oarsmen. To reflect the more informal nature of the Pacific islands, Prince Philip had tried to keep the amount of ceremonial to a minimum during each of the visits but the Samoans were more insistent and, in the end, he yielded to their request for 'Full Dress'. The move came as a surprise to Lord Mountbatten who hadn't brought any of his medals or decorations. Fortunately, he was entitled to wear the same medals as Prince Philip so he was able to borrow his nephew's set of medals together with a Garter Sash and his OM to ensure that he met the Samoans' request. Not having any spare medals Prince Philip borrowed FORY's set of medals! When he landed, Prince Philip was met by the Samoan Head of State, His Highness Malietoa Tanumafili II, for the welcoming ceremonies. At the end of the day's programme Prince Philip stayed overnight in HH Malietoa Tanumafili II's house which was once owned by Robert

Louis Stevenson. The second day of the visit was dominated by demonstrations of local sports, including the Samoan version of cricket called *kirikiti*. Although the game follows the basic principles of cricket there are a number of differences. For example, the ball is made of natural rubber and the bat is more like a three-sided club. The routine of the game itself is very relaxed, with team numbers only limited by mutual agreement, while the ball is bowled from whichever end it finishes up at. That evening His Highness and the Samoan Cabinet came on board for a dinner which was rounded off by the Minister of Justice playing the piano in the Royal Drawing Room while the rest of the Samoan party sang as only Pacific islanders can sing! Following a further morning of engagements ashore on 4 March the Yacht set sail for Fiji.[15]

The Yacht's approach to Lakeba, Fiji on 6 March was dogged by strong winds and heavy rain, so when the pilot was embarked off the reef it was decided that the Yacht would remain underway rather than at anchor as planned. Once the worst of the weather had subsided the Royal party were able to go ashore, taking the Barge for the first part of the journey, before being transferred to an outrigger canoe inside the reef for the final stages. When Prince

Lord Mountbatten indulges in a little dancing with a chieftain's daughter on Raratonga.

Philip's canoe touched the beach it was lifted out of the water by 20 strong men, who then carried the canoe across the beach and placed it on the grass so that Prince Philip could step ashore. There he was greeted by the Fijian Prime Minister, Sir Kamisese Mara and Lady Lala Mara. Having opened a new Junior Secondary School in the Prime Minister's native village Prince Philip and his party sat down to a sumptuous feast under a specially built U-shaped shelter, as Admiral Trowbridge recalled:

'There were a number of dogs that were making a nuisance of themselves. After they had been taken away I asked the Prime Minister, "What are dogs called in Fiji?"

"Well," he said, "it's very straight forward. They are called "come 'eres"."

"Oh yes," I replied, but it didn't sound very straight-forward to me so I said, "I still don't get it."

So he explained that until the middle of the nineteenth century there weren't any dogs in Fiji. When the missionaries arrived in Fiji they brought dogs with them but the Fijians didn't have a word to describe the new animals so when they kept hearing the missionaries shouting "come here, come here" the Fijians decided to call dogs "come 'eres."'

The continuous rain failed to dampen the evening's atmosphere, which culminated in *Britannia*'s departure from Lakeba to the sound of 'Isa Lei' sung by the Fijians on the beach.[16]

The next morning the Royal party landed in Kadavu and were taken on a tour of the island, while the RM

Band came ashore to perform a concert for the ladies of the island. The short passage ashore in local canoes presented more of a challenge to the Bandsmen because they had to keep hold of their instruments and music stands as the canoes negotiated the surf. Once ashore the RM Band were taken to the middle of the village, as Lieutenant Colonel Mason remembers:

'They put out some chairs for us and we were about ready to start when the head lady turned to me and said that before you start we would like you to drink kava. I had drunk it before so I knew what to expect. There is a set routine as to how one is expected to drink it so I turned to the young men in the Band and said, "Do exactly what I do and whatever happens drink it, no matter what the taste!" Kava is always brought by a young girl who brings the drink in a half coconut and kneels down to offer up the drink. You then have to clap your hands three times, pick up the kava, drink it straight down, hand the coconut back, and clap your hands three times again, then off she goes. Kava tastes a bit like soapy water with a slight minty taste. The Band all drank their Kava and we played the first number. I was about to start the next number when this lady said that she would like us to drink Kava again. Every time we stopped we went through this routine again. After this had happened a couple of times I turned to the lady and said that if this was alcoholic we couldn't keep going. She said that it wasn't but the ladies would be offended if we didn't drink Kava so thereafter we just kept going. While Kava isn't alcoholic, it is a paralysing drug which anaesthetises the tongue. After about half an hour we couldn't play anymore because of the affects of the Kava that we had been given so we were all taken for a tour of the island instead.'

From Kadavu the Yacht weighed anchor in the evening for Lautoka. Once again the weather became a problem in the early hours of 8 March. The transit of the Navula Passage was delayed until after dawn because heavy rain squalls reduced the visibility below the level needed to make the passage. More bad news followed when it was confirmed that the bad weather of the last few days had developed into Cyclone Thelma which was approaching the Yacht's position from the north west. In view of the situation the Yacht changed course for Nandi Bay to ride out the storm. An hour after the Yacht dropped anchor Lord Mountbatten, together with Lord and Lady Brabourne, were landed ashore to begin their journey back to the UK. By the following morning the weather had moderated, so the Yacht weighed anchor and entered Lautoka for Prince Philip to host a lunch and present Duke of Edinburgh Gold Awards on the Verandah Deck.[17]

From Fiji the Yacht sailed for Prince Philip's visit to the Solomon Islands culminating in the call on Bougainville Island on 17 March when the Yacht slipped through the reef and into the bay of Kieta just as the sun was setting. The visit coincided with an interesting period in the island's history because the tranquil Pacific island was in the middle of being brought into the twentieth-century's industrial age. This historic transformation was caused by the discovery of large deposits of gold and copper ore 1500 feet up in the island's hills. To extract these valuable resources, all of the necessary infrastructure was being put into place as part of a £200 million development programme, which included the construction of a new port and homes for 10,000 people. On the second day of his visit Prince Philip went to see the new Paanguna copper mine for himself, before returning to the Yacht for another sunset transit through the reef as Britannia began the last leg of a fascinating voyage which had taken her across 9588 miles of the Pacific Ocean since His Royal Highness embarked in Balboa.[18]

Prince Philip was given an enthusiastic welcome, when the Yacht reached Madang on 20 March, by local people in highly decorated boats as well as the crowds lining the jetties. The following morning Prince Philip was taken to the village of Siar near Madang where the Royal party watched a re-enactment of an significant part of Siar's history. Before the First World War the northern part of New Guinea was administered by the Germans. In 1912 the Siar villagers rose up against their German rulers in protest against their harsh methods which resulted in the Germans moving their troublesome subjects 50 miles away along the coast. In 1914 a small party of villagers were secretly making their way back to Siar to see what was going on and collect food supplies when they were intercepted by a British warship which offered them a tow. During this passage the British Captain explained that the villagers had nothing to fear from their former German masters who had been ousted from New Guinea and that they could in fact return to Siar. Before they parted the Captain presented the villagers with a White Ensign which they treasured until it was burnt by the Japanese when they invaded in 1942. This whole story was dramatically performed by the villagers with the warship being represented by a merchant vessel displaying a sign saying 'English warship'.

After the Second World War, when Australia became responsible for the administration of New Guinea, the villagers asked the Australian District Commissioner if he could supply them with a replacement White Ensign. He apparently had great difficulty explaining that he could only supply them with an Australian Flag, which they reluctantly accepted. When Admiral Trowbridge became aware of this he was only too pleased to present the village with a new White Ensign from Britannia's own flag locker.

On 22 March Prince Philip left the Yacht at Madang to fly to Australia for the beginning of his Tour of Australia[19] which enabled Britannia to begin her long voyage back across the Pacific via Kwajalein Atoll, Pearl Harbour, San Francisco and Esquimalt, to arrive in Vancouver on 30 April ready for the embarkation of The Queen, Prince Philip and Princess Anne on 3 May, at the start of their Tour of the Canadian west coast. Shortly, after the Royal Family embarked the Yacht sailed for Victoria. As the Yacht left Vancouver she passed a gathering of yachts from the local clubs which included 32 boats owned by the flag officers of the participating yacht clubs.[20]

The jetties were packed for that evening's arrival in Victoria, as Admiral Trowbridge recalled:

'I impressed upon the Yachtsmen that this was going to be a difficult entry and they got their heaving lines further than ever. Unfortunately, one of the lines hit a woman in the crowd who had turned out to see us. When we got alongside I yelled out from the Bridge to bring the lady and her husband on board. The Canadian liaison officer strongly advised me against this saying, "For God's sake don't do that, that's admitting liability."

So I asked him, "what are you talking about?"

"Oh," he said, "in this country everyone sues everybody for everything." However, the couple came on board and I apologised for the incident. They had come a long way to see The Queen and told me to forget about it which was kind of them but it was the type of incident that could have reflected badly on the Royal Family if it had been mishandled.'

While FORY was entertaining his guests, the Royal Family went ashore to undertake their first formal event of the Tour by meeting the Mayor of Victoria and the Mayors of the neighbouring municipalities in City Hall. The following morning the Royal Family visited the Parliament buildings in Victoria before splitting up to make separate visits. The Queen and Prince Philip were driven to Ladysmith and Nanaimo, where they watched a bathtub regatta, while Princess Anne was flown to Tojino to visit a beach camping site. On completion of that night's dinner the Yacht slipped to spend the night at sea, before landing the Royal Family at Patricia Bay to carry on their programme ashore while the Yacht sailed back to Vancouver.[21]

Having visited the heart of British Columbia the Royal Family returned to the Yacht on the afternoon of 6 May in time for that night's dinner.[22] When the guest list was drafted the Canadian Prime Minister Pierre Trudeau, suggested that the President of the Student Council known simply as Steve should be invited, as Captain Bird explains:

'Steve was an extreme left winger and he had made it quite clear to the press what he was going to say to The Queen when he came on board. When the time of the dinner approached all of the guests had arrived except Steve. The Private Secretary and the Master of the Household arrived by the gangway to decide if they were going to wait for Steve. As they were making their decision a ghastly old banger painted in gaudy colours full of students complete with a banner "Steve for King" above it appeared. Out of this van erupted Steve in regalia that just passed for evening dress – not quite an orthodox dinner jacket!

'Looking on in dismay at this spectacle one of the officials remarked, "We really can't have someone like that to dinner with The Queen!"

Prince Philip had arrived by this time and said, "If we have invited him to dinner, then to dinner he must come."

I watched Steve come up the gangway on his own and I could see the step falter a bit as the spectacle of the Yacht began to hit him. As he arrived at the top of the gangway The Queen's Equerry, Lieutenant Commander Jock Slater appeared and said, "Oh there you are. You're a bit late The Queen was getting a bit worried you weren't coming. Come on I'll present you to The Queen." I am told that at dinner he was subdued and boring and the speech he was going to make was stillborn and never given. But it was a good example of the effect the mystique of the Yacht and Royalty had on people.'

Over the next six days the Royal Family continued their round of public engagements visiting New Westminister, Comox, Westview, Twin islands, Comox (for a second time), Victoria and finally, Vancouver, where the Royal Family disembarked on 12 May to fly back to the UK.[23]

The voyage home included calls at San Diego and Balboa, prior to making the Yacht's fastest transit of the Panama Canal to record a time of six hours which enabled *Britannia* to reach Bermuda earlier on 2 June than was originally envisaged.[24] The brief visit to the island provided the opportunity for a little entertaining, as Admiral Trowbridge recalled:

'Among those at the cocktail party held on board in Bermuda were a dozen members of the House of Lords sailing team who were on the island for a week's racing against the Royal Bermuda Yacht Club. Usually, the guests invited to a cocktail party on board *Britannia* were given the privilege of a guided tour and were greatly impressed by what they saw. Most favourable comment was normally reserved for the Engine Room where the standard of excellence could scarcely be believed by some. After the tour the wife of a well-known MP asked me how it was we were able to keep the Engine Room looking so immaculate. With a twinkle in my eye I told her, "Well you see we have two Engine Rooms. One for making the ship go and the other for showing to visitors."

"Ah, I see. Thank you," she said. Two nights later we attended a cocktail party given by the Royal Bermuda Yacht Club. I had barely finished shaking the hand of the Commodore and his officers when I was almost physically set upon by the MP's wife. "You horrid man, I hate you!" she shouted. "Your story about the two Engine Rooms in *Britannia* has made me the laughing stock of the whole of Bermuda for the last two days!" And off she stormed. A couple of gin and tonics later she and her husband apologised to me, and the hatchet was finally buried a couple of months later at Cowes when they invited me on board their yacht. However, we all learn from experience and I never told the two Engine Room story again!'

Two days later the Yacht slipped from Bermuda and set sail for Portsmouth, where she arrived on 14 June.[25]

Shortly after the Yacht's return to Portsmouth FORY

was told that the Labour MP for West Fife, Willie Hamilton, had asked The Queen if he could visit *Britannia*. Over the years Willie Hamilton had been a fierce critic of *Britannia*, constantly asking questions about her costs in Parliament. Rather than allow him to visit on his own The Queen granted permission for a Parliamentary Delegation of six MPs to see the Yacht for themselves in Portsmouth on 29 July 1971. The delegation included Mrs P Fenner, Mr P Goodhart, Mr J Barnett, Mr R Sheldon, Mr K Speed and of course Mr W Hamilton.[26] The MPs were met and personally shown around the Yacht by Admiral Trowbridge, as he explains:

'I had already told the Yachtsmen, who knew all about Willie Hamilton, that any questions should be answered by giving an honest opinion of what they thought. The delegation came on a lovely sunny day and I rather liked Willie. He obviously learned a lot and was very pleasant to everyone. As he was leaving the Wardroom after an excellent lunch he said how very grateful he was for the opportunity to see for himself how ordinarily pleasant the Royal Apartments were and not a bit ornately plush as he had always understood. Later on the facts speak for themselves and I don't think I ever had to answer another derogatory Parliamentary question from Willie in the whole of my time as FORY, although he did continue to be very rude about the Royal Family. A couple of years after his visit he wrote an autobiography and we were all rather touched to see that the photograph on the dust cover was one of me receiving him when he came on board.'

Before the Yacht's traditional commitments of Cowes Week and the Western Isles Cruise, *Britannia* acted as the venue for Princess Anne's 21st birthday on 2 August. Describing the background to the decision to hold her party on board the Yacht, Princess Anne said:

'When the arrangements for my 21st birthday party were being discussed the only place I really wanted to have it was in the Yacht. It would have to be in Portsmouth just before the beginning of Cowes Week because my birthday would be when we were on the Western Isles Cruise. It worked very well and we discovered that there was a dance floor under the carpet in the Royal Dining Room. It had been there since she was built but it was probably the first time that it had been used, and possibly the last, which was a shame.'

When the party finished in the early hours of 3 August the Yachtsmen worked through the night to put the Royal Apartments back to normal and ensure that *Britannia* was ready to sail on time for Cowes Week. At the end of their

time at Cowes Week Prince Philip, The Prince of Wales and Princess Anne were taken in the Barge on 6 August to the Royal Southern Yacht Club. Once ashore they joined in the welcome for the yachtsman Chay Blyth who had just arrived in Southampton at the helm of the 59-foot ketch *British Steel*. His return marked the successful conclusion of his attempt to become the first man to sail alone non-stop around the world westwards against the prevailing winds and currents.[27]

Three days later *Britannia* sailed from Portsmouth to Southampton where The Queen, accompanied by Prince Philip, The Prince of Wales, Princess Anne, Prince Andrew and Prince Edward embarked for the Western Isles Cruise.[28] As Princess Anne approached her 21st birthday she began to appreciate her time on board the Yacht in a different way, as she explains:

'We found as children that there was so much to do, we expended so much energy that we wouldn't describe our time in the Yacht as a rest. I appreciated later in life that it was a place to go where I could do as much or as little as I wanted and I could do it in utter confidence that it would remain private. That was perhaps one of the most underrated achievements of the Yacht and the men who served in her.'

Once the Yacht reached the west coast of Scotland the Royal Family were able to enjoy their privacy ashore, as Admiral Trowbridge recalled:

'It had been decided to have a picnic lunch on a small island just off the Laxford River. The Queen and Prince Philip were having tea with the Duchess of Westminister and were about to start their lunch when I heard the noise of a motor boat approaching. I couldn't see it so I left the Royal party and walked over the sand dunes to see where the boat was going. I was just in time to see an open boat with about 30 people on board who were about to land on the beach. So I ran down to the beach and explained to them that just over the sand dunes the Royal Family were having a picnic lunch and that I hoped they wouldn't intrude. Realising the situation the people aborted their landing and went off up the coast.'

Having explored the Scottish West Coast the Yacht anchored in Scrabster Bay on 15 August so that the Royal Family could spend the afternoon with The Queen Mother and celebrate Princess Anne's birthday. The following morning the Yacht arrived in Aberdeen to disembark the Royal Family before returning to Portsmouth on 19 August.[29]

After the short docking period during August and

Princess Anne talks to Rear Admiral Trowbridge as she returns on board the Yacht in Bangkok.

(© British Crown Copyright / MOD)

September, the Yacht sailed from Portsmouth on 5 October for The Queen's State Visit to Turkey. The visit included a trip on 22 October to the Dardenelles where The Queen, Prince Philip and Princess Anne landed to look round the former battlefields of the First World War and lay wreaths at the many war memorials. The next morning the Yacht sailed through the Bosphorus to the entrance to the Black Sea, where she turned round and headed back to Istanbul for the final three days of the visit. In a move contrary to normal practice the escorting frigate HMS *Hermione* left Istanbul on 25 October before the Royal Family had left Turkey by air. The unusual arrangements were necessary because the Montreux Convention banned the transit of the Dardenelles by warships at night. The Yacht finally arrived back in Portsmouth on 2 November to prepare for The Queen's Tour of South East Asia.[30]

The extensive spring Tour meant another early start as the Yacht sailed from Portsmouth on 28 December for

Thailand via Madeira, Cape Town and Singapore. *Britannia* arrived at Sattahip on 8 February 1972 and The Queen, together with Prince Philip and Princess Anne, embarked the next morning, as Admiral Trowbridge recalled: 'I asked Prince Philip if they had had a good journey out? He replied, "as good a journey as one could expect to have by air!" That doesn't mean to say that it was a good journey.' Within an hour of their embarkation the Yacht sailed for Bangkok where she arrived on 10 February. The passage up the Bangkok River was especially memorable for the large number of flag-waving children who were assembled at every riverside town and school.[31]

The white elephant is a sacred animal to the people of Thailand. During the course of The Queen's programme ashore in Bangkok she was due to feed the Senior White Elephant in one of the city's public squares, as Admiral Trowbridge remembers:

'The Queen's visit was being televised and everyone who was able to do so was watching it on board the Yacht. Just before The Queen was due to arrive at the square the TV started to show images of the huge crowds being kept back by lots of soldiers and policemen. All of this noise and commotion was clearly upsetting the elephant, which began very slowly to pore the ground. Then, as we were watching, the elephant slowly backed towards a police car and with great dignity quietly sat down on it. You have never seen four people get out of a car so quickly! Sadly, The Queen never did feed the elephant as it was sent away in disgrace.'

Following the dinner for The King and Queen of Thailand on 12 February, the British Royal Family disembarked to continue the inland part of their State Visit, before rejoining the Yacht in Sattahip on 15 February to leave Thailand and sail to Singapore for the next stage of the Tour.

Half an hour after the Yacht's arrival in Singapore on 18 February, The Queen, together with Prince Philip and Princess Anne, landed to begin their shore programme.[32] During the Yacht's stay in Singapore the Royal party was joined by Lord Mountbatten who remained on board for the rest of the Tour of South East Asia. The Royal programme culminated with the State Banquet on board for the President and Prime Minister of Singapore on 20 February, before the Yacht sailed out of the harbour to the sound of a Singapore pipe band.[33] The next day was spent cruising the Straits of Malacca as the Royal party took the opportunity to unwind a little before the start of the State Visit to Malaysia. When the Yacht arrived in Port Klang on 22 February the Royal party left to begin the inland part of their visit, and the following day *Britannia* sailed to Labuan, where the Royal party rejoined the Yacht on 26 February. From there they continued their Malaysian State Visit with a call at Mangalum Island before reaching Kota Kinabalu on 28 February. This visit was particularly moving for Lord Mountbatten because during the day's programme ashore he visited the room where his wife, Countess Mountbatten, had died in 1960. That night *Britannia* sailed for the next day's visit to Brunei. As part of the welcoming ceremonies the Royal Family travelled in the Golden Chariot which was used for the coronation of the Sultans of Brunei. The 18-foot long carriage with seats on three different levels was drawn by 120 soldiers of the Royal Brunei Malay Regiment. The day-long tour finished with a State Banquet for the Sultan and his family before the Yacht sailed that night for Kuching.[34]

Following the brief call at Kuching the Yacht sailed back to Singapore where she arrived on 5 March. One of those waiting on the quayside in Singapore was The Queen's Lady-in-Waiting, Lady Susan Hussey. Although she had accompanied The Queen on board *Britannia* before, it was the first time that Lady Susan Hussey had actually witnessed the arrival of the Yacht as an ordinary spectator. Describing her impressions of the spectacle of the Yacht's arrival and comparing it to what it was like to be on board for that type of occasion she said:

'On the jetty there was a huge crowd and there were bands playing. Suddenly, round the spithead came the sight of this amazing ship with the Royal Marine Band playing on the top deck, flags flying, and The Queen and The Duke of Edinburgh on deck waving to the crowds. It was so proud making, beautiful and British. I felt very moved by this sight and judging by the cheering and waving so did vast numbers in the crowd – many people had tears in their eyes. Equally, these arrivals were moving for those of us on board. It's immaculate, like a perfect stage setting and it's hard to believe that you are there because it's so unreal. My main worry in my early days on board the Yacht was where I should be or, much more importantly, not be, so as not to spoil this great picture for the people waiting to see The Queen and the Yacht. I didn't want to make it look untidy by being in the wrong place and I was very afraid of offending naval etiquette of which I knew nothing!'

For those working deep inside the Yacht entering these dramatic locations could be frustrating at times, as The Queen's Chef, Lionel Mann recalls:

'Usually I was working down in the galley whenever we entered port. FORY always insisted that the scuttles were all closed because it looked a mess if one was open and others weren't. We weren't even supposed to stand next to the scuttles because it might show up on a photograph which irritated us no end as we were bottled up and couldn't even look out – but that was the way it was. If we weren't working we could change and go up to another deck and watch our arrival.'

During this second visit to Singapore the Royal party visited the ANZUK force which was made up of units from Australia, New Zealand and the UK. The force had been set up following the British Government's decision in 1968 to withdraw its military forces from the Far East. The new ANZUK force had come into being on 1 November 1971 when the British Far East Command ceased to exist and, at the time of The Queen's visit, comprised two RN frigates, one frigate from both the RAN and RNZN, and aircraft from the RAF and RNZAF. Shortly after The Queen and Prince Philip landed to visit the Commonwealth War Graves Cemetery at Kranji, Princess Anne left for Teugah to be flown back to the UK.

The Queen, followed by Prince Philip and Princess Anne, disembarks from the Yacht in Singapore. Note the Yachtsmen have manned ship for Her Majesty's disembarkation.

On completing their programme ashore, The Queen returned to the Yacht, while Prince Philip joined the escorting frigate HMS *Cleopatra* for the passage to Kelong in the Singapore Straits. There the Royal party watched the fishermen gathering the evening's catch, before resuming the passage to Malacca, where *Britannia* arrived the following morning.

As part of their shore programme in Malacca the Royal party saw a demonstration of both Malay and Chinese weddings, conducted according to the appropriate ancient customs. Meanwhile the Yacht weighed anchor and sailed for Port Klang, where she arrived in the afternoon. From Port Klang, the Yacht visited the Sembilan Islands on 7 March, followed by Penang, the Maldives and Gan before sailing for the Seychelles on 15 March. Once again this part of the Tour was a good example of how *Britannia* enabled The Queen to visit remote island communities which would have been much harder to achieve without the Yacht. During the voyage across the Indian Ocean some members of the Household were given the opportunity to visit the escorting frigate HMS *Arethusa* by jackstay transfer. One of those to go across was Lady Susan Hussey. Describing the experience she said:

'It was a very strange sensation for me as an ordinary civilian, married woman to be trussed up in a cage-like thing and slung from one ship to another! It was quite an adventure and I was greeted by the officers of *Arethusa* with a glass of champagne. We had a meal on board and a look round the frigate which was just as much fun for the Ship's company as it was for us I think, not least because they saw some new faces.'

Shortly before the Yacht reached North Cousin Island of the Seychelles on the afternoon of 19 March Lord Mountbatten transferred to *Arethusa* to be taken to the island of Mahe. While Lord Mountbatten was taken around Mahe before his flight home, The Queen and Prince Philip went ashore to visit the bird sanctuary on North Cousin Island, prior to making their own visit to Mahe the next day. Following their tour of the island the Yacht weighed anchor for Mauritius where they received an enthusiastic welcome on 24 March. When *Britannia* entered Mauritius she passed two Soviet survey vessels which were dressed overall and had manned ship in honour of the Royal couple. The final visit of this extensive Tour began with The Queen and Prince Philip travelling to the Mauritian Parliament, where Her Majesty delivered a speech from the throne.[35] After two very busy days ashore the Royal couple finally left *Britannia* early on the morning of 26 March to fly back to the UK via Kenya, as Admiral Trowbridge recalled: 'The Queen told me before she left

that it was the longest continuous time that she had ever spent in *Britannia* and how very much she had enjoyed the pleasant restful cruise across the Indian Ocean. She expressed the hope that she could do it again one day.'

Two days later *Britannia* began her own voyage home via Simonstown, St Helena and Madeira, before arriving at Spithead late on 30 April. Before the Yacht weighed anchor the next morning the Yachtsmen were joined by their families who had been brought out for the voyage up into Portsmouth harbour. Having spent over two weeks back in harbour it was time for the Yacht to begin her busy programme of Royal duty closer to home, beginning with the voyage to Rouen in mid May to collect The Queen and Prince Philip and bring them back to Portsmouth after their State Visit to France. A day after their return, *Britannia* sailed on 21 May to take Princess Anne to the Channel Islands. It was the first time that the young Princess had used the Yacht on her own, as Admiral Trowbridge explains: 'I really felt for the poor girl because practically everyone she met was old enough to be her father or mother if not her grandfather or grandmother.' The Tour began with a visit to Jersey on 22 May, followed by Guernsey the next day. As Princess Anne recalled, the weather deteriorated while she was undertaking her engagements ashore in St Peter Port:

'We had a dinner in St Peter Port. When we came back in the Barge the crew were all wearing lifejackets and they had put out lifejackets for all of us inside the Barge. It was the only time I ever saw this happen. By this time it was dark so I never saw the size of the waves – which was fortunate. We were hoisted inboard in the Barge, which was quite exciting, and a good demonstration of the Yacht's seamanship.'

The weather continued to cause problems and resulted in the programme for Sark and Alderney, on 25 May, being heavily curtailed, with Princess Anne returning on board at 1910. Soon after, the Yacht weighed anchor for Portsmouth and made her way home through the poor weather, which failed to improve, as Princess Anne remarked:

'The overnight passage back from Alderney was quite rough. There was one lurch followed quickly by another one and perhaps the stabilisers got out of sink because the Yacht simply kept going over and everything on the table in my cabin took off. There was a huge rushing sound followed by a crash and I kept going down the bed – but not off it! After that the Yacht seemed to settle back into its rhythm and I drifted back to sleep.'

The Yacht reached Portsmouth the following morning.

At the end of July the Yacht attended Cowes Week, followed by the Western Isles Cruise. Before the Yacht headed north she entered the River Dart on 31 July for The Queen to pay her first visit to BRNC since she had assumed the title of Lord High Admiral in 1964. Having fulfilled a number of civic engagements within Dartmouth, Her Majesty was driven the short distance up the hill to BRNC where she took Lord High Admiral's Divisions and presented The Queen's Sword and telescopes. In the afternoon The Queen, Prince Philip and Princess Anne, were taken to Waddington Beach where they saw the Royal Dart Yacht Club's junior sailing week. In the evening the Yacht sailed out of the Dart, escorted by the College's Picket Boats and Fairy Huntresses, as she began the voyage north via the Isle of Man, where the Royal Family undertook further public engagements before beginning the private part of the cruise. When *Britannia* returned to Portsmouth at the end of the Western Isles Cruise on 11 August, the preparations for the major refit began to get underway.

Although the refit was aimed principally at improving the living conditions of the Yachtsmen, the Government were still wary about how the cost of *Britannia*'s latest refit would be exploited by her critics. One of the aspects of *Britannia* that had always attracted criticism was the validity of her secondary role as a hospital carrier. The Parliamentary Under Secretary of State (RN), Keith Speed MP, felt that it could be very useful politically to exercise the conversion plans and present the public with firm evidence that she could be converted if needed. The first of the conversion schemes was drawn up in September 1954 and required 48 hours to be implemented, following the delivery of the majority of the stores required. This plan required virtually no structural work to be undertaken and initially enabled 180 patients to be carried. When this scheme was revised in 1966 the patient capacity was increased through the decision to use 2-tier bedstead cots, instead of conventional hospital beds and mattresses as had been originally envisaged. This change increased the capacity to 240 patients (42 on the Shelter Deck, 110 on the Upper Deck, 39 on the Main Deck and 49 on the Lower Deck).

The plans for the second more extensive conversion were first drawn up in August 1957 and were known as the 10-day scheme. To provide an increased capacity of 255 patients (40 on the Shelter Deck, 98 on the Upper Deck, 37 on the Main Deck and 80 on the Lower Deck), some structural work would be required, including the cutting of arched openings to improve the movement of stretcher cases and the conversion of a number of cabins

to provide an X-ray Room, Dispensary and Dental Surgery. Although this plan offered a greater patient capacity, *Britannia* would still only have been capable of offering patients first aid and life-saving measures. Therefore, when the 48-hour plan was revised to provide a similar capability, the 10-day plan effectively became redundant. By 1972 there were no naval plans to use *Britannia* as a hospital carrier in a general war situation, although it was still possible that she could be used in those circumstances. However, it was felt more likely that she would be employed either in a limited war, or in the aftermath of a major unexpected disaster, in the hospital carrier role. It was for this scenario that it was decided to practice the conversion of *Britannia* from a Royal Yacht.

It was felt that the period of de-storing, before *Britannia* entered dockyard hands, would provide the best opportunity for the exercise to be held. So on 8 September Admiral Trowbridge initiated the conversion procedure and soon trucks loaded with beds began to appear at the dock side. To keep the cost of the exercise down, the scope of the conversion was limited to the removal of the furniture and carpets from the Royal Apartments and the

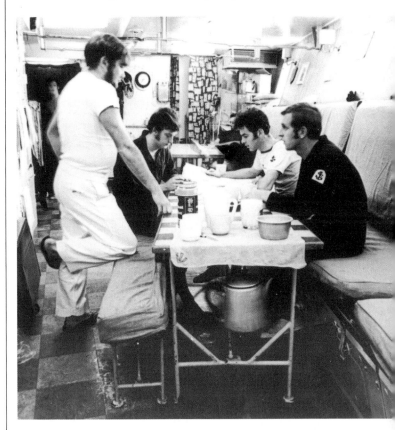

Britannia's major 1972/73 refit was aimed at improving the living conditions of the Yachtsmen. As part of this work bunks were fitted to replace the hammocks which had previously been used by the Yachtsmen.

fitting of the beds, which were produced from naval stores. Without the embarkation of medical stores and staff, the work was completed within 24 hours, thus successfully demonstrating that a limited conversion could be carried out quickly in an emergency.

On 2 October 1972 *Britannia* entered dockyard hands to begin her modernisation refit which was due to be completed on 6 July 1973. The timing of the refit had been a major task for Admiral Trowbridge since he became FORY because, at that stage, nothing had been firmed up in the MOD. Luckily, Admiral Trowbridge found an ally in the form of a previous Commander of the Yacht who had by then become the Vice Chief of the Naval Staff. Vice Admiral T Lewin was able to lobby within Whitehall to ensure that *Britannia* received her modernisation. Because of the sensitive nature of the costs involved for the refit, MOD went to extraordinary lengths to ensure that the work remained within the clearly defined budget of £1.7million.

The principle objective of this major refit was to upgrade the quality of the accommodation for the Royal Yachtsmen. When the Parliamentary delegation had visited the Yacht during the previous July they had commented about what they felt was a poor standard of accommodation for the Yachtsmen. As part of the upgrading work air conditioning was installed, together with dining halls, recreation spaces and refurbished bathrooms. However, from the historical point of view, it was the change from hammocks to full bunk sleeping which was the most significant change. By 1972 *Britannia* had become the last ship in the RN in which the sailors still slept in hammocks. Whilst this fact was not unusual for the older Yachtsmen, who had experienced similar conditions on other warships, it was a culture shock for some of the younger Yachtsmen who joined shortly before the refit, as 'Swampy' Marsh (later Mr Marsh MVO RVM) recalls:

'By then the RN didn't train Ratings how to fold or make a hammock. When I joined the Yacht that summer I was taken down to the stores and presented with bits of canvas and string. As I stood there looking at this collection of bits they said, "That's your bed!" I was lucky because for the first few nights I slept in a bunk. The first few times I slept in the hammock were unforgettable!'

Inevitably there was a change of personnel during the course of the refit and one of the Naval Officers who joined at this time was the new Assistant Navigating Officer Lieutenant Charles Howeson RN (later Commander C Howeson RN). On joining the Yacht he went to see the Commander who offered him some unusual but very sound advice, as he explains:

'Commander Balfour told me, "We don't do things in quite the normal way. The Yacht is run by the senior Yachtsman and not the Officers, which you will find rather different from any other ship you have ever served in. The reason is that they have been here longer than any of the Officers who come and go and therefore there is a level of continuity that is unique in the RN. It's a continuity that's based upon such excellence that it can't be improved upon. You will take the blame if something goes wrong and you will monitor and no doubt you will learn a lot. However, as far as the Yacht is organised and run on a day-to-day basis you don't get involved in that. That is done by the Yachtsmen at Chief Petty Officer level starting with the Coxswain." I left his cabin and felt this appointment was going to be very different.'

As the Yacht neared the end of her refit the Yachtsmen were able to progressively move back on board *Britannia* and experience the new, improved living conditions. As Admiral Trowbridge observed, there was an interesting reaction to the changes:

'When the Yachtsmen returned to this new set-up they didn't like it a bit. The old cosiness that they had been used to for years wasn't there. Some of the Yachtsmen made remarks along the lines, "what's the Navy coming to?" It was fascinating to watch. However, they soon realised that this was a vast improvement and the old frets packed up very quickly.'

After nearly a year in dockyard hands the Yacht emerged from Portsmouth on 9 July 1973 to begin a week of post-refit trials which were successfully completed so that she was ready for Cowes Week at the beginning of August. Admiral Trowbridge felt that the short passage across the Solent would be an ideal opportunity for the press to see the scope of the recent work for themselves and hopefully generate some well-informed articles. Thus, when *Britannia* sailed from G Moorings off Whale Island on 3 August, 20 members of the press were embarked.[36] It was a significant milestone in Buckingham Palace's relations with the press because it was the first time that they had been on board the Yacht for a passage in UK waters. It was also the first time that the press were given access to the Yachtsmen's quarters. The timing of this event was particularly topical because Buckingham Palace had just announced that *Britannia* was going to be used for the honeymoon of Princess Anne and Captain Mark Phillips. Although FORY had been informed of these plans beforehand he was keen to see the announcement made prior to the press day, so that he could concentrate upon presenting what had been achieved by the refit, rather than fielding questions about whether she was going to be used by the Royal couple or not. Although the reporters were not given access to the Royal Apartments the gamble worked and the following morning a series of positive articles appeared in the national newspapers. One reporter who peered through the curtains of the Royal Apartments from outside and described what she saw ended her article by asking, 'how could the Royal Family be accused of extravagance in furnishing *Britannia*?' As Admiral Trowbridge later remarked, 'the Yachtsmen couldn't have put it better if they had written it themselves.'

Prince Philip arrived in Cowes two days later to find that gale force winds had led to the cancellation of all the races except those for the Admiral's Cup on 5 and 6 August. However, he was able to go racing with Prince Andrew in *Yeoman XIX* on 7 August before leaving the following morning. Shortly afterwards the Yacht weighed anchor for Avonmouth and arrived there on 9 August. Both Princes Andrew and Edward had remained on board for the passage round the coast. When the Yacht arrived in Avonmouth they were taken ashore to visit SS *Great Britain* and the recently commissioned Type 82 destroyer HMS *Bristol*, which interestingly was commanded by the next FORY Captain Hugh Janion. After The Queen and Prince Philip had joined separately in the evening they hosted a dinner party followed by a reception, before the Yacht headed back out to sea on 10 August to begin the Western Isles Cruise.[37] As the Navigating Officer at the time, later Rear Admiral Sir Patrick Rowe KCVO CBE, explains, the Royal Family's choice of where to go was greatly assisted by a new book:

'While we were in refit we organised a helicopter from RNAS [Royal Naval Air Station] Culdrose to take the First Lieutenant, Lieutenant Commander Ian Aston Johnson to photograph all the likely looking beaches around the Western Isles. These were then given to me to decide which beaches would be accessible from the sea. We kept a record on board of which beaches the Royal Family had visited before and naturally they always wanted to go somewhere new. We therefore compiled a great catalogue of photographs of beaches on deserted islands that were accessible from the sea. At the start of the cruise itself the only forward planning consisted of ensuring that the Yacht was at the point of disembarkation at the appointed time. Other than that we took it day by day and the Admiral would go aft with the charts and discuss the options with the Royal Family.'

In a change to the usual routine the Royal Family left the Yacht in Dundee on 16 August to travel to Balmoral for the summer break.[38]

After a couple of months back in Portsmouth, *Britannia* sailed on 30 October at the start of another major six-month global deployment. During the coming months she would be used for the honeymoon of Princess Anne and Captain Phillips, followed by Royal duty in support of the Commonwealth Games in New Zealand, and then a Tour of Australia, Indonesia and several Pacific Islands. After a relatively uneventful passage the Yacht arrived in Barbados on 12 November.

On the morning of the Royal wedding, on 14 November, the Yachtsmen listened to the service on the radio. Because of the time difference between Barbados and the UK it was only 0815 when FORY led the Wardroom in a toast to the Royal couple in Champagne. The following evening the Princess and Captain Phillips arrived on board. Large crowds had turned out to welcome the Royal couple to the West Indies and, as a result, their journey from the airport took half an hour longer than

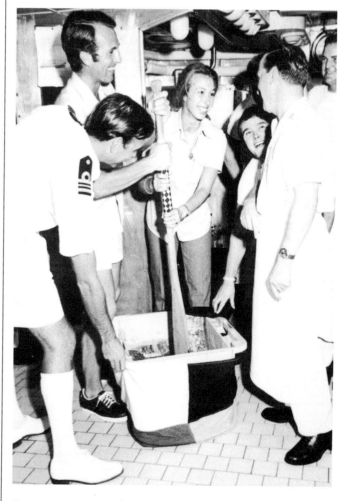

Princess Anne and Captain Mark Phillips stir the Christmas pudding during their honeymoon. (© British Crown Copyright / MOD)

planned. When the Yacht sailed 40 minutes later she left the accompanying RFA *Blue Rover* behind to catch up on her programme of maintenance, which had slipped as a result of her recent participation in a number of major fleet exercises. When FORY had discussed the situation with her Captain they agreed that *Blue Rover* would rendezvous with the Yacht in a week's time.[39] In the meantime the Yacht began a cruise around the West Indies, as Admiral Trowbridge explains:

'The whole of the West Indies seemed to be swarming with reporters from every newspaper and TV channel in the world. Our task was to thwart the endeavours of all these people from getting anywhere near the Royal couple when they were ashore picnicking or swimming. We had done a great deal of homework into identifying isolated patches of beach on various islands. It was quite impossible to hide the Yacht among the islands because there were light aircraft constantly flying around to find out where we were. We would land the Royal couple at 1100 in one of the motor boats and they would stay ashore until they wanted to return at about 1500. They were in communication the whole time with *Britannia* and the Yachtsmen stayed inshore with them picnicking 300 yards away further down the coast. In *Britannia* we steamed off 20 or 30 miles away in the direction from where they were and put the Barge down and sent it off as if we were landing the Royal couple somewhere else. This strategy worked thanks more to the fact that it was windier than usual and there was quite a lot of sea running most of the time. I heard afterwards that there were all types of boats with photographers who knew where the Royal couple had landed. They had set off from the nearest town and got so sea sick that they gave up and turned back.'

After nearly a fortnight cruising the Caribbean the Yacht entered the Panama Canal on 28 November, as the Deputy Supply Officer at the time later Commander G Creedy LVO RN recalled:

'In places the canal passes quite close to built-up areas, and at one point a young Panamanian lad was seen running along the bank shouting, "Where's the Princess? I want to see the Princess."

As it happened, Her Royal Highness was on the upper deck looking at the countryside and wearing a sun hat, a T-shirt and a pair of shorts, so she called back, "It's me. I'm the Princess." The boy refused to believe her – after all, she wasn't dressed in a ballgown with long white gloves and a diamond tiara, so she clearly couldn't be a real princess!'

After a brief stop in Rodman US Naval Base the Yacht sailed that night for the Galapagos Islands. Two days later the customary Crossing-The-Line ceremony was held with a twist as King Neptune's Guard were dressed as four brides and four grooms. The grooms were wearing a dress uniform resembling that of Captain Phillips's cavalry regiment! Princess Anne was presented with a carved wooden fish to remind her of her 'fisherman' husband, and Captain Phillips was consigned to the bears as a novice.[40] On 1 December the Yacht dropped anchor in Academy Bay off Santa Cruz Island. In recent years the Yacht had become a regular visitor to the islands as this was her third visit to the Galapagos since 1970. During the Royal couple's three days in the islands they saw much of the local wildlife including the giant tortoises and the marine iguanas. The Yacht's second honeymoon cruise came to an end early on 4 December when the Princess and Captain Phillips were taken ashore to the island of Baltra to begin their journey back to the UK.[41] In the afternoon the Yacht headed west and set course for Pitcairn Island, where she arrived on 12 December. Soon after the Yacht dropped anchor off the remote island a small party of islanders came on board bringing a selection of locally made items to begin a brisk trading session on the forecastle. The items included wooden sharks, fish, birds and vases as well as the island's stamps and first day covers. Some of the Yachtsmen took the opportunity to go ashore and look round the island while a small party of women and their children came on board in the afternoon to watch the film *Jungle Book* and have tea. While the Yachtsmen were enjoying this brief call, *Blue Rover* caught up with the Yacht and then sailed on ahead towards Raratonga. After a very enjoyable day the Yacht weighed anchor to catch up with *Blue Rover*.[42]

That night as the Yacht began to close in on *Blue Rover* she was clearly visible on the horizon when the lights suddenly went out about 2230. Those on watch on the bridge wondered what had happened. When *Blue Rover* contacted the Yacht by radio it became clear that the tanker had suffered a major engine room fire and the Yacht increased speed to provide assistance. As Commander Creedy explains, word soon got round the Yacht of *Blue Rover*'s plight and the Yachtsmen pulled together to do what they could:

'I realised that my Department would need to supply foam so I tried to contact the Duty Stores Accountant by telephone to tell him to open up the appropriate stores and find all the canisters of foam and get them ready. I was unable to find him because he had beaten me to it. Having heard about the situation he went off his own initiative down to the store and was already pulling out the canisters of foam by the time I found him in the store room. It was subsequently decided to send across food parcels to *Blue Rover* so I went to the galley to see how things were going. I found the Coxswain and the Chief Cook buttering bread as fast as they could go to make sandwiches. There was nothing else for the Coxswain to be doing so there he was helping his friend in the galley make the sandwiches. This was typical of the way the Yachtsmen would always pitch in and do much more than simply their job.'

By the time the Yacht reached *Blue Rover* the fire itself had been extinguished by drenching the engine room with CO_2 but she was left without any power, as Admiral Trowbridge continues:

'We sent over our complete emergency party on arrival and luckily the weather was better than at any time since our departure from the UK. As soon as the fire was out my main concern was that here I was 1200 miles from the nearest port in Tahiti with not enough fuel on board either to get there towing *Blue Rover* or even to get there on my own. Although *Blue Rover* was full of fuel she had no means of getting it over to the Yacht except in buckets! As it turned out *Blue Rover* had a donkey engine that hadn't been used for years on the upper deck. If it could be made to start it could move fuel over to us very slowly via a hose over the stern. Therefore as soon as it was light the next morning all efforts were made to see if this piece of ancient equipment would work. We could only stand and watch from the bridge as the engineers from *Britannia* tried to make it work. On board the Yacht we could see the smoke rings going up in the air before we heard any sound, so there was three or four rings in the air followed by pop, pop, pop, stop. This seemed to go on for hours until the moment came when it didn't stop. As soon as the engine was working we hauled out the hose and connected it up on the forecastle and got cracking. We finished fuelling before dark and passed the tow to get underway by 2015.'

However, by 14 December the winds had freshened and as the Yacht tried to increase her speed from 8.7 knots to 9 knots the tow parted. It took about half a day to change the nylon line for a heavier steel line from *Blue Rover*'s stores. When the tow resumed there were no further problems and FORY was able to convene the Board of Inquiry to firmly establish the cause of the fire. Thus each morning after breakfast a team, headed by the Commander, went across to *Blue Rover* to undertake the investigation work. By the time the Yacht reached Tahiti on 19 December the Board had established that *Blue Rover* had been extraordinarily fortunate and that when the fire had started all of the correct actions had been taken. The fire itself had been started by a fractured pipe on the port engine spraying fuel on to the exhaust of the starboard engine. Whilst the prompt actions of the Ship's company had physically saved *Blue Rover* the damage was so extensive that it wasn't entirely clear whether she would be refitted or scrapped. Nevertheless FORY felt that *Blue Rover*'s Captain and the Ship's company had done everything they could to get the tanker back up to standard and of course if it hadn't been

Princess Anne and Captain Mark Phillips take a closer look at one of the large tortoises found on the Galapagos Islands.

for the fractured pipe they would have succeeded. It later transpired that the Yacht's feat of towing *Blue Rover* 1200 miles to Tahiti was the longest impromptu tow to have taken place in the RN since the Second World War. As for *Blue Rover* she was subsequently refitted for further service with the Royal Fleet Auxiliary Service.

Obviously, these events affected the Yacht's programme and the visit to Raratonga was reorganised for 21 to 23 December. This meant that the Yacht would be at sea on Christmas Day rather than at Fiji as originally planned. Worst still the Yacht would cross the International Dateline on Christmas Day so technically it wouldn't exist in the Yacht. Therefore, it was decided to keep Christmas Day and lose Boxing Day instead. This fact was heralded by Daily Orders, which began with the announcement, 'Today is 27th December – Boxing Day has been cancelled owing to lack of interest!' All of the Christmas traditions and customs were observed on board, including carols on the forecastle and rounds by FORY, while the youngest Yachtsman was dressed up as the Admiral. After four days in Suva, the Yacht sailed for Auckland on 30 December 1973 and spent New Year's day at sea. When the Yacht arrived in Auckland on 3 January 1974 the Yachtsmen soon set about the task of repainting the Yacht's hull. Following the Yacht's transatlantic crossing it had become clear that something had gone wrong when *Britannia* was repainted at the end of the refit. The crazing and blistering was now so bad that there was no alternative but to com-

RFA Blue Rover *seen from on board the Yacht while she was being towed by* Britannia *to Tahiti following her major engine room fire.*   (© British Crown Copyright / MOD)

pletely repaint the hull from stem to stern before she could begin the next period of Royal duty with Prince Philip. The day after *Britannia* reached Auckland the First Lieutenant rang up the paint's manufacturers in the UK and arranged for a fresh supply of paint to be flown out as soon as possible.[43] During the period alongside the Yachtsmen briefly stopped work on 7 January to celebrate the 20th Anniversary of the Yacht being commissioned when the Keeper & Steward, Lieutenant Connell, who was the senior member of the Yacht's company to have served on board continuously since 1954, cut a specially baked cake on the forecastle.[44] After analysis by a chemist who was flown out from the UK it was firmly established that the paint had peeled because it had been applied during poor weather conditions towards the end of the refit. Despite the fact that the weather conditions weren't right when the paint was applied the decision to proceed had been taken because of everyone's determination that the refit would be completed on time and within budget. Ironically, this obsession with time and cost had led to the additional expense of having to fly out a new batch of blue paint, which was specially produced, as well as hiring additional contractors to help the Yachtsmen paint the hull when the Yacht reached Lyttleton on 17 January. By the time Prince Philip embarked on 22 January *Britannia* looked pristine and was ready for Royal duty. Two days later Prince Philip opened the Commonwealth Games and, over the following days, attended various events of the Games.[45] On 29 January the frigate HMS *Jupiter* entered Lyttleton with The Prince of Wales who was serving on board as a Seaman Officer.[46] The following day Prince Philip travelled to Christchurch to meet The Queen, Princess Anne and Captain Phillips who had arrived in New Zealand by air.[47] As well as spending time at the Games the Royal Family undertook a busy programme of social engagements both ashore and on board. On 1 February The Queen hosted a dinner followed by a reception for 250 guests, as Commander Creedy observed:

'It was much easier to have the VIPs to dinner and then be joined by others for drinks afterwards, than to hold a cocktail party and have to persuade everyone to leave before dinner except those invited to stay. All the officers were on duty for these receptions, and there was a well-practised routine. The guests were presented to The Queen and Prince Philip by the Master of the Household and then an officer would go up to them and guide them firmly away from the doorway, make sure they had a drink from a tray held by one of the Stewards, talk to them for a minute or two, perhaps introduce them to someone else, and then go back for another couple. In this way we ensured that there was no crowd of guests hovering near their Royal hosts and causing a bottleneck. Along with members of the Royal Household, we would continue to help entertain the guests throughout the party.'

On 2 February The Queen closed the Commonwealth Games. The following morning the Royal Family began the rest of their Tour of New Zealand, calling first at Whangerai, and then Waitangi on 6 February. It was there that the Prime Minister, Norman Kirk, embarked from the famous Maori war canoe, which was paddled by 150 Maoris and had last been used in 1940. This part of the Tour was significant because, as part of the celebrations to mark New Zealand's first National Day, the Prime Minister asked The Queen to formally sign the bill that approved her position as The Queen of New Zealand. At the end of this historic day The Prince of Wales returned to HMS *Jupiter* to resume his duties.[48]

From Waitangi the Yacht sailed to Auckland where Lord Mountbatten joined the Royal party. The Yacht then headed north to begin the Tour of the Pacific Islands including Norfolk Island and Pentacost Island, where the Royal Family watched a local display of land diving on 16 February which ended with tragic results. The Pentacost islanders have performed the head down jump for many generations as a form of celebration known as *Gol*, which roughly translates into fun. The islanders normally perform the jump after the first yam harvest at a site deep within the jungle away from the tourists. However, the islanders agreed to make an exception for The Queen and

erect a jump tower of some 80 feet near the beach at a time of the year when they don't normally jump. Two lengths of lianas are tied around the ankles of the jumper to the tower and they are carefully measured so that they nearly reach the ground when they are fully stretched. When the time comes to jump the crowd starts chanting louder and louder which helps to whip up an air of expectation. The man then jumps off the platform and is brought to a halt by the lianas very close to the soft ground before jumping to his feet. Sadly, the third jumper wasn't so lucky, as Prince Philip explains:

'The jumper volunteered to take the place of one who had gone sick at the last moment. The "old men" tried to dissuade him on the grounds that the vines had been measured for the other man and were not suitable for him. Unfortunately, they eventually let him jump and their fears were justified.'

The lianas did not break but he received fatal head injuries when he hit the ground and was quickly taken to hospital where he died a few days later. Despite the obvious risks of land diving the jumper was one of only a few recorded deaths caused by land diving. The Royal Family returned to *Britannia* and the Yacht sailed for Santo, before heading off to the Solomon Islands that night.

The following evening there was a very memorable ship's concert entitled 'Round The World In Eighty Ways', as Admiral Trowbridge explained:

'It was quite outstanding because the first act was carried out by the entire Royal Household and the mem-

The Queen on a walkabout during her visit to the New Hebrides.

(© British Crown Copyright / MOD)

bers of the Royal Family embarked. This was something that had never happened before and the theme of the act was to show the Yachtsmen what happens when The Queen arrives by air and is then greeted by the locals before joining *Britannia* and sailing away. Another of the highlights was The Queen's Private Secretary, Martin Charteris, who gave a superb address in Pidgin English. He had ERII written on his bald head which was visible whenever he bowed. The house was brought down by Princess Anne and a couple of the younger girls in the office doing a magnificent hula dance. It finished off with me turning up with a couple of hula girls to find that the Yacht had sailed without me!'

Lord Mountbatten also led a *haka*, which is a Maori war dance. He performed the actions and shouted the words of a *haka* he had learned while serving as Flag Lieutenant to Rear Admiral Sir Lionel Halsey during the Tour of Australia and New Zealand by The Prince of Wales in 1920.

During the Tour of the Solomon Islands, the Royal Family visited Guadalcanal, Gizo and Bougainville Islands, before arriving in Rabaul in Papua New Guinea on 23 February. At the end of the visit to Papua New Guinea The Queen had been due to fly south to Canberra and then begin a short Tour of South and West Australia, with Prince Philip rejoining the Yacht at Darwin. However, The Queen felt that she should be back in London in case important decisions needed to be made after the British General Election, which had been called by Edward Heath for 28 February 1974. Therefore, The Queen flew from Port Moresby down to Canberra,

where she opened the Australian Parliament on 28 February, before catching a flight back to the UK where she arrived in the early hours of 1 March. In the event The Queen took the right decision because the result of the General Election was very close with neither party winning a clear working majority. Although the Conservatives had won five less seats than the Labour Party, Edward Heath didn't immediately resign as Prime Minister and tried in vain to form a coalition Government with the Liberal Party. After a weekend of talks Edward Heath had failed to reach a deal so he resigned on 4 March thus clearing the way for Harold Wilson to become the next Prime Minister. At the time of her departure the future of the Tour looked uncertain because there was some doubt about whether The Queen would return to Australia.[49] In the meantime Prince Philip undertook the planned programme around Australia without The Queen, while Princess Anne and Captain Phillips flew back to the UK. Lord Mountbatten remained on board for an extra couple of days before flying to Singapore on 1 March to undertake further engagements prior to rejoining the Yacht in Darwin. While the Royal Family were carrying out their various separate programmes, the Yacht sailed for Darwin on 2 March and arrived there four days later to await the return of Lord Mountbatten and Prince Philip on 8 and 9 March respectively. Following a day of engagements ashore in Darwin for His Royal Highness the Yacht sailed for Bali on 10 March. During the passage Prince Philip took the opportunity to walk round the Yacht and talk to many of the Yachtsmen.

On 14 March the Yacht reached Bali and anchored to await the embarkation of The Queen who had flown back from London. After a day of engagements ashore in Bali, which culminated in a dinner for Indonesian Ministers, the Yacht sailed for Tanjong Priok, the port of Jakarta, where she arrived on 18 March to formally begin The Queen's State Visit to the Republic of Indonesia. The Queen and Prince Philip, together with Lord Mountbatten, lived ashore for the duration of the State Visit. It was while they were living ashore that news reached the Yacht in the early hours of 21 March that Princess Anne and Captain Phillips had been held up in The Mall by a gunman who had shot the Princess's driver and detective as well as a policeman and another man. Despite trying to pull the Princess from the car his kidnap plan failed and he was subsequently arrested. After some initial confusion about where to contact The Queen's Private Secretary, Sir Martin Charteris, he was given the news on the Yacht, which he broke to The Queen and Prince Philip by telephone.

While the Yacht was berthed in Tanjong Priok three packing cases arrived on the jetty for the Director of Music on 22 March. During their stay at the Presidential Palace in Jakarta The Queen and Prince Philip attended a concert laid on for them which included some music played on anklungs. Prince Philip managed to arrange for a set to be delivered to the Yacht because he thought it would provide a challenge for the RM Band and an interesting party piece. Anklungs follow the principles of tubular bells so that when each bell is rattled it produces a note. The principle difference is that anklungs are made from bamboo. Lieutenant Colonel Mason recalled:

'The three packing cases contained the anklungs with 80 bamboo bells in all to produce a full range of notes. I laid them out on the deck to make sure that we knew what they were and marked each bell with the appropriate note. I invited The Queen to then come out and have a look at her set of anklungs when she returned that afternoon. She said, "They look very nice. Please can you play them at tonight's dinner in the Embassy." We had to hurriedly write sheets of music out and each Bandsman had a couple of these anklungs and when it came to his bit he rattled it. We played a couple of tunes that night. When we returned to the UK I used them in a concert in the Guildhall, Portsmouth. They subsequently deteriorated because of the change in climate between Indonesia and the UK!'

Normally, during the course of a State Visit The Queen hosted a return banquet on board *Britannia*. However, President Suharto's Military Secretary was so concerned about the President's safety during the journey through the rough suburbs to where *Britannia* was berthed that he tried to get the plans changed. In the end after a series of protracted negotiations, during which the official used every excuse possible before finally admitting his real concerns, the banquet was held in the British Embassy. The change of venue created a lot of additional work for everyone, not least the Master of the Household who had to arrange for everything required that night to be moved 10 miles from the Yacht to the Embassy. Despite this the banquet proved to be a successful climax to the Royal

The Queen is presented with a gift during her visit to the Solomon Islands with Prince Philip.

Rear Admiral Richard Trowbridge celebrates the 21st Anniversary of the Yacht's commissioning with the six members of the Yacht's company who had served continuously in the Yacht during that time. (© British Crown Copyright / MOD)

Family's long overseas Tour. The following evening they left Jakarta by air to fly back to the UK. Shortly, before The Queen's aircraft took off, the Yacht began her own long journey home calling at Singapore, Mauritius, St Helena, Dakar and Casablanca, to reach Portsmouth on 3 May. In a deployment which had already witnessed several major changes, the planned call at Simons Town on the way home was cancelled as a result of the new Labour Government refusing permission for the visit. Although the visits to St Helena and Casablanca were organised as substitutes for the Simons Town visit there wasn't a Yachtsman on board who wasn't disappointed by the Government's decision. The year's Royal duty ended with Cowes Week and the Western Isles Cruise during August before the Yacht entered dockyard hands for routine maintenance.

The New Year began with celebrations to mark the Yacht's 21st birthday on 8 January 1975. As part of the celebrations there was a cake cutting ceremony performed in front of the Yachtsmen, followed by the presentation of tankards to the six men who had continuously served on board the Yacht since she was first commissioned in 1954[50]. To provide the rest of the Yachtsmen with a souvenir of this milestone the Coxswain Fleet Chief Petty

Officer Norrell arranged for a silver medallion to be struck. Each medallion was given a serial number with number one being presented to The Queen.

At the end of the month the Yacht left Portsmouth for her deployment to the Caribbean, Central America and the USA. Having crossed the Atlantic via Madeira and Antigua, the Yacht arrived in Nassau on 16 February. Four days later The Queen and Prince Philip embarked for the final stages of their Caribbean Tour, during which they had already visited Bermuda and Barbados.[51] The following morning the Royal couple undertook a busy programme of engagements ashore, including the opening of the Central Bank before returning to the Yacht after lunch, prior to her sailing for Cozumel and their next State Visit.[52] Originally, the Yacht was to have sailed to Vera Cruz for The Queen and Prince Philip to fly on to Mexico City for the start of their State Visit. However, the Mexican Government didn't want The Queen's first view of Mexico to be Vera Cruz, which had become a very run down area. Instead the Mexicans wanted The Queen to disembark at the island of Cozumel but, when FORY consulted the Atlantic Pilot, he was concerned by what he read. The Pilot said that in the month of February Cozumel was likely to have at least half a dozen Force 8 or 9 gales. Despite this warning the Mexicans still pressed for the visit to begin at Cozumel. Thus the arrangements were made accordingly and the Yacht arrived off the island on 24 February. As Admiral Rowe explains, the charts for Cozumel weren't entirely accurate:

'I took morning stars and worked out that we were two hours away from Cozumel. Two hours later there was no sign of Cozumel – it wasn't where it was charted. Luckily, the escort HMS *Tartar* had a decent radar set and told me that they had a contact on their radar 30 miles to the west which they thought was Cozumel. So we set off at high speed to catch up the lost time. When we arrived it was blowing a gale and we had to run down wind into uncharted waters, which I had expected to be deeper. During our approach to the anchorage the forecastle party suddenly rang me to ask, "should we be able to see the bottom?" I immediately looked over the side and could see the crabs scuttling away as the shadow of the Yacht came over them. I rang down full astern and it took ages for us to start going astern. Not helped by the Engine Room phoning the Bridge to ask if we really meant "full astern". It was the closest I ever came to running the Yacht aground!'

The bad weather looked as though it would disrupt the plans for The Queen and Prince Philip's disembarkation. It had been envisaged that they would be taken ashore in the

Barge, where they would board the waiting VC10 at the airport for the flight to Mexico City. However, before that could happen all the Royal luggage needed to be taken ashore and originally this was due to have been done by boat. In view of the weather conditions it was decided that The Queen's luggage would be flown ashore by Wasp helicopter from the Royal Escort HMS *Tartar*. With the issue of the Royal luggage resolved, FORY still had to take the difficult decision about how The Queen and Prince Philip would be taken ashore. On the one hand Admiral Trowbridge wanted to ensure that The Queen was able to carry out her programme and yet he was personally responsible for her safety. Describing the dilemma and the course of action he took Admiral Trowbridge said:

'At 0430 we were about 3 miles off the coast in a flat calm waiting for it to get light. As dawn broke at 0600 it was blowing a near gale, steep choppy sea, uncomfortable swell, and all in all very unpleasant. We got a motor boat away in very marginal conditions, which found the jetty that The Queen was supposed to use completely out of the question and awash. We discovered, by looking at the chart, that a couple of miles up the coast there was a small yacht harbour so we sent a motor boat to investigate. They reported that providing we could get in it would be possible. I was then faced with the most difficult decision of the whole of my time as FORY. A constant stream of information was reaching the bridge from back aft saying there were somewhere between a million and a million and a half spectators lining the streets of Mexico City where The Queen was expected later on. What were we going to do? Would I say yes, or no? I said I would make my decision in time for The Queen to be landed at the time she expects to go or not. My main concern was that The Queen would have to board the Barge at deck level together with the rest of us and then be lowered and slipped. In those days the Barge had no disengaging gear. Opinion aft was split, as some said yes while others said no. With a mental toss up, "will it, won't it", I sent a message back aft saying I was ready to land Her Majesty and that I considered that we could get ashore safely. At the upper deck level we all got on board the Barge and it was levelled a few feet above the water. With the excellence that one comes to expect from the Barge's crew and exactly the right roll of the ship as we dipped into the sea the last bit of the shackles were disengaged and we were off – much to my relief! We got in safely and the tiny harbour was full of yachts and cheering Americans who were astonished that we had risked coming in. The Queen thanked me for getting her ashore on time under very difficult conditions. All in all it was a very tricky few hours operating on the borders of safety. I think we were extremely lucky the price paid was one broken wrist and one of the motor boat crew washed overboard and then quickly recovered with only a brief dunking – it could have been very much worse.'

To celebrate the Yacht's 21st birthday a limited number of medallions were produced to mark the event. The Coxswain, Fleet Chief Petty Officer E V Norrell presents the first medallion to Her Majesty.

(© British Crown Copyright / MOD)

The dramatic lowering of the Royal Barge during the visit to Cozumel at the start of The Queen and Prince Philip's State Visit to Mexico.   (© British Crown Copyright / MOD)

Three quarters of an hour after The Queen and Prince Philip went ashore the Yacht sailed for Vera Cruz where she arrived on 26 February ahead of the next day's Sea Day.[53] It was the first time that a Sea Day had been held in the Yacht since the original events off Brazil in 1968. Shortly, before the Yacht's departure from the UK, Buckingham Palace had announced the news that she was going to be used for a Sea Day to try and help promote British industry. Interestingly, the press reacted very negatively to the news. When the journalists tried to find out who was funding the event there seemed to be some confusion. Buckingham Palace was under the impression that the DTI were paying while DTI thought that the British Overseas Trade Board were footing the bill. It was a fascinating foretaste of the future conflicts over which Government Department would pay for *Britannia's* replacement. Despite the controversy in the press the Sea Day itself was very successful, as Admiral Trowbridge explains:

'We sailed at 1000 and the weather couldn't have been better. Everything went well. Our escort HMS *Tartar* provided a superb display firing her guns, dropping depth charges, and helicopter exercises. Peter Thornycroft, who was part of the British delegation, told me later that as a direct result of that Sea Day Vosper Thornycroft sold a number of patrol boats to the Mexican Navy. However, despite the success of the day going back into harbour was typical of Mexican inefficiency. Although we had the best pilot in Vera Cruz on board there were no tugs and despite his best efforts to get some nothing happened for about 20 minutes. We could see a couple of pairs of tugs shifting a huge slab-sided merchantmen around the harbour a few hundred yards away. As a result of me being rather rude to our Mexican liaison officer he went away and got one of our civilians on board who turned out to be the Minister for Marine. He – splendid fellow – got in touch with the shore authorities and within a minute two slab-sided vessels were left drifting and four tugs were steaming towards us. They made an excellent job of getting us alongside.'

About two hours after the guests for the Sea Day had disembarked, The Queen and Prince Philip returned to the Yacht to host the return State Banquet for the President of Mexico. Two days later, in the morning The Queen and Prince Philip visited one of the two fishery protection vessels which had been built in the UK for the Mexican Navy before The Queen travelled alone to the airport to fly home. After his visit to the Mexican Naval Academy in the afternoon Prince Philip returned to the Yacht for the passage to Belize.[54] During his Tour of Central America, between 1 and 19 March, Prince Philip visited Belize, Honduras and Costa Rico before flying back to the UK.

When this spring deployment was being planned, the period between Prince Philip's departure on 19 March, and The Queen's embarkation in Jamaica on 26 April presented FORY with a major PR challenge. It wasn't worth sailing back to the UK because a day or so after the Yacht docked in Portsmouth she would have to turn round and sail back across the Atlantic. However, the Yacht couldn't be seen to be simply swanning about the Caribbean for a month, as the press would pick up on this very quickly. Therefore, FORY had to come up with a credible plan, which included two weeks' self-maintenance in Bermuda and an additional visit in the area. New Orleans seemed to be the popular choice on board the Yacht so FORY managed to speak to the Foreign Secretary, Jim Callaghan, who told him to go ahead and make the arrangements. Callaghan felt that such a visit could be a useful method of generating some goodwill in the USA. Furthermore, he said that if the press tried to make trouble he would explain the facts of the situation to them personally. Thus, from Costa Rico, the Yacht headed north for New Orleans, where she arrived on 24 March for a week-long visit. The Americans took the Yacht to their hearts and made the Yachtsmen extremely welcome. From New Orleans the Yacht headed south again, to arrive in Bermuda on 9 April for 10 days of routine maintenance before sailing for Jamaica and anchoring off Kingston on 23 April. Three days later The Queen and Prince Philip embarked for the Commonwealth Heads Of Government Meeting (CHOGM).

In addition to receiving each of the Commonwealth leaders for an individual audience on board the Yacht during the course of CHOGM The Queen also hosted a major dinner on 29 April. Twenty Prime Ministers, seven Presidents and five deputies, as well as the Secretary General of the Commonwealth, attended the dinner on board. With the Yacht lying at anchor off Kingston each of the leaders had to be taken by boat out to *Britannia*, as Commander Creedy recalled:

'I had a truly fascinating half hour coming face to face with so many national leaders – some of whom were instantly recognisable and others less so. Amongst the former category were Harold Wilson, Pierre Trudeau of Canada, Archbishop Makarios of Greece, Mrs Ghandi of India and Kenneth Kaunda of Zambia. I was on the jetty leading the VIPs to the appropriate boats to take them out to the Yacht. Everything seemed to be going smoothly when a resplendently uniformed African (glittering with gilt oak leaves on his cap, aiguillettes

The Governor of the Isle of Wight, Lord Mountbatten, escorts The Queen Mother during her visit to Cowes.

(© British Crown Copyright / MOD)

The Royal Escort HMS Tartar puts on a show for the embarked businessmen during the Sea Day held off Vera Cruz.

(© British Crown Copyright / MOD)

Prince Edward is 'promoted' to Able Seaman by Rear Admiral Trowbridge during Cowes Week as the Commander and Coxswain look on.   (© British Crown Copyright / MOD)

on his shoulder and medals on his chest) strode on to the jetty accompanied by a gentleman in plain clothes. I instantly identified them mentally as General Gowon of Nigeria plus bodyguard. I gave the General a smart salute and invited him to follow me to a boat, whereupon he said, "Thank you very much. This is President Stevens of Sierra Leone, and I'm his ADC [Aide-de-Camp]!" The real General Gowon arrived a few minutes later in Nigerian national dress.'

At the end of their four-day visit The Queen and Prince Philip left Jamaica on 30 April by air for their visits to Hong Kong and Japan.[55] The next morning Britannia sailed for the UK, arriving in Portsmouth on 14 May.

On 27 May The Queen Mother joined Britannia in Portsmouth for her visit to the Channel Islands. Having visited Guernsey and Jersey, the Yacht headed back towards the mainland and anchored off Sandown on 31 May, where the Governor of the Isle of Wight, Lord Mountbatten came on board, as Admiral Trowbridge remembered: 'Lord Mountbatten was greatly thrilled to embark in the Yacht wearing his uniform as Captain General of the Royal Marines. Because he had never worn this uniform on board the Yacht before he wanted Snaps to take his photograph as he arrived to escort The Queen Mother.' After a day of engagements in Cowes The Queen Mother returned to the Yacht for the night. The

following morning she toured Britannia to meet many of the Yachtsmen before the Yacht weighed anchor for Portsmouth at lunchtime.[56] When the Yacht reached Portsmouth The Queen Mother disembarked to HMS Vernon, as Commander Creedy recalled:

'As The Queen Mother stepped ashore the Barge lurched slightly and she almost stumbled; in regaining her balance The Queen Mother dropped her handbag, which fell into the water between the Barge and the jetty. Hugh Slade, the Royal Barge Officer, quickly bent down and retrieved it before it sank. He was about to return the dripping bag to its owner when he thought better of it and instead handed it to Lady Jean Rankin, the Lady-in-Waiting. A couple of days later Hugh Slade received a hand-written letter of thanks from The Queen Mother enclosing a silver propelling pencil.'

Admiral Trowbridge's final duty as FORY was to take the Yacht to Cowes Week at the beginning of August. The Queen had decided it wasn't appropriate for her to undertake a Western Isles Cruise in view of the poor economic state of the country. Thus Admiral Trowbridge concluded his seagoing career on 9 August when he brought Britannia back into Portsmouth at the end of Cowes Week. This change of plan also meant that Admiral Trowbridge was the first FORY not to be knighted by The Queen on board the Yacht. Instead he received his KCVO during his farewell audience with The Queen at Buckingham Palace on 31 July.[57]

LT. CMDR. G.J.T. CREEDY.
D.S.O. 1973 - 1975

Each of the officers were presented with a 'Gonk' made by the shipwright. Each Gonk was personalised to reflect the officer's specialisation. In this case coins and a tankard were added to the Gonk presented to Lieutenant Commander Creedy when he finished his appointment as the Deputy Supply Officer.   (© Richard Johnstone-Bryden)

Chapter Eight

THE JUBILEE TOURS

Rear Admiral Sir Hugh Janion KCVO 1975–1981

After 40 years in the Royal Navy, Rear Admiral Sir Richard Trowbridge KCVO retired, both as FORY and from the service, on 11 September 1975. He was succeeded by Rear Admiral Hugh Janion who had first joined the RN in 1937. Admiral Janion had an active career during the Second World War serving in the battleship HMS *Rodney* followed by the cruiser HMS *London* escorting convoys to Russia. In 1943 he was sent to the Mediterranean in the destroyer HMS *Brocklesby* to participate in the Allied landings at Sicily and Salerno as well as operations in the Adriatic during 1944. Following his service in the Malayan emergency and the Korean War, Admiral Janion specialised as an Air Direction Officer, serving in the aircraft carriers HMS *Indomitable*, HMS *Glory*, HMS *Centaur*, and HMS *Ark Royal* which proved a lucky ship as he was promoted to Commander when he left her for the first time, and to Captain on the second occasion. In between his appointments to *Ark Royal*, he commanded the minesweeper HMS *Jewel*. As a Captain he commanded the frigate HMS *Aurora* and went to Northwood on the staff of Commander-in-Chief Fleet as Captain of the Fleet. In 1973 he became the first Captain of the Type 82 destroyer HMS *Bristol*, before being promoted to Rear Admiral in July 1975. Describing Admiral Janion as FORY, his last Commander, later Vice Admiral Sir Michael Moore KBE LVO, said: 'he had such immense style and he would wander around the Yacht and know everyone's name and everything about them. He had a great heap of experiences and a never-ending fund of stories, which he told with a delightful sense of humour and fun.' As Commander Creedy, who served in the Yacht

as the Supply Officer, explains, Admiral Janion remained cool and collected under the most testing of circumstances:

'During The Queen's Tour of the Middle East in 1979 we were coming into a port assisted by local tugs. One of the tug skippers was either overcome by the situation or let down by his command of English; either way he was still pushing hard after he had been instructed to stop pushing and pull us astern. From my position near the bridge I watched with horror as the jetty approached noticeably faster than usual. I thought to myself, "this is going to be embarrassing; I hope there won't be too much damage."

'At that moment I heard Admiral Janion's voice, as calm as if he had been asking someone to pass the salt, "Full astern both engines. Hard a' starboard." As the propellers bit into the water the Yacht shuddered and, rapidly losing her forward momentum, tucked herself neatly alongside the jetty with the gentlest of bumps against the fenders. One could almost hear the collective exhalation of breath as the expected crash failed to materialise.'

Within a week of becoming FORY, Admiral Janion took the Yacht to sea for the first time on 17 September when she sailed from Portsmouth to undergo sea training at Portland. During Admiral Janion's time as the Captain of HMS *Bristol* she had suffered a major boiler room fire while at anchor off Milford Haven in 1974. The fire caused extensive damage on board and would have resulted in the loss of the ship if it hadn't been for the prompt actions of her Ship's company. Not surprisingly, Admiral Janion placed a very high emphasis on safety and he wanted to ensure that the Yachtsmen were fully versed in the latest safety drills. The whole regime at Portland was geared towards working up operational warships, so *Britannia* had historically only ever spent a short time at Portland as part of her work-up routine because her training requirements were very different to those of a warship. Therefore, during the Yacht's three days of exercises in the Portland area, Flag Officer Sea Training's Staff concentrated upon seamanship exercises, such as damage control and ceremonial procedures, such as manning ship and dressing ship.[1] On completion of the Yacht's time at Portland she sailed to participate in a naval exercise, before returning to Portsmouth on 2 October to prepare for the forthcoming refit.[2] Interestingly, the issue of whether *Britannia* should be converted to run on diesel instead of Furnace Fuel Oil (FFO) was considered. Because there were still a number of warships, both in the RN and other NATO navies, that ran on FFO the conversion issue hadn't yet become a matter of urgency. The idea was quickly dropped when doubts were raised about whether the thinner diesel would leak out of the Yacht's riveted fuel tanks.

The refit itself was completed by mid April 1976 and, once the post-refit trials had been completed, she was ready to sail from Portsmouth on 19 May for The Queen's State Visit to Finland. Having embarked The Queen and Prince Philip in the Port of Mariehamn on 24 May, the Yacht arrived the next morning at Helsinki for the beginning of the visit. During their time in Finland the Royal couple lived ashore in the Presidential Palace in Helsinki, before rejoining the Yacht in Turku for the final part of their programme. This culminated in the floodlit departure of the Yacht on 28 May and the next day's passage through the Kiel Canal, which was watched by large and enthusiastic crowds. Despite the poor weather the banks were dominated by long lines of people following the Yacht in their cars.[3] Once *Britannia* entered the North Sea, she headed for the River Thames, where Prince Philip disembarked at Gravesend on 1 June, followed later in the morning by The Queen, who left at Tilbury before the Yacht sailed back to Portsmouth.[4]

Two weeks later the Yacht left Portsmouth for her deployment to North America via the Azores and Bermuda, where The Queen and Prince Philip embarked on 3 July. After the reception and Beat Retreat, *Britannia* sailed that night for the USA and, the next morning, a church service was held in the Royal Dining Room to mark the bicentenary of America's Independence from the UK.[5] Two days later *Britannia* made her way up the Delaware River to berth in Philadelphia. Once alongside, The Queen and Prince Philip landed, to be taken away in a large motorcade to begin their shore programme, beginning with the inauguration of the Bicentary Bell at the Independence National Historical Park, before going on to tour the older parts of the city. In the afternoon the Royal couple returned to the Yacht for a reception attended by 37 of America's 52 Governors, as the Commander (E), later Captain R A Worlidge LVO RN recalls:

'What impressed me was what a genuine honour they all felt it was to be presented to The Queen. They were also enthralled with the Yacht itself. When the Governors and their wives left 35 people came on board for an investiture followed by a further 250 people streaming on board before the end of the ceremony for a reception. It was a pretty mammoth organisation dealing with about 350 people within two hours to go to different functions.'[6]

Early the next morning the Yacht sailed, to berth in the Philadelphia Navy Yard for that morning's disembarkation of The Queen and Prince Philip for their flight to Washington, where they were received by President and Mrs Ford at the White House. Meanwhile, once the Yacht had taken on more fuel she sailed for New York where she berthed at Bayonne Military Ocean Terminal on the morning of 8 July. Half an hour later 100 guests and 12 members of the press were embarked for the Sea Day, organised by the British Overseas Trade Board to foster improved commercial links between the UK and the USA. The American guests included the heads of the airlines TWA and PANAM, the senior executive of Woolworths, as well as 26 chief executives of American transnational corporations whose combined assets were worth over $66 billion. The Sea Day was a great success and the Yacht made a very positive impression on the American guests, as Captain Worlidge explained: 'one gentleman said to me, "You know you are the only nation in the world who could pull this off and get such an influential gathering of men together and make it such an outstanding success. They wouldn't have come for anyone else."' The following morning the Royal couple returned to *Britannia* after their Washington visit prior to the passage up into the heart of New York to berth at Pier 88, which was once used by famous liners such as *Queen Elizabeth* and *Queen Mary*. Describing the Yacht's arrival, Captain Worlidge continued:

'It was a subdued entrance as the police kept all boats at least ½ mile clear, instead of our customary 40 yards. Any boat that dared to come near was either warned off by the coastguard craft or buzzed at the height of about 10 feet by a helicopter. An aircraft appeared flying a banner saying "English, get out of Ireland" and was immediately escorted away by two helicopters and reported to have been arrested. The Americans were clearly taking the security very seriously. The Queen disembarked half way up the harbour to go to the battery, and we then forged on to make an extremely difficult alongside with a 4-knot ebb tide on to a hollow pier.'

The Queen and Prince Philip returned, late afternoon, for that night's dinner and reception, as Captain Worlidge observed:

'We sailed at midnight for the most memorable trip up the Eastern River round Manhattan Island. It was just like a fairytale with the thousands and thousands of lights, and going under numerous bridges. The first bridge we went under, Brooklyn Bridge, we only had 6-foot clearance, which was quite exciting. This excitement went on for about two hours. I had never seen anything like it. Naturally, we were floodlit, so we must have made a superb sight from the shore.'[7]

Having rounded Manhattan Island, the Yacht sailed for Newport, Rhode Island, where she arrived the following morning. While the Royal couple were away undertaking engagements ashore, preparations were underway for that evening's visit of President Ford, as the Royal Cypher Officer, later Commodore A J C Morrow CVO RN, explained:

'As part of the shore-side liaison team I had to ensure that the President was going to have the right communications available during his time on board. I therefore had a number of conversations with the President's security and communications staff. Initially, they weren't very happy that we didn't allow any weapons on board but we soon overcame the problem because they realised that from a security point of view while the President and The Queen were ashore it was their problem and while they were on board it was our problem. However, the issue of communications presented more of a challenge not least the hot line. A black telephone was provided by the Yacht with the cable to connect it to a junction box on the jetty. I agreed with

President and Mrs Ford and their daughter Miss Susan Ford are welcomed on board Britannia *by the Commander during the Yacht's visit to Newport, Rhode Island on 10 July 1976.*

(© British Crown Copyright / MOD)

The Yacht is berthed astern of the US Navy's oldest commissioned warship the 179-year-old USS Constitution *during* Britannia's *visit to Boston.*

(© British Crown Copyright / MOD)

the Admiral that this telephone would be placed in The Queen's Sitting Room. When the President's staff saw the arrangements they couldn't believe that we undid the carpet in both The Queen's Sitting Room and the area leading to it so that there were no unsightly wires showing.'

However, once the cable and telephone were in place there were a few minor teething problems, as Fleet Chief Petty Officer Dick Field, later Mr R Field RVM, recalled:

'At first I couldn't get it to work so I tried dialling out and nothing happened. Eventually, I was holding the phone to my ear and I said, "I can't get anything on this," to which a voice on the other end said, "We're on listening watch all the time. We are never off this phone!"'

At 2015 the President, together with Mrs Ford and his daughter Susan arrived and were greeted by the Yacht manning ship, a distinct honour for a visiting President. As Captain Worlidge remembers: 'it was a most impressive performance with outriders, bullet proof cars and

Secret Service men. As the President's car drew up the following car's doors opened and the security men leapt from the running boards and surrounded the President's car looking outwards before any doors were opened.' The President posed for photographs with his family at the bottom of the brow, before stepping on board. As he did so, he received the unprecedented honour of being piped on board in plain clothes. This honour was accorded to the President at the express wish of The Queen, to mark the bicentenary of the American Declaration of Independence, and to highlight the respect held by the British for the office of the President of The United States of America. While the President and the other Government officials attended the State Banquet held in the Royal Dining Room, the Wardroom entertained the remaining officials who couldn't be accommodated within the Royal Dining Room, as Commodore Morrow explains:

'The Presidential aides all had their walkie talkies and were constantly checking in with their counterparts to ensure that everything was OK. They were getting a bit jittery towards the end of dinner because they wanted to be in a position to go ashore with the President the moment he was ready to leave. They couldn't believe it when suddenly the Commander announced that the President was going to depart in five minutes. One of them was fascinated by this and asked us how this was possible. We explained that one of the staff in the Royal Dining Room would let the Wardroom know when something like this would happen. One of the staff went to the Wardroom area where they would look through one of the scuttles and put his thumb up as the signal. This was passed to the Commander who knew exactly what was going on. It was so important to the silent running of *Britannia* – a simple thumbs up was enough.'

Looking back on his visit to the Yacht President Ford, later recalled:

'Mrs Ford and I had two memorable visits to the Royal Yacht *Britannia* as guests of Her Majesty and Prince Philip. On this occasion, we hosted The Queen and Prince Philip at a State Dinner in Washington DC as an occasion of the America's Bicentennial. The Queen subsequently invited the Fords to a reciprocal State Dinner on *Britannia*. This was a most memorable dinner.'

Following the President's departure, the Yacht sailed overnight for The Queen's visit to Boston the next morning.[8] As the Yacht entered Boston Harbour she was greet-ed by the sight of the US Navy's oldest commissioned vessel, the 179-year-old USS *Constitution*, which had been towed out from her permanent berth to fire a 21-gun salute in honour of The Queen. As part of their shore programme the Royal couple attended morning service in Old North Church, which was originally built by the Church of England in 1730. In the evening the Yacht sailed for The Queen's Tour of Canada, arriving in Halifax on 13 July, where The Queen and Prince Philip left the Yacht to spend the night ashore before flying inland to begin their programme. Meanwhile, the Yacht sailed shortly before midnight to begin her passage up through the St Lawrence Seaway to Montreal. Since the Yacht's last visit to the St Lawrence Seaway in 1967 the local pollution laws for the Seaway had been significantly changed and *Britannia* no longer met all of the requirements for pumping out sewage. Obviously, something had to be done, but there hadn't been enough time during the refit at the beginning of the year to fit holding tanks. Therefore, it was decided to embark portable toilets for use by the Yacht's company for the duration of the Yacht's time on the Seaway so that she complied with the regulations.[9]

The Yacht arrived in Montreal on 16 July and, later that evening, The Queen, Prince Philip and Prince Andrew embarked ahead of the next day's opening of the Montreal Olympics by The Queen. The Yacht's company were unable to get tickets for the Opening Ceremony, so they watched the live coverage on the TV sets that had

The Prince of Wales and Prince Andrew walking up the brow followed by Prince Edward in Montreal.

Prince Edward helps to rig a sailing dinghy during the Royal Family's 1976 Western Isles Cruise.

(© British Crown Copyright / MOD)

been lent to the Yacht. Over the next nine days the Royal Family attended various events at the Games which had an added personal interest through the participation of Princess Anne in the Equestrian 3-Day Event. Her Royal Highness had a bad fall during the event, but re-mounted and finished the course. At the end of two very busy Tours, the Royal party, which had been joined by The Prince of Wales and Prince Edward on 23 July, flew back to London at midnight on 25 July. After a further day alongside, the Yacht began her passage back down the St Lawrence Seaway to St John's Newfoundland, where she stopped for a day to take on fuel, before heading back across the Atlantic Ocean. Because of the timing of the North American visits, the Yacht headed straight for Scotland, to undertake the Western Isles Cruise, before finally returning to Portsmouth on 17 August for the next day's Families Day. Once the Yacht's company returned from Summer leave, the preparations got underway for one of the Yacht's busiest years, in which *Britannia* played a pivotal role in supporting The Queen's programme to celebrate her Silver Jubilee.

To meet the tight programme, it was necessary for the Yacht to sail from Portsmouth on 28 December to begin her sixth circumnavigation of the world. As *Britannia* steamed towards Madeira, the Yacht's company gathered on the Verandah Deck shortly before midnight on New Year's Eve to witness the New Year being rung in on the Yacht's bell. After a brief stop at Antigua, the Yacht sailed through the Panama Canal on 15 January 1977. The pilot

for the transit was Captain Makibbin who had taken the Yacht through the canal before. The occasion was especially memorable for the Captain because he was about to retire and *Britannia* was to be one of his final jobs. During the transit it transpired that the Captain was very partial to kippers which were very hard to come by in the Canal Zone. Thus when the Captain disembarked he was presented with a box of kippers as a farewell present. Two days later the Yacht sailed from Rodman Naval Base to begin her passage across the vast expanse of the Pacific Ocean, via Tahiti, Raratonga and Palmerston Island, before arriving in Paga Pago on 6 February.

Four days later The Queen and Prince Philip embarked, after their 23-hour flight from London, to begin the Silver Jubilee Tour of the Pacific and Australasia. One of those who accompanied The Queen on board the Yacht was the new Assistant Private Secretary, later The Rt Hon. Lord Fellowes GCB GCVO QSO. The Tour was to be his first experience of *Britannia*. Looking back on how he thought the Yacht enhanced The Queen's visits he remarked:

'The Yacht was an invaluable adjunct to a Tour, in that it afforded The Queen, Prince Philip, and the Household a wonderful background. It wasn't somewhere for them to relax because the Yacht was, in every sense, a floating office, and one did a lot of hard work on board. When I joined the Yacht after a few days ashore, I would find bags of work waiting from London.

The Queen would often go straight to her office and start working. Therefore the idea that it was a floating Palace, or a luxury liner, is really nonsense. It was comfortable, it was beautiful, great fun and there was a certain excitement of being at sea, or even alongside, because it was a tremendous magnet for people to come and look at it. By the time I joined the Yacht, the days of month-long cruises along the Pacific Ocean were over. Already, The Queen was flying out to meet the Yacht somewhere, sail for a couple of days, use her again, and then depart into the interior. Therefore, the original *raison d'etre* of the Yacht, which was to carry The Queen from A to B, to C, to D, had already gone. That increasingly became the case until towards the end of the Yacht's service, when there was practically no travelling in the Yacht. It was always a question of using her in key locations. Instead, the Yacht added value to a State Visit by adding style and there was nothing like her anywhere else in the world. Foreign Heads of State, whether they were of the traditional monarchical mould, or presidents, were tremendously struck by being entertained in unique style. For example, in 1983 when the Reagans spent their 31st wedding anniversary on board the Yacht, their party ended with their Chief of Staff playing the piano wearing a Marine helmet, while Ronald and Nancy Reagan sang 'True Love' holding hands. There aren't many palaces where that would have happened but there was something special about the Yacht that enabled that to occur without embarrassment – it was spontaneous, and terrific fun.'

Later in the morning of 10 February the Yacht sailed for Apia, arriving there in the evening, where she received an enthusiastic aquatic welcome, including some of the long war canoes known as *fautasi* which were paddled by up to 50 men. That night The Queen hosted a dinner attended by the Head of State HH Malietoa Tanumafili II. Before the Yacht sailed the next afternoon The Queen received some of the local Chiefs, as the Commander of the Yacht, later Rear Admiral C H Layman CB DSO LVO, recalled:

'Anyone who is invited to meet The Queen always turns up early and so these Chiefs were waiting for The Queen to arrive. While they waited for The Queen they stood on the recently tarmaced jetty and gently sank into the tarmac. By the time The Queen came back on board and the Chiefs were invited to come on board, the beautiful teak decks ended up with black tarmac footprints all over them!'

On completion of farewells, *Britannia* sailed for Tonga, crossing the International Dateline on the way, thus 13 February didn't exist on board.

On 14 February the Yacht arrived in Tonga, where The Queen and Prince Philip were welcomed by The King and

The Queen stands next to HH Malietoa Tanumafili II for Her Majesty's formal welcome to Apia, Western Samoa.

The Queen and Prince Philip on deck for Britannia's *departure from Suva, Fiji at the end of another successful visit.*

(© British Crown Copyright / MOD)

Queen of Tonga, before being taken to the Royal Palace. After their brief return to the Yacht, The Queen and Prince Philip were the guests of honour at the feast held at Mala Pangai which was also attended by some of the Yacht's officers, as Captain Worlidge remembered:

'We were all seated in a series of shelters in the grounds of the Palace, 30 guests to a shelter. The food was displayed on low tressle tables on the ground – the tables some 36 feet long and 4 feet wide and covered by nets, I had never seen so much food – 17 tables absolutely laden with suckling pigs, crayfish, lobsters, all sorts of fish, yam, turkey, chicken, tara, water melon, pineapple, bananas, mangos and so on. The food was all prepared by the local villages and ceremonially brought to the feast. Being that it was such a feudal system, the nobles detail off certain people to give so much, and

from then on there is no argument. For The King's daughter's wedding 2000 of the 4000 pigs in the kingdom were slaughtered for the feast. However, the food doesn't get wasted, as it is all distributed after the event. Needless to say, we didn't make any impression on the spread. I sat between the Secretary to the Prime Minister and The King's Chaplain, who were both fairly large men and kept egging me on to eat up. Having shown an interest in a lobster I got a whole one passed my way – cracking it up by hand – a half a turkey and so it went on. The method of cooking the meat and fish using traditional Polynesian ground ovens was absolutely delicious and gave the food a slightly smoked taste. The feast ended with fruit salad and ice cream. Drinks were either coconut milk or passion fruit juice.'

The feast was followed by a display of Tongan dancing and singing. For those left behind on the Yacht, The King of Tonga sent across cooked pigs and boxes of fruit. The day was rounded off by a dinner and reception before the Yacht sailed that night to the accompaniment of a Tongan choir watched by The Queen and Prince Philip from the Verandah Deck as *Britannia* slipped into the night bound for Fiji.[10]

Two days later *Britannia* anchored off Suva for The Queen's visit to Fiji, which began with the traditional *Cavuikelekele* ceremony before the Royal couple landed for their programme ashore. On the second day of their visit, the Royal couple flew to the Fijian island of Vanua Levu for their first visit, before returning to the Yacht in the evening for the dinner attended by the Governor General and the Prime Minister of Fiji. During both the dinner, and the subsequent departure of *Britannia*, a choir accompanied by a band from the Royal Fiji Military forces and the Royal Fiji Police force played on the wharf.[11]

As *Britannia* steamed towards New Zealand, the Yacht's company staged the traditional ship's concert for The Queen and Prince Philip, as Captain Worlidge recalled:

'The stage was rigged on the forecastle with complete side-screens and awnings and it made a very good little theatre. The theme was a take off of *Sailor* (the BBC TV series about HMS *Ark Royal*, which was the first of the modern "fly-on-the-wall" TV documentaries) with a TV film crew who wandered round the Yacht filming and meeting various turns. They were supplemented by a driver of the Governor's car who kept on appearing and trying to deliver a box to the Headmaster of the Royal Allotments (Master of the Household), and other such twisted lines. There is no doubt that the Yachtsmen adored this sort of thing, as they turned on an extremely slick show, which was masterminded by the Wardroom. The Queen thoroughly enjoyed the concert; she has such an enormous sense of fun and laughed with the rest of us. I was one of the performers and I must say, appearing in front of the Royal Family about 6 feet away was not nearly as terrifying as I thought it would be. The Royal Family and Household had their legs pulled fairly hard, as did most of us, and all seemed to take it in the right spirit. The show ended with the driver eventually opening the box, which said, "Happy Birthday Prince Andrew" (which it was). The Queen and Prince Philip came into the Wardroom after the show and stayed until midnight, it was a great compliment to us.'

The Yacht arrived at Auckland on 22 February to begin a very busy Tour as the Yacht visited eight ports within 14 days. To meet the demands of the tight programme the Yacht sailed at high speed between ports while The Queen and Prince Philip carried out their engagements ashore. It was estimated, by the time *Britannia* sailed for Australia on 7 March, that a third of the New Zealand population had seen something of the Tour. As *Britannia* made her way across the Tasman Sea towards Australia,

The Queen and Prince Philip flew on ahead to Canberra before rejoining the Yacht in Newcastle. Unfortunately, the Yacht's arrival was overshadowed by trade union wrangling over berthing party rights. To get round the problem the RAN authorities used a Sea Cadet line handling party in place of union members. Like the previous visits to Australia, each of the port arrivals was characterised by large and enthusiastic aquatic welcomes, of which Sydney's was the most impressive as the vast natural harbour was filled with boats of every description which had turned out to greet Her Majesty. When *Britannia* entered the harbour on 13 March the Prime Minister of Australia, Malcolm Fraser, was embarked, as Admiral Layman explained:

'The forecastle party was being a bit slow about passing a line down to the tug which seemed to be ready to take it. So I said to the forecastle officer on the radio, "Pass it down now you'll find the natives quite friendly." Malcolm Fraser turned round and said, "You never know!"'

A BBC film crew record Britannia's *entry into Sydney escorted by a large number of small boats.*

The Yacht's RM Band Beat Retreat at the end of the night's reception given by The Queen and Prince Philip during their visit to Liverpool as part of The Queen's Silver Jubilee Tour. The Royal Escort HMS Tartar *can be seen clearly in the background.*

(© British Crown Copyright / MOD)

For the cricket fans among the Yacht's company the highlight of the Australian Tour was undoubtedly the Centenary Test Match in Melbourne. Interestingly, the final outcome of the match was the same as a century before, with Australia wining by 45 runs. The Tour concluded with the visit to Freemantle on 28 March and The Queen and Prince Philip's departure on 30 March to fly back to London. Three days later the Yacht sailed to begin a swift voyage back to the UK via Diego Garcia, the Suez Canal, Malta and Gibraltar, before arriving back in Portsmouth on 6 May.

Most of May was taken up with repainting work to ensure the Yacht looked her best for her busy round of engagements in home waters in support of The Queen's Silver Jubilee. The UK Tour for the Yacht began with a week in the Pool of London, including the lunch given

by The Queen on 9 June during the Royal progress up the River Thames. From London the Yacht returned to Portsmouth for a week, before beginning the tour of the West Coast and Wales which included visits to Liverpool, Holyhead, Milford Haven, Barry and Cardiff. Among the guests to visit the Yacht in Cardiff was Prime Minister Jim Callaghan, who was also the MP for Cardiff South East.

The Yacht sailed from Cardiff on 25 June for Portsmouth, in time for the Fleet Review to be held off Spithead on 28 June. In the 24 years since The Queen's Coronation Fleet Review the size of the RN had continuously contracted. The battleship had finally passed into history and the RN's final conventional fixed wing carrier HMS *Ark Royal* was beginning the last phase of her final commission. The heavy cruiser was also about to disappear from the RN, with both HMS *Tiger* and HMS *Blake* about to be paid off. However, despite these impending cuts, the RN still managed to assemble an impressive collection of 101 warships and 2 hovercraft, including the Anti Submarine Warfare (ASW) carrier HMS *Hermes* and the destroyers HMS *London* and HMS *Glamorgan*. In addition there were 79 ships from 17 other countries representing the navies of the Commonwealth, NATO, CENTO and EEC nations including the Australian carrier HMAS *Melbourne* and the New Zealand frigate HMNZS *Canterbury*.

The Royal Family joined the Yacht the night before the Fleet Review in Portsmouth. The following morning the Prime Minister's tour of the Yacht was interrupted at 1000 when he was asked to join FORY in his cabin. The RN promotion list had been brought forward from the end of June to the day of the Fleet Review, as Admiral Layman explains:

'When I arrived in FORY's cabin I was met by the Prime Minister who said, "I am very pleased to tell you that you have been promoted to Captain." He then went on to say, "I am particularly delighted to tell you that because I am normally only allowed to make Bishops!"'

The Commander wasn't the only officer on board the Yacht to received good news because Commander Worlidge was also promoted to Captain, while Lieutenant Commanders Jones and Taylor were selected for promotion to the rank of Commander. By the time the Yacht

sailed at 1100 The Queen and Prince Philip had been joined by a distinguished party, including The Prime Minister, the Chief of the Defence Staff, Admiral of the Fleet Sir Edward Ashmore, the First Sea Lord, Admiral Sir Terence Lewin and Lord Mountbatten.

Half an hour later the Yacht anchored at the head of the Fleet for the lunch, which was attended by the Admiralty Board and the Flag Officers present at the review. After lunch the Yacht weighed anchor to begin the review of 7 miles of ships split into 10 separate review lines. As the Yacht passed each ship, their Ship's company gave three cheers for Her Majesty who acknowledged their salute from the Verandah Deck. On completion of the review the Yacht once more anchored at the head of the Fleet for the flypast of the FAA. Unfortunately, the murky conditions meant that only the helicopters performed their flypast. That night The Queen and Prince Philip were the

The Silver Jubilee Fleet Review off Spithead, 28 June 1977. Britannia leads HMS Birmingham and RFA Engadine as The Queen reviews the Fleet.

(© British Crown Copyright / MOD)

From left to right: A rather damp departure from Newcastle for the Navigating Officer, Lieutenant Commander Franklyn, FORY, and the pilot.

(© British Crown Copyright / MOD)

principle guests at the dinner hosted by Commander-in-Chief Fleet, Admiral Sir Henry Leach, in *Ark Royal*. The following morning the Yacht returned to Portsmouth, where The Queen and Prince Philip disembarked

Nearly two weeks later the Yacht sailed to begin The Queen's visit to the East Coast. The Queen and Prince Philip joined the Yacht in Felixstowe on 11 July, after completing their engagements in Norfolk and Suffolk during the day. Over the next three days the Yacht visited Grimsby, Hull, and Newcastle where the Yacht received its most enthusiastic welcome in home waters on 15 July. Throughout *Britannia*'s one and a half hour passage up the Tyne, people watched her progress from every vantage point, including the Ship's company of the Type 42 destroyer *Newcastle* which was still being fitted out by Swan Hunter, as Commodore Morrow recalled: 'some of the spectators were holding wonderful placards like "Welcome Your Majesty To Geordie Land" and "Howway The Queen Wot Cheor Bonny Lass" It was a tremendous out pouring of affection.' Following a busy morning of engagements ashore The Queen left for London after lunch, while *Britannia* remained alongside for the weekend, prior to returning to Portsmouth. Throughout her stay in Newcastle, *Britannia* acted as a tremendous magnet, with people coming to see the Yacht from the Tyne Bridge and the opposite bank.[12]

At the end of July *Britannia* arrived off Cowes for the annual regatta followed, at the beginning of August, by

Prince Philip at the helm of Yeoman XIX *belonging to Sir Owen Aisher during Cowes Week.*

(© British Crown Copyright / MOD)

The Queen's Tour of the South Coast, visiting Torbay, Plymouth, Falmouth, Lundy Island and Avonmouth. From Avonmouth, the Yacht crossed the Irish Sea where, on 10 August, The Queen transferred to the Royal Escort HMS *Fife* to be flown in a helicopter for the first time. The use of the Wessex from The Queen's Flight was felt necessary for The Queen's brief visit to Hillsborough Castle, Northern Ireland for a garden party and investiture. In the afternoon she returned with Prince Philip to HMS *Fife* and was transferred back to the Yacht. By then the Royal Squadron had anchored off Bangor for that night's reception held on board. When the last guests had been landed the Yacht weighed anchor for Portrush, where she anchored the following morning. Once again The Queen went ashore in a Wessex from HMS *Fife* to visit the new University of Ulster for a thorough tour and a garden party, before returning to the Yacht, via HMS *Fife*, in the afternoon. On completion of that evening's reception for people of outstanding achievement in Northern Ireland the Yacht weighed anchor for a normal Western Isles Cruise. Although the four days of informal cruising provided the Royal Family with a much needed break in an extremely hectic year, it was tinged with some sadness for The

Queen's Private Secretary, Sir Martin Charteris, who was enjoying his final days on board before his retirement. To mark the event FORY presented Sir Martin Charteris with a silver Armada Dish in front of the Yacht's company on the forecastle on 14 August.

Looking back at what the Yacht meant to him Sir Martin Charteris later wrote to Admiral Janion:

'This letter is written during the last night that I spend in HMY *Britannia* as The Queen's Private Secretary. I've been as happy in this ship as anywhere else I have ever been. Here one is surrounded by people who are as dedicated as I am to the service of The Queen and that is a good place to be. I was enormously touched yesterday by what you said and by the splendid gift given to me by the Officers and Royal Yachtsmen. I own nothing I value more. My thanks yesterday were inadequate because in moments like that it is not easy to find the right words. Perhaps you could let everyone know how truly grateful I am.'

The Queen receives a very enthusiastic welcome from local yachtsmen for her visit to Falmouth in Britannia.

(© British Crown Copyright / MOD)

The Queen steps on board a Wessex of The Queen's Flight on board HMS Fife for her visit to Hillsborough Castle, Northern Ireland. It was the first time Her Majesty had flown in a helicopter

(© British Crown Copyright / MOD)

During the Yacht's visit to Scrabster towards the end of the 1978 Western Isles Cruise The Queen Mother returned on board with the Royal Family for a brief visit. Shortly after coming on board Her Majesty was shown this impressive 20-pound conger eel caught from the forecastle by Sgt Fleming of the RM Band.

(© British Crown Copyright / MOD)

When the Yacht returned to Portsmouth on 18 August she had completed her first ever extensive tour of the UK, steaming 4264 miles within 11 weeks, and visiting 28 different places.

Following summer leave, at the end of September the Yacht sailed from Portsmouth to begin the last of The Queen's Silver Jubilee Tours. *Britannia* arrived at Nassau on 15 October, having already called at the Azores, Bermuda, and Freeport on the way. Four days later The Queen and Prince Philip arrived in Nassau in the afternoon at the end of their visit to Canada. The next day was taken up with a programme of engagements, including the opening of the Bahamian Parliament and hosting a dinner and reception on board the Yacht. By the time of the Yacht's departure at 2345 the Police Band, together with the Junkanoo men and women dressed as the Crown Jewels and Beefeaters, had gathered on the jetty to provide a memorable send off for The Queen. After spending a day in the British Virgin Islands the Yacht sailed for Antigua, where The Queen visited English Harbour on 28 October to see the progress being made to restore the former dockyard once used by Lord Nelson, and Admiralty House, once occupied by The Duke of Clarence, later King William IV. From there, *Britannia* sailed for Mustique and, as she steamed across the Caribbean on 29

October, The Queen and Prince Philip went for a walk around the Yachtsmen's messes. During the course of their tour the Coxswain, Fleet Chief Petty Officer Norrell, presented them with the first of the commemorative Silver Jubilee Medallions to be produced by the Yacht.[13]

The next morning *Britannia* anchored off Mustique where The Queen and Prince Philip went ashore to spend the day with Princess Margaret. From there the Yacht sailed to Barbados and along the way she was passed over by Concorde which had flown out from London to bring The Queen and Prince Philip home, as Dixie Deane recalled:

'FORY inquired about the possibility of communicating with Concorde so I asked British Airways to give me the relevant frequencies which they readily supplied. Our first contact with Concorde was shortly after take off from Heathrow. Some time later they asked for our exact position. The next thing I heard was that they had us in sight so I informed FORY who was aft with the Royal Family on the Verandah Deck. FORY asked if I could ask the pilot to do a low flypast along the starboard side, which they did. The photographer captured Concorde between The Queen and Prince Philip and the image was later used by British Airways on the front cover of their magazine.'

When the Royal Family later joined Concorde one of the air hostesses remarked that she had never flown round in a circle quite so close to the sea before! After two and a half days of engagements ashore the Royal couple flew from Barbados to London in Concorde on 2 November. In her farewell message to FORY The Queen acknowledged the key role played by the Yacht in her Silver Jubilee year when she said:

'Prince Philip and I wish to thank you and all Royal Yachtsmen for your outstanding contribution to the celebration of my Silver Jubilee. Our visits both at home and overseas were made all the more comfortable and impressive by the presence of the Yacht. We appreciate that this has meant a great deal of hard work. God speed your passage home and may you have a happy Christmas. Splice the Mainbrace!
ELIZABETH R.'

Once The Queen Mother had disembarked the Yacht weighed anchor for Aberdeen. The Royal Family gathered on the Verandah Deck to watch the Yacht steam past The Queen Mother's Caithness home, the Castle of Mey.

(© British Crown Copyright / MOD)

The Yacht began her own journey home on 5 November and arrived back in Portsmouth on 18 November to conclude one of the Yacht's busiest years. The year 1978 started at a much slower pace, with a period in dry dock for routine maintenance, followed by the inevitable sea trials and work up, before sailing from Portsmouth on 17 May for The Queen's State Visit to West Germany. Having crossed the North Sea and sailed up the Kiel Canal, the Yacht arrived in Kiel on 19 May to await the embarkation of The Queen and Prince Philip on 24 May. After their dinner ashore at the Kieler Schloss, The Queen and Prince Philip joined the Yacht for its westward transit of the Kiel Canal. As the Yacht made its way towards Bremerhaven on 25 May, 51 guests were embarked by motor boat for a lunch. Describing the scene in the Royal Dining Room as the guests sat down for lunch the Foreign Secretary at the time, later The Rt Hon. the Lord Owen CH, remarked:

'Looking around the table I saw the Admirals from the West German Navy dressed in uniform sitting down to eat as guests of Her Majesty and I felt that there was something very final about the reconciliation between our two nations. It appeared to me that we had come full circle in our relations with both countries enjoying a very settled and stable relationship. The attempt to stage a demonstration by West German warships, albeit severely curtailed by the fog, added another dimension to the visit and placed it very firmly within a NATO context.'

In the afternoon *Britannia* arrived in Bremerhaven for that night's return State Banquet which was held on board for the President of the Federal German Republic to mark the end of a successful State Visit. The next morning *Britannia* sailed at 0545 for Breman where the Royal couple disembarked to fly back to the UK.[14] The brief State Visit was for the new Commander of the Yacht, later Captain David Hart-Dyke CBE LVO RN, his first experience of *Britannia* in action, as he explains:

'After many years in destroyers and frigates, everything about the Yacht seemed different. How refreshing it was to join an immaculately maintained ship with no armament and a superbly professional crew. The Yacht's company, a happy and finely tuned team, strove for perfection in their work of supporting many Royal duties and State Visits – all of it carried out in the glare of the world's media, so there was plenty of scope for mistakes and adverse publicity. I well remember the pressures of straining to get everything right and the need to plan to the smallest detail when preparing for Royal duty. But

what fun we had too and how privileged we were to serve and work closely with many members of the Royal Family. I felt that *Britannia*'s role was just as important as that of a warship, at least in peacetime. It was evident to us all that in projecting British interests all over the globe the Yacht was unique and the envy of the world. To observe at close quarters the impression that she made when visiting countries around the world and entertaining their heads of state was unforgettable. In political goodwill achieved and trade agreements signed the importance of these visits to the nation was enormous, and in value-for-money terms *Britannia* seemed to be worth every penny.'

After a few days in Bremerhaven the Yacht returned to Portsmouth on 31 May.

During the previous year's extensive Tour of the UK The Queen had been unable to visit the Channel Islands and so this rather unfortunate omission was corrected at the end of June. Originally, The Queen and Prince Philip were due to join the Yacht alongside in Portsmouth but fears of disruption to the Yacht's departure, caused by the ongoing industrial action of the trade unions, meant that *Britannia* was moved from her moorings at Whale Island to No. 3 Buoy in the harbour where the Royal couple joined on 26 June shortly before she sailed.[15] During their three days in the Islands The Queen and Prince Philip visited Jersey, Guernsey, Sark and Alderney before returning to Portsmouth on 30 June.

On 28 July the Yacht sailed from Portsmouth to anchor off Cowes for the regatta. Two days later The Prince of Wales, Princess Anne and Lord Mountbatten embarked.

'At the age of 78 Lord Mountbatten was as sharp as ever; he sat in an armchair in the Wardroom one afternoon and talked about his remarkable life. Like The Queen and Prince Philip he was related through Queen Victoria to virtually all the European Royal Families of the century, and it was fascinating to hear his reminiscences. Little did we imagine that some of us would be attending his funeral a year later,' Commander Creedy remarked.

At the end of Cowes Week the Yacht sailed on 2 August for Falmouth, where The Prince of Wales disembarked the next day, before the Yacht headed north for Greenock. There, The Queen and Prince Edward embarked for the start of the traditional Western Isles Cruise, which lasted until the 14 August. Although The Queen was accompanied on these cruises by a scaled down Household, there was always still an amount of official business to be conducted, as Lord Fellowes explains:

'In good weather, the Western Isles Cruise was as near heaven as one can get. Deck tennis on a lovely day in the Western Isles, followed by a swim and a picnic lunch – life doesn't get much better! On the other hand, poor weather presented more of a challenge as there was always a lot to do. The other two Private Secretaries had by then gone on holiday and thus I was getting all the work from Whitehall, who were winding up their affairs, before going on leave themselves. Therefore, my main memory of the Western Isles Cruises was a mixture of bliss and trying to work, in sometimes rather rough weather, producing a box for The Queen every evening, feeling slightly queasy. However, if we are going to ask someone to be a Head of State until an indefinite age, you need to give them some form of recompense. The Western Isles Cruise was a wonderful way of capping the first eight months of a very busy life. Once The Queen got to Balmoral there was all the work from London, people to stay and the responsibility of being a large landowner, etc.'

As part of the preparations for the forthcoming Tour of the Gulf, a trial embarkation of The Queen's Rolls Royce was conducted in Portsmouth on 6 September. Despite the success of these trials, it was decided not to embark the Rolls Royce for the Tour. Thus the trials were the last time that a Rolls Royce was embarked in the Yacht's garage, which by then had become a Bosun's locker and beer store for the Yachtsmen.[16] During the autumn of 1978 the Yacht wasn't required by the Royal Family so in October she was deployed to the Mediterranean to participate in Naval exercises. The deployment enabled the Yacht's company to attend the Trafalgar Day Ceremony at the Trafalgar Cemetery in Gibraltar on 21 October. The following morning after the Yacht had sailed from Gibraltar a brief memorial service was held on the Verandah Deck with Cape Trafalgar visible in the background. FORY read Nelson's prayer and then cast a wreath into the sea in memory of Lord Nelson and the other men who had given their lives 173 years earlier. Three days later the Yacht returned home to Portsmouth.

On 11 January 1979 the Yacht sailed for The Queen's Tour of the Gulf. As well as marking the start of another important deployment for *Britannia*, it was the Yacht's Silver Jubilee and the event was toasted in Champagne at midday by a select group including the Coxswain and the NAAFI Canteen Manager, Mr Douglas Jackson, who had both served continuously on board since January 1954.[17] The voyage to Kuwait took just under a month with stops at Gibraltar, Alexandria, and the island of Khor Al Quwai. On 12 February The Queen and Prince Philip arrived in Kuwait having flown from London in Concorde. The Queen's Tour was unique because Arab

As part of the preparations for The Queen's visit to the Middle East a trial embarkation of The Queen's Rolls Royce was conducted in Portsmouth.

(© British Crown Copyright / MOD)

countries don't normally respect ladies of rank so in effect The Queen became an 'honorary man' for the next three weeks. The Tour came at a very difficult time for the region, with the overthrow of the Shah in Iran, and the formation of an Islamic Republic under the leadership of Ayatollah Khomeini. By undertaking the Tour at this time The Queen was able to clearly demonstrate to the other nations in the Gulf that the British Government would stand by them and not jump ship.

After the visits to Kuwait and Bahrain, the Yacht arrived in Damman in Saudi Arabia on 18 February. The next day the Royal party arrived from Riyadh in Concorde to embark for that night's return State Banquet for King Khalid Ibn Abdul Aziz Al Saud. The Queen was accompanied by the Foreign Secretary at the time, later The Rt Hon. the Lord Owen CH. Soon after he arrived on board, Lord Owen used the Yacht's communication facilities to send an important signal, as he recalled:

'The British Government had stood with the Shah quite deliberately. While others had argued that the UK should cut its losses, I felt it would enhance our relations with the other Gulf states to demonstrate loyalty and go down with "the sinking Shah". I then wanted to be very early on recognition so it was agreed once we had received a favourable report from our man in Tehran we would recognise them. The cable came into the Yacht so I sent the response back using the Yacht's facilities to recognise the new regime in Iran. I found it very easy to be in the Yacht because I was fully "locked

in" to the Foreign Office telecommunications so I received all of the cables and was kept fully up to date. Thus the Yacht was just as much an office for the accompanying Minister as it was for The Queen.'

Describing that night's return State Banquet Lord Owen said:

'The King of Saudi Arabia was by then an old man. It was quite clear that he thoroughly enjoyed being on board the Yacht. At the end of the meal Prince Philip escorted him off the Yacht and down to his car. The whole of the quayside had been cleared for the visit and resembled a large empty car park. The Queen was standing up on deck to wave good-bye to The King and we saw this old man put his hand out with his stick waving to The Queen as he was driven across this vast, empty space. It was a wonderful sign of a person who had been totally enchanted by the whole experience."

Once the last of the guests had disembarked the Foreign Secretary left to fly back to the UK and was relieved by the Foreign Office Minister, Frank Judd MP for the rest of the Tour.

One of the most remarkable aspects of this Tour was the range of gifts presented to The Queen and Prince Philip by each of the rulers. The Royal couple presented each of their hosts with a handsome silver salver engraved with a profile of the Yacht. In return they received a treasure chest of gifts including three Persian carpets, as Prince Philip explains:

'The first of these carpets was presented by the Sheikh of Kuwait. I suggested putting it in the saloon. When we got to Bahrain, I just happened to mention to the Ruler that we were standing on a carpet given to The Queen by Kuwait. Another carpet appeared within hours. I repeated this tactic later on and the third appeared. They now grace the new private Chapel in Windsor Castle!'

The most valuable gift of the Tour was the pair of gold camels and palm trees given to The Queen by Sheikh Rashid of Dubai. This was retained on board for use during state banquets in the Royal Dining Room. The Queen flew home from Oman on 2 March, while Prince Philip remained on board a further two days before flying to the Soviet Union. The Yacht sailed shortly afterwards, calling at Naples and Palma before reaching Portsmouth on 30 March 1979.

On 11 May *Britannia* left Portsmouth for The Queen's State Visit to Denmark. The day after the Yacht's arrival in Frederikshaven on 14 May The Queen and Prince Philip embarked. Within an hour of their arrival the Yacht sailed for Copenhagen, where she secured to a buoy the next morning. Since the last State Visit earlier in the year the Labour Government led by Jim Callaghan had been defeated at the General Election on 3 May. Thus one of Lord Carrington's first duties on becoming Foreign Secretary was to accompany The Queen to Denmark, where he observed the impact the Yacht had on the Danish people, as he remembered:

'Whenever the Yacht was given a major refit the cost of the work was always criticised by a small but vocal minority in the press. Unfortunately, I don't feel that these people understood for one moment what an enormous effect the Yacht had on people abroad when they saw her. The sight of *Britannia* entering Copenhagen harbour with The Queen's Court Flags flying and the RM Band playing on deck had a tremendous effect on people's regard not just for the Royal Family but for the nation as a whole. This was further enhanced by the ability of The Queen to entertain in her own residence which left people with the impression at the end of a State Visit that Britain was an important country and her voice mattered on the international stage.'

After the return State Banquet for Queen Margarethe on 17 May, Queen Margarethe transferred to the Danish Royal Yacht HDMY *Dannebrog* prior to the two Royal Yachts sailing in company overnight to Aarhus Harbour where The Queen and Prince Philip undertook further engagements ashore. After that night's dinner and reception, the two yachts made a floodlit departure and sailed to Helsingor, where The Queen and Prince Philip disembarked the next morning to spend a private weekend with the Danish Royal Family before flying home. *Britannia* arrived back in Copenhagen in the afternoon for a three-day visit prior to returning to Portsmouth on 24 May.

On 1 June The Queen Mother joined the Yacht in Portsmouth for her visit to the West Coast of Scotland.

The Queen bids farewell to the Amir of Bahrain before boarding Concorde to fly on to Saudi Arabia for the next part of her Middle East Tour.

(© British Crown Copyright / MOD)

The Queen Mother's visit to Dover Castle to be formally installed both as Constable of the Castle and Lord Warden of the Cinque Ports. On Her Majesty's arrival the Deputy Constable of the Castle surrendered the keys of the Castle to Her Majesty.   (© British Crown Copyright / MOD)

Shortly afterwards, the Yacht sailed to begin the passage to the RN submarine base at Faslane, arriving there on 3 June. That night Her Majesty hosted a dinner party, before going ashore the following morning to visit the submarine base, including a tour of the Polaris nuclear submarine HMS *Resolution*. The Queen Mother returned at lunchtime for the passage to the Isle of Cumbrae, where she went ashore in the afternoon for a visit to the Marine Biological Station at Millport. Her short Tour ended on 5 June with a visit to the new British Steel ore terminal at Hunterston. Unfortunately, Her Majesty was unable to see the machinery in operation before she flew back to London because of the inter-union dispute at the plant. That afternoon the Yacht sailed for Portsmouth.[18]

At the end of July the Yacht sailed for the Thames to embark The Queen Mother and sail to Dover. The ceremony of Shepaway to install Her Majesty as Lord Warden of the Cinque Ports, Admiral of the Cinque Ports and Constable of Dover Castle on 1 August was performed in St Mary's Church within Dover Castle. At the moment when The Queen Mother was formally installed a 19-gun salute was fired from the castle. On the 19th gun the Flag of the Lord Warden of the Cinque Ports was broken at the mizzen mast in the Yacht. The ceremony was followed by a lunch for the Mayors and Barons of the Cinque Ports in the Maison Diere. In the afternoon Her Majesty returned to the Yacht to watch the Red Arrows over Dover Harbour at 1800. The eventful day was rounded off by the Yacht's floodlit departure from Dover just after midnight during the fireworks display from the castle. The next

Princess Alexandra and her family take part in an impromptu concert by the Yacht's RM Band on the forecastle during their voyage back to Portsmouth.

(© British Crown Copyright / MOD)

morning *Britannia* berthed in Portsmouth where the Royal party disembarked.[19]

Within 24 hours of her return from Dover, the Yacht was heading out from her home port again, this time for Cowes Week, followed by the Western Isles Cruise. When the Yacht arrived in Aberdeen on 15 August all of the Royal Family disembarked, except Princess Alexandra, The Hon. Angus Ogilvy and their children James and Marina, who remained on board for the passage south back to Portsmouth. During the two-day voyage home they took part in various aspects of Yacht life including the concert given by the RM Band on the forecastle. Ten days after the Yacht's return to Portsmouth the nation was shocked by the assassination of Lord Mountbatten by the IRA. At his funeral service in Westminister Abbey the Yacht was represented by FORY and 18 members of the Yacht's company.[20] A week after Lord Mountbatten's funeral the Yacht entered dry dock in Portsmouth to begin her refit, which was to last until mid April 1980, when she sailed for the usual round of post-refit trials and work up.

On 7 July 1980 The Queen Mother joined the Yacht shortly before she sailed from Portsmouth. As the Yacht made her way through the Solent, she reduced her speed to rendezvous with a gathering of small boats which had assembled off Yarmouth to mark Her Majesty's 80th birthday. As *Britannia* steamed past the boats, Her Majesty appeared on the Verandah Deck to acknowledge their welcome. The following morning the Yacht berthed in Dover for The Queen Mother to make her first visit to the Cinque Ports since she was installed as the Lord Warden of the Cinque Ports in the previous year. Over the course of the three-day visit to Dover The Queen Mother visited each of the Cinque Ports, returning to *Britannia* for the night. The short visit was rounded off with a dinner on board for the Mayors of the Cinque Ports, before *Britannia* made a floodlit departure from Dover on 10 July. The next day the Yacht sailed up the Thames, pausing briefly off Gravesend to embark Princess Margaret, Viscount Linley and Lady Sarah Armstrong-Jones, before passing through Tower Bridge to moor in the Pool of London. As Admiral Moore explains, The Queen Mother's disembarkation from the Yacht led to the setting of a new precedent:

'It was laid down in the Yacht's routine that as the member of the Royal Family disembarked at the end of their time in the Yacht their flags were struck. When Admiral Janion returned from accompanying The Queen Mother ashore he said to me, "It's not right, we must change the routine because it would be much nicer if her Standard was still flying until she was disembarked from the Barge, and left the jetty." So the routine was changed.'

The Yacht remained in London until 15 July when she sailed for Portsmouth, returning there the following morning.[21]

Four days later the yacht sailed for Brest, where she was to be used in support of a visit abroad by The Prince of Wales for the first time. His Royal Highness joined the

As Britannia's *refit comes to an end one of the dockyard painters works on the Royal Coat of Arms on the bow.*

(© British Crown Copyright / MOD)

Yacht in Brest on 21 July to host a dinner and reception. On the second day of his visit, His Royal Highness visited the French ballistic missile submarine base at Ile Longne, before returning to *Britannia* in the afternoon for the overnight passage back to Portsmouth.[22] On 31 July *Britannia* crossed the Solent for Cowes Week, followed as usual by the Western Isles Cruise.

The Yacht's autumn deployment to the Mediterranean began on 30 September when she sailed for La Spezia to join in with the NATO exercise Display Determination on 6 October. On arrival the Yacht took charge of a convoy being protected by an Italian escort group. The objective of the exercise was to prove NATO's ability to defend, reinforce and re-supply the southern region. However, the Yacht's other commitments soon intervened and, on the second day of the exercise, she detached to practice some manoeuvres with HMS *Apollo* for the forthcoming Sea Day off Naples where she arrived on 9 October. A week later 80 businessmen embarked for the Sea Day organised by British Invisibles on 16 October to promote the financial services of the City of London. The party from London was headed by the former Governor of the Bank of England, Lord O'Brien and, according to British Invisibles, generated $100 billion of business for the UK.[23]

The day after the businessmen left, The Queen and Prince Philip flew from Rome to Naples to join the Yacht for the rest of their Italian State Visit. Having visited Naples and the ruins of Pompeii on 18 October, the Royal couple returned to the Yacht later in the afternoon ahead of that night's dinner and reception. As ever the arrivals and departures were all recorded by the Yacht's Photographer, who in 1980 was Leading Airman (phot.) Gordon Ford, later Lieutenant Commander Gordon Ford RN. Describing this work he said:

'The photographic work on board the Yacht wasn't exactly demanding technically providing that one wasn't nervous. If one didn't like working with people it certainly wasn't the right job. I had to be able to talk myself into places that I wasn't really supposed to be in because I was never issued with Royal rota passes. The press were issued with these passes and I was just expected to be there. If any security men tried to stop me I would simply ask for the name of their superior because The Queen will want to know where the photographs were. Equally, The Queen's own security men were never too far away and providing they were happy no one stopped me. I was never given any transport either but the press usually gave me a lift because they assumed that I would know what the next major event

was. The reality was that they were in fact better briefed and given a full itinerary whereas I was expected to find out by asking or through Daily Orders. I was the only person on board the Yacht who was allowed to have a camera but I never went aft unless the Royal Family knew I was going to be there.

'My job was to record the events but in a different way to the press. The press were always looking for someone to fall over and break their leg, etc. Every time there was a dinner on board the principal guests would be photographed just before they went into dinner. I was never told how many principal guests there would be and thus I never knew if I needed a wide-angle lens or a standard lens. This was made worse by the fact that I was only given 30 seconds for the photograph and I wasn't allowed to talk to them. On a Haselblad with a wide-angle lens you can't focus so I had to learn the distances. The first couple of times I was doing this Prince Philip would take the mick out of me and I would think that he was having a go at me. But then it dawned on me what he was doing, because he would make everyone look at me and smile thus making my job easier. While the guests went down to dinner I would process the film, produce the best print and frame it. The photograph would then be sent up to The Queen's Sitting Room. She would nip out and sign it so that when the principal guests left the ship they had a signed picture of the occasion.'

As usual the night's programme of official entertainment was concluded with the Beat Retreat ceremony on the quayside. The P&O liner SS *Oriana* was berthed close to the Yacht and her Captain had deliberately delayed the liner's time of sailing so that all of the passengers could watch the Yacht's RM Band in action. On completion of the ceremony *Britannia* made a floodlit departure during the fireworks display over Naples.[24] From Naples, the Yacht headed south west for The Queen's State Visit to Tunisia, followed by the State Visit to Algeria. The Algerian visit coincided with the aftermath of the recent earthquake in El Asnam, and as part of their programme, The Queen and Prince Philip visited some of the victims in the Mustapha civil hospital. In a further gesture of support the Master of the Household, Vice Admiral Sir Peter Ashmore, presented the Algerian Foreign Secretary with a cheque for £510 for the El Asnam earthquake fund on the night of the dinner on board on 26 October. The money had been raised through donations from The Queen, Prince Philip, their Household and the officers and men of the Royal

Squadron. The following morning The Queen and Prince Philip left to fly to Morocco for the start of their State Visit. Meanwhile, the Yacht sailed within an hour of the Royal couple's departure to arrive in Casablanca where they rejoined the Yacht for the return State Banquet on 29 October.[25] The Moroccan State Visit provided the new Foreign Office Minister Douglas Hurd MP, later The Rt Hon. Lord Hurd of Westwell CH CBE, with quite a test of his diplomatic skills as he recalled:

'The King of Morocco sent his Lord Chamberlain to ask if The Queen could postpone the time of the dinner on board the Yacht by one hour. I received this message and went to see Her Majesty. She said that she couldn't do this because there was no way of informing the other guests of the revised time but please inform The King that she would understand if The King was delayed. The King arrived on board the Yacht with some Princes who hadn't been invited in quite a rage because his suggestion hadn't been acted upon. With The Queen he conducted a fairly inane conversation about personalities because I think he was quite afraid of her. However, with me, because he was in a furious rage he started hissing in French, "I am not being treated like a gentleman, it's all going wrong, and that steel mission we were discussing on the train this morning I won't receive it because I haven't got time and what's more your Ambassador must be out of Morocco tomorrow." I was quite inexperienced and I didn't know what to do so I discussed the matter with Prince Philip. He told me to stay cool, keep smiling and do nothing. It was absolutely right because in the morning everything was OK and The Queen knighted the Ambassador in question.'

The King even went to Casablanca airport to personally say farewell to The Queen and Prince Philip before they boarded their flight back to London on 30 October. Three days later the Yacht sailed for Portsmouth, arriving there on 5 November, to conclude Admiral Janion's seagoing career. During his time as FORY, the Yacht had steamed 102,912 miles, visited 158 different ports in 44 countries and worn a Royal Standard for 36 separate tours.[26]

The Queen and Prince Philip are driven away to begin their State Visit to Morocco. (© British Crown Copyright / MOD)

Chapter Nine

ENTERING THE SATELLITE AND DIESEL AGE

Rear Admiral Sir Paul Greening GCVO 1981–1985

The Yachtsmen lined the taff rails to bid farewell to Rear Admiral Hugh Janion when he left *Britannia*, after being succeeded as FORY by Rear Admiral Paul Greening at noon on 4 February 1981. Admiral Janion was taken ashore in number one motor boat, to be met by a vintage Rolls Royce flying his flag to take him on the first part of his journey into retirement after 44 years in the Royal Navy.

Admiral Janion's successor joined the RN in 1946 and was given his first command nine years later when he became the Commanding Officer of the *Ham* Class minesweeper HMS *Asheldham*. In 1963 he was promoted to the rank of Commander and appointed as the Senior Officer Second Minesweeping Squadron and Commanding Officer of HMS *Lewiston*. He was later given command of the frigates HMS *Jaguar* and HMS *Aurora* before becoming the Captain of Britannia Royal Naval College (BRNC) in 1976. From there he was promoted Rear Admiral in November 1978 when he became the Naval Secretary.

Unfortunately, Admiral Greening's arrival was over-shadowed a week later, when several Yachtsmen were discovered to be active homosexuals and therefore had to be discharged in line with the RN's policy at that time. The

tabloid press had a field day and thus *Britannia* came under the media spotlight for all the wrong reasons. It was a sad chapter within the Yacht's history. However, on 3 March, *Britannia* slipped her Portsmouth moorings to begin sea trials at Portland, which provided a welcome opportunity for the Yacht's company to focus on *Britannia*'s forthcoming programme and put the events of the previous weeks behind them. For Admiral Greening it was his first opportunity to take her to sea, as he recalls: 'it was a good opportunity to get the feel of the Yacht. We spent a period at Portland during which time a strong off-shore wind seemed to be blowing every time I wanted to come alongside!' The Sea Training staff also visited the Yacht, as Admiral Moore explains:

'No one apart from the Keeper & Steward and his staff were allowed in the Royal Apartments unless carrying out rounds when members of the Royal Family were not embarked. I took Commander Sea Training, Commander Morgan, round the Royal Apartments and he turned to me and said, "There are no fire extinguishers." I opened up behind a cubby hole and produced some. He looked at these, noted where they had come from but was wise enough not to comment that they should be on display and readily available.'

With the sea trials successfully completed, it was soon time for the year's first Royal duty when The Queen Mother embarked in Portsmouth on 8 April 1981. Shortly afterwards, the Yacht sailed for Dartmouth, where she arrived the next morning in very misty conditions. Despite the weather FORY decided to press on and enter the River Dart and, as the Yacht did so, the fog lifted to enable *Britannia* to secure to two buoys in front of BRNC. It was The Queen Mother's first visit to BRNC in a Royal Yacht since she accompanied the late King in 1939 on board *V&A*. During the day Her Majesty visited Dartmouth, after which she took the salute at the Lord High Admiral's Divisions at the College. In the evening Her Majesty hosted a dinner which was concluded by the RM Band performing Beat Retreat, much to the delight of both the guests and the people of Dartmouth watching from the shore. As the sun rose the following morning the Yacht slipped out of the Dart and headed west towards Falmouth, where she spent three days while The Queen Mother carried out engagements in the area. During the voyage back to Portsmouth on 13 April Her Majesty took the opportunity to walk round the Yacht. Unfortunately, the planned Solent cruise for the next day's Families Day didn't take place because the dockyard tug men were on strike.[1]

Two weeks later *Britannia* left Portsmouth for Harwich to embark The Queen and Prince Philip for their visit to Norway and the Shetland Islands. After a rather rough crossing of the North Sea, the Yacht arrived in Oslo on

FORY between 1981 and 1985, Rear Admiral Sir Paul Greening GCVO.

(© British Crown Copyright / MOD)

The Yacht's officers hired a vintage Rolls Royce so that Rear Admiral Janion could begin his journey into retirement in style.

(© British Crown Copyright / MOD)

The Queen, Prince Philip and King Olav of Norway seen during the Royal visit to the Shetland Isles.

(© British Crown Copyright / MOD)

5 May to an impressive aquatic welcome staged by the Royal Norwegian Yacht Club. Once *Britannia* had anchored in view of Akerhus Fortress, the Crown Prince Harold arrived alongside in the Norwegian Royal Barge *Stjernen* to escort The Queen and Prince Philip ashore, where they were received by King Olav and the Crown Princess. The Royal party visited the Resistance Museum before going on to the Royal Palace for lunch when The Queen presented the Crown Prince with his commission as an Honorary Colonel in the Royal Marines. The Royal couple lived ashore at the Royal Palace during the visit, but they returned to the Yacht on the evening of 6 May for the return State Banquet which was attended by King Olav, as well as the Crown Prince and Princess. While The Queen and Prince Philip continued their programme ashore, on 7 May *Britannia* sailed from Oslo for the passage to Stavanger, where she arrived the next morning. In the afternoon The Queen and Prince Philip were joined by King Olav as they embarked for the overnight passage across the North Sea to the Shetland Islands. As The King stepped aboard *Britannia* his Standard was broken alongside that of The Queen, much to the delight of the large crowd that had gathered to witness the Yacht's imminent departure.[2]

The Royal party were greeted with low cloud and fine drizzle as *Britannia* entered Sullom Voe in the Shetland Isles to anchor off the impressive oil terminal. Several of the large tankers present had dressed overall in honour of the visit and soon the Royal party went ashore for a thorough tour of the Oil Terminal, before taking lunch in the

The Queen Mother inspects Lord High Admiral's divisions at Britannia Royal Naval College, Dartmouth.

(© British Crown Copyright / MOD)

accommodation ship *Rangatiri*. Meanwhile, the Yacht weighed anchor and steamed round to Lerwick, where the Royal party rejoined at the end of their shore programme for the dinner on board. The next morning the Royal party disembarked to pursue their separate programmes, with Prince Philip flying back to London, and King Olav flying on to the Orkney Islands before returning to Norway. The Yacht returned to Portsmouth on 13 May.[3]

On 27 July 1981 *Britannia* sailed from Portsmouth at the beginning of another major global deployment, in which she would embark The Prince and Princess of Wales for their honeymoon in the Mediterranean, before going on to support The Queen and Prince Philip's Tours of Australia and New Zealand. However, before she headed south, the Yacht sailed to Portland for a series of trials, and to disembark FORY who was going to remain in the UK to attend the Royal wedding in St Paul's Cathedral on 29 July, before flying out to join the Yacht in Gibraltar ahead of the Royal couple. The planning of the honeymoon had been underway since the public announcement of the engagement on 21 February 1981. Initially, it had been planned that the honeymoon cruise would be in the West Indies on the Yacht's way out to Australia via the Panama Canal. However, this would have required the services of an accompanying RFA tanker, which would have flown in the face of the Government's economy drive on public spending. Thus the Palace changed the plans and it was decided to have the honeymoon cruise in the Mediterranean. Although this option removed the potential for public criticism of cost of the honeymoon, it did create a major challenge for the Admiral to shield the Royal couple from the expected media attention, during a period when the Mediterranean was at its most crowded. Equally, the change of plan presented an immediate diplomatic problem over where the Royal couple should join the Yacht. Locations in Portugal, Tangiers and Spain were discussed, before it was decided on the advice of the Foreign Office to use Gibraltar. While this choice was welcomed by the people of Gibraltar, it immediately created major difficulties in the UK's diplomatic relations with Spain. Describing the atmosphere on board the Yacht, as she headed south towards Gibraltar, the Second Lieutenant, later Captain Richard Cosby LVO RN, said: 'it was a flat moment when we sailed from Portsmouth just as the country was preparing for the Royal wedding at home and therefore we felt rather left out. We headed quietly south and met some Russian warships off Brest which we photographed early one morning.'

In the absence of FORY the Commander assumed command of the Yacht for the voyage to Gibraltar, where she arrived on 31 July 1981, watched by FORY who embarked by boat shortly before she secured alongside. During the morning of 1 August the dockyard in Gibraltar was opened to the public who flocked down to the quayside to see the gleaming Yacht.[4] Describing the Royal couple's arrival in the afternoon Captain Cosby said:

'As usual we had a good radio link up with The Queen's Flight to ensure that we received as much information as possible on their arrival so that we knew their latest arrival time. I had never seen so many small craft gathered together in one place. The Prince and Princess arrived in a Triumph Stag and we manned ship for their arrival. They came up the Royal Brow and gave a reception on board for those who had helped with the arrangements in Gibraltar. At 1845 we slipped on time and made our way through the huge

The Prince and Princess of Wales watch the tremendous aquatic escort as Britannia *sails from Gibraltar.*

The Prince and Princess of Wales hosted a private dinner for President Sadat of Egypt and his wife before the Yacht steamed through the Suez Canal.

number of boats. The noise of boats' sirens and cheering was so great that it was very difficult to communicate my orders to the Yachtsmen on the quarterdeck without shouting, which I had to avoid as it was so close to where the Royal couple were standing on the Verandah Deck.'

The Yacht cleared Gibraltar just as the sun was setting and, under the cover of darkness, *Britannia* made her way into the Mediterranean. The planning of the Yacht's programme was left fairly open until 12 August, when the Yacht had to be in Port Said because The Prince of Wales had invited President Sadat on board for a dinner. Apart from that the honeymoon was treated like a Western Isles Cruise, with FORY going aft each evening to discuss the next day's destination. Remarkably, the Yacht managed to dodge the press until they reached Ithaka. Having enjoyed a pleasant evening anchored off the island the Royal couple attended the Wardroom barbecue on a deserted beach after which they decided that they wanted to spend the next day there. However, word had soon got round about the Yacht's presence and by the morning helicopters and a number of boats started to appear so the Yacht weighed anchor, as Admiral Greening recalled:

'It was very satisfying that as we departed we passed a ferry coming from the mainland which had many members of the press embarked who waved to us as we steamed in the opposite direction! We had more luck with our next stop off the north-west corner of Crete where we found a totally uninhabited area with a small bay which was a perfect place for bathing and a picnic. We had one beach for The Prince and Princess and another beach where about 100 Yachtsmen went ashore to have a swim and barbecue. In the middle of the morning over the hill behind the beach came two very attractive, blonde, Scandinavian girls. These poor girls had been told that if they walked in the direction of this bay they would find a deserted area where they could camp and spend the day. You can imagine their amazement when they came over the hill and found 100 Yachtsmen! Needless to say they were very well looked after and had a marvellous day and waved us away in the evening.'

After nearly a fortnight cruising the Mediterranean, the

Yacht reached Port Said on 12 August. As the Yacht arrived she received a tremendous welcome from the local population who turned out in force to watch her secure to two mooring buoys in front of the old Customs House. That evening President Sadat and his wife embarked for a private dinner with the Royal couple. At 2300 the Yacht made a floodlit departure to enter the canal at the head of that night's southbound convoy, as Admiral Greening remembered:

> 'In the course of the dinner The Princess of Wales told President Sadat that during the time in the Mediterranean she had discovered how much she enjoyed mangos. As a result on the way down the canal the whole convoy of 40 ships which we were leading was halted while a boat came alongside loaded with mangos as a present from the President to the Princess.'

The Yacht completed her transit of the canal the following afternoon and entered the Red Sea, sailing on to Hurghada, Egypt, where the Royal couple disembarked on 15 August to begin their long journey to Balmoral for the rest of their honeymoon. Three days later the Yacht entered Djibouti to take on fuel. The next morning the Yacht's officers turned out at 0515 to say farewell to the Commander.[5] In the afternoon the Yacht resumed her

At the end of their honeymoon The Prince and Princess of Wales are taken ashore in the Royal Barge to disembark at Hurghada, Egypt. (© British Crown Copyright / MOD)

On the final night of their honeymoon on board Britannia *the Yachtsmen put on a ship's concert for The Prince and Princess of Wales.* (© British Crown Copyright / MOD)

passage east, with further stops at Colombo and Singapore, before reaching Fremantle on 12 September. There, the Yacht's company were invited to Government House to attend a reception hosted by the Governor of Western Australia, Rear Admiral Sir Richard Trowbridge who had retired as FORY in 1975. Interestingly, Admiral Trowbridge was the last person to be sent out from the UK to be the Governor of an Australian State. From Fremantle, the Yacht steamed on to Melbourne, arriving there on 22 September for the Commonwealth Heads Of Government Meeting (CHOGM). The Queen embarked on 26 September, and three days later began the process of receiving each of the Commonwealth Heads of Government for a 20-minute audience in her Sitting Room on board the Yacht including the UK Prime Minister, Margaret Thatcher. It was Margaret Thatcher's first visit to the Yacht so she was given a guided tour, after which she became a great Yacht supporter! With so many visiting Heads of Government it was important to ensure

that the correct formalities were observed, as Captain Cosby explained:

'We developed an elaborate system which entailed Dixie Dean being sent a couple of miles away from the Yacht with his radio, a pair of binoculars and a programme waiting to see which car was approaching first. He then called us up on the radio with the information to check it was what we were expecting and make sure the right flags were flying and those back aft knew who was arriving next.'

As ever it was important for the Yacht's company to maintain their high degree of attention to detail, especially when Her Majesty was receiving the Commonwealth Heads of Government for their separate audiences, as Captain Cosby continues:

'On Royal duty we didn't go aft unless we had a particular reason especially as on this occasion I knew The Queen was in her Sitting Room talking to one of the Commonwealth Heads. I went to check the dress ship flags because I thought they had become fouled. I was carefully tiptoeing across the Royal Deck with my telescope under my arm as I was the Duty Officer. I got half way across the deck and I heard this giggle. My first thought was that it had come from one of the secretaries. I was just about to turn round and ask her to be quiet when something in my mind told me not to and I realised it was The Queen, together with her Private Secretary, who was watching me and chuckling. With a big smile she immediately said, "Who's been tiptoeing across *my* deck?" The Yachtsmen subsequently drew a cartoon in honour of the event!'

Prince Philip briefly joined The Queen between 30 September and 1 October when he left to fly to Singapore for a series of engagements.

On completion of the CHOGM the Yacht sailed on 2 October for Hobart and the start of The Queen's Tour of Australia. Three days later the Yacht reached Hobart, where Prince Philip rejoined Her Majesty having flown back from Singapore. After a day of engagements in Hobart, the Royal couple disembarked from the Yacht on 7 October to continue their Tour of South and Western Australia, while the Yacht steamed across to Lyttleton, where they rejoined the Yacht on 12 October. During The Queen's Tour of New Zealand the Yacht visited Lyttleton, Auckland and the Bay of Islands. As before, while the Yacht was steaming between ports the Royal couple continued their programme of engagements in land before rejoining the Yacht at the next port. The Tour concluded in Auckland on 20 October when The Queen and Prince

FORY escorts the British Prime Minister, Mrs Thatcher. It was the Prime Minister's first visit to the Yacht, and after her audience with The Queen Mrs Thatcher was taken for a tour of the Yacht. (© British Crown Copyright / MOD)

Philip left to fly to Sri Lanka for their State Visit. Two days later, the Yacht sailed from Auckland to begin her long voyage home via Brisbane, Darwin, Singapore, Colombo, Djibouti, the Suez Canal and Gibraltar, before arriving in Portsmouth on 11 December.

The New Year began with a routine work up at Portland and in the English Channel between 17 and 24 March 1982, before the Yacht's company went on Easter leave at the end of the month. While they were away Argentina invaded the Falkland Islands on 2 April, triggering an immediate international crisis leading to the Falklands War. As the news broke, work began immediately in the UK to assemble a Task Force to retake the Falklands. Initially, it looked as though *Britannia* would be sent to the South Atlantic to perform her secondary role as a casualty evacuation ship for the first time. Obviously, such a move would quash the persistent derisory comments that her secondary role was merely a sop to public opinion. However, doubts about the Yacht's suitability began to emerge not least the fact that, apart from the flagship HMS *Hermes*, the Yacht would be the only ship in the Task Force running on FFO and to provide it for the Yacht as well would have created major logistical problems. Equally, it wasn't clear how the Argentineans would conduct themselves in war. It was quite possible

that they would view the prospect of sinking the Yacht as a high priority. In such circumstances the value of having *Britannia* would be quickly outweighed by the diversion of valuable resources to protect her from attack. As a result, it was reluctantly decided on 6 April not to send *Britannia* to the Falklands and instead requisition the P&O's educational liner SS *Uganda*, which was much more suitable for the conditions in the South Atlantic for use as a hospital ship. The decision was a major blow to the Yacht's company who wanted to play their part in the forthcoming conflict. The decision was also disappointing from a PR perspective as it handed easy ammunition to the critics of the Yacht.

Despite the events occurring in the South Atlantic it was decided that *Britannia* should continue to fulfil her programme of Royal duty, beginning with her part in Prince Philip's visit to mark the 40th Anniversary of the St Nazaire Raid. The daring raid was an early example of Allied combined operations and used the old flushdeck destroyer HMS *Campletown* on the night of 27 March 1942 to ram the gates of the large dry dock at St Nazaire which was capable of taking the German battleship *Tirpitz*. The following morning the delayed action fuses on board the destroyer triggered the 3 tons of explosives to put the dry dock out of action. The lock gates of the St Nazaire Basin

Prince Philip talks to some of the veterans of the St Nazaire raid during the commemorations to mark the 40th Anniversary of this dramatic wartime operation.

FORY looks on as members of the Commando Association drop a wreath into the sea in memory of those who lost their lives in the St Nazaire raid.

(© British Crown Copyright / MOD)

were also disabled in a similar manner by a Motor Torpedo Boat (MTB). In an unprecedented gesture Prince Philip invited the St Nazaire veterans to take passage in the Yacht from Portsmouth to St Nazaire for the commemorations. When the Yacht sailed from Portsmouth on 22 April the first wave of Task Force ships had already sailed for the South Atlantic, but the dockyard was still working hard to prepare further ships for war service.

Two days later the Yacht secured to the south lock at St Nazaire ahead of the day's commemoration events at the Commando Memorial at St Nazaire. Prince Philip arrived direct from London at St Nazaire in the morning and went straight to the Commando Memorial to join the veterans for a service of remembrance and parade. After a lunch on board *Britannia* for the St Nazaire Society Prince Philip attended the memorial service at La Baule cemetery before leaving to fly back to Heathrow. The Yacht's second day in St Nazaire began with a church service held on the Verandah Deck attended by the veterans. On completion of the Society's reception in the Royal Apartments, 55 members of the outward party of veterans changed places with another 55 members for the voyage back to Portsmouth. Thus, when the Yacht sailed that evening, her upper deck was once more full of veterans for the two-day voyage home.[6]

On 7 June the Yacht sailed to Dover, where she arrived the next morning ahead of The Queen Mother's embarkation for a programme of events in the area in her capacity as Lord Warden of the Cinque Ports. At the end of the second day in Dover The Queen Mother was presented with a gift, as Lieutenant Commander Ford recalled:

'I got a knock on the door of the dark room and I was told that The Queen Mother wanted me up in the ante room. So I grabbed the camera and went. When I arrived I saw what was happening and set myself up. When The Queen Mother saw that I was ready she took the Rose Bowl out of its box and looked directly at me and said, "Snaps isn't this a wonderful present." She wasn't asking me the question because she wanted my opinion. It was so that she could include the two WRNS who had presented her with this rose bowl. As a result they would have a nice photograph which I thought was very nice of her.'

Once the RM Band had Beat Retreat at the end of the reception, the Yacht sailed to begin the overnight passage back to Portsmouth. As *Britannia* headed west it soon became clear that she would be sailing through the Solent at the same time as the liner *QEII*, which was bringing back the survivors from HMS *Coventry*, HMS *Ardent* and HMS *Antelope*, all of which had been sunk in the Falklands War. It was decided to meet up with the liner in the Western Solent as she made her way towards Southampton. Early the next morning the two ships made their way through the Needles Channel to be greeted by a large number of boats and press helicopters which had turned out to welcome the famous liner home from war. As both ships sailed up the Solent the survivors of the three warships lined the decks of *QEII* to give The Queen Mother three cheers as the liner steamed past the Yacht. In a mark of respect to the survivors the Yachtsmen were fallen in at attention while Her Majesty acknowledged the survivors' cheers from the Verandah Deck. The two ships then went their separate ways as *QEII* sailed into Southampton and *Britannia* entered Portsmouth.[7]

At the end of July the Yacht was at Cowes Week for Prince Philip. During the Yacht's period of Royal duty at the regatta the First Lieutenant was flown out to the Pacific to perform a reconnaissance trip ahead of the forthcoming Pacific Tour. Explaining the reason for the trip Captain Cosby said:

'I was given a pack of questions from FORY, the Commander and the Navigator which had to be answered so that the plans for the Tour could be finalised. My brief was to look at the various jetties – in particular their state of repair and their suitability for either the Yacht or the Barge. I also had to look at the steps that were going to be used to see whether they were slippery, the right height for the Barge, where mooring lines would be secured, and would anywhere need painting. I also had to check the depth of water around the jetties as well as further out where the Yacht might have to anchor. For example, at Nauru there was only a small harbour with an inadequate breakwater. It was surrounded by a coral reef with one narrow channel running through it but there was no protection from the prevailing south easterly winds. This meant that the Barge would probably have a very rough trip down this narrow channel through the reef. There wasn't likely to be any shelter in the harbour and there was always a big swell there too. The problem was do we use the Barge or should we use the flat-bottomed Activity? I also had to look at whether it was shallow enough for the Yacht to anchor: there were a great many unknowns and details required – including the dimensions of the ceremonial canoes in which The Queen and Prince Philip and the Household would be conveyed ashore

from *Britannia*'s starboard after ladder in the lagoon at Tuvalu. The trees that we selected on the recce would have to be wide enough to give sufficient girth when cut, to provide enough freeboard to minimise The Queen's step-down from the lower platform of the ladder to her flower bedecked throne in the canoe.'

The Yacht returned to Portsmouth at the end of Cowes Week on 3 August and immediately began the final preparations for the Pacific Tour, which meant there wasn't enough time for a Western Isles Cruise. A week later the Yacht sailed for Australia, calling at Gibraltar, Colombo, Singapore and Darwin, before arriving at Townsville on 23

The survivors from the ships' companies of HMS Coventry, HMS Ardent *and HMS* Antelope *gather on the decks of the liner QEII to give three cheers to The Queen Mother. Her Majesty acknowledges their cheers on the Verandah Deck.*

(© British Crown Copyright / MOD)

September. Four days later Prince Philip embarked for the two-day passage to Brisbane, as Admiral Greening recalls:

'When Prince Philip embarked at Townsville he brought with him his brand new Private Secretary, Brian McGrath, later Sir Brian McGrath GCVO. The Royal Wine Steward was apprehensive as amongst the new Private Secretary's many admirable qualities he was a "Master of Wine". The Stewards concerns were justified when on the very first night at dinner he announced that the wine was corked! Much to Prince Philip's amusement.'

His Royal Highness opened the XII Commonwealth Games on 30 September.[8] Over the next week Prince Philip undertook a programme of engagements, principally in connection with the Games. Prince Philip was joined by The Queen on 6 October for the final stages of the Games culminating in the Closing Ceremony on 9 October. Later that afternoon the Yacht sailed for Port Moresby, while The Queen and Prince Philip continued their Australian programme by travelling to Canberra, before flying out to join the Yacht in Port Moresby on 13 October for their two-day visit to Papua New Guinea, followed by a one-day visit to Honiara in the Solomon Islands.[9]

During the voyage to Nauru the Wardroom celebrated Trafalgar Night a day early on 20 October.[10] The Wardroom were joined for the evening by The Queen and Prince Philip, as the Senior Engineer, later Commander John Prichard RN, recalls:

'The Commander told me as the latest Naval Officer to join the Yacht I should give the Grace for the Trafalgar Night dinner. The Grace had to be original so I spent a long while writing it and said, "Oh God, who made Lord Nelson a great leader in war and peace and blessed him with a sense of fun and enjoyment of life, we thank Thee for the opportunity to celebrate his life as he would have wished with happiness, good food and good wine. For these blessings we are most grateful. Amen." It was well received so you can imagine my horror when the Commander turned to me after dinner and said, "Grace John." I wasn't expecting to have to give a second Grace as well so all I could think of was, "For what we have received may the Lord make us truly thankful."

The Queen said, "Well! If you can't do better than that we'll have to get a padre on board!"'

The following morning the Yacht appeared off the small independent island Republic of Nauru. As the island was so steep and the water so deep the Yacht had to remain underway for the whole 12-hour visit. Despite its size the island was enjoying a period of relative prosperity thanks to its large natural deposits of phosphate. After a full day of engagements ashore the Royal couple returned to the Yacht in the evening. Later on they went forward to watch the proclamation by the Herald of King Neptune's Court ahead of the next day's Crossing-The-Line ceremony, before returning aft to host that night's dinner for some of the island's residents, including the President of Nauru, Hammer De Roburt.[11] When the last of the guests disembarked the Yacht sailed for a one-day visit to Tarawa in Kiribati on 23 October, followed by the voyage to Funafuti. When the Yacht arrived off Funafuti for the Tuvalu visit on the 25 October she entered the Lagoon for The Queen and Prince Philip to go ashore in the Activity Boat. For the final stages of their landing the Royal couple, and the Household, were transferred to separate canoes which, as they touched the beach, were lifted out of the water and carried, accompanied by dancers and singers, to the town centre where The Queen and Prince Philip stepped out to watch the welcoming ceremonies. Having hosted a reception on board for 150 local people the Royal couple's first day in Funafuti was rounded off with a traditional Polynesian feast, followed by a colourful display of local dancing by teams from each of the islands that make up Tuvalu. After a second day ashore, which included a visit to the Maritime School at Amatuku, the Yacht sailed for Suva, Fiji, where the Yacht arrived on 30 October. Once they had been welcomed ashore the Royal couple travelled to M'bau Island to visit the ancient site of Fijian culture, before going on to a lunch hosted by the Governor General, followed by a display of local dancing. After the State Banquet in the evening Prince Philip left Fiji for Japan to carry out a series of engagements in connection with the World Wildlife Fund (WWF), leaving The Queen to return to the Yacht. The Queen's Tour ended with a day of functions on board the Yacht, beginning with a lunch, followed in the evening by a dinner and reception, prior to Beat Retreat. Once the RM Band had re-embarked the Yacht sailed serenaded by a choir of 200 on the jetty for Lautoka, where The Queen disembarked on 1 November to fly back to London.[12]

Two days later the Yacht's long voyage home began with the short passage to Apia, Western Samoa, where the Yacht arrived on 4 November. The day of the Yacht's arrival proved to be rather more eventful than planned, as Admiral Greening explained: 'I was watching the football match in which the Yacht were playing the locals when someone came rushing up to tell me that the jetty we were alongside was on fire!' Captain R Love RN, who was the Electrical Officer at the time, continues:

'I was the duty Engineer Officer and one of the men came in to tell me that there was a fire. "Where?" I asked.

"Oh, it's all right, Sir, it's on the jetty."

'We looked at this jetty and there was a warehouse full of sisal, coconut, oil and rubber, which was all on fire. The local fire brigade weren't very well equipped and our real fear was that there was a huge oil tank which could blow up if the fire continued to spread. As a precaution I ordered that the notice for sailing should be reduced and the main engines be brought to immediate notice for sea. I then mustered all those on board and organised a fire party under the Chief Stoker. We gathered the Yacht's equipment that could be sensibly spared, organised teams and a plan of attack and got stuck in. The Western Samoan fire brigade then arrived, but were short of equipment, people, and did not have any breathing apparatus. They were obviously very relieved to have our help. It took a good hour or so to extinguish the fire.'

Meanwhile Admiral Greening returned to the Yacht to see the unfolding situation for himself, as he recalled:

'I rushed back to find that the Yachtsmen had got the whole thing in hand and were fighting the fire. The next day I had a letter from the Prime Minister of Western Samoa thanking us for our help and telling me how much we had taught the Apia Fire Brigade in the process.'

Thankfully, the rest of the voyage home proved to be much less eventful with stops at the Marquesa Islands, Rodman Naval Base at the Panama Canal and the British Virgin Islands, before reaching Portsmouth at the end of a round-the-world tour on 10 December.

The beginning of the New Year heralded the start to another major deployment, with *Britannia* leaving Portsmouth on 25 January 1983 to cross the Atlantic and sail through the Panama Canal for The Queen's State Visit to Mexico. The Yacht reached Acapulco on 16 February, ahead of The Queen and Prince Philip's embarkation the next day. The Queen and Prince Philip's only engagement on the day of their arrival was an open-air dinner at San Diego Fort for 400 guests hosted by the President of Mexico. On their return the Yacht made a floodlit departure for Lazaro Cordenas for the next day's visit to the steel town that was being developed thanks to a loan from the UK which had been made at very beneficial rates. From there the Yacht sailed on to Puerto Vallarta for the final stage of the visit culminating in the return State Banquet on board the Yacht on 20 February. As usual the evening's official entertainment was rounded off with the ceremony of Beat Retreat. When the Tour was being organised the Mexicans said that they wanted to participate in the ceremony in some way. It was eventually decided that the RM Band would play first and then the Mexican Band would play their part. The ceremony would then conclude with the firing of a 42-gun salute in honour of The Queen and the President by a Mexican battery. When the moment came

While the Yacht was berthed in Long Beach the local area was hit by flash flooding and the water was too deep on the roads for the official cars. The only solution was for one of the American officials to go into the dockyard and commandeer this yellow school bus to take The Queen and Prince Philip to their next engagement.

(© British Crown Copyright / MOD)

for the Royal salute there was tremendous noise as smoke and flames billowed out of the ancient muzzle-loading guns. However, after the seventh gun had been fired the gun crews decided to stop because the guns had set fire to the surrounding bush and they thought it was too dangerous to continue with the salute! The Yacht sailed that night.[13]

With the official part of the Mexican visit over, the Yacht anchored off the Mexican State of Baja California Sur on 22 February for The Queen and Prince Philip to make an informal visit and attend a private lunch with the Governor of State at his private beach. In the afternoon Britannia resumed her passage. The following morning the Yacht anchored off the Bahia de Ballenas (the Bay of Whales) so that The Queen and Prince Philip could spend the day whale watching. In the evening the Yacht weighed anchor for San Diego. The Queen's visit to the West Coast of America was a Royal Visit, rather than a formal State Visit, which began on 26 February when they arrived at San Diego for a day of engagements, including lunch on board the aircraft carrier USS Ranger in the US Naval Base.[14]

The next morning the Royal couple continued their programme ashore while the Yacht made a fast passage along the coast to Long Beach, where she arrived in the afternoon. That night The Queen and Prince Philip attended a glittering show biz dinner hosted by Mrs Reagan in Hollywood at the 20th Century Fox film studios. The event was filled with show business personalities, such as Frank Sinatra, Bob Hope, Betty Davies and George Burns, to name but a few. Sadly, by the time of the return dinner party on board the Yacht on the second night the weather had taken a distinct change for the worse. When The Queen and Prince Philip returned from their engagements ashore FORY discussed that night's planned departure for San Francisco. In view of the atrocious weather forecast he felt it was inadvisable to sail that night, firstly due to the discomfort that would be encountered at sea and because there was little chance of landing the Royal couple by Barge at Santa Barbara or reaching San Francisco on time to meet the programme for the next part of the Tour.

The Royal couple readily agreed with FORY's advice and the US tour officials began work immediately to re-arrange the travel plans so that The Queen and Prince Philip would be flown to Santa Barbara for the next day's engagements, which included lunch with President and Mrs Reagan at their ranch in the mountains. The weather overnight vindicated FORY's advice and by the morning the local area had been hit by flash floods. Shortly before the Royal couple were due to disembark, a message

reached Britannia to say that the water on the roads leading to the Yacht was too deep for the cars which were due to collect the Royal party. Therefore, one of the US officials went out into the dockyard and commandeered a very tatty looking yellow school bus which was the only vehicle with a high enough wheel base capable of getting through the water. One of the officials wasn't entirely sure that the bus driver, who clearly hadn't shaved for a few days, realised quite who he was ferrying to the airport. That said he managed to get the Royal party through the floods and ensured that they reached the airport for their flight. In the evening The Queen and Prince Philip were joined by Mrs Reagan when they returned to the Yacht for the night. Again the weather intervened and it was decided that the Royal party would fly on to San Francisco and stay in a hotel so that The Queen could carry out her programme as planned, while the Yacht would sail as soon as possible for San Francisco. Thus on 2 March the Royal party disembarked, and an hour later the Yacht sailed in improving conditions.[15]

Two days later the Yacht entered San Francisco Bay and sailed below the world famous Golden Gate Bridge just as The Queen and Prince Philip flew overhead in the Presidential Boeing 707 on their way to an engagement up country. In the afternoon the Royal couple returned prior to hosting a dinner and reception on board the Yacht attended by President and Mrs Reagan.[16] When the last guests had disembarked, The Queen held a small informal reception for the Reagans, as Admiral Greening remembers: 'the Reagans stayed on board for the night and after the main reception finished The Queen organised a little party to celebrate the Reagans 31st wedding anniversary.' Mrs Nancy Reagan continues:

'The Queen and Prince Philip went out of their way to make it a very special time. The crew gave us a large card, which everyone had signed and we were taken on a complete tour of the Yacht, which was fascinating. We had a lovely dinner and were given a silver cigarette box with a nice inscription on the top (in order to keep it we had to buy it because of our laws). And then there were the toasts. When it came to Ronnie he said, "I know I promised Nancy everything in the world when I married her, but how can I ever top this?"'

The next morning the President and Mrs Reagan accompanied The Queen and Prince Philip ashore to continue their programme while the Yacht sailed to Seattle arriving on 7 March for the Royal couple to embark at the end of a very successful visit. From Seattle, the Yacht headed north to Victoria for The Queen and Prince Philip's short visit to British Columbia, before they flew back to the UK from Vancouver on 11 March.[17] Three days later the Yacht started the voyage home via San Diego, the Panama Canal and Antigua, reaching Portsmouth on 14 April.

During the Yacht's month alongside in Portsmouth she was fitted with a new satellite communications system.[18] FORY had been arguing for some time that the Yacht should be fitted with this system but MOD had always blocked his requests because of the cost. However, when the ships taken up from trade for the Falklands War returned to Portsmouth they were stripped of all additional equipment, which had been fitted so that they could communicate with the Fleet, before they were returned to their owners. Thus, there was an amount of spare communications equipment and the Yacht was finally allocated a satellite communications system. Before the system was installed, FORY altered some photographs of the Yacht to show both The Queen and Prince Philip how the equipment would change her profile. They approved the modifications, and shortly afterwards the contracted company installed the system, as Admiral Greening explains:

'I went up to watch it being set up. To my surprise it looked very smart and clean. I said to the man working on it that it didn't look as though it had spent several months down in the South Atlantic. He smiled and said, "Don't tell anyone but when we were told that we were to install one of the systems which had previously been used in a merchant ship for the Falklands War in *Britannia* we decided that she should be given a new one."'

On 21 May *Britannia* sailed for Stockholm after The Queen embarked in Portsmouth for the voyage across the North Sea and up the Kiel Canal. Three days later the Yacht dropped anchor off the island of Gotland where Prince Philip joined Her Majesty after his week in Zambia and Zimbabwe for the Royal Agricultural Society of the Commonwealth. The next morning The Queen and Prince Philip were joined by The Duke and Duchess of Halland for the final stages of the approach to Stockholm. When the Yacht had anchored the Royal party disembarked into the Swedish Royal Pulling Barge *Vasa Orgen*. Unlike *Britannia*'s Barge, this Barge was a relic from another age, being propelled by 18 young oarsmen under the command of a Swedish Naval Officer, resplendent in his cocked hat and frock coat. During the course of The Queen and Prince Philip's visit they lived ashore in the Swedish Royal Palace.[19]

While the Royal couple undertook their programme ashore, *Britannia* was used on 26 May for a Sea Day spon-

sored by British Invisibles. Although the holding of Sea Days on board the Yacht was still an occasional event it was clearly being seen as another effective method of employing the Yacht for the benefit of the nation. The development of *Britannia*'s commercial role was advanced slowly to ensure that the institution of Monarchy wasn't devalued in the drive to promote the UK's economic interests. The first Sea Days, held in 1968 and 1975, clearly demonstrated that the Yacht had the unique ability to attract important foreign businessmen and government ministers who would not necessarily attend similar presentations held in either prestigious hotels or the local Embassy.

British Invisibles' Gaye Murdoch made the detailed arrangements both for this event and the other Sea Days that they held on board the Yacht. Explaining why she felt the Yacht was such a useful asset for the promotion of UK business abroad, and exactly what was achieved by these events she said:

To celebrate the 31st wedding anniversary of President and Mrs Reagan, The Queen organised a private party on board the Yacht. Afterwards President and Mrs Reagan stayed on board for the night.

'The Yacht generated so much good will I would often come across people after an event who would tell me that they still remembered their reception on board. The fact that it was The Queen's home appealed to everyone. That was the essential difference between holding an event in any conference hall or art gallery and holding one on board the Yacht. Nobody declined an invitation, not least because they were curious – that didn't matter because once these people were on board that was our opportunity to sell to them. However, the great difficulty with the Yacht was determining exactly how much she made from each Sea Day. *Britannia's* great contribution was that these days provided contacts for the future. It was a great calling card because everyone would want to come to a Sea Day from government ministers downwards. Of course once we sailed we had a captive audience, which was unique. Not all of the Sea Days were designed to be commercial; some of them were designed to be a showcase and therefore it wasn't such a hard sell. There is no doubt that over the years the Yacht earned millions for Britain and was the envy of all our competitors. However, because the financial sector is so competitive we would find that if we tried to find out accurate figures we were told by many companies that their contracts hadn't been formally signed and thus they couldn't discuss figures at that time. So it wasn't uncommon for the results to take up to five years to emerge.'

The following evening The Queen and Prince Philip returned to the Yacht to host the return State Banquet for The King and Queen of Sweden, before going ashore to spend the night in the Royal Palace, and then flying back to Scotland the following morning. *Britannia* remained in Stockholm for a further two days before sailing on 30 May for the UK[20] where she called at Portland for half an hour on 2 June.[21] From Portland the Yacht continued to head west and cross the Atlantic to arrive in Halifax on 10 June to be used four days later in support of The Prince and Princess of Wales's Tour of eastern Canada. Their two-week Tour included visits to Nova Scotia, New Brunswick, Newfoundland and Prince Edward Island. At St John's, Newfoundland, on 24 June, Their Royal Highnesses attended the opening ceremony of the celebrations to commemorate the 400th Anniversary of Sir Humphrey Gilbert taking possession of Newfoundland in the name of Queen Elizabeth I. In the evening what looked like half the population of St John's gathered by the jetty to watch the RM Band Beat Retreat on a fine moonlit night. The crowds stayed on to watch the Yacht's departure an hour later. As

Britannia made her way out of the harbour she passed a large iceberg which had run aground near the harbour entrance. It made an impressive sight when it was illuminated by one of the Yacht's 20-inch spotlights.[22] Their Royal Highnesses left the Yacht on 29 June in Charlottetown to fly on to Edmonton for their final engagements prior to flying back to the UK. After a brief refuelling stop at St John's Newfoundland the Yacht began her passage back across the Atlantic to arrive in Portsmouth on 7 July.

At the end of July the Yacht attended Cowes Week, followed by the Western Isles Cruise. Unusually, the weather was extremely good during the cruise, which included another milestone in the history of *Britannia*. With her imminent conversion to run on diesel, she carried out her final FFO RAS at 0630 on 10 August. The event was marked by the cutting of a commemorative cake by FORY and the Senior Engineer, Lieutenant Commander Prichard. At the end of the cruise the Yacht returned to Portsmouth on 17 August. The next day she sailed for the Families Day, which included 'air attacks' by Hunters based at RNAS Yeovilton.

When the Yacht's company returned from summer leave, preparations got underway in earnest for the refit, with *Britannia* entering dry dock on 29 September and being docked down the following day.[23] The issue of whether the Yacht should be converted to run on diesel had been discussed a number of times during the previous decade but it had always been dismissed on the grounds that it would be too difficult and expensive. However, the issue had been brought to a head by the Falklands War when it became clear that her continued use of FFO undermined her ability to usefully perform her secondary role as a casualty evacuation ship. As part of the conversion the internal arrangements of the funnel were revised with the removal of the elaborate soot cleaning system and its replacement by smaller uptakes, thus saving 5 tons of top weight! Another long-standing issue to be rectified by the refit was the installation of two sewage treatment plants. The need for this equipment had been first highlighted in 1977 when the Yacht had to embark portable toilets for the transit of the St Lawrence Seaway. Interestingly, when the ventilation system was cleaned internally a May 1953 edition of the *Daily Mirror* was found inside some trunking which contained details of the ceremonial arrangements for The Queen's Coronation!

Work was also carried out to improve the living facilities for the Yachtsmen. This included the fitting of a new sound reproduction equipment system, which was the prototype of the system to be installed in the RN's Type 23 frigates. As the Yacht approached the final stages of the refit during February 1984 the engineers flashed up the boilers, which caused a surprising reaction, as Commander Prichard recalled:

'When we flashed up we found that, as the boiler uptakes heated up, soot from the diesel fuel, which was of a different consistency from the FFO soot we were used to, came out of the funnel looking like black butterflies which floated down on to the deck. Unfortunately, these "black butterflies" were acidic when wet and thus stained the deck. We soon learnt that we had to flash up quickly to minimise the problem because once everything was up to the right temperature it was no longer a problem.'

At the end of March 1984 *Britannia* emerged from refit and undertook the usual round of post-refit trials and work up, beginning with the passage to Devonport to collect the Royal Barge on 30 March. The acceptance of the Barge from the Dockyard attracted considerable press interest because it was the first time that the Barge had not been refitted by Portsmouth Dockyard. While the Barge was being hoisted on board, the Yacht continued her work up, as exercises to approach a buoy were carried out.[24] The next day *Britannia* left Plymouth Sound to continue her work up off Portland, before reaching Portsmouth on 6 April.

On 29 May The Queen Mother joined the Yacht in Portsmouth for her visit to the Channel Islands beginning with Guernsey the next morning where Her Majesty received a 21-gun salute on arrival. A single muzzle-loader operated by a gun crew dressed in eighteenth-century costumes was used for the occasion and took no less than 10 minutes to complete the salute.[25] During her three-day visit to the islands Her Majesty also visited Alderney, Sark and Jersey, prior to the Yacht's return to Portsmouth on 2 June. With the approach of the 40th Anniversary of the D Day landings at Normandy The Queen Mother held a reception in the evening for 200 veterans. The following morning she attended a thanksgiving service in Portsmouth Cathedral before leaving the Yacht in the afternoon to open the D Day museum in Southsea and travel back to London.[26]

Two days later The Queen and Prince Philip embarked in the Yacht. She sailed overnight towards the Normandy coast and entered the Caen Canal at 0500 on 6 June. Despite the early hour the Yacht's arrival was greeted with cheers and loud applause. Over an hour later the Yacht passed the famous Pegasus Bridge and received another enthusiastic welcome from the small crowd that had gathered by the famous café there. By 0700 the Yacht had berthed in the Basin de Calise Caen, which had

been refurbished specially for the occasion with laid turf and planted flowers and palm trees. At 1100 the Royal couple landed to visit the tomb of William the Conqueror in the former Abbey before returning to the Yacht to host a lunch for The King of the Belgians, The King of Norway, The Queen of the Netherlands and the Grand Duke of Luxembourg. As each Head of State arrived they were piped on board and their Standard was broken, resulting in the flying of five Royal Standards at the same time. After lunch the Royal party dispersed in the afternoon to attend the various D Day remembrance services in the area and at 1600 the Yacht sailed back through the canal to anchor off the remains of the Mulberry Harbour at Arrommanches. There the Yacht formed part of the Naval presence off the beach, while The Queen and Prince Philip visited the D Day museum and addressed the assembled veterans. At the end of their engagements the Royal couple left to fly back to the UK. Shortly afterwards the Yacht weighed anchor for Portsmouth.[27]

Towards the end of the month *Britannia* sailed from Portsmouth for The Queen's Tour of Canada, stopping at Ponta Delgada and Bermuda for fuel. While the Yacht was making her way up the gulf of St Lawrence early on 9 July, she received a message from Buckingham Palace. The message stated that the Tour would be postponed until the autumn because of the general election called by the Canadian Prime Minister, Pierre Trudeau, and that a public announcement to that effect would be made shortly. Thus the Yacht turned round and headed back to Portsmouth where she arrived on 19 July.[28]

On 2 August *Britannia* sailed to Southampton where the Royal Family embarked for the Western Isles Cruise. On the way north the Yacht stopped at Liverpool on 4 August to witness a parade of the sailing ships participating in the final leg of the Tall Ships Race. That night the Yacht caught up with one of the sailing ships, as Commander Prichard remembers:

'The Band were playing jazz music for The Queen in the Royal Dining Room. As we approached the *Kruzenshtern* The Queen said to the Bandmaster, "Shall we go out on to the waist and give them some music? What can you play?"

He replied, "Well it's a jazz evening so why not 'Tiger Rag'?" The Royal party all went out on to the waist as we sailed past the *Kruzenshtern* and the RM Band belted out "Tiger Rag" while The Queen waved. The Russians looked absolutely astounded with what was going on!'

Two days later the Yacht suffered from a total steam failure, shortly after RFA Blue Rover began to pump fuel across to Britannia at the start of a RAS early in the morning. The Yacht had suffered a similar problem when she underwent trials to test the new fuelling arrangements off Portland in June. Following that incident FORY ordered an immediate investigation and the experts from MOD concluded that it was a one off glitch. Because of the nature of Britannia's programme she hadn't undertaken another RAS since then so the total steam failure came as an unpleasant surprise, as Commander Prichard explains:

'We were at special sea dutymen and I was in the Engine Room. There was a broadcast from the Boiler Room, "flame out, both boilers total steam failure!" I rang the Bridge and got a disbelieving answer from the Engineering Officer, Commander Peter Mansfield, when I told him what had happened.'

Admiral Greening continued:

'Fortunately we managed to swing away from Blue Rover and everything parted before we came to a complete halt. It took us another hour and a half to get going again. Luckily, we had enough fuel to get us to Aberdeen so we didn't need to connect up again. Later in the day The Queen turned to me and asked, "Why did it all suddenly go so quiet early this morning?"'

When Britannia returned to Portsmouth at the end of the cruise on 13 August, she berthed alongside RFA Olmeda at the oil fuel jetty to carry out a controlled experiment to find out exactly what happened. As before, about 40 seconds after Olmeda began to pump fuel, the Yacht suffered another total power failure. It was firmly established that the problem was caused by the difference in viscosity between FFO and diesel. This led to air being blown through a balance line and into the boilers when the tanker started to pump. The heavier FFO had prevented that happening. The problem was solved simply by closing a valve on the balance line.[29]

On 10 September Britannia sailed from Portsmouth once more to head across the Atlantic to support The Queen's delayed Tour of Canada. During the course of the Tour Britannia steamed up the St Lawrence Seaway as far as Toronto, before The Queen and Prince Philip flew back to London from Toronto Airport on 4 October. At the end of her passage back down the St Lawrence Seaway Britannia called at Sydney, Nova Scotia on 9 October where FORY was inducted as a member of the Order of Sou'wester, which is an unusual honour also shared at the time by the Captain of the Cunard liner QEII. That evening the Yacht sailed for Gibraltar under the Commander, Commander McKnight, as FORY had to

return to London to discuss the arrangements for forthcoming tours.[30] Following an uneventful crossing of the Atlantic, FORY rejoined the Yacht in Rosia Bay on 17 October, prior to her entry into Gibraltar that morning.[31]

Two days later Britannia sailed for Ancona, where The Queen Mother embarked on 24 October. The next day the Yacht berthed in Venice at lunchtime for Her Majesty's four-day visit. The waterways of Venice were too shallow for the Barge, so two water taxis were hired and used as temporary Royal Barges. As Admiral Greening recalled, these weren't the only unusual craft to be used for Royal duty during the visit:

'The Queen Mother's Household had been determined there wasn't going to be a gondola involved in this trip. Although the press kept asking for The Queen Mother to go in a gondola we thought that we had got away with it. However, on the last day The Queen Mother was visiting a church and when she came out sitting at the steps was a gondola together with the gondolier standing in an appropriate rig who had been hired by the media. It was therefore difficult to say no and thus The Queen Mother agreed to go down into the gondola and do a little round trip for the benefit of the media. Her Majesty said that someone must go with her and as it was considered to come under the heading of seagoing I was nominated by the Household! We did a little trip around a block, which was an extraordinary event. By the steps where we embarked there was chaos with the world's press and yet as we got around the corner of the building there was absolute peace and quiet until right at the back of the building we went round there was a veranda. Two nuns were standing on this veranda who at first looked absolutely astonished to see us going past before they became hysterical with excitement. This was followed by peace again until we turned the corner and were confronted by the chaos created by the press around the steps where we had started.'

After The Queen Mother flew home, the Yacht sailed for Portsmouth via Gibraltar.

At the beginning of December the Yacht sailed round to London and passed through the completed Thames Barrier for the first time on her way to the Pool of London on 4 December. Two days later The Queen, Prince Philip, The Prince and Princess of Wales, Prince Andrew, Princess Margaret and The Duke and Duchess of Gloucester embarked for a reception held for people connected with maritime affairs.[32] After nearly a week in London the Yacht began her overnight passage back to Portsmouth on the afternoon of 10 December.

The Yacht's spring deployment to the west coast of

Africa and the Mediterranean began on 26 February 1985 when she sailed for Madeira, for the first fuel stop on her way to the Gambia River, where she arrived on 7 March. Two days later Prince Philip arrived 24 hours ahead of schedule because his aircraft couldn't land in Senegal as planned due to a dust storm. Prince Philip wasn't able to communicate with the Yacht to let them know about the change of plan. Thus his unannounced arrival led to some quick thinking, as Admiral Greening explains:

'It was the Navigating Officer's birthday so some of the Wardroom decided that they would take one of the Yacht's boats up the river for a banyan. I couldn't go because I had to attend an engagement with the High Commissioner in the afternoon so I decided to go for a swim in the morning. Just as I had finished my swim one of the Chief Petty Officers came down the beach and enquired if I knew that Prince Philip had arrived. I dashed back to the Yacht much to Prince Philip's amusement. Fortunately, the Duty Lieutenant Commander had done his job well with the Yacht dressed overall and flying Prince Philip's Standard. Equally fortunate, was that the Keeper & Steward hadn't gone on the banyan so he could open up the Royal Apartments. The Wardroom had a nasty shock because they came back in good heart about tea time and as they turned the corner saw the Yacht dressed overall flying Prince Philip's Standard.'

The following morning His Royal Highness landed to begin his three-day programme in the Gambia with a visit to a wildlife reserve on the border between the Gambia and Senegal. Although Prince Philip's visit was principally concerned with his work for the WWF, his programme culminated in a dinner for the President and Vice President of the Gambia on board the Yacht on 12 March. The next morning Prince Philip landed early to fly on to Dakar. Half an hour later the Yacht sailed for Dakar Harbour, where she arrived in the afternoon. During the voyage from Banjul the Commander transferred to the Royal Escort HMS Boxer to gain experience of handling a Type 22 frigate in preparation for his forthcoming appointment as the first Captain of HMS Brave. The Yacht left Dakar on 14 March for the bird sanctuary at Banc d'Arguin, which Prince Philip visited two days later,

The Queen Mother is taken for a short trip in a Gondola during her visit to Venice. (© British Crown Copyright / MOD)

having been transferred to *Boxer* and flown ashore in her Lynx helicopter.[33]

The following morning the Yacht arrived in the unsheltered waters of Nouadhibou Harbour in Mauritania. The sight that greeted the Royal party was stark to say the least, with the low lying terrain dominated by a number of wrecked vessels and the tail of an aircraft sticking out of the water. The Soviet Ilyushin aircraft had ended up in the water when it failed to stop at the end of the runway. The scene was completed by some small ships from the Soviet bloc lying at anchor. In the afternoon Princess Alexandra and the Hon. Angus Ogilvy joined the Yacht and would remain on board until *Britannia* reached Portugal.[34] Over the coming days *Britannia* headed north, visiting the Salvagen Islands and Madeira, prior to reaching Setubal on 24 March, when Princess Alexandra and her husband left for London. The next day The Queen embarked in the evening and the Yacht sailed that night for Lisbon, where Her Majesty formally began her State Visit to Portugal the next day. While the Royal couple were visiting Sintra on 27 March the Yacht embarked 110 Portuguese and British businessmen for a Sea Day aimed at promoting UK technology.[35] As usual the State Visit was rounded off with a return State Banquet, held on board on 28 March. The Queen and Prince Philip then left Portugal by air to fly home. Two days later the Yacht left Lisbon for Gibraltar for a fortnight of maintenance, before sailing into the Mediterranean and the next stage of her deployment, beginning with the embarkation of The Prince and Princess of Wales in the Sardinian port of Olbia on 19 April for their Italian visit.

Soon after the embarkation of Their Royal Highnesses the Yacht began the overnight passage to La Spezia for the start of their Tour of Italy on 20 April. Once in La Spezia, Their Royal Highnesses left by car for Milan to carry out the inland part of their Tour. The Yacht played a more prominent role in the later stages of the Tour, when she took Their Royal Highnesses from Civitavecchia to Trani and Bari on the east coast of Italy. From there the Yacht sailed to Venice, where she arrived on 4 May. The Royal couple followed the example of The Queen Mother and, on the first day of their visit, went for a short trip in a gondola, much to the obvious delight of the assembled media. On the second day of their visit, Their Royal Highnesses were joined by their sons the 2-year-old Prince William and the 7-month-old Prince Harry who had been flown out in an aircraft of The Queen's Flight. Many of the guests for that night's dinner and reception chose to arrive by gondola on a beautifully clear, moonlight night. Once the last of the guests had left

after the Beat Retreat, the Yacht made a dramatic flood-lit departure watched by large crowds ashore.[36] During the voyage back to Olbia the Yacht celebrated a significant event on 8 May with a small party to celebrate the completion of the Yacht's 750,000 mile. The event was attended by some of the longest serving Yachtsmen on board, as well as Their Royal Highnesses, with the specially baked cake being cut by the Coxswain, Warrant Officer Norrell and The Princess of Wales.[37] The following morning the Yacht berthed in Olbia and Their Royal Highnesses disembarked to fly back to the UK. At lunchtime *Britannia* began her own homeward journey, via Gibraltar, to reach Portsmouth on 16 May.

On 6 June The Queen Mother joined the Yacht in Portsmouth for a Tour, which included visits to Falmouth, the Scilly Isles and finally Plymouth. At the Scilly Isles the weather took a turn for the worse before that night's dinner,[38] as Admiral Greening explained:

'The Yacht was anchored in the bay and many of the guests were arriving either very wet or seasick or both. We were forced into a situation where we managed to get the men off the boats at the ladder but then the ladies in their evening dresses had to be hoisted in the boats and I am afraid that many of them found the whole thing rather upsetting! When the time came for dinner there were a number of empty seats. The PMO had opened up a sort of casualty ward in the Equerries Room. Queen Elizabeth in a way rather enjoyed it as she never suffered from the sea. She told me the next day with some glee that every time she looked up she saw the PMO leading off some poor lady. It was a great relief to me when we managed to get them all off ashore in one piece, which took some time because we couldn't take too many at a time as the boats had to be hoisted between trips, which led to a busy and exhausting evening for the boat's crews.'

When the last of the guests had made it ashore the Yacht weighed anchor for the overnight passage back to Portsmouth.

A week later the Yacht entered dry dock for repainting, and emerged in time to attend Cowes Week at the beginning of August, followed by the Western Isles Cruise. At the end of the cruise the Yacht berthed in Aberdeen on 15 August. Before The Queen left, she invested Rear Admiral Greening with the KCVO to mark his imminent retirement as FORY. Thus Rear Admiral Sir Paul Greening brought the Yacht into Portsmouth for the last time on 18 August 1985 to bring his Naval career to a close, six weeks short of 40 years. In his four and a half years as FORY the Yacht had steamed some 115,000 miles.

Chapter Ten

THE ADEN EVACUATION

Rear Admiral Sir John Garnier
KCVO CBE 1985–1990

Rear Admiral Sir Paul Greening's time as FORY came to an end on 12 September 1985 when he was succeeded by Rear Admiral John Garnier CBE LVO. At noon Admiral Greening, together with Lady Greening, disembarked from the Yacht and boarded the elegant steam pinnace that the Yachtsmen had borrowed for the beginning of the Admiral's journey into retirement. However, this wasn't to be the end of Admiral Greening's association with *Britannia* because at the beginning of the New Year he was due to relieve Vice Admiral Sir Peter Ashmore as the Master of the Household.

For Rear Admiral Garnier his appointment as FORY was a return to familiar territory as he had served in the Yacht as a Season Officer under Vice Admiral Sir Conolly Abel Smith between 1956 and 1957. He had also accompanied The Queen on board *Britannia* during his time as her Equerry between 1962 and 1965. As a Commander he commanded the frigates HMS *Dundas* and HMS *Minerva*, before becoming the Executive Officer of the assault ship HMS *Intrepid*. He was subsequently promoted to the rank of Captain and became the last Commanding Officer of the *County* Class destroyer HMS *London* in 1981. Following his appointment as the Director of Naval Operations and Trade, he was promoted to the rank of Commodore in 1985 to become the Commodore Amphibious Warfare. From there he was promoted to Rear Admiral prior to becoming FORY.

For Admiral Garnier there was little time to acclimatise to his new role, as within a fortnight the Yacht sailed for the Caribbean and CHOGM, which was held in the Bahamas where The Queen joined the Yacht on 11 October in Nassau. As The Queen's Assistant Private Secretary at the time, later The Rt Hon. Lord Fellowes GCB GCVO QSO, explains, just because The Queen was over 4000 miles away from London the flow of red boxes didn't stop:

'At the core of each delivery of mail to the Yacht was a number of red plastic or canvas pouches containing The Queen's work and the Private Secretary's work. We arranged for the Councillors of State to undertake some of the Queen's routine work in her absence. The Councillors of State are the four immediate members of The Queen's family, next most senior to HM and Prince Philip, which towards the end of the Yacht's time consisted of Queen Elizabeth The Queen Mother, The Prince of Wales, The Princess Royal and The Duke of York. They were entitled to sign certain documents. They could hold audiences and see Ambassadors, but there were certain things they couldn't deal with, such as the political side of life, honours, and most of the things to do with The Queen's 15 other Realms. Therefore, the residual business of The Queen's that came out from London was roughly like her daily work in London, without some of the more mundane and routine business. We also had a system where we didn't have Cabinet Papers sent to her every day, or Foreign Office telegrams, but they would come out in summary form, perhaps on a weekly basis. Thus the work in these bags could range from a couple of hours, down to half an hour on an easy day, on top of the busy daily schedule of the tour itself.'

After three days of engagements ashore in the Bahamas, The Queen began the process of receiving the various Heads of the Commonwealth in her Sitting Room in the Yacht on the afternoon of 15 October. Over the next three days Her Majesty granted a 20-minute audience to each Head of Government, including the British Prime Minister, Margaret Thatcher. Prince Philip arrived in Nassau to join The Queen on 16 October, having flown direct from Melbourne at the end of his Australian visit. While Her Majesty continued to grant further audiences, Prince Philip pursued his own programme ashore, including a visit to the Nassau Yacht Club's sailing regatta in

FORY between 1985 and 1990, Rear Admiral Sir John Garnier KCVO CBE.

Montego Bay on 18 October. That evening the Royal couple hosted a reception for the Commonwealth Foreign Ministers, prior to the Yacht making a floodlit departure for St Kitts to begin The Queen's Tour of the Caribbean.[1] During the course of the Tour The Queen visited 14 islands within 16 days.

Like previous tours of the Caribbean, the programme moved at a rapid pace with a day of engagements ashore, followed by an overnight passage to the next island ready for the following day's activities. Without the presence of *Britannia* it wouldn't have been possible for The Queen and Prince Philip to maintain this schedule. When The Queen left the Yacht to fly home from Trinidad on 3 November she fully acknowledged the important role that *Britannia* had played in the Tour with the signal she sent to FORY:

'It would be difficult to exaggerate the value of the Royal Yacht during the recent Commonwealth Tour of the Caribbean. It is obvious that the people of these islands have happy memories of their association with Great Britain. The behaviour and bearing of the Officers, Yachtsmen and members of the Royal Marine Band have helped remind them of all that is best in the old mother country. This has made our job in the islands that much more effective and, I hope more memorable. I know it has meant a great deal of work for everyone but it was worth every bit of it.'[2]

The next day the Yacht sailed from Trinidad to begin the voyage back to Portsmouth, where she arrived on 16 November. While the Yacht's company were preparing for their next major deployment, news reached *Britannia* of Vice Admiral Sir Conolly Abel Smith's death on 4 December 1985. FORY and the Coxswain travelled to Scotland for his funeral on 10 December. As a mark of respect colours were flown at half mast in the Yacht during the period of the funeral service and committal.[3]

The Yacht's departure on New Year's Eve for Australia was slightly delayed by winds of 30 knots which had eased enough by late morning to enable *Britannia* to sail out of Portsmouth.[4] However, that wasn't to be the last bad weather encountered by the Yacht on her outward voyage because by the next day *Britannia* was battling against winds of up to 70 knots and 50-foot high waves. Thankfully, the weather began to ease as she reached Gibraltar, where she berthed on 4 January 1986 for a well-earned respite in her battle against the elements, while she took on fuel for the next leg of her voyage, which she began later that day. As the Yacht headed east, intelligence was received on board advising FORY that in view of Libya's growing support of terrorist attacks it would be prudent to keep as far from the Libyan coast as possible during her transit of the Mediterranean. Thus the Yacht passed between Malta and Sicily, maintaining an easterly heading until she reached Crete, when she headed south towards Port Said and sailed through the Suez Canal on 11 January.[5]

As the Yacht made her way down the Red Sea a civil war was erupting in South Yemen triggered by the Marxist leader, President Ali Nasser Mohammed, ordering several of his former colleagues to be assassinated. This led to fighting between Government troops and rebels from other Marxist factions. In London the British Government were discussing how to evacuate British nationals trapped by the fighting in South Yemen. *Britannia*'s close proximity to South Yemen coupled with the fact she was a non combatant ship of the Royal Navy made her a very attractive candidate to be used as part of the British rescue operation which was given the code name of Operation Balsac. As the Defence Secretary at the time, later The Rt Hon. Viscount Younger of Leckie KT KCVO TD DL, explains:

'The issue was would the MOD permit *Britannia* to be converted into a casualty evacuation ship. The Queen had given her full backing to the idea. Those against the suggestion said it would be very difficult to achieve and it would take a lot of time to put her back to normal. Those in favour stated that she had been in service for over 30 years and here was an actual situation where she could be usefully employed in her secondary role which would bring nothing but good publicity.'

The Defence Secretary agreed with the latter sentiments, and so a signal was sent by MOD to the Yacht on the evening of 14 January ordering her to head for Aden. In addition to diverting *Britannia*, MOD sent orders to Mombasa for HMS *Newcastle*, HMS *Jupiter* and RFA *Brambleleaf* to sail for Aden, followed by the redeployment of HMS *Hydra* from her surveying duties off East Africa on 17 January.

When the signal arrived on board the Yacht the Wardroom were in the middle of a delicately balanced darts match against the Petty Officer's mess. FORY was informed that an urgent message had arrived for his attention so he left the room to examine its contents. Immediately FORY began sending for each of the senior officers to discuss the situation and agree a plan of action for the coming hours and days. Interestingly, in the Journal of HM Yachts kept by the Commander (S) on behalf of FORY, it was noted that unusually no precedent existed in the previous experience of the Yacht on how to cope with the unfolding situation![6] From the initial information it looked as though the Yacht would be required to embark about 200 people which immediately raised the issue of where to accommodate them. The only realistic option was to house them in the Royal Apartments, so the Keeper & Steward was ordered to clear the Royal Dining Room and the Royal Drawing Room overnight. Some of the furniture was moved up to Verandah Deck level while the remainder was stored in a few of the Household cabins. Up forward the Royal Charthouse was rigged as the Operations Room and the Yacht's company went on to a war footing as they were split into two watches to enable a

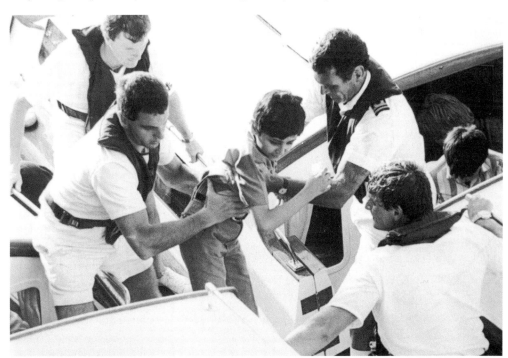

A refugee is transferred between boats as part of the relay between the beach and Britannia *to speed up the evacuation from Aden.*

(© British Crown Copyright / MOD)

24-hour routine to be worked throughout the emergency. However, FORY later discovered that once the first of the refugees had been embarked some of the off duty Yachtsmen were going down to the Royal Apartments to help care for the refugees. Thus he had to ensure that once the Yachtsmen finished their watch they actually went down to their messes to get some sleep!

Being the closest of the British ships sent to Aden, the Yacht arrived outside South Yemen's territorial waters at first light the next morning, with instructions to maintain a low profile out of sight of land until the situation ashore became clearer. FORY had hoped that he might be able to carry out a very straightforward evacuation by steaming into Aden and embarking the evacuees and sailing out again. However, those hopes were quickly dashed when contact was made with the Sri Lankan registered British merchant ship MV *Pacific Universal*, which had managed to leave Aden Harbour the previous day. Despite the outwardly calm scene that greeted the Yacht on the horizon *Pacific Universal*'s Master informed FORY that heavy fighting had been taking place in and around the harbour. He also confirmed the harbour was covered by heavy artillery and that aircraft had attacked the airport.[7] Faced with this new information FORY had to reconsider his options and plan a new way forward. His first major challenge was to establish who exactly should be contacted to gain official permission to enter South Yemen's territorial waters. Despite the chaos ashore the Yacht couldn't just steam into South Yemen's territorial waters and carry out a rescue mission without official permission to do so.

Until further information could be obtained, the Yacht held her position offshore where she was joined some distance away by the French destroyer *De Grasse* and the Soviet ships *Boris Chilikin* (AOR), a *Ropucha* class landing ship and an *Ugra* class submarine support ship.

In the early hours of 17 January, HMS *Newcastle*, HMS *Jupiter* and RFA *Brambleleaf* of the Armilla Patrol arrived at their holding position 30 miles to the south of Aden to await further orders. Later in the morning the British Ambassador in Aden, Arthur Marshall, managed to establish contact with the Yacht through *De Grasse*, as the Ambassador's equipment was incapable of direct communication with the Yacht. In his message Arthur Marshall said that the fighting appeared to have died down in the harbour but the situation ashore was still critical. Later in the afternoon, Arthur Marshall passed a further message to FORY via *De Grasse* that *Britannia* had permission to begin the evacuation of the first refugees. However, there still appeared to be confusion about who was exercising tactical command of South Yemen's territorial waters as when the Yacht steamed towards Khormaksar beach to start picking up refugees she was challenged by the Soviets to say that after all permission hadn't been given for the Yacht to enter territorial waters. FORY, however, disregarded this statement as being just a repetition of a number over the previous 24 hours.

Thus at 1825 the Yacht began her passage towards the coast as the sun was setting. To enable easy identification of *Britannia* a large Union Flag was broken at each mast and her superstructure was floodlit to provide a curious but patriotic sight that brought a lump to the throats of the British waiting on the beach. Over an hour and a half later the Yacht dropped anchor a mile off Khormaksar beach. Shortly afterwards FORY sent the first of the Yacht's boats ashore under the command of the Boatswain, later Commander R Easson RN, to make contact with the British Embassy staff on the beach, as he recalled:

'Although it was dark there were a lot of people on the beach waiting to come off. Once ashore I took on the role of Beach Master and had to organise the people on the beach. Some of the people were wandering around in a daze, while others hadn't slept or eaten for days. We didn't have time to send supplies ashore because our efforts were directed entirely towards getting people off the beach. Surprisingly, the first person I met as I arrived on the beach was a man called Pat Curtis who I had known when he served in the Fleet Air Arm! We initially thought that the Activity Boat was the best boat for the job because it was fast, but in fact we got into real trouble once we got close to the shore as it was so shallow and there was a lot of surf. This caused the boat to pitch round and it was very difficult to keep its bows on to the beach. As a result we had to abandon our first attempt and call in the jolly boats. With the jolly boat we were able to lay a kedge anchor out and place the bow on shore while we were getting people out. At one point the rate at which we could take people off was getting quite slow so we decided to organise a relay where the larger motor boats came to about half distance and took off people from the jolly boats thus enabling the jolly boats to go back and pick up more people off the beach.'

Within half an hour of the Activity Boat being launched, the first of the refugees were brought on board *Britannia*. As each person arrived they were given a blanket and taken to the Verandah Deck for hot soup and a snack before being led to the temporary registration point, which had been set up in the Verandah. Once each person's details were noted they were shown to the make shift dormitories in the Royal Apartments.[8] During that night's evacuation operation, which lasted for three and a quarter hours, a total of 152 people of 26 nationalities were rescued, plus one French dog! (When the news of the dog's rescue reached HMS *Newcastle* her chippies made a wooden lamp post which was sent across to the Yacht a few days later.) During the night the Soviet ships, which had also been engaged in rescue operations off Khormaksar beach, weighed anchor leaving *Britannia* as the only ship off the beach at daybreak. Shortly before sunrise the evacuation was restarted, as a large crowd gathered on the beach in excess of the anticipated numbers. Soon the first signs of the cease-fire disintegrating began to emerge as fighting broke out close to the beach, leading to a temporary suspension of the evacuation when sniper fire started to straddle the Yacht's boats.

The operation resumed for over half an hour until 0909, when the first tanks approached the beach. Describing what he could see from *Britannia*'s Bridge Admiral Garnier

The details of each refugee were taken at the temporary registration point set up in the Verandah as part of the hasty conversion from Royal Yacht to evacuation ship.

(© British Crown Copyright / MOD)

*To keep the refugees fed,
the cooks worked some very
long shifts during the Aden
crisis.*

said, 'it was a little like watching the Royal Tournament because we could see the rebel tanks coming in from one side and firing over the top of the Yacht's boats while Government tanks were responding from the other side.' In view of the deteriorating situation FORY was left with no other option than to suspend the operation during which a further 279 people were saved including the Ambassador. Once the boats had been recovered the Yacht weighed anchor and headed out of territorial waters. The 160 people left behind on the beaches ran for cover as the rebel forces launched their final attack on Aden while FORY waited for the next opportunity to evacuate the remaining refugees. When the Yacht reached international waters the Captain of *De Grasse* was most insistent that the 81 French and francophile nationals were to be transferred from *Britannia* to FNS *Jules Verne*. The transfer was complete by 1110 and within an hour the Yacht was back off the beach. As she paused offshore, there were shells landing in the water between the Yacht and the shore, and it was clear that the fighting showed no signs of dying down. So FORY decided to take the remaining 350 refugees across the Gulf of Aden to Djibouti on the East African coast, where she arrived at 2259.

As the senior British officer present, FORY had been given command of the British evacuation operation so when the Yacht took the first group of refugees to Djibouti he temporally left HMS *Newcastle*'s Captain, Peter Erskine in command of the mission. While the Yacht was away Captain Erskine managed to establish contact with the remaining British nationals in Yemen and discovered that a group of 200 people were moving towards Zinjibar. Thus when the Yacht sailed from Djibouti on the morning of 19 January she headed past Aden towards Zinjibar for that night's evacuation operation, as Commander Easson explains:

'We arrived off Zinjibar in the dark and there were 209 people waiting to be picked up. It was only thanks to the headlamps of cars that we could see anything. The rebels who were guarding them had commandeered all the vehicles. They got quite nasty at one point and I thought that the only way we could get people off without anybody being hurt was to send for a lot of supplies from the Yacht which I could give to the rebels to calm them down. The next boat that came in was topped up with cigarettes, chocolates and drinks and I said, "here is all these supplies just let the people go," which they did and we spent the next few hours taking them off.'

By 2200 all of the refugees had been rescued and *Britannia* headed out once more into international waters to meet up with the frigate HMS *Jupiter*. Although *Britannia* had been given clearance to enter territorial waters the rebels still wouldn't allow any grey ships to approach the coast including the RFA tanker *Brambleleaf* which was fired upon when she tried to sail towards Khormaksar beach on 18 January. Therefore, once the refugees had been embarked the Yacht steamed into international waters, where she joined up

The Queen and Prince Philip together with other members of the Royal Family gather for the traditional informal family photograph on the Verandah Deck during the final Western Isles Cruise. (© British Crown Copyright / MOD)

The Royal Coat of Arms on Britannia's bow. (© Richard Johnstone-Bryden)

The Duke of Edinburgh and King Constantine of Greece together with their crew on board the yacht Yeoman XXVIII which they raced during Cowes Week 1993. (© British Crown Copyright / MOD)

This fine binnacle was first mounted in the Royal Yacht Royal George when she was built in 1817 and has been moved to each successive Royal Yacht. The bell was presented to The Queen by the Elder Brethren of Trinity House and is dated 21 October 1953. Above the bell is the Royal Coat of Arms which were first mounted in V&A (II) in 1845.

(© Devonport Management Ltd)

The Royal Drawing Room as seen by visitors to Leith.

(© Yacht Events Ltd)

The Royal Apartments were
designed by Sir Hugh
Casson. They are elegant,
deliberately understated and
beautifully proportioned.
This is the Royal Dinning
Room.

Everyone who has visited
Britannia remembers the
Engine Room. Quite simply,
it is a gleaming yet
functional showpiece of
engineering. It was
maintained in immaculate
condition throughout the
Yacht's 44-year service.

ABOVE: *The Fleet Review held off Spithead to mark the 50th Anniversary of D Day on 5 June 1994. The Yacht can be seen on the left engulfed by an armada of small boats as she approaches the Cunard liner QEII.* (© British Crown Copyright / MOD)

OPPOSITE PAGE ABOVE: *The marine artist, Geoff Hunt, was lucky enough to be invited on board HMS Illustrious for the Fleet Review to mark the 50th Anniversary of D Day on 5 June 1994. From his grandstand view on board the carrier Geoff was able to capture Britannia participating in this historic event through some rough pencil sketches and by taking photographs. Geoff later remarked: 'The camera records all the complexity, but the eye records what is essential for the artist's purpose.'*

(Reproduced by kind permission of Geoff Hunt RSMA)

OPPOSITE PAGE BELOW: *To bring the evening's reception on board* Britannia *to a close the Yacht's RM Band perform the ceremony of Beat Retreat on the quayside so that the Band can be clearly seen by the guests.* (© British Crown Copyright / MOD)

Britannia moored in the Pool of London for the commemorations to mark the 50th Anniversary of V J Day on 19 August 1995.

Flying her 412-foot long paying off pennant Britannia begins her final voyage under her own power as she departs from the Pool of London on 21 November 1997.

Flying her paying off pennant Britannia is escorted by various small boats as she approaches Portsmouth on 22 November 1997.

Britannia's last day at sea as she approaches her new home of Leith under tow on 5 May 1998.   (© Forth Ports plc)

Britannia alongside her permanent moorings at Leith's Ocean Terminal.   (© Forth Ports plc)

with *Jupiter* at 2300 to transfer the evacuees so they could be taken to Djibouti on board the frigate, thus allowing the Yacht to remain off Aden to rescue more people.

Early the next morning FORY managed to establish contact with the Aden Port Captain, Captain Saeed Yafai and begin negotiations for the final phase of the evacuation. These discussions continued into the morning of 21 January when the Yacht was granted permission to approach Little Aden and take off further British nationals. During the intervening 36 hours the situation for those ashore grew more serious as they began to run out of food and water. By late morning the Yacht had embarked a further 15 British nationals before taking up station off Khormaksar. In an attempt to improve communications between the French and Soviet ships FORY invited both nations to send a liaison officer to the Yacht. The Soviet's accepted his invitation and sent across MV *Vinnitsa*'s Second Officer, Sergi Yatchuk, who was known on board simply as Boris.[9]

Despite some promising signs of a French/Soviet plan beginning to emerge in the afternoon it wasn't until 22 January that real progress was made. Unfortunately, the swell had become too rough for another beach recovery mission so it was decided to direct the refugees to Little Aden where the rescue operation resumed in the afternoon. By sunset the operation was in full swing with a steady stream of people being recovered by both the Yacht and Soviet ships. Further along the coast the Cunard cargo ship MV *Diamond Princess*, which had been chartered by MOD on 21 January, berthed in Mukalla on 22 January and managed to embark 248

evacuees, before she sailed at 0300 the next morning.

Meanwhile, off Little Aden the Yacht rescued a further 227 people before work stopped for the night at 2300. *Britannia*'s last day of operations began on the morning of 23 January, when the rescue work resumed off Little Aden. By lunchtime the Yacht's work was completed with the recovery of a further 200 people, enabling her to weigh anchor and head for Djibouti. Within half an hour of sailing news reached the Yacht that another Briton had arrived at the beach to be evacuated. *Britannia* turned round to rescue the Yemen-born London bus driver Saleh Ali who had been staying with his family when the war broke out. He later described his feelings about the sight of *Britannia* reaching the coast to the press saying: 'when I saw the launch coming in, with its White Ensign fluttering in the wind, I was very happy inside and there were tears in my eyes. The Queen's yacht turned back for me, just for me. I can't believe it!' Once Saleh Ali had been embarked the Yacht set course again for Djibouti where she arrived that night to disembark the refugees.

When *Britannia* reached Djibouti her role within the Aden crisis came to an end, thus enabling her to resume the voyage to New Zealand on 24 January which was critical for the Yacht to stand any chance of meeting her commitments in support of The Queen's programme. Despite the pressure of bringing the Yacht back up to the high standards expected for her Royal role the Yacht's company were able to reflect with pride on the work they had undertaken in Aden. Although FORY's brief had been to rescue British subjects it clearly would have been inhumane to have left the other refugees behind so the

The large open spaces of the Royal Apartments were ideal to shelter all of the refugees during their short stay on board the Yacht. Here a group of refugees have gathered in the Royal Drawing Room.

(© British Crown Copyright / MOD)

To improve the communications between the French and Soviet ships, Admiral Garnier suggested that both nations should send a liaison officer to the Yacht. The Soviets took up FORY's suggestion and sent Second Officer Sergi Yatchuk who is seen here talking to Admiral Garnier.

(© British Crown Copyright / MOD)

Yacht's boat crews saved everyone who could reach them. During her involvement in the Aden crisis *Britannia* rescued 1082 of the 1379 people of 55 nationalities saved by British ships during Operation Balsac. For *Britannia* her involvement in the crisis proved very useful politically because it clearly demonstrated that she could be quickly converted to perform her secondary role as a casualty evacuation ship. Although her secondary role was more commonly given the title of hospital ship, the contingency plans held by MOD for *Britannia* clearly show that she was never intended to act as a fully-fledged hospital ship. Instead MOD had always planned that she would be used to move casualties from a war zone back to a safe haven where they could receive further medical attention. Her large open spaces in the Royal Apartments coupled with the high number of boats that she carried made her ideal for this role and it was these capabilities that stood her in good stead for the Aden crisis.

Britannia's exploits had become headline news around the world and soon a steady stream of congratulatory signals began to arrive on board, including messages from The Queen, the Prime Minister and the Foreign Secretary, as well as the Chief of the Defence Staff and the Defence Secretary. The task of returning the Royal Apartments to normality was achieved by the Keeper & Steward's team, before the Yacht's stop at Colombo for fuel on 29 January. The refugees had been very careful during their time on board and nothing was either scratched or damaged. Having made further short stops at Singapore and Darwin,

Britannia was on her way to Cairns when she received a distress call from the 29-foot motor cruiser, *African Queen*, stating that the engines had seized and she was taking on water. As *Britannia* approached *African Queen*, FORY sent a boat across with a three-man team, consisting of Chief Petty Officers Mace and Cook and Petty Officer Turner, to see what if any help they could provide. Within two hours they managed to get both engines running when the crew, Mr Heinz Zimmer, suddenly collapsed. He was transferred immediately to the Yacht where he was examined by the PMO, Surgeon Commander Tim Douglas-Riley, who recommended that he should be sent to a hospital as soon as possible. Faced with the prospect of completing the rest of his voyage alone in an unreliable boat the owner, Mr Kevin Ross, decided to join the Yacht. Before he did so, the Yacht guided him by radar to a point about ½ mile offshore where he anchored the motor cruiser and retrieved what he could, prior to being collected by one of the Yacht's boats. The next morning a helicopter of the Cairns State Emergency Service flew out to *Britannia* to transfer Mr Zimmer to hospital. The transfer was completed in trying conditions with 15 to 20 knots blowing across the deck at the time. When the Yacht reached Cairns that evening it was the first chance many of the Yacht's company had had to go ashore since they left the UK and it was their only chance to have a rest ahead of the forthcoming period of Royal duty.

Despite the disruption caused to the Yacht's programme by her diversion to Aden, she was just one day late when she arrived in Auckland on 23 February. Normally, such a delay would have been totally unacceptable. However, The Queen was very understanding because she fully appreciated that the Yachtsmen needed a short break, after a long yet eventful outward voyage, before undertaking a hectic period of Royal duty. When The Queen and Prince Philip embarked later that afternoon they were accompanied by a very familiar face who was returning to the Yacht for the first time in his new role as the Master of the Household. Describing his new role Rear Admiral Sir Paul Greening said:

'Although it was wonderful to be back in the Yacht, it was very different not least because I was no longer in naval uniform and lived in the opposite end of the Yacht. As the Master of the Household I ran the domestic aspects of the Royal organisation. I was responsible for the entertaining and anything that could be classed as housekeeping. I did that in Buckingham Palace, Holyrood House, Windsor Castle and the Royal Apartments in the Yacht. As far as the Yacht was concerned I looked after the allocation of cabins and the staff were brought on board from the Palace. The major events in the Yacht were much smaller than those organised in Buckingham Palace. For example, in Buckingham Palace there might be a reception for 500 people whereas in the Yacht we couldn't host more than 200 people. Obviously, there was a limited amount of space in the Yacht so there was always a certain amount of scene shifting particularly for commercial occasions. The Yachtsmen enthusiastically got involved in this process volunteering for furniture moving or washing up, etc.'

The Tour of New Zealand also presented The Queen's new Assistant Private Secretary, later Sir Kenneth Scott KCVO CMG, with his first opportunity to experience life on board the Yacht, as he explains:

'In the Palace I saw The Queen every morning for about half an hour to discuss the business and that was about it for the day. On board *Britannia* I was almost made to feel part of the family which was wonderful. During these trips I would be in direct personal contact with the embarked members of the Royal Family for each meal which did of course mean that I got to know them very well. It took a little bit of getting used to but it was great fun.'

In New Zealand, the Yacht supported the Royal couple's visit to Auckland and Lyttelton, before they flew onto to Canberra on 2 March to begin their Australian Tour. The Yacht sailed half an hour after they disembarked, and arrived in Melbourne on 6 March, when The Queen and Prince Philip rejoined at 2200. Half an hour later the Yacht made a floodlit departure to begin the overnight voyage to Western Port where, in the afternoon, The Queen and Prince Philip were taken ashore in the Barge despite the wind blowing a steady 40 knots. Once ashore the Royal couple were driven to HMAS *Cerberus*, where The Queen presented a new Queen's Colour to mark the 75th Anniversary of the foundation of the Royal Australian Navy (RAN). Interestingly, Prince Philip was wearing the uniform of a RAN Admiral of the Fleet. On completion of the garden party the Royal couple returned to the Yacht, which weighed anchor for Adelaide. While on passage the Royal party got up early on the morning of 9 March to observe Halley's comet at 0600, which unfortunately was not at its most impressive because it was only visible between patch-

A helicopter of the Cairns State Emergency Service hovers over the Yacht's forecastle ready to winch up Mr Zimmer for the flight to the hospital in Cairns.

(© British Crown Copyright / MOD)

es of cloud. At lunchtime *Britannia* arrived off Glenelg where the first settlers in South Australia landed. Sadly, the weather wasn't as kind as it had been to the original settlers and the conditions were extremely marginal to land the Royal couple in the Barge. However, The Queen did not want to disappoint the local people so she insisted that an attempt should be made. Despite the very best efforts of The Queen's Coxswain it was decided to abandon the attempt and return to the Yacht. Once the Barge had been recovered *Britannia* steamed rapidly round to the passenger terminal in Adelaide so that The Queen and Prince Philip could continue with their programme as planned.[10]

The morning of 10 March should have been a day of rest for the Royal party but, in view of the problems in reaching Glenelg on the previous day, the Royal couple landed to carry out the engagements that they would have

The Adelaide Sea Day was the first trade event to be held on board the Yacht in a Commonwealth country. To reflect this fact the traditional demonstration was performed by the Australian frigate HMAS Darwin.

(© British Crown Copyright / MOD)

undertaken the day before. Two days later the Yacht hosted the first Sea Day to be held in a Commonwealth country. The event was sponsored by British Invisibles and was held while The Queen and Prince Philip were undertaking further engagements ashore. The principle difference, between this event and those held elsewhere, was that the demonstration was performed by a ship from the RAN rather than the RN. This reflected the normal policy for tours in Commonwealth countries, when the Royal Escort was provided by the host nation rather than the RN. As Admiral Garnier explains, the Sea Day had some very useful effects:

'I was talking to Ken Williams, the President of the Australian CBI, about the value of the Sea Day. He told me that as far as he was concerned it had been a wonderful catalyst because it had made him address the issue of invisible trade. He explained that he had undertaken a considerable amount of research, which was now available for other companies in Australia. Without the Sea Day he wouldn't have otherwise addressed the issue.'

The Royal couple concluded their Tour on 13 March by hosting a lunch on board for the Governor General of Australia, HE the Rt Hon. Sir Ninian Stephen, and the Australian Prime Minister, Bob Hawke. In the afternoon The Queen and Prince Philip disembarked to fly home.[11]

Four days later *Britannia* began her long voyage home, via Fremantle, Port Hedland, Singapore, and Djibouti. As a result of the US bombing of Libya on the night of 14 April, the Yacht's level of security was significantly raised as she anchored in Port Suez four days later. Because the US F111 bombers were launched from USAF bases in the UK there were fears that either the Libyans, or terrorists, might try to launch an attack against *Britannia* while she was in Egyptian waters or the Mediterranean. Once the Yacht entered the Mediterranean on 19 April, she immediately headed north towards Crete under the protection of RAF Phantoms which maintained a combat air patrol until *Britannia* reached the NATO fuelling jetty at Souda Bay, Crete. From Crete to Sicily, the frigate HMS *Aurora* took over escort duties as the Yacht headed east at 20 knots. Further protection was provided over the horizon by the US Navy's carrier USS *America* and her battle-group. USS *America* sent aircraft to check the Yacht's position visually every two hours. Finally, from Sicily through to the Straits of Gibraltar, the destroyer HMS *Southampton* and the frigate HMS *Brazen* provided the final escort. Having reached the Atlantic, *Britannia* headed north again on her own, to reach Portsmouth on 29 April. By then the engineers had calculated that, in the period since she left Portsmouth on 31 December 1985, the propellers had each turned 29 million revolutions, while the engines had burned 7000 cubic meters of diesel and produced 8400 tons of water![12] Just over a week after

Britannia's voyage home through the Mediterranean came shortly after the US bombing of Libya. Because the American bombers took off from bases in the UK there was a fear that Britannia might provide an attractive target for a revenge attack either by the Libyans or terrorist groups. To counter this threat the Yacht was provided with increased protection during her passage through the Mediterranean including air cover provided by this RAF Phantom.

(© British Crown Copyright / MOD)

Britannia's return, she entered dry dock for maintenance and repainting work, ahead of another hectic round of engagements planned for the second half of the year. While the Yacht was in dry dock, it was announced on 10 June in the *London Gazette* that Lieutenant Easson had been awarded The Queen's Commendation for bravery in recognition of his hazardous work as the Beach Master during the Aden crisis.[13]

On 19 July the Yacht left Portsmouth for the Azores to undertake her fourth (and what would be her final) honeymoon cruise. The security of the honeymoon destination for Prince Andrew and Sarah Ferguson had been well preserved until a few days before when the news was leaked from Portugal.[14] Despite the leak, many of the press refused to believe where the Yacht was heading. The Yacht arrived off the Azores on 23 July. Back in the UK, it was the wedding day of Prince Andrew and Sarah Ferguson. Before the ceremony The Queen announced that she would create Prince Andrew The Duke of York, thus granting him the title once held by her father until he became King George VI. After the wedding ceremony, and subsequent reception held at Buckingham Palace, the Royal couple flew out to join the Yacht, which was lying

Britannia managed to dodge the press throughout The Duke and Duchess of York's honeymoon. The one exception was when the Yacht entered Ponta Delgada for Their Royal Highnesses to thank the authorities and local people for preserving their privacy. As Britannia approached the port this microlight carrying a cameraman made a number of low passes.

(© British Crown Copyright / MOD)

at anchor in Victoria Bay, Terceira Island. To mark the embarkation of The Duke and Duchess of York, The Queen had instructed the Yachtsmen to man ship for their arrival. As they boarded the Yacht they were met by FORY and a small party from the Band who played 'Congratulations' and 'The Grand Old Duke of York'. Within two hours the Yacht had weighed anchor to begin the cruise around the Azores.[15] Describing what it meant to him to be able to have his honeymoon on board the Yacht The Duke of York said, 'the privilege of having her for our honeymoon was wonderful. After all the organisation of the things that we had had to do to be able to have those four or five days of complete peace and quiet was fantastic.'

The programme during the cruise resembled a typical Western Isles Cruise, with FORY going aft each evening to discuss the next day's destination with the Royal couple. While Their Royal Highnesses were ashore, many of the Yachtsmen took the opportunity to pursue some fishing as the PMO, later Surgeon Captain Tim Douglas-Riley RN remembered:

'One day while many of us were fishing from the fore-castle one of the Yachtsmen came up to me and said, "I've got a bit of trouble with the wife, Sir."
   "Oh yes?"
   "I've seemed to upset her."
   "Oh dear, how have you done that?"
   "Well I think it's that letter I wrote."
   "What was in the letter you wrote?"
   "I told her it's the best honeymoon I have ever been on!"'

The decision to hold the honeymoon cruise in the waters around the Azores worked well because there were only a few flights into the islands, which were often overbooked. The Portuguese authorities were particularly helpful in stopping the media from getting on these flights, so the press didn't catch up with the Yacht until she arrived off Ponta Delgada. As the Yacht approached Ponta Delgada on 28 July, she received a taste of what might have happened, when a cameraman in a microlight made a number of very low passes over *Britannia*. As the Yacht entered the harbour, about 50 members of the press were waiting to catch their first glimpse of the Royal couple, who appeared on the Verandah Deck for a photo call. The visit to Ponta Delgada was made at the request of Their Royal Highnesses who wanted to personally thank the authorities and local people for all that they had done to preserve their privacy during the honeymoon.[16] That night *Britannia* sailed from Ponta Delgada for the voyage back to the UK for Prince Philip to attend Cowes Week.

The Yacht's arrival in the Solent on 2 August attracted considerable media interest as the honeymoon couple were still on board. The weather dictated a change of plan so, instead of anchoring off Cowes, the Yacht continued up into Portsmouth Harbour where she secured to No. 3 Buoy to disembark The Duke and Duchess of York and embark the Royal party for Cowes Week.[17] The following morning the Yacht sailed back across the Solent to Cowes Roads, where she remained until 6 August when she sailed to Southampton. There she embarked the Royal Family for the Western Isles Cruise and headed back into the Solent that night. In view of the deteriorating weather, FORY decided to spend the night anchored off Lymington. While at anchor a red distress flare was spotted in the early hours of the morning. The flare had been fired by the yacht *Suva* which had suffered an engine failure. The starboard jolly boat was lowered to provide assistance if required and was subsequently relieved by the Yarmouth lifeboat.[18] Later in the morning, *Britannia* weighed anchor to begin the voyage north towards her birth place of Clydebank, where she arrived on 9 August.

An hour after the Yacht's arrival in Clydebank, The Queen went ashore to name the oil rig Mr Mac that had been built for Transworld in the former John Brown & Co shipyard. By 1986 the Yard was owned by the French company UiE Shipbuilding Ltd. Despite the title, the yard no longer built ships on the site, instead concentrating on the construction of modules for oil rigs, as well as some complete oil rigs. After further engagements in the area, The Queen returned to the Yacht in the afternoon prior to her departure for Mingary Bay and Her Majesty's visit to the Ardnamurchan lighthouse on 11 August. The lighthouse is situated on the westernmost part of the Scottish mainland and provided the Royal party with good exercise as they climbed the 152 steps to reach the top of the lighthouse. Although there had been unfounded speculation in the press that Her Majesty had suffered a heart flutter earlier in the year she completed the climb without any difficulty thus squashing any such suggestions. On her way back to the Yacht, Her Majesty paid a short call on the Northern Lighthouse Board Vessel *Pharos* to complete her formal engagements. In the after-

noon *Britannia* weighed anchor for the private part of the Western Isles Cruise.[19] Describing why the regular cruise among the Western Isles was so important to The Queen, The Duke of York said:

'The Yacht was a place of sanctuary for The Queen – more so than any of us. She got a week or 10 days of sanctuary from anything that was going on. That little bit of tranquillity made up for all the other things that she has to do and not having that week of sanctuary must be a terrible loss for The Queen. It was a chance for her to have her family around her in her environment.'

As usual the Western Isles Cruise culminated with a visit to the Castle of Mey for the Royal Family to visit The Queen Mother on 15 August. Soon after their arrival, the PMO was summoned to examine The Queen Mother, who appeared to have a fish bone stuck in her throat, so she was evacuated by helicopter to the hospital in Aberdeen. The next morning the Yacht berthed in Aberdeen for the Royal Family to disembark and travel to Balmoral for the summer break. Before she left, Her Majesty undertook a tour of the harbour and visited the port control. *Britannia* returned to Portsmouth on 18 August for the Yacht's company to prepare for the historic State Visit to China by The Queen and Prince Philip.[20]

Britannia began that historic voyage on 1 September, stopping on the way at Gibraltar to take on more fuel, before sailing through the Suez Canal on 12 September. During her passage through the Red Sea, *Britannia* had

The Queen and Prince Philip share a joke with the Coxswain, Warrant Offtcer Ellis Norrell, during the Western Isles Cruise.

(© British Crown Copyright / MOD)

THE ROYAL YACHT BRITANNIA

The Coxswain presents a birthday cake to Princess Anne on behalf of the Yachtsmen watched by Her Royal Highness's daughter Zara Phillips during the Western Isles Cruise.

(© British Crown Copyright / MOD)

been due to take on fuel from RFA *Brambleleaf*, but she developed a fault so the Yacht made her first visit to Aden since the crisis at the beginning of the year,[21] as Admiral Garnier recalled:

'I went ashore to see the British Ambassador Arthur Marshall and have a look round some of the more battered parts of Aden much of which had been patched up. There was an air of normality with only a few military personnel in evidence. I came back on board at 1100 with the Marshalls who went straight down to the Warrant Officers and Chief Petty Officers mess for coffee. They had a lot of friends on board especially as he took so much trouble to telephone so many relatives when he returned to the UK following the evacuation. Typical of his kindness too he brought 300 postcards on board so that anyone could send one home if they wished. We then had a reception on the Verandah Deck about noon and there was a good turn out from the local diplomatic corps including the Soviet and Chinese Ambassadors and the Port Captain, Captain Saeed Yafai.'

Although the circumstances and background relating to this specific reception were unusual, the Yacht normally held a reception for local people whenever she visited a foreign port for more than a day when she wasn't on Royal duty. These events provided a good opportunity for people to see the Yacht for themselves, as the Engineering Officer at the time, later Captain C Page RN, explains:

'These receptions were hosted on board by FORY and the Wardroom and would include a tour of *Britannia*. People were always staggered by the cleanliness of the Yacht and the general friendliness as well as the high calibre of people who served on board. They were also amazed by the open way in which they talked to guests. Obviously, those who served in the Yacht were used to talking to members of the Royal Family and as a result they had developed a very easy way of talking to people in the very highest echelons of the world's establishments from presidents downwards. When people were shown the outside of the Royal Apartments the usual reaction was one of surprise at their modesty. Usually people expected to see a "wedding cake" and yet they found a relatively comfortable and simple place where the Royal Family felt at home and could live.'

After further refuelling stops at Colombo, Singapore and Hong Kong, *Britannia* berthed in Shanghai on 11 October. Three days later 36 British businessmen embarked immediately after colours for the Sea Day sponsored by the British Overseas Trade Board. The event was attended by 65 Chinese guests including Government Ministers and Industrial leaders as well as members of the Chinese media.[22] The Yacht spent the day cruising the waters of the Yangtze River which provided an excellent opportunity for the British businessmen to discuss their projects with the Chinese guests, as Admiral Garnier observed:

'At lunch I was sitting next to a businessman who was trying to get a slice of a £4 billion contract for a new steel mill not far from Shanghai. He told me that he had been in China for six months and all the people he wanted to see were on this table, including the Minister, the Mayor and the Project Manager. He went on to say it would have taken him another six months to a year to have done that without the Sea Day!'

On 15 October The Queen and Prince Philip arrived in Shanghai to embark in the Yacht ahead of that night's return State Banquet. The State Visit was an important milestone in the improving relationship between the two nations, following the signing of the Hong Kong agreement in December 1984. The visit was given an added historical significance because it was the first time that a reigning British Monarch had travelled to China. The Foreign Secretary, later The Rt Hon. the Lord Howe of Aberavon CH QC, accompanied The Queen throughout the State Visit as a member of the Royal party. His arrival in Shanghai in The Queen's motorcade provided quite a contrast to his first visit to Shanghai, as he explains:

'I first visited Shanghai as a guest of the Chinese Government in 1978, together with my wife and Sir Leon Brittan. The Cultural Revolution had taken place the year before and we were escorted by Roger Garside from the Foreign Office. We wanted to walk around the city ourselves without our Chinese escort, so we eventually broke ranks and told the driver, who had taken us, that we were going to walk back to our hotel through the old city and that they would find us when they got back there. It was still a very beleaguered, imprisoned country, or so it seemed. To then be back there eight years later, being driven as part of The Queen's cavalcade to the Royal Yacht, was quite extraordinary. As we approached the Shanghai waterfront, there were thousands of Chinese people holding torches and peering in at the extraordinary spectacle of The Queen in her car. The Chinese leaders were inclined to use cars with darkened windows, which were diven at high speed. Therefore, the sight of The Queen being driven slowly in a car with clear windows was a new experience for the Chinese people. When we arrived at the harbour, it was a very special moment to see Britannia in that setting, where she

When Britannia returned to Aden the Yachtsmen were greeted by visible reminders of the fighting earlier in the year.

(© British Crown Copyright / MOD)

looked absolutely perfect for the occasion. As soon as I got on board the Yacht I went down to my cabin and sent a postcard to Roger Garside saying, "When we were here eight years ago, you would never have imagined that I would be sitting here, writing a postcard from this ship in this place at this time, with HM The Queen." It represented a truly historic moment and the use of *Britannia* for this type of occasion helped Britain to "punch above her weight" on the international stage.'

The principal guest at that night's State Banquet was President Li. It was reported that it was the first time the President had been outside Peking for many years. Thus it was a mark of the importance that the Chinese Government attached to The Queen's visit that he made the journey to Shanghai to dine on board the Yacht. Once the final guests had landed, The Queen and Prince Philip disembarked to spend the night at the Xi Jiao Guest House. At midnight *Britannia* slipped and began the passage back down the Yangtze River to head out to sea for Canton where, after passing just 80 miles from the centre of a tropical storm, she arrived on 18 October. The Queen and Prince Philip embarked in the afternoon, ahead of that night's reception. As the Yacht prepared to sail, a display of traditional Chinese dancing and singing was staged on the quayside. As the display reached its climax the Yacht made a floodlit departure to round off another successful State Visit.[23]

The Yacht reached Hong Kong late on 19 October and remained underway overnight, before anchoring the next day for the Royal party's day of rest. The Queen's short visit to the colony began on 21 October with the ceremonial entry, and concluded two days later when she flew back to the UK. Prince Philip remained on board for an additional day of engagements before flying back to China for a further visit in support of the WWF. Within an hour of His Royal Highness's departure, the Yacht sailed for the Persian Gulf to be used in support of The Prince and Princess of Wales's visit to Oman and Saudi Arabia between 10 and 19 November. At the end of their two visits, the Royal couple remained on board for the initial stages of the voyage home, with the Princess leaving at Hurghada on 21 November, and The Prince of Wales departing when *Britannia* reached Cyprus on 24 November. As soon as His Royal Highness disembarked, the Yacht's company began preparing the Yacht for the long refit ahead. By the time *Britannia* berthed in Gibraltar on 28 November the Royal Apartments resembled a warehouse, with all of the loose items already packed into boxes for storage. When the Yacht reached

Portsmouth on 4 December, she was taken straight to No. 3 Basin to continue with the de-storing operation. The requirement to remove as much as possible from the Yacht led to some interesting discoveries, such as a quantity of plates from previous Royal Yachts which had remained undisturbed since they were transferred from V&A in 1953. Many of the historic artefacts were transferred to Windsor Castle for storage, and the whole operation was completed by 19 December.

The year 1987 began with the short passage from Portsmouth to Devonport, where she arrived on 7 January. By then the Yacht had been in service for 33 years and was in need of a major refit to extend her service into the 1990s. It was assumed she would receive a further modernisation at that stage to enable her to serve into the twenty-first century, when she would be replaced by a new Royal Yacht. Explaining the decision to refit *Britannia* rather than replace her the Defence Secretary, at the time Viscount Younger, said:

'We looked at how long *Britannia* could remain in service if we refitted her and the effect of doing so. The conclusion was that it was worth giving her another refit not least because there was no consensus on what would replace her. It was felt that a decision to replace *Britannia* would be highly controversial and that if a further refit was a cost-effective option it should be taken. I wish now with the benefit of hindsight that I had been firmer and said let us build a new Royal Yacht.'

While the actual decision to refit *Britannia* was welcomed by the Yacht's company, the location where the work was carried out was not. When the long refit was first being planned it was clear that neither Portsmouth or Devonport in Plymouth would have the capacity to refit the Yacht. Therefore, it was expected that the work would be carried out as a commercial contract, with the most likely candidate being Vosper Thornycroft at their Southampton yard. This choice would have minimised the travelling for the Yachtsmen. Unlike their counterparts in the general service the members of the Royal Yacht Service served continuously at sea and thus did not enjoy the benefits of a shore job between seagoing appointments. To balance this fact it had been understood that the Yacht would always be refitted by Portsmouth Dockyard thus enabling the Yachtsmen to spend as much time as possible with their families between periods of Royal duty. However, a reduction in the number of ships in the RN in mid 1986 led to the sudden availability of capacity within Devonport Dockyard. Fearing that a fall in the dockyard's workload might lead to redundancies the Unions brought pressure to bear on the Government to award the contract for *Britannia*'s refit to Devonport. They argued the move would safeguard jobs and act as a clear sign of the Government's confidence in Devonport Management Ltd (DML) when they took over responsibility for the Dockyard in April 1987. Faced with this change in circumstances it would have been very difficult politically for the Government to award the contract to Vosper Thornycroft. To try and counter the disappointment of this decision Admiral Garnier worked hard to ensure that the Yachtsmen received some recompensed losing some of their at home time. He arranged for the Yachtsmen to receive free accommodation and food, and assistance with travel expenses between Portsmouth and Devonport, which are some 170 miles apart.

Once the Yacht entered dry dock on 13 January the remaining removal work began in earnest, as many parts of the Yacht were completely stripped to enable the replacement of approximately 20 miles of old wiring. Elsewhere within *Britannia*, about 7000 square yards of asbestos was removed, while 145 tonnes of additional ballast were fitted to meet the latest stability requirements. Externally, the teak decks were removed because, after 33 years of scrubbing and polishing, their thickness had been reduced from 2 inches to just 1 inch in many places. In recent years water had seeped down on to the steel deck below the teak through the wooden dowels that covered the steel securing studs. This had led to severe corrosion which needed to be repaired prior to the fitting of 14 miles of new teak planks. Due to the constant painting

between periods of Royal duty, the paint on the superstructure had built up to a considerable thickness in places. As a result about 25 tonnes of paint had to be removed, when both the hull and superstructure were blasted back to bare metal and repainted. Like other ships in the RN, while she was being built the Yacht had received various items of equipment that had been used in previous warships. Not surprisingly, some of these items, as well as more modern equipment, were becoming worn out. For example, the water distillers had been present during the Dardenelles Campaign in 1915 on board the battleship HMS *Queen Elizabeth*, which was subsequently sold for scrap in 1948, having served throughout the Second World War.[24]

Despite *Britannia*'s period of enforced inactivity while she was in dockyard hands, the planning of her future programme was already underway. A decision about whether to use the Yacht to support a State Visit would be made in principle about a year in advance of it taking place, as Lord Fellowes explains:

'By then we would have already heard from the Foreign Office about what they would like The Queen to do over the ensuing 12 to 18 months. I would then approach FORY to discuss possible dates and how it related to his other commitments. The Queen and Prince Philip would then finally decide whether or not to take the Yacht. To make this decision, they would look at the political implications, and the sort of pro-

As part of the 1987 refit, the Royal Apartments were completely stripped as this view of the staircase to the Verandah Deck clearly shows.

gramme that had been suggested for them. Being a sailor, Prince Philip would be far more adept at working out the sailing times than anyone else would be. Once they had made the decision, there was a process of firming up the plans with the host country, not least how best to use the Yacht.'

As the work continued on board the Yacht, the Royal Family were keen to see the progress of the refit, so a number of visits by members of the Royal Family were organised, beginning with Prince Philip's visit on 13 March.[25] Further visits were made by The Prince of Wales,

Externally all of the teak decks were removed and subsequently replaced. Here the fore deck has been stripped back to the metal structure.

(© British Crown Copyright / MOD)

The Duke and Duchess of York, and The Princess Royal with Peter and Zara Phillips. As Admiral Garnier explains, these visits provided a great boost to the morale of the Yachtsmen: 'we were very honoured to have so many visits and most grateful that they should take such an active interest. It was indicative though of how precious the Yacht was to all members of the Royal Family.'

After 10 months in dock, *Britannia* finally began the first of her post-refit sea trials on 12 October. These trials were concluded a few hours early on 15 October to ensure that *Britannia* was securely alongside in Devonport when the infamous hurricane swept across southern England during the early hours of 16 October 1987. Having survived the hurricane unscathed, the work to return the Yacht to service continued with a visit by Sir Hugh Casson on 17 October to inspect the refurbished Royal Apartments.[26] His confirmation that the colour scheme

matched his original specification provided a useful boost to confidence ahead of the contract acceptance date for the refit on 3 November. Before signing the appropriate paperwork to accept the Yacht back into service, FORY, accompanied by Director General Ship Refitting, Rear Admiral David Sherval, and the Managing Director of DML, Mike Leece, carried out a formal inspection of the Yacht. At midday they hosted a press conference to deal with the intense media interest surrounding the scope of the refit and its cost. Clearly the cost of such a major refit was bound to attract criticism from certain quarters so it was important for the facts to be presented to the press as early as possible. This plan worked and the subsequent media coverage was very positive, just as it had been when she emerged from her modernisation in 1973.[27]

Ten days later *Britannia* returned to Portsmouth, where the furniture and paintings were replaced in the Royal Apartments to complete the refit work. The year 1988 heralded a return to Royal duty, as *Britannia* sailed from Portsmouth on 6 January to begin another major global deployment. The crossing of the Atlantic was dominated by bad weather, especially as the Yacht headed towards Bermuda when she was hit by a violent swell from the north east, accompanied by rapidly increasing winds. These conditions struck *Britannia* in the early of hours of the morning on 17 January and within half an hour the Yacht experienced a number of severe rolls of over 30 degrees. By 0600 it was decided to heave to and wait for

the weather conditions to ease as the winds had reached hurricane conditions and were regularly gusting over 60 knots. After lunch the weather appeared to be moderating so FORY decided to run down the sea during the remaining hours of daylight to make progress towards Bermuda. As darkness fell the Yacht hove to again for the night, before repeating the procedure the following morning.[28] Thus the sight of Bermuda appearing over the horizon on 19 January was welcomed by all on board. After *Britannia* berthed in Bermuda the first signs of corrosion were discovered around the scuttles. During the major refit all of the scuttles were removed for the first time as the hull was stripped back to bare metal. Unfortunately, when they were put back into position something had gone wrong with the re-sealing process and they proved to be a cause for concern throughout this deployment.[29]

From Bermuda the Yacht sailed to Barbados, where Princess Margaret came on board for dinner with FORY and the officers in the Wardroom on 29 January. The following day Prince Philip arrived for the night before disembarking to Costa Rica, where he was to visit conservation projects before re-embarking in the Yacht on 10 February in Costa Rica, by which time the Yacht had steamed through the Panama Canal and berthed in Puerto Caldera. Prince Philip hosted a dinner for the President of Costa Rica, President Arias, before the Yacht sailed for the five-day visit to the Galapagos Islands. During the course of the visit all of the Yachtsmen were

The morale of the Yacht's company was boosted by the various visits made to Britannia *by members of the Royal Family during the course of the refit. FORY escorts The Duke and Duchess of York as they look round the Yacht to view the progress of the refit.*

given the chance for at least one visit ashore and those who took up the opportunity were absolutely enthralled by the unique wildlife and scenery of the islands. When the Royal party disembarked on 18 February to fly back to London they took the Lord High Admiral's verge with them, which was being lent to BRNC for Lord High Admiral's divisions.[30] Half an hour later *Britannia* weighed anchor for Los Angeles, where she arrived on morning of 26 February ahead of that afternoon's embarkation of The Duke and Duchess of York who had flown direct from the UK. Explaining why *Britannia* made a real difference to their visit The Duke of York said:

'The Yacht made a complete difference to what was a major visit to America. It meant that we didn't have to use hotels and deal with staff we didn't know. It gave us

At last Britannia *begins to resemble her old self as she is eased out of a massive, covered dry dock in Devonport Dockyard.*   (© Devonport Management Ltd)

the ability to entertain people in circumstances and conditions that were unique. We were moored across from the American battleship USS *Missouri*. We held an evening reception which included the normal ceremony of Beat Retreat performed by the RM Band. *Missouri*'s Ship's company had built a stand on board in order for their guests to watch the Beat Retreat which was extraordinary.'

In addition to their programme of engagements associated with the UK/LA '88 Festival, The Duke of York officially welcomed all of the guests for the Sea Days held on board on 29 February and 2 March before disembarking to continue his programmes ashore. This marked a significant development in *Britannia*'s commercial role, which was becoming firmly established as her true secondary role. It was the first time that a member of the Royal Family had been directly involved in a Sea Day because, previously, they were all held while the embarked member of the Royal Family was undertaking engagements ashore.[31]

The Duke and Duchess's visit culminated with a flight out to the US aircraft carrier, USS *Nimitz* on 3 March. During their day on board one of the world's biggest warships, they had the chance to observe the exciting if dramatic environment of an aircraft carrier's flight deck while aircraft were being launched and recovered. The following morning, the Royal couple went for a walk round the Yacht's mess decks before disembarking to fly home. After lunch *Britannia* sailed for the next stage of her deployment, with stops at Pearl Harbor and Pago Pago, before reaching Nuku 'alofa in Tonga on 25 March. During the visit FORY hosted a reception, which was due to be rounded off as usual by the ceremony of Beat Retreat performed by the RM Band. During the week before the reception, the local media had built up a sense of anticipation among the local people. Sadly, the weather intervened at the last moment, as the Director of Music at the time, later Captain E P Whealing MVO RM, explains:

'On the night it was pouring with heavy rain. I spoke to the Admiral and said, "There is no way that the Band can perform Beat Retreat." We went out on to the waist and watched the rain absolutely pouring down. The Admiral turned to me and said, "The decision is yours." I explained that if we went ahead the instruments would be completely saturated and ruined. As our next performance was due to be in front of The Queen in Sydney this would be disastrous as there was nothing that could be done beforehand. Thus because we as a band were always aiming for our next Royal performance I was unable to take any other decision in the circumstances.'

Britannia sailed from Tonga on 28 March and headed south to Sydney where she arrived on 2 April to undertake a self-maintenance period. During this visit FORY hosted a dinner attended by former FORYs, Rear Admiral Sir Joseph Henley and Rear Admiral Sir Paul Greening. From Sydney the Yacht headed round to Brisbane to await the embarkation of The Queen and Prince Philip for their Tour to mark the 200th Anniversary of the arrival of the first settlers in Australia. However, the day before they were due to arrive, protesters supporting an Aboriginal group paddled underneath the jetty to slip past the police security and spray 'End The Killing Times' in red paint on the port bow. Once clear of the Yacht the protesters telephoned the press and soon the story became headline news around the world. Despite this interest the Yachtsmen managed to thwart the attempts of photographers trying to get their photograph by painting out the graffiti before sunrise so the story quickly died. Although

no lasting physical damage had been done to the Yacht it did represent a significant breach of security.[32]

On 29 April Prince Edward embarked in the morning and, as he stepped aboard, his Standard was broken in the Yacht for the first time. Later in the morning he left to attend The Duke of Edinburgh International Award Scheme Forum at the Parliamentary Annex. The Queen and Prince Philip joined the Yacht in the afternoon, ahead of that evening's dinner and reception. The following morning they were taken in the Barge to the River Strape and the site of World Expo 88. When The Queen opened the exhibition she caught the mood of local people with her opening speech when she said, 'though this is

The actress Joan Collins is greeted by the Commander as she embarks for a reception hosted by The Duke and Duchess of York during the Yacht's visit to Los Angeles.

often called the sunshine state I prefer it by its original name Queensland.' World Expo 88's first day proved a success, with over 100,000 people visiting the exhibition.[33] Having attended a further meeting of The Duke of Edinburgh Award Scheme Forum with his father, Prince Edward flew back to the UK on 1 May. In the afternoon *Britannia* sailed to take The Queen and Prince Philip to Sydney for their two-day visit, which included The Queen's opening of Darling Harbour's inner harbour, and the New South Wales Library, as well as visiting the First State 88 Exhibition. On 5 May *Britannia* made a floodlit departure from Sydney at 2345 with the RM Band playing on deck, before heading north to Newcastle where she arrived on the morning of 7 May. As she steamed up the river into Newcastle, The Queen and Prince Philip were given a rousing welcome by the crews on board the ships of the first fleet re-enactment which were berthed alongside. The Queen and Prince Philip landed to perform engagements in the area, before flying on to to Canberra.[34] *Britannia*'s role within the Tour had come to a close, and three days later, she began the voyage towards the Mediterranean, where she would support The Queen Mother's visit to southern Italy.

Britannia reached the Sicilian port of Catania on 19 June where The Queen Mother joined the next day. Interestingly, Her Majesty had invited the designer of the Royal Apartments, Sir Hugh Casson, and his wife to join her for the duration of the Tour. After the visits to Catania and Syracuse, *Britannia* reached Palermo on 22 June, where she was joined by the Type 42 destroyer HMS *Edinburgh* in which The Duke of York was serving as a watch keeping officer. An hour and a half later both ships sailed for Salerno where they anchored the next morning. Her Majesty went ashore in the Barge to visit the British military cemetery, as well as visiting the temples and museum at Paestum, before returning to *Britannia* for lunch.[35] As the time approached to begin the passage to Naples there were a few tense moments on board HMS *Edinburgh*, as His Royal Highness recalled:

'We wrapped a piece of rope around the port shaft which stopped us from going anywhere. The Yacht gave us 20 minutes while they were getting their anchor up to sort ourselves out. A diver was quickly sent over the side and he managed to get the rope off the shaft so we were able to sail on time. Thus Queen Elizabeth would never have known that we were disabled for some time. I was then the Officer Of The Watch when we followed the Yacht. She was very difficult to follow because her speed and ours wouldn't match and there was a constant battle to keep on station. The Yacht's acceleration was very dif-

ferent to ours and it seemed like an eternity for her to get up to speed. After lunch we performed the customary steam past the Yacht always carried out by the escorting warship. I had of course seen many steam pasts from on board the Yacht and the really impressive ones were when the escort has got her engines opened up and then performs a tight turn back on to station at speed. I discussed this with Captain Ross and I advised him that he needed to create white water and plenty of noise.'

The Captain heeded the advice and performed an impressive steam past before the Royal Squadron reached Naples in the afternoon. In the evening The Duke of York embarked in the Yacht to join the reception and dinner, before returning to *Edinburgh*, which sailed at 2315 to rejoin the RN's Task Group 'Outback 88' which was headed by the aircraft carrier HMS *Ark Royal*. The warships were on their way to Australia for the Bicentennial Naval Salute to be held in Sydney as part of the year-long celebrations to mark the 200th Anniversary of the settlement in Australia. At the end of Her Majesty's three-day visit to Naples she flew back to the UK. Forty minutes after Her Majesty departed the Yacht sailed for Portsmouth, arriving there on 1 July to conclude a very successful deployment which had lasted nearly seven months.

Within three weeks the Yacht was off again, this time to participate in the celebrations to mark two very different events from British history. The first of these events celebrated the tercentenary of Prince William of Orange landing in Torbay to depose King James II. Prince William was married to James II's daughter and had been invited by seven politicians from both the Whig and Tory parties to assist with their efforts to remove her father from power. On 15 November 1688 Prince William landed in Torbay, leading his army, virtually unopposed, to London, and James II fled the country into exile. An extraordinary meeting of Parliament, known as the Convention Parliament, was called and declared the Throne vacant, offering it to Prince William and his wife Mary who were jointly crowned in 1689. Three hundred years on, the event was marked by two days of Anglo-Dutch celebrations on 20 and 21 July. The Queen and Prince Philip were joined by The Prince of Orange, heir to the Dutch Throne, who stayed on board the Yacht ahead of the re-enactment of Prince William's landing, held in Brixham on 21 July.

In the afternoon, the Yacht sailed to Plymouth for the celebrations to mark the 400th Anniversary of the defeat of the Spanish Armada, which included an Armada Night dinner for the Royal couple in the Wardroom of HMS *Drake*, and a visit to Devonport Naval Base the next morning. The Yacht returned to Portsmouth without The Queen and Prince Philip.[36] At the end of July the Yacht attended Cowes Week and then sailed north early in August for the Western Isles Cruise. When the Yacht arrived in Aberdeen on 15 August, The Queen and Prince Philip met a number of survivors from the recent Piper Alpha Oil Rig disaster before leaving for Balmoral. The voyage back to Portsmouth marked the retirement of the Coxswain, Warrant Officer Ellis Norrell MVO RVM, more widely known as Norrie to those who have served in the Yacht. He handed over the duties of Coxswain to Warrant Officer Tatlow on 17 August. By that stage he was the last man to have served in the Yacht since she was first commissioned and had become the longest serving Yachtsman in *Britannia*. To mark his long service he was entertained to drinks in the Wardroom, followed by lunch with FORY, before the Yacht's return to Portsmouth the next day.[37]

Britannia sailed from Portsmouth for the State Visit to Spain on 10 October. Five days later the Yacht berthed in Barcelona for the Sea Day on 16 October, which was sponsored by British Invisibles. The official side of the State Visit was rounded off by the return State Banquet held on board the Yacht on 21 October. That night *Britannia* sailed for Majorca to begin the private part of the visit, as Sir Kenneth Scott explains:

'The King of Spain managed to persuade The Queen to add a weekend visit to Majorca on to the end of the State Visit. I had carried out the recce for the State Visit and made all the arrangements for Madrid, Saville and Barcelona but I wasn't allowed to make any plans for the weekend. I was told The King would organise it all. When we arrived in Majorca we had no idea what was going to happen next. As soon as we had moored alongside and lowered the brow I went ashore to see the British Consul and The King's ADC who were standing on the jetty to ask them, "What happens next?" The ADC told me that as soon as the land telephone lines had been connected The King would ring The Queen and discuss the programme for the weekend. So I went back on board and told The Queen this.

Some of the Yacht's company take the opportunity to buy a few souvenirs from a local market during the visit to Cochin.

King Juan Carlos is taken for a thorough tour of the Yacht.

(© British Crown Copyright / MOD)

She said, "As soon as The King has phoned me I will tell you what we have arranged so that you can tell the people down below." So I went back down to the jetty to explain this to the British Consul and just as I finished there was some cheering at the end of the jetty and a small car appeared with The King at the wheel. Seeing this I rushed back on board to tell Her Majesty that The King was about to arrive and I reappeared back on deck together with the British Ambassador, Lord Nicholas Gordon-Lennox. The King got out of the car and looked up saying, "Nicky, I come on board now or I come back in half an hour?" So we invited him on board and the two Royal couples went off to discuss the arrangements. About quarter of an hour later the four of them appeared and got into The King's car and went off!'

At the end of the afternoon The Queen and Prince Philip returned to the Yacht for the night. The next morning Prince Philip landed to join the Spanish Royal Family on board their Royal Yacht *Fortuna* for the short passage to Illa de Cabrera. *Fortuna* was a very different vessel to *Britannia*. The 85-foot aluminium *Fortuna* is powered principally by a gas turbine engine to give her a top speed of 45 knots. She was designed by Don Shead, built by Palmer and Johnston of Wisconsin, USA in 1979 and commissioned the following year in Spain.

In the evening the Spanish Royal Family came across to *Britannia* for the evening, as Admiral Garnier recalled:

'The King and Queen, Princess Irene and The Duke and Duchess of Badajoz asked if they could have a thorough tour of the Yacht and meet some of the Yachtsmen. They also made unannounced visits to the Wardroom and CPOs mess. There was a barbecue for 10 on the Verandah Deck. The King, Duke and Duchess left for *Fortuna* at 2330 for the passage back to Palma, while Queen Sophia and Princess Irene stayed on board for the passage back.'

Britannia arrived back in Palma the next morning and, three hours later, King Juan Carlos and Queen Sophia arrived at the jetty to personally escort The Queen and Prince Philip to the airport for their flight home. Two days later *Britannia* sailed for Portsmouth where she berthed on 31 October.

1989's programme began with the Yacht's arrival in the Pool of London on 27 February. Two days later the Yacht received a call from members of the House of Lords and the House of Commons Defence Study group, as Admiral Garnier explains:

'Their visit was part of the group's defence work. It coincided with questions about the future of the Yacht and the possibility of its replacement. Despite visits like this it wasn't possible to get people to accept that the Yacht, through its Sea Days, was making a lot more money than her capital costs and running costs. Equally, they failed to appreciate that through the Sea Days the Yacht contributed to the costs of new hospitals and other important projects. If she was looked at from the overall UK perspective the contribution that was made by the Yacht vastly outweighed its running costs. However, in political terms she wasn't seen as desirable.'

In the evening The Queen hosted a reception for the winners of Her Majesty's Industry awards. On her final full day on the Thames the Yacht hosted a River Day on 9 March for important financiers and Ambassadors which was attended by The Duke of Kent. The following afternoon *Britannia* sailed for Portsmouth.[38]

On 22 May The Queen joined the Yacht in Portsmouth for her visit to the Channel Islands, having already visited the wreck of the *Mary Rose* and the preserved ironclad HMS *Warrior* on public display within the dockyard.[39] During The Queen's second day in the islands the Yacht met up with HMS *Edinburgh*, in which The Duke of York was serving as a Watch Keeper, as The Duke of York remembers:

'The previous Wednesday I had been sent for by the out-going First Sea Lord, Admiral Sir William Staveley, to see him to say farewell. We were operating off Portland at the time and I was transferred to HMS *Cornwall*, which was about to enter the harbour. As we entered Portland I saw a Type 21 frigate doing some saluting drills. I asked what was going on and I was told that she was practising for Royal Escort duties. It didn't mean anything at the time so I went ashore and drove to London. I saw The Queen that evening and while we were chatting she said that she was going to the Channel Islands the following week in the Yacht. "Oh really, that's interesting because we're going down to the Channel Islands next week in HMS *Edinburgh*."

"What are you doing down there?" The Queen asked.

"We are doing fleet navigating training."

"Oh, we must meet up."

"Yes, what a good idea. I am sure there is a possibility of meeting up somewhere." Although I was wondering how. I rejoined my ship in Portsmouth on the Monday morning. I went to see the Captain and asked him if he was aware that the Yacht was going to be in the Channel Islands this week.

"No," he said.

"Well I spoke to The Queen on Thursday evening and she said we must meet up." The Captain said all right and I left it for the day. When The Queen joined the Yacht in Portsmouth she said to Admiral Garnier, "I understand HMS *Edinburgh* is going to be in the Channel Islands this week. We must meet up."

The Admiral said, "I am sure this can be arranged," at which point a flash signal was sent to *Edinburgh* inquiring what we were doing in the Channel Islands and requested our nav track. The operational orders for the fleet training week and for the Yacht had both been despatched to Flag Officer Portsmouth's office but the two had not been over laid so neither knew they were going to be in the same piece of water. Normally, such clashes were avoided so it was only because of my conversation with The Queen that anyone knew. We made the arrangements to meet up. On the actual day I had just finished my watch so I went down to the Wardroom to have a cup of tea. Knowing that we were due to see the Yacht shortly I went back up to the

The 85-foot Spanish Royal Yacht Fortuna.

(© British Crown Copyright / MOD)

The Queen stirs the Yacht's Christmas pudding while Prince Philip adds the all important ingredient!

(© British Crown Copyright / MOD)

The Queen and Prince Philip watch the steam past executed by HMS Edinburgh *during their visit to the Channel Islands. The event clearly provided an ideal opportunity for Her Majesty to photograph the ship in which The Duke of York was serving at the time.*

(© British Crown Copyright / MOD)

bridge. The Captain turned to me and said, "Had we sailed round the corner to find the Yacht moored with The Queen embarked without my prior knowledge I wouldn't have believed you if you had pleaded innocence of the crime of not telling me!" We were allowed to man ship by division in half blues which I think is unique in the Yacht's history.'

At the end of the short visit *Britannia* returned to Portsmouth on 26 May without The Queen, who flew back to London from Jersey. Shortly after the Yacht's return, FORY left to attend the funeral of former FORY Rear Admiral Sir Patrick Morgan who had died on 20 May. During the period of the funeral service, colours on board the Yacht were flown at half mast.[40]

On 3 June The Queen Mother embarked for the Yacht's visit to Dover for Her Majesty to undertake engagements in her capacity as the Lord Warden of the Cinque Ports. From Dover, the Yacht sailed across the Channel to Caen for The Queen Mother to participate in the commemorations on 6 June to mark the anniversary of the D Day Landings at Normandy in 1944. On completion of the ceremonies, Her Majesty flew home. The Yacht sailed back down the Caen Canal on 7 June and was saluted by a number of veterans who were fallen in at the famous Pegasus Bridge.[41] July started on a sad note, when news was received on board of the death of the former FORY Vice Admiral Sir Peter Dawnay. FORY attended his funeral on 11 July and colours were once more lowered to mark the passing of another former FORY.[42]

At the end of the month *Britannia* anchored in Cowes Roads for Cowes Week, which was especially memorable, thanks to a rather unfortunate incident on 1 August, as Admiral Garnier observed:

'After lunch I was relaxing on the Verandah Deck with Princess Alexandra, Sir Angus Ogilvy and Guy Acland watching the afternoon's racing which was exciting thanks to a stiff breeze and a strong tide. We were well placed to witness the yacht *Scorcher* owned by Dr Cox get entangled in *Britannia*'s White Ensign and remove it together with most of the Ensign Staff. It was all cut clear to avoid further damage. Thus *Scorcher* had to go into harbour with the Yacht's White Ensign flying free from the mast head. It provided a field day for the press and we were expecting headlines such as "Dr Coxs It Up", but most went for "What A Scorcher!" We managed to get the spare ensign staff rigged very quickly so there was no embarrassment to us.'

The next day *Britannia* returned to Portsmouth and, two days later, embarked the Royal Family for the Western Isles Cruise.

The autumn deployment to the Far East began on 5 September, when *Britannia* left her Hampshire home port. Having already stopped at Gibraltar and sailed through the Suez Canal, the Yacht entered Aden on 22 September to refuel. While the Yacht was alongside, the terrible news reached *Britannia* of the IRA bomb that had exploded at the Royal Marines School of Music at Deal killing 10 Bandsmen. The Yacht sailed as planned the next day and, as she headed east on 24 September, special prayers and a silence were held as part of the Sunday church service. During the afternoon the full casualty list was received on board which brought home the full extent of the tragedy. Despite the depressing news, the RM Band went ahead with their concert as planned at

The Duke of York introduces the 1-year-old Princess Beatrice to some of the Yachtsmen during the Western Isles Cruise.

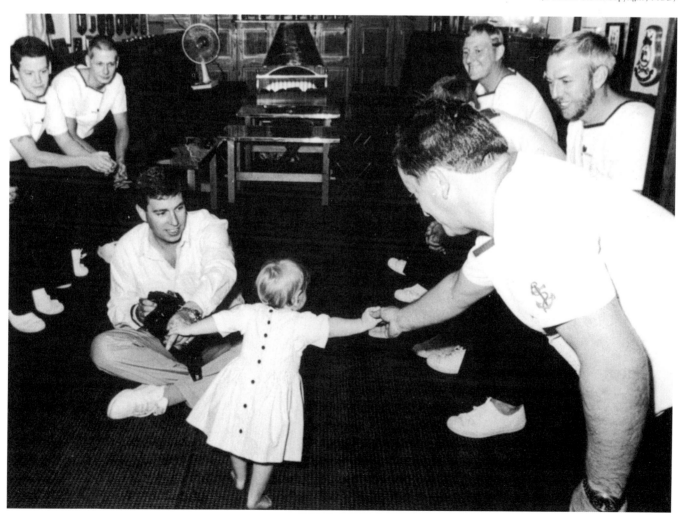

1700, which was much appreciated by the Yachtsmen who turned out in large numbers to support the Bandsmen. It also provided an opportunity to announce the disaster fund and give an advance warning of fund raising. One of the dead Bandsmen was Musician Simons who was known to many on board as he had been a regular member of the Yacht's RM Band until 1986. On 1 October a memorial service was held on the foredeck. This was later followed by a number of fund raising activities, which generated a total of £1911 towards the fund for the dependants of those who had been killed.[43]

The Yacht's period of Royal duty began with back-to-back State Visits by The Queen and Prince Philip to Singapore and Malaysia, followed by being the venue for the dinner in Lamut Naval Base in Malaysia for CHOGM delegates. When The Queen left Kuala Lumpur on 21

This is just one of the fund raising events held on board the Yacht following the bombing of the Royal Marines School of Music at Deal. The money raised was donated to the specially formed fund to support the dependants of those who had been killed.

(© British Crown Copyright / MOD)

October, Prince Philip returned to the Yacht to begin his own visit to Indonesia in support of the WWF and that night *Britannia* sailed from Port Klang. Early the next morning Admiral Garnier was woken up at 0600, as he remembers:

'The *Vigia XXX* had been spotted on fire. *Vigia XXX* was at anchor with smoke billowing out. I sent the First Lieutenant and a team across to take stock and find out if there were any casualties on board that needed assistance. However, they found that there wasn't anyone on board and it was clear that the fire had been burning for some time in view of the buckled superstructure. As there was no life at risk and we had no time for delays we left her to burn away. We contacted the shore authorities to inform them of *Vigia XXX* before we got underway again to resume our programme.'

During the course of Prince Philip's Tour the Yacht visited Indonesia, Malaysia and Brunei before he concluded his Tour with a visit to Tengku Abdul Rahman State Park in Sabah, Malaysia on 1 November. Prince Philip then flew back to the UK. That night the Yacht sailed for Hong Kong to support the visit by The Prince and Princess of Wales. At the end of the visit His Royal Highness remained behind on the Yacht to attend the Remembrance Day Service at the Cenotaph in the colony, before flying home on 13 November. On the same day *Britannia* began her own journey home, to reach Portsmouth on 18 December.

Britannia's deployment to the West Coast of Africa began on 15 February 1990 when she left Portsmouth for Lagos, via Las Palmas, Freetown and Abidjan. The continuation of the deployment was thrown in some doubt, shortly after the Yacht left Freetown on 5 March, when a leak, caused by a crack the size of a pin hole, was discovered in one of the port boiler's tubes during a routine inspection. When the boiler was shut down, further cracks were discovered and contact was made with MOD in Bath, who recommended that the Yacht should return to Portsmouth immediately. However, FORY felt that, in view of the Yacht's importance to the forthcoming visit by The Prince and Princess of Wales to Lagos and Douala, it was unthinkable for the Yacht to simply turn back for Portsmouth unless it was absolutely necessary. Thus the Yacht pressed on for Abidjan as planned, where she was met by two experts from Bath who examined the problem. Their inspection revealed that the starboard boiler's pipes were OK and that it would be safe to carry on with *Britannia*'s programme as planned and rectify the faults when she returned to the UK.[44] Although this verdict represented good news, it meant that handling the Yacht in certain conditions would be more challenging because only half her power was available, and that facilities such as air conditioning would be less effective than normal. Adjustments to the programme were made to accommodate this reduction in power and, as a result of most careful operation and monitoring of the one boiler by the technical departments, *Britannia* returned to the UK on 8 April without any delaying incidents.

Having restored full power to the Yacht during a short period in dockyard hands, *Britannia* sailed from Portsmouth for The Queen's State Visit to Iceland on 20 June. Four days later the Yacht berthed in Reykjavik to await the embarkation of The Queen and Prince Philip the next day. The Queen's Royal party included the well-known Icelander Magnus Magnasson of *Mastermind* fame and the Foreign Office Minister, later The Rt Hon. the Lord Waldegrave of North Hill, whose sister is The Queen's Lady-in-Waiting Lady Susan Hussey, also a member of the Royal party for this trip. When he went down to his cabin on board the Yacht, Lord Waldegrave was in for quite a shock, as he recalls:

'All the luggage was flown ahead in a RAF Tristar which dropped off our luggage in Iceland before flying on to Canada with a group of Royal Marines who were being flown out for a NATO exercise. When I arrived on board the Yacht I went down to my cabin to change for a black tie dinner with the Prime Minister of Iceland, etc. When I reached the cabin there was a combat uniform of a Royal Marines Sergeant carefully laid out on the bed by a presumably very surprised footman who obviously thought this is a very strange Minister. This Royal Marine was obviously somewhat larger than me and I didn't think that combats were quite on for the dinner! So my first test was to go round to the cabin of my sister, Lady Susan Hussey and ask for help. With typical efficiency the Yacht somehow found another dinner jacket that fitted me. I often wondered what the unfortunate Royal Marine who arrived in Canada with my dinner jacket thought when he found it!'

During the course of this short visit, Lord Waldegrave was able to see the contribution that *Britannia* made to a State Visit to a small country like Iceland, as he explains:

'On a trip like this the Yacht was ideal because I am not too sure where The Queen could have stayed in Iceland. Importantly, the presence of the Yacht meant that we had a piece of British territory with us which enabled us to do our own entertaining in a way that would not have been possible in our Embassy in Iceland. The wonderful backdrop of the Yacht dressed overall dominating the small harbour of Reykjavik had a tremendous pulling power with crowds of at least 12,000 people coming to see not only The Queen but also the Yacht itself which represented a significant proportion of their population. During the Icelandic summer it never gets dark so although the Royal Marine band waited until midnight to perform Beat Retreat it was still as light as day which must have been unique in the history of the Yacht.'

At the end of the State Visit to Iceland, The Queen and Prince Philip left Reykjavik on 27 June on board a Canadian Forces Boeing 707 for a visit to Canada. The following morning *Britannia* began the voyage home reaching Portsmouth on 2 July.

The Queen and Prince Philip joined the Yacht in Portsmouth late on 26 July, for the next day's celebrations to mark the 150th Anniversary of the founding of the Cunard Steamship Company. To mark the event The Queen reviewed a selection of Cunard ships anchored in the Solent, headed by the famous liner *QEII*, from the Verandah Deck. Shortly before the Yacht anchored at the western end of the review line, Concorde led a fly-past over the Solent, which included both civilian and naval aircraft. The Royal couple then transferred to *QEII* in the Barge for a celebratory lunch on board, and later sailed to Southampton on board the liner.[45] Three days later The Queen Mother joined the Yacht in Portsmouth for the passage round to London. As the Yacht made her way down the Solent she slowed down for Her Majesty to review a gathering of 2000 yachts and motor boats to mark her 90th birthday. The Yacht reached the Pool of London on 1 August and Her Majesty disembarked in the afternoon to visit the east end of London. In the evening she returned on board for the family dinner, hosted by The Queen, to celebrate her birthday which was attended by 25 members of the Royal Family. The evening was rounded off by a major fireworks display over the Thames. The Queen Mother stayed on board overnight before leaving the following morning.[46] Within an hour of doing so the Yacht sailed for Cowes where she arrived the next day. At the end of Cowes Week the Yacht returned to Portsmouth on 8 August for a few hours to embark the Royal Family for the Western Isles Cruise which concluded on 16 August in Aberdeen. Four days later Admiral Garnier brought the Yacht into Portsmouth for the last time as FORY to conclude his seagoing career.

Chapter Eleven

THE RETURN TO SOUTH AFRICA

Rear Admiral Sir Robert Woodard KCVO 1990–1995

Rear Admiral Robert Woodard's imminent appointment as the next FORY was heralded in the traditional manner when his flag was hoisted in the aircraft carrier HMS *Illustrious* on 18 September 1990. Later in the morning Admiral Woodard stepped aboard his temporary flagship for coffee, before walking across the Dockyard to *Britannia* and relieving Rear Admiral Sir John Garnier KCVO CBE as FORY. For Admiral Garnier's journey into retirement the Yachtsmen had organised a horse-drawn landau which was preceded by the RM Band.[1]

Admiral Woodard joined the Royal Navy in 1958 specifically to fly. He served in the aircraft carriers HMS *Ark Royal*, HMS *Eagle*, HMS *Victorious* and HMS *Bulwark*; flying jet attack aircraft and commando helicopters. Before his promotion to Commander he commanded 771 and then 848 naval air squadrons. He then went on to command the Type 21 frigate HMS *Amazon* as a Commander and the Type 42 destroyer HMS *Glasgow* as a Captain before returning ashore to command the Naval Air Station at Portland HMS *Osprey*. Before becoming FORY Admiral Woodard served as Commodore Clyde with responsibility for the facilities used by the RN's nuclear submarines and in the NATO appointment of COMCLYDENORLANT.

A week after assuming command of the Yacht, Admiral Woodard took her out of Portsmouth for the first time as she set sail for the Caribbean. Describing how *Britannia*'s handling characteristics differed from the modern gener-

ation of gas turbine warships that he had previously handled, Admiral Woodard said:

'My overriding impression was the amount of anticipation needed for every manoeuvre. For example, when I stopped the engines to bring her slow astern I did this with ¼ mile in hand. In HMS *Amazon* I could stop her from 36 knots in three times her own length compared with *Britannia* which could stop in five times her own length from 6 knots! All of these characteristics were comprehensively written up to help one plan where she was going to stop. However, she was much more vulnerable to wind and tide because she was under their influence for longer. Once her speed dropped below 6 knots steerage was lost and therefore the way to take charge of *Britannia* was through the use of large amounts of power. She didn't respond to clever touches of light power. It took a little while to realise how much power I needed and how brave I had to be whilst manoeuvring.'

On her way across the Atlantic, the Yacht called at Ponta Delgada on 30 September to refuel. If possible the Yacht always stopped at Ponta Delgada during a transatlantic crossing because it was a NATO refuelling stop which meant the cost of fuel to the Yacht was cheaper than international fuel prices. The island also had an added draw for the Admiral because his mother had recently retired there but hadn't finished moving all of her things. As Admiral Woodard explains:

'I arranged with the Master of the Household to stow her dining table and a sideboard in the Royal Apartments during the voyage from Portsmouth. At this stage the Yachtsmen hadn't had the chance to get to know me as I had only been in command for about a week. One can therefore imagine that they were taken aback to see soon after we reached Ponta Delgada the arrival of an old, rusty, open-topped wagon alongside. They were perhaps even more surprised to see furniture being unloaded from the Royal Apartments and being taken away. Doubtless, they thought the new Admiral was up to no good!'

When *Britannia* left Ponta Delgada on 1 October she continued her passage to Barbados, where she embarked The Princess Royal [Princess Anne was declared The Princess Royal on 13 June 1987] on 12 October for her visits to Barbados and Trinidad before flying on to Jamaica on 17 October. Once FORY had received confirmation that the Princess's aircraft had safely taken off, the Yacht sailed for Brazil, calling first at Recife, before reaching Rio on 28 October, ahead of the following day's Sea Day sponsored by British Invisibles.[2] The event led to mutual benefits between the UK and Brazil, as Admiral Woodard observed:

'British businessmen came out to convince the Brazilian Government that in their bankrupt state they could be rescued if our bankers and insurers showed them the way and did the work for them. All the money they earned would of course be taxable and the tax was counted as money made by *Britannia*. Therefore, it was tax on deals that actually happened on the day that counted towards the average of £700 million a year during my final three years as FORY.'

As usual the Sea Day included music from the embarked RM Band during the break for drinks which was also enjoyed by some of those on the beach, as Captain Whealing remarked: 'we were steaming off Copacabana beach so I thought we would play some Latin American music which went down very well with our guests. Apparently the people on the beach could also hear our music and many of them were dancing to it as we steamed past.' After a further two days in Rio, the Yacht began the voyage home via Fortaleza, Dakar, Funchal and Falmouth, to arrive in Portsmouth on 30 November. Within a fortnight the Yacht headed out of Portsmouth for a three-day visit to London to conclude her programme for the year.

In April 1991 *Britannia* retraced her voyage of the previous autumn, when she once more headed out from Portsmouth and across the Atlantic Ocean to Brazil. Having called at Fortaleza and Belem, the Yacht anchored off the Brazilian Naval Base at Val de Cais on 26 April to embark 26 business leaders for a forum held in the Royal Drawing Room. The businessmen were joined by the Minister for Overseas Development, Lynda Chalker, and The Prince of Wales who hosted a lunch for the delegates. When the delegates left in the afternoon the President of Brazil embarked to join His Royal Highness for an Environment seminar, as *Britannia* continued to cruise up the Amazon River.[3] Describing the challenge of navigating the world's most famous river Admiral Woodard said:

'The Amazon is incredibly wide yet very shallow in places whilst deep enough in other places. Because of the silting up and the various floods it was difficult to predict the channel so we had an Amazonian Indian pilot on board who would point diagonally across the river to show us where to go and we hoped he was right because the water was very muddy!'

FORY between 1990 and 1995, Rear Admiral Sir Robert Woodard KCVO DL.

Unfortunately, the Yacht's progress up the river was limited by the fact that she had to return to the Brazilian Naval Base at Val de Cais to disembark the Brazilian President. He had originally planned to spend the night on board but his advisors felt it would be unwise for him to do so as his critics would claim he was enjoying a pleasure cruise with The Prince of Wales while his people endured the economic crisis gripping Brazil. Thus the President left the Yacht after dinner and the seminar concluded the following afternoon while the Yacht was at anchor off Belem. Shortly after the seminar finished His Royal Highness disembarked to fly home.

On 28 April the Yacht weighed anchor for Barbados, to embark the British High Commissioner ahead of the visit to Dominica on 3 May where His Excellency hosted The Queen's Birthday party on board. This was an important event because The Queen wanted to thank the Dominican Government for its unequivocal support in the United Nations for British actions in both the Falklands War and the Gulf War. As an independent member of the Commonwealth, Dominica has a vote in the United Nations so their help on both occasions proved very useful. By allowing the High Commissioner to host The Queen's Birthday party on board the Yacht it provided a clear public acknowledgement of Dominica's support for the UK. The visit also highlighted another facet of FORY's role, when he was required to act as an ambassador for The Queen. Shortly after the Yacht had berthed in Dominica, Admiral Woodard went ashore to pay calls on the President, HE Sir Clarence Seignaret GCB OBE, and then the Prime Minister, Eugenia Charles,[4] who was known as the Iron Lady of the Caribbean, as Admiral Woodard recalls:

'Paying my official call I was kept waiting by the Prime Minister although I could see through the crack of the door that she had no one with her. When I went in to see her she asked me how many times had I been there? How many times had the Yacht been there? How many times had my predecessors been there? I answered her questions but the point she was trying to make was that the Yacht didn't visit often enough. She then explained that the Dominicans were predominately Roman Catholic. Attempting to show some knowledge I replied, "I imagine that's because for a time you were a French Colony."

She responded, "Your schoolboy history doesn't impress me at all! Now when are you seeing The Queen next?"

I told her, "In four days time."

"Well, because we're predominately Roman Catholic we need the Pope here. The Pope's aeroplane is too big to land in Dominica so I have decided that the only way the Pope can come here is in *Britannia*. So you are to ask The Queen, when you next see her, if she will lend *Britannia* to the Pope to enable him to visit as we want to see him." So I pulled a handkerchief from my pocket and tied a knot to which she asked, "What are you doing?"

"Very important questions Prime Minister, I tie a knot in my handkerchief. When I undress at night I take my handkerchief out, undo the knots and put them in my note book." She howled with laughter, asking me to sit down and offered me a drink. When she came on board for lunch later that day as I was trying to present the Commander to her she ignored him saying, "Show me your handkerchief!" so I pulled it out. There was still only one knot in it to which she remarked, "You haven't had a very busy morning have you?"

When I returned there in 1993 with Prince Philip she came up to me at lunchtime asking, "Show me your handkerchief Admiral," so I pulled it out.

This time I had purposefully tied 11 knots in it and I remarked, "I have had a hell of a morning Prime Minister," which she found very amusing.'

The Yacht sailed from Dominica on 6 May and headed north west for the US port of Miami, where she arrived four days later to support the Florida leg of The Queen and Prince Philip's State Visit to America. Before their embarkation on 17 May the Yacht was alleged to have violated the harbour's strict environmental regulations which caused real difficulties for Admiral Woodard, as he explains:

'The authorities spotted some soap suds appearing from the stern so the Harbour Pollution Officer came on board demanding to see me personally, walking straight past the Commander who tried to stop him. He blew into my cabin to announce, "There is a $10,000 fine on you and you sail within two hours because you are polluting my harbour."'

Obviously, this was a very unfortunate situation but, as The Queen was due to host a dinner that night as part of her State Visit, it was impossible for FORY to comply with the Sheriff's ruling. After further discussions FORY had to ask for high level intervention from officials at the White House to resolve the situation. Despite their assistance it wasn't quite the end of the matter, as Admiral Woodard continues:

'In a quiet moment after The Queen had embarked she asked me how everything had gone so I told her about the problem with the harbour authorities and that he insisted that the fine stood. She was concerned as to how I might pay the fine, so I said, "Well, I have had a bright idea if you don't mind. You know the little mixture bottles for ginger ale and tonic of which we have a lot after each reception. I wondered Ma'am if we could possibly fill those with your bath water and sell them for $1000 each. We wouldn't have any difficulty selling them at all." She thought it was extremely funny but needless to say we didn't do it.'

Despite the earlier difficulties with the authorities, the dinner itself went ahead and was a great success. The guests included President Clinton as well as all of the surviving former US Presidents namely President Ford, President Carter, President Reagan and President Bush. On completion of Beat Retreat the Yacht made a floodlit departure.

The following afternoon the Yacht anchored off Loggerhead Key, where The Queen and Prince Philip,

accompanied by the senior Household officials, went ashore for a picnic. Just as they were about to sit down and eat their food FORY was telephoned by the Commander to say that he had received a message from the East Midlands Police Force stating that they had been given an anonymous tip off about the planting of a bomb on board the Yacht 4 feet below the waterline. It was claimed that the bomb would detonate in an hour's time. Despite strict security before the Yacht's departure from Portsmouth, and during her subsequent visits, a search was initiated just in case, as Admiral Woodard recalled:

'These things must be taken seriously so the Commander initiated the standard checking procedure. I told the Commander, "When you are happy just carry on and unless I hear an explosion or you ring me back

The RM Band performs for the American guests at the end of the Miami Sea Day.

I will imagine that all will be well for our return." I then went back to have my supper. The Queen enquired as to what the call was about so I said, "Nothing Ma'am." Unconvinced with my answer she asked again so I told her. She responded by explaining that it was very difficult to know whether to take these things seriously or not and then asked me what would happen if a bomb did go off. I replied, "I don't think you will notice the difference Ma'am because we are in only 4 feet of water so if she sinks we can probably live on board but we will be there for some time – a luxury hotel stuck on the bottom." But those were the moments that showed how Her Majesty has to view those wretched things.'

The message proved to be a hoax. The Royal party returned on board that night for the overnight passage to Cayo Costa for the second day of rest for the Royal party, before resuming their programme of public engagements on 20 May, when Britannia berthed in Tampa Harbour. During The Queen's visit she met General Norman Schwarzkopf, who had commanded the Allied forces during the Gulf War, and invested him with an honorary knighthood. From Tampa the Royal couple disembarked from the Yacht to continue inland for the rest of their State Visit while the Yacht hosted a Sea Day the next day before sailing for Bermuda on 27 May.[5]

As the Yacht headed towards Bermuda on 28 May, a person was spotted floating in a lump of hollowed out, expanded polystyrene. A boat was launched to investigate. It turned out to be a 21-year-old Cuban textile worker, Lazaro Sandoval, from a town just outside Havana. Like many other Cubans before him the man was fleeing from the Communist regime on the island and trying to reach the USA where he would claim political asylum. He was prepared to risk his life, paddling across the Straits of Florida on a small polystyrene raft. Despite being at sea for three days and running out of food and water the young man was found to be in reasonable health. Britannia headed back towards Miami, where Lazaro Sandoval was transferred to a US Coastguard Cutter, and Britannia resumed her voyage to Bermuda where she took on more fuel for the transatlantic crossing to Ponta Delgada.[6] The Yacht headed across to Faro, where she embarked The Duke and Duchess of Kent on 9 June. With Their Royal Highnesses on board, the Yacht sailed to spend the following day at sea, prior to the ceremonial entry into Lisbon to mark the beginning of their visit on 11 June. The weather provided a last minute surprise for Admiral Woodard just as Britannia was about to berth, as he remarked:

'The conditions were very good with light airs as Britannia glided up the middle of the harbour. Just as we started to turn the wind suddenly increased in strength. By the time we had completed half the turn the wind had strengthened to 15 knots and subsequently to 25 knots as we came alongside. As a matter of ceremony all the flags are hoisted to dress overall the moment the first line is ashore. Because of the conditions I had left everything as late as I could and went very firmly astern to stop her in the allocated position to hand the lines to the jetty – it was one of my better manoeuvres! However, the moment this happened the flags were hoisted which had the effect of raising three spinnakers and we were off as the lines parted, etc., with the wind blowing us 5 knots sideways! I went round again and told the Yeoman not to raise the flags until we were firmly secured. Thankfully, it was the only time I ever had to go round again!'

On the second day of their Lisbon visit, the Duchess of Kent went ashore to pursue her programme ashore, while His Royal Highness remained on board to host the Sea Day, entitled 'Finance in the 1990s', which was attended by 100 delegates. In the evening Their Royal Highnesses rounded off their visit by hosting a reception, before flying back to the UK the next morning. Britannia sailed for Portsmouth on 14 June, arriving there three days later.[7]

Nearly a month later the Yacht sailed for Milford Haven, pausing on the way to embark The Duke of York at Portland. The visit had been planned at relatively short notice so it wasn't included within FORY's pre-year forecast for fuel. As Admiral Woodard explains, the discussions surrounding his request for fuel were a foretaste of the future conflicts over expenditure in a post Cold War environment where the defence budget was becoming progressively smaller:

'I needed 300 tons of fuel to get up there and back so the Navigator rang up Commander-in-Chief Fleet's office and informed them of the additional requirement for fuel. The Navigator came and told me that Commander-in-Chief Fleet had refused the request. So I contacted the Commander-in-Chief Fleet and said, "I don't understand. This is a Royal engagement and it is to be undertaken." To which I was told, "Bad luck it wasn't in the original forecast for the year and there isn't the fuel." I explained that we're only talking about 300 tons of fuel, which I could probably reduce to 260 tons. They said, "You're not listening. Which frigate do you want us to keep alongside?" It was an absolute refusal. However, I found out that Amoco were a major sponsor of the Tall Ships Race so I phoned up the Chief Executive who had never heard of FORY. He thought I was pulling his leg when I explained that I was the Admiral in charge of *Britannia* and I needed some fuel. He really didn't believe it to begin with. He asked, could I get up there? If so, it would be waiting for us.'

Having solved the fuel problem, the Yacht arrived in Milford Haven on 13 July to enable His Royal Highness to carry out his programme ashore in the afternoon. The next day's programme began with the parade of sail, headed by the frigate HMS *Juno*. The Yacht slipped her buoy mid morning to take up her position for the afternoon's race starts. Once the last of the tall ships had crossed the start line, the race officials were disembarked to enable the Yacht to sail for Portland to drop off His Royal Highness before returning to Portsmouth.[8]

At the beginning of August the Yacht was used by Prince Philip for Cowes Week, followed by the regular Western Isles Cruise, before the Yacht returned to Portsmouth on 21 August. A month later *Britannia* sailed from Portsmouth for a week's visit to London, beginning on 24 September. One of the political difficulties of *Britannia*'s role was that she spent a great deal of her time deployed in foreign waters and thus out of sight from the British public. This resulted in the very unfortunate situation that the public usually only heard about *Britannia* when a politician was criticising the cost of her latest refit. Therefore, Admiral Woodard was determined to try and change this situation by ensuring that the Yacht spent about a week in London each year during his time as FORY so that she could be seen in operation, both by the public, and the key decision makers who would ultimately decide her future. During the course of these visits the Admiral would plan four or five major events of which at least one or two would be Royal and the others would be commercial. On the second day of *Britannia*'s London visit she hosted a seminar, sponsored by British Invisibles, entitled 'London and Tokyo – Financial Partnership In The New Europe'. Princess Alexandra joined the delegates for lunch which provided the unique set of circumstance for a gathering of FORYs with Rear Admiral Sir Paul Greening as the Master of the Household, Rear Admiral Sir John Garnier as the Private Secretary to Princess Alexandra, and of course Admiral Woodard as the current FORY[9]. Because of the tight programme that year some of the Yachtsmen were sent home on leave at the beginning of the visit so the Yacht returned to Portsmouth with a skeleton crew on 27 September.

A few days later the Yacht left Portsmouth to begin her deployment to Canada to support the visit of The Prince

and Princess of Wales. Having taken the usual route via Ponta Delgada, *Britannia* arrived at a very foggy Halifax on 12 October, before beginning her voyage up the St Lawrence Seaway to Toronto, where she arrived nine days later. On 22 October Prince William and Prince Harry embarked ahead of their parents who arrived the following evening. This wasn't the first time the young Princes had accompanied their parents on a visit in the Yacht.

While The Prince and Princess of Wales were undertaking their official engagements ashore, various activities were organised for the Princes, including a visit to the Canadian destroyer HMCS *Ottawa*. During the Yacht's passage to Kingston, Ontario on 27 October The Royal party went for an informal walk round the Yacht, culminating in the young Princes being invited to stir the Christmas pudding. Shortly afterwards the Princes disembarked in the Barge to Oshaua Marina to be taken back to

A Yachtsmen is lowered in a Bosun's chair having removed the bolt to enable the fore mast to be scandalised during the Yacht's passage up the St Lawrence Seaway.

Toronto for the flight home. The following morning the Yacht berthed in Kingston for Their Royal Highnesses to fulfil their public engagements before flying back to the UK on 29 October. Within two hours of their departure the Yacht started her own journey home, to reach Portsmouth on 12 November.[10]

Soon after the Yacht's return, she entered dockyard hands for a short refit which was completed in time for her to sail on 15 May 1992 for Palermo, where The Queen and Prince Philip would embark ahead of their visit to Malta. The visit was timed to coincide with the 50th Anniversary of the siege of Malta during the Second World War. In an unprecedented gesture King George VI awarded the George Cross to the island on 15 April 1942 which was accompanied by the following citation: 'To honour her brave people I award the George Cross to the island fortress of Malta, to bear witness to a heroism and a devotion that will long be famous in history.' In circumstances reminiscent of their first arrival on board *Britannia* in 1954, the battlements surrounding Grand Harbour were packed with people who had turned out to welcome the Royal couple back to the island where they had once lived while Prince Philip was serving in the Mediterranean Fleet. As the Yacht slipped in to Grand Harbour on 28 May she was followed by a large number of small boats. The next day the Royal couple attended the dedication service in Valletta for the Siege Bell Monument, which was designed by Michael Sandle. Standing 50 feet high, the bell tower dominates the entrance to Grand Harbour to provide a fitting memorial to the 7000 servicemen who died in the defence of Malta during the Second World War. The existence of this impressive monument was due to the tireless efforts of Admiral of the Fleet, Lord Lewin. In the evening The

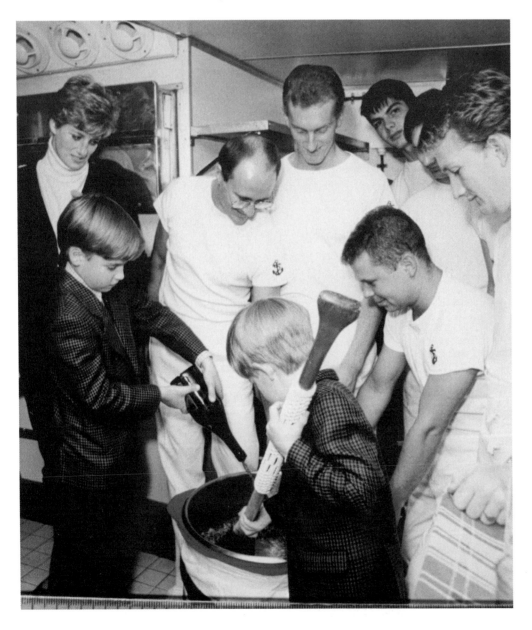

The Princess of Wales looks on as Prince Harry stirs the Yacht's Christmas pudding and Prince William adds the rum.

(© British Crown Copyright / MOD)

Queen hosted a State Banquet on board the Yacht for the President and Prime Minister of Malta. Large crowds gathered around the harbour to watch the Yacht sail out of Grand Harbour early on 30 May as she headed to the north of the island for The Queen and Prince Philip to carry out engagements ashore in Gozo, before making the overnight passage to Palermo, where the Royal couple left the Yacht on 31 May. Later that afternoon *Britannia* sailed out of Palermo and that night the Master of the Household, Rear Admiral Sir Paul Greening, was dined out before his retirement.[11]

The following morning the Yacht berthed in Civitavecchia Harbour ahead of the Sea Day sponsored by British Invisibles on 2 June. Describing the routine of a typical Sea Day, the Commander of the Yacht, later Captain R Cosby LVO RN, said:

'Seminars were held in the Royal Dining Room. The day would begin with the Master of the Household who would welcome the delegates to the Yacht on behalf of Her Majesty. FORY would then welcome them on behalf of the Yacht and outline the programme for the day before going up to the Bridge to take charge of the departure. After this the Yacht would sail and if necessary would maintain a course downwind to make it as comfortable as possible. After the initial presentations coffee would be served on the Verandah Deck with the RM Band playing incidental music. The escort would

The Yacht passes the impressive Siege Bell Monument, Valletta, Malta as local people gather at every vantage point to see The Queen and Prince Philip's arrival on board Britannia.

(© British Crown Copyright / MOD)

close the Yacht to perform a small demonstration such as firing a few guns or launching the helicopter for a display. This would be followed by lunch in the Royal Dining Room. To stop people from thinking they were (or weren't) on the top table 12 big round tables seating 10 people each were available to be used for lunch. People would be grouped together depending on their business interests so that they could continue their discussions over lunch. An officer would sit at each of the tables to help open up the conversation or re-start it if things went a bit quiet. In the afternoon the seminars continued. These Sea Days were great fun but very hard work especially for the Yachtsmen who were involved in the constant scene shifting as the Royal Apartments were adapted to the different stages of the Sea Day.'

From Civitavecchia the Yacht sailed via Gibraltar for Bordeaux to support The Queen and Prince Philip's State Visit to France. During her passage across the Bay of Biscay the Yacht received an unwelcome signal from Commander-in-Chief Fleet informing FORY that he was to make a 10 per cent cut in his budget as part of the latest round of defence cuts. Despite the imminent period of Royal duty, the proposals on how the cuts were going to be achieved were required in a matter of days. When the cuts were subsequently approved in December 1992 the Yacht's company was reduced by 5 per cent including 2 Officers and 11 Yachtsmen.[12] By 1992 *Britannia's* operating costs were paid for from a ring-fenced budget within the headquarters budget of Commander-in-Chief Fleet which enabled the Yacht's finances to come under closer scrutiny, as Admiral Woodard explains:

'The creation of a formal, controlled budget meant that the Yacht was no longer in charge of its own destiny; outside forces could have a controlling influence and, for the first time, the anti Yacht lobby within the RN could get hold of statistics with which to make mischief, and they did! A classic example of the exterior controlling influence was the demand from Commander-in-Chief Fleet to reduce the Yacht's company. The Yacht had been running for nearly 40 years at that stage, and the Yacht's company was finely honed to the task, which incidentally, was increasing rapidly in the wake of the very successful commercial programme. It is also worthy of note that some 178 of the 226 Yachtsmen could be members of the Royal Yacht Service and thus could not, reasonably, be cut. Therefore, the cut had to be taken from the Ocean Compliment from which the new members of the Royal Yacht Service would be recruited. Thus it is very easy to see the knock on effects of an apparently reasonable request! The refusal for fuel for the Tall Ships Race was another symptom of the same set up. The change to external financial control was, in my view, the beginning of the end for *Britannia*.'

However, despite Commander-in-Chief Fleet's signal the Yacht's programme had to go on regardless with The Queen hosting the return State Banquet on board for President Mitterrand on 11 June. After the reception and Beat Retreat the French President had a surprise, as Admiral Woodard recalled:

'President Mitterrand fooled us all by letting off an amazing fireworks display on the other side of the river. One of the things that only people in the know knew was that when there were, for example, 300 people on the port side of the Yacht they would be balanced by lowering boats on the starboard side. On this occasion the Barge had been swung right out and was quite near the water to hold the Yacht level with 300 people. The instant the Royal Marines finished and the lights went out, off went the fireworks on the other side of the Yacht and off went 300 people running across the deck. The Yacht took on the most alarming list so the Officer of the Watch let the Barge slip to take the weight off which helped a bit. However, the Yacht started to rock back so the boats on the other side were then lowered but when the Yacht moved back again those boats rested on the jetty and they were weightless. In all there were three huge rolls before the Yacht settled down.'

Two days later the Yacht sailed for Portsmouth.

A week after the return from Bordeaux, the Yacht sailed for Leith to be used for two separate commercial events hosted by the Scottish Secretary, Ian Lang on 26 June. To assist the principal event, 'Doing Business In Europe', The Princess Royal embarked to attend lunch with the delegates.[13] Three days later the Yacht sailed for Portsmouth, stopping on the way at Newcastle for a four-day visit. At the end of the month *Britannia* attended Cowes Week. Describing some of the preparations before Cowes Week, Captain Cosby said:

'Josephine Terry had inherited Uffa Fox's house in Cowes. In the spring if the Yacht was in Portsmouth we would go on a 'Terry's Lunch Party Run'. Unusually, we were sometimes allowed to take the Barge to carry out her annual trials at the same time. The whole Wardroom would go across for the lunch which was also attended by the Cowes Harbour Master and other local characters. We would always return the hospitality with a reciprocal lunch on board the Yacht. About six weeks before Cowes Week we would receive a delegation from the Combined Cowes Clubs to discuss the final arrangements including the movements of the Royal Family during the week. Yet another very pleasant meeting and lunch party – and all in the name of duty!'

As usual Prince Philip's visit to Cowes Week was followed by the Royal Family's cruise among the Western Isles.

The autumn programme began on 30 September, when the Yacht sailed for the West Country with visits to Dartmouth and then Falmouth. Within a week of the Yacht's return to Portsmouth, she sailed for Stockholm for the Sea Day sponsored by British Invisibles on 21 October. By now there was a clear step change in *Britannia*'s commercial role, which was becoming an important part of the Yacht's annual programme as the number of events began to steadily increase. Despite the growing importance of these events the planning had to be undertaken within the constraints placed by *Britannia*'s Royal duties. Because these events were held within the Royal Apartments, the detailed arrangements for the Sea Days were handled by the Master of the Household and his office within Buckingham Palace. In 1992 Rear Admiral Sir Paul Greening retired from this post and was relieved by Major General Sir Simon Cooper KCVO. Describing the process of how these events were arranged, General Cooper said:

'We took the lead in arranging the Sea Days because once we heard from FORY where the Yacht was going to be it was up to us to talk to various organisations like British Invisibles and DTI. As a result of these discussions we then began to arrange where each event was going to take place, how long it could last, etc. As part of this process the DTI had to weigh up the priorities of the various interested claims on the Yacht and we had to make a decision about what could be achieved while trying to ensure that everyone had their fair share. When we planned these events we had to ensure that we didn't over stretch the Yachtsmen. We were conscious of the fact that if we asked the Yachtsmen to run a reception, followed by lunch, an afternoon briefing and a dinner for five days in succession, as the various agencies hoped we would, it would drive them into the ground because they worked hard during these events. Another risk of running too many events in the same place in quick succession was the possibility of Yacht fatigue setting in. As can be appreciated there were a number of different interests who in some cases might be trying to attract the same people to their events. Thus whilst these important people might be very pleased to come to an event in the Yacht for the first time they may be less enthusiastic after say three visits in the same week!'

At the end of the Yacht's short visit to Stockholm she sailed for Portsmouth on 23 October.

At the beginning of December *Britannia* headed north from Portsmouth for her second visit of the year to the Scottish port of Leith, where she arrived on 9 December. The following afternoon Princess Margaret embarked ahead of The Queen, Prince Philip, The Prince and Princess of Wales and The Princess Royal who all embarked on 11 December. That night The Queen hosted a State Banquet for the visiting Heads of Government attending the EC Summit being held in Edinburgh.[14] At the end of the event the British Prime Minister, John Major, asked FORY if he could go and thank the Yachtsmen for their help behind the scenes with the evening, as Admiral Woodard recalled:

'For any state occasion there had to be upwards of 60 volunteers to make it happen. For example, at the end of a Banquet there was usually a reception for about 200 people so all of the Royal Dining Room had to be cleared back into an empty room with two bars in under 20 minutes. The Prime Minister asked, "Should I ask Her Majesty if I could do this?"

I said, "No because by the time you have got to The Queen to ask her it will be time for people to start leaving and you have to be there. So just come with me and I will tell her that you asked. It is more important that they see you but don't delay as we go through the Royal Dining Room because I want to take you to the washing up place where the real chaps are."

At this stage in an evening there would be a Chief Petty Office Electrician doing the washing, a Chief Petty Officer Seaman drying, and a senior Royal Marine shoving the things through the hatch to be stowed in the silver room or china pantry. When we arrived in the washing room my writer from the Admiral's office was there with his hands in the sink. By that stage he had been a Leading Writer for 15 years and had no intention of going anywhere else. He looked up without any reaction and carried on with what he was doing. I introduced him and he said, "Hello Prime Minister, you must be a permanently unhappy man."

The Prime Minister bridled at that and asked, "What do you mean by that?"

He said, "Well, backing Chelsea."

"What's wrong with Chelsea?"

"Load of idiots!"

The Prime Minister smiled and then came out with

the whole league tables and how they stood. The chaps were amazed. They stopped what they were doing and gathered round him. There was the Prime Minister telling them how it was all going – an amazing fund of knowledge. As we walked back across the Royal Dining Room he turned to me and said, "Now I realise why the Yacht is special."'

The following morning the members of the Royal Family disembarked separately to pursue their individual programmes and, three days later, the Yacht sailed for home.

The New Year began with another transatlantic crossing for the visit to the Mexican island of Cozumel, where The Prince of Wales embarked on 18 February 1993 at the end of his visit to Mexico to host a reception. That night the Yacht weighed anchor for Kingston, where His Royal Highness hosted a further reception on 21 February, prior to flying back to the UK. The following night Britannia sailed for St Lucia, stopping on the way at Martinique. When the deployment was being planned FORY circulated the offer to host a Sea Day during the visit to St Lucia, because the Yacht was due to be there for a week before Prince Philip's embarkation. The offer was readily accepted by the Caribbean Trade Association CARITAG which is made up of UK companies that want to trade into the Caribbean rim. The event was held on 4 March and proved to be a great success, as Admiral Woodard observed:

'One man came up to me half way through the reception and said, "Excuse me Admiral have you got a bottle of champagne? I have just landed a wonderful contract."

So I said, "Yes of course, tell me more."

"It's just perfect. I run a small business in the Midlands and we produce sausage-making machines and I have just sold one to Jamaica."

"A sausage machine!"

"Don't laugh, the order for this sausage-making machine is worth £1 million to my company. When it is delivered it will be making sausages for the British yachts in the Caribbean."

The order was only possible because of Britannia's presence, which enabled him to talk to the right people. His company was one of 30 companies who had put their year's profits into coming out to try and sell, which was brilliant.'

Six days later Prince Philip joined the Yacht and held a dinner that night for the Governor General and Prime Minister of St Lucia, before the Yacht sailed to begin His Royal Highness's Tour of the Caribbean. Over the next 10 days Prince Philip undertook visits to eight separate countries of the Commonwealth on behalf of The Queen, at the request of the Foreign Office. With the Yacht coming under closer scrutiny from the media in the UK, journalists seized on this Tour and some of the tabloids came out with banner headlines such as 'Prince Philip Swans In Caribbean At Tax Payers Expense'. This style of reporting, which completely missed the point of the Tour, played straight into the hands of Britannia's band of small, but constantly vocal, critics at home. But despite the negative reporting, the Tour was a great success, with Prince Philip receiving an enthusiastic welcome at each of the islands. At the end of the Caribbean Tour the Yacht headed north west to the port of Palm Beach, where she arrived on 24 March. Prince Philip was joined during the day by Prince Edward before they attended a charity reception in support of The Duke of Edinburgh's Award Scheme at the Breakers Hotel. The following morning Their Royal Highnesses disembarked to fly back to the UK. The rest of the visit to Palm Beech was used to promote Scottish interests, with the Scottish Secretary hosting a reception in support of The Whisky Association at lunchtime, and a trade day on 26 March which was focused on attracting inward investment to Scotland, as Admiral Woodard continues:

'The major companies of Silicon Valley were looking to set up new operations in Japan before they attended the trade day in the Yacht. Ian Lang opened the event by making a speech for about an hour without a note. He started very cleverly by saying that he was standing on one of the best bits of Scottish equipment going – the Yacht. He then went on to say that Scotland would welcome them and open their way into Europe. His department would pay their legal fees and give them vast subsidies to set up in Scotland. I know that one of the firms had already signed a contract to set up in Japan but cancelled it opting for Scotland instead all as a direct result of that day with Ian Lang.'

On completion of the trade day the Yacht began the voyage home, via Bermuda and Ponta Delgada, to arrive in Portsmouth on 8 April.

A month later the Yacht sailed from her Hampshire home port to begin a short tour in home waters, beginning with four days in London, followed by the voyage to Sunderland where The Queen and Prince Philip embarked for their Tour of the east coast, with visits to Hartlepool, Hull and Great Yarmouth where they disembarked on 20 May. After three days back in Portsmouth, the Yacht sailed on 24 May to head round to the west coast for Holyhead, where King Harald of Norway and Prince Philip embarked on 26 May ahead of the next day's

Fleet Review off Liverpool. The review was held to mark the 50th Anniversary of the Battle of the Atlantic which was the longest running campaign of the Second World War. During the war Liverpool was home to the HQ of the Western Approaches' Naval Command, as well as being the main convoy port throughout the war. To commemorate the conflict, warships from the allied nations who fought against the German Navy attended, including the Russian Navy which sent the *Sovremenny* class destroyer *Gremyashchy*. Ten merchant ships were also present to remember the 28,000 merchant sailors who were lost in the Atlantic. The weather conditions were quite simply appalling, as the event became the first Fleet Review to be held in a Force 8-plus gale, which evoked memories of the atrocious conditions regularly endured by those who fought the prolonged campaign against the German U-Boats.

Although the weather might have seemed fitting, it did present major problems for the organisers, not least the large amount of boat running which was required to get people out to the ships before the review began. The types of boats carried by most of the warships, which were due to take on guests for the review, were quite unsuitable for ferrying guests in those conditions, so much of this work was undertaken by the Yacht's two 30-foot motor launches which really came into their own. To ease their increased workload it was decided to embark the press, who had been due to join in the frigate HMS *Active*. During the course of the review, the weather was so bad that the Elder Brethren of Trinity House, who were embarked in their vessel *Mermaid*, had to surrender their ancient right of preceding the Yacht for the first time and tuck in astern of *Britannia*. Without the presence of the Yacht the Fleet Review could have very easily turned into a major PR disaster for the RN. Despite the challenges presented by the weather, the Yacht was able to carry on regardless and the event was a very successful start to a five-day programme of commemorative events, during which the Yacht was berthed in front of the famous Liver

Britannia encounters rough seas as she passes the Russian Sovremennyy *class destroyer* Gremyashchy *during the Fleet Review off Liverpool to mark the 50th Anniversary of the Battle of the Atlantic.*

(© British Crown Copyright / MOD)

Building. At the beginning of June the Yacht entered Portsmouth to undergo a short period of maintenance in the Dockyard.

The work was completed to enable *Britannia* to sail on time for Cowes Week on 29 July which was followed by the Western Isles Cruise. The autumn deployment began on 16 September, when the Yacht left Portsmouth to begin the passage to Istanbul to support the visit to Turkey by The Prince of Wales. His Royal Highness joined the Yacht on 6 October, while she was at anchor off the Turkish city of Istanbul. Two days later His Royal Highness became the most senior member of the Royal Family to be involved in a Sea Day on board the Yacht, when he welcomed the delegates to the Sea Day sponsored by British Invisibles. In his welcoming address The Prince of Wales spoke about some of the opportunities that existed for closer financial links between the UK and Turkey. After lunch, His Royal Highness disembarked, and the next day *Britannia* weighed anchor for Piraeus, where she arrived on 11 October. The visit to Piraeus was originally planned around a Sea Day for British Invisibles which was due to be attended by The Duke of Kent, but in view of the Greek General Election, which was called at short notice, the Sea Day was cancelled.[15]

Britannia sailed from Piraeus on 14 October for Larnaca, where The Queen and Prince Philip joined on 18 October for CHOGM, which was held in Limassol where the Yacht berthed two days later. While Her Majesty attended the CHOGM conference His Royal Highness disembarked to fly to the Adriatic to visit some of the ships enforcing the UN's Naval blockade of the former Yugoslavia and attend the Trafalgar Night dinner on board the frigate HMS *London*. Back in Cyprus the Yacht provided Her Majesty with neutral territory so that she wasn't seen to be favouring either half of the island during the conference. As usual, The Queen granted a 20-minute audience to each of the Commonwealth leaders in her sitting room on board the Yacht. Prince Philip returned from the Adriatic on 21 October in time for the State Banquet held by The Queen for the Commonwealth leaders. As CHOGM was coming to a close, the first effects of an outbreak of salmonella were beginning to surface on board the Yacht. By the time The Queen and Prince Philip disembarked on 24 October, over 60 of the Yacht's company were suffering and it was quite clear that *Britannia* would be unable to continue with her programme until the outbreak was dealt with. As many as possible of those suffering from salmonella were sent to the RAF hospital at Akrotiri.[16] To contain the problem *Britannia* remained at anchor in Akrotiri Bay and was placed in quarantine. The cause of the outbreak was subsequently traced to a batch of Scotch eggs.

Thus, after five days at anchor, the Yacht was finally able to get underway for the Gulf but, because of the delay, *Britannia* had to steam at full power all the way to make up for the lost time, with the exception of her passage through the Suez Canal, where she had to comply with the slower mandatory speed limit. When she emerged from the canal the next day she resumed her high-speed passage and was able to maintain full power until she reached Dammam on the morning of 8 November. As the Yacht approached the harbour, FORY gave the order to reduce speed for the Yacht's entry into the harbour. The fact that *Britannia* was able to complete such a passage clearly showed that her engines were not worn out as some of her critics were trying to claim in the argument over her future. Admiral Woodard later remarked that if he had had to slow down at any point to allow either shafts or bearings to cool down he would not have been able to reach Dammam ahead of the arrival of The Prince of Wales. As it was the Yacht only arrived alongside a few hours before His Royal Highness rather than the usual couple of days. On the night of his embarkation His Royal Highness hosted a dinner that was attended by HH Prince Mohammed Bin Falid, who is a son of The King of Saudi Arabia and the Governor of the Eastern Province. The next morning His Royal Highness left the Yacht for his visit to Kuwait, while *Britannia* sailed to Abu Dhabi where The Prince of Wales re-embarked on 10 November. The second day of His Royal Highness's visit began with the welcoming of delegates to the Energy Seminar on board, before disembarking to continue his engagements ashore, which included a visit to the Dubi International Air Show accompanied by FORY. In the evening His Royal Highness concluded his visit with a dinner for HM Sheikh Khalifa. When the last of the guests had disembarked, His Royal Highness invited the officers for drinks in the Royal Drawing Room, where FORY presented him with a birthday card together with the two brushes and a paint scraper he had used during his first voyage in the Yacht in 1954.[17]

Twenty minutes after His Royal Highness disembarked from the Yacht on 12 November, *Britannia* sailed for Bombay, where she berthed three days later. During her four-day visit the Yacht was the venue for the signing of a number of important contracts worth a combined total of £1.5billion.[18] These contracts had been generated as a result of John Major's visit to India the year before. However, the Indian Government's high levels of bureaucracy means that the process of getting a contract signed can drag on for years, so the presence of *Britannia* imposed a firm deadline for these contracts to be signed. Thus quite a lot of Indian red tape was cut to speed up the negotiation process, resulting in the contracts being signed on the appointed date on board *Britannia* in the presence of the Foreign Secretary, Douglas Hurd and his Indian counterpart. Without this level of pressure it is quite likely that a number of those contracts may never have come to fruition, while others would have taken much longer to conclude. On 19 November *Britannia* began the voyage home via Aden, Crete and Gibraltar.

For the second year running the New Year began with a transatlantic crossing for the Yacht, with stops at Ponta Delgada and Bermuda for fuel, before reaching New York early on the morning of 10 February 1994. The Yacht's arrival coincided with an extremely cold spell of weather, as Admiral Woodard explains:

'As we came gliding into New York harbour the pilot said, "You're going to dock at Pier 88."

So I asked, "Where's that?" and he pointed. '"But hey, that's inland."

"No Admiral, that is ice!"

It was the coldest weather in a lifetime and the whole of the Hudson had frozen over. As we got into the ice and it broke up it was quite horrifying to look over the bridge wing and see huge great lumps of ice going past with red and blue paint on them. Then quite suddenly I heard a yelp that we were losing steam. The cooling water for the steam turbine generators goes through filters and the little chips of ice blocked the filter thus stopping the flow of cooling water. The generators shut down because they were about to overheat and we lost everything, the lighting, steering motors, fuel pumps, etc. There we were stuck in the middle of New York harbour with nothing. Then our sturdy little generator nicknamed "chitty chitty bang bang" lit up to give us some lighting and enabled us to re-flash the boilers. (This generator was believed to be the oldest seagoing operational diesel in existence and it had originally been fitted in 1943 as a propulsion engine in HM Submarine *Vampire*.) A Coastguard Cutter with an ice-breaking bow was despatched to clear a channel and we were manoeuvred into our berth where we froze solid for six days.'

The weather continued to deteriorate after the Yacht's arrival as snow began to fall heavily on 11 February, bringing New York's traffic to a stop and resulting in the closure of the city's three airports. This affected the Yacht's delicately balanced plans for the visit as people started to arrive early or late for events which began to merge into each other. Because of the travel problems people were also turning up direct from the airport with their luggage, which caused further problems as the Yacht was normally pushed to accommodate one coat per person for a 200-person reception. However, the Yachtsmen rose to the

Is Britannia *the first Royal Yacht to have its own snowman? The extremely cold spell of weather endured by the Yacht during her visit to New York provided an opportunity for FORY and the Master of the Household to build one on the Verandah Deck.*

(© British Crown Copyright / MOD)

challenge with guests being led to all sorts of strange places on board to make them happy. The very low temperatures also led to the cancellation of the Beat Retreat. During the rehearsal the temperature was −5°F and the brass instruments seized up because the moisture created when blowing into the instrument froze, thus seizing up the valves. The Director of Music, later Captain David Cole MVO RM, went to see FORY who wasn't initially convinced until Captain Cole arranged for a demonstration to show him the problem. However, Captain Cole was determined not to disappoint his guests so he decided to stage a 'Staircase' Beat Retreat. The display began with the RM Band coming down the main staircase in pairs in complete silence followed by the Director of Music who came to a halt at the bottom of the staircase. The Band then sounded a fan fare, followed by a march or local tune, before concluding with the national anthem. At the end of the ceremony the band then left via the main staircase to provide the signal for the guests to depart.

It was during this visit that a very well-known actress came on board and walked into the Royal Dining Room and said, "Gee that's really dowdy." She had been expecting to see an interior dominated by chandeliers and gold!

Once again the visit provided another clear example of the pulling power of Britannia, as the Supply Officer, later Captain N Wright LVO RN, observed:

'At the dinner concluding a very high level British Invisibles financial seminar chaired by the Governor of The Bank of England, Sir Edward George, the leader of the US delegation Mr William Donaldson, then Chairman of the New York Stock Exchange remarked that it was the first weekend he had spent in New York for years simply because his wife had said this was one dinner she wasn't going to miss! This was interesting because it underlined the fact that people wouldn't have stayed in New York for the weekend if the event had been held ashore in a major hotel.'

After six very cold days in New York the Yacht slipped to begin her passage back through the frozen expanse of New York Harbour which caused a new set of problems. As the Yacht slipped into the Gulf Stream the sea temperature rose by 14°F within 22 minutes leading to leaks in 74 pipes. The mess caused by these leaks, together with the dirt left by people coming on board in snow boots, meant that the Yacht's company had a steep slope to climb if the Yacht was going to be ready for The Queen and Prince Philip's embarkation a week later off Belize City. Needless to say the Yachtsmen pulled through, and by the time the Royal couple embarked on 22 February the Yacht was up to her usual high standards.

Two days later the Yacht weighed anchor for Grand Cayman, which turned out to be a very special voyage within the long and varied history of the Yacht. As Britannia steamed across the Caribbean on 25 February she joined the ranks of an elite group of ships when, in position 18° 46' North, 84° 45' West, she completed a million miles. To mark this rare achievement The Queen and Prince Philip went down to the Engine Room to attend a special ceremony where Her Majesty cut a red ribbon which had been tied between the throttles and then cut a cake baked for the occasion. As a more permanent reminder of the occasion all of the Yacht's company were presented with a certificate stating they were in the Yacht when she steamed through the million-mile barrier.

A day later the Yacht dropped anchor off George Town for the Royal couple's visit to Grand Cayman. As part of the Royal couple's programme ashore they visited the local museum, as Admiral Woodard recalls:

'We went into a small room and were met by the Curator of the Museum who was proud to announce that he was descended from the original inhabitants of the island. Prince Philip seized on this and said, "So your forebears were pirates?"

"Indeed they were, Sir, and I'm proud of it." The Queen then looked at the Coral Room while I joined Prince Philip to look round the Wreck Room. There we were greeted by another man who was pleased to announce that he was a direct descendent of the original islanders, so Prince Philip asked him if his ancestors were also pirates. Again, like the curator, this second man was proud to confirm that his forebears were pirates. Back home the tabloids had a field day with headlines such as "Prince Philip insults Cayman Islanders by calling them all pirates." Once again the press had whipped things up and missed the point. The islanders were actually very proud of their pirate heritage and in fact Prince Philip couldn't have been nicer to them.'

After a second day ashore on Grand Cayman the Yacht weighed anchor for the two-day visit to Jamaica, which was followed by the visit to the Bahamas, where the Tour concluded on 8 March when the Royal couple flew back to the UK. On her way back to the UK, the Yacht paid her last call to the RN Dockyard in Bermuda HMS Malabar, which was due to close on 1 April 1995.[19] Having made a further stop at Ponta Delgada, the Yacht berthed in Portsmouth on 23 March.

The next phase of the Yacht's 1994 programme centred around engagements in home waters. When the original long-term plans were being formulated back in 1992, the

Yacht was due to undergo a short refit in the middle of 1994. However, the prospect of *Britannia* being out of action during the commemorations to mark the 50th Anniversary of D Day was unthinkable so the date of the refit was postponed until the end of the year. In the meantime the Yacht's series of home engagements started with a visit to Southampton to act as the venue for the launch of the new Marine Safety Agency and the Coastguard Agency on 10 May by the Minister for Aviation and Shipping, Lord Mackay of Ardbrecknish. This was followed later in the month by a visit to Pembroke Dock and Swansea in support of The Prince of Wales who hosted events on board in aid of the Welsh Tourist Board, The Prince's Trust and the Welsh Development Agency. When the Yacht sailed from Swansea on 26 May she headed for Southampton where she was used by Prince Philip the next day to review a flotilla of ships and yachts which had gathered in the Solent for the Hampshire Remembers D Day Review. On completion the Yacht returned to Portsmouth, where His Royal Highness disembarked.[20]

The embarkation of Princess Margaret on 4 June began a remarkable couple of days for the Yacht where she played a central role within the commemorations to mark the 50th Anniversary of the D Day landings. As the day went

on The Queen, Prince Philip, The Queen Mother and The Princess Royal all arrived in Portsmouth ahead of President and Mrs Clinton who spent the night on board.[21] The following morning began with the Drum Head Church Service on Southsea common attended by the Royal party while HMS *Illustrious* led 14 warships out of Portsmouth Harbour to take up their positions at Spithead for the Fleet Review. Their sailing times were carefully calculated so that the ships passed the Southsea War Memorial during the Drum Head service to provide their own dramatic mark of respect. To reflect the involvement of the US forces in the Normandy landings the RN warships were joined for the review by the aircraft carrier USS *George Washington* and the last of the wartime Liberty ships *Jeremiah O'Brien*.

Meanwhile, in Portsmouth The Queen and Prince Philip returned to the Yacht to welcome each of the Heads of State and Government as they embarked for the Fleet Review. By the time *Britannia* sailed, her unique

The Yacht is surrounded by an armada of small boats as The Queen reviews the Fleet in the Solent which has gathered to mark the 50th Anniversary of the D Day landings.

(© British Crown Copyright / MOD)

gathering of VIPs included The King of Norway, Prince Bernard of the Netherlands, the Presidents of the USA, Poland, The Czech Republic, Slovakia, The Prime Ministers of Canada, Australia, New Zealand and the Defence Minister of Greece, as well as the British Prime Minister and Foreign Secretary. As *Britannia* passed the Southsea War Memorial at 1242 she was over flown by the first aircraft leading a 10-mile long flypast. Eleven minutes later the Yacht approached the first of the two review lines, followed by an armada of small boats whose wake turned the blue waters of the Solent into a choppy sea. At the head of the Fleet the two liners *QEII* and *Canberra* lay at anchor with their decks lined with veterans who waved at the Yacht as she approached. On completion of the review President Clinton disembarked to USS *George Washington* before the Yacht headed out of the Solent into the English Channel for the trip to France. On the way she was over flown by 18 RAF Hercules aircraft, en route to drop 1000 paratroopers in the vicinity of Pegasus Bridge. An hour later *Britannia* rendezvoused with an international flotilla for a wreath-

Large crowds turned out to watch the Yacht's voyage up the Caen Canal, including the site of the original Pegasus Bridge.   (© British Crown Copyright / MOD)

laying ceremony in the Channel that culminated with the flypast of a solitary Lancaster bomber which dropped a million poppies alongside the liner *Canberra* as a tribute to the men who died during the landings.

When *Britannia* arrived at Ouistreham Lock in the evening Admiral Woodard was faced with a difficult dilemma, as he explains:

'When we arrived there was a high cross wind blowing which normally would have ruled out our entry into the lock because we would be blown sideways as we entered. However, with all those VIPs on board and crowds along the jetty one had to make certain it wasn't possible. As we entered the funnel to the locks the wind just dropped away from 25 knots on the beam to about 7 knots in the lock which was a huge relief!'

Once the Yacht had berthed in Ouistreham Lock The Queen hosted a dinner for her guests before they disembarked. When the last of the VIPs had left, *Britannia* began the passage through the Caen Canal with the Royal Family assembled on the Royal Bridge from where they acknowledged the cheers of those gathered by Pegasus Bridge and the Café Goudree which was the first building to be liberated on 6 June 1944.[22]

Describing the following day's events, Sir Brian McGrath recalled:

'The Queen and Prince Philip were due to disembark at 1030 to join President Mitterand at the War Memorial and Cemetery near Bayeux where a large number of war veterans were assembled. As it was a cold, damp morning it was obviously important to arrive on time, as the veterans had been assembled early. Just when The Queen was expecting to disembark, a message came through that President Mitterand had been delayed an hour – and this was the first engagement of the day! I remember Her Majesty sinking into a chair in despair as the timings for the whole day's events were now at risk, which included the problem of a rising tide at Arromanches in the late afternoon. When we finally arrived at the Cemetery we made it quite clear to the veterans that it was not Her Majesty's fault that they were kept waiting so long in the cold and drizzle. By cutting time here and there during the day the march past by 6000 veterans did take place on the beach at Arromanches in the nick of time before the tide could engulf the marchers! One of the cuts agreed was the removal of the cheese course during the official lunch which was certainly a sacrifice by our French hosts especially as we were in Normandy!'

In the evening The Queen, Prince Philip and Princess Margaret returned to the Yacht before she began the passage back down the Caen Canal, escorted by the minesweeper HMS *Cottesmore* which was commanded by The Duke of York. Describing their arrival at Ouistreham Lock His Royal Highness recalled:

'We were due to go into the lock with the Yacht but this was changed at the last minute so we entered the second lock thus sitting opposite the Yacht and I remember having a conversation across the lock with The Queen. I had a piper with me from an Irish Regiment and The Queen shouted across, "Is that one of your Pipers?"

"Yes," I replied. '

"Well tell him, for God's sake play." So the piper was thunder struck to be asked to play by The Queen from another ship but he played happily away.'

Once the Yacht entered the English Channel, HMS *Cottesmore* steamed past before detaching from the Royal Squadron and being relieved by the destroyer HMS *Edinburgh* for the overnight voyage back to Portsmouth, where she berthed the next morning.[23]

Ten days later the Yacht sailed to Helsinki where she arrived on 21 June for three days of commercial duties. On the second day British Invisibles sponsored a Sea Day. The event was attended by the President of the Board of

Trade, Michael Heseltine, who joined to address the delegates before the Yacht sailed, as Admiral Woodard remembered:

'When Michael Heseltine arrived he asked me how long did we have from the gangway before we reached the reception?

"About a minute."

"Well you've got a minute to justify the Yacht."

So I stopped and said, "We've got much more than a minute if we don't walk but I believe the Cabinet have already met. I won't ask you now what went on but if you want me to justify the Yacht in a minute the best I can say is if you've got a goose laying golden eggs how stupid it is to let it die of starvation while you argue over who pays the feed!"'

The following day the Yacht undertook further commercial duties. When the last of the delegates disembarked, the whole of the Yacht's company were assembled in the Royal Dining Room to be addressed by FORY. Admiral Woodard began by reading verbatim the statement that was about to be made by the Defence Secretary, Malcolm Rifkind, in the House of Commons. The statement contained the news that *Britannia* would not be given another major refit and that she would be paid off in 1997.[24] Although the statement signalled the beginning of the end for *Britannia* it failed to answer the question of whether a replacement would be built. The Yacht's company greeted the announcement with a mixture of sadness and disbelief but they remained optimistic that the Government would make an early announcement about a successor. However, the failure of the Government to deal with the issue at this point led to a vacuum, which continued to cast a long shadow over the Yacht during her final years in service.

Despite the uncertainty caused by this announcement the Yacht's company still had a valuable job to perform. Thus *Britannia* sailed from Helsinki on 24 June and headed back across the North Sea for her visit to London, which began on 28 June with two days of commercial events moored in London's Docklands. From there she was moved up river to the Pool of London for further events, which included the reception hosted by the Lord Mayor of London to celebrate the centenary of Tower Bridge. This was followed on 1 July by a reception and dinner hosted by The Duke of York in support of The King George's Fund for Sailors (KGFS).[25] The event was the brainchild of Admiral Sir Brian Brown who became the Chairman of the KGFS when he retired from the RN. As a previous Deputy Supply Officer in the Yacht he had seen the effect that

As Britannia's commercial role continued to expand the Yacht also hosted trade events in London including this event in London's Docklands by Canary Wharf.

(© British Crown Copyright / MOD)

Britannia had in attracting important people to Sea Days. Admiral Brown thought that this effect would be very useful for generating awareness of the charity's activities, as he explains:

'The impact that the Yacht had on people was profound. From a charitable point of view she was a powerful tool that could be used in support of maritime charities. It was an aspect of the Yacht that was beginning to be exploited more successfully during her final years in commission to the great benefit of seafarers and their dependants in need. Obviously, the Yacht couldn't be used as a direct source of fund raising – one couldn't charge for tickets to a dinner on board. However the sort of people that we could invite who would snap up the tickets were the sort of people who would hopefully give us considerable support or be available to help if they were asked. We certainly received substantial sums of money from individuals after such events. I can remember one person saying to me while he was waiting to take the boat back to the shore, "Brian I would like to give you a donation for KGFS and I am going to send you a cheque for £25,000."'

At the end of another successful visit to the Thames *Britannia* sailed on the morning of 4 July and returned to her home port the following morning.

In a break with tradition the Yacht's attendance at Cowes Week at the end of July wasn't followed by the Western Isles Cruise because The Queen and Prince Philip were due to fly to Canada in mid August for the Commonwealth Games in Vancouver.[26] When the Yacht's company returned from their summer leave they began the preparations in earnest for the historic State Visit to Russia before the Yacht's departure on 3 October. On the morning of 15 October the Yacht entered the River Neva for the final stages of the voyage to St Petersburg. As the Yacht approached the Russian city the Yacht's company were given an insight into how rapidly the circumstances of the Russian Navy had changed from the height of the Cold War only a few years before, as Admiral Woodard remarked:

'All the warships of the Baltic fleet were draped with strings of washing. The ships' companies hadn't been paid for three months so their families were left with no alternative but to move on board as they were evicted from their rented homes. On the starboard side there were old submarines lying on their side with the hatches open filling up with the tide. While on the portside were old merchant ships which had rusted through and were flooding with the tide under rusty gantries. These ships encroached a long way into the navigable river it was a sad sight.'

When *Britannia* arrived in St Petersburg the Yacht berthed at the exact location where, 77 years earlier, the Russian cruiser *Aurora* fired her gun at the start of the Russian Revolution. To commemorate the event the embankment was re-named the embankment of the Red Fleet. Interestingly, before the Revolution it had been called the English Embankment because that was where the English church stood, as The Queen's Deputy Private Secretary at the time, Sir Kenneth Scott KCVO CMG recalled:

'When I travelled to St Petersburg for the reconnaissance trip I visited the Mayor (his assistant for foreign relations was Vladimir Putin – now the Russian President – who was helping with the arrangements for the visit). I said to the Mayor, "Thank you for this wonderful berth for *Britannia*. Before the revolution of course it was called the English Embankment. Wouldn't it be nice to call it that again?"

"What a good idea," said the Mayor. So by the time the Yacht arrived the embankment had reverted to its former name.'

During the passage to Russia the Yacht was joined by the Type 42 destroyer HMS *Glasgow* which had once been commanded by FORY. When The Queen embarked, *Glasgow* would formally take on the role of Royal Escort. So once the two ships had berthed *Glasgow*'s Commanding Officer, Commander R L Twitchen and his officers came on board to be briefed on the role of the Royal Escort by the Commander of the Yacht, later Captain H B Daglish LVO RN, as he explains:

'The brief covered the important aspects of doing the job because it was very different from their normal operational role not least that they were in many ways

The Yacht's Commander, Commander H B Daglish, meets the Commanding Officer of the Russian escort RNS Bespokoynyy as a group of officers from the Yacht are taken for a guided tour of the Russian warship.

(© British Crown Copyright / MOD)

going back to the ways of the "old Navy". This meant that they had to be very pukka about everything, which was different from the modern age where the greater emphasis was on getting operational and capable. However, the sailors reacted very well to it, because it was different, and there was a sense of honour, responsibility and pride in being The Queen's escort.'

On 16 October a group of officers from the Yacht were invited on board their Russian escort RNS *Bespokoynyy* for a guided tour – an act that only a few years earlier would have been unthinkable.[27] The *Sovremennyy* class destroyer had entered service in 1992 and was one of the Russian Navy's latest warships. As the group of British officers walked round they were taken back by what they saw, remarked Captain Daglish:

'In a capability sense the ship was very impressive, but it was very noticeable that the sailors had a very sullen, dejected look about them. While we were in the Engine Room I looked through a door and saw a sailor, sitting on a very hard metal seat, who was a picture of abject depression. When we left the Executive Officer who had been our host asked me, "What do you think about the cleanliness of my ship?"

This presented me with a problem because it was actually not very clean and rather rough so I bought a bit of time by saying, "Of course she is an operational ship and not to be compared with *Britannia* as they have very different roles." Commander Simon Lister, our interpreter, translated this while I struggled to think of something diplomatic. "But I admire what you achieve with the number of men that you have." In the boat back to the Yacht I turned to Simon and said, "I hope he didn't take offence."

He responded, "No he didn't, but he knew what you meant!"'

Three days later The Queen and Prince Philip arrived to begin their historic two-day visit to the former capital of Imperial Russia. On her arrival The Queen became the first British Monarch to visit the country since before the Russian Revolution which resulted in the murder Tsar Nicholas II and his family. Interestingly, both The Queen and Prince Philip are directly related to the Russian Imperial Family. On the second day of their visit the Royal couple visited some of St Petersburg's historical sites linked to its Imperial past, including the impressive Winter Palace, and the Fortress of Peter and Paul which houses the marble tombs of the Tsars of Russia. After their lunch with the Mayor at the Marinsky Palace the Royal

couple travelled to Piskaryovskoya Cemetery. There they joined President Yeltsin for a Remembrance Service to honour those who died during the German siege of the city in the Second World War. In the evening the short visit concluded with a State Banquet on board the Yacht for President Yeltsin which was followed by Beat Retreat and a brief farewell ceremony on the jetty.[28]

When the ceremony finished The Queen stepped back on board the Yacht and *Britannia* sailed as the first fireworks were fired from the opposite bank to provide a dramatic send off. The departure from St Petersburg presented FORY with his biggest challenge of the trip. The 2-knot current running down the River Neva meant that *Britannia* had to steam at a minimum speed of 8 knots to maintain steerage whilst negotiating a number of tight bends made more hazardous by a lack of navigation lights and various wrecks along the banks of the river. In an attempt to reduce the risk posed by the night-time departure FORY sent the Navigating Officer out in a motor boat the night before at the same time as *Britannia* would leave. The exercise proved very worthwhile, as Admiral Woodard recalls:

'When we sailed there were pitch black holes but we were able to fix our position using the various back lit bus stops and other features the Navigator had found the night before. We had a rather shocking moment because the pilot claimed to speak English but he didn't say too much. I asked him, "Have we got water to port?" We were coming up to a turn with a slight swing on.

He replied, "Dar dar."

Two minutes later the Commander came running on to the bridge and said, "Sir, you should know that the pilot has just come up to me and asked me which side is port!"'

Despite the drama the Yacht reached Helsinki the next day where The Queen and Prince Philip disembarked to fly home. Without *Britannia*'s presence in St Petersburg The Queen's visit would have been more difficult to arrange from the point of view of security. *Britannia* provided an important contribution to a very historic and successful visit by The Queen, which is sometimes overlooked because it was followed quite quickly by the visit to South Africa. A day later the Yacht sailed for Copenhagen for a four-day visit before returning to Portsmouth on 31 October.

Three weeks later the Yacht entered dry dock to begin the delayed refit, from which she emerged in the New Year in time to sail on 21 February 1995 for her second historic State Visit within six months. Before she sailed, the Yacht's company was joined by a BBC film crew who were making a TV documentary about the Yacht's 85th and final State Visit.[29] When it was completed the programme revealed many aspects of the Yacht's routine, from the meticulous preparation prior to the embarkation of The Queen and Prince Philip through to the lighter moments of life on board such as the inter-mess quizzes.

The Yacht reached South Africa on 17 March when she berthed in Simons Town to await The Queen and Prince Philip who arrived by helicopter two days later. That night the Yacht sailed for the overnight passage around the Cape of Good Hope. By dawn the distinctive profile of Table Mountain was beginning to emerge over the horizon as the Yacht headed towards Cape Town in the morning sunshine. As she entered harbour with The Queen's Standards flying it seemed unbelievable that this was the last time *Britannia* would be used for a State Visit. The impact of her arrival was clear for all to see as thousands of South Africans gathered around the port to witness The Queen's arrival. As Her Majesty stepped ashore to be greeted by President Mandela the assembled crowds all cheered – it was a truly remarkable moment in history.

Incredibly, this moment nearly didn't happen because, when the plans for this visit were being drafted, The Queen rejected the option of using *Britannia*. She felt that the cost of sending *Britannia* to South Africa for only four days of Royal duty would be prohibitive. However, FORY was able to persuade The Queen to reconsider her decision when he was able to present a programme of commercial events which could be organised off the back of the State Visit. These additional commitments suddenly transformed the viability of using the Yacht so The Queen readily agreed to her deployment. That morning's arrival not only confirmed the wisdom of using *Britannia*, but also The Queen's own judgement in deciding to press on with the plans for the State Visit despite the doubts raised by the Foreign Office over the timing. Although the Foreign Office was sure that President Mandela would be very polite and hospitable to The Queen, they weren't sure how the black South Africans would react. In the event their fears seemed over cautious because many of the South Africans remembered The Queen's last visit to South Africa in 1947 when she accompanied her parents on board HMS *Vanguard*. The Queen's arrival in Cape Town provided her with the chance to return to the city where, 48 years earlier, she had spent her 21st Birthday. It was the first time that the heir to the British Throne had come-of-age in one of the Dominions. To mark the event the young Princess had made a special broadcast dedicating herself to the service of the British Commonwealth and Empire. In addition to her solemn commitment, the speech contained a special message for the South African people when she said that even though she was 6000 miles away from where she was born she still felt herself to be at home. Seizing on this history the South Africans gave The Queen wherever she went, the welcome, not of a visiting Head of State, but as an old friend returning.

While The Queen and Prince Philip continued their programme inland, the Yacht sailed for Durban on the afternoon of 21 March, arriving there three days later. Despite the gloomy wet conditions a large crowd had turned out to see the Yacht sail into port. The Royal couple returned to *Britannia* in the afternoon ahead of that night's return State Banquet for President Mandela.[30] Once again the Yacht provided the right setting for the climax to another successful State Visit. During the visit the Foreign Secretary, later The Rt Hon. Lord Hurd of Westwell CH CBE, accompanied The Queen as her Minister in attendance. Explaining why he felt the Yacht provided the right environment for this type of major event Lord Hurd said:

'The Yacht had that balance between simplicity and formality which was extremely effective. The fact that The Queen and Prince Philip enjoyed their time in the Yacht clearly communicated itself. Foreign visitors felt that they were extremely privileged to be on board, but not in a grand way. There they were on The Queen's Yacht surrounded with things that were personal to her and they were being made to feel at home in a way which wasn't as grand as Buckingham Palace but was in a way even more remarkable. That and the Beating the Retreat by the Royal Marines worked very well.'

The following morning The Queen and Prince Philip stepped ashore to begin their final day of engagements. When they returned in the afternoon Admiral Woodard went to take his leave of Her Majesty as he approached the end of his time as FORY. When she received him in her sitting room The Queen rewarded Admiral Woodard by investing him with the KCVO. In the evening the Royal couple disembarked to attend a performance at the Durban Playhouse before going on to the airport to catch their flight back to the UK. About five minutes before The Queen and Prince Philip took off, the Yacht sailed for Cape Town to undertake four days of commercial events. On completion of the last event, *Britannia* slipped out of Cape Town and headed past the Cape of Good Hope for the fifth time that month, to arrive in Simons Town on 31 March. When *Britannia* berthed in the evening it signalled the end of Rear Admiral Sir Robert Woodard's seagoing career.[31]

Chapter Twelve

HISTORIC TIMES

Commodore Anthony Morrow CVO RN 1995–1997

In a break with tradition, the South African Naval Base at Simons Town provided the setting for the departure of the final Admiral to command *Britannia* and hold the position of Flag Officer Royal Yachts. Before he stepped ashore on 1 April 1995, to be taken into retirement in a horse-drawn carriage, Rear Admiral Sir Robert Woodard KCVO was relieved by Commodore Anthony Morrow RN. For Commodore Morrow it was his third appointment to *Britannia* having served as the Royal Barge Officer from 1965 to 66 and as the Royal Cypher Officer from 1976 to 78.

Commodore Morrow joined the Royal Navy in 1962 and after his first appointment to the Yacht he served in HMS *Eagle* and minesweepers in the Far East and Persian Gulf. He qualified as a Signals Officer in 1972 and after his second appointment to the Yacht he commanded HMS *Lindisfarne*, followed later by command of the Type 21 frigate HMS *Active*. As a Captain he commanded the RN's Communications and Navigation School before returning to HMS *Active* as Captain 4th Frigate Squadron. From there he became Assistant Chief of Staff Plans and Policy to the Commander-in-Chief at Northwood prior to being appointed in command of *Britannia*.

The appointment of Commodore Morrow was a historic event because it was the first time since before the First World War that the Royal Yacht Service had been commanded by an officer below the rank of Rear Admiral. *Britannia* had always been commanded by an Admiral because the role of FORY went beyond the normal responsibilities of a ship's Commanding Officer. First and foremost FORY was directly responsible for the personal safety of the Sovereign while embarked in the Yacht. As part of this duty FORY would exercise tactical command when the Yacht was being escorted by other ships. To avoid any unnecessary difficulties it was important that FORY was the most senior officer within the Royal Squadron, which meant that in practice he had to be above the rank of Captain. FORY was also a member of the Household and had full responsibility for the planning, as well as the execution, of *Britannia*'s programme. FORY was responsible for the selection, promotion, training and administration of those ratings who were part of the Royal Yacht Service. In the absence of the Royal Family, FORY was also required to take on a diplomatic role at times, which included the hosting of functions for members of foreign Royal families, presidents, prime ministers and high commissioners.

The decision to appoint an officer in the rank of Commodore to relieve Admiral Woodard stemmed directly from the 1992 defence review 'Options For Change' which reviewed the senior posts in all three services. Since *Britannia* joined the Fleet in 1954, the number of seagoing jobs held by Flag Officers had been reduced to just two appointments, including the position of FORY. In view of this trend, and the Government's drive to clip the defence budget wherever possible, the decision was taken to appoint a Commodore to head the Royal Yacht Service and command the Yacht when Admiral Woodard retired, thus saving £7000 per year. At the time of this announcement it was seen as a long-term decision because the question of whether *Britannia* would be replaced had not been settled. It was presumed that if a new Royal Yacht was commissioned she would be commanded by a Commodore. However, this long-term thinking wasn't clear to the outside world and there were many people who viewed the change in status with concern when it was announced in September 1994, as Admiral Woodard explains:

'Shortly after the announcement I received a letter from the Prime Minister of Dominica, Dame Eugenia Charles. She asked, "Why on earth this should be? What are the views of The Queen because she must be very disappointed." Dame Eugenia was also very concerned because the outward signs to her and others in the Commonwealth were that the appointment was a downgrading in the importance of the Yacht and perhaps there was a reason behind that.'

Despite these concerns, Commodore Morrow does not feel that he suffered any major adverse effects by not being an Admiral, as he explains:

'I do not believe that during my time in command of Britannia there were any difficulties because I was a Commodore. I have no doubt that had my position been one of an Admiral it might have made a slight difference from time to time. However, I tackled a number of problems throughout my time in Britannia when I had to deal with very senior people and always received the support this position deserved. For example, I successfully managed to argue for Britannia's programme to run to the end of 1997.'

Once the news of Commodore Morrow's appointment had been made public he was able to begin his preparations to take command. To reflect the change in rank, the title of Flag Officer Royal Yachts would disappear and be replaced with the term Commodore Royal Yachts which was abbreviated to CORY. This left the issue of what uniform Commodore Morrow would wear for ceremonial occasions. In 1994 the RN was moving towards the establishment of the substantive rank of Commodore to bring the service in line with both the Army and the RAF, as well as Britain's Allies. Previously, the rank of Commodore, which has been described as the most anomalous of Naval ranks, was a non substantive rank in the RN for senior Captains serving in particular jobs. When they completed their specific appointment, if they were not promoted, the officer reverted to the rank of Captain. Approval was given in 1824 for the introduction of two classes of non substantive Commodore and both grades continued to be used until 1958 when the designation of 1st Class was

dropped. Since then the uniform regulations had been changed by Admiral Sir Edward Ashmore who restricted the requirement for a full dress uniform to full Admirals, the Naval Secretary, the Defence Services Secretary and FORY. Because CORY would be expected to undertake the same range of duties as his predecessors in Britannia the Second Sea Lord approved the re-introduction of the ceremonial day coat for CORY with the shoulder straps for Commodore 1st Class. However, the two rows of gold oak leaves on the cap peak were not adopted from the uniform of a Commodore 1st Class.

Following discussion as to the most appropriate date when Commodore Morrow would take command of Britannia it was agreed that Admiral Woodard would stay for the State Visit to South Africa and be relieved by Commodore Morrow after The Queen's departure. He would bring the Yacht home to prepare her for the rest of

Britannia's final Commanding Officer, Commodore Anthony Morrow CVO RN.

(© British Crown Copyright / MOD)

the 1995 programme. The day of Commodore Morrow's arrival marked the beginning of a short maintenance period in Simons Town, as he recalls:

'I felt it was important for me to talk to the Yacht's company on the changeover day. I wanted to keep it brief because I knew that they would be wanting to get away for some well-earned leave during the maintenance period for which many of the Yachtsmen's families had flown out to see them. There was a sense of change, the Admiral had gone and now there was a Commodore. It was important to reassure them that with my arrival things were not going to change. With those opening words I dedicated myself to ensure that not only would *Britannia* have three honourable years of final service but together we would give her an appropriate, proper and proud send off when the time came to decommission her.'

The Duke and Duchess of Kent acknowledge the cheers of the crowds gathered along the banks of the Kiel Canal to see the Yacht.

(© British Crown Copyright / MOD)

The Defence Secretary, Malcolm Rifkind, hosted a lunch on board the Yacht for his opposite number in the South African Government on 10 April before *Britannia*'s departure for the UK. Despite the short notice of the request for this event it was important that the Yacht be available for such a function, not least because it would provide an ideal opportunity for the Defence Secretary to see the Yacht for himself. When the last of the lunch guests had disembarked, CORY was able to spend some time with the Defence Secretary, which provided a good opportunity to discuss the issue of *Britannia*'s future, as Commodore Morrow continues:

'The Defence Secretary clearly wanted to find out how we in *Britannia* saw things panning out with respect to her demise. He was able to see the excellent condition that *Britannia* was in not least that she was not a ship falling apart at the seams and that she still had a considerable amount of life left in her. Although I had only just joined the ship I felt very comfortable arguing the case for the Yacht and could justify what I was saying because I knew the ship well. I remember him asking me how long a life *Britannia* still had left. I made it quite clear that I felt she could continue in service following a refit for another five to seven years beyond 1997.'

Once Malcolm Rifkind disembarked, the Yacht began the voyage home, which included commercial events in Tema and Dakar, before the Yacht berthed in Portsmouth on 5 May.

At the end of May the Yacht sailed for Falmouth where she embarked The Queen and Prince Philip before sailing around Land's End and up to the Welsh Coast for their visit to Solva and Pembroke Dock on 1 June. The Yacht sailed to make the short overnight passage to the Severn Estuary for the following day's visit to Avonmouth, where the Royal couple left the Yacht. Three days later *Britannia* sailed for Portsmouth, arriving there on 6 June.[1] Nearly a fortnight later she left for Germany, where she arrived on 19 June to embark The Duke and Duchess of Kent in the Kiel Canal at Rendsburg. Their Royal Highnesses were attending the celebrations to mark the centenary of the canal's opening. In 1895 the Royal Yacht *Osborne* attended the original opening ceremony and the attendance of her successor a century later proved to be very popular with the German people. It was estimated that on 20 June about one million people turned out to see the Yacht at some point along the 30 kilometres between Rendsburg and Kiel where she arrived in the afternoon. As the Yacht approached her berth in Kiel several thousand people watched from the various vantage points while bands were playing on the quayside, including the band of the Royal Dragoon Guards. After a day of engagements in the Kiel area on 21 June Their Royal Highnesses flew back to the UK. Two days later the Yacht sailed for Dundee where she berthed on 26 June to support the visit by The Prince of Wales.[2] This visit included a dinner in support of the 'Locate in Scotland' initiative and a lunch in aid of the Scottish Tourist Board. Within an hour of the departure of His Royal Highness on 27 June, the Yacht sailed for Portsmouth.

At the end of July the Yacht crossed the Solent to anchor in Cowes Roads for the annual regatta. During Cowes Week speculation was again rife in the press about the future of the Yacht. The Government's continued lack of direction about the future of *Britannia*, and whether she would be replaced, created the right environment for sections of the media to speculate about what was happening. CORY had already had a number of meetings with officials from MOD and they were in the process of establishing what the options were before drawing up some firm plans.

'It was important to me that MOD knew what we were all talking about. Very few of the Civil Servants had any real experience of *Britannia* or knowledge of the ship so it was very important that they realised fully what was involved. I needed to take the opportunity to prepare the case to answer any number of questions. Sadly, we had some very unfortunate leaks at this stage about what was going on. The press were there hawking for decisions from the Government. During this Cowes Week there were headlines such as "Palace anger over sell off inventory issued by Whitehall". This was a foretaste of how things would progress. Everywhere we went there were questions about *Britannia*'s future, whether there would be a replacement and what would happen to the ship,' Commodore Morrow remarked.

At the end of Cowes Week the Yacht returned to Portsmouth on 3 August, for the Royal Family's embarkation the following day for the start of the Western Isles Cruise. Among those joining the Yacht before The Queen was Miss Sophie Rhys-Jones who had been invited on board for the first time by Prince Edward. The Palace was keen to ensure that she arrived discreetly so that her presence didn't provide the trigger for a great deal of speculation within the press. After all, the cruise was a private event and they wanted to keep it that way. The cruise followed very much the standard pattern but in magnificent weather. It included a meeting with The Princess Royal and Captain Laurence in their yacht *Blue*

Doublet. At the end of the cruise the Yacht berthed in Aberdeen on 14 August, where the Royal Family disembarked. Rather than proceeding to Portsmouth to start summer leave, the Yacht left Aberdeen that afternoon for the Pool of London for *Britannia* to play a key role in the commemorations to mark the 50th Anniversary of VJ Day. On the evening of 19 August 16 members of the Royal Family embarked prior to an impressive flypast of aircraft over the Thames which culminated in a salute by a lone Spitfire. After the evening's reception for veterans the guests gathered on deck to watch the fireworks display which stretched from Wapping to Westminster and was rounded off by four of the Yacht's Bandsmen sounding sunset from the upper span of Tower Bridge. Unusually, the weather was so hot that the Yacht's company went into 'whites' for the duration of the Yacht's stay in London. In addition to the ceremonial duties the visit provided the opportunity for further commercial events, including a Gulf Day Seminar organised by British Invisibles and chaired by the Governor of the Bank of England, Eddie George. Within an hour of The Queen and Prince Philip disembarking on 21 August, the Yacht sailed for the overnight passage back to Portsmouth where she berthed the next morning for the Yacht's company to begin their summer leave.[3]

A month later the Yacht left Portsmouth for an autumn deployment to the Mediterranean, which was built entirely around commercial commitments in Piraeus and Lisbon. On the return to Portsmouth the Wardroom were able to hold the annual Trafalgar Night dinner in the very waters where the famous battle had been fought 190 years earlier. A week after the Yacht returned to Portsmouth on 30 October, she entered dockyard hands for a short refit which lasted until the New Year.[4]

The Yacht sailed for three days of training at Devonport on 19 February 1996, before heading off across the Atlantic, via Ponta Delgada and Bermuda. Despite running through bad weather across the notorious Bermuda triangle the Yacht arrived off Palm Beach on 12 March only to find the port was closed to all shipping due to a severe current running across the harbour entrance and breaking seas over the bar. Thus *Britannia* spent the night at anchor off the coast waiting for the weather to improve before being allowed into Palm Beach the following morning. Two days later Prince Philip embarked after lunch to host a reception for supporters of The Duke of Edinburgh Award scheme, followed in the evening by a fund-raising dinner ashore for the scheme in the Breakers Hotel, before flying home the next morning. On 18 March the Yacht sailed for visits to Savannah and Baltimore, followed by Boston, where she arrived on 28

March. The Duke of York embarked on 31 March and the next day hosted a reception for the launch of a joint radio project between the BBC World Service and the US public broadcasting radio station WGBH. In the evening His Royal Highness hosted a further reception in aid of the British Olympic Association, before flying home on 2 April. After further receptions in aid of the Welsh Tourist Board and the British American Business Consulate, the Secretary of State for Wales, The Rt Hon. William Hague MP, hosted a dinner for the Welsh Development Agency.[5] Describing why he felt the use of *Britannia* for this type of event provided British industry with a major advantage over its competitors, William Hague said:

'It was a very special place to be invited to. Corporate chief executives in America wouldn't have known me, or what the Secretary of State for Wales did. Nonetheless, they all came including some who flew into Boston from the mid west just for the evening so we easily filled every available place. They would not have done that for a Secretary of State for Wales if we had held the meeting in a prestigious hotel or the Consulate General's house. When they had arrived I gave a speech in the Royal Drawing Room about why they should invest in Wales and then they were shown around the Yacht. This was followed by a dinner in the Royal Dining Room at which I gave a further speech and this was followed by one from the Mayor of Boston. This was another example of the Yacht's drawing power because the Mayor of Boston wouldn't have normally included a visiting minister from another country within his programme especially as it coincided with election time in Boston. His attendance was useful because it gave added credibility to the occasion. For the guests it was a very memorable occasion. I was convinced that the Yacht was a great asset in encouraging inward investment into Britain when you were trying to convince people overseas about the nation's qualities. To add to that some of the status and atmosphere of Britain as seen by the world, which *Britannia* did, I thought helped to make a very powerful combination. I certainly met potential investors into the UK which I wouldn't have been able to have done without the use of the Yacht. It was part of the Government's successful campaign of attracting investment in the UK. The Yacht allowed a more subtle form of salesmanship because if we gathered the same people together in a hotel or Embassy the building wouldn't have been of interest so we would have to talk the whole time about the purpose of the evening. The Yacht enabled us to give them the same message but do

it in a way that they would enjoy which is usually a more effective method. It was also extremely cost effective in terms of a minister's time because to meet the same number of people on an individual basis would take a couple of weeks whereas if we could get them together on board the Yacht for one evening it was more effective.'

Five days later the Yacht sailed from Boston to head north for her sixth and final journey up the St Lawrence. A voyage up the St Lawrence is one of those events that taxes any ship handler and this passage proved to be no exception with every conceivable kind of weather from ice, to snow, to rain and cross winds. However, the Yacht arrived at Toronto as planned on 15 April for that afternoon's reception for British Invisibles. After a further two days of receptions the Secretary of State for Scotland, later the Rt Hon. Lord Forsyth, hosted a dinner on 18 April to support moves to gain inward investment for Scotland.

'*Britannia* was invaluable for this kind of event. We wanted to have the top business leaders in attendance and an invitation to dinner on the Royal Yacht is seldom refused particularly where spouses are included. The evening was a huge success and when the band of the Royal Marines performed Beat Retreat on the quayside even the press officers were in tears. Fighting for inward investment is a hugely competitive business in which getting the investors attention is crucial. *Britannia* gave us an edge over everyone else. I could think of many arguments in support of *Britannia* but this experience alone would have been enough to persuade me that the Yacht was an invaluable resource for our country and ought to have been refitted or replaced.'

Having successfully completed another round of commercial engagements, the Yacht began the passage back down the St Lawrence on 22 April, which provided a baptism of fire for the new Navigating Officer, Commander Jeremy Blunden, who joined while the Yacht was berthed in Toronto. Once again the Yacht's transatlantic crossing was dogged by bad weather. After a brief stop in Ponta Delgada on 3 May to refuel, the Yacht resumed her voyage home and, over the next three days, the weather continued to deteriorate. At lunchtime on 6 May the Yacht was hit by two exceptionally large waves in quick succession which swamped the forecastle while she was steaming at 16.5 knots. With a gap of just 15 seconds between waves there wasn't enough time for the water to drain away from the forecastle before the second deluge of water landed. The pressure of the water on the bulwarks, as the bow came back up after the second wave, caused a 16-foot section of the starboard sacrificial bulwark to be ripped off. Although *Britannia* looked somewhat the worse for wear when she made her way into Portsmouth on 7 May her arrival went unnoticed.[6]

Two days later the Yacht hosted a meeting for the Chiefs of Staff in Portsmouth while the Dockyard carried out the repairs to her bulwarks, which involved the use of riveting on one of HM ships for possibly the last time. On 21 June the Yacht sailed for the Isle of Man to embark The Prince of Wales three days later for his historic visit to Northern Ireland. Having crossed the Irish Sea overnight, the Yacht berthed in Belfast on the morning of 25 June for the first time since The Queen Mother's visit to the province in 1958. The visit came at a difficult time for Northern Ireland as the peace process was being tested to the limit. The IRA's 17-month cease-fire had come to an end on 9 February 1996, an hour before the organisation detonated a bomb at Canary Wharf in London. Only 10 days before His Royal Highness reached Belfast, the IRA had blown up the centre of Manchester. Despite these atrocities His Royal Highness's visit went ahead and included a reception and dinner on board to attract inward investment to Northern Ireland. That night the Yacht made a floodlit departure for the overnight voyage to Portrush. The following morning His Royal Highness disembarked in the Barge, before the Yacht began the passage up the narrow River Foyle to berth in Londonderry for that evening's reception in aid of the Northern Ireland Tourist Board hosted by the Prince. During the course of the visit CORY discussed *Britannia*'s future with the Northern Ireland Secretary, Sir Patrick Mayhew, who was accompanying His Royal Highness. Like the other Government Ministers he had spoken to, Commodore Morrow found that Sir Patrick Mayhew was supportive of *Britannia*'s retention or replacement.

'That sentiment was typical of what we were seeing at the time. It was very hard to come to terms with the lack of decision while giving leadership to one's people in the Yacht. As always the Yachtsmen deserve huge credit for managing all this – another example of what they had had to tolerate and accept in the very long life of this great ship,' remarked Commodore Morrow.

After two remarkable and highly successful days in Northern Ireland, His Royal Highness disembarked on 27 June to fly back to the British mainland, while the Yacht sailed later in the day for Portsmouth.[7]

Once back in Portsmouth preparations were made for a short visit by The Queen Mother who joined the Yacht in

Commodore Morrow escorts The Queen Mother as she embarks in the Yacht for the last time.

(© British Crown Copyright / MOD)

Portsmouth on 5 July shortly before she sailed to Marchwood for Her Majesty to launch the restored RAF rescue launch HSL102. The meticulous restoration of the 64-foot wartime HSL102 had taken an estimated 40,000 man hours to complete and within a few hours of her launching she was able to perform a high speed pass down the starboard side of the Yacht off Fawley. By then Her Majesty had returned to the Yacht and she was heading towards Falmouth for The Queen Mother's visit the next day. A busy visit culminated in a reception on board and the RM Band performing Beat Retreat on the jetty in front of 500 spectators. On 7 July the Yacht sailed from Falmouth back towards Portsmouth which provided an opportunity for Her Majesty to have a final walk around the Yacht and talk to the Yachtsmen before she arrived in Portsmouth the next day. Although The Queen Mother was only on board for a few days, the visit was organised as a result of her conversation with CORY during the Royal Family's visit to the Castle of Mey as part of the Western Isles Cruise in 1995. Her Majesty enquired about 'Dear Britannia' to which CORY said that it would be wonderful if she could make another voyage in the Yacht. He saw that in the programme for 1996 there would be an opportunity for a brief visit which would enable the Queen Mother to make what would probably be her final visit to Britannia.[8]

After a short trip to Amsterdam in mid July for two days of commercial events attended by The Duke of Kent the Yacht sailed across the Solent at the end of July for Cowes Week. Although the full 1997 programme had yet to be confirmed, it was already clear that Britannia's 1996 visit to Cowes was almost certainly going to be her last. Commodore Morrow explained that 'it was very much a traditional Cowes Week in terms of the guests who attended. However, there was a tremendous feeling of sadness that this was going to be her last appearance. My abiding memory was the strength of feeling of farewell to Britannia.' On the morning of 7 August it was time for the Yacht to take her leave of Cowes when she slipped from the buoy and executed a tight turn to the west, before turning again to begin a ceremonial steam past Cowes. It seemed as though all of Cowes had turned out to say farewell to the Yacht with an escort of at least 200 small craft accompanying Britannia. As she passed the Royal Yacht Squadron a 35-gun salute was fired to represent Britannia's 35 visits to Cowes. Prince Philip, Prince Edward and Prince Michael of Kent acknowledged the tremendous send off from the Verandah Deck.[9] Later in the day The Queen joined the Yacht in Portsmouth for the start of the Western Isles Cruise. When the Yacht returned to Portsmouth on 19 August she underwent a short maintenance period a head of her final major deployment in the New Year.

When the options for the deployment to the Far East were being examined, Commodore Morrow hoped that it would be possible for Britannia to undertake a final circumnavigation of the world. He felt this would be the most appropriate way for the Yacht to leave the international stage, providing of course that all the Royal and commercial commitments could be met. Britannia had, however, already visited the USA in the first half of 1996, so it would be unlikely for further Royal visits to be planned there for the beginning of 1997. Without a vital US visit, it became necessary to concentrate upon building a programme around engagements in the Middle East and India, for which there was tremendous support for both Royal and commercial duties, before going on to make the Yacht's first visits to Japan and Korea.

Britannia's final year in commission began on a very uncertain note with the Government showing no signs of making a decision about either her future, or whether she would be replaced. Despite this continued state of limbo the Yacht's company carried on and completed the final preparations before the Yacht sailed on 20 January 1997 amid great interest from the media. Two days later, having just crossed the Bay of Biscay, CORY received signals in the morning from both Commander-in-Chief Fleet and Buckingham Palace to inform him that the Defence Secretary, Michael Portillo, was going to make a statement in the House of Commons. That afternoon, just as the Defence Secretary arrived at the despatch box to deliver his statement, CORY addressed the Yachtsmen. He began by reading Michael Portillo's announcement, which set out the Government's intention to build a new purpose-built Royal Yacht to replace Britannia. The new Yacht would be funded by the Government, built in a British shipyard, manned by the RN and fly the White Ensign. In addition to her Royal role the new Yacht would have the firm secondary role of promoting the UK's economic interests. It was hoped that the new Royal Yacht would be commissioned in time for The Queen's Golden Jubilee in 2002. Not surprisingly, the Yachtsmen were thrilled by the news, which they had been waiting to hear for two and a half years. Suddenly, they could look forward to a future beyond the end of 1997 and prepare for a new era in the long and distinguished history of British Royal Yachts. The statement also clarified the future of Britannia by confirming the decision to decommission her at the end of the year and that she would not be sold to a new owner for private use. However, the Government would be prepared to consider proposals for a prestigious use of Britannia within the UK, providing that she could be maintained in good condition.

Otherwise, the Government felt it would be better to scrap *Britannia* rather than allow her to deteriorate.

Within 24 hours, Michael Portillo's announcement turned out to be the opening shots in the Battle of *Britannia* which would rage until the end of the year. Neither the Leader of the Opposition, Tony Blair, nor the senior members of his Shadow Cabinet, had any direct experience of *Britannia* so they failed to grasp the importance of the Yacht's contribution to the nation, both diplomatically and economically. Instead they viewed the Government's announcement as a golden opportunity to score short-term political points in the run up to the General Election which had to be held by the middle of May. Sadly, the Government failed to learn from history and examine how the construction of *Britannia* had been approved. In spite of announcing the building of *Britannia* in the run up to the 1951 General Election, Clement Attlee had avoided the risk of it becoming a political issue by gaining the support of the opposition leaders *before* an announcement was made. The Conservative Government made a critical error of judgement that gave the Labour party the freedom to oppose the funding of a new Royal Yacht and turn it into a major election issue which proved to be popular with the voters.

While the politicians argued over whether a new Royal Yacht should be built and who was going to pay for it, the Requirements Working Group was formed in MOD to produce the detailed operational requirement for the new Royal Yacht. Commander John Prichard, who had served in *Britannia* as the Senior Engineer under Rear Admiral Sir Paul Greening, was appointed to lead the group. Two other sub groups were formed, the Design Working Group at MOD Abbey Wood for ship construction and engineering aspects, and the Complement Working Group from the Directorate of Naval Manpower to determine the size and composition of the complement. In addition a third sub group dealing with the aesthetic

Prince Philip and Prince Edward watch the tremendous send off given to Britannia *from Cowes. In addition to the large numbers of small boats that turned out to escort the Yacht many people lined the shore to watch* Britannia's *final exit from Cowes Week.*

aspects of the design and overall appearance was formed using civilian expertise in design and fitting out of passenger ships and large yachts. The project was expected to take five years to produce the replacement for *Britannia* with the new Yacht being commissioned in time for The Queen's Golden Jubilee Fleet Review at Spithead on 26 June 2002. Once in service the new Royal Yacht was to be capable of undertaking all of the duties performed by *Britannia* based on the 1991 'Indicative Design' for a Royal Yacht.

The 1991 design had been prepared amid great secrecy by a team from Bath. Unfortunately, this team did not include any naval personnel, let alone any one with previous *Britannia* experience, or a representative from Buckingham Palace. This quickly became apparent when Commander Prichard examined the design, which was woefully inadequate. The 1991 design was smaller than *Britannia* with a length of 90 metres, a Yacht's company of just 50 and accommodation for a Royal party of only 20. Among the design's many omissions there wasn't even accommodation for the RM Band, who were expected to fly out from the UK to join the Yacht for each period of Royal duty. The team from Bath had been completely fooled by the dropping of the requirement to embark the Royal Family for long ocean passages. They missed the point that the Yacht's busiest times were always when she was in harbour, when a relatively large Yacht's company was required to perform all of the tasks associated with a typical Royal programme. In contrast, the embarkation of the Royal Family for long ocean passages introduced only a slightly higher workload for the Yacht's company over their standard duties when at sea. The team from Bath also proposed other dubious ideas to help reduce the Yacht's company, such as the use of contract caterers for state banquets and trade days. Although the idea was financially attractive it ignored issues such as the quality of the food and of course the security aspect of having to vet all of the people who would wait on The Queen and another Head of State. Having reviewed the 1991 design and its shortcomings Commander Prichard realised that a larger, more capable design would have to be produced if it was to meet the broad requirements that had been set out by the Government. As Commander Prichard began his work he soon discovered that the project had its critics inside MOD, as he explains:

'It was evident from the first day that there was considerable antipathy to the project within MOD, including some senior Naval Officers. The Civil Servant allocated to the project from RP Navy (who held the purse strings and therefore had a major influence) said to me on the first day that not only did he not believe that there should be a new Royal Yacht, but he did not believe in the Monarchy! Not a good start!'

Meanwhile, *Britannia* continued to head east having already visited Malta and Hodeida in Yemen, before arriving in Aden on 7 February. That night the Yacht's football team found themselves the centre of attention when they arrived at the city's football stadium for a friendly game against the local team. When they walked on to the pitch they were amazed to find a crowd of 8000 football fans who had paid to see the game. It was soon apparent that the local side included some members of the Yemeni international football team. Flattered but undaunted the Yachtsmen managed to achieve a level score at half time. As they stepped back on to the pitch for the second half the Yachtsmen were somewhat taken back to find the rest of the game was being televised. The concluding half proved to be more disappointing for the Yachtsmen as the heat began to take its toll and the Aden team finished ahead at 7 goals to the Yachtsmen's 2. However, its not every sailor that goes for a kick about with international footballers and finds himself on live TV! On the second day of the visit the Yacht hosted a trade day, which was attended by the President of Yemen – significantly on the day Ramadan ended.[10]

The following morning the Yacht sailed for the Gulf for a busy round of commercial duties in Dubai, Doha and then Kuwait City, where The Prince of Wales embarked on 21 February for his visits to Kuwait, Saudia Arabia and Qatar. Describing what he felt the Yacht brought to this and other visits, The Prince of Wales remarked:

'It made such a difference to have the Yacht in which to hold receptions rather than having a reception in either a hotel or a British Embassy. Whenever she arrived somewhere it was a major event and gave the visit something extra which is hard to define, particularly in financial terms. However, she created a tremendous amount of goodwill and her Yacht's company were marvellous ambassadors for the country wherever they went.'

His Royal Highness left the Yacht in Doha on 26 February to fly on to Bangladesh for his visit. A day later the Yacht sailed for the next round of commercial duty in Pakistan.

Once the Yacht completed her transit of the Straits of Hormutz on 28 February, she took up station alongside RFA *Bayleaf* for a routine RAS. With about five minutes to go before the RAS was completed, the Yacht experienced difficulties which prevented the rudder from being turned more than 10 degrees to port. This resulted in a minor collision with *Bayleaf*, as Commodore Morrow explains:

'This was a pure accident and no one's fault. It was caused by misalignment on the steering that conspired after a period of time to prevent the Yacht from being steered accurately. The conditions at the time of the collision were calm and benign, so much so that when the Yacht came in at a very narrow angle to the side of the tanker very little damage was done. Superficially, the amount of damage looked much worse than it actually was. Clearly, the repair work was going to be important but the damage would not affect the Yacht's ability to remain at sea nor would it affect the planned programme.'

Britannia reached Karachi on 2 March as planned, where the initial repairs were completed to enable her to continue with the hectic commercial programme without interruption in Pakistan, India, Thailand and Malaysia. Once the programme of commercial engagements in Singapore City was completed she entered Sembawang ship repair yard for a planned maintenance period which included further work to complete the repairs to the damage caused by the collision with *Bayleaf*.

The period in Sembawang provided an opportunity for CORY to fly back to the UK to discuss outstanding issues which needed to be dealt with for the rest of 1997, including the autumn programme, the decommissioning, the future of *Britannia* and the new Royal Yacht. One of the risks whenever the Yacht was away for long periods was that there was no one left in the UK to argue the case for the Yacht's interests. Therefore Commodore Morrow felt that it was necessary to return at this time and discuss these issues with the appropriate departments to determine the best way forward notwithstanding the timing of this visit coinciding with the immediate aftermath of the General Election and the defeat of the Conservative Government. While the issue of *Britannia* and her replacement had become key election issues it was too soon to see exactly how the new Labour Government were going to deal with these. Meanwhile, *Britannia* sailed from Singapore on 6 May under the command of the Commander arriving in Bangkok on 9 May where CORY rejoined the next day.

Two days later *Britannia*'s round of commercial duties resumed with two contract signing ceremonies in the Royal Drawing Room followed by a dinner for British Invisibles attended by the Deputy Prime Minister of Thailand and the Minister of Industry. Unfortunately, the well-documented but very typical amount of debris in

When The Prince of Wales disembarked in Doha he inspected this guard of honour.

(© British Crown Copyright / MOD)

The Governor of Hong Kong, Chris Pattern, looks back at Hong Kong as he comes on board the Yacht in-between the handover ceremonies during the final day of British rule in the colony.

(© British Crown Copyright / MOD)

Bangkok's harbour caused major problems for the engineers as this blocked the inlets. While they managed to just about keep the generators going, the air conditioning system experienced a total failure resulting in temperatures reaching an uncomfortable 40°C! Despite these unpleasant conditions, the visit was a great success and everything returned to normal when the Yacht sailed for Manila on 14 May, enabling the engineers to return to normal water circulation.[11] After a brief stop at Manila the Yacht's commercial programme concluded with visits to Japan and Korea, before heading to Okinawa where the Yacht's company completed preparations for their historic visit to Hong Kong. As Commodore Morrow recalled:

'*Britannia*'s first ever visit to Japan was a huge success. Princess Alexandra and Sir Angus Ogilvy were able to use the Yacht for their planned visit while a very demanding commercial programme was undertaken and coincided with the Royal programme whenever possible. The Korean visit was commercial but again of significant value in furthering British interests in this important industrial nation.'

Early on the morning of 23 June, *Britannia* met up with HMS *Plover* of the Hong Kong Squadron, which escorted the Yacht into Hong Kong's Victoria Harbour to commence the final week before the end of British rule in the colony. Five days later The Prince of Wales embarked at the start of his visit, representing The Queen at the events to formally return the colony to China. On the second day of his visit His Royal Highness hosted a dinner which was attended by many of the VIPs who had flown out for the next day's handover ceremony, including the US Secretary of State, Madeline Albright, the President of Fiji, Sir Kiamese Mara, and former British Prime Ministers, Baroness Thatcher and Sir Edward Heath. The Prime Minister, Tony Blair, flew out to Hong Kong for the handover day itself and was received by His Royal Highness on board the Yacht after lunch.[12] When the Prime Minister emerged from his meeting with The Prince of Wales there was an opportunity for Commodore Morrow to give Tony Blair a brief tour of the Yacht, as he recalls:

'There was only just time for a very brief visit so I was keen that Mr Blair could at least see the Engine Room while we discussed the Yacht's general condition. I informed him that *Britannia* was about to begin her longest and fastest continuous passage that night and that I had no doubts about her timely arrival in Portsmouth on 1 August. I felt that at least he left *Britannia* that afternoon better informed about our issues than when he arrived to call on The Prince of Wales.'

Just over an hour after the Prime Minister disembarked, the last British Governor of Hong Kong, Chris Patten, and his family embarked briefly before leaving again in the evening for the farewell ceremony held in the new purpose-built stadium adjacent to the Yacht. While the farewell events got under way ashore the Yacht's company prepared for that night's departure, as Commodore Morrow explains:

'The departure from Hong Kong was really just another event in the life of *Britannia*. There was nothing from the Yacht's point of view that was different to a state farewell with The Queen embarked. For over 40 years *Britannia* had done very much the same with arrivals and departures firmly in the public eye at key moments in history such as the State Visit to Cape Town in 1995. At my standard leaving harbour briefing which I carried out with Commander (N), I drew the Yachtsmen's attention to the fact that this particular departure was very much going to be in the public eye and televised across the world. We were not going to break any records in leaving Hong Kong: we just needed to do it properly, quietly and calmly.'

Shortly before midnight the final handover ceremony began in the Convention Centre. After The Prince of Wales delivered his speech, the Union Flag and the Hong Kong Flag were lowered in the colony for the last time. This was followed by the playing of the Chinese National Anthem and the raising of the Chinese Flag together with the Flag of the Special Administrative Area, as Hong Kong was now termed by the Chinese. At 0022 His Royal Highness and the former Governor of Hong Kong embarked in the Yacht to complete the British withdraw-

al from the former colony. The timing of *Britannia*'s departure had caused a certain amount of uncertainty with the authorities in Hong Kong because the Chinese wanted to ensure that the Yacht would sail the moment The Prince of Wales and Chris Patten embarked. They found it hard to understand that it could take up to half an hour for the Yacht to leave the wall dependent upon the time taken for the removal of gangways, cables and lighting. When the time came, everything went smoothly, enabling the Yacht to sail at 0045 as she was taken gently off the berth by two tugs. As the Yacht sailed away from the jetty the RM Band were up on the Royal Deck where they had erected a PA system to carry the music as far as possible, playing 'Jerusalem' and 'Rule Britannia'. Once clear of the jetty the Yacht took up her position at the head of the Royal Squadron to lead HMS *Chatham*, HMS *Peacock*, HMS *Starling*, HMS *Plover* and RFA *Sir Percival* proudly out of Hong Kong watched by the eyes of the world. Soon the bright lights of Hong Kong faded over the stern as the squadron headed out into the night en route to Manila.[13].

Later that morning, when darkness had given way to the grey murk of daylight, the Yacht met up with the 17 ships of the RN's Task Group Ocean Wave '97 who were operating off Hong Kong under the command of Rear Admiral Alan West DSC. The Task Group had formed up in two columns to allow the Yacht to pass between them. As the Yacht did so The Prince of Wales and the former Governor watched from the Verandah Deck. His Royal Highness was given three cheers by the Ship's company of

The morning after! HMS Illustrious leads the RN's Task Group Ocean Wave '97 out of the gloom to meet up with the Yacht. The event provided an interesting contrast to the emotive events of the night before when Britannia *took The Prince of Wales and the former Governor of Hong Kong, Chris Pattern, away from Hong Kong on completion of the handover ceremonies.*

each ship as the Yacht steamed past. On completion of the steam past, seven of the warships detached to pursue their individual programmes, while the remaining warships accompanied the Yacht overnight as she steamed to Manila, where she arrived on 3 July to disembark The Prince of Wales and the Patten family. A few hours later the Yacht sailed out of Manila to begin her fastest passage to the Suez Canal. During the voyage to Port Suez King Neptune paid his final visit to the Yacht as she crossed the equator for the last time on 11 July at 0930.[14] When the Yacht anchored at Port Suez 10 days later Commodore Morrow was able to send the following signal to the First Sea Lord, Admiral Sir Jock Slater.

The return to the UK from the Far East provided a last chance for King Neptune to pay his customary visit when the Yacht crossed the Equator on 11 July.

(© British Crown Copyright / MOD)

'Be pleased to inform the Members of the Navy Board that on anchoring in Suez Bay this morning *Britannia* has completed the longest continuous and fastest passage of her 43-year service. In company with RFA *Olna* from passing Singapore, the passage from Manila to Suez at 6673 nautical miles was completed at an average speed of 15.6 knots. Joined by HMS *Fearless* on the equator at 78° East, the group conducted three triple ship replenishments of fuel, the last of which on the 20 July is believed to be the final such replenishment with all steam-powered ships in the Royal Navy. For *Britannia* this has been but part of her fast return passage from Hong Kong to Portsmouth (over 10,000 miles) which will see her at sea for every day of this month: another first. Once completed, this will be a remarkable achievement. With more to come it has been a singular pleasure to witness the pride and professional manner with which this passage has been undertaken.'

Once the Yacht passed through the Suez Canal on 22 July she resumed her passage towards her final port of call outside UK waters arriving at Gibraltar on the morning of 28 July for a seminar organised by British Invisibles. As usual the guests were welcomed by the Master of the Household, Major General Sir Simon Cooper, who reminded guests that this was the last such event to be held on board the Yacht. Describing the atmosphere during that evening's event and what he felt British industry was about to lose with the imminent passing of the Yacht, The Hon. Peter Benson, Chairman, International Privatisation Group, Coopers & Lybrand, remarked:

'It was in a way depressed because we recognised it was the end of an era and that we were losing something we would never get back. The Yacht was the most fantastic draw in that people we could never get without the Yacht always accepted an invitation for a trade event on board. I had known a number of trade days held around the world in hotels where we couldn't get an audience but we never failed with *Britannia*. It was the Royal Yacht; it was something utterly special and unique. It had a quality, an ambience from the beginning and we got the audiences as a result. In terms of benefits it wasn't a case that I gave a talk about the set of skills I was selling and then someone came up to me afterwards saying please sign a contract – it didn't work like that normally. It was much more about name recognition. For example, someone would come up to me some time after a trade day saying that we had met at an event on board the Yacht and that they thought we could work together in various areas. We lost something very special by giving her up. The short sightedness of politicians as to such things is quite remarkable at times.'

On completion of the evening's reception the RM Band Beat Retreat in front of 1000 spectators before the Yacht sailed at 2300 amid a spectacular farewell fireworks display launched from the harbour breakwater.[15]

Four days later the Yacht steamed up Spithead and into Portsmouth just as CORY had predicted when he spoke to the Prime Minister on board in Hong Kong. When she berthed in the Dockyard the Yacht had completed a remarkable deployment which had seen her undertake 28 visits to 17 countries and host over 100 Royal, commercial and diplomatic events. It was a fitting way for Britain's most travelled and capable Royal Yacht to bow out from the international stage. However, this was not quite the end of the story because six days later the Royal Family embarked for the beginning of their traditional Western Isles Cruise. During the course of the 11-day cruise 19 members of the Royal Family spent time on board the Yacht. Despite everyone knowing that this was the last time the Royal Family was going to enjoy a pri-

vate cruise in the Yacht it was nonetheless a happy time. As usual the Yacht headed round the west coast of Scotland on an ad hoc basis anchoring off secluded beaches for the Royal Family to go ashore for barbecues and long walks. A final Royal concert party took place much to the complete enjoyment of the Royal party. There was also the traditional stop off Scrabster for the Royal Family to call on The Queen Mother at the Castle of Mey and another splendid fireworks display before the Yacht reached Aberdeen on 17 August where the Royal Family disembarked for Balmoral. Two days later the Yacht returned to Portsmouth for the Yachtsmen to take their summer leave ahead of the UK Tour in the autumn.

While the Yacht had been in the Far East new doubts had been raised about both *Britannia*'s future and that of the new Royal Yacht following the Labour Party's election in

The final Western Isles Cruise began as normal with The Queen meeting some of the Yachtsmen's families on the quayside in Portsmouth before Her Majesty embarked in the Yacht.

(© British Crown Copyright / MOD)

By October 1997 MOD had made good progress with its own design for a future Royal Yacht. This design incorporated many of the lessons learned through experience in Britannia *and had the potential to produce a Royal Yacht that would stand the test of time.*

(© British Crown Copyright / MOD)

May. During August the press carried stories about the Government considering various schemes to refit the Yacht for further service but no firm announcements were made either way thus helping to fuel the air of uncertainty. At the same time MOD continued to evaluate the various proposals that were submitted by organisations hoping to preserve *Britannia*. By August MOD had reduced the 30 proposals, that had been received at the beginning of March, to a list of just six organisations which had presented credible plans. To help these organisations move their ideas forward CORY showed representatives from each organisation around the Yacht during the summer leave period to enable them all to begin their work from a common base line.[16]

Despite the change of Government MOD continued its work to produce the design for a new Royal Yacht. By the beginning of October the team had prepared an initial design for a Royal Yacht of 104 metres, manned by a Yacht's company of 125 (including the RM Band) with accommodation for a Royal party of 34. The reduced Yacht's company was possible thanks to the incorporation of modern machinery and surveillance systems. It proved

difficult to significantly reduce either the Supply Department or the Seaman Department as their respective workloads remained largely unchanged from that experienced in *Britannia*. However, the 1997 design did correct one of *Britannia*'s major shortcomings by increasing the range of the new Royal Yacht to 6000 miles, compared to *Britannia*'s 2000-mile range, thus eliminating the requirement for an accompanying RFA tanker on major deployments. The 1997 design also included a Conference Room with the latest presentation facilities capable of taking 100 delegates that fitted neatly below the enlarged Verandah Deck which was capable of taking a light helicopter. Crucially, the 1997 design looked like a Royal Yacht, unlike many of the private designs that had appeared in the press over the previous few years, some of which looked like overgrown 'sunseekers'. While many of these designs were innovative, they had been proposed by people who had been misled by the term Royal Yacht. The 1997 design was different because, like *Britannia*, it had the presence of a ship which was important if she was going to create a sense of occasion whenever she made a ceremonial entry into port to begin a State Visit. Although the external appearance was far from finalised it had the makings of a profile that would continue to look elegant in a further 40 years. After all, this was a key ingredient of *Britannia*'s success. Even after 43 years *Britannia*'s profile did not seem out of place in the modern world. She looked elegant and distinctive – not dated.

Initial estimates suggested that the 1997 design could be built for £80 million, including a full outfit of stores and spares. This figure could have been significantly reduced if the companies supplying equipment were allowed to advertise that their equipment was installed in the Royal Yacht.

However, having considered the Royal Yacht issue since taking office, the Labour Government finally made its mind up and announced on 10 October that there would not be a new Royal Yacht, nor would *Britannia* be refitted. This statement finally brought the subject of *Britannia* to a close. While the news came as little surprise to the Yacht's company, who had seen their hopes raised and dashed on countless occasions, it was still a major disappointment to them. While Tony Blair's Government had taken the final decision on both *Britannia* and her successor, the demise of the Royal Yacht lies principally with the previous Conservative Government who could have dealt decisively with the issue in 1994. Although the standing of the Royal Family had taken a pounding in the eyes of the general public during the early 1990s, the

building of a new Royal Yacht could have been clearly justified at that time. Around 1994 *Britannia*'s programme included a number of high profile events within home waters, such as her participation in the Battle of the Atlantic commemorations off Liverpool in 1993, and the commemorations of D Day in 1994. These, coupled with the historic State Visits to Russia and South Africa, as well as her growing economic role, clearly demonstrated the excellent value and need for building a new Royal Yacht and could be used to counter the poorly informed arguments that the Royal Yacht was merely an extravagance enjoyed by the Royal Family at the tax payers' expense. Instead the Government was divided on the issue. According to John Major's autobiography the main opposition towards building a new Royal Yacht came from Chancellor Kenneth Clarke who felt that such a move would backfire and damage public support for the Royal

The Queen and Prince Philip photographed for the last time with the entire Yacht's company.

(© British Crown Copyright / MOD)

Family. By failing to show clear leadership on the issue John Major, who states in his autobiography that he was a supporter of the Royal Yacht, allowed the issue to drift unguided for two and a half years. During this period the issue became clouded as the debate moved on from whether there should be a new Royal Yacht to how the construction and running of *Britannia's* successor was going to be funded. When the Conservative Government finally made up its mind to order the new Royal Yacht it did so in the worst possible circumstances by failing to consult the Opposition and announce its decision in the run up to a General Election. Whilst being incredibly short sighted, the reaction of the Labour party was unsurprising and virtually sealed the fate of the new Royal Yacht before the issue could become the focus of a more reasoned and bipartisan discussion.

In addition to dismissing all of the options to provide a Royal Yacht beyond the end of the year, the Government also announced the six options being considered in the search for a new role for *Britannia* once she paid off. This list was subsequently extended to include the ideas put forward to display her on the Manchester Ship Canal. The other proposals included a bid by her home port of Portsmouth to berth her close to HMS *Warrior* and a submission from Glasgow to place her in the grade A listed No. 3 Govan Dry Dock as an example of Clyde shipbuilding. There were also three separate bids to preserve her in London, as well as a proposal to exhibit her in Leith. With the confirmation that *Britannia* was going to be decommissioned, the Admiralty Board advised that she should die with dignity and be scrapped. It was a view shared by many who had served in the Yacht who did not wish to see a ship renowned for her immaculate appearance suffer an undignified fate by slowly deteriorating. This view was subsequently reinforced by The Princess Royal and *Britannia's* designer, Sir John Brown, who both felt that *Britannia* should share the same fate as her illustrious namesake and be scuttled. Explaining her views The Princess Royal remarked:

'Because *Britannia* was so special and in that way personal it was a travesty to have her hanging about. I know the public say, "oh no we should be able to look at her." Well that is a fair argument but if you are asking for my opinion ships shouldn't have to suffer that level of indignity!'

With her naval career drawing to a close, *Britannia* set out from Portsmouth on 20 October to begin the final operational stage of her long life with a very important Tour of the UK. Describing the background to this final Tour, Commodore Morrow said:

'From my early discussions with the Navy it was felt that if she went to Hong Kong that would be the end. They argued that the budget did not allow for *Britannia* after August because they had accepted that we would do Hong Kong, come back for the Western Isles Cruise and then finish. I questioned this view because the original statement said that *Britannia* would be taken out of service at the end of 1997. That meant December. I felt that there was no point having *Britannia* sitting in Portsmouth still in full commission from September to November when she could still be usefully employed. I had put my proposals forward to The Queen that *Britannia* could be available for an autumn tour of the UK before her decommissioning took place in December. With the Yacht out of the UK for most of 1997 it would naturally be most fitting to complete her service in this manner.'

The Tour was organised so that the Yacht would complete a clockwise circumnavigation of the UK as she visited eight major ports. Members of the Royal Family would join the Yacht for most of the stops beginning with The Princess Royal in Devonport. This was followed by the embarkation of Prince Edward in Cardiff, and a short visit to Belfast, before steaming up the Mersey to Liverpool, where Princess Alexandra and The Duke of Kent would embark for separate events. From there the Yacht headed north to make an emotional return on 31 October to the river of her birth. The Princess Royal, together with her husband Captain Laurence, embarked in the evening to begin four days of public engagements in Glasgow. As Her Royal Highness observed, the visit made a big impact on the city:

'It underlined the quality and care with which she was built as well as the feelings in Glasgow about her. Practically everyone who came aboard asked why is she going? I suppose many people hadn't stopped to think about her until she was going and they didn't think about the role she was playing until she was going. Unfortunately due to the way in which the system works it was too late by then to ask such questions.'

On the third day of her visit to Glasgow the Yacht's 96-year-old designer, later Sir John Brown, returned to his creation for the first time since she left John Brown's shipyard in 1954 and met Her Royal Highness. Describing his feelings about seeing the Yacht again after so many years, Sir John Brown commented:

'I was quite impressed by the condition in which she had been maintained. The decks had been beautifully kept. When she left on 3 November a small group of us went to the point at the John Brown shipyard where she had been built to watch her leave the Clyde for the first time. As she passed Commodore Morrow saluted us by a sound of her horn. It was sentimentally very touching.'[17]

Having steamed around the north of Scotland, the Yacht headed south, calling at Aberdeen and Newcastle for further Royal visits, before arriving in the Pool of London on 13 November. The following day The Queen, Prince Philip, and The Prince of Wales embarked for a lunch attended by the serving Chiefs of Staff as well as former Chiefs of the Defence Staff and former First Sea Lords. Among the distinguished gathering were Admiral of the Fleet, Lord Lewin and Admiral Sir Jock Slater who had both served in the Yacht. During the rest of the London visit the Yacht was used to accommodate members of the European Royal Families who were attending the events to celebrate the Golden Wedding Anniversary of The Queen and Prince Philip. Once the last of the Royal guests had disembarked on 21 November the thoughts of the Yacht's company turned towards *Britannia's* final voyage, which would begin that night. From about 1630 crowds began to gather along the Embankment and across Tower Bridge waiting with anticipation for the moment when *Britannia* would slip the two mooring buoys and begin her floodlit passage down the River Thames.[18]

The moment to slip finally came an hour later as the paying off pennant was hoisted, as Commodore Morrow explains:

'Naval tradition required the flying of a paying off pennant on the last Sunday in harbour before decommis-

As part of Britannia's *valedictory Tour of the UK she visited the east coast port of Newcastle.*

sioning. That was always going to be difficult because of the publicity surrounding the Yacht and where she was going to be as well as the sense of it all. So we decided that we would leave London flying our paying off pennant and enter Portsmouth the following morning with the pennant flying. The design parameters were that it should to be one and a half times the length of the ship plus the number of years in commission in feet. This meant that the resulting pennant would have been a considerable length so we had decided it would be more sensible to make it the length of the Yacht – 412 feet. It was hoisted just before sailing but after the most dramatic thunderstorm over London. It was an evening charged with emotion with large numbers of people watching in disbelief paying their last respects to Britannia. We had a quiet night steaming towards Portsmouth, a subdued evening. I had a wander around the mess decks meeting the Yachtsmen as we all reflected on the sadness of this final night at sea.'

The following morning dawned bright and sunny as Britannia met up with ships off Portsmouth, including the Type 42 destroyer HMS Southampton wearing the flag of

Britannia's seagoing career comes to an end as she enters her home port of Portsmouth for the final time on 22 November escorted by the destroyer HMS Southampton.

(© British Crown Copyright / MOD)

Commander-in-Chief Fleet, Admiral Sir Michael Boyce KCB CBE. Despite being the end of November a large number of private boats turned out to give Britannia a superb aquatic welcome as she returned to Portsmouth for the very last time. As she approached the harbour the numbers of boats continued to increase while Ridley's Round Tower at Southsea was packed with large numbers of people paying their farewell respects. The Yacht entered harbour at 1055, when she was over flown by a Lynx, Sea King, and Sea Harrier of the Fleet Air Arm as well as a BAe146 of the Royal Squadron. Once Britannia was in the harbour, she turned and Commodore Morrow brought her alongside South Railway Jetty. At 1135 he gave the order to ring off main engines. That was it: Britannia's seagoing career was over after 44 years having steamed 1,087,623 miles. Without doubt everyone involved just could not believe this day had arrived and that Britannia's service was finally at an end.[19]

Chapter Thirteen

UNCHARTED WATERS

Decommissioning and Subsequent Preservation

With *Britannia*'s seagoing days at an end it now looked as though 1997 was going to finish as it had begun for the Yacht with a huge question mark over her future. With just one day to go before her decommissioning, the Government announced on 10 December that five of the seven bids to preserve her had been eliminated. This meant that *Britannia* would escape the scrapman's blowtorch and she would end her days in either Manchester or Leith.

The Queen is piped on board the Yacht for the last time to begin the day's events to mark the decommissioning of Britannia.   (© British Crown Copyright / MOD)

Despite the press frenzy to resolve the future of the Yacht, when the moment actually came to conclude her service as a Royal Yacht, *Britannia* was given the kind of send off usually reserved for a prominent statesman or Head of State. Looking back on this treatment Commodore Morrow remarked:

'It was a very great tribute to the Yacht and those who had served in her and everything that she stood for. The fact that the day was given very positive television coverage with tributes appearing in the press said something that I believe journalists could never say. Much

The decommissioning day began with members of the Royal Family visiting the various messes. Here Prince Philip talks to some of the officers in the Wardroom.

of the press had been so miserable in its criticisms of *Britannia* over the years, yet in the end they felt that there really was something very special about this ship and that was their tribute.'

Early on the morning of 11 December the media gathered in force at Portsmouth Dockyard to record the day's events, beginning with the arrival of the Royal Family led by The Queen and Prince Philip who embarked in *Britannia* soon after 1100. Fourteen members of the Royal Family travelled to Portsmouth for the paying off ceremony – clearly underlining the strong personal bond between the Royal Family and the Yacht. The only notable absentee was The Queen Mother who did not want to see the Yacht pay off.

Shortly after their arrival on board, the Royal Family split into three groups to walk round the Yacht and say good-bye to the Yachtsmen personally. On completion of their tour the Royal party adjourned to the Royal Apartments for lunch where they were joined by The First Sea Lord, Admiral Sir Jock Slater and Lady Slater, The Secretary of State for Defence, the Rt Hon. George Robertson and Mrs Robertson, former FORYs and their wives as well as the widows of former FORYs. By the time the first members of the Royal party disembarked after lunch to witness the paying off ceremony, the two stands on the jetty were full with about 2200 former Royal Yacht Officers and Yachtsmen together with their families. Around the country millions watched live on television as

The Queen was piped ashore for the last time at 1501 before taking up her place in the Royal Box for the start of the decommissioning service.[1]

The service was essentially based on a typical Sunday service held on board the Yacht when she was at sea and was conducted by the three principal Naval Chaplains, namely The Chaplain of the Fleet, The Venerable Simon Golding QHC, The Principal Chaplain of the Church of Scotland and Free Churches, The Reverend Dr Charles Stewart QHC Bsc BD Mth and The Principal Roman Catholic Chaplain, The Reverend Monsignor Noel Mullin QHC VG, as well as CORY. The Royal Marine Band provided the finale with their Beat Retreat ceremony culminating in the Ceremony of Sunset. For this CORY left his place in the Royal Box to take up position to salute *Britannia* as the Flag of the Lord High Admiral, the Union Flag and the White Ensign were lowered for the last time at 1537. Thus from that moment onwards she was no longer in commission and would be known simply as *Britannia*. The only visible reminder of her former status was the Royal Standard, which continued to fly from the main mast as The Queen was still present. However, the Royal Marine Band had one last surprise for everyone as they brought the service to an end, as Captain Cole explains:

'The Drum Major and I marched up to The Queen and saluted her and turned. Coming away the Yacht was on our right and normally we would have marched straight off. However, as a Band we had talked about what we wanted to do next. We marched off and halfway down the Band struck up "Auld Land Syne" and we saluted the Yacht. We hadn't told anyone not even CORY – it was our tribute to the Yacht.'

Although the press highlighted The Queen and The Princess Royal both shedding tears during the ceremony they weren't the only ones, as Dick Field, who had retired from the Yacht as a Fleet Chief Petty Officer, recalls: 'when the Band played that final tune it got to all of us and if the press had swung their cameras around they would have caught another 2000 former Royal Yacht Officers and Yachtsmen doing exactly the same thing. It was the worst day of our lives.' Lord Fellowes continues, 'It was a very moving occasion because everyone was saying good-bye to something they all loved, from The Queen downwards.'

The Queen visits the Chief Petty Officers mess.

(© British Crown Copyright / MOD)

Although the ceremony was in many ways a very sad occasion for those present it was also an opportunity to reflect with pride on the achievements of 44 years of service. These feelings were perhaps best summed up by The Queen and Prince Philip in their farewell message to the Yacht's company when they said:

'Together with members of my family, Prince Philip and I join you today to pay tribute to *Britannia* and give our thanks to all who have been part of her Company. Looking back over forty-four years we can all reflect with pride and gratitude upon this great ship which has served the country, the Royal Navy and my family with such distinction. *Britannia* has provided magnificent support to us throughout this time, playing such an important role in the history of the second half of this century. Steaming over one million miles she has proudly carried out over seven hundred Royal visits at home and overseas as well as numerous highly successful commercial programmes. Her achievements are a great testament to those who designed and built her and to those craftsmen and artisans who have main-

tained her with such dedication over all these years.

'In recognising *Britannia*'s marvellous service, we pay particular tribute to the Officers and Royal Yachtsmen who have served in her. My family and I extend our heartfelt thanks to all these men for their unfailing loyalty, dedication and commitment to the Royal Yacht Service. While many of the present Royal Yacht's company will return to the Royal Navy to continue their naval service and others come to the end of their service, we wish you every success in your future endeavours. We would also wish to thank the wives and families who have quietly but strongly supported the Royal Yacht over the years and often during the periods of long absence.

'It is with sadness that we must now say good-bye to *Britannia*. It is appropriate that with this final event she bows out in the style which is so typical of the manner in which her business has always been conducted.'

Once the ceremony was complete the Royal Family went for a very informal walkabout mixing with former Yachtsmen and their families before taking tea with them in one of the adjacent covered buildings. Since *Britannia*'s arrival nearly three weeks beforehand these buildings had been specially prepared for this event by the Yachtsmen. Later that night Rear Admiral Sir Robert Woodard took a final look round his former command, as he recalls:

'I walked around her on that evening and she was cold. She was as gleaming as ever but cold and empty. There was a Mary Celeste feeling about it. Once a Ship's company has left a ship it doesn't have a soul. The life of a ship is the Ship's company and that was why *Britannia* was so special. It was extraordinary to walk ashore and feel that was the last time – good-bye *Britannia*.'

At the beginning of the following week the process of preparing *Britannia* for disposal got underway in earnest. The phased reduction of the Yacht's company began immediately and *Britannia* was moved by tugs into No. 3 Basin on 16 December[2] so that she could be de-stored and de-fuelled. Normally, the operational commanding officer of an HM ship would have left quite quickly but Commodore Morrow elected to stay on to supervise the handover. The First Sea Lord granted permission for his broad pennant to continue to fly from the fore mast despite *Britannia*'s change in status. Three days after the cold move to No. 3 Basin all of the galleys were shut down for the last time with the Wardroom having had their last meal together as a mess at lunchtime.[3] When the main Christmas leave expired on 12 January 1998 the final 130 Yachtsmen who had been living on board *Britannia* began to move into accommodation in HMS *Nelson*. The administrative staff also left *Britannia* to use the four portakabins alongside as their offices to co-ordi-

By the end of February 1998 the last members of the Yacht's company had finished the de-storing process. Thus their duty was over and Commodore Morrow signed the Yacht over to the Disposal and Reserve Ships Organisation witnessed by the Naval Base Commander, Commodore Iain Henderson, in the Royal Dining Room.

(© British Crown Copyright / MOD)

Commodore Morrow says farewell to the final members of the Yacht's company as he leaves Britannia *for the last time as her Commanding Officer.*

(© British Crown Copyright / MOD)

nate the final weeks of activity. During that first week the de-storing continued with the return of items such as bedding, galley equipment and trophies.[4] In the last week of January the fuel tank cleaning was finished before they were filled with fresh water as ballast and all the on board facilities were closed down including the fire fighting services[5]. By the first week of February the Royal Apartments had been completely emptied and the clean-ing parties began to work through *Britannia*.[6] All too quickly the handover day approached and on 23 February the handover rounds began at 1000. CORY and the Naval Base Commander, Commodore Iain Henderson CBE ADC RN inspected *Britannia* finishing in the Royal Dining Room at 1035 where they signed the documenta-tion to transfer responsibility of *Britannia* to the Disposal and Reserve Ships Organisation. Commodore Morrow and the remaining Yachtsmen had completed their duty and thus at 1055 Commodore Morrow left *Britannia* for the last time having symbolically turned off the power to *Britannia* and thrown the keys into the basin.[7]

For the next six weeks *Britannia* awaited her fate in Portsmouth Dockyard until George Robertson finally announced on 8 April 1998 that the Forth Ports bid to berth her in Leith had won. Explaining his decision in an interview that evening with Kit Fraser for BBC Radio Scotland George Robertson said:

'I had to make a difficult decision between two very close schemes, one could say a perfect orange/a perfect apple because they were very different but both very good but Leith got it on two marginal grounds. One is that they'd had a slightly more imaginative scheme involving the use of some of the state rooms for very special occasions and secondly because Leith has got that ocean-going tradition that fits in with *Britannia*'s million mile background and of course, for centuries it has that Royal tradition of yachts and ships that have brought Royal families over these centuries into Edinburgh. On both these grounds, we believe that this is the right decision for both the preservation and the presentation of what is actually a national treasure.'

Describing his reaction to the news and the work that now lay ahead Forth Ports' Property Director, Terry Smith said:

'Although we had been prepared for the possibility that we could win it was impossible to prepare for a moment like that. *Britannia* is such a national asset with so much history that I felt a very heavy weight of responsibility when the announcement was made. I also felt a great level of pride that a small Scottish company had been able to put forward such a bid and be successful and it was beyond belief. We now relished the opportunity to carry out our plans and I felt it was important that she should be opened to the public as early as possible with a target of 15 to 20 weeks after the transfer of ownership. There then followed a period of intense activity not least putting all the legal work in place such as the formation of a charitable trust.'

As part of this work a Board of Trustees had to be formed and their choice was based on their areas of expertise rather than their ability to open doors. It was important to the success of *Britannia*'s preservation that the Board looked credible and would be accepted by both the public and Buckingham Palace. Viscount Younger was approached to become the Chairman of The Former Royal Yacht *Britannia* Trust. As a former Secretary of

State for Scotland and Defence Secretary he had a wealth of background knowledge which would prove very useful to the Trust especially in its early days. When Viscount Younger accepted the position he did so on one condition as he recalls:

'I said that I would accept on the condition that they would agree to a credible naval input to what was done which in turn would mean that there should be a naval component in the Board and ex Yachtsmen in the working crew. This was important so that when we said for example, go and polish a port hole they would know how to polish a port hole. This they readily agreed to.'

This in due course resulted in the appointment of Rear Admiral Neil Rankin CB CBE as the Naval Trustee. During his time in the RN Admiral Rankin commanded the aircraft carrier HMS *Ark Royal* and was later appointed as the Flag Officer Portsmouth. Explaining why he felt the preservation of *Britannia* was, in the end, a positive move, Admiral Rankin said:

'I think an advantage of having *Britannia* open to the public is that they can now appreciate that the Royal Yacht was not the luxury vessel they assumed the Royal Family were enjoying at their expense. Most people who visit express astonishment at the austerity of the Royal accommodation and the modest fitting out of the ship; the most impressive aspect of the Royal Yacht was her immaculate presentation, the efficiency of her operation and the dedication of her Yacht's company. Whenever I visit *Britannia*, I speak to those going around her; very few of them ever appreciated how much she actually did for Great Britain in terms of trade and promotion and now, having learned, view the vessel in a new light.'

To provide advice on the care of historic paintings and artefacts on board *Britannia* the Director for National Galleries in Scotland, Sir Timothy Clifford was also asked to become a Trustee. Terry Smith and Edinburgh's Lord Provost, The Rt Hon. Eric Milligan, completed the line up of Trustees. Discussing the challenges that he felt the new Trust would have to face Viscount Younger remarked:

'The biggest challenge always was and still is the maintenance. On a ship maintenance is everything and it requires a lot of hard work. *Britannia* had a pretty large crew for her size, which meant she was kept pretty well perfectly. Therefore, this is going to be a perpetual battle. The second challenge was how far should we alter her to comply with her new role as a spectacle and in so doing depart from her previous role as an active ship.

It was rather painful to do but one really had to accept that she was now going to be a spectacle rather than an active ship. We had to decide to what extent sentiment, ourselves, and ultimately the Palace would be prepared to agree to certain things taking place.'

As part of their early priorities Terry Smith's team had to begin discussions with The Queen's Private Secretary, Sir Robert Fellowes, to establish which items of furnishing would be made available, as Lord Fellowes explained:

'Everyone was conscious that if she was going to be preserved and shown off she must have a core of what was originally there to make an honest presentation. While The Queen and Prince Philip took some of the things that were very personal to them which they owned they allowed enough to stay to provide a good impression of what was there.'

Another issue that had to be addressed was how *Britannia* was going to be moved from Portsmouth to Leith. Forth Ports had hoped that it would have been possible for *Britannia* to make the voyage under her own power. Sadly, a number of practical issues made this impossible. First, *Britannia* had been disabled during the necessary disposal period. Secondly her fuel tanks had been emptied and filled with water to preserve her stability, which would have necessitated work to clean the tanks before they could be refuelled. Finally, the men needed to man her for the journey had been dispersed since her decommissioning. The only option left open was to tow her to Leith

where work was already underway to prepare for her arrival and subsequent display. The biggest part of this work was the construction of a purpose-built £1.25 million visitor centre which was designed by Sir Terence Conran and Campbell & Co. of Edinburgh.

Less than a month since the announcement of her fate, *Britannia* was formally handed over by Mike Robinson of the Disposal Sales Agency to Terry Smith of The Former Royal Yacht *Britannia* Trust at 1220 on 1 May 1998 at Portsmouth Dockyard. As part of the package the Trust had purchased all of the spares and stand alone stores for *Britannia* which were held at various locations around the country. While they didn't have to purchase the spares they saw it as a good investment towards *Britannia's* long-term preservation – not least there were many unique items which couldn't have been acquired from anywhere else. That afternoon *Britannia* was moved off her lay up berth inside No. 3 Basin into the entrance lock by MOD tugs. She was then taken in tow by the German tug *Fair Play* as she was eased out of the Dockyard for the last time.

The decision to use a German tug for the tow attracted a lot of criticism in the press but Forth Ports had little choice other than to use a foreign tug without incurring delays to their programme. Expanding on the reasons for this decision Terry Smith said:

'We had gone out to the European market to find the best tug available for the tow. We had tried to book a British one but they were all booked up a long way in

The beginning of a new era in Britannia's *life as Terry Smith (right) of The Former Royal Yacht* Britannia *Trust accepts the Yacht on behalf of the Trust from Mike Robinson of the MOD Disposal Sales Agency.*

(© British Crown Copyright / MOD)

The lifeless hull of Britannia *leaves Portsmouth under tow for Leith.*   (© British Crown Copyright / MOD)

advance so we booked the German tug *Fair Play*. The crew were very good and the voyage went like clockwork.'

Despite attempts to keep the departure as low key as possible word soon got round Portsmouth that she was about to leave and about 1000 people gathered around the Round Tower to see her off. The sight that greeted them was very different from her final arrival just six months before when she had been surrounded by a flotilla of yachts and motor boats while her RM Band continued to play and her long paying off pennant gently fluttered in the breeze. As she left Portsmouth for the last time to begin a new life the mood was very different. She was now plain *Britannia*, the powerless empty hulk – a dead ship. As Terry Smith explains he didn't feel this was the right time to try and get maximum publicity:

'The paying off ceremony had been a very moving event and we wanted to keep the tow from Portsmouth as low key as possible and get her into Leith to start the restoration work in earnest. Since the decommissioning the maintenance had been kept to the minimum and we felt that extensive exposure at that stage would have created a lot of disappointment.'

For the next five days *Britannia* made her way slowly up the east coast of the UK towards Leith reaching a top speed of no more than 10 knots at times. For safety reasons the tow had to be 'a dead tow', which meant that nobody was on board during the voyage to Scotland.

Instead, Terry Smith joined the crew on board *Fair Play*. Describing the passage he said:

'On the tug there wasn't a great deal to do other than look out and watch *Britannia*, which was very solitary. Over the five days we received a number of messages of goodwill from the various Coastguard units and local shipping. It was decided to use a 600-metre hawser between *Britannia* and the tug. Thus she was so far behind that at times it looked as though she was making her own way north. At times depending upon the prevailing conditions she was abreast of the tug. At night there were moments when the effects of the moonlight made it look as though the lights had come on. It was moments like these that were very moving and the tug crew felt this as well. Coming out of the straits of Dover we encountered very rough weather as the winds reached Force 8 at times and there was the possibility that we would need to seek shelter in the Thames Estuary. However, when the time came to make the decision everything looked fine so we decided to press on. As we passed the Bass Rock there was a beautiful sunrise to herald the start of *Britannia*'s last day at sea.'

Soon the isolation of the 560-mile passage north was broken by the appearance of press boats and a helicopter which came out to record *Britannia*'s arrival at her new home port on 5 May. A small welcoming ceremony was held to mark the occasion before she was placed in dry dock on 8 May to begin her £2.5 million conversion into a tourist attraction.

The coming months witnessed a period of intense activity as everyone worked hard to ensure that she was ready to receive her first paying visitors on 19 October. To ensure that those involved in *Britannia*'s preservation achieved a high level of accuracy and authenticity with her presentation, Commodore Morrow was invited by Terry Smith to advise the preservation team. Thus over the coming months until she opened to the public he became a frequent visitor to Leith. Because *Britannia* was considered locally as a prestige project, companies were prepared to pull out all the stops and thus deadlines that normally would have been impossible were met. The project manager for the refit was Iain Jones who first saw *Britannia* shortly after she was placed in dry dock. Talking about his initial impressions when he saw her he said:

'I thought what a great pity that she had been reduced to this. She still had a certain amount of majesty about her and I was greatly thrilled to have the opportunity to walk through her. I had this vision that the Royal Apartments would have gold fittings and be very opulent but I was surprised by how understated they were.'

Another visitor to the ship at this time was Bob Downie who had just been appointed as the future Director of *Britannia*. Describing his own impressions Bob Downie said, 'she looked like the inside of a house after the removal men have been. She was fairly dark because there was only temporary power on board. I did however sense what a privilege it was to take command of such an important piece of British naval history.'

Another early appointment was David Campbell of the design consultants Campbell & Co. His brief was to develop the visitor centre, be involved in the refurbish-

ment of the interiors and devise a route for visitors to see as much of *Britannia* as possible. This last task was more challenging because of Forth Ports' original commitment to make *Britannia* fully accessible to the disabled. Explaining the philosophy of his approach to *Britannia*'s exhibition David Campbell said:

'Previously, we had worked on castles and other historic buildings so we felt that if *Britannia* had been a building she would have been given a Grade A status. We therefore approached our work as if she was a Grade A listed building. To that extent our philosophy was to be as non interventionist as possible and to do as little to the fabric of the vessel as was needed. There was also a great deal of research to be done not least to make a complete inventory of all the items that had been on board. We compiled this through lists from the Royal Collection and by looking at photographs taken on board while she was in service. We then tried through Forth Ports to recover as many of these items as possible. About 80 per cent of the furniture came back, although there were some significant absentees such as the dining room table and chairs. To fill these gaps we approached the long-established Edinburgh furniture makers Whytock & Reid. They made most of the missing items of furniture such as sofas and some small tables. A chance meeting in an Edinburgh model shop led to the building of a replica model of HMS *Magpie* to be placed in Prince Philip's Sitting Room. We later received news that Prince Charles was prepared to let us have the bookcase back which had

Britannia *approaches her new home port of Leith under tow.*

(© Forth Ports plc)

originally been in *V&A*. Thanks to Commodore Morrow we knew the types of books that had previously been in it which included a set of James Bond books. In the Sun Lounge there were plastic basket chairs which we as designers liked because they were very fashionable in the 1950s and firmly placed *Britannia* in time as well as showing that the Royal Family are not just interested in antiques.'

Britannia's change in status from an active ship to a museum ship brought with it new requirements for the display of items from the Royal Collection. As part of their standard loan agreement the Royal Collection required their items to be displayed in gallery conditions despite the fact that when she was in service the items would not have been kept that way. To ensure that these requirements are met a number of monitors for humidity, etc., have been placed around *Britannia* which are regularly checked. In addition to obtaining these items on loan Forth Ports also managed to arrange for the loan of artefacts from the MOD Collection and the Wardroom Trust to complete the interior displays. The Wardroom Trust, which has The Prince of Wales and Commodore Morrow as Trustees, was formed specifically to keep the contents of the Royal Yacht's Wardroom together so that they could be passed to the Wardroom of a future Royal Yacht. Until that can be achieved the Trust agreed to the display of its artefacts on board *Britannia*.

To avoid the problem of people walking through The Queen's former Bedroom it was decided to remove whole sections of the walls and insert glass panels keeping to the rhythm of the surrounding panels.

(© Iain Jones)

Workmen create a new opening in Britannia's hull to provide access for the Engine Room.

(© Iain Jones)

As work began to retrieve as many of her original arte-facts as possible, decisions had to be taken about the contents of the visitor centre and the manner in which *Britannia* herself would be displayed. It was decided to use the visitor centre to explain the roles of *Britannia* and highlight key events within her history as well as to display items, such as the wheelhouse, and the Barge, which were difficult to present on board. The biggest dilemma of this whole process was the issue of how the Royal Apartments should be presented. It was clear that the public would be most curious about this area of the ship. The issue broke new ground because the sleeping quarters of a reigning British Monarch had not been exhibited to the public before and thus great sensitivity was required. Everyone agreed that the thought of people walking through the bedrooms would be inappropriate and allowing people to peek through the door would have caused congestion. So it was decided to remove whole sections of the wall and insert glass panels keeping to the rhythm of the surrounding panels. As David Campbell recalls it led to some interesting comments after she was opened to the public. 'I remember after we opened watching two old ladies. One turned to the other and said, "You would had thought The Queen would have some curtains." The glazed panelling had worked so well that they didn't realise that it was new!' Whilst tact had governed the policy over the Royal Apartments, the issue of access dictated the way in which the Engine Room could be shown. If Forth Ports were going to keep their promise of making the visitor route accessible to all, a radical solution was needed for the Engine Room. In the end it was decided to cut a new access into the side of the hull and allow visitors to look at the Engine Room through a glass panel. The only disadvantage of this solution is that the access is only about 6 inches above the waterline so if the wind reaches more than Force 5, the doors have to be closed to preserve the watertight integrity of the hull. The position of the wheelhouse also presented access difficulties but its smaller size meant that it could be removed and re-assembled within the visitor centre.

While she was in dry dock, Iain Jones's team concentrated on the work that needed to be done below the waterline. This included blasting the hull back to bare metal and applying a full recoat after blanking off the openings no longer required, such as the holes for the stabilisers. The removal of historic equipment presented a few problems as Iain Jones remarked:

'There was a great deal of concern about the craning off of the *Royal George* Binnacle, so a beautiful metal structure was fabricated to safely remove it. Some time after this was done, we were removing redundant equipment from *Britannia* when we found a packing case which we opened up only to find it contained the structure which the RN had used for removing the binnacle when she was in refit.'

All of the underwater fittings were blanked off.

(© Iain Jones)

As the work progressed there was tremendous interest from the press which resulted in a total ban of cameras on board from day one. The only exceptions to this rule were the naval architects who needed to record specific stages of the work. While the press were excluded from *Britannia* one exception was made to allow Tom McKendrik to make a TV documentary for the BBC covering both her history and her preservation. Whilst the press had to be kept off *Britannia*, Iain Jones was worried about keeping all of her artefacts on board and counter the threat posed by souvenir hunters among the 300 tradesmen working on board. It wasn't practical to search everyone coming off *Britannia* but signs were put up informing workers that they would be subjected to random searches. If a worker was asked to open up his toolbox and he refused, his employers were immediately informed to remove him from the job. This stopped the removal of larger items although a number of small tally plates and other minor items still vanished during the course of the refit.

Once *Britannia* emerged from dry dock on 9 July 1998 she was berthed alongside Edinburgh Dock so that the portside of the hull could be painted. The environment of Leith docks presented a few hiccups with dust discharges from other ships ruining the finish of the paint a couple of times, while having a number of consecutive dry days was also a problem. People later commented that the new paint on the hull was marginally different to her original blue. In the interests of authenticity International Paints were asked to conduct a chemical analysis of the original paint and they achieved a chemical match. However, in practice when the paint was applied it didn't match shade for shade, which was probably due to the method of application. When she had been painted in Portsmouth Dockyard the paint was always applied by brush but time and money meant that in Leith it had to be sprayed on. The other source of controversy was the gold leaf band that some journalists thought was now yellow. Forth Ports were advised by the MOD that in refits over the years, the band had been changed to a gold paint specification, which was exactly the same paint used in the restoration.

Once *Britannia* was out of dry dock the issue of which flags were to be flown needed to be considered. As a decommissioned vessel there were no previous guidelines to follow for *Britannia*, but it was eventually decided that she would fly the Union Flag at the bow, the Flag of St Andrew at the fore mast, The Union Flag at the main mast, the EU Flag at the mizzen and the Red Ensign at the stern. The choice of the EU Flag caused some controversy when she opened to the public so it was later decided to create a house flag using the Yacht's unofficial badge displayed on a plain blue background. The Red Ensign was

Britannia on her temporary exhibition moorings in Leith.

(© Yacht Events Ltd)

also subsequently exchanged for the defaced Blue Ensign of the Royal Forth Yacht Club. Another issue which required attention was how the staff on board would be dressed. It was felt inappropriate to design a naval style uniform as that could have seemed disrespectful. Equally, dressing them in a blazer and slacks could have made the staff look more like security guards than guides. In the end Bob Downie decided that he wanted to have a more regimental look for his staff and opted for a tartan based uniform. *Britannia* didn't have her own tartan so a new one was designed by the Royal Family's kiltmakers Kinloch Anderson using the colours of gold, blue, white and red. Not surprisingly, the tartan was called 'The Royal Yacht *Britannia* Tartan'. This took time to produce and, in the interim, the staff used the 'Leith Tartan', which had been specifically designed for the 1995 Tall Ships Race, until the new tartan became available in October 1999.

As Bob Downie's team prepared to greet their first guests, they received a useful boost to their training when a small team of former Yachtsmen returned to *Britannia* for the first time since she was decommissioned. Commodore Morrow had assembled the team to provide advice and guidance about specific aspects of *Britannia* to help the Trust maintain her in an authentic manner. These new skills were first put into practice during the preview week, with the first four days directed towards the shareholders of Forth Ports. This was a way of thanking the company which had made the Leith bid for *Britannia* a reality, while the fifth day was an open day for the media.

Interestingly, it was the corporate market rather than the general public who were the first to see *Britannia*. Ford of Great Britain secured the honour of hosting the first banquet on board on 16 October. Bob Downie and his team couldn't have asked for a better start in their bid to firmly establish *Britannia* as a premier corporate entertainment facility. To ensure that the 'Britannia Brand' was not devalued the number of corporate events is limited to just 75 per year. Obviously, with this type of activity there is no standard package as each event is tailored to the client's individual requirements, but the options include a fireworks display or the Beat Retreat ceremony performed on the quayside by a pipe or military band. All of the catering for each event is done on board by the two full-time chefs who work in the former Royal Galley. The former Wardroom galley is now used for making bread, pastries and sweets while the former ship's galley accommodates the dishwashers.

On Monday, 19 October 1998 it was time for members of the public to walk round the UK's first preserved former Royal Yacht. She had become the first visitor attraction in Scotland to introduce a system of entry by pre-booked tickets only. This system was initially adopted to regulate the flow of people and avoid long queues. The tabloids instantly assumed that the absence of these queues meant that *Britannia* was a flop but this was not the case because within two days of the ticket hotline opening 30,000 tickets had been sold. At the end of the first month 33,000 people had visited *Britannia* and there were advance orders for a further 35,000 tickets and over 40,000 reservations made on behalf of coach groups.

Although a great deal had been achieved in a very short time, Bob Downie felt that it would not be possible to stock and open a professional gift shop within the time scale of the refit without franchising the shop to an established company with retail experience. Jenners department store in Edinburgh seemed the logical choice and they agreed to take on the franchise and develop the range of merchandise available. It was the first time in Jenners' 160-year history that they had opened another outlet outside their Princes Street location in Edinburgh. Operating under the title of 'The *Britannia* Collection by Jenners' the shop was opened on 23 November to complete the visitor centre. As a result of the success of this operation Jenners have subsequently opened branches in Edinburgh airport and, more recently, at Loch Lomond.

At the end of the first year it was clear that *Britannia*'s preservation had been a great success. On the corporate side major companies such as Jaguar, Lloyds TSB and HMV UK Ltd hosted events on board while 436,619 members of the public paid to look round her. These figures made *Britannia* the fourth most visited attraction in Scotland while Group Leisure magazine granted her their prestigious Best New Attraction 1998/1999 award. A report prepared by the economic development consultants Segal Quince Wicksteed Ltd revealed that during her first year *Britannia* generated over £12 million of new spending in the Edinburgh and Lothian economy with an average of £24 being spent in the area by each visitor. The maintenance team had also proved that they could maintain *Britannia* in her new role as they began to learn some of her quirks. For example, the starboard side is in much better condition than the portside. They also began to undertake long-term preservation work such as chipping the inside faces of any rusty bulwarks back to metal and repainting them. The areas around the scuttles in the hull, which had always given some problems with rust since they were removed and refitted during the 1987 refit, were also worked on. Obviously, as *Britannia* is open to the public all through the year this work has to be done in full view of the public, which has led to some people saying that *Britannia* is being poorly preserved. What these people do not realise is the difference between her two roles and the corresponding levels of exposure. When *Britannia* was in commission she was always immaculate whenever she was on Royal duty, which was usually no more that a fortnight at a time. In between these periods of duty the Yacht's company were busily painting and polishing *Britannia* to keep her up to standard. Even during Royal duty this process would continue albeit at a lower level out of the public eye. Therefore in her current role where she is open to the public throughout the year it is impossible for *Britannia*'s maintenance team to conduct their essential work without being seen by the public. On some days people will see parts of the ship being stripped down or primed prior to repainting.

One of *Britannia*'s features that caught the imagination

of the public was the fact that she once carried a Rolls Royce. During the bidding process Terry Smith had been keen to see a Rolls Royce return to the Yacht and had made a formal request to obtain one of the original cars that had been embarked. His request was declined but early in 2000 Terry Smith found a suitable alternative when he came across a 1964 Rolls Royce Phantom V which was for sale. The car had been discovered in an

The fact that a Rolls Royce used to be embarked in the Yacht for Royal tours caught the imagination of the public. The Trust's request to borrow one of the Roll Royce cars embarked in the Yacht was turned down. Fortunately the Trust found a suitable alternative early in 2000. The owner kindly agreed to lend the car to the Trust and it was craned on board in May 2000. The new Ocean Terminal can be seen taking shape in the background.

(© Forth Ports plc)

American barn in a terrible condition by the Real Car Company who re-imported it to the UK. Its new owner Gary Gifford then spent about a year restoring the car to its former glory. Interestingly, the car had originally been used by HRH Princess Alexandra and still had a number of its original features including the blue Royal roof light and the glass partition in the centre of the car. Being a strong Royalist Gary Gifford was happy to agree to the loan of the car for display inside the garage on board the Yacht. Under very careful supervision the £150,000 car was craned on board at the beginning of May 2000.

In February 2001 *Britannia*'s success as a visitor attraction was further underlined by the Scottish Tourist Board's award of its prestigious five star rating to *Britannia*. This made her only the third tourist attraction in Edinburgh to have reached this standard. *Britannia*'s achievement is perhaps more impressive because it was the first time that she had been formally assessed by the Scottish Tourist Board. In Scotland the grading system judges an attraction by its overall quality rather than simply the facilities. Therefore, they look at the customer care such as the cleanliness, the interaction, appearance and behaviour of the staff and the experience provided by a visit to the attraction. February 2001 also saw a change in the way the shop was managed when Jenners' lease expired. An attraction like *Britannia* needs to have control of its own shop as this is a very useful source of additional income. When the lease expired the Trust appointed a merchandising manager to specifically develop the range of merchandise while a shop manger was hired to manage and run the shop itself.

After nearly three years on display *Britannia*'s permanent moorings at Leith's £120 million Ocean Terminal had been completed and were finally ready to receive her. To prepare for the move *Britannia* was closed to the public on 23 September 2001 and three days later she was carefully manoeuvred by two tugs across the dock to her new berth. The Barge was moved ahead of *Britannia* at 0300 on 13 September and placed in a new berthing pool alongside *Britannia*'s moorings, which is covered by a glass canopy.

The first visitors were able to see the re-vamped *Britannia* experience when she re-opened to the public on 4 October 2001. In sharp contrast to the original temporary facilities the new site had been planned with the full benefit of the experience gained since 1998, as well as advice from the Scottish Tourist Board. The layout of the new smaller visitor centre, which is located on the second floor of the Sir Terence Conran designed Ocean Terminal, was planned so that visitors were provided with a clearly planned route and obvious locations to purchase their tickets and collect their audio tour handset.

Britannia *is towed across the basin in Leith Docks from her temporary exhibition moorings to her permanent home at Ocean Terminal in September 2001.*

(©Forth Ports plc)

As part of the temporary exhibition, the Barge was put on display in a covered berthing pool. The Barge was later moved to Ocean Terminal with the Yacht.

(©Yacht Events Ltd)

On board *Britannia* the move provided the opportunity to open new sections to the public. Early research among the visitors showed that people wanted to see more of the ship – in particular where the Yachtsmen had lived. It was therefore decided to open the forward part of the main deck. This allowed visitors to see the PO and CPO's messes, the Marine Barracks, the Junior Rates mess area, the Sick Bay, the Laundry, the Post Office and the NAAFI. The principal challenge presented by opening up these areas was to maintain a logical one way route that did not require significant alterations to the structure of the ship. However, the making of a further two access points could not be avoided and, like the access point made for the Engine Room, they were made to blend in with the style of the double doors in the aft part of the hull which were an original feature of *Britannia*. Internally, an opening had to be cut through one bulkhead and one item of machinery had to be moved to gain access to the junior Yachtsmen's mess. Despite the limited nature of this work it does clearly highlight the difficult balancing act between authenticity and providing access to people of all levels of mobility.

The opening of these new areas meant that the audio tour needed to be updated. Originally, the tour was available in five languages – English, French, German, Italian, Spanish, and a children's version in English aimed at

The Chief Petty Officers mess was one of the new areas to be opened up to the public as part of the move to Ocean Terminal.

(© Yacht Events Ltd)

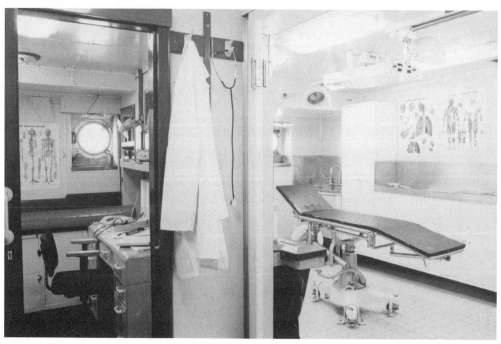

The Sick Bay was also opened in October 2001.

(© Yacht Events Ltd)

5–11-year-olds. The children's version was about half the length of the adult's commentary, which caused problems with children wanting to move on before their parents. To solve this the new version needed to be the same length as the adult tour. However, it was important that the new tour was not boring and did not include too much jargon and other things children could not understand. To get round this the tour contains basic factual information about each area followed by a short interactive section along the lines of 'can you see the monkey behind the Wardroom bar?' The range of languages was also increased with the introduction of Japanese and Dutch versions of the tour. It was also felt that the signs on board could be enhanced to improve people's orientation and make the route itself as clear as possible. To achieve this the signs for the audio tour on each deck were colour coded and 'no entry' signs across ladders were changed to 'the tour continues this way' to reassure people that they were walking in the right direction.

The move to Ocean Terminal does of course limit the amount of major future development that can be undertaken on board. Although there are still additional areas that could be opened up to the public these are in truth unlikely to add real value to the average person's visit to *Britannia*. Therefore, Bob Downie and his team are concentrating on the finishing touches which help to give *Britannia* a 'lived in' feel, thus achieving the highest lev-

ABOVE & BELOW: Britannia *on her permanent moorings at Leith's Ocean Terminal.*   (© Richard Johnstone-Bryden)

The fulfilment of Forth Port's original vision for the preservation of Britannia, *as the liner* The World *pays a visit to Leith's Ocean Terminal thus presenting* Britannia *within the centre of a working port.*

(© Forth Ports plc)

els of authenticity. For example, at Christmas time the various messes are decorated with festive decorations, just as they would have been when she was in service. A book of music has been placed on the piano in the Drawing Room. A CD player has been placed discreetly in the Drawing Room so that piano music can be played quietly in the background while in the Royal Marine barracks music is also played.

In January 2002 *Britannia* reached another major milestone when the total number of visitors since she first opened to the public in 1998 reached 1,000,000. This provided further proof of the continued attraction of *Britannia*. The annual figures for visitor numbers has varied with a peak of 436,619 visitors in the first year but it now appears to have settled around 270,000–300,000 visitors per annum. Despite 2001 being a tough year for tourism throughout the UK, which was heavily affected first by the outbreak of foot-and-mouth disease, and then by the terrorist attacks in New York on 11 September, *Britannia* still managed to attract a total of 250,000 visitors. The move to Ocean Terminal and opening up the new areas has proved a great success and in 2002 *Britannia* attracted just over 300,000 visitors.

A Final Note From the Author

In researching for this book I enjoyed two visits to *Britannia* in Leith. On the first occasion she was on her initial moorings and by the time of my second visit she had been moved across the basin to her present berth at Ocean Terminal. I was impressed by the commitment and efforts of all those involved in her preservation. Although many were sceptical about the success of preserving *Britannia*, The Royal Yacht *Britannia* Trust has gone to great lengths to make sure her preservation will stand the test of time and is doing a good job. These efforts have been rewarded by the number of visitors and their comments as well as the awards received by the Trust as detailed within this chapter. Presenting *Britannia* to the public was always going to require a major diplomatic balancing act between respecting her Royal heritage and giving the public a chance to see as much of the Yacht as possible. On the whole the Trust has managed to walk this fine line and achieve the objective stated by two successive Governments of preserving *Britannia* in a dignified manner. The way in which the inside of the ship has been presented is excellent and authentically represents so much of the former detail. Externally *Britannia* is being well maintained by the standards of preserved ships notwithstanding the huge difference in numbers of those undertaking this maintenance. Despite *Britannia's* change of status from The Royal Yacht to a preserved Royal Yacht, she continues to be a fitting memorial to the proud traditions of the Royal Yacht Service.

HMY BRITANNIA: THE DETAILS

Appendix I

Commanding Officers
Dates in Command

Note that dates are written as day/month/year.

Captain J S Dalglish OBE RN 7/1/54–28/4/54
Vice Admiral Sir Conolly Abel Smith GCVO CB 28/4/54–30/1/58
Vice Admiral Sir Peter Dawnay KCVO CB DSC 30/1/58–25/1/62
Rear Admiral Sir Joseph Henley KCVO CB 25/1/62–9/3/65
Rear Admiral Sir Patrick Morgan KCVO CB DSC 9/3/65–1/9/70
Rear Admiral Sir Richard Trowbridge KCVO 1/9/70–11/9/75
Rear Admiral Sir Hugh Janion KCVO 11/9/75–4/2/81
Rear Admiral Sir Paul Greening GCVO 4/2/81–12/9/85
Rear Admiral Sir John Garnier KCVO CBE 12/9/85–18/9/90
Rear Admiral Sir Robert Woodard KCVO 18/9/90–1/4/1995
Commodore A J C Morrow CVO RN 1/4/95–11/12/97

Appendix II

Key Dates

Ordered: 5 February 1952
Keel laid: 16 June 1952
Launched: 16 April 1953
Commissioned: 11 January 1954
Decommissioned: 11 December 1997
Sold: 1 May 1998
Opened to the public: 19 October 1998

Appendix III

Dimensions and Statistics
On Completion 1954

Length overall (LOA):	412ft 3in
Length waterline (LWL):	380ft
Beam:	55ft
Draught:	
light condition:	14ft
normal load condition:	15ft 9in
extreme deep condition:	16ft 4½in
Height of masts from the waterline:	
fore mast:	117ft 11½in
main mast:	122ft 11½in
mizzen mast:	102ft 11½in

Load displacement:	4715 tons
Gross tonnage:	5769 tons
Propulsion:	Single reduction geared turbines
Shaft horse power:	12,000
Speed on trials at 12,000 shp:	22.75 knots
Continuous seagoing speed:	21 knots
Endurance:	
Carrying 330 tons of FFO:	2000 miles at 20 knots
	2400 miles at 15 knots
Carrying full capacity 490 tons of FFO:	3100 miles at 20 knots
	3560 miles at 15 knots
Pennant number:	A00 (never displayed)
Royal Yacht role:	
Complement:	21 Officers
	250 Royal Yachtsmen
Capacity for receptions:	250 guests
Capacity for State Banquets:	56 guests
Hospital ship role:	
Naval medical complement:	8 medical and dental officers
	5 nursing sisters
	47 male ratings
Patient capacity:	200 patients
Ship's boats:	1 x 40ft Royal Barge
	2 x 35ft medium speed motor boats
	1 x 32ft motor cutter
	2 x 27ft jolly boats
	2 x 16ft fast motor dinghies
	2 x 14ft sailing dinghies

Armament

2 x 3pdr Mark 1 Saluting Guns

These guns were removed during October 1954 as part of the desire to reduce *Britannia*'s topweight. The guns were carried for the sole purpose of firing the morning and evening gun. The Queen had previously decided not to continue the custom during the Coronation Naval Review and thus had no objection to the custom lapsing in *Britannia*.

Appearance

Hull:	Bluebottle blue
Boot topping:	Scarlet
Gold line around hull:	Gold leaf 5½in wide
Upperworks:	White
Masts and funnel:	Buff

The Royal Coat of Arms was carried on the bow and the Royal Cypher at the stern.

Summary of Activities 1954–1997

State Visits: 85

Overseas visits to non Commonwealth countries with The Queen embarked, but not on a State Visit: 162

Visits to Commonwealth countries by The Queen: 90

Visits in UK waters by The Queen: 162

Visits to Commonwealth countries by other members of the Royal Family: 133

Visits to non Commonwealth countries by other members of the Royal Family: 226

Visits in UK waters by other members of the Royal Family: 110

Major exercises: 10

Minor exercises: 18

Sea Days/Seminars/Diplomatic/Royal events/Reception: 186

Fleet Reviews: 8

Other reviews/Royal events at sea: 1

Families Days: 10

Operational commitments: 1

Miles Steamed Per Year

1954: 17,646	1976: 16,464
1955: 20,576	1977: 42,241
1956: 40,688	1978: 10,075
1957: 24,521	1979: 20,035
1958: 6773	1980: 10,367
1959: 40,132	1981: 32,909
1960: 22,363	1982: 29,856
1961: 19,945	1983: 31,247
1962: 13,077	1984: 23,186
1963: 29,134	1985: 23,991
1964: 44,499	1986: 59,118
1965: 5793	1987: 2340
1966: 33,459	1988: 39,232
1967: 12,591	1989: 26,149
1968: 22,285	1990: 28,716
1969: 6154	1991: 25,615
1970: 40,150	1992: 11,614
1971: 42,156	1993: 36,062
1972: 29,489	1994: 18,924
1973: 16,625	1995: 25,071
1974: 24,288	1996: 16,716
1975: 21,805	1997: 32,983

Total distance steamed 1954–1997: 1,087,623 miles

Appendix IV

Costs

Construction £2,098,000

September 1954–December 1954 refit £67,000

October 1955–March 1956 refit £69,000

September 1957–January 1958 refit £163,000

November 1960–March 1961 refit £208,000

March 1962–January 1963 refit £60,500

December 1964–April 1965 refit £324,000

August 1967–November 1967 refit £234,000

August 1969–December 1969 refit £474,000

October 1972–July 1973 refit £1,782,000

January 1976–April 1976 refit £1,379,000

September 1979–April 1980 refit £5,100,000

Annual Costs Including Refits (where published)

1963/64: £366,700	1983/84: £8,905,000
1964/65: £713,700	1984/85: £5,843,000
1965/66: £475,900	1985/86: £6,943,000
1966/67: £490,300	1986/87: £4,749,000
1967/68: £664,800	1987/88: £22,364,000
1968/69: £518,000	1988/89: £9,542,000
1969/70: £943,500	1989/90: £6,998,000
1970/71: £776,000	1990/91: £9,272,000
1971/72: £895,000	1991/92: £12,458,000
1972/73: £1,882,000	1992/93: £8,361,000
1973/74: £1,654,000	1993/94: £8,397,000
1974/75: £1,516,000	1994/95: £11,424,000
1975/76: £2,453,000	1995/96: £8,423,000
1976/77: £2,140,000	1996/97: £10,446,000
1977/78: £3,100,000	1997/98: £7,463,000
1978/79: £2,100,000	1998/99: £88,000
1979/80: £1,900,000	

(excludes the amount for the 1979/80 refit costing £5.1million)

BIBLIOGRAPHY

Reference has been made to the following books and documents during the research for this book.

Voyage Round The World 1956–1957, privately printed by HMY *Britannia*, 1957.

Britannia 1959, privately printed by HMY *Britannia*, 1959.

Westabout 1962–63, privately printed by HMY *Britannia*, 1963.

Her Majesty's Yacht Britannia Antipodes 1970, privately printed by HMY *Britannia*, 1970.

HM Yacht Britannia Silver Jubilee Tours 1977, edited by Lt Cdr A J C Morrow RN, privately printed by HMY *Britannia*, 1977.

HM Yacht Britannia 1954–1997, Bishops Printers Ltd, 1997.

The Tour Diary of Prince Philip's 1956/57 World Tour.

The Tour Diary of Prince Philip's 1959 World Tour.

The Tour Diary of Prince Philip's 1971 Pacific Tour.

The Ship's Book – HMY *Britannia*.

The Journal of HM Yachts 19th January 1935–15th November 1956.

The Journal of HM Yachts 16th November 1956–16th December 1960.

The Journal of HM Yachts 1st January 1961–30th June 1964.

The Journal of HM Yachts 1st July 1964–8th August 1968.

The Journal of HM Yachts 8th August 1968–18th January 1972.

The Journal of HM Yachts 24th January 1972–17th March 1977.

The Journal of HM Yachts 17th March 1977–11th February 1981.

The Journal of HM Yachts 11th February 1981–10th March 1984.

The Journal of HM Yachts 12th March 1984–24th April 1986.

The Journal of HM Yachts 25th April 1986–23rd June 1988.

The Journal of HM Yachts 24th June 1988–29th November 1990.

The Journal of HM Yachts 29th November 1990–5th June 1994.

The Journal of HM Yachts 6th June 1994–3rd December 1996.

The Journal of HM Yachts 3rd December 1996–23rd February 1998.

The Personal Journal of Rear Admiral J H Adams CB LVO.

Private letters by Captain H H Owen RN.

Private letters by Captain I R Bowden LVO RN.

The Royal Yacht Britannia – Inside The Queen's Floating Palace, by Brian Hoey, Patrick Stephens Ltd, 1995.

The Royal Yacht Britannia – Life Onboard The Floating Palace, by Andrew Morton, Orbis Publishing Ltd, 1984.

Royal Yachts, by Paymaster Cdr C M Gavin RN, Rich & Cowan Ltd, 1932.

The Story of the Britannia, by E P Statham, Cassell, 1904.

The Life Story of a Fish, by Captain J S Dalglish CVO CBE RN, Adelphi Press, 1992.

The King's Ships: Volume 1, by H S Lecky, Horace Muirhead, 1913.

Royal Standard Red Ensign – With The Queen in the Gothic, by Sir David Aitchison KCVO, Pall Mall Press Ltd, 1958.

The Queen's Coronation Review – Spithead June 1953, by Cdr Thomas Woodrooffe RN, Pitkins, 1953.

Coronation Naval Review – Spithead 15th June 1953, Overseas Tankship (UK) Ltd, 1953.

HMS Vanguard Crossing The Line Royal Tour 1947, printed privately, 1947.

HMS Vanguard And The Royal Voyage To South Africa, HMSO, 1947.

Mountbatten – The Official Biography, by Philip Ziegler, Guild Publishing, 1985.

The Royal Dragon, by R L Hewitt, Routledge and Kegan Paul Ltd, 1958.

British Royal Yachts – A Complete Illustrated History, by Tony Dalton, Halsgrove, 2002.

Royal Yachts of Europe – From the Seventeenth to the Twentieth Century, by Reginald Crabtree, David & Charles, 1975.

Annal of our Royal Yachts 1604–1953, by J E Grigsby, Adlard Coles Ltd, 1953.

The Royal Yacht *Britannia* – Audio Tour Script.

The National Maritime Museum Royal Yachts, by G P B Naish, HMSO.

Britannia Royal Naval College Dartmouth, by Revd B K Hammett MA RN, Pitkin Pictorials, 1992.

The Luxury Yacht – From Steam to Diesel, by Reginald Crabtree, David & Charles, 1973.

King George V – His Life and Reign, by Harold Nicolson, Constable & Co. Ltd, 1952.

King George VI – His Life and Reign, by John W Wheeler-Bennett, Macmillan & Co., 1958.

Majesty – Elizabeth II and The House of Windsor, by Robert Lacey, Hutchinson & Co., 1977.

Philip – An Informal Biography, by Basil Boothroyd, Longman Group Ltd, 1971.

The Duke: A Portrait of Prince Philip, Tim Heald.

The Royal Family in Africa, by Dermot Morrah, Hutchinson & Co., 1947.

Edward Seago – The Other Side of the Canvas, by Jean Goodman, Collins, 1978.

Fiddler on the March – A Biography of Lt Col. Sir Vivian Dunn KCVO OBE FRAM RM, by Derek Oakley, Royal Marines Historical Society, 2000.

Conflict of Loyalty, by Geoffrey Howe, Pan Books, 1995.

Rock of Exile – A Narrative of Trista da Cunha, by D M Booy, J M Dent & Sons Ltd.

Vanguard To Trident – British Naval Policy since WWII, by Eric Grove, US Naval Institute, 1987.

Conway's All The World's Fighting Ships 1860–1905, Conway Maritime Press, 1979.

Conway's All The World's Fighting Ships 1906–1921, Conway Maritime Press, 1985.

Conway's All The World's Fighting Ships 1922–1946, Conway Maritime Press, 1980.

Conway's All The World's Fighting Ships 1947–1995, Conway Maritime Press, 1995.

The National Geographic Volume CXII Number 5.

NOTES

These reference codes are the documents the author has relied on from The Royal Archives.
Note that dates are written as day/month/year.

Chapter One

1 RA/PS/GVI/332/01
2 RA/PS/GVI/332/01
3 RA/PS/GVI/332/02
4 RA/PS/GVI/332/07
5 RA/PS/GVI/332/09
6 RA/RY/Admiral's Diaries/30/06/36
7 RA/RY/Admiral's Diaries/01/07/36
8 RA/RY/Admiral's Diaries/12/11/36
9 RA/PS/GVI/332/14
10 RA/PS/GVI/C332/16
11 RA/PS/GVI/C332/17
12 RA/PS/GVI/C332/16
13 RA/PS/GVI/C332/22
14 RA/PS/GVI/C332/23
15 RA/PS/GVI/C332/29
16 RA/PS/GVI/C332/31
17 RA/PS/GVI/PS00317/136
18 RA/RY/Admiral's Diaries/20/7/39
19 RA/RY/Admiral's Diaries/21/7/39
20 RA/RY/Admiral's Diaries/22/7/39
21 RA/RY/Admiral's Diaries/22/7/39
22 RA/RY/Admiral's Diaries/23/7/39
23 RA/RY/Admiral's Diaries/24/7/39
24 RA/RY/Admiral's Diaries/8/8/39
25 RA/RY/Admiral's Diaries/9/8/39
26 RA/RY/Admiral's Diaries/10/8/39
27 RA/PS/GVI/C332/53
28 RA/RY/Admiral's Diaries/7/9/39
29 RA/PS/GVI/PS07643/27
30 RA/RY/Admiral's Diaries/16/9/39
31 RA/RY/Admiral's Diaries/19/9/39
32 RA/RY/Admiral's Diaries/23/9/39
33 RA/PS/GVI/PS07643/11
34 RA/PS/GVI/PS07643/13,15,16
35 RA/PS/GVI/PS07643/27
36 RA/PS/GVI/PS07643/29
37 RA/PS/GVI/PS07643/32
38 RA/PS/GVI/PS07643/37/2
39 RA/PS/GVI/PS07643/37/2
40 RA/PS/GVI/PS00317/154
41 RA/PS/GVI/PS07643/37/4
42 RA/PS/GVI/PS07643/38
43 RA/PS/GVI/PS07643/38
44 RA/PS/GVI/PS07643/39
45 RA/PS/GVI/PS07643/40
46 RA/PS/GVI/PS07643/41
47 RA/PS/GVI/PS00317/162
48 RA/PS/GVI/PS07643/49
49 RA/PS/GVI/PS07643/51
50 RA/PS/GVI/PS07643/51
51 RA/PS/GVI/C332/16-/50
52 RA/PS/GVI/C332/16-/60
53 RA/PS/GVI/C332/16-/60
54 RA/PS/GVI/C332/16-/49/A
55 RA/PS/GVI/C332/16-/60
56 RA/PS/GVI/C332/16-/62
57 RA/PS/GVI/C332/16-/67
58 RA/PS/GVI/C332/16-/68
59 RA/PS/GVI/C332/16-/67
60 RA/PS/GVI/C332/16-/67
61 RA/PS/GVI/C332/16-/73
62 RA/PS/GVI/C332/16-/75

Chapter Two

1 RA/PE105/File No.8 SS *Gothic*/ Letter
   to Basil Sanderson 8/2/52
2 RA/PE105/File No.8 SS *Gothic*/ Letter
   from Naval Construction Department
   28/5/52
3 RA/PS/QEII/PS12140.0/ Cabinet
   Minute 19/5/52
4 RA/PS/QEII/PS12140.0/ Letter from
   Michael Adean 20/5/52
5 RA/RY/Admiral's Diaries/2/2/53
6 RA/PS/QEII/PS16700.7/ Letter to
   Lascelles 23/6/52
7 RA/PS/QEII/PS16700.7/ Letter from
   Lascelles 24/6/52
8 RA/PS/QEII/PS16700.0/ Letter from
   Lascelles 17/3/53
9 RA/RY/Admiral's Diaries/16/4/53
10 RA/PS/QEII/PS16700.0/ Note from the
   Admiralty about the five proposed
   names. (Also from minute of
   Admiralty Ship's Names Committee
   held by RN Historic Branch.)
11 RA/PS/QEII/PS16700.0/ Letter from
   Lascelles 5/11/52
12 RA/RY/Admiral's Diaries/16/4/53
13 RA/PS/QEII/PS10040.0 Letter to
   Lascelles 2/12/52
14 RA/PS/QEII/PS10040.0
15 RA/PS/QEII/PS10040.0 Letter to
   Lascelles 5/1/53
16 RA/PS/QEII/PS10040.0 Response to
   the letter from A/F McGrigor
17 RA/RY/Admiral's Diaries/8/6/53
18 RA/RY/Admiral's Diaries/14/6/53
19 RA/RY/Admiral's Diaries/15/6/53
20 RA/RY/Admiral's Diaries/15/6/53
21 RA/RY/Admiral's Diaries/16/6/53
22 RA/RY/Admiral's Diaries/26/10/53
23 RA/RY/Admiral's Diaries/9/11/53

24 RA/RY/Admiral's Diaries/8/1/54
25 RA/RY/QEII/PS16700.0 (1988-1997)/
   Memo from FORY 16/6/93
26 RA/RY/Admiral's Diaries/15/2/54
27 RA/RY/Admiral's Diaries/26/2/54
28 RA/RY/Admiral's Diaries/14/4/54
29 RA/RY/Admiral's Diaries/23–27/4/54
30 RA/RY/Admiral's Diaries/28/4/54
31 RA/RY/Admiral's Diaries/30/4/54
32 RA/RY/Admiral's Diaries/1/5/54
33 RA/PS/QEII/PS16700.0/ Letter from
   Lascelles 14/10/53
34 RA/RY/Admiral's Diaries/4/5/54
35 RA/RY/Admiral's Diaries/7/5/54
36 RA/RY/Admiral's Diaries/14/5/54
37 RA/RY/Admiral's Diaries/15/5/54
38 RA/RY/Admiral's Diaries/16/5/54
39 RA/RY/Admiral's Diaries/19/5/54
40 RA/RY/Admiral's Diaries/20/5/54

Chapter Three

1 RA/RY/Admiral's Diaries/29/5/54
2 RA/RY/Admiral's Diaries/9/7/54 &
   10/7/54 & 11/7/54
3 RA/RY/Admiral's Diaries/30/7/54
4 RA/RY/Admiral's Diaries/5/8/54
5 RA/RY/Admiral's Diaries/17/8/54
6 RA/RY/Admiral's Diaries/18/8/54 &
   23/8/54
7 RA/RY/Admiral's Diaries/24/8/54 &
   30/8/54 & 31/8/54
8 RA/RY/Admiral's Diaries/16/12/54
9 RA/RY/Admiral's Diaries/18/1/55
10 RA/RY/Admiral's Diaries/29/1/55
11 RA/RY/Admiral's Diaries/9/2/55
12 RA/RY/Admiral's Diaries/26/2/55
13 RA/RY/Admiral's Diaries/7/3/55 &
   8/3/55
14 RA/RY/Admiral's Diaries/10/3/55
15 RA/RY/Admiral's Diaries/13/3/55
16 RA/RY/Admiral's Diaries/15/3/55 to
   22/3/55
17 RA/RY/Admiral's Diaries/22/3/55 to
   1/4/55
18 RA/PS/QEII/PS16700.0 (1954–1968)
   Letter from VA Abel Smith to Sir
   Michael Adeane & RA/RY/Admiral's
   Diaries/4/4/55
19 RA/RY/Admiral's Diaries/18/6/55
20 RA/RY/Admiral's Diaries/23/6/55
21 RA/RY/Admiral's Diaries/26/6/55
22 RA/RY/Admiral's Diaries/28/6/55

23 RA/RY/Admiral's Diaries/30/6/55 & 5/7/55 & 7/7/55
24 RA/RY/Admiral's Diaries/29/7/55
25 RA/RY/Admiral's Diaries/4/8/55 & 5/8/55
26 RA/RY/Admiral's Diaries/6/8/55
27 RA/RY/Admiral's Diaries/7/8/55 & 8/8/55
28 RA/RY/Admiral's Diaries/9/8/55
29 RA/RY/Admiral's Diaries/12/8/55
30 RA/RY/Admiral's Diaries/13/8/55 & 15/8/55
31 RA/RY/Admiral's Diaries/3/10/55
32 RA/RY/Admiral's Diaries/12/10/55
33 RA/RY/Admiral's Diaries/13/10/55
34 RA/RY/Admiral's Diaries/14/10/55 & 17/10/55
35 RA/RY/Admiral's Diaries/19/10/55
36 RA/RY/Admiral's Diaries/21/10/55
37 RA/RY/Admiral's Diaries/1/3/56
38 RA/RY/Admiral's Diaries/10/3/56
39 RA/RY/Admiral's Diaries/26/3/56
40 RA/RY/Admiral's Diaries/29/5/56
41 RA/RY/Admiral's Diaries/4/6/56
42 RA/RY/Admiral's Diaries/8/6/56
43 RA/RY/Admiral's Diaries/10/6/56
44 RA/RY/Admiral's Diaries/11/6/56 to 17/6/56
45 RA/RY/Admiral's Diaries/20/6/56 & 27/6/56
46 RA/RY/Admiral's Diaries/30/6/56 & 1/7/56 & 2/7/56 & 3/7/56
47 RA/RY/Admiral's Diaries/3/8/56 & 9/8/56 & 11/8/56
48 RA/RY/Admiral's Diaries/18/8/56
49 RA/RY/Admiral's Diaries/19/8/56 to 22/8/56
50 RA/RY/Admiral's Diaries/21/9/56 to 23/9/56
51 RA/RY/Admiral's Diaries/8/10/56
52 RA/RY/Admiral's Diaries/16/10/56
53 RA/RY/Admiral's Diaries/1/11/56
54 RA/RY/Admiral's Diaries/10/11/56
55 RA/RY/Admiral's Diaries/10/12/56
56 RA/RY/Admiral's Diaries/31/12/56
57 RA/RY/Admiral's Diaries/12/1/57
58 RA/RY/Admiral's Diaries/21/1/57
591 RA/RY/Admiral's Diaries/17/5/57
60 RA/RY/Admiral's Diaries/18/5/57
61 RA/RY/Admiral's Diaries/21/5/57
62 RA/RY/Admiral's Diaries/23/5/57 & 25/5/57
63 RA/RY/Admiral's Diaries/27/5/57 to 29/5/57
64 RA/RY/Admiral's Diaries/10/8/57

Chapter Four
1 RA/RY/Admiral's Diaries/30 & 31/1/58

2 RA/RY/Admiral's Diaries/21 & 25/3/58
3 RA/RY/Admiral's Diaries/27, 28 & 29/3/58
4 RA/RY/Admiral's Diaries/5/5/58
5 RA/RY/Admiral's Diaries/8 & 10/5/58
6 RA/RY/Admiral's Diaries/12/5/58
7 RA/RY/Admiral's Diaries/26/7/58
8 RA/RY/Admiral's Diaries/27/7/58
9 RA/RY/Admiral's Diaries/28/7/58
10 RA/RY/Admiral's Diaries/7/8/58
11 RA/RY/Admiral's Diaries/9/8/58
12 RA/RY/Admiral's Diaries/10/8/58
13 RA/RY/Admiral's Diaries/11 & 13/8/58
14 RA/RY/Admiral's Diaries/18/8/58
15 RA/RY/Admiral's Diaries/20/8/58
16 RA/RY/Admiral's Diaries/8/10/58
17 RA/RY/Admiral's Diaries/23 & 24/4/59
18 RA/RY/Admiral's Diaries/28/4/59
19 RA/RY/Admiral's Diaries/26/6/59
20 RA/RY/Admiral's Diaries/1 & 2/7/59
21 RA/RY/Admiral's Diaries/15/1/60
22 RA/RY/Admiral's Diaries/19/2/60
23 RA/RY/Admiral's Diaries/7/5/60
24 RA/RY/Admiral's Diaries/6/3/61
25 RA/RY/Admiral's Diaries/23/4/61
26 RA/RY/Admiral's Diaries/27/4/61
27 RA/RY/Admiral's Diaries /28 & 29/4/61
28 RA/RY/Admiral's Diaries/29 & 30/4/61
29 RA/RY/Admiral's Diaries/5/5/61
30 RA/RY/Admiral's Diaries/6/5/61
31 RA/RY/Admiral's Diaries/7/5/61
32 RA/RY/Admiral's Diaries/20 & 22/5/61
33 RA/RY/Admiral's Diaries/25/5/61
34 RA/RY/Admiral's Diaries/5/6/61
35 RA/RY/Admiral's Diaries/18/9/61
36 RA/RY/Admiral's Diaries/27/9/61
37 RA/RY/Admiral's Diaries/3/10/61
38 RA/RY/Admiral's Diaries/20/11/61
39 RA/RY/Admiral's Diaries/23/11/61
40 RA/RY/Admiral's Diaries/25/11/61
41 RA/RY/Admiral's Diaries/1/12/61
42 RA/RY/Admiral's Diaries/2/12/61
43 RA/RY/Admiral's Diaries/5 & 6/12/61
44 RA/RY/Admiral's Diaries/15/12/61

Chapter Five
1 RA/RY/Admiral's Diaries/25/1/62
2 RA/RY/Admiral's Diaries/1/2/62
3 RA/RY/Admiral's Diaries/12 & 13/2/62
4 RA/RY/Admiral's Diaries/28/3/62
5 RA/RY/Admiral's Diaries/27, 28 & 30/4/62 & 29/6/62
6 RA/RY/Admiral's Diaries/27/7/62
7 RA/RY/Admiral's Diaries/7/8/62
8 RA/RY/Admiral's Diaries/10–13/8/62
9 RA/RY/Admiral's Diaries/5/10/62
10 RA/RY/Admiral's Diaries/4 & 7/12/62

11 RA/RY/Admiral's Diaries/25/12/62
12 RA/RY/Admiral's Diaries/1/1/63
13 RA/RY/Admiral's Diaries/7/1/63
14 RA/RY/Admiral's Diaries/8/1/63
15 RA/RY/Admiral's Diaries/10/1/63
16 RA/RY/Admiral's Diaries/15/1/63
17 RA/RY/Admiral's Diaries/16/1/63
18 RA/RY/Admiral's Diaries/20/1/63
19 RA/RY/Admiral's Diaries/3/2/63
20 RA/RY/Admiral's Diaries/14/5/63 & 21/6/63 & 4/7/63
21 RA/RY/Admiral's Diaries/6/7/63
22 RA/RY/Admiral's Diaries/8/7/63
23 RA/RY/Admiral's Diaries/7/1/64
24 RA/RY/Admiral's Diaries/3/2/64
25 RA/RY/Admiral's Diaries/8/2/64
26 RA/RY/Admiral's Diaries/12/2/64
27 RA/RY/Admiral's Diaries/1 & 2/4/64 & 13/4/64
28 RA/RY/Admiral's Diaries/27–30/6/64
29 RA/RY/Admiral's Diaries/1–3/7/64 & 10/7/64
30 RA/RY/Admiral's Diaries/17/7/64
31 RA/RY/Admiral's Diaries/3/8/64
32 RA/RY/Admiral's Diaries/8/8/64
33 RA/RY/Admiral's Diaries/11, 14–16/9/64
34 RA/RY/Admiral's Diaries/18–28/9/64
35 RA/RY/Admiral's Diaries/3/10/64
36 RA/RY/Admiral's Diaries/5 & 6/10/64
37 RA/RY/Admiral's Diaries/10 & 11/10/64
38 RA/RY/Admiral's Diaries/13 & 20/10/64
39 RA/RY/Admiral's Diaries/28 & 29/10/64
40 RA/RY/Admiral's Diaries/2/11/64
41 RA/RY/Admiral's Diaries/3 & 4/11/64
42 RA/RY/Admiral's Diaries/9 & 13/11/64
43 RA/RY/Admiral's Diaries/18/11/64 & 2/12/64
44 RA/RY/Admiral's Diaries/14 & 15/12/64
45 RA/RY/Admiral's Diaries/18/1/65

Chapter Six
1 RA/PS/QEII/PS16700.7/Letter to Sir Michael Adeane 10/9/64
2 RA/PS/QEII/PS16700.7/Letter to Sir Michael Adean 12/9/69
3 RA/RY/Admiral's Diaries/28/3/65
4 RA/RY/Admiral's Diaries/30 & 31/3/65
5 RA/RY/Admiral's Diaries/12/5/65
6 RA/RY/Admiral's Diaries/14–19/5/65
7 RA/RY/Admiral's Diaries/26/5/65
8 RA/RY/Admiral's Diaries/28/5/65
9 RA/RY/Admiral's Diaries/30/5/65
10 RA/RY/Admiral's Diaries/23–28/6/65

11 RA/RY/Admiral's Diaries/1/7/65
12 RA/RY/Admiral's Diaries/25 & 26/7/65
13 RA/RY/Admiral's Diaries/31/7/65
14 RA/RY/Admiral's Diaries/9/8/65
15 RA/RY/Admiral's Diaries/10/8/65
16 RA/RY/Admiral's Diaries/11 & 18/8/65
17 RA/RY/Admiral's Diaries/19 & 20 & 30/1/66
18 RA/RY/Admiral's Diaries/7/4/66
19 RA/RY/Admiral's Diaries/9 & 10/4/66
20 RA/RY/Admiral's Diaries/12 & 14/4/66
21 RA/RY/Admiral's Diaries/15/6/66 & RA/PS/QEII/PS16700.0 (1954–1968) Letter from Rear Admiral Morgan 20/6/66
22 RA/RY/Admiral's Diaries/4/8/66
23 RA/RY/Admiral's Diaries/1/5/67
24 RA/RY/Admiral's Diaries/2/5/67
25 RA/RY/Admiral's Diaries/3/5/67
26 RA/RY/Admiral's Diaries/4–5/5/67
27 RA/RY/Admiral's Diaries/28/6/67
28 RA/RY/Admiral's Diaries/1–3/7/67
29 RA/RY/Admiral's Diaries/4/7/67
30 RA/RY/Admiral's Diaries/5 & 10/7/67
31 RA/RY/Admiral's Diaries/11/7/67
32 RA/RY/Admiral's Diaries/13/7/67
33 RA/RY/Admiral's Diaries/15/7/67
34 RA/RY/Admiral's Diaries/22–26/7/67
35 RA/RY/Admiral's Diaries/13, 14 & 16/8/67
36 RA/RY/Admiral's Diaries/8, 10, 13, 17 & 19/5/68
37 RA/RY/Admiral's Diaries/17–28/6/68 and the Sea Day program glued into the Admiral's Diary.
38 RA/RY/Admiral's Diaries/2, 8 & 10/8/68
39 RA/RY/Admiral's Diaries/16 & 19/8/68
40 RA/RY/Admiral's Diaries/14 & 18/10/68
41 RA/RY/Admiral's Diaries/29/10/68 & 1 & 2/11/68
42 RA/RY/Admiral's Diaries/3 & 5/11/68
43 RA/RY/Admiral's Diaries/11–19/11/68
44 RA/RY/Admiral's Diaries/6/12/68
45 RA/RY/Admiral's Diaries/16/5/69
46 RA/RY/Admiral's Diaries/26/6/69 & 1–5/7/69
47 RA/RY/Admiral's Diaries/Second booklet glued into the Admiral's Diary after entry for 29/7/69
48 RA/RY/Admiral's Diaries/27 & 28/7/69
49 RA/RY/Admiral's Diaries/29 & 30/7/69
50 RA/RY/Admiral's Diaries/19/1/70
51 RA/RY/Admiral's Diaries/8/2/70
52 RA/RY/Admiral's Diaries/11/2/70
53 RA/RY/Admiral's Diaries/7/3/70
54 RA/RY/Admiral's Diaries/10/3/70
55 RA/RY/Admiral's Diaries/11 & 12/3/70
56 RA/RY/Admiral's Diaries/15/3/70
57 RA/RY/Admiral's Diaries/22/3/70
58 RA/RY/Admiral's Diaries/24/3/70
59 RA/RY/Admiral's Diaries/26–30/3/70
60 RA/RY/Admiral's Diaries/12 & 13/4/70
61 RA/RY/Admiral's Diaries/16/4/70
62 RA/RY/Admiral's Diaries/20 & 21/4/70
63 RA/RY/Admiral's Diaries/23, 24, 28 & 29/4/70
64 RA/RY/Admiral's Diaries/29, 30 & 31/7/70
65 RA/RY/Admiral's Diaries/2, 7, 10 & 20/8/70

Chapter Seven

1 RA/RY/Admiral's Diaries/15/1/71 & 3–5/2/71
2 RA/RY/Admiral's Diaries/7/2/71
3 RA/RY/Admiral's Diaries/8/2/71
4 RA/RY/Admiral's Diaries/9/2/71
5 RA/RY/Admiral's Diaries/10/2/71
6 RA/RY/Admiral's Diaries/11/2/71
7 RA/RY/Admiral's Diaries/12/2/71
8 RA/RY/Admiral's Diaries/14/2/71
9 RA/RY/Admiral's Diaries/15/2/71
10 RA/RY/Admiral's Diaries/16/2/71
11 RA/RY/Admiral's Diaries/18/2/71
12 RA/RY/Admiral's Diaries/21/2/71
13 RA/RY/Admiral's Diaries/26/2/71
14 RA/RY/Admiral's Diaries/27 & 28/2/71
15 RA/RY/Admiral's Diaries/1–4/3/71
16 RA/RY/Admiral's Diaries/6/3/71
17 RA/RY/Admiral's Diaries/7–9/3/71
18 RA/RY/Admiral's Diaries/17 & 18/3/71
19 RA/RY/Admiral's Diaries/20–22/3/71
20 RA/RY/Admiral's Diaries/3/5/71
21 RA/RY/Admiral's Diaries/3,4/5/71
22 RA/RY/Admiral's Diaries/6/5/71
23 RA/RY/Admiral's Diaries/12/5/71
24 RA/RY/Admiral's Diaries/28/5/71
25 RA/RY/Admiral's Diaries/14/6/71
26 RA/RY/Admiral's Diaries/29/7/71
27 RA/RY/Admiral's Diaries/2, 3 & 6/8/71
28 RA/RY/Admiral's Diaries/9/8/71
29 RA/RY/Admiral's Diaries/15, 16 & 19/8/71
30 RA/RY/Admiral's Diaries/22 & 25/10/71 & 2/11/71
31 RA/RY/Admiral's Diaries/8–10/2/72
32 RA/RY/Admiral's Diaries/18/2/72
33 RA/RY/Admiral's Diaries/20/2/72
34 RA/RY/Admiral's Diaries/29/2/72
35 RA/RY/Admiral's Diaries/24/3/72
36 RA/RY/Admiral's Diaries/3/8/73
37 RA/RY/Admiral's Diaries/5–10/8/73
38 RA/RY/Admiral's Diaries/16/8/73
39 RA/RY/Admiral's Diaries/15/11/73
40 RA/RY/Admiral's Diaries/30/11/73
41 RA/RY/Admiral's Diaries/4/12/73
42 RA/RY/Admiral's Diaries/12/12/73
43 RA/RY/Admiral's Diaries/4/1/74
44 RA/RY/Admiral's Diaries/7/1/74
45 RA/RY/Admiral's Diaries/22 & 24/1/74
46 RA/RY/Admiral's Diaries/29/1/74
47 RA/RY/Admiral's Diaries/30/1/74
48 RA/RY/Admiral's Diaries/6/2/74
49 RA/RY/Admiral's Diaries/27/2/74
50 RA/RY/Admiral's Diaries/8/1/75
51 RA/RY/Admiral's Diaries/20/1/75
52 RA/RY/Admiral's Diaries/21/1/75
53 RA/RY/Admiral's Diaries/25 & 26/2/75
54 RA/RY/Admiral's Diaries/27/2/75 & 1/3/75
55 RA/RY/Admiral's Diaries/30/4/75
56 RA/RY/Admiral's Diaries/31/5/75 & 1/6/75
57 RA/RY/Admiral's Diaries/31/7/75

Chapter Eight

1 RA/RY/Admiral's Diaries/18–22/9/75
2 RA/RY/Admiral's Diaries/23/9/75 & 2/10/75
3 RA/RY/Admiral's Diaries/24–28/5/76
4 RA/RY/Admiral's Diarie /1/6/76
5 RA/RY/Admiral's Diaries/3 & 4/7/76
6 RA/RY/Admiral's Diaries/6/7/76
7 RA/RY/Admiral's Diaries/7–9/7/76
8 RA/RY/Admiral's Diaries/10/7/76
9 RA/RY/Admiral's Diaries/11–13/7/76
10 RA/RY/Admiral's Diaries/14/2/77
11 RA/RY/Admiral's Diaries/16 & 17/2/77
12 RA/RY/Admiral's Diaries/15/7/77
13 RA/RY/Admiral's Diaries/19–29/10/77
14 RA/RY/Admiral's Diaries/17–31/5/78
15 RA/RY/Admiral's Diaries/23 & 26/6/78
16 RA/RY/Admiral's Diaries/6/9/78
17 RA/RY/Admiral's Diaries/11/1/79
18 RA/RY/Admiral's Diaries/1–5/6/79
19 RA/RY/Admiral's Diaries/27/7/79–2/8/79
20 RA/RY/Admiral's Diaries/16 & 27/8/79 & 5/9/79
21 RA/RY/Admiral's Diaries/7–16/7/80
22 RA/RY/Admiral's Diaries/20–25/7/80
23 RA/RY/Admiral's Diaries/6, 7, 9 & 16/10/80
24 RA/RY/Admiral's Diaries/17 & 18/10/80
25 RA/RY/Admiral's Diaries/25–29/10/80
26 RA/RY/Admiral's Diaries/5/11/80 & 4/2/81

Chapter Nine

1 RA/RY/Admiral's Diaries/8–14/4/81
2 RA/RY/Admiral's Diaries/5–8/5/81
3 RA/RY/Admiral's Diaries/9–13/5/81

4 RA/RY/Admiral's Diaries/31/7/81 &
   1/8/81
5 RA/RY/Admiral's Diaries/12–19/8/81
6 RA/RY/Admiral's Diaries/22–27/4/82
7 RA/RY/Admiral's Diaries/8–11/6/82
8 RA/RY/Admiral's Diaries/30/9/82
9 RA/RY/Admiral's Diaries/6–13/10/82
10 RA/RY/Admiral's Diaries/20/10/82
11 RA/RY/Admiral's Diaries/21/10/82
12 RA/RY/Admiral's
   Diaries/23/10/82–1/11/82
13 RA/RY/Admiral's
   Diaries/17/2/83–20/2/83
14 RA/RY/Admiral's Diaries/22–26/2/83
15 RA/RY/Admiral's
   Diaries/27/2/83–2/3/83
16 RA/RY/Admiral's Diaries/4/3/83
17 RA/RY/Admiral's Diaries/5–11/3/83
18 RA/RY/Admiral's Diaries/17/5/83
19 RA/RY/Admiral's Diaries/21–25/5/83
20 RA/RY/Admiral's Diaries/27–30/5/83
21 RA/RY/Admiral's Diaries/2/6/83
22 RA/RY/Admiral's Diaries/24/6/83
23 RA/RY/Admiral's Diarie /29 & 30/9/83
24 RA/RY/Admiral's Diaries/30/3/84
25 RA/RY/Admiral's Diaries/30/5/84
26 RA/RY/Admiral's Diaries/2 & 3/6/84
27 RA/RY/Admiral's Diaries/5 & 6/6/84
28 RA/RY/Admiral's Diaries/9/7/84
29 RA/RY/Admiral's Diaries/13/8/84
30 RA/RY/Admiral's Diaries/9/10/84
31 RA/RY/Admiral's Diaries/17/10/84
32 RA/RY/Admiral's Diaries/6/12/84
33 RA/RY/Admiral's Diaries/13/3/85
34 RA/RY/Admiral's Diaries/17/3/85
35 RA/RY/Admiral's Diaries/27/3/85
36 RA/RY/Admiral's Diaries/4 & 5/5/85
37 RA/RY/Admiral's Diaries/8/5/85
38 RA/RY/Admiral's Diaries/11/6/85

Chapter Ten
1 RA/RY/Admiral's Diaries/11–18/10/85
2 RA/RY/Admiral's Diaries/3/11/85
3 RA/RY/Admiral's Diaries/5 & 10/12/85
4 RA/RY/Admiral's Diaries/31/12/85
5 RA/RY/Admiral's Diaries/6–11/1/86
6 RA/RY/Admiral's Diaries/14/1/86
7 RA/RY/Admiral's Diaries/15/1/86
8 RA/RY/Admiral's Diaries/17/1/86
9 RA/RY/Admiral's Diaries/21/1/86
10 RA/RY/Admiral's Diaries/6–9/3/86
11 RA/RY/Admiral's Diaries/13/3/86
12 RA/RY/Admiral's Diaries/29/4/86
13 RA/RY/Admiral's Diaries/10/6/86
14 RA/RY/Admiral's Diaries/19/7/86
15 RA/RY/Admiral's Diaries/23/7/86
16 RA/RY/Admiral's Diaries/28/7/86
17 RA/RY/Admiral's Diaries/2/8/86

18 RA/RY/Admiral's Diaries/7/8/86
19 RA/RY/Admiral's Diaries/9–11/8/86
20 RA/RY/Admiral's Diaries/15–18/8/86
21 RA/RY/Admiral's Diaries/16/9/86
22 RA/RY/Admiral's Diaries/14/10/86
23 RA/RY/Admiral's Diaries/15–18/10/86
24 RA/RY/Admiral's Diaries/3/11/87
25 RA/RY/Admiral's Diaries/13/3/87
26 RA/RY/Admiral's Diaries/12–17/10/87
27 RA/RY/Admiral's Diaries/3/11/87
28 RA/RY/Admiral's Diaries/17 & 18/1/88
29 RA/RY/Admiral's Diaries/19/1/88
30 RA/RY/Admiral's Diaries/18/2/88
31 RA/RY/Admiral's Diaries/29/2/88 &
   2/3/88
32 RA/RY/Admiral's Diaries/21 & 28/4/88
33 RA/RY/Admiral's Diaries/29 & 30/4/88
34 RA/RY/Admiral's Diaries/1–7/5/88
35 RA/RY/Admiral's Diaries/22/6/88
36 RA/RY/Admiral's Diaries/19–22/7/88
37 RA/RY/Admiral's Diaries/15–18/8/88
38 RA/RY/Admiral's Diaries/2&9/3/89
39 RA/RY/Admiral's Diaries/22/5/89
40 RA/RY/Admiral's Diaries/26/5/89
41 RA/RY/Admiral's Diaries/3–7/6/89
42 RA/RY/Admiral's Diaries/1 & 11/7/89
43 RA/RY/Admiral's
   Diaries/22/9/89–1/10/89
44 RA/RY/Admiral's Diaries/5–11/3/90
45 RA/RY/Admiral's Diaries/26 & 27/7/90
46 RA/RY/Admiral's
   Diaries/30/7/90–2/8/90

Chapter Eleven
1 RA/RY/Admiral's Diaries/18/9/90
2 RA/RY/Admiral's Diaries/1, 12, 17 &
   28/10/90
3 RA/RY/Admiral's Diaries/26/4/91
4 RA/RY/Admiral's Diaries/3/5/91
5 RA/RY/Admiral's Diaries/18, 20, 21 &
   27/5/91
6 RA/RY/Admiral's Diaries/28/5/91
7 RA/RY/Admiral's Diaries/9–14 & 17/6/91
8 RA/RY/Admiral's Diaries/12–15/7/91
9 RA/RY/Admiral's Diaries/25/9/91
10 RA/RY/Admiral's Diaries/23,
   27–29/10/91
11 RA/RY/Admiral's Diaries/28–31/5/92
12 RA/RY/Admiral's Diaries/16/2/93
13 RA/RY/Admiral's Diaries/26/6/92
14 RA/RY/Admiral's Diaries/11/12/92
15 RA/RY/Admiral's Diaries/6, 8 &
   14/10/93
16 RA/RY/Admiral's Diaries/18, 20, 21 &
   24/10/93
17 RA/RY/Admiral's Diaries/8–11/11/93
18 RA/RY/Admiral's Diaries/16/11/93
19 RA/RY/Admiral's Diaries/12/3/94

20 RA/RY/Admiral's Diaries/10, 23, 24,
   26 & 27/5/94
21 RA/RY/Admiral's Diaries/4/6/94
22 RA/RY/Admiral's Diaries/5/6/94
23 RA/RY/Admiral's Diaries/6 & 7/6/94
24 RA/RY/Admiral's Diaries/23/6/94
25 RA/RY/Admiral's Diaries/24, 28 &
   30/6/94 & 1/7/94
26 RA/RY/Admiral's Diaries/5/8/94
27 RA/RY/Admiral's Diaries/16/10/94
28 RA/RY/Admiral's Diaries/19 &
   20/10/94
29 RA/RY/Admiral's Diaries/21/2/95
30 RA/RY/Admiral's Diaries/21 & 24/3/95
31 RA/RY/Admiral's Diaries/25, 28 & 31/3/95

Chapter Twelve
1 RA/RY/Admiral's Diaries/29–31/5/95 &
   1, 2, 5 & 6/6/95
2 RA/RY/Admiral's Diaries/18–21, 23 &
   26/6/95
3 RA/RY/Admiral's Diaries/8 &
   17–22/8/95
4 RA/RY/Admiral's Diaries/21/10/95 &
   6/11/95
5 RA/RY/Admiral's Diaries/12, 13, 15, 16,
   28 & 31/3/96 & 1–3/4/96
6 RA/RY/Admiral's Diaries/3, 6 & 7/5/96
7 RA/RY/Admiral's Diaries/21 &
   24–27/6/96
8 RA/RY/Admiral's Diaries/5–8/7/96
9 RA/RY/Admiral's Diaries/10–14/7/96 &
   7/8/96
10 RA/RY/Admiral's Diaries/7 & 8/2/97
11 RA/RY/Admiral's Diaries/12/5/97
12 RA/RY/Admiral's Diaries/2 &
   28–30/6/97
13 RA/RY/Admiral's Diaries/30/6/97
14 RA/RY/Admiral's Diaries/1, 3
   &11/7/97
15 RA/RY/Admiral's Diaries/28/7/97
16 RA/RY/Admiral's Diaries/25–31/8/97
17 RA/RY/Admiral's Diaries/31/10/97 &
   1–3/11/97
18 RA/RY/Admiral's Diaries/13, 14 &
   21/11/97
19 RA/RY/Admiral's Diaries/22/11/97

Chapter Thirteen
1 RA/RY/Admiral's Diaries/11/12/97
2 RA/RY/Admiral's Diaries/16/12/97
3 RA/RY/Admiral's Diaries/18/12/97 &
   19/12/97
4 RA/RY/Admiral's Diaries/12/1/98
5 RA/RY/Admiral's
   Diaries/26/1/98–30/1/98
6 RA/RY/Admiral's Diaries/2/2/98–6/2/98
7 RA/RY/Admiral's Diaries/23/2/98

GLOSSARY

Activity Boat. A flat bottomed dory which had the ability to be safely run up sandy beaches. It was especially useful during the Western Isles Cruise when it was used to take the Royal party ashore for picnics and barbecues.

banyan: An informal and relaxed tropical picnic held ashore.

bilges. The bilge is the bottom part of the hull either side of the keel which meets the sides. In most types of vessel the bilge meets the side in a curve and this part of the hull is known as the turn of the bilge.

binnacle. The wooden housing of the ship's compass and its correctors.

British Invisibles. A private sector organisation promoting the international activities of UK based financial institutions and professional and business services. British Invisibles has close links with the Government.

brow. A narrow platform forming a gangway between ship and shore; it is called a gang-plank when laid between ship and ship.

capstan. A cylindrical barrel which is fitted on a vertically mounted spindle. The capstan is used for handling ropes/cables under heavy loads such as raising the anchor. Capstans are normally mounted on the centre line of the ship and driven by either steam or electricity.

catamarans – ngawalas. A vessel with two parallel hulls joined together. Ngawalas are a type of fast sailing catamaran built in Zanzibar.

Cinque Ports. An association of towns on the Channel coast of England, mainly for juridical purposes, originally composed of five ports, Dover, Hastings, Romney, Hythe and Sandwich. The association was subsequently enlarged through the addition of the towns of Rye and Winchelsea. The Cinque Ports were charged until the sixteenth century with providing the Crown with ships and men in the event of war. In return for this commitment the Cinque Ports were granted charters

guaranteeing them certain privileges in tolls and fishing and in maritime jurisdiction covering the waters of the eastern English Channel. Following the establishment of a permanent Royal Navy by Henry VII and Henry VIII the influence of the Cinque Ports declined. The most recent Lord Warden of the Cinque Ports was HM Queen Elizabeth The Queen Mother.

clear lower deck. This order is given to signal the requirement for all sailors to assemble on the upper deck for a particular purpose such as an address by the Commanding Officer.

Cod Wars. Naval operations off Iceland in support of the British fishing industry known colloquially as the Cod Wars. The first Cod War resulted from Iceland's declaration of a 12-mile fishing limit, and lasted from September 1958 to March 1961. The second concerned the 50-mile limit, with naval protection being provided between May and November 1973. The third Cod War lasted from November 1975 to May 1976 and was a continuation of the 50-mile dispute reactivated by Iceland's declaration of a 200-mile limit.

dhow. A generic term that covers the lateen-rigged sailing coasters native to the Red Sea, Persian Gulf and Indian Ocean.

dress ship. The procedure to decorate a ship with flags to mark either a national or local celebration such as a major regatta or public holiday. A ship is dressed overall when she flies a continuous line of flags from her jackstaff via the mast heads to the ensign staff. A ship is dressed when she flies flags at her mastheads.

The Duke of Edinburgh Scheme. The Duke of Edinburgh Scheme was launched in the UK in 1956 with His Royal Highness as Chairman of the Trustees and Sir John Hunt as its First Director. The Scheme became international in 1961 and now has programmes in over 100 different countries. Nearly five million young people have taken part in the Scheme world-wide.

echo sounder. A navigational instrument for measuring the depth of water using the

principle of sonar. By using a vertical sonar pulse and measuring the time taken between emission of the signal and the receipt of the echo off the bottom, the depth of the water can be accurately calculated.

Ensigns. The national flag as worn by ships of a nation. For British ships three Ensigns are used namely the White Ensign, Blue Ensign and the Red Ensign. The White Ensign is used by ships of the RN in commission, Shore Establishments of the RN and by yachts of the RYS. The Blue Ensign is used by naval auxiliary vessels. The Red Ensign is used by vessels of the Merchant Navy and any non naval British vessel. Some Yacht Clubs have approval for their yachts to use the Blue Ensign or Red Ensign defaced with their badge in the bottom right-hand corner.

Gemini. A small inflatable boat powered by an outboard engine.

International Date Line. A line running essentially along the longitude of 180°. The line is slightly adjusted to ensure that the island groups that lie along the longitude are not divided by the International Date Line. It is on this International Date Line that the time zones of +12 hours and -12 hours meet and the date changes.

jackstay. A rope or wire secured firmly between two points and used as a support. For example, during a Replenishment At Sea (RAS) the fuel line is suspended from a jackstay between the tanker and the ship being refuelled.

jolly boat. This was the old naval term applied to the pair of open motor whalers embarked in *Britannia*. These general purpose work boats were used for a variety of tasks.

kedge anchor. A light or secondary anchor normally used for pointing the ship/boat in some required direction. For example, a kedge anchor could be used for hauling and holding the stern of an anchored ship/boat against wind and tide to keep clear of a regatta course. Before the advent of steam, ships were often moved in harbour by laying out anchors ahead successively and 'kedging' up to them.

liberty boat / liberty men. Liberty is the sailor's name for those given permission to go ashore for the day or night. Thus those going on leave are known as liberty men while the boat they are taken ashore in is known as the liberty boat.

mules. The progress of a ship through the locks of the Panama Canal is controlled by a number of locomotives, known as mules, running on railway lines alongside each lock. Lines are passed from the ship to locomotives on both sides of the lock. The lines are adjusted so that the ship remains in the centre of the lock while the mules pull the ship through.

outrigger. A counterpoising log of wood rigged out from the side of a native canoe in the Pacific and Indian Oceans to provide additional stability when carrying sail in a stiff breeze.

paying off pennant. Since before the Napoleonic Wars it has been the custom for HM ships to fly a 'paying off pennant' at the main truck when they leave their fleet to return to their home port to pay off. The pennant is displayed by a ship coming back from a foreign deployment when entering or leaving harbours during her passage home, and by a ship in home waters on leaving for and arriving at her home port. It is also the custom for a ship to fly this pennant on the Sunday preceding her departure, or, if already in her paying-off port, on the Sunday preceding the day on which she pays off.

Roaring Forties. The area in the south Indian Ocean between latitudes of 40° and 50° South where the prevailing wind blows from the west.

tot. Every rating in the RN over the age of 20 (except an Apprentice under training) was entitled to be issued with one tot (⅛ of a pint) of rum a day or to be given a cash allowance (grog money) instead. The day's tot had to be drunk before rounds on the day of issue as the saving of rum was forbidden. The tot was issued for the last time on 31 July 1970. However, rum is still occasionally distributed on board HM Ships when the order 'Splice the mainbrace' is given by a member of the Royal Family. In *Britannia* at the end of a successful Royal tour the embarked member of the Royal Family would usually send FORY/CORY a congratulatory signal which included the order 'Splice the mainbrace' to reward the Yachtsmen for their hard work.

LIST OF ABBREVIATIONS

AC	Companion of the Order of Australia
ADC	Aide-de-camp
ANZUK	Australian New Zealand United Kingdom force
ASW	Anti Submarine Warfare
BAe	British Aerospace
BBC	British Broadcasting Company
BEM	British Empire Medal
BOAC	British Overseas Airways Corporation
BRNC	Britannia Royal Naval College
CB	Companion of the Order of the Bath
CBE	Commander of the Order of the British Empire
CENTO	Central Treaty Organisation
CERA	Chief Engine Room Artificer
CH	Companion of Honour
CHOGM	Commonwealth Heads Of Government Meeting
CMG	Companion of the Order of St Michael and St George
CO	Commanding Officer
COMCLYDENORLANT	Commander Clyde North Atlantic
CORY	Commodore Royal Yachts

CPO	Chief Petty Officer
CSI	Companion of the Order of the Star of India
CVO	Commander of the Royal Victorian Order

The four Heads of Department in *Britannia* were referred to as Commander (E) or (L) etc. The letter in brackets denoted their Department as listed below:

Commander (E)	Engineering Officer
Commander (L)	Electrical Officer
Commander (N)	Navigating Officer
Commander (S)	Supply Officer
DCVO	Dame Commander of the Royal Victorian Order
DL	Deputy Lieutenant
DML	Devonport Management Ltd
DSC	Distinguished Service Cross
DSO	Distinguished Service Order
DTI	Department of Trade and Industry
EC	European Community
EEC	European Economic Community
EU	European Union
ERD	Army Emergency Reserve Decoration

FAA	Fleet Air Arm		OBE	Officer of the Order of the British Empire
FFO	Furnace Fuel Oil		OM	Order of Merit
FIDS	Falkland Island Dependency Survey		P&O	The Peninsular and Oriental Steam Navigation Company
FNS	French Naval Ship			
FORY	Flag Officer Royal Yachts		PANAM	Pan American Airlines
GCB	Knight / Dame Grand Cross of the Order of the Bath		PMO	Principal Medical Officer
			PO	Petty Officer
GCVO	Knight / Dame Grand Cross of the Royal Victorian Order		PR	Public Relations
			PTI	Physical Training Instructor
GMT	Greenwich Mean Time			
GRP	Glass Reinforced Plastic		QC	Queen's Counsel
			QEII	Cunard Liner *Queen Elizabeth II*
			QSO	Companion of The Queen's Service Order (New Zealand)
HDMY	His / Her Danish Majesty's Yacht			
HE	His / Her Excellency			
HH	His / Her Highness		UK	United Kingdom
HM	His / Her Majesty		UN	United Nations
HMA	His / Her Majesty's Ambassador		US	United States
HMAS	His / Her Majesty's Australian Ship		USAF	United States Air Force
HMCS	His / Her Majesty's Canadian Ship		USN	United States Navy
HMNZS	His /Her Majesty's New Zealand Ship		USS	United States Ship
HMS	His / Her Majesty's Ship			
HMY	His / Her Majesty's Yacht		RAN	Royal Australian Navy
HQ	Head Quarters		RAS	Replenishment At Sea
HRH	His / Her Royal Highness		RCAF	Royal Canadian Air Force
			RCMP	Royal Canadian Mounted Police
INS	Indian Naval Ship		RCNC	Royal Corps of Naval Constructors
IRA	Irish Republican Army		RFA	Royal Fleet Auxiliary
ISC	Island Sailing Club		RM	Royal Marines
			RMS	Royal Mail Ship
K&S	The Keeper & Steward of the Royal Apartments		RN	Royal Navy
KBE	Knight Commander of the British Empire		RNAS	Royal Naval Air Station
KCB	Knight Commander of the Bath		RNC	Royal Naval College
KCMG	Knight Commander of St Michael and St George		RNS	Russian Naval Ship
KCVO	Knight Commander of the Royal Victorian Order		RNVR	Royal Naval Volunteer Reserve
KG	Knight of the Order of the Garter		RNZAF	Royal New Zealand Air Force
KGFS	King George's Fund for Sailors		RNZN	Royal New Zealand Navy
KT	Knight of the Order of the Thistle		RVM	Royal Victorian Medal
			SS	Steam Ship
LA	Leading Airman		SRE	Sound Reproduction Equipment
LVO	Lieutenant of the Royal Victorian Order			
			TD	Territorial Efficiency Decoration
MBE	Member of the Order of the British Empire		TM	Their Majesties
MOD	Ministry Of Defence		TRH	Their Royal Highnesses
MP	Member of Parliament		TWA	Trans World Airlines
MTB	Motor Torpedo Boat			
MV	Motor Vessel		V&A	HM Yacht *Victoria & Albert* (III)
MVO	Member of the Royal Victorian Order		VJ Day	Victory over Japan Day
NAAFI	Navy, Army and Air Force Institute		WRCNS	Women's Royal Canadian Naval Service
NATO	North Atlantic Treaty Organisation		WRNS	Women's Royal Naval Service
NMM	National Maritime Museum		WWF	World Wildlife Fund

INDEX

HMY BRITANNIA

GENERAL ARRANGEMENTS
PROFILE AND SECTIONS

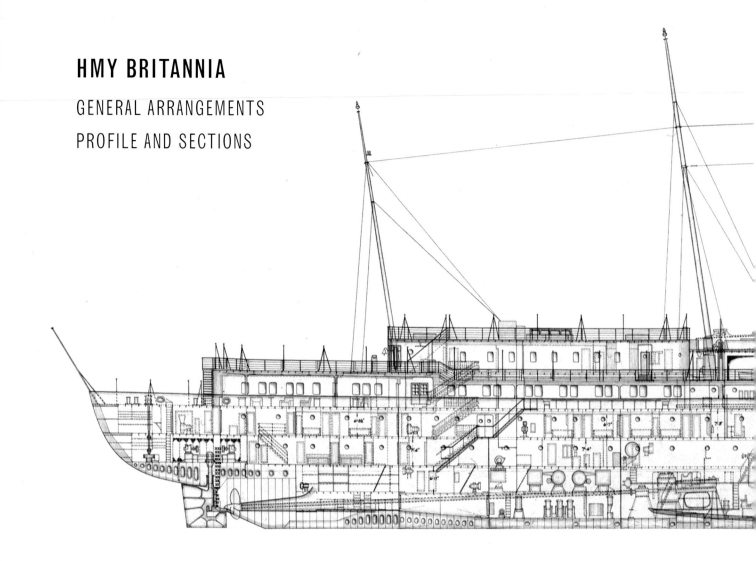

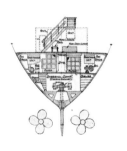

SECTION AT 180 STATION
LOOKING AFT

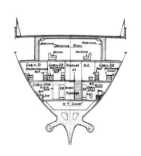

SECTION AT 170 STATION
LOOKING AFT

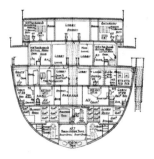

SECTION AT 142 STATION
LOOKING AFT

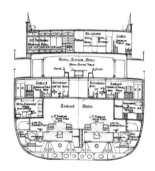

SECTION AT 115 STATION
LOOKING AFT